*The Papers of*
George Washington

# The Papers of
# George Washington

Theodore J. Crackel, *Editor in Chief*

Philander D. Chase, *Senior Editor*

Frank E. Grizzard, Jr., *Senior Associate Editor*

Edward G. Lengel and Beverly H. Runge, *Associate Editors*

David R. Hoth and Christine Sternberg Patrick
*Assistant Editors*

## Revolutionary War Series
# 16

*July–September 1778*

*David R. Hoth*, Editor

## UNIVERSITY OF VIRGINIA PRESS

CHARLOTTESVILLE AND LONDON

This edition has been prepared by the staff of
*The Papers of George Washington*
sponsored by
The Mount Vernon Ladies' Association of the Union
and the University of Virginia
with the support of
the National Endowment for the Humanities and
the National Historical Publications and Records Commission.

The preparation of this volume has been made possible by
grants from the Norman and Lyn Lear Foundation and
the National Trust for the Humanities and a gift from
Philip G. and Michelle L. LeDuc of Seattle, Washington.

The publication of this volume has been supported by
a grant from the National Historical Publications
and Records Commission.

UNIVERSITY OF VIRGINIA PRESS

*First published 2006*

The paper used in this publication meets the
minimum requirements of ANSI/NISO Z39.48-1992
(R 1997) (Permanence of Paper).

Library of Congress Cataloging-in-Publication Data

Washington, George, 1732–1799.
 The papers of George Washington, Revolutionary
War series.
 Includes bibliographical references and indexes.
 Contents: v. 1. June–September 1775 — 2. Sep-
tember–December 1775 — [etc.] — v. 16. July–
September 1778.
 1. United States—History—Revolution, 1775–
1783. 2. Washington, George. 1732–1799—Ar-
chives. 3. Presidents—United States—Archives.
I. Crackel, Theodore J.; Hoth, David R. II. Revolu-
tionary War series. III. Title.
E312.72 1985 973.3 87-403730
ISBN 0-8139-1040-4 (v. 1)
ISBN 978-0-8139-2579-0 (v. 16)

# Contents

Contents                                            xv

# Maps

# Introduction

The summer of 1778 was a time of enormous optimism for GW and other supporters of the American cause. The welcome news of a French alliance in May had been followed by the British evacuation of Philadelphia in mid-June and capped by what the Americans believed to be a glorious victory at the Battle of Monmouth on 28 June. It seemed possible that the British, weakened by the loss of "at least 2000 Men & of their best Troops" in the march through New Jersey (GW to John Augustine Washington, 4 July), might even abandon their remaining strongholds at New York City and Newport, R.I., for Canada or the West Indies.

As this volume, which covers the period from 1 July to 14 September 1778, opens, GW, having concluded that he could not seriously hinder the British evacuation from New Jersey to New York, was putting his army in motion to take up a position better suited to the defense of the Hudson River. Even before that movement was completed, GW received welcome news of the arrival on the American coast of a powerful French fleet commanded by the Comte d'Estaing. For once GW would be planning a campaign in which an American ally, and not the British, controlled the sea lanes.

GW's preferred alternative was clearly to capture the main British army at New York, and he stationed his army at White Plains, where it could cooperate with the French navy in joint operations against the city. However, he also anticipated the possibility of an attack on the British forces at Rhode Island and directed Maj. Gen. John Sullivan to prepare for such an eventuality, authorizing him to "immediately apply in the most urgent manner, in my name" for an additional 5,000 men (GW to Sullivan, 17 July). As it turned out, the pilots determined that it was inadvisable for the larger French ships to attempt to enter New York Harbor, so GW detached two brigades and some of his most trusted generals to assist Sullivan in the attempt to take Newport, and d'Estaing's fleet sailed east to support that operation.

In consequence, the most crucial activity of the summer campaign would depend on the diplomacy, energy, and strategy of someone other than GW. If Sullivan and d'Estaing succeeded in capturing Newport, they would cement the French and American alliance with a glorious victory and, by taking a second British army, might force the British to sue for peace. With American expectations of ultimate success raised to a high pitch, GW could only pepper Sullivan with letters conveying what little useful intelligence he could gather from New York, offering suggestions about what Sullivan might do to improve the chances for victory, encouraging Sullivan's diligence and energy, and above all, pleading for information: "Even if nothing material should happen in the course of a day or two, just to hear that all is well will be a relief to me" (GW to Sullivan, 4 Aug.).

Unfortunately, the venture, which began with glowing reports of high morale and good understanding among allies, degenerated into disappointment and recriminations as weather and circumstance combined to defeat the objects of the American expedition. On 10 August, as Sullivan was preparing to attack, Admiral Richard Howe's British fleet from New York, strengthened with the first arrivals of a naval reinforcement from England, appeared off Rhode Island, and d'Estaing sailed away to meet them. Then both fleets and armies were battered by a massive three-day storm. When d'Estaing appeared again on 20 August, it was only to announce that his fleet would withdraw to Boston for repairs. Sullivan's position thus became untenable. He could not hope to reduce Newport without the aid of the French fleet, and the narrow window of French maritime superiority was closing. Although Sullivan continued siege operations for another week in hopes of a prompt French return, by the 28th he decided to withdraw to the northern end of the island, and after an inconclusive battle with pursuing British troops on 29 August, Sullivan, advised by GW of British reinforcements, successfully withdrew to the mainland.

The summer of promise had ended in nothing. Instead of celebrating victory, GW was carefully trying to soothe French feelings wounded by Sullivan's protests of their withdrawal and to ensure that American trust in the French alliance would not be severely damaged by the unexpected failure of the Rhode Island expedition. With the arrival of more of the reinforcing fleet, the British once again had control of the sea and the initiative. Although GW asked a council of war on 1 September to consider whether his army might make an assault on New York City while the British forces there were reduced by the troops sent to trap Sullivan on Rhode Island, his generals were agreed that such a project was foolish. As the volume closes, GW is withdrawing his army to positions better suited to a defensive response to British actions, whether directed against the French fleet at Boston or the American posts on the Hudson River.

Although the Newport expedition dominates this volume, other important events occurred during the period. A mixed force of Loyalists and Indians destroyed the American settlement at Wyoming in Pennsylvania, and New York frontier communities also became increasingly concerned about the possible threat from Loyalist-Indian allies. In mid-

July, GW detached the 4th Pennsylvania Regiment and a part of the rifle corps to assist in frontier defense, but the larger detachments to Rhode Island left him unable to offer more help.

Courts were held to consider Maj. Gen. Charles Lee's recent behavior at the Battle of Monmouth and Maj. Gen. Arthur St. Clair's role in the loss of Ticonderoga in 1777, with Maj. Gen. Philip Schuyler's trial for Ticonderoga awaiting the completion of St. Clair's. The necessary engagement of generals on those courts exacerbated the chronic shortage of qualified general officers, and GW continued to press Congress to fill vacancies more promptly.

He also pressed Congress for completion of the army reorganization, and by mid-September the members of Congress sent to camp to join with GW as a reorganization committee had begun considering a number of long-standing disputes about the ranks of officers.

Precisely because GW's strategic decisions had given the main active roles to others, this volume is particularly revealing of his diplomatic skills, whether in dealings with the French, with Congress, or with his subordinate officers. The advice that GW sent to Sullivan also provides useful information about the military precepts that he tried to follow. Moreover, his awareness of the importance of intelligence and his efforts to obtain it are well displayed, even though the results fell short of what he and Vice Admiral d'Estaing desired.

# Editorial Apparatus

Transcription of the documents in the volumes of *The Papers of George Washington* has remained as close to a literal reproduction of the manuscript as possible. Punctuation, capitalization, paragraphing, and spelling of all words are retained as they appear in the original document. Dashes used as punctuation have been retained except when a period and a dash appear together at the end of a sentence. The appropriate marks of punctuation have always been added at the end of a paragraph. Errors in spelling of proper names and geographic locations have been corrected in brackets or in annotation only if the spelling in the text makes the word incomprehensible. When a tilde is used in the manuscript to indicate a double letter, the letter has been silently doubled. Washington and some of his correspondents occasionally used a tilde above an incorrectly spelled word to indicate an error in orthography. When this device is used, the editors have silently corrected the word. In cases where a tilde has been inserted above an abbreviation or contraction, usually in letter-book copies, the word has been expanded. Otherwise, contractions and abbreviations have been retained as written, although a period has been inserted after every abbreviation. When an apostrophe has been used in a contraction, it is retained. If the meaning of an abbreviation or contraction is not obvious, it has been expanded in square brackets: "H[is] M[ajest]y." Superscripts have been lowered. Editorial insertions or corrections in the text also appear in square brackets. Angle brackets ⟨ ⟩ are used to indicate illegible or mutilated material. A space left blank in a manuscript by the writer is indicated by a square-bracketed gap in the text [    ]. Deletions from manuscripts are generally not indicated, although if a deletion contains substantive material, it appears in a footnote. If the intended location of marginal notations is clear from the text, they are inserted without comment; otherwise they are recorded in the footnotes. The ampersand has been retained and the thorn transcribed as "th." The symbol for per (⅌) is used when it appears in the manuscript. The dateline has been placed at the head of a document regardless of where it occurred in the manuscript. Some documents of a routine nature have been omitted; more information on this policy and a list of items omitted are in the appendix to this volume.

Where multiple versions of a document are available, the document closest to the one received by the addressee is printed. The other versions have been collated with the selected text, and significant variations are presented in the annotation. In the case of general orders, the Varick transcript has been selected, except when the orders exist in the writing of GW or one of his aides. Copies of the army general orders in division, brigade, and occasionally regiment orderly books have been examined for significant variations, which are reported in the annotation.

Since GW read no language other than English, incoming letters written to him in foreign languages were generally translated for his information. Where this contemporary translation has survived, it has been used as the text of the document. If there is no contemporary translation, the document in its original language has been used as the text.

All of the documents printed in this volume, as well as any documents omitted, the original foreign language documents (where otherwise not provided), and a number of ancillary materials, will ultimately be available in an electronic edition of the GW papers. To learn more about the electronic edition, visit the Web site of The Papers of George Washington (www.gwpapers.virginia.edu) or of the Rotunda, the digital imprint of the University of Virginia Press (rotunda.upress .virginia.edu).

In the Revolutionary War series, the titles of the documents include current military ranks of persons on duty with the contending armies or mobilized militia units.

Individuals mentioned in the text are identified usually at their first substantive mention and are not identified at length in subsequent volumes. The index to each volume indicates where an identification appears in an earlier volume of the Revolutionary War series.

## Symbols Designating Documents

| | |
|---|---|
| AD | Autograph Document |
| ADS | Autograph Document Signed |
| ADf | Autograph Draft |
| ADfS | Autograph Draft Signed |
| AL | Autograph Letter |
| ALS | Autograph Letter Signed |
| D | Document |
| DS | Document Signed |
| Df | Draft |
| DfS | Draft Signed |
| L | Letter |
| LS | Letter Signed |
| LB | Letter-Book Copy |
| [S] | Used with other symbols to indicate that the signature on the document has been cropped or clipped. |

# Repository Symbols and Abbreviations

| | |
|---|---|
| CSmH | Henry E. Huntington Library, San Marino, Calif. |
| Ct | Connecticut State Library, Hartford |
| CtHi | Connecticut Historical Society, Hartford |
| CtY | Yale University, New Haven, Conn. |
| DLC | Library of Congress |
| DLC:GW | George Washington Papers, Library of Congress |
| DNA | National Archives |
| DNA:PCC | Papers of the Continental Congress, National Archives |
| FrPBN | Bibliothèque Nationale, Paris, France |
| FrPNA | Archives Nationales, Paris, France |
| ICHi | Chicago Historical Society |
| InU | Indiana University, Bloomington |
| LNHiC | The Historic New Orleans Collection, New Orleans, La. |
| M-Ar | Massachusetts Archives Division, Boston |
| MBU | Boston University, Boston |
| MdAA | Maryland Hall of Records, Annapolis |
| MdAN | U.S. Naval Academy, Annapolis |
| MdHi | Maryland Historical Society, Baltimore |
| MH | Harvard University, Cambridge, Mass. |
| MHi | Massachusetts Historical Society, Boston |
| MiU-C | William L. Clements Library, Ann Arbor, Mich. |
| MWA | American Antiquarian Society, Worcester, Mass. |
| N | New York State Library, Albany |
| Nc-Ar | North Carolina State Department of Archives and History, Raleigh |
| Nh-Ar | New Hampshire Division of Records Management and Archives, Concord |
| NhHi | New Hampshire Historical Society, Concord |
| NHi | New-York Historical Society, New York |
| Nj-Ar | New Jersey State Archives, Trenton |
| NjMoNP | Washington Headquarters Library, Morristown, N.J. |
| NjP | Princeton University, Princeton, N.J. |
| NN | New York Public Library, New York |
| NNC | Columbia University, New York |
| NNebgGW | Washington's Headquarters (Jonathan Hasbrouck House), Newburgh, N.Y. |
| NNGL | Gilder Lehrman Collection at the New-York Historical Society, New York |
| NNPM | Pierpont Morgan Library, New York |
| NNU-F | Fales Collection, New York University, New York |
| OMC | Marietta College, Marietta, Ohio |

PEL           Lafayette College, Easton, Pa.
PHarH         Pennsylvania Historical and Museum Commission,
                 Harrisburg
PHi           Historical Society of Pennsylvania, Philadelphia
PPAmP         American Philosophical Society, Philadelphia
PPRF          Rosenbach Foundation, Philadelphia
P.R.O.        Public Record Office, London
PWacD         David Library of the American Revolution, Sol
                 Feinstone Collection, on deposit at PPAmP
R-Ar          Rhode Island State Library, Rhode Island State
                 Archives, Providence
RG            Record Group (designating the location of documents
                 in the National Archives)
RPJCB         John Carter Brown Library, Providence, R.I.
ScHi          South Carolina Historical Society, Charleston
ScU           University of South Carolina, Columbia
ViFaCt        Fairfax County Courthouse, Fairfax, Va.
ViHi          Virginia Historical Society, Richmond
ViLoCt        Loudoun County Courthouse, Leesburg, Va.
ViMtV         Mount Vernon Ladies' Association of the Union
ViW           College of William and Mary, Williamsburg, Va.

# Short Title List

André, *Journal.*      John André. *Major André's Journal: Operations of the British Army under Lieutenant Generals Sir William Howe and Sir Henry Clinton, June 1777 to November 1778.* 1930. Reprint. New York, 1968.

Baldwin, *Revolutionary Journal.*      Thomas William Baldwin, ed. *The Revolutionary Journal of Col. Jeduthan Baldwin 1775–1778.* 1906. Reprint. New York, 1971.

Baurmeister, *Revolution in America.*      Carl Leopold Baurmeister. *Revolution in America: Confidential Letters and Journals, 1776–1784, of Adjutant General Major Baurmeister of the Hessian Forces.* Trans. and annot. Bernhard A. Uhlendorf. New Brunswick, N.J., 1957.

"Beatty Journal."      "The Journal of Captain William Beatty, of the Maryland Line, 1776 to 1780." *Historical Magazine and Notes and Queries concerning the Antiquities, History, and Biography of America,* 2d ser., 1 (Jan. 1867), 79–85.

"Brigham Diary."      Edward A. Hoyt, ed. "A Revolutionary Diary of Captain Paul Brigham, November 19, 1777–September 4, 1778." *Vermont History,* 26 (1966), 3–30.

Burgoyne, *Diaries of Two Ansbach Jaegers.*      Bruce E. Burgoyne, trans.

and ed. *Diaries of Two Ansbach Jaegers, Lt. Heinrich Carl Philipp von Feilitzsch and Lt. Christian Friedrich Bartholomai.* Bowie, Md., 1997.

Butterfield, *Adams Diary and Autobiography.* L. H. Butterfield et al., eds. *Diary and Autobiography of John Adams.* 4 vols. Cambridge, Mass., 1961.

Campbell, *Bland Papers.* Charles Campbell, ed. *The Bland Papers: Being a Selection from the Manuscripts of Colonel Theodorick Bland, Jr., of Prince George County, Virginia.* Petersburg, Va., 1840.

Coldham, *American Loyalist Claims.* Peter Wilson Coldham. *American Loyalist Claims.* Washington, D.C., 1980.

*Conn. Public Records.* *The Public Records of the State of Connecticut . . . with the Journal of the Council of Safety . . . and an Appendix.* 17 vols. Hartford, 1894–2001.

Custis, *Recollections.* George Washington Parke Custis. *Recollections and Private Memoirs of Washington.* New York, 1860.

Cutler, *Rev. Manasseh Cutler.* William Parker Cutler and Julia Perkins Cutler, eds. *Life Journals and Correspondence of Rev. Manasseh Cutler, LL.D., By His Grandchildren.* 2 vols. Cincinnati, 1888.

Davies, *Documents of the American Revolution.* K. G. Davies, ed. *Documents of the American Revolution, 1770–1783 (Colonial Office Series).* 21 vols. Shannon, Ireland, 1972–81.

Davis, *Memoirs of Aaron Burr.* Matthew L. Davis. *Memoirs of Aaron Burr, with Miscellaneous Selections from his Correspondence.* 2 vols. 1836–37. Reprint. New York, 1971.

*Delaware Archives.* *Delaware Archives.* 5 vols. Wilmington, 1911–19. Reprint. New York, 1974.

*Diaries.* Donald Jackson and Dorothy Twohig, eds. *The Diaries of George Washington.* 6 vols. Charlottesville, Va., 1976–79.

*Documentary History of Maine.* Maine Historical Society. *Documentary History of the State of Maine.* 24 vols. Portland, Maine, 1869–1916.

Döhla, *Hessian Diary.* Johann Conrad Döhla. *A Hessian Diary of the American Revolution.* Trans. and ed. Bruce E. Burgoyne. Norman, Okla., and London, 1990.

Doniol, *Histoire de la participation de la France.* Henri Doniol. *Histoire de la participation de la France à l'établissement des États-Unis d'Amérique: Correspondance diplomatique et documents.* 5 vols. Paris, 1886–92.

Duffy, *Ethan Allen and His Kin.* John J. Duffy et al., eds. *Ethan Allen and His Kin: Correspondence, 1772–1819.* 2 vols. Hanover, N.H., 1998.

Ewald, *Diary.* Johann Ewald. *Diary of the American War: A Hessian Journal.* Trans. and ed. Joseph P. Tustin. New Haven and London, 1979.

*Extrait du journal d'un officier de la marine.* *Extrait du journal d'un officier de la marine de l'escadre de M. le comte d'Estaing.* N.p., 1782.

Field, *Angell Diary.*　　Edward Field, ed. *Diary of Colonel Israel Angell, Commanding the Second Rhode Island Continental Regiment during the American Revolution, 1778–1781.* Providence, 1899.

*Franklin Papers.*　　William B. Willcox, Leonard W. Labaree, Whitfield J. Bell, Jr., et al., eds. *The Papers of Benjamin Franklin.* 37 vols. to date. New Haven, 1959–.

Godfrey, *Commander-in-Chief's Guard.*　　Carlos E. Godfrey. *The Commander-in-Chief's Guard, Revolutionary War.* Washington, D.C., 1904.

*Greene Papers.*　　Richard K. Showman et al., eds. *The Papers of General Nathanael Greene.* 12 vols. to date. Chapel Hill, N.C., 1976–.

Griffin, *Stephen Moylan.*　　Martin I. J. Griffin. *Stephen Moylan, Muster-Master General, Secretary and Aide-de-Camp to Washington, Quartermaster-General, Colonel of Fourth Pennsylvania Light Dragoons and Brigadier-General of the War for American Independence. . . .* Philadelphia, 1909.

Gruber, *Peebles' American War.*　　Ira D. Gruber, ed. *John Peebles' American War: The Diary of a Scottish Grenadier, 1776–1782.* Mechanicsburg, Pa., 1998.

Hammond, *Rolls of Soldiers.*　　Isaac W. Hammond, ed. *Rolls of the Soldiers in Revolutionary War. . . .* 4 vols. New Hampshire Provincial and State Papers, vols. 14–17. Concord and Manchester, N.H., 1885–89.

Hammond, *Sullivan Papers.*　　Otis G. Hammond, ed. *Letters and Papers of Major-General John Sullivan, Continental Army.* 3 vols. Collections of the New Hampshire Historical Society, vols. 13–15. Hanover, N.H., 1930–39.

Hastings, *Clinton Papers.*　　Hugh Hastings and J. A. Holden, eds. *Public Papers of George Clinton. . . .* 10 vols. 1899–1914. Reprint. New York, 1973.

"Heath Papers."　　William Heath. "The Heath Papers." Parts 1–3. *Collections of the Massachusetts Historical Society,* 5th ser., 4:1–285; 7th ser., vols. 4 and 5. Boston, 1878–1905.

Hening.　　William Waller Hening, ed. *The Statutes at Large: Being a Collection of All the Laws of Virginia from the First Session of the Legislature in the Year 1619.* 13 vols. 1819–23. Reprint. Charlottesville, Va., 1969.

Hinman, *Historical Collection.*　　Royal R. Hinman, comp. *A Historical Collection, from Official Records, Files &c., of the Part Sustained by Connecticut, during the War of the Revolution.* Hartford, 1842.

"Inman's Narrative."　　"George Inman's Narrative of the American Revolution." *Pennsylvania Magazine of History and Biography,* 7 (1883), 237–48.

JCC.　　Worthington C. Ford et al., eds. *Journals of the Continental Congress.* 34 vols. Washington, D.C., 1904–37.

Jones, *Loyalists of New Jersey.*     Edward Alfred Jones. *The Loyalists of New Jersey: Their Memorials, Petitions, Claims, Etc. from English Records.* Collections of the New Jersey Historical Society, vol. 10. Newark, 1927.

"Journals of Henry Duncan."     Henry Duncan. "Journals of Henry Duncan, Captain, Royal Navy, 1776–1782." Ed. John Knox Laughton. *The Naval Miscellany,* vol. 1. *Publications of the Navy Records Society,* 20 (1902), 105–219.

*Kemble Papers.*     Stephen Kemble. *The Kemble Papers.* 2 vols. Collections of the New-York Historical Society, vols. 16–17. New York, 1884–85.

*Lafayette Papers.*     Stanley J. Idzerda et al., eds. *Lafayette in the Age of the American Revolution: Selected Letters and Papers, 1776–1790.* 5 vols. to date. Ithaca, N.Y., 1977–.

Laurens, *Army Correspondence.*     Laurens, John. *The Army Correspondence of Colonel John Laurens in the Years 1777–8. Now First Printed from Original Letters to His Father, Henry Laurens, President of Congress; with a Memoir by Wm. Gilmore Simms.* New York, 1867.

*Laurens Papers.*     Philip M. Hamer, George C. Rogers, Jr., David R. Chesnutt, et al., eds. *The Papers of Henry Laurens.* 16 vols. to date. Columbia, S.C., 1968–.

Ledger A.     Manuscript Ledger in George Washington Papers, Library of Congress.

Ledger B.     Manuscript Ledger in George Washington Papers, Library of Congress.

Ledger C.     Manuscript Ledger in Morristown National Historical Park, Morristown, N.J.

*Lee Papers.*     Charles Lee. *The Lee Papers.* 4 vols. Collections of the New-York Historical Society, vols. 4–7. New York, 1872–75.

Lesser, *Sinews of Independence.*     Charles H. Lesser, ed. *The Sinews of Independence: Monthly Strength Reports of the Continental Army.* Chicago, 1976.

Lydenberg, *Robertson Diaries.*     Harry Miller Lydenberg, ed. *Archibald Robertson, Lieutenant-General Royal Engineers: His Diaries and Sketches in America, 1762–1780.* New York, 1930.

Kidder, *History of the First New Hampshire Regiment.*     Frederic Kidder. *History of the First New Hampshire Regiment in the War of the Revolution.* Albany, 1868.

*Mackenzie Diary.*     *Diary of Frederick Mackenzie, Giving a Daily Narrative of His Military Service as an Officer of the Regiment of Royal Welch Fusiliers during the Years 1775–1781 in Massachusetts, Rhode Island and New York.* 2 vols. Cambridge, Mass., 1930.

*Maryland Convention Proceedings, December 1775.*     *Proceedings of the*

*Convention of the Province of Maryland, Held at the City of Annapolis, on Thursday the Seventh of December, 1775*. Annapolis, [1776].

*Maryland Convention Proceedings, June 1776*.    *Proceedings of the Convention of the Province of Maryland, Held at the City of Annapolis, on Friday the Twenty-first of June, 1776*. Annapolis, [1776].

*Maryland Convention Proceedings, August 1776*.    *Proceedings of the Convention of the Province of Maryland, Held at the City of Annapolis, on Wednesday the Fourteenth of August, 1776*. Annapolis, [1776].

*Mass. Resolves*, May 1777–April 1778.    *Resolves of the General Assembly of the State of Massachusetts-Bay, Begun and Held at Boston, in the County of Suffolk, on Wednesday the Twenty-eighth Day of May. . . .* [Boston, 1778].

Meng, *Despatches of Gérard*.    John J. Meng, ed. *Despatches and Instructions of Conrad Alexandre Gérard, 1778–1780*. Baltimore, 1939.

Miller, Lockey, and Visconti, *Highland Fortress*.    Charles E. Miller, Jr., Donald V. Lockey, and Joseph Visconti, Jr. *Highland Fortress: The Fortification of West Point during the American Revolution, 1775–1783*. [West Point, N.Y., 1988].

Moore, *Materials for History*.    Frank Moore, *Materials for History, Printed from Original Manuscripts*. New York, 1861.

*N.C. State Records*.    William L. Saunders, Walter Clark, and Stephen B. Weeks, eds. *The State Records of North Carolina*. 30 vols. Raleigh and various places, 1886–1914.

"Newport in the Hands of the British."    "Newport in the Hands of the British. A Diary of the Revolution." *Historical Magazine, and Notes and Queries Concerning the Antiquities, History and Biography of America*, 4 (1860), 1–4, 34–38, 69–72, 105–7, 134–37, 172–73.

*Pa. Archives*.    Samuel Hazard et al., eds. *Pennsylvania Archives*. 9th ser., 138 vols. Philadelphia and Harrisburg, 1852–1949.

*Pa. Col. Records*.    *Colonial Records of Pennsylvania*. 16 vols. Harrisburg, Pa., 1840–53.

*Pa. Laws, Nov. 1776–Mar. 1777*.    *Laws Enacted in a General Assembly of the Representatives of the Freemen of the Common-Wealth of Pennsylvania. Begun and Held at Philadelphia the Twenty-eighth Day of November, A.D. One Thousand Seven Hundred and Seventy-six, and Continued by Adjournments to the Twenty-first Day of March, A.D. One Thousand Seven Hundred and Seventy-seven*. Philadelphia, 1777.

*Papers, Colonial Series*.    W. W. Abbot et al., eds. *The Papers of George Washington, Colonial Series*. 10 vols. Charlottesville, Va., 1983–95.

*Papers, Confederation Series*.    W. W. Abbot et al., eds. *The Papers of George Washington, Confederation Series*. 6 vols. Charlottesville, Va., 1992–97.

*Papers, Presidential Series*.    W. W. Abbot et al., eds. *The Papers of George

*Washington, Presidential Series.* 12 vols. to date. Charlottesville, Va., 1987–.

*Papers, Retirement Series.*        W. W. Abbot et al., eds. *The Papers of George Washington, Retirement Series.* 4 vols. Charlottesville, Va., 1998–99.

*Papers of John Adams.*        Robert J. Taylor, Gregg L. Lint, et al., eds. *Papers of John Adams.* 13 vols. to date. Cambridge, Mass., and London, 1977–.

"Popp's Journal."        Joseph G. Rosengarten, ed. "Popp's Journal, 1777–1783." *Pennsylvania Magazine of History and Biography,* 26 (1902), 25–41, 245–54.

Prechtel, *Diary.*        Johann Ernst Prechtel. *A Hessian Officer's Diary of the American Revolution.* Trans. and ed. Bruce E. Burgoyne. Bowie, Md., 1994.

"Price Diary."        William S. Pattee. "Items from an Interleaved Boston Almanac for 1778, Being a Diary of Ezekiel Price." *New England Historical & Genealogical Register,* 19 (1865), 329–38.

Prince, *Livingston Papers.*        Carl E. Prince et al., eds. *The Papers of William Livingston.* 5 vols. New Brunswick, N.J., 1979–88.

Reed, *Joseph Reed.*        William Bradford Reed. *Life and Correspondence of Joseph Reed.* 2 vols. Philadelphia, 1847.

*Remembrancer.*        *The Remembrancer; or, Impartial Repository of Public Events.* 17 vols. London, 1775–84.

Ritchie, "New York Diary."        Carson I. A. Ritchie, ed. "A New York Diary of the Revolutionary War." *New-York Historical Society Quarterly,* 50 (1966), 221–80, 401–46.

Sabine, *Smith's Historical Memoirs, 1778–1783.* William H. W. Sabine, ed. *Historical Memoirs from 26 August 1778 to 12 November 1783 of William Smith, Historian of the Province of New York. . . .* New York, 1971.

*St. Clair Court Martial.*        *Proceedings of a General Court Martial, Held at White Plains, in the State of New-York, By Order of His Excellency General Washington, Commander in Chief of the Army of the United States of America, For the Trial of Major General St. Clair, August 25, 1778. Major General Lincoln, President.* Philadelphia, 1778.

*Sandwich Papers.*        G. R. Barnes and J. H. Owen, eds. *The Private Papers of John, Earl of Sandwich, First Lord of the Admiralty, 1771–1782.* 4 vols. Publications of the Navy Records Society, vols. 69, 71, 75, 78. London, 1932–38.

*Scudder Journal.*        William Scudder. *The Journal of William Scudder, an Officer in the Late New-York Line, Who was Taken Captive by the Indians at Fort Stanwix. . . .* [New York?], 1794.

Scull, *Montresor Journals.*        G. D. Scull, ed. *The Montresor Journals.* Collections of the New-York Historical Society, vol. 14. New York, 1882.

Shepherd, *Va. Statutes at Large.*        Samuel Shepherd, ed. *The Statutes at*

*Large of Virginia from October Session 1792, to December Session 1806, Inclusive.* 3 vols. Richmond, 1835.

Simcoe, *Operations of the Queen's Rangers.* John Graves Simcoe. *Simcoe's Military Journal. A History of the Operations of a Partisan Corps, Called the Queen's Rangers, Commanded by Lieut. Col. J. G. Simcoe, during the War of the American Revolution.* 1844. Reprint. New York, 1968.

Smallwood, *Trials.* *Proceedings of Several General Courts-Martial, Held, By order of Brigadier-general Smallwood on the Trials of Col. J. Carvil Hall, and Capt. Edward Norwood.* Annapolis, 1779.

Smith, *Letters of Delegates.* Paul H. Smith et al., eds. *Letters of Delegates to Congress, 1774–1789.* 26 vols. Washington, D.C., 1976–2000.

Stark, *Memoir of John Stark.* Caleb Stark. *Memoir and Offical Correspondence of Gen. John Stark, with Notices of Several Other Officers of the Revolution. . . .* 1860. Reprint. Boston, 1972.

Stevens, *Facsimiles.* Benjamin Franklin Stevens, ed. *B. F. Stevens's Facsimiles of Manuscripts in European Archives Relating to America, 1773–1783. With Descriptions, Editorial Notes, Collations, References and Translations.* 25 vols. London, 1889–98.

*Susquehanna Company Papers.* Julian P. Boyd and Robert J. Taylor, eds. *The Susquehanna Company Papers.* 11 vols. Ithaca, N.Y., and London, 1930–71.

Symmes, *Gilbert Diary.* Rebecca D. Symmes, ed. *A Citizen-Soldier in the American Revolution: The Diary of Benjamin Gilbert in Massachusetts and New York.* Cooperstown, N.Y., 1980.

Syrett, *Hamilton Papers.* Harold C. Syrett et al., eds. *The Papers of Alexander Hamilton.* 27 vols. New York, 1961–87.

Tallmadge, *Memoir.* Benjamin Tallmadge. *Memoir of Col. Benjamin Tallmadge, Prepared by Himself, at the Request of His Children.* 1858. Reprint. New York, 1968.

Van Rensselaer, *Annals of the Van Rensselaers.* Maunsell Van Rensselaer. *Annals of the Van Rensselaers in the United States, Especially as They Relate to the Family of Killian K. Van Rensselaer, Representative from Albany in the Seventh, Eighth, Ninth and Tenth Congresses.* Albany, 1888.

"Vaughan Journal." Virginia Steele Wood, ed. "The Journal of Private Zebulon Vaughan Revolutionary Soldier 1777–1780." *Daughters of the American Revolution Magazine,* 113 (1979), 101–14, 256–57, 320–31, 478–85, 487.

"Vernon Papers." "Papers of William Vernon and the Navy Board, 1776–1794." *Publications of the Rhode Island Historical Society,* 8 (Jan. 1901), 197–277.

*Va. House of Delegates Journal 1793.* *Journal of the House of Delegates of the Commonwealth of Virginia; Begun and Held at the Capitol, in the City of Richmond, on Monday, the Twenty-First Day of October, One Thousand Seven Hundred and Ninety-Three.* Richmond, 1793.

*Va. State Council Journals.* H. R. McIlwaine, Wilmer L. Hall, George H. Reese, and Sandra Gioia Treadway, eds. *Journals of the Council of the State of Virginia.* 5 vols. Richmond, 1931–82.

Vt., *Rolls of Soldiers.* John E. Goodrich, ed. *Rolls of the Soldiers in the Revolutionary War 1775 to 1783.* Rutland, Vt., 1904.

Ward, "Colonel Samuel Ward." John Ward. "Colonel Samuel Ward, of the Revolutionary War." *New York Genealogical and Biographical Record,* 6 ( July 1875), 113–23.

Whinyates, *Services of Francis Downman.* F. A. Whinyates, ed. *The Services of Lieut.-Colonel Francis Downman, R.A., in France, North America, and the West Indies, between the Years 1758 and 1784.* Woolwich, England, 1898.

"Wild Journal." "The Journal of Ebenezer Wild (1776–1781), who served as Corporal, Sergeant, Ensign, and Lieutenant of the American Army of the Revolution." *Proceedings of the Massachusetts Historical Society,* 2d ser., vol. 6 (1890–91), 79–160.

The Papers of George Washington
Revolutionary War Series
Volume 16
July–September 1778

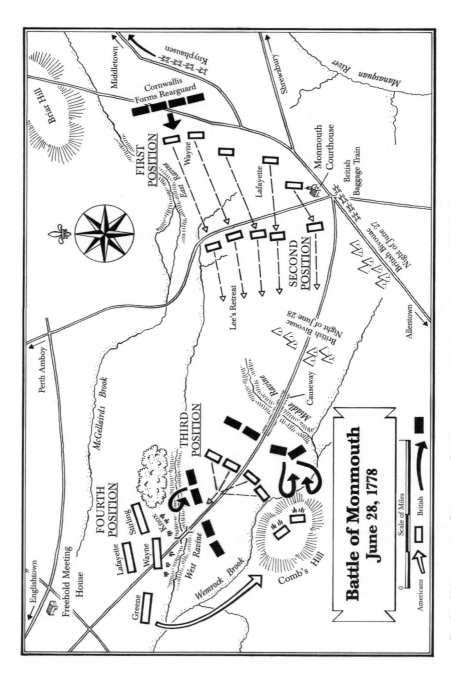

*Battle of Monmouth, 28 June 1778. (Illustrated by Rick Britton. Copyright Rick Britton 2005)*

# General Orders

Head Quarters Spotswood [N.J.] Wednesday July 1st 1778.
Parole                                                                     C. Signs

The General will beat at twelve ôClock, troop at half past twelve and the march begins at one; The Troops are in the mean time to take as much Sleep and Refreshment as possible that they may be the better prepared.

A General Court-Martial whereof Lord Stirling is appointed President will sit in Brunswick tomorrow (the hour and place to be appointed by the President) for the Trial of Major General Lee— Brigadier Generals Smallwood, Poor, Woodford & Huntington and Colonels Grayson, Johnson, Wigglesworth, Febiger, Swift, Angell, Clark and Williams are to attend as Members—All Evidences and Persons concerned are to attend.[1]

Varick transcript, DLC:GW.

1. The court-martial of Maj. Gen. Charles Lee arose out of his behavior at the Battle of Monmouth and his correspondence with GW in the aftermath of that battle. He was formally charged with "disobedience of orders, in not attacking the enemy on the 28th of June, agreeable to repeated instructions"; "misbehaviour before the enemy on the same day, by making an *unnecessary, disorderly*, and *shameful retreat*"; and "disrespect to the Commander-in-Chief, in two letters dated the 1st of July and the 28th of June" (*Lee Papers*, 3:2). For the proceedings of the court-martial, which concluded on 12 Aug. by finding Lee guilty on all three counts, see ibid., 3:1–208. Evidence gathered against Lee at this time includes a statement of 1 July by David Forman, which asserts that Lee "appeared irresolute and confused" while he missed several early opportunities to attack the British, that during the retreat Lee's "frequent and contradictory orders" led to "the greatest confusion amongst the Troops," and that "Genl Lee from the whole of his conduct appeared determined to avoid fighting" (DLC:GW). A letter of 2 July from an unknown correspondent to GW's aide-de-camp Richard Kidder Meade identifies witnesses to "prove that Genl Lee ordered the second line to retreat early in the day," to "testify to some disrespectful expressions both relative to the orders for attack and the consequences of it," and to "prove his countermanding his Excellencys orders for bringing up the second line . . . and snearing at the notion of the enemys *retreat* as mentioned in his Excellencys message" (DLC:GW).

# From Major John Jameson

Sir                                                    Middletown [N.J.] July 1st 1778

The Enemy left this place last night about ten OClock the Rear is now about three miles below this place on the Road leading to Sandy hook. I am Your Excellency's most Obt Servant

John Jameson

ALS, DLC:GW. A notation on the cover indicates that this letter was sent "𝄞 Dragoon."

## To Henry Laurens

Sir                                                    English Town [N.J.] 1st July 1778

I embrace this first moment of leisure, to give Congress a more full and particular account of the movements of the Army under my command, since its passing the Delaware, than the situation of our Affairs would heretofore permit.

I had the honor to advise them, that on the appearances of the enemy's intention to march thro' Jersey becoming serious, I had detached General Maxwells Brigade, in conjunction with the Militia of that State, to interrupt and impede their progress, by every obstruction in their power; so as to give time to the Army under my command to come up with them, and take advantage of any favorable circumstances that might present themselves.[1] The Army having proceeded to Coryell's ferry and crossed the Delaware at that place, I immediately detatched Colo. Morgan with a select Corps of 600 Men to reinforce General Maxwell, and marched with the main Body towards princetown.[2]

The slow advance of the Enemy had greatly the air of design, and led me, with others, to suspect that General Clinton desirous of a general Action was endeavouring to draw us down into the lower Country, in order by a rapid movement to gain our Right, and take possession of the strong Grounds above us. This consideration, and to give the troops time to repose and refresh themselves from the fatigues they had experienced from rainy and excessive hot Weather, determined me to halt at Hopewell Township, about five Miles from princetown, where we remained till the Morning of the 25th On the preceding day I made a second detatchment of 1500 chosen troops under Brigadier Genl Scott, to reinforce th⟨os⟩e already in the vicinity of the Enemy, the more effectually to annoy and delay their march.[3] The next day the Army moved to Kingston, and having received intelligence that the Enemy were prosecuting their Rout towards Monmouth Court House, I dispatched a thousand select men under Brigadier General Wayne, and sent the Marquis de la Fayette to take the command of the whole advanced Corps, including Maxwells Brigade and Morgans light Infantry; with orders to take the first fair opportunity of attacking the Enemy's Rear.[4] In the evening of the same day, the whole Army marched from Kingston where our Baggage was left, with intention to preserve a proper distance for supporting the advanced Corps, and arrived at Cranberry early the next morning. The intense heat of the Weather, and a heavy storm unluckily coming on made it impossible to resume our march that day without great inconvenience and injury to the troops. Our advanced Corps being differently circumstanced, moved from the position it had held the night before, and took post in the evening on the Monmouth Road, about five Miles from the Enemy's Rear, in expectation of attacking them next morning on their march. The main Body having remained at Cranberry, the advanced Corps was found to be too remote, and too far upon the Right to be supported either in case of an attack upon, or from the Enemy, which induced me to send orders to the Marquis to file off by his left towards English Town,[5] which he accordingly executed early in the Morning of the 27th.

The Enemy in marching from Allen Town had changed their disposition and placed their best troops in the Rear, consisting of all the Grenadiers, Light Infanty, and Chasseurs of the line. This alteration made it necessary to increase the number of our advanced Corps; in consequence of which I detatched Major General Lee with two Brigades to join the Marquis at English Town, on whom of course the command of the whole devolved, amounting to about five thousand Men.[6] The main Body marched the same day and encamped within three Miles of that place. Morgans Corps was left hovering on the Enemy's right flank, and the Jersey Militia, amounting at this time to about 7 or 800 Men under General Dickinson on their left.

The Enemy were now encamped in a strong position, with their right extending about a Mile and an half beyond the Court House, in the parting of the Roads leading to Shrewsbury and Middletown, and their left along the Road from Allen Town to Monmouth, about three miles on this side the Court House. Their Right flank lay on the skirt of a small wood, while their left was secured by a very thick one, a Morass running towards their Rear, and their whole front covered by a wood, and for a considerable extent towards the left with a Morass. In this situation they halted till the morning of the 28th.

Matters being thus situated, and having had the best information, that if the Enemy were once arrived at the Heights of Middletown, ten or twelve Miles from where they were, it would be impossible to attempt any thing against them with a prospect of success I determined to attack their Rear the moment they should get in motion from their present Ground. I communicated my intention to General Lee, and ordered him to make his disposition for the attack, and to keep his Troops constantly lying upon their Arms, to be in readiness at the shortest notice.[7] This was done with respect to the Troops under my immediate command.

About five in the Morning General Dickinson sent an Express, informing, that the Front of the Enemy had began their march. I instantly put the Army in motion, and sent orders by one of my Aids to General Lee to move on and attack them, unless there should be very powerful Reasons to the contrary; acquainting him at the same time, that I was marching to support him, and for doing it with the greater expedition and convenience, should make the Men disencumber themselves of their packs and Blankets.[8]

After marching about five Miles, to my great surprize and mortification, I met the whole advanced Corps retreating, and, as I was told, by General Lee's orders without having made any opposition, except one fire given by a party under the command of Colo. Butler, on their being charged by the Enemy's Cavalry, who were repulsed. I proceeded immediately to the Rear of the Corps, which I found closely pressed by the Enemy, and gave directions for forming part of the retreating troops, who by the brave and spirited conduct of the Officers, aided by some pieces of well served Artillery, checked the Enemy's advance, and gave time to make a disposition of the left Wing and second line of the Army upon an eminence, and in a wood a little in the Rear, covered by a morass in front. On this were placed some Batteries of Cannon by Lord Stirling, who commanded the left Wing, which played upon the Enemy with great effect, and seconded by parties of Infantry detached to oppose them, effectually put a stop to their advance.

General Lee being detached with the advanced Corps, the command of the Right Wing, for the occasion, was given to General Greene. For the expedition of the march, and to counteract any attempt to turn our Right, I had ordered him to file off by the new Church two Miles from English Town, and fall into the Monmouth Road, a small distance in the Rear of the Court House, while the rest of the Column moved directly on towards the Court House.[9] On intelligence of the Retreat, he marched up and took a very advantagious position on the Right.

The Enemy, by this time, finding themselves warmly opposed in front made an attempt to turn our left Flank; but they were bravely repulsed and driven back by detached parties of Infantry. They also made a movement to our Right, with as little success, General Greene having advanced a Body of Troops with Artillery to a commanding peice of Ground, which not only disappointed their design of turning our Right, but severely enfiladed those in front of the left Wing. In addition to this, General Wayne advanced with a Body of Troops and kept up so severe and well directed a fire that the Enemy were soon compelled to retire behind the defile, where the first stand in the beginning of the Action had been made.

In this situation, the Enemy had both their Flanks secured by thick Woods and Morasses, while their front could only be approached thro' a narrow pass. I resolved nevertheless to attack them, and for that purpose ordered General Poor with his own and the Carolina Brigade, to move round upon their Right, and General Woodford upon their left, and the Artillery to gall them in front:[10] But the impediments in their way prevented their getting within reach before it was dark. They remained upon the Ground, they had been directed to occupy, during the Night, with intention to begin the attack early the next morning, and the Army continued lying upon their Arms in the Feild of Action, to be in readiness to support them. In the mean time the Enemy were employed in removing their wounded, and about 12 OClock at Night marched away in such silence, that tho' General Poor lay extremely near them, they effected their Retreat without his Knowledge. They carried off all their wounded except four Officers and about Forty[11] privates whose wounds were too dangerous to permit their removal.

The extreme heat of the Weather—the fatigue of the Men from their march thro' a deep sandy Country almost entirely destitute of Water, and the distance the Enemy had gained by marching in the Night, made a pursuit impracticable and fruitless. It would have answered no valuable purpose, and would have been fatal to numbers of our Men, several of whom died the preceding day with Heat.

Were I to conclude my account of this days transactions without expressing my obligations to the Officers of the Army in general, I should do injustice to their merit, and violence to my own feelings. They seemed to vie with each other in manifesting their Zeal and Bravery. The Catalouge of those who distinguished themselves is too long to admit of particularizing individuals: I cannot however forbear mentioning Brigadier General Wayne whose good conduct and bravery thro' the whole action deserves particular commendation.

The Behaviour of the troops in general, after they recovered from the first surprize occasioned by the Retreat of the advanced Corps, was such as could not be surpassed.

All the Artillery both Officers and Men that were engaged, distinguished themselves in a remarkable manner.

Inclosed Congress will be pleased to receive a Return of our killed, wounded and missing. Among the first were Lieut. Colo. Bunner of Penna and Major Dickinson of Virginia both Officers of distinguished merit and much to be regretted.[12] The Enemy's slain left on the Feild and buried by us, according to the Return of the persons assigned to that duty were four Officers and Two hundred and forty five privates. In the former number was the Honble Colo. Monckton.[13] Exclusive of these they buried some themselves, as there were several new Graves near the feild of Battle. How many Men they may have had wounded cannot be determined; but from the usual proportion the number must have been considerable. There were a few prisoners taken.[14]

The peculiar Situation of General Lee at this time, requires that I should say nothing of his Conduct. He is now in arrest. The Charges against him, with such Sentence as the Court Martial may decree in his Case, shall be transmitted for the approbation or disapprobation of Congress as soon as it shall have passed.

Being fully convinced by the Gentlemen of this Country that the Enemy cannot be hurt or injured in their embarkation at Sandy Hook the place to which they are going, and unwilling to get too far removed from the North River, I put the Troops in motion early this morning and shall proceed that way, leaving the Jersey Brigade, Morgans Corps and other light parties (the Militia being all dismissed) to hover about them—countenance desertion and to prevent their depredations as far as possible. After they embark, the former will take post in the Neighbourhood of Elizabeth Town—The latter rejoin the Corps from which they were detatched. I have the Honor to be with the greatest Respect Sir Yr most obt Servt

Go: Washington

LS, in Tench Tilghman's writing, DNA:PCC, item 152; Df, DLC:GW; copy, NNebgGW; copy, DNA:PCC, item 169; Varick transcript, DLC:GW. This letter was read by Congress on 7 July (see *JCC*, 11:672). On 4 July, with Congress not in session, Laurens sent a copy of the letter to John Dunlap for publication; it was printed in an extra of Dunlap's *Pennsylvania Packet* (Philadelphia) on 6 July and subsequently appeared in other newspapers.

1. See GW to Brig. Gen. William Maxwell, 25 May. GW had advised Congress of the detachment in his first letter to Laurens of 28 May.

2. See General Orders, 22 June, and GW to Maj. Gen. Philemon Dickinson, that date.

3. See GW to Brig. Gen. Charles Scott, 24 June.

4. See GW to Maj. Gen. Lafayette, 25 June. For some of the intelligence, see Dickinson to GW, 25 June, and Maj. Gen. Steuben to GW, that date. The orders detaching Brig. Gen. Anthony Wayne's troops have not been identified.

5. See GW to Lafayette, 26 June (second letter).

6. See GW to Maj. Gen. Charles Lee, 26 June.

7. The specific nature of these orders, which GW gave to Lee at a meeting on the afternoon of 27 June, was the subject of testimony at Lee's court-martial (see *Lee Papers*, 3:2–6).

8. See Dickinson's first letter to GW of 28 June. For the testimony of GW's aide Richard Kidder Meade about the orders to Lee, see ibid., 3:6–8.

9. This order has not been identified.

10. At this place in the draft, Robert Hanson Harrison wrote a clause that is not in the LS: "The Troops advanced with great spirit to execute their orders."

11. Harrison wrote "fifty" on the draft.

12. The enclosed return, in Tench Tilghman's writing, reported 8 officers, 1 sergeant, and 60 men killed; 18 officers, 10 noncommissioned officers, 1 adjutant, and 132 men wounded; and 5 sergeants and 127 men missing, noting that "Many of the missing dropt thro' fatigue and have since come in" (DNA:PCC, item 152). Rudolph Bunner commenced service in January 1776 as a captain in the 2d Pennsylvania

Regiment, which was reorganized and redesignated the 3d Pennsylvania Regiment in 1777. He was promoted to major in June 1777 and to lieutenant colonel in August 1777.

13. Henry Monckton (1740–1778), a younger brother of Lt. Gen. Robert Monckton, was appointed an ensign in the 1st Regiment of Foot Guards in December 1760 and rose to become lieutenant colonel of the 45th Regiment of Foot in July 1771. In May 1776 he was appointed to command the 2d Battalion of Grenadiers.

14. The preceding sentence does not appear in Harrison's draft, which reads instead: "Nor can the amount of the prisoners taken be ascertained as they were sent off in small parties, as they were captured, and the returns not yet made." British general Henry Clinton reported his casualties in the 28 June battle as 65 killed, 59 dead of fatigue, 170 wounded, and 64 missing (Davies, *Documents of the American Revolution*, 13:320).

*Letter not found*: from Col. David Mason, 1 July 1778. On 1 July, Mason wrote GW: "I this Day by favr of Mr John Sewall Junr of Gloster wrote You." No other letter of that date from Mason to GW has been found.

## From Colonel David Mason

Sir                                           Wsburg [Va.] July 1st 1778
I this Day by favr of Mr John Sewall Junr of Gloster wrote You[1] & did not at that time Expect so favrable & Speedy an Opportunity of Sending on a Small Detachment of Men as now offers, Captain Tayler of [     ] Ship Sets Sail this Evening for the Head of Elk,[2] on Board the sd vessel Lt Thellaball of the 15th regt goes with Twenty six Men, Numbers of them the Blackest of Rascalls, Particularly John Bates—Wm Lyon & Alexander McGrigger all Deserters, Bates I woud have Tryed Here as Your Excellency had Hond me with a Commn for appointing of Genl Courts Martial[3]—but we coud not Collect Office[r]s Sufficient for his Tryal, I had the witness's which are John Balmer & ⟨Joshua⟩ Butler to Prove his Desertion & Seduction of them & others and Carrying with them Several Stand of arms & Accoutrements, Lyon is a deserter and has been with the Enemy & in service agt us, by his own Confessison, but whether it can be Proved if he denys it, I am not able to Acqt you, He is a Fellow of the Basest of Characters has Murdered a Man & almost another, but unfortunately for us, we cannot Prove it by any white Person, McGrigger Deserted from the Northwd & I think from Your Camp, Lieutt Thillaball has been Detained Here for Sometime Past in the Lower Parts of this State Near Norfolk for the Purpose of Apprehending of a Number of Deserters in that Quarter but without any Great Success, He has done Everything in his Power & is a very Active vigilant Officer, his Expences has Greatly Exceeded his Wages & I shoud hope woud in Some Measure be Reimbursed as he is of Slen-

der Circumstances[4] I am to Acqt Your Excellency that I shall continue Here a Few Days, to Collect all the Men I Possably can as I Expect several Brot to me this week & shall b[y][5] some Speedy & Safe Conveyance Forwd them to Head Quarters—And as You Have been plased to Signifie Your Pleasure of my Resigning on Account of the Situation of my Family,[6] I do with the Great Candour Assure your Excellency it is with the Utmost Reluctance that I am Constrained to do it & so Accept of your Promise, and shall take the Liberty so soon as I can Adjust a few Matters Here to Inclose your Excellency my Commission & Hope it will be received. I Most Sincerely congratulate You on the Repossession of the City of Philadelphia & the Glorious Prospect we have of Success in our Present Contest, with wishing Every Happiness that Life can Afford & a Safe Return to your Friends & Country I Remain Sir Your Excellencys Mo[s]t Obedt Humble Servt

David Mason Colo. 15th regt

ALS, DLC:GW.

1. Mason's previous letter of this date has not been found. John Seawell, Jr. (1760–1806), was later a justice of the peace in Gloucester County, Virginia.

2. Mason may have been referring to Capt. Richard Taylor (c.1748–1825) of the Virginia navy, who at this time commanded the *Tartar*. Taylor, of Caroline County, was commissioned in March 1776 and commanded the cruiser *Liberty* and the schooner *Hornet* before the *Tartar*. He served to the close of the war. In 1794 Taylor moved to Kentucky.

3. GW had sent the commission with his letter to Mason of 16 April.

4. Robert Thelaball of Norfolk County was commissioned an ensign of the 15th Virginia Regiment in February 1777 and promoted to 2d lieutenant in March of that year. In September 1778, Thelaball was ordered to rejoin his regiment, and he apparently resigned about that time.

5. Mason wrote "be."

6. Mason was alluding to GW's letter to him of 19 May.

## From Brigadier General William Maxwell

Sir                          English Town [N.J.] 1st July 1778 ½ after 7 oclock

I have the pleasure to Inform your Excellency that the Letter which accompanys this was delivered a little way below this place a few minutes ago, by a Capt. Murray one of General Clintons Ade D. Camps,[1] I was surprised that he was not stoped sooner but the Militia did not know Your Excellencys former Orders I suppose and I suppose they purposely eluded Coll Morgan. He delivered General Clintons Compliments to the Generals of our Armey and to the officers in General for their polite behaviour to the Prisoners that fell into our hands. I am sorry they got up so far without being stop'd.

I leave a guard here and set off to morrow Morning between 2 and 3 oclock⟨.⟩ I am Your Excellencys Most obedient Humble Servant.

Wm Maxwell

N.B. A number of Applications is made to me by the distressed Inhabitants for leave to go in to the Enemy to endeavour to get their Horses or cattle, but thir horses in particular. I cannot give them leave without your Excellencys approbation. I hope you will favour me with an answer to morrow respecting it.

This is all the Horse man I have which is one of the 9 months men.[2]

ALS, DLC:GW.

1. Thomas Murray was probably carrying Gen. Henry Clinton's letter to GW of this date, which reads: "I had the honour of receiving Your Excellency's dispatch of the 20th of last Month Yesterday afternoon, with the several inclosures therein. that address'd to their Excellencies the King's Commissioners I shall forward by the earliest opportunity" (P.R.O., 30/55, Carleton Papers). Murray (c.1749–1816) served as a junior officer of the 55th Regiment of Foot from 1765 until he was promoted to captain of the 48th Regiment of Foot in October 1773. Clinton's general orders of 20 June 1778 had directed that he be obeyed as an aide-de-camp (*Kemble Papers*, 1:596). Murray, who transferred to the 16th Regiment of Foot in February 1780, became major of the 84th Regiment of Foot in February 1781 and was placed on the half-pay establishment when that regiment was disbanded in 1783. While on half pay, Murray was promoted within the army line to lieutenant colonel in 1790, colonel in 1795, and major general in 1798. He was appointed colonel of the 7th Royal Garrison Battalion in December 1802.

2. This sentence was written on the back of the page containing the other text. An address to GW was also on that side of the page.

## To Lieutenant Colonel Holt Richeson

Sir                                                  [Spotswood, N.J., 1 July 1778]

Having received information that the State of Virginia has determined to fill up her Regiments by Recruits,[1] I desire that you will immediately proceed thither with such Officers of the 3d 7th 11th and 15th Virginia Regiments as can be spared, to superintend the recruiting Service. Upon your arrival at Williamsburg, you are to apply to his Excellency the Governor for your instructions by which you will be informed whether and upon what terms you are to enlist the Men. You are to abide strictly by those instructions, both as to time of enlistment and the Bounty to be given. You are to consider the Officers of the above Regiments under your direction, and you are to appoint them to such Counties as they may be best acquainted with, and have the most influence in. You are to furnish me from time to time with an account of your success and you will forward the Recruits to Camp under the Care of Officers as fast as they are raised. Given at Spotswood New Jersey the 1st day of July 1778.

Go: Washington

DfS, in Tench Tilghman's writing, DLC:GW; Varick transcript, DLC:GW. The docket of the draft indicates that the same instructions were given to Maj. Ralph Faulkner of the 2d Virginia Regiment. Similar instructions for recruiting the 1st, 5th, and 9th Virginia Regiments had been given to Lt. Col. Robert Ballard on 18 June.

1. See John Parke Custis to GW, 29 May, and notes.

## General Orders

Head-Quarters Brunswick [N.J.] Thursday July 2nd 1778.
Parole                                                    C. Signs

The Army is to remain on it's ground tomorrow—The commanding Officers of Regiments under the direction of their Brigadiers are to avail themselves of this Opportunity for collecting all their Straglers— The baggage is to be got up and the Waggons arranged in their proper order.

The men are to wash and cleanse themselves, they are to be conducted to bathe in squads by non commissioned Officers who are to prevent their bathing in the heat of the day, or remaining too long a time in the water.

Officers are to exert themselves in restraining their men from stragling, injuring Fences, Fruit Trees &c. They are to have the orders of the 30th ultimo relative to marauding read to the men and use every means to guard against this infamous Practice.

Baron Steuben will have a pro tempore command of Woodford's, Scotts and the North Carolina Brigades.

The General Court Martial ordered to sit this day for the trial of Major General Lee will sit tomorrow eight ôClock at the house of Mrs Voorkees in the Town of New-Brunswick[1]—Members the same as yesterday except Coll Shepard, *vice* Coll Johnson.

The Brigadiers and Officers Commanding Brigades will order General Courts Martial to sit in their several Brigades for the trial of their own Prisoners.

Such Officers as are under Arrests may be tried by said Courts Martial if they choose.

Two orderly Serjeants from each Brigade to attend the Grand Parade at Guard mounting which will be on the road near the Orderly-Office leading to Head-Quarters.

The troop to beat at six ôClock & the guards to be on the Parade precisely at seven.

Two Light Dragoons are to attend Lord Stirling whilst President of the General Court Martial.

The Deputy Commissary of Cloathing has a few shirts by him— Commanding Officers of Regiments will apply for such of their men as are intirely destitute; he has also shoes in store, a few Over-halls, Breeches Vests and Blankets which may be drawn this afternoon or tomorrow.

Varick transcript, DLC:GW.

1. In the 1770s the widow Voorhees (or Van Voorhees) kept the tavern commonly known as Whitehall on Albany Street in New Brunswick, New Jersey.

## From John Beatty

Sir,                                        Princeton [N.J.] July 2d 1778

Inclosed you have a List of the Prisoners capturd during the Enemys march thro this state & now lodged in the goal at Trenton [1]—whether any yet remains in the Provost, I cannot ascertain, having receiv'd no returns from the Provost marshall.

Nine of these call themselves Deserters, but as no proof appears, that they intentionally fell into our Hands, shall detain them as Prisoners of War. They are all hearty, Hale Fellows, should be glad to know whether I shall include them in the Exchange now about to take place.

Capt. Nesbitt on Parole in this town is very desirous of going to Philada, where he says he has a number of Friends [2]—I told him, I could not comply with his request, Untill Your Excelly was made aquainted with it. I am Sir your most Obedient & very Humb. Servt

Jno. Beatty
Com: gen. of Prisoners

ALS, DLC:GW.

1. The enclosed return by Deputy Commissary of Prisoners George Tudor, dated 2 July, listed forty-six prisoners at Princeton, twenty-seven prisoners at Trenton, and one man "on Parole at Duyckins Mills on the North Branch of Raritan." Beatty's note on the document added, "I am rather Inclined to believe, there are none in the Provo. as these were march'd up last Tuesday, Except 27—part of whom were those taken by Coll Morgan—which arrived here Sunday Evening" (DLC:GW).

2. Beatty was apparently referring to Lt. Albert Nesbit of the 17th Regiment of Foot, who had been captured on 27 June (see "Inman's Narrative," 243). Tudor's return lists Captain Nesbit as belonging to that regiment. Nesbit was exchanged on 16 March 1780 ("Exchange of Prisoners Settled with Col: Beatty 9 Septr 1779 at Elizabeth Town," DNA: RG 93, Revolutionary War Rolls, 1775–1783).

## From William Gordon

My dear Sir                                        Boston July 2. 1778

I just catch a few minutes before the post goes off to acquaint you that Lord Chatham is dead—that no troops whatsoever are coming either from G.B. or Ireland—that tho' an English fleet of 1–90 guns 9–74 & 1–64 may be sailed from St Helens, a powerful provision has been made for counteracting them when they are upon the American coast; their opposers may possibly be at the Rendezvous before them. A vessel arrived from France yesterday.[1] My prayers are daily offered for your Excellency's success; & tho' you have not met with so early or so full a support as you had a right to expect, I hope Clinton's army will by your military skill be speedily rendered as harmless as Burgoynes. With great esteem I remain your Excellency's sincere friend & very humble servant

William Gordon

ALS, DLC:GW.

1. The news of a British fleet "in the Road of St. Helens, near Portsmouth," England, was contained in a letter of 18 May from the American commissioners in Paris, which was published in Boston newspapers of this date. The letter was apparently brought by Capt. Joseph Chapman, who left Nantes, France, in late May. Chapman also brought news that Lord Chatham had died, that "No reinforcements have been sent, nor are to be sent to the armies at Philadelphia or New York," and "that a Fleet of 21 Sail of Men of War, sailed from Nantz on the 13th April, for America" (see *Independent Chronicle. And the Universal Advertiser*, 2 July, and *Continental Journal, and Weekly Advertiser*, 2 and 9 July; see also *Boston-Gazette, and Country Journal*, 6 July).

## From Colonel Daniel Morgan

Sir                    Middletown [N.J.] 2d [July][1] 78 9 oclock

I came to this place early Yestorday Morning—the enemy had left it the night before—thair main body is encampd about three miles from the *Town* thair rear within a mile, we are in full vew of each other—I am and have been, ever since I come out, at a great Loss for light horse, having *none onaxt* [annexed] to me—Genl scott sent me a serjant and six, whose horses ware tierd and was Rather an encumbarance, as thay could scarcely Raise a gallop Major *Jameson* was here yesterday I applied to him for a few, he sent Capt. *Harison*—who staid with me about two hours, when Colo. *Moylan* sent for ⟨him⟩ and his party—Moyl⟨an⟩ certainly has reasons for so doing but sir you know that cavalry is the Eyes of the infantry—and without any, my situation must not be very pleasing being, in full Vew of the enemys whole army.[2]

my advance engaged thair rear yesterday thay reinforced and sent a colume on each flank we retreated to a hill this end of the town—thay retreated to thair own ground, a few ware killd—I had one slightly wounded—but had no horse till coronet Dorsy luckily come up.[3] I am with esteem your most obedient and Hble servt

Danl Morgan

ALS, DLC:GW.

1. Morgan wrote "June," but the letter was docketed "2 July," and the troop positions date the letter in July. GW's aide-de-camp John Laurens reported Morgan's intelligence in a letter of this date to his father, Henry Laurens (Laurens, *Army Correspondence*, 201).

2. GW's aide Richard Kidder Meade replied to this letter on 3 July, informing Morgan: "His Excellency received your favor dated yesterday, & desires me to request that you will join this army immediately on your finding that you can no longer do them (the Enemy) injury. Should they be on the Hook, it is taken for granted that there is no annoying them, in which case you will march this way. You will be pleased to desire Colo. Gist to conduct himself in the same manner" (NN: Myers Collection).

3. Larkin Dorsey (1744–1822), formerly a cadet in Col. William Smallwood's Maryland Regiment and a second lieutenant in the Baltimore Artillery Company, became a cornet in the 4th Continental Dragoons in January 1777. He resigned in September 1778.

## From Colonel Stephen Moylan

Sir                         [Bound Brook, N.J.] Thursday 2d July 1778
the inclosed note, reachd me this morning as it is not wrote by any of your Excellencys familly, and So very Contradictory to the orders I received yesterday, I realy have my doubts whether it ought to be obeyd or not,[1] I have Sent orders to the different parties that are now out to come in this evening, they ought to have at least a fortnights rest, before they begin to march and if your Excellency woud approve of it I woud reccommend Shrewsbury, and its environs for that purpose, it is inhabited by the disaffected who as I am informd have large quantitys of grain and the pasture there, is exceeding fine[2] the enemy are now four miles from Midletown I expect they will be embarkd to morrow or next day, Morgans & Gists men, with the parties of Horse, have Saved a fine Country from being pilaged, I shall wait your further orders by the bearer, and am allways Sir your most ob. & most H. St

                                              Stephen Moylan

ALS, DLC:GW. The cover, which indicates that the letter was carried "by a Dragoon," is docketed in part, "Ansd 3d"; the reply has not been found.

1. The enclosure, a letter from Dragoon Lt. Zebulon Pike written from Englishtown, N.J., on 1 July, informed Moylan that "it is his Excellenceys Pleasure the horse Should all follow the Main body of the Army Which marcht from this this morning for which Purpose he desires You to Collect them this day and march them tomorrow Morning take the Same Rout the body of the Army doth" (DLC:GW). The earlier orders to Moylan have not been identified.

2. On 5 July, Commissary General of Forage Clement Biddle wrote to Moylan from GW's camp at Brunswick, N.J., "If the cavalry should halt to refresh themselves I am of opinion they can be best furnished with hay and pasture on the plain below the Mountain from Middlebrook to the Scotch Plains" (Griffin, *Stephen Moylan*, 77–78).

# From Major General Stirling

Sir                                              July 2d 1778 at Guests [Brunswick, N.J.] [1]
   The enclosed I recived yesterday evening and took the liberty of opening them least they might require some immediate arrangement.[2] the Rear of the Army is up, in much better order than I could have expected. I am this moment going to the Court Martial after a little retardment as your Excellency will see by the enclosed Note & Answer.[3] I have sent Col: Bur to Elizabeth Town to make some enquiries.[4] I am your Excellency's Most Obt Humble Servt

Stirling,

ALS, DLC:GW.
   1. Stirling may have been staying at the house of New Brunswick tanner Henry Guest (c.1727–1815), then at the corner of Livingston Avenue and New Street.
   2. These enclosures have not been identified.
   3. Stirling enclosed a letter of this date from Maj. Gen. Charles Lee and his reply (both DLC:GW). Lee expressed "confidence" in Stirling's "integrity and honour" but added: "as I have been told that You had the imprudence (for if it is a fact, certainly was an imprudence) already to give an opinion—I think it more eligible for many reasons that Monsr de Calb shoud be President instead of yourself." Stirling replied: "It Certainly is not a fact, that I have Given an Opinion on any thing that you stand Charged with; It was Indeed impossible I should; for to this moment I know not the Charge upon which you are to be tryed. After this declaration if you have any Objection, I willingly shall decline an Office the most disagreable I could in the Course of my duty have met with."
   4. On 4 July, Stirling received a report from Lt. Col. Aaron Burr and acknowledged it in the following words: "On showing it to General Washington, he approves of the progress of your inquiries, and desires they may be continued. But he particularly desires me to *send off this express to you*, to request that you will endeavour to get all the intelligence you possibly can from the city of New-York: What are the preparations of shipping for embarcation of foot or horse?—what expeditions on hand?—whether up the North river, Connecticut, or West Indies? For this purpose you may send one, two, or three trusty persons over to the city, to get the reports, the newspapers, and the truth, if they can" (Davis, *Memoirs of Aaron Burr*, 1:129). On 6 July, Stirling wrote Burr again, acknowledging another report and requesting that Burr "direct your letters with such intelligence as you may procure, to his Excellency General Washington who will be on the line of march with the Army." In a postscript, he continued: "Genl Washington desires me to Add that he wishes you would employ three four or more persons to go to Bergen heights Weeahacks, Hosbouck or any of the heights there about Convenient to observe the motions of the Enemy's Shipping and to give him the Earliest intelligence thereof; wether up the River particularly; in short every thing possible that Can be Obtained" (MWA: Burr Papers). Burr continued on this assignment until at least 8 July, when GW's aide-de-camp Tench Tilghman wrote to him: "His excellency desires me to inquire whether you have received any information of the enemy's movements, situation, or design? He will leave this place about 4 o'clock this afternoon, before which he will expect to hear from you" (Davis, *Memoirs of Aaron Burr*, 1:130).

# General Orders

Head Quarters Brunswick Landing [N.J.] July 3rd 1778.
Parole                                    C. Signs

Coll Craige and Majors Nichols and Vaughan are appointed to superinte[n]d the Hospitals in Pennsylvania—They will call at the Orderly-Office tomorrow morning for Instructions.

Vaults for Necessaries are to be immediately sunk, the Offal at the slaughtering pens to be buried and the dead horses removed or buried.

### After Orders.

Tomorrow, the Anniversary of the Declaration of Independence, will be celebrated by the firing thirteen Pieces of Cannon and a *feu de joie* of the whole line; The Army will be formed on the Brunswick side of the Rariton at five ôClock in the afternoon on the ground pointed out by the Quarter Master General—The Soldiers are to adorn their Hats with *Green-Boughs* and to make the best appearance possible—The disposition will be given in the orders of tomorrow—Double allowance of rum will be served out.

The General Court Martial whereof Major General Lord-Stirling is President will assemble tomorrow morning at the time and place mentioned in yesterdays Orders—Members the same as heretofore, except Colonel Irvin, vice, Coll Grayson.[1]

Varick transcript, DLC:GW.

1. In an orderly book of Brig. Gen. Jedediah Huntington's brigade, the orders continue: "The Post office is kept at Brunswick at the house of Mrs Graham in Albany Street a few days [doors] above white Hall. The Post will set out on Monday Morning early" (NHi). Lt. Col. Aaron Burr's orderly book replaces the last sentence of that text with "A Southern Post will set out on Sunday Morning Early" (NHi).

# To Colonel Theodorick Bland

Dear Sir                    Head Quarters Brunswic [N.J.] 3d July 1778

I have been favd with your two letters of the 5th ulto. As it was not possible for Capt. Medici to procure Horses at the prices to which he had been at first limited, I think you did right in advising him to purchase upon the best terms he could, without limitation: but I do not think that you should advance him any money. He will, with more propri⟨ety draw it⟩ from the State to which he belongs. ⟨There are⟩ some Horse Accoutrements arrived fro⟨m Fra⟩nce at Portsmouth New England, but how many, or what kind, I do not know. I would therefore have you still procure all you can in Virginia. I have ordered the above accoutrements to m⟨eet⟩ me at the North River,[1] and therefore I desire that you may send forward the Men and Horses as fast as the first are cloathed and the last fit for service, and I will accoutre them th⟨ere.⟩

⟨Lieut.⟩ Lewis is certainly intitled to a Captaincy ⟨from the da⟩te of Major Lee's promotion, but what reason Capt. Jones has to complain, I cannot conceive, unless it be, that Congress, on account of the extraordinary merit of Capt. Lee and the officers who served under him last Campaign, have promoted them in a separate Corps.[2] Had Capt. Lee been promoted in the Regiment, Capt. Jones would then have had reason to think himself injured.

It was the pleasure of Congress that Capt. Lee's former troop should make part of his presen⟨t⟩ Corps, and therefore I can say nothing about it, further than that in the inlistment of Men for your Regiment, you must make provision for that deficiency.

I should have been exce⟨edingly happy⟩ had the settlement of the Rank of th⟨e officers of Ho⟩rse been agreeable to all parties. You m⟨ust be⟩ sensible that it is not in my power to do more than I have done, or to alter the determination of the Board of Officers to whom it was left.[3]

You are mistaken as to ⟨the⟩ Colonels of the other Regiments of Cavalry having filled up the vacancies in their Regiments: They have only taken an account of such Gentlemen as are willing and qualified to serve, and I sh⟨all be g⟩lad that you would do the same.

I have just recd yours ⟨of the 1⟩4th ulto with the Returns inclosed and am Dear Sir Your most obt Servt

                                                          Go: Washington

LS, in Tench Tilghman's writing, in private hands; Df, DLC:GW; Varick transcript, DLC:GW. Where the LS is mutilated, the text in angle brackets has been taken from the draft.

1. See GW to William Heath, this date.
2. For Congress's resolution of 7 April promoting Henry Lee to major, see *JCC*, 10:314–15.
3. For the determination of cavalry ranks by a board of general officers ordered in November 1777, see John Sullivan to GW, 24 Nov. 1777, n.1. On receipt of this letter, Bland wrote Henry Laurens to lay his claim to a higher rank before Congress (Bland to Laurens, 18 July, DNA:PCC, item 78).

## To Major General Horatio Gates

Sir                          Brunswick [N.J.] 3d July 1778. [      ] OClock

My last to you was upon the 29th June. I have the pleasure to inform you, that the loss of the Enemy, in the action of the 28th, was more considerable than we at first apprehended. By the Returns of the officers who had charge of the burying parties, it appears, that they left 245 non commd and privates on the Feild, and 4 Officers, one of whom was the

Honble Col: Monkton of the Grenadiers. Our loss was 7 officers and 52 Rank and File killed and 17 officers and 120 R. & f. wounded. Among the former were Lt Colonel Bunner of pennsylvania and Major Dickinson of Virginia, the only Officers of Rank. There were several fresh Graves and burying holes found near the feild, in which, the Enemy put their dead before they quitted it. These were exclusive of the 245 before mentioned. We have made upwards of one hundred prisoners, including forty privates and four officers left wounded at Monmouth Court House. The number of their wounded we can only guess at, as they were employed in carrying them off during the action, and untill midnight, when they stole off, silent as the grave.[1] Finding that the Enemy had, during the Action, pushed their Baggage to Middle town, and that they, by marching off in the Night after the engagement, would gain that place before there was any possibility of overtaking their Rear, I determined to give over the pursuit. From the information of General Forman, and several Gentlemen well acquainted with the Country, I found it would be impossible to annoy them in their embarkation, as the neck of land, upon which they now are, is defended by a narrow passage, which, being possessed by a few men, would effectually oppose our whole force. Besides this consideration, I thought it highly expedient to turn towards the North River. I marched from the English town the 30th last month, and arrived here yesterday with the whole Army, except Maxwells Brigade and Morgans Corps, who are left upon the Rear of the Enemy to prevent their making depredations, and to encourage desertion, which still prevails to a considerable degree.

The march from English Town was inconceivably distressing to the Troops and Horses, the distance is about twenty Miles thro' a deep sand, without a drop of Water, except at south River, which is half way. This, added to the intense heat, killed a few and knocked up many of our Men, and killed a number of our Horses.[2] To recruit the former upon the airy open Grounds near this place, and to give the Qr Mr General an opportunity of providing the latter, will occasion a short halt, but you may depend that we will be with you as soon as possible.

My present intention is to cross the North River at King's ferry, but should you be of opinion, that it will be in the power of the Enemy to hinder our passage, be pleased to inform me, as it would be loosing much time to be obliged to turn up from thence and march thro' the Clove. The Rout by King's Ferry is so much the shortest and best, that if the passage could be kept open by throwing up Works and mounting some Cannon upon them, I think it would be worth while having it done. But this I leave to your determination. I am Sir Your most obt and hble Servt

Go: Washington

LS, in Tench Tilghman's writing, NHi: Gates Papers; Df, DLC:GW; Varick transcript, DLC:GW. A "Copy of Letter Genl Washington to Gen. Gates," dated "Camp Wite Plains July 6th 1778," exists as a manuscript in M-Ar: Revolution Letters, 1778, and variants were published in contemporary newspapers, such as the *Continental Journal, and Weekly Advertiser* (Boston), 16 July. That document was apparently derived from this letter, although it is not a verbatim copy. As Gates was at White Plains on 6 July and GW was not, the dateline evidently refers to the date of copying and not to the date of the letter.

1. On the draft, which is in Tilghman's writing, the preceding two sentences were added in the left margin, and the second is in GW's writing.

2. Lt. Thomas Blake of the 1st New Hampshire Regiment recorded the effects of the weather in his journal for 1 July: "the weather being so excessively hot (the road being for the most part through Pitch pine plain) . . . near one-third of the men were so overcome that they were obliged to stop; many were not able to march until the cool of the evening, and some so overcome they were obliged to be conveyed in waggons" (Kidder, *History of the First New Hampshire Regiment*, 43).

## To Major General William Heath

Head Quarters, near Brunswick [N.J.]

Dear Sir                                    3d [July] 1778.

I received your favor of the 22d Ultimo by the hands of Captain Horton.

It is a melancholly consideration that in the execution of our duty an officer of the convention should suffer so unfortunate a fate.[1] However your conduct in the affair will meet general approbation.

I have attended to Ensign Ponds memorial and accept of his resignation.

In my last of the 24 Ulto I gave you the course of the enemy—we came up with them near Monmouth Court house, when an action ensued—The several contentions during the day were sharp and severe. We remained in full possession of the ground—of 245 dead, and several wounded which they had not time to carry off—Our loss in rank & file is 60 killed and near 130 wounded.[2] About midnight they decamped, retreating in great silence and rapidity, and gained a position which made any further pursuit impracticable.[3]

In one of your late letters you mention the arrival of a vessel with military stores, among which are horse accoutrements[4]—I desire that the latter may be sent forward to the North River with all possible dispatch. I am, Sir, your most obedient and very hble servt

Go: Washington

LS, in James McHenry's writing, MHi: Heath Papers; Df, DLC:GW; Varick transcript, DLC:GW. Although the LS is dated 3 June, the draft and Varick transcript are dated 3 July, and the content of the letter suggests it must have been written in July. GW signed the cover of the LS. Heath wrote GW that he received this letter on 12 August.

1. GW was referring to the shooting of Lt. Richard Brown by an American sentry.

2. The draft reports "52 killed and 120 wounded," which are the numbers given in GW's letter to Maj. Gen. Horatio Gates of this date. The larger number reported in the LS includes artillery casualties.

3. At this point on the draft, McHenry wrote but crossed out a sentence: "Consequences truely valuable and important will attend the advantage gained in this instance over the flower of the British army."

4. See Heath to GW, 9 June.

## To Major General Lafayette

Dear Marquis,               Head Quarters Brunswick [N.J.] July 3d 1778

I have received your letter on the subject of the corps raising by Col: Armand.[1]

You are sensible that it rests solely with Congress to determine the existence of a new corps and decide in an affair of this nature, If they should think proper to give their sanction to Col. Armand in the business he is engaged in, and in which by your representation he has made so considerable a progress, I assure you, it will be intirely agreeable to me, not only because I should be glad to see Col. Armand himself provided for; but because the corps he is raising may furnish means of employment to a number of the foreign officers who are hitherto unemployed. I am My Dear Marquis Yr Most Obedt serv.

Df, in Alexander Hamilton's writing, DLC:GW; Varick transcript, DLC:GW.

1. Lafayette had written GW on 2 July: "I have Receiv'd one other letter from Clel Armand where he Aquaints me of his arrival at Congress, and where he says that his Corps amounts alréady to about two hundred men provided it may be accepted by Congress and the expense of raising it approuv'd by them—the Clel adds that a letter from you on the subject will much advance the expedition of his affair, as the gentlemen in Congress will certainly know if the matter is agreable to your excellency—for my part besides the esteem I have for that gentleman's Caracter, and affection I entertain for his person, I believe the Corps may prouve very useful to the Service first by its own exertions and merit, Secondly by giving Room to many stranger officers who Can not be employ'd in the line of the Several States" (PEL).

*Letter not found*: to Col. Stephen Moylan, 3 July 1778. The docket on Moylan's letter to GW of 2 July reads in part, "Ansd 3d."

## General Orders

Head-Quarters Brunswick [N.J.] Saturday July 4th 1778.

Parole                                                    C. Signs

At three ôClock this afternoon a Cannon will fire at the Park as a signal for the troops to be put under Arms and formed ready to march—At four another signal Cannon for the Right to march by the Right over the Bridge to the Ground which shall be shewn them to form on—At half past four a third signal Cannon for the Left Wing to march by the Right and follow the Right Wing—At five a fourth Signal for the second Line to form on the ground which shall be shewn them— After the Army is formed upon a signal by order of the Commander in Chief, thirteen Pieces of Cannon will be discharged, after which a single Cannon which will be a signal for a runing fire to begin on the right of the Army and be continued to the left with Musquetry and Cannon. At the Conclusion of which, on a signal three Cheers will be given, "Perputual and undisturbed Independence to the United States of America."[1]

Previous to forming the Army the commanding Officers of Corps will see that their men draw their charges and that such as cannot be drawn be discharged under the Eye and direction of proper Officers.

As blank Catridges are not to be procured the officers will be careful that their men charge their pieces with their worst Catridges after having taken the balls out of them, and that the Balls thus taken out be delivered to the Regimental Quartr Masters, who are to deliver them to the Quarter Masters of Brigade and they to the Commissary of Military stores—A March beat on the left will be a signal for the troops to retire by the left to their respective Encampments.

The Commander in Chief presents his Compliments to the General Officers and Officers commanding Brigades, The Commissary, Muster Master and Judge Advocate Generals with the Surgeon General of the Hospital & desires the pleasure of their Company to dine with him at three ôClock this afternoon.

The Left Wing of the Army is to march precisely at half after three ôClock tomorrow morning by the Left—The Quarter Master General will give the Route, Encampments and halting days.

The baggage and stores belonging to this Wing are to follow in their proper order.

No Member of the General Court-Martial now sitting at the request of Major General Lee is to march with the above division, and if there are any Evidences in the said Division for or against him they are to remain and attend the Court. Their Names to be given in to the Judge Advocate.

Varick transcript, DLC:GW.

1. In his diary for this date, Pvt. Elijah Fisher recorded a brief description of this celebration and added that "At Night his Exelency and the gentlemen and Ladys had a Bawl at Head Quarters with grate Pompe" (Godfrey, *Commander-in-Chief's Guard*, 280).

## From Major David Salisbury Franks

Philadelphia 4th July 1778

General Arnold being very unwell has ordered me to Answer your Excellency's Letter of 30th June. he will give every Assistance in his Power to General Portail.

Col. Hartly's Regiment came here three days since and is detained agreable to your Excellency's Order. Congress having given no directions for any other disposition.

The General's wound continues in a fair Way, but he has been afflicted for some days with a violent Oppression in ⟨the⟩ Stomach, he is however much better this Morning & hopes soon to be well.

| | |
|---|---|
| The Number of British deserters | 136 |
| The Number of Foreigners | 440 |
| | 576 |

This Account is taken from the Town Majors Return.[1] I have the Honor to be with the greatest Respect Your Excellencys most obedient, most humble Servant

Davd S. Franks

This Morning a Duel was fought between Generals Cadwallader & Conway the latter was shot thro' the Head & 'tis suppos'd will not recover.[2]

ALS, DLC:GW. The letter was docketed in part, "from Genl Arnold Ansd"; see GW to Benedict Arnold, 6 July. David Salisbury Franks (c.1740–1793) was one of Arnold's aides-de-camp. For a summary of his activities during the war, see his letter to GW of 12 May 1789 (*Papers, Presidential Series,* 2:278–81).

1. The town major at Philadelphia was Lewis Nicola.

2. According to Richard Henry Lee's letter to Francis Lightfoot Lee of 5 July, Maj. Gen. Thomas Conway, "having been informed of some disrespectful words spoken of him by Gen. Cadwallader," challenged him, "and they met on the Common yesterday morn. They threw up for the first fire & Cadwallader won it. At a distance of 12 paces he fired and Shot Conway thro the side of the face, on which he fell & was carried off the field. He is supposed not to be in danger unless an unforeseen inflamation should produce it" (Smith, *Letters of Delegates,* 10:223).


## To Patrick Henry

Dear Sir                         Head Quarters Brunswic [N.J.] 4th July 1778

I take the earliest opportunity of congratulating you on the success of our Arms over the British on the 28th June near Monmouth Court House. I have, in a letter to Congress, given a very particular account of the Maneuvres of both Armies preceding the action, and of the Action itself; and as this will be published I must take the liberty of referring you to it for the matter at large[1]—The Enemy left 245 dead upon Feild and 4 officers among whom was Colo. Monckton of the Grenadiers, the above were buried by us, but we found, besides, several Graves and burying holes in which they had deposited their dead before they were obliged to quit the Ground. Our loss amounted to 60 Rank and file killed and 130 Wounded. We lost but two Officers of Rank Lt Colo. Bonner of Penna and Major Dickinson of the 1st Virginia Regt The former of these Gentlemen is unknown to you, but the latter ought much to be regretted, by his friends and Countrymen as He possessed every qualification to render him eminent in the Military line. Capt. Fauntleroy of the 5th was unfortunately killed by a random Cannon Ball. We made upwards of one hundred prisoners while the enemy remained within our reach, but desertions since they lef Philada have been prodigious, I think I may, without exaggeration assert, that they will lose near one thousand Men in this way before they quit Jersey, and that their Army will be diminished two thousand by killed, wounded, deserters and fatigue. I have the Honor &c.

Df, in Tench Tilghman's writing, DLC:GW; Varick transcript, DLC:GW.

1. GW's letter to Henry Laurens of 1 July was published in Dixon and Hunter's *Virginia Gazette* (Williamsburg) of 17 July.

## From Colonel John Lamb

Sir                                    Farmington [Conn.] 4th July 1778

Inclos'd you have an Extract, from Genl Gates's Orders bearing Date 4 June; From which it appears, that, I am superceded (by an inferior Officer) in the Command of the Artillery, in the Middle Department.[1]

From your Excellency's known Character, for Justice, and generosity; and a full conviction, that, you will never give your sanction, to so flagrant an Act of injustice, I am induced (tho' reluctantly) to trouble you at this time, on so disagreable a Subject. And shall Esteem it a singular favor, to be honour'd with a Line (for my information) respecting the true State of this matter. I am with the greatest Respect your Excellency's Most Obdt Hume Servant.

Copy, in Lamb's writing, NHi: Lamb Papers. Lamb enclosed this letter in one of the same date to Brig. Gen. Henry Knox for delivery to GW. Knox received the letters on 19 July, when he wrote Lamb that he would deliver Lamb's letter to GW (both letters, NHi: Lamb Papers).

1. The enclosure has not been identified, but Lamb quoted the offending extract in his letter to Col. William Malcom of this date: "Lt Colo. Ebenezer Stevens, by the direction of Congress, and the approbation of his Excellency Genl Washington, is appointed to the Command of the Artillery, in ⟨the⟩ Northern, and Middle Departments." Lamb added, "Good Heaven if this be the base, and cruel

treatment, we are to meet with, for sacrificing our Property, destroying our health, risqueing our Lives, and bleeding in the defence of our Country, it is high time, for every Man of Spirit to quit a Service, where superior Officers, may insult with impunity, and where maltreatment, is to be the only reward, he is to receive, for bravely doing his duty, as an Officer, and Soldier" (NHi: Lamb Papers; for the full text of Maj. Gen. Horatio Gates's general orders of 4 June, see Gates orderly book, 20 Aug. 1777–16 July 1778, NN: Emmet Collection).

## To William Livingston

Head Quarters near Brunswick [N.J.]
Dear Sir,                                                      July 4th 1778.

I had the honour to inform you on the ground of action of the advantage over the Enemy on the 28th Ult.[1] I could not then be particular in their killed, as the burying parties were not come in. They have returned 245 killed. Besides the Enemy left behind them at Monmouth Court House, 4 wounded Officers and 40 privates exclusive of those we took on the field of battle. The prisoners taken since the Enemy entered the Jerseys amount to about 100.

Our loss considering the severity and sharpness of the different contentions is very inconsiderable. We have 60 rank and file killed and 133 wounded. Not knowing where to find you the letter alluded to above could not be sent.[2] I have now the honor to inclose it. and am dear Sir with much respect & esteem &c.

Go: Washington.

Copy, MHi: William Livingston Papers; Df, DLC:GW; Varick transcript, DLC:GW.
    1. This letter has not been found.
    2. On the draft, James McHenry originally wrote, "I find the inclosed by some mistake or other has not been forwarded," but he corrected the text to its present language.

## From Colonel William Richardson

General Smallwood's Quarters
May it please your Excellency                                  July 4th 1778

It is irksome to call your attention to a subject with which you have been already so often troubled, but my very disagreeable situation will, I hope, apologize for requesting your interposition toward settling the Rank of the Maryland Officers, the uncertain State of which gives great uneasiness to many, is productive of frequent Warmths & Heartburnings among us, and has Occasioned several good Officers to quit the Service. I am not unapprized of your frequent directions to General Smallwood to have it done, whom I believe has taken much pains to effect it: but in vain. Indeed, to be plain with your Excellency, it is not likely that it ever will, nor proper that it ever should be settled by the Maryland Officers who are all, more or less, involved in the dispute. I think a more eligible Mode (should it meet your approbation) will be to appoint a board of three or more General Officers unconnected with the Maryland Officers, to hear & determine upon the premisses: this will Certainly be allowed by all parties to be the most impartial way of deciding it.

I apprehend the dispute, when once set about, may soon be ended, since it chiefly depends on a Single Point I.E. whether the Flying Camp Officers have Rank with provincial Officers or not? This point being once fixed, the Principle will then be laid down, by which most of our Claims are to be determined. here I beg leave to remark that the Convention of our State, at the time of raising the flying Camp, ranked the Officers on a line with those of the State Regiment then under Command of Colo. Smallwood—that is to say Flying Camp Colonels to Command the Lieutenant Colonel of the State Regiment, & so on downward—this General Smallwood knows to be true. I would also observe that by a resolution of Congress all Flying Camp Officers have Rank with the Officers of their State Battalions respectively.[1]

While I am honored with a Commission in the Service of my Country I wish to be within the line of my duty, but I cannot think of taking Command untill my Rank is Ascertained: I should therefore be happy to have it done soon; but if it Cannot, I wish to retire to my Family; relinquishing my Pay until the matter Can be settled. I have the Honor to be with profound respect Your Excellency's most obedient And most Humble Servt

W. Richardson

ALS, PHi: Gratz Collection; Sprague transcript, DLC:GW.

1. Richardson's intended references are not clear. The Maryland convention resolution establishing the flying camp, 25 June 1776, did not address the relative ranks (*Maryland Convention Proceedings, June 1776*, 5–7). A subsequent resolution of 16 Aug. 1776 directed that the flying camp brigadier general be subject to then-colonel Smallwood (*Maryland Convention Proceedings, August 1776*, 6). In GW's general orders of 18 Aug. 1778, he appointed a board of general officers to settle the rank of the Maryland line, and that board's report of 7 Sept. placed Richardson fourth among the seven Maryland colonels (DNA: RG 93, War Department Collection of Revolutionary War Records, Revolutionary War Rolls, Maryland). On 13 April 1779 another board appointed to settle continuing complaints about the Maryland arrangement specifically ruled against Richardson's claims, arguing that the Maryland resolutions of 14 and 15 Jan. 1776, establishing Smallwood's independent corps and giving its officers precedence over higher-ranking militia officers, "gave the Field Officers of Colo. Smalwood's Battalion, the right of Commanding any Field offi[c]er of whatsoever Rank in the Flying Camp, or in the Militia belonging to the State" (DNA: RG 93, War Department Collection of Revolutionary War Records, Revolutionary War Rolls, Maryland; see also DNA:PCC,

item 173; for the resolutions, see *Maryland Convention Proceedings, December 1775,* 42–54).

## To John Augustine Washington

Dear Brother,                         Brunswick in New Jersey July 4th 1778.
Your Letter of the 20th Ulto came to my hands last Night[1]—before this will have reached you, the Acct of the Battle of Monmouth propably will get to Virginia; which, from an unfortunate, and bad beginning, turned out a glorious and happy day.

The Enemy evacuated Philadelphia on the 18th Instt—at ten oclock that day I got intelligence of it, and by two oclock, or soon after, had Six Brigades on their March for the Jerseys, & followed with the whole Army next Morning—On the 21st we compleated our passage over the Delaware at Coryells ferry (abt 33 Miles above Philadelphia) distance from Valley forge near 40 Miles—From this Ferry we moved down towards the Enemy, and on the 27th got within Six Miles of them.

General Lee having the command of the Van of the Army, consisting of fully 5000 chosen Men, was ordered to begin the Attack next Morning so soon as the enemy began their March, to be supported by me— But, strange to tell! when he came up with the enemy, a retreat commenced; whether by his order, or from other causes, is now the subject of enquiry, & consequently improper to be discanted on, as he is in arrest and a Court Martial sitting for tryal of him. A Retreat however was the fact, be the causes as they may; and the disorder arising from it would have proved fatal to the Army had not that bountiful Providence which has never failed us in the hour of distress, enabled me to form a Regiment or two (of those that were retreating) in the face of the Enemy, and under their fire, by which means a stand was made long enough (the place through which the enemy were pursuing being narrow) to form the Troops that were advancing, upon an advantageous piece of Ground in the rear. hence our affairs took a favourable turn, & from being pursued, we drove the Enemy back, over ground they had followed us, recovered the field of Battle, & possessed ourselves of their dead. but, as they retreated behind a Morass very difficult to pass, & had both Flanks secured with thick Woods, it was found impracticable with Men fainting with fatiegue, heat, and want of water, to do any thing more that Night. In the Morning we expected to renew the Action, when behold the enemy had stole off as Silent as the Grave in the Night after having sent away their wounded. Getting a Nights March of us, and having but ten Miles to a strong pass, it was judged inexpedient to follow them any further, but move towards the North River least they should have any design upon our posts there.

We buried 245 of their dead on the field of Action—they buried several themselves—and many have been since found in the Woods, where, during the action they had drawn them to, and hid them—We have taken five Officers and upwards of One hundred Prisoners, but the amount of their wounded we have not learnt with any certainty; according to the common proposition of four or five to one, their should be at least a thousand or 1200—Without exagerating, there trip through the Jerseys in killed, Wounded, Prisoners, & deserters, has cost them at least 2000 Men & of their best Troops—We had 60 Men killed—132 Wounded & abt 130 Missing, some of whom I suppose may yet come in. Among our Slain Officers is Majr Dickenson, & Captn Fauntleroy, two very valuable ones.

I observe what you say concerning voluntary enlistments, or rather your Scheme for raising 2000 Volunteers; & candidly own to you I have no opinion of it—these measures only tend to burthen the public with a number of Officers without adding one jot to your strength, but greatly to confusion, and disorder—If the several States would but fall upon some vigorous measures to fill up their respective Regiments nothing more need be asked of them, but while these are neglected, or in other words ineffectually & feebly attended to, & these succeedaniums tried, you never can have an Army to depend upon.

The Enemy's whole force Marched through the Jerseys (that were able) except the Regiment of Anspach, which, it is said, they were affraid to trust, & therefore sent them round to New York by Water, along with the Commissioners; I do not learn that they have received much of a reinforcement as yet—nor do I think they have much prospect of any, worth Speaking of, as I believe they stand very critically with respect to France.

As the Post waits I shall only add my love to my Sister[2] and the family, & Strong assurances of being with the sincerest regard & Love— Yr Most Affecte Brother

Go: Washington

Mr Ballendines Letter shall be sent to New York by the first Flag.[3] I am now moving on towards the No. River.

ADfS, DLC:GW.

1. This letter has not been found.

2. GW was referring to his sister-in-law, John's wife, Hannah Bushrod Washington.

3. This letter has not been identified. The correspondent may have been John Ballendine (d. 1782), at this time of Fairfax County, a promoter, builder, and operator of a series of mills, ironworks, and canals in Virginia, with whom GW had a variety of dealings.

## From Brigadier General William Winds

Dear General                    Hd Qrs Elizabeth Town [N.J.] July 4th 1778

I am happy in having it in My power to Inform you, from What I think pretty Good Authority, that there has not lately been any Material Movements of the Enemy about New York or the Islands Dependant on it, no troops are Yet Come from Middletown to Either of the above places, Nearly the Whole Strength of the Enemy on York Island are said to be Collected at & Near Kings Bridge.

A Person Who lately Made his Escape from New York By swiming across the North River, Informs me he has Counted all the Troops on York Island, & Declares, there are not 2000 Men Including Delanceys Corps. I Expect soon to be Able to Give your Excellency a particular Account of the strength & position of the troops on Staten Island.

I have heard that 600 or 700 Prisoners have been landed there from Philadelphia of Which I shall soon be better Informed than at present. I am Respectfully Your Excellencys Most Obdt Hume servt

Wm Winds B:G:

ALS, DLC:GW. GW's aide Robert Hanson Harrison replied to this letter on 5 July, writing Winds: "His Excellency received your favor of the 4th Instant and thanks you for it. He has nothing of a particular nature, either to communicate or to request and only wishes, as before, your vigilance & attention to the movements of the Enemy & the earliest advices of them or of any other material occurrences" (DLC:GW).

## General Orders

Head Quarters Brunswick Landing [N.J.] July 5th 1778.

Parole Paris—                          C. Signs Peace. Plenty.

The Right Wing of the Army is to march at three ôClock tomorrow morning under the Command of Majr General Baron de Steuben— The Route, halting places and Encampments will be given by the Qr Mastr Genl.

Any Officers of the Right Wing who may have Evidence to give to the Court Martial sitting for the trial of Major General Lee are to remain in Camp that they may attend.

The Park of Artillery is to move with the Right Wing. The sick of the Right Wing are to be sent to the Barracks in the City of Brunswick this Evening. All Invalids who are able to march with the Army and carry their Arms not to be sent—Three Commissioned Officers from the Wing are to be left to superintend the sick which shall be left.

Varick transcript, DLC:GW.

## From Brigade Major Matthias Halsted

Sir                                        Elizabeth Town [N.J.] July 5. 1778

Brigdr Genl Winds having rode out of town last Evening & previous to his Going, Directed me to Communicate to your Excellency every Intelligence I Might Recieve from Staten Island in his Absence, Now Affords me the Honor of Informing you that I have the following Account from a person Who left the Island last Night & In Whom Genl Winds places much Confidance. the Prisoners Mentioned by Genl Winds Yesterday, to have been landed on Staten Island were Carried to New York & Landed there, no troops had Got up from Middle town last Evening, nor were they Expected soon, the report there is that the transports are taking on board the baggage & heavy Waggons, to bring them up to New York, & that the light Waggons were to remain with the Army, Which is shortly to Go in pursuit of Your Excellency & the American Army, In Consequence of positive Orders for that purpose brought by the last Packet, lately arrived, The Distruction of the American Army to be their only Object thus far he was Informed by two Captains seperately, both of Whom told him they had the Information from Br. Gl Campbell (Comdt there.) My Informant Also Adds that bread is Extreemly Scarce at New York & on the Island, that the troops on the Island have not recieved one ounce of flour or bread for above a Week past. he Confirms the following Account of their Fortifications on the Island & the Number & position of their troops Which we had had Nearly before.

On the Heights of Richmond town there is a large fort said to be unfinished, another said to be Compleat on the High Ground at the Narrow & three Redouts in the Hill Near the Watering place Northwestwardly from it,[1] Which are all the fortifications on the Island, the troops as follows, 400 or 500 foreigners lay Contigious to the fort & Redouts at the Eastern part of the Island; one Batallion of the 71st lay along the Kills,[2] said to be 400 strong; the three Corps (formerly five) Dignified with the title of Jersey Volunteers, who Do not Amount to 400 Effective Men, Guard to the westward of the Dutch Church as far as the blazing star, from thenc[e] to the West End is Guarded by the Militia, Whose Numbers are small & the Greatest part Much Disaffected to them of late; about 150 British Troops lay at Richmond town Who Work on the fort there, I believe the Above Estimate Rather to Exceed than fall short of their Real Strength, tho they say they have above 2000 Effective Men on the Island.

Should I learn anything further from the Enemy In the Absence of Genl Winds I will Imediately Communicate it to your Excellency, & you May be Assured that Nothing Will be wanting to Obtain the best

Intelligence, Either in his absence or Presence. I have the Honor to be with the Greatest Respect Your Excellencys Most Obdt Humle servt

M. Halsted Majr Brigd. To Br. Gl Winds

ALS, DLC:GW. The cover was docketed as a letter from Brig. Genl. William Winds of the New Jersey militia. Matthias Halsted (c.1746–1835) had served as an ensign and quartermaster in the 1st New Jersey Regiment from November 1775 to August 1776. After his service as a militia brigade major under Winds, he served as an aide-de-camp with the rank of major for Maj. Gen. Philemon Dickinson.

1. The British began constructing Fort Richmond (Fort Izzard), centrally located on the island about five miles southwest of the Narrows, in July 1776 and abandoned the fort in 1782. The redoubt on Signal Hill at the Narrows was rebuilt from an American redoubt called Flagstaff Fort. The Watering Place was the area around current Tompkinsville, near the northeast tip of Staten Island.

2. Kill Van Kull, also called the Kills, is the channel between Staten Island and Bergen Point (Bayonne), New Jersey.

## From Brigadier General William Maxwell

Monmoth 2 miles below the Court House [N.J.]

Sir                                                           5th July 1778

I have to Inform your Excellency that the main body of the Enemy lyeth about 3 miles below middleton on a chain of Heights, that reaches from the bay to Shrewsberry River, which is verry narrow and not come[-]at[-]able. By several accounts they have been busy embarquing since the night before last, (that is their Baggage only & possably some of their Artillery[)]. We have no certainty of any Troops having gone on board though some of the Deserters said there was 3 Regts immediately Imbarked when they tutched the Shore.[1] Coll Morgan lyeth about middleton in the day time, and moves a little way back in the nights, the day before yesterday he sent me 4 Prisoners & several Deserters I had in all that day near 20 & yesterday 5 which was the lowest besides they are going to the North, South, and every way.

They have been under great apprehensions of your following them but I suppose they are easie on that head before this no doub⟨t⟩ knowing where your are. A Doctor Muir came to one of my Pickets the day before yesterday with two two horse Waggons loaded with stores for the Wounded Office⟨rs.⟩[2] He had a list of the Articles and some Instructions from the Augt General with a Sample of Blarney, which they lavish away profusely in times of their distress; but a sparing of both that and good manners in their prosperity. I sent Coll Shrieve to them and informd them that if they wanted their Waggons should go back, there was two of mine to take up their Stores, that they might take up the two servants they had brought if they pleased, but that neither Servant, driver, nor Waggon, that was at, or would go to the Prisoners should return again while the Enemy stayed in the Jersey; yet your Excellency will see by the Inclosed with what ease Mr Kidd the former Doctor applyeth to Coll Beattie for leave for the whole to return;[3] I thought proper to put this in a clear light that your Excellency, nor Coll Beattie might not be deceived; they shall have every asistance in my power, but they shall not have it their own way; I will send Waggons for any necessary they want, or their own Waggons, but they shall be my Drivers I should be glad to know where I shall send the Prisoners to I have and whether I have any Bussiness to send off any of these at the Court House if they are fit to go; one of them I am told has endeavoured to make his Escape. I am your Excellencys Most Obedt Humble Servant

Wm Maxwell

ALS, DLC:GW.

1. According to a journal kept by British brigadier general James Pattison, the British army began embarking their artillery, provisions, baggage, and horses on 1 July and embarked the troops on 5 July (Ritchie, "New York Diary," 263–64).

2. Maxwell was probably referring to James Muir, who appears on a 1778 list of British officers in North America as an established mate of the Philadelphia hospital and on a 1779 list as a mate at New York.

3. The enclosure has not been identified. Alexander Kidd, like Muir, had served as a hospital mate in Philadelphia.

## From Brigadier General John Stark

Honoured Sir · Albany 5th July 1778

last night came to hand your favour of the 20th May, Informing of General Sullivans desire, that I should Join him this Campeign—had it been the pleasure of Congress, to have ordered me to that place, I should thot myself very happy, to serve a Campeign with that Worthy Officer.

and would still be glad to Join him if it should be thot for the good of the service—I Look upon myself in a Very disagreeable situation, pened up in a poor City, very little Employ Except to Guard the Frontiers, no Troops to do it with but some Militia, who are Engaged but for a month at a Time—here I cannot gain any great Advantage to the Publick, nor any Honor to myself[1]—Notwithstanding, I shall Cheerfully comply with any Instructions, or orders, Congress may think proper to Intrust me with—the good of the common cause is my ambition. I am Sir with Great Respect Your Very Humbl. Sevt.

L, DLC:GW. The letter is docketed in part, "from Genl Starke."

1. Stark expressed his opinions more forcefully in a letter of this date to Maj. Gen. John Sullivan: "this is a Cursed place & people. . . . we can do but Little on our

part we have no troops but Militia & they turn out like drawing a Cat by the tail if they are safe they dont care if the Devil had all their Neighbours" (Hammond, *Sullivan Papers*, 2:86–87).

## General Orders

Head-Quarters Brunswick [N.J.] Monday July 6th 1778.
Parole                                                                                      C. Signs
The second Line is to march at three ôClock tomorrow morning under the Command of Major General De la Fayette.

The Director General of the Flying Hospital is desired to make as exact a return as he can of the sick and wounded from the time of the Army's crossing the Delaware and deliver it in at Head-Quarters as speedily as possible.[1]

The General Court Martial of which Lord-Stirling is President is to adjourn to one ôClock tomorrow afternoon and meet at Morristown where the Evidences will attend.[2]

The sick of the Second Line are to be dispos'd of as mentioned in yesterday's orders relative to the Right-Wing—A sufficient number of Officers to superintend them, also Orderlies and Camp Kettles are to be left with them.

The Army marching by Divisions.

Varick transcript, DLC:GW.
1. The director general of the flying hospital was John Cochran.
2. GW altered this order in a letter of 7 July to Major General Stirling and the members of the court: "On further consideration of the adjournment of the Court Martial to Morris Town, It appears to me that the matter is liable to many great and almost insuperable objections. Should the Court remain there, it would be necessary for more Officers to be drawn distantly from the Army than could be prudently spared; and the frequent occasions there will be of calling on the same Witnesses on the several and often on the same points in question would cause such a detention of them as might be very injurious. From these considerations I am induced to change the place of the Court's setting & to request that they will adjourn from Morris Town to pyramus Church which will be immediately in the route of the Army. The Court will be pleased to notifye General Lee of the removal and the Witnesses in such way as they shall deem most proper" (Df, DLC:GW). In consequence, when the court met at Morristown on 8 July, it adjourned to meet at Paramus, N.J., on 10 July (*Lee Papers*, 3:30).

## To Major General Benedict Arnold

⟨D⟩ear Sir                                                        Bruns⟨wic [N.J.] 6t July 1778⟩
I received your fav⟨or of the 30th Ulto⟩ and thank you much for your ⟨kind and⟩ affectionate congratulations. As yo⟨u will⟩ have seen before

this, the account of ⟨the⟩ Action transmitted to Congress,[1] I shall ⟨only⟩ add, since that was given, most of ⟨the⟩ Enemy have been found dead in ⟨the⟩ woods near the field of action and on ⟨their⟩ route according to report; and that de⟨sertions⟩ yet prevail in a pretty considerable degree.

I have also been favoured with M⟨ajor⟩ Franks's Letter of the 4th and was sorry to f⟨ind⟩ you had been afflicted with a viole⟨nt⟩ oppression in your Stomach. I hop⟨e you⟩ are relieved from it & shall also be ⟨happy⟩ to hear that your leg is in a very fa⟨ir way⟩ of recovering.

Sr Henry Clinton had really su⟨ffered⟩ in his march through Jersey. From desertion—&c, I am firmly persuaded his Army has ex⟨perienced⟩ a diminution of Two Thousand men at le⟨ast⟩ since it left philadelphia. I am My Dr Sir with great esteem & regard Yr Obligd & Affect. Hb⟨le Sert⟩

Go: Washin⟨gton⟩

P.S. Our left wing moved yesterday morning and our right this on the rout to the North river.

LS, in Robert Hanson Harrison's writing, NHi; Df, DLC:GW; Varick transcript, DLC:GW. Where the LS is damaged, text has been supplied in angle brackets from the draft.

1. See GW to Henry Laurens, 1 July.

## From Major General Horatio Gates

Sir,                                                      White plains July 6th 1778.

This moment I had the Honour to receive Your Letter, dated Brunswick the 3rd Instant; and do most heartily Congratulate Your Excellency, upon the glorious News it Contains. I shall Order Colonel Hay to have every thing in readiness, for passing Your Army Cross the River at Kings Ferry.

Inclosed I have the Satisfaction to send Your Excellency, the latest, and best Intelligence from New York.[1] I have the honor to be, Sir, Your Excellency's Most Obedt Humble Servant

Horatio Gates

LS, DLC:GW; Df, NHi: Gates Papers.

1. Gates enclosed an examination of Polly Mitchell, who had left New York on 3 July. She stated: "That M. Gen. Tryon's Division, consisting of about 600 Men, were posted on Long Island, at the Head of the Flye, between New-Town & Flushing—That his Quarters were at Waters's, and Delancey's at Furman's. That ten or twelve Wagons were employed, the other Day, in carrying Gen. Tryon's Baggage to New-York, where it was generally supposed he would soon embark it for Great Britain. That they were endeavouring to raise a Troop of Light Dragoons at Jamaica.

That a British Regiment was encamped at Brooklyn. That they were busy in repairing the Works on Brooklyn Heights—That two new Redoubts were erected on the Bedford Road—That two Anspach Regiments were posted on Long-Island, opposite Hell-Gate—That a Party is employed in the Woods, near Herrick's on Long-Island, in cutting Timber for Block houses, & framing them. That since Major Monckrief & Mr Bache were taken from Flatbush, they have kept strong Guards there, & will not suffer any of our Prisoners to be out of their Houses at Night— That a Majority of the Inhabitants on the Island are our firm Friends, & wait, with great Impatience, for an Opportunity of Joining our Army.

"That there were no more Troops in the City of New-York than were barely sufficient for the ordinary Guards—That there was a Generally a tolerable plenty of fresh Provisions in the Markets—That the Citizens were healthy—that they, as well as the Officers of the Army, were exceedingly distressed on Account of the gloomy State of their Affairs, and particularly the late Action in New-Jersey—that between 4 & 500 of the B. Army, wounded, had been brought into the City & it was currently reported that they had near 400 killed—That the B. Army was encamped on the Heights of Neversink, and were soon expected in New-York—That all the Ships, Boats & Craft in the Harbour, had been impressed, & sent to Sandy Hook the Day before she left the City. That the Commissioners had arrived, and Gov. Johnstone was frequently insulted by the Name of Rebel in the Streets. That many warm Tories affirmed and believed that the Commissioners had Authority to withdraw the Fleets & Armies, in order to settle a Peace—That few supposed the Campaign would be continued—if it was, the Scenes of Action would certainly be in the States of N. York & Connecticut. That they were not embarking, in the Harbour of N. York, any Cannon, military Stores, Horses &c.—That Bunker's, or Bayard's Hill was demolished—That the Grand Battery was in no State of Defence—That there was an Encampment at Greenwich; but could not ascertain the Number of Men there—That they had made no Alteration in the Works at Paulus Hook, neither had they thrown up any new ones there—That Lt Col. Trunbull, with between 2 & 300 of the New Levies, was posted there—That she dined lately with a Captain of Transport, in Appearance a good Whig, who sailed from England in April last— That he informed her two thousand Recruits would be all the Reinforcement the British Army would receive this Year—That a Ship arrived, a few Days ago, from England in which came two Letters flatly contradictory to each other—One mentioned that a War between France & England was inevitable—the other that there was not the least Prospect of it. That the Refugees from Philadelphia, particularly, were constantly visiting our Prisoners, in the City, and shewing them every Mark of Humanity. That they flattered themselves this Conduct would regain them the Esteem & Affection of their Countrymen—That our Prisoners confined in ships were treated with the most rigorous Severity, and die in great Numbers" (DLC:GW).

## From Major General William Heath

Dear General                                 Head Quarters Boston July 7th 1778
    I have been honored with yours of the 17th Ultimo.
    Captain Robert Davis left this place to join the Army some three or four weeks since. I believe General Glover & his Brigade Major Fosdick are much better acquainted with his conduct and services while here, than I am.

The Military Stores which arrived at Portsmouth from France in the Dutchess of Grammond I have ordered to this place on their way to the Arsenals where they will be sent as fast as they arrive. There are a number of Carbines and pistols for the Dragoons and some wall peices, if the light Horse are not fully supplied with those necessary Arms, they will be ready to forward from Springfield by the time your Excellency's pleasure is signified to Colo. Cheever at that place.[1]

We are momently waiting the arrival of the News of some interesting Event having taken place with you; may it be honorary to yourself and happy to your Country—which is the earnest wish of him who has the honor to be With great respect Your Excellency's Most Obedt Humble Servt

W. Heath

LS, DLC:GW; ADfS, MHi: Heath Papers.
1. Heath had reported the arrival of the *Duchesse de Grammont* at Portsmouth, N.H., on 5 June in his letter to GW of 9 June.

## To Henry Laurens

Sir                         Camp near Brunswic [N.J.] July 7th 1778

I have the Honor to inform you, that on sunday morning[1] the left wing of the Army moved towards the North river—The right followed yesterday; and the second line which forms the rear division, is also now in motion. I shall advance, as fast as I can, consistently with the circumstances of the weather and the health of the Troops.

The Enemy, from the advices of our parties of observation, were nearly, if not all embarked yesterday. They have continued to desert upon all occasions.

I should be extremely happy if the Committee, appointed to arrange the Army, would repair to it, as soon as possible.[2] Congress can form no adequate idea of[3] the discontents prevailing, on account of the unsettled state of rank, and the uncertainty in which Officers are, as to their future situation. The variety of hands, in which the power of granting of Commissions and filling up vacancies is lodged, and other circumstances have occasioned frequent instances of younger Officers commanding their seniors, from the former having received their Commissions and the latter not; and these not only in the line of the Army at large—but in their own Brigades and even in their own Regiments. This it will be readily conceived is necessarily productive of much confusion, altercation and complaint and requires the speediest remedy. I have the Honor to be with great respect & esteem Sir yr Most Obedt servant

Go: Washington

P.S. By accounts from Monmouth more of the Enemy's dead have been found; It is said the number buried by us & the Inhabitants exceeds three Hundred.

LS, in Robert Hanson Harrison's writing, DNA:PCC, item 152; Df, DLC:GW; copy, DNA:PCC, item 169; Varick transcript, DLC:GW. GW signed the cover, which was docketed in part, "Read 9" (see *JCC*, 11:676).
    1. The previous Sunday was 5 July.
    2. Congress, by a resolution of 4 June, had empowered GW, "with the advice and assistance of the honble. Joseph Reed and Francis Dana, Esqs. or either of them," to implement the new army arrangement (ibid., 11:570). Reed had gone to camp immediately, but the work of arrangement had been interrupted by the departure of the army from Valley Forge. Congress responded to this request by resolving on 9 July that the committee should go to GW's headquarters and commence work "without delay" (ibid., 11:676).
    3. On the draft, which is otherwise in Harrison's writing, Alexander Hamilton completed the paragraph from this point. However, Harrison subsequently wrote for insertion the words that follow "the latter not" and complete that sentence.

## From Henry Laurens

Dear Sir.                 Philadelphia 7th July 1778.
    I have had the honor of presenting to as many Members of Congress as have been convened in this City since the adjournment from York, Your Excellency's several favors of the 28th & 30th June & 1st Inst: & at their special Instance have caused them to be printed for the information of the public.[1]
    I arrived here on Tuesday last, but hitherto have not collected a sufficient number of States to form a Congress, consequently I have received no Commands.[2] Your Excellency will therefore be pleased to accept this as the address of an Individual intended to assure you Sir of my hearty congratulations with my Country Men on the success of the American Arms under Your Excellency's immedeate Command in the, late Battle of Monmouth & more particularly of my own happiness in the additional Glory atcheived by Your Excellency in retrieving the honor of these States in the Moment of an alarming dilemma.
    It is not my design to attempt encomiums upon Your Excellency, I am as unequal to the task as the Act is unnecessary, Love & respect for Your Excellency is impressed on the Heart of every grateful American, & your Name will be revered by posterity. Our acknowledgements are especially due to Heaven for the preservation of Your Excellency's person necessarily exposed for the Salvation of America to the most imminent danger in the late Action; that the same hand may at all times

guide & Shield Your Excellency is the fervent wish of Dear sir Your much obliged & faithful humble servant[3]

Henry Laurens

ALS, DLC:GW; LB, ScHi: Henry Laurens Papers. A notation on the letter book indicates that this letter was carried "by [Joseph] Gray."

1. There was no favor of 30 June; Laurens meant GW's letter of 29 June (see Laurens to GW, 8 July). On 4 July, Laurens wrote John Dunlap, editor of the *Pennsylvania Packet* (Philadelphia), asking him to publish the three letters, and they appeared in a special one-page issue of the *Packet* dated 6 July.

2. The previous Tuesday was 30 June. The Continental Congress, which had been adjourning from day to day since 2 July, reconvened on this date (*JCC*, 11:671–72).

3. GW wrote Laurens on 11 July, acknowledging this letter and continuing: "My warmest acknowledgements are due for the indulgent terms in which you express your sense of my conduct, in our late rencounter, with the British army. Not to be pleased with the approbation and esteem of any of the virtuous and discerning part of my countrymen would indicate a want of sensibility; but I assure you, my dear Sir, there is no man on whose good opinion & friendship, I set a higher value than on your's; and every fresh instance, I receive of them, cannot fail of affording me the most sincere & genuine satisfaction. At the sametime, it is both a pleasing and humiliating consideration to me, that the partiality of my friend⟨s⟩ greatly overates the importance of my Services" (ALS, DLC: John and Henry Laurens Papers).

## Lieutenant Colonel Alexander Hamilton to Colonel Stephen Moylan

*7 July 1778.* Conveys GW's wish that Moylan "collect the *whole of the cavalry*, without delay, as well the unarmed as the armed, and after a little refreshment, and getting the horses shod &c. proceed moderately towards the North river to join the army." Cavalry "accoutrements" that arrived "to the Eastward" were "ordered immediately on—These will meet us shortly, it is to be hoped on the North River and will serve to supply deficiencies."

ADfS, DLC:GW; Varick transcript, DLC:GW.

## From Brigadier General James Mitchell Varnum

Sir                                                    Peekskill [N.Y.] 7th, July 1778.

I arrived here Yesterday morning on my Way from Rhode Island. I found Mrs Varnum in a distressed Situation, having been robbed of every Article Cloathing, except a morning undress which she had on. I am detained here by a severe Inflamation in the Face, occasioned by a Cold after drawing a troublesome Tooth. I hope to join my Brigade soon, but fear I shall be laid by for several Days. Genl Sullivan is in Command of but few Troops, and the Enemy there have been rein-

forced by a part of Browns Corps from New York.[1] There are universal
Complaints against the Commissary of Prisoners in that Department,
"Mr Mershroe," Tis said he demands Money for procuring Exchanges,
and effects them out of Turn; That he carries on an illicit Commerce
with the Enemy, & makes his Residence principally in Newport with the
worst of Tories.[2] I am, with great Respect, your Excellency's most obdt,
& very humble Servant,

J.M. Varnum.

ALS, DLC:GW.

   1. Brig. Gen. Montfort Browne's provincial regiment (The Prince of Wales American Volunteers), numbering about four hundred men, had joined the British forces at Rhode Island on 11 and 12 June (see *Mackenzie Diary*, 1:299–300).

   2. Persistent reports that "indulgence of paroles hath been granted to the prisoners of the convention of Saratoga, in consideration on money paid and received for the same," led Congress on 27 Oct. 1778 to appoint a special committee to investigate (*JCC*, 12:1065; see also Henry Laurens to William Heath, 10 Oct., and to the Massachusetts Council, 29 Oct., in Smith, *Letters of Delegates*, 11:45, 146). Deputy Commissary of Prisoners Joshua Mersereau, however, retained his post.

## From Major General Benedict Arnold

Dear General,                       Philadelphia July 8th 1778.

   Yesterday I had the honor of your Excellency's favour of the 6th and
am very happy to hear the Enemy have suffered so very considerably in
their march thro' the Jerseys—I make no doubt this Campaign will be
crown'd with success, & that your Excellency will soon enjoy in peace
the Laurels you have with so much perseverence, toil & hazard reaped
in the Iron field of War.

   My extreme illness has prevented my writing as often as I wished; at
present I am entirely free from the disorder in my stomach; my wound
is in a p[r]omising way and pretty free from pain.

   I presume General Portail will return to Philada again, no measures
will be taken respecting the Works here & those to be constructed untill I receive your Excellency's instructions on the subject.

   Three hundred prisoners of War will go from this tomorrow morning on their way to New York, and as many the last of this week—The
whole number of deserters arrived here is upwards of Six hundred—I
have the honor to be with the greatest respect, most Affectionately &
Sincerely Dr General your Excellency's Obedt Humble servant

B. Arnold

Since writing the above an Express is arriv'd to Congress from France
by the way of Boston, with intelligence that on the 15 of April a French

fleet sailed from Tolu [Toulon] consisting of twelve sail of the Line, seven Frigates & four Xebecs—which we may hourly expect to arrive in this or Chesepeak Bay—By this express dispatches have come for the Admiral & Monsieur Gerard[1]—Count De Esteen commands the fleet.

Admiral Keppel sailed the 24 of April from St Helens with eleven sail of the Line.

May 5th 17 Sail of the Line were in the Brest road eight others were to join them in a few days exclusive of Frigates.

B. Arnold

ALS, DLC:GW.

1. When he was nominated in March 1778 as France's first minister to the United States, Conrad-Alexandre Gérard (1729–1790) was serving as commissioner of boundaries in the French department of foreign affairs. He remained as minister until September 1779.

*Letter not found*: from Lt. Col. Francis Barber, 8 July 1778. On 9 July, GW wrote Barber: "I was this afternoon favoured with your Letter of the 8th Inst."

## From Vice Admiral d'Estaing

Sir,                                                          At sea the 8th July 1778

I have the honor of imparting to Your Excelly the arrival of the King's fleet; charged by his Majesty with the glorious task of giving his allies the United States of America the most striking proofs of his affection. Nothing will be wanting to my happiness if I can succeed in it; it is augmented by the consideration of concerting my operations with a General such as Your Excellency. The talents and great actions of General Washington have insured him in the eyes of all Europe, the title, truly sublime of deliverer of America. Accept Sir, the homage that every man—that every military man owes you; and be not displeased, that I solicit, even in the first moment of intercourse, with military and maritime frankness, a friendship so flattering as yours. I will try to render myself worthy of it by my respectful devotion for your country; it is prescribed to me by orders, and my heart inspires it.

I have the honor of rendering accot to Congress of the letter I write to Your Excellency.[1] Mr Dr *Chouin*, Major of infantry in the King's service has orders to present you this—I pray you to grant the most extensive confidence to all this officer shall tell you on my part. He is a near relation to Mr Sartine.[2] This Minister has been long since known for his attachment to the common cause. 'Tis less the desire of pleasing a statesman, honored with the confidence ⟨of the⟩ King which has determined me to send you Mr Chouin, than an opinion of his military knowlege—the clearness of his ideas and the precision with which he will communicate mine. I beseech you to grant him your kindness. I have the honor to be with respect Sir Yr Excellency's Most humble & most Obedient servant

Estaing

Translation, DLC:GW; LS (in French), DLC:GW; Df (in French), FrPNA: Marine, B4, I46; copy (in French), FrPNA: Marine, B4, I46; copy (extract in French), FrPBN. Robert Hanson Harrison docketed the LS, in part, "recd 17. ansd the 17. a Duplicate copey recd before." The duplicate enclosed with d'Estaing's letter of 13 July was received on 14 July.

1. D'Estaing's letter of this date to President of Congress Henry Laurens told him: "I have the Honour to write to General Washington and shall send successively to his Camp Two Officers with offers to combine my movements with his" (*Laurens Papers*, 14:6).

2. Although appointed a major in 1776, André-Michel-Victor, marquis de Choin (Chouin; 1744–1829), had been employed in the French marine ministry before becoming d'Estaing's aide-de-camp and in October 1778 the maréchal général des logis for his troops. Antoine-Raymond-Gualbert-Gabriel de Sartine (1729–1801), a former head of the Paris police, was appointed the French minister of marine and the colonies in 1774. He remained in office until 1780. At this point the extract in the French archives includes a phrase omitted from the LS: "ministre du Roy chargé du département de la Marine."

## From Henry Laurens

Sir                                   Philadelphia 8th July 1778

I beg leave to refer to a private Letter of yesterday by Gray, in which I acknowledged the receipt of Your Excellency's Letters to Congress of the 28th & 29th Ulto & 1st Inst. I should have added the 21st Ulto which came to hand the 2d Inst.

With some difficulty a Congress was collected yesterday, Your Excellency's Letters were immediately taken under consideration & the House unanimously Resolved a Vote of thanks for Your Excellency's approved conduct from the time when the Army left Valley forge Camp to the conclusion of the Battle of Monmouth a Certified Copy of which I have the honor & particular happiness of transmitting within the present Cover.

I have likewise the pleasure of conveying an Act of the same date for thanking the Gallant Officers & Men under Your Excellency's Command who by their conduct & valor distinguished themselves in that Battle.[1] I have the honor to be With the highest Esteem & Regard—Sir Your Excellency's Most obedient & Most humble servant

Henry Laurens.<br>President of Congress—

ALS, DLC:GW; LB, DNA:PCC, item 13. The ALS is docketed in part, "ansd 12." A notation on the letter-book copy indicates that the letter was carried "by Major Putnam."

1. The enclosed resolutions, on a single page signed by Secretary of Congress Charles Thomson, are in DLC:GW (see also *JCC,* 11:672–73).

## From John Cleves Symmes

Sussex Court house [Newton, N.J.]

May it please Your excellency,                                    8th of july 1778

I wish I may not be thought troublesome, but by the Information I get at this place by other Means than what Your Excellency will see by the Inclosed deposition,[1] I must Conclude the enemy are formidable, tis said that there are 300 Regular troops, 1500 Indians and a Large body of Tories which Compose the enemies force, I need not suggest to Your Excellency the apprehesions of the Inhabitants in the Minisinks and their wishes of support, there are not 300 Men as Yet in Arms at the Minisinks,[2] Numbers of the Militia of this County are on service bel⟨o⟩w, and none of the first Battalion of the County are even warned to assemble; to all appearance the Crissis will be over before I can procure the Amunition from Easton. I have the honor to be, sir, Your Excellencies Most Obedient humble Servant

John Cleves Symmes

P.S. I am now seventeen Miles from the Minisinks. Many families have come Over this day.

ALS, DLC:GW. The cover indicates that the letter was sent "pr Express."

1. Symmes had taken the deposition on this date from Solomon Avery of Norwich, Connecticut. Avery testified "that he Left Wioming on the Susquehannah, the night after the Action on the third Inst. at that place, that Col. [Zebulon] Butler met the Enemy with 400 men, that at first the enemy did not present a more extensive front than the Inhabitants, but the Enemy after the action had Continued for some time, drew up a second line in the rear of Col. Butler as extensive and to appearance as numerous as the body they had in front, when Col. Butler gave way and being on the Bank of the Susquehannah Many fell and were Drown'd, the number of those who Escaped did not exceed thirty men; this Deponent also saith that when he was on the Mountain to the east of the Settlement he saw the Settlement all on fire, this deponent further saith that of 5000 souls he supposes 2000 have perished in the Carnage, that when he past Col. Strowds on the 7th Inst. at Fort Pen (a viliage so called) express came in with information that the enemies Van was at Lackawack, a Settlement 14 miles west of the Delaware, Upon the Upper Road from Goshen to Wioming" (DLC:GW; see also Avery's report of 15 July, printed in *Connecticut Gazette; and the Universal Intelligencer* [New London], 17 July).

2. Symmes was evidently referring to the community of Minisink (now Montague), N.J., on the east side of the Delaware River above Minisink Island, about fifty-five miles east of Wyoming, Pennsylvania. In his report of the Wyoming battle, Loy-

alist John Butler wrote to Lt. Col. Mason Bolton on 8 July that "The settlement of Schohary or the Minisinks will be my next objects, both of which abound in corn and cattle, the destruction of which cannot fail greatly distressing the rebels" (Davies, *Documents of the American Revolution*, 15:166). Butler, however, may have been referring to the town of Minisink in Orange County, N.Y., or more generally to the Minisink region along the Delaware River above the Water Gap in New York, New Jersey, and Pennsylvania.

## From Brigadier General William Winds

Head Quarters Elizabeth Town [N.J.]
Dear General                                        July 8. 1778
   I am happy in the present Oppertunity of Informing you from the Authority of a Gentleman of Veracity, Who left long Island the Night before last & New York Yesterday: from long Island he saw the Whole of the british fleet leave Middletown & Come into the Narrows, after Which they Divided Into three Divisions, one of Which Landed their troops on Staten Island, another on Long Island, the third at New York, he thinks the Divisions Nearly Equal & is well Assured the troops were all Landed last Night,[1] he Asserts that Yesterday there was the Greatest Confusion Imaginable among the British troops at New York, the Occasion uncertain.
   A flagg boat to & from Staten Island this Day Discovered a large new Encampment on the Hills Near the Watering place, which Alone would satisfie me that troops were lately landed there. Your Excellencys Most Obdt Humb. servt

                                                    Wm Winds

ALS, DLC:GW.
   1. British general Henry Clinton's general orders for 5 July had directed: "The First & Second Brigades of British are to Encamp near the watering place, on Staten Island, but are not to land Until they Receive their Tents. The 16th & 17th Regiments of Dragoons & the Three Provincial Troops, the Guards, Flank Companies of 22nd & 43rd & Marines Queens Rangers & all the Hessian Corps are to be posted on New York Island, the Rest of the Army will be Station'd Near Utrecht on Long Island" (Brigade of Guards Orderly Book, DLC:GW; see also *Kemble Papers*, 1:603). Brig. Gen. James Pattison's record of British movements reports the same locations but a different distribution of troops for the British landings of 6 July: "The 16th & 17 Regiments of Dragoons, the 3rd. and 4th Brigades of British Infantry & all the Provincial Corps, except the Queen's Rangers, at New Utrecht, where the Infantry encamp'd, but the Regiment of Dragoons . . . proceeded to Jamaica.
   "The 1st. & 2nd. Brigades of British Infantry desembark'd on Staten Island.
   "The Brigade of Guards, Queen's Rangers, Hessian Grenadiers & the Brigades of Sterne & Walworth, encamp'd on different Parts of N. York Island" (Ritchie, "New York Diary," 265; see also Scull, *Montresor Journals*, for another report of the British dispositions).

## To Lieutenant Colonel Francis Barber

Dr Sir                                    [Newark, N.J.] July 9: 1778

I was this afternoon favoured with your Letter of the 8th Inst.[1] While you are at Elizabeth Town, I wish you to obtain the best intelligence you can from time to time of the Enemy's situation and of any movements, they may seem to have in view. For this purpose you will employ the persons you mention, or such others as you may judge necessary. Whatever expences you are at, upon this occasion, will be repaid on the earliest notice.

I am extremely happy to hear your wound is in so favourable a way.[2] I hope it will be better every day. Tho I wish for your services, I would not have you to rejoin the Army before your condition will admit of it, with the most perfect safety. I am Dr Sir Yr Most Obedt servt

Go: Washington

LS, in Robert Hanson Harrison's writing, owned (1986) by Mr. Joseph Rubinfine, Pleasantville, New Jersey. GW signed the cover of the LS.

1. Barber's letter to GW of 8 July has not been found.
2. Barber had been wounded at the Battle of Monmouth on 28 June.

## From John Brown

Dr Sr                                    Providence July 9th 1778

I being a Small part Concern'd in a prize Ship Arived at the port of Boston with a Cargo of Maderia wine and haveing lately ben told that Good wine was not to be bot at or near Your Camp, have taken the Liberty to present You with a Butt Qt 157 Gs. which was picked out by Collo. More, as the Best in the whole Cargo which Consisted of about 29,000 Gallons the Same was well Cassed up and Forworded by Thoms Chace D.Q.M. Genl as pr Copy of his Recept Inclosed,[1] I wish it Safe to Your hands, & Hartily Congrattulate You on the Late Signel Success of our Arms in the Jerseys and Most Sincearly wish You a Continuation of the Devine Favour and that You May Long Live to Injoy this most Happey Free and Independent Empire which You have in a Very Great Meisure ben the Cause of Establishing. I am with the Graitest Respect Dr Sr Your Most Obt Humble Servt

John Brown

P.S., the Butt is Marked on the Bulge, JB to GW.

ALS, DLC:GW.

1. The enclosed receipt, dated June 1778, indicates that Thomas Chase sent the wine to Fishkill, N.Y., to be forwarded to GW by Udny Hay (DLC:GW). A butt of

wine for GW was received at Fishkill on 29 July (receipt of Josiah Nichols, that date, NN: George Washington Papers). The prize ship was probably the brig "laden with wine" that arrived at Boston on 13 June after being captured by the Rhode Island privateer *Blaze-Castle* (*Boston-Gazette, and Country Journal*, 15 June).

## To Major General Horatio Gates

Sir                                           Newark [N.J.] 9th July 1778

I yesterday met yours of the 6th on the march to this place, at which, the front division of the Army arrived in the morning. They halt this day and will march again at one OClock tomorrow Morning. The other divisions follow at a days distance. I am glad to hear that every thing will be ready at Kings ferry to transport the Army and hope that measures will be taken to keep the passage open should the Enemy attempt to interrupt it—Since my last,[1] we have discovered a number more of their dead, near Monmouth; the buried now amount to upwards of three hundred. The number of deserters, to every quarter, will be near if not quite one thousand. I am with Respect Sir Yr most obt and hble Servt

Go: Washington

LS, in Tench Tilghman's writing, NHi: Gates Papers; Df, DLC:GW; Varick transcript, DLC:GW.

At "Sun Sett" on this date, Gates wrote Brig. Gen. John Glover, "I have the pleasure to send You a Copy of a Letter I this moment received from His Excellency General Washington," and he sent orders about the escort for the grand army's crossing at King's Ferry to Colonel La Radière, Capt. John Winslow, and the officer commanding the detachment from West Point (all, NHi: Gates Papers).

1. See GW to Gates, 3 July.

## From Brigadier General Peter Muhlenberg

Sir.                                           [New Jersey] July 9th 1778.

Colo. Josiah Parker of the 5th Virginia Regt returnd to Camp, since the temporary Arangement of the 1st 5th & 9th Regiments made by Your Excellencys Order,[1] so that there is at present no Command for him, except he should supersede Colo. Richd Parker, who now Commands the Regt who has made the whole Winters Campaign, & takes great pains to put the Regt in good Order—Colo. J. Parker wishes to know Your Excellencys pleasure with regard to himself that he may act accordingly. Your Excellencys Most Obedt humble Servt

P: Muhlenberg.

ALS, DLC:GW.
1. For discussion of the temporary arrangement of these Virginia regiments, see GW to Muhlenberg, 18 June, and note 1.


## From Brigadier General William Winds

Head Quarters Elizabeth Town [N.J.]

Dear General                                                    July 9. 1778

At this Critical Juncture I Cannot Delay a Moment In transmiting to your Excellency, Every Interesting piece of Intelligence, that Comes to My Ear, leaving it to you to Compare them with Accounts you may recieve through Other Hands & Make a proper Digest of the Whole.

Two Men returned last Night to this place from Staten Island, one of them was Yesterday in New York, they had two Days to Collect the Intelligence Which follows—Nine Regiments are landed on Staten Island from Middletown, Who are Encamped on the Heights Near the Watering place, the Numbers landed at New York, are far Short of those on Staten Island, but the pieces of Dislocated Carriages &c. landed there is Immense, tis said, there were the pieces of 1500 Waggons, besides Other Carriages, on & near the Warfs, & Yesterday there was Nothing Doing towards puting them together. The Grea[te]st part of the British troops from New Jersey landed on Long Island, all the British General Officers were Assembled at New York supposed to be In Council, This Agrees with the report Made by the Officer Who went from here to Staten Island with a flag Yesterday, (vizt) that He was Informed by the Officer Who recd him that the Generals Were Gone to New York, Wherefore he Could not Accomplish the Business he went on.

One of the first abovementioned Men Declares that he was in a friends House on Staten Island, When some British Officers Came in & took the room Next the one he was in, that he overheard their Conversations, part of Which was as follows, one of them Acknowledged the Regt he belonged to had lost upwards of 80 Men in their March through New Jersey: by Desertion, Capture, Killed In Action, & Died by the Heat, Another Allowed the loss of his Regiment to be Great but Did not Mention Numbers, they Agreed that they Never saw Men so Much fatigued as their Army In General, & that it would take some time Yet to recover it. that they Should Do Nothing More untill the Arrival of another Packett, Which they feared Would bring Orders for their Going to the West Indies, but if not, they Should Make some Other Grand push, Altho they Could not see any Advantage that Could possibly Arise from such a Measure, tho Great Evils May. a Violent hot press in New York the Night before last in Which they picked up about 400 Men &

forced them on board the Men of War, among them Many who were no seamen.[1]

I have now to Acknowledge the Rect of Your Excellencys favr Through Col: Tilghman, Which Came to hand since the Above was wrote[2] Your Excellency May rely on Recieving Every piece of Intelligence that I Can possibly Collect. I am Dr Genl Your Most Obdt Humb. servt

Wm Winds

Inclosed are two late New York Papers for your Excellencys Amusement.[3]

ALS, DLC:GW.

1. British officer Stephen Kemble wrote in his journal for 8 July: "Advice received that the Andromeda had been off the Capes of Delaware, and saw ten Sail of the line, French. Lord Howe proposed to the Transports to turn out Seamen Volunteers to Man the Fleet, 1,000 offered in a few hours for the Service" (*Kemble Papers*, 1:155). Brig. Gen. James Pattison's journal of military operations noted that "a hot press of Seamen began . . . but was soon put a stop to, upon a sufficient Number of Men from the Transports turning out as Volunteers to serve in the Fleet" (Ritchie, "New York Diary," 265).

2. The "favr Through Col: Tilghman" has not been found.

3. The enclosed newspapers have not been identified.


## From Henry Laurens

sir.                                                 Philadelphia 10th July 1778

I had the honor of writing to Your Excellency by Major Putnam the 8th Inst.[1]

Congress while sitting before Noon received intelligence of the following import.

Mr Blair McLenahan said he had seen a Capt. Selby or Selwin off Chincoteague who had fallen in with the French Fleet Eastward of Bermuda—the Admiral had taken him on board & enjoined him to pilot the ffleet to this Coast, the ffleet arrived near Chincoteague in the Evening of the 5th Inst. there they found the Ship Lydia of 26 Guns from New York on a Cruise—she was sunk by a french Frigate of 36 Guns— On Monday Capt. selby was sent on Shoar in order to procure Pilots he engaged six to go on board the French ffleet upon Wednesday—the Fleet consisted of the Admiral Count d'Estaing of 90 Guns— 2 Ships of 80—8 of 74—1 of 64.—4 of 36. & said to have 12000 Men—they had taken a Ship of 18 Guns from Providence before they had made the Land.[2]

War was to be declared against England by France & Spain on the 19th May—they had originally intended for Delaware but hearing that the Enemy were gone to New York they required Pilots to conduct them to Sandy Hook, they had then six Months provision on board.

Your Excellency will perceive by the inclosed printed paper that a Fleet had been prepared at Portsmouth in order to intercept or annoy this Fleet[3] of which 'tis possible the Count d'Estaing may be ignorant as he sailed from Toulon the 15th April 'tis possible also that a Check may have been put upon that by a Fleet from Brest, be that as it may, Count d'Estaing should be apprized of this important circumstance & also of the strength of the British Marine power in New York, which from the best accounts we have been able to collect is made up of the following Ships—

| Boyne | 70 Guns. | Centurion | 50. | Roebuck | 44. |
|---|---|---|---|---|---|
| Eagle | 64. | Experiment | 50. | Phœnix | 44. |
| St Alban | 64. | Preston | 50. | & many Frigates | |
| Ardent | 64. | Renown | 50. | | |
| Sommerset | 64. | Chatham | 50. | | |
| Trident | 64. | Isis | 50. | | |
| | | Vigilant formerly 64. | | | |

I shall endeavor to reach Count d'Estaing with the necessary advices on the Coast of New Jersey or off the Capes of Delaware[4]—Your Excellency will, if he shall have proceeded nearer Sandy Hook endeavor to meet him with a Letter where it may reach him, & you will also concert measures for improving the force under Your Excellency's immediate Command & that under the direction of Major General Gates, in the present critical conjuncture.

Your Excellency will also if you have a more exact Account of the British Fleet at New York make proper corrections upon the list above enumerated. I have the honor to be With the highest Esteem & Respect Sir Your Excellencys Most obedient & most humble servant

Henry Laurens,
President of Congress

It is almost unnecessary to intimate to Your Excellency the propriety of opening & keeping up a correspondence with the Admiral Count d'Estaing.

ALS, DLC:GW; LB, DNA:PCC, item 13. A note on the letter-book copy indicates that this letter was carried by Levellin Barry.

1. Daniel Putnam (1759–1831), a son of Maj. Gen. Israel Putnam, was commissioned a lieutenant in the 20th Continental Infantry Regiment in January 1776 and became a major and his father's aide-de-camp in May of that year. He was returning to Hartford, Conn., with Laurens's acknowledgment of a letter from Israel Putnam to Congress.

2. The preceding Monday was 6 July. For another report of Blair McClenachan's information, with more detail about the engagement with the *Lydia*, see *Royal Ga-*

*zette* (New York), 22 July. Other hearsay reports of the 5 July engagement appeared in the *North-Carolina Gazette* (New Bern), 24 July. When Vice Admiral d'Estaing's squadron left Toulon, it consisted of the *Languedoc*, of 90 guns; *Tonnant*, of 84 guns; *César*, *Zélé*, *Hector*, *Guerrier*, *Marseillais*, and *Protecteur*, of 74 guns; *Vaillant*, *Provence*, *Fantasque*, and *Sagittaire*, of 64 guns; and the *Chimère*, *Engageante*, *Flore*, *Alcmene*, and *Aimable*, of 26 guns, with about 9,500 seamen and 1,000 soldiers. The *Flore* returned to France before the fleet reached American waters. "Capt. Selby," who had joined the French fleet by 27 June, may have been William Selby, Jr., of Pitts Landing, Virginia. The fleet took the merchant ship *Charlotte*, out of New Providence Island in the Bahamas, on 30 June (see *Extrait du journal d'un officier de la marine*, 9).

3. Laurens enclosed a copy of a letter from the American commissioners in France of 18 May, which was read in Congress on 8 July and ordered published (*JCC*, 11:675). Printed in the *Pennsylvania Packet or the General Advertiser* (Philadelphia) of 9 July, the letter gave intelligence "that eleven British ships of war, viz. One of 90 guns, nine of 74, and one of 64 guns, are in the road of St. Hellens, near Portsmouth, bound for North America" and asked that the recipients publish the information and inform the French fleet.

4. For Laurens's letter to d'Estaing of this date, see *Laurens Papers*, 14:12–14.


## From Theodosia Bartow Prevost

Hermitage [Ho-Ho-Kus, N.J.]
Friday morning, eleven oclock [10 July 1778]
Mrs Prevost Presents her best respects to his Excellency Genl Washington—requests the Honour of his Company—as She flatters herself the accommodations will [be] more Commodious than those to be procured in the Neighbourhood⟨.⟩ Mrs Prevost will be particularly happy to make her House Agreeable to His Excellency, and family.[1]

AL, owned (1978) by Mr. William Miller, Old Saybrook, Connecticut. Theodosia Bartow Prevost (1746–1794) was the wife of James Marcus Prevost (1736–1781), a major in the First Battalion of the British 60th (Royal American) Regiment with a North American rank of lieutenant colonel. After his death, she married Aaron Burr in 1782.

1. GW made his headquarters at the Hermitage, about two miles north of Paramus, N.J., 11–14 July 1778. An entry in GW's military family expense account indicates that on 14 July, £4.10 was given to Prevost's servants by GW's order (DLC:GW, ser. 5, vol. 28).


## To John Cleves Symmes

Sir                                    Paramus [N.J.] 10th July 1778
I recd yours of the 8th instant near this place, and am extremely sorry to hear of the melancholy stroke that has fallen upon the Wyoming settlement. I have lately made a very considerable detatchment from the Army to go to Fort Pitt to quell the Indian disturbances in that

quarter,[1] and from the loss of Men in the late Action near Monmouth and the numbers that have fallen down thro' fatigue in the excessive heat, I could not, but in a case of the greatest emergency, spare any more. What I shall therefore advise at present is for you and the Gentlemen in your Neighbourhood, to gain the most exact intelligence of the Enemy's Number, Situation and intention. I am of opinion that now they have struck the meditated Blow they will retire and not attempt to penetrate the Country, but should they seem seriously to persist, I will, upon hearing from you again, afford what force I can, to give them a check—In the mean time all possible opposition should be given by the Militia remaining above. I shall discharge those on service below. I am &c.

Df, in Tench Tilghman's writing, DLC:GW; Varick transcript, DLC:GW.
    1. For discussion of the Indian depredations near Fort Pitt and GW's detachment of troops to that post, see Timothy Pickering to GW, 19 May, and GW to Pickering, 23 May.

## From John Cleves Symmes

Sir.                              Minisinks [N.J.] the 10th of july 1778.
    I have the honor to transmit to Your Excellency an Examination of Jacob Wise, who says Many things of the Intentions and Movments of the Enemy, the Substance of which Your Excellency will have Inclosed.[1]
    It would be vain in me to Comment or infer. I beg leave only to Mention to your Excellency that the Militia come in but slow, we have not three hundred men on the River and an extent of 30 Miles frontier. our safety at present depends on the delays of the Enemy, which we cannot expect will protect us long. I should think myself too officious were I to expostulate with your Excellency on our situation.
    The distressed Inhabitants from Wioming are passing this post by hundreds in the Most forlorn Condition; Perhaps no Age has produced a paralel of Cruelty.
    John Devee (now present) who Escaped the battle assures Me that 360 Men fell in the Action who now lie Unburied. I have the honor to be, Your Excellencies humble servant

                                        John Cleves Symmes

ALS, DLC:GW. A notation on the cover indicates that this letter was sent "pr Express."
    1. In the enclosure, dated 10 July, Jacob Wise, "one of the Number of those who cut of[f] Wioming on the 3rd & 4th Inst.," testified "that he left the body of the Enemy on the 5th who were then Making Up the River with the plunder of the Settlement laden in Canoes, that there were six or seven hundred Indians, thinks

the Number of the Tories did not exceed two hundred, that there were no Regular troops with them, that they were Commanded by Col. [John] Butler and a Senakees Chief [Sayenqueraghta]; that one of the block house Garrison Capitulated, Upon terms of having life and property spared, but that the Indians Imediately seized all their property: This Examinant further saith that he left the detachment Commanded by Col. Brant on the Delaware about fourteen days since, that Brant hath about one thousand Indians in his party and two hundred Tories, that their Rendouzvous was at Quago 46 miles above Coshethton and 80 miles from the Upper end of Minisinks, This Examinant says that he Understood (since the Reduction of Wioming) that Col. Butler was to March across from the Susquehannah to join Brant and proceed down the Delaware; That the despotick Conduct of the Indians and the destress which he suffered among them Induced this Examinant to leave them. That he hear'd the Indians had 250 scalps and that they Complained because they Could not get the scalps of the Drowned" (DLC:GW).

## To Jeremiah Wadsworth

Sir,                                      On the March [Paramus, N.J.] 10th July 1778.
   Having received information that there is a quantity of fat Cattle and Sheep in the district called Barbadoes neck[1]—which by their situation are exceedingly exposed to the enemy, and are besides the property of persons disaffected to the United States—I hereby authorise you to take all such Cattle and Sheep as may not be absolutely necessary for the use of the families settled in that neighborhood—paying the value of them—and secure them for the use of the Army. Given at Head Quarters this 10th day of July 1778.

Df, in John Laurens's writing, DLC:GW; Varick transcript, DLC:GW. A purported ALS of this letter was offered for sale in 1943 by William Todd of Mount Carmel, Conn., who noted: "On third page is an order from Wadsworth to Royal Flint, Asst. Commissary General, 'to immediately wait on Major General, the Marquis Lafayette with his Excellency's letter' and the request he carry out the order. Suggests Flint go with the party and that they cross 'a little this side of Shyler's House where I observed a large snow [a small ship resembling a brig].'"
   1. The New Barbadoes Neck was the name given to the peninsula formed by the Hackensack and Passaic rivers in the neighborhood of present-day Kearney, New Jersey.

## From Brigadier General William Winds

                                      Head Quarters Elizth Town [N.J.]
Dear General                                      July 10. 1778
   The Account I had the Honor of Sending you yesterday is Confirmed in Every Material Circumstance by the Capt. & Hands onboard the flagg of Truce provision sloop Who Came Yesterday from New York with this addition that there was a Meeting of the Merchants of New York on

Wednesday last,[1] to Consult on What would be best to be Done on the Evacuation of New York, to know how many & who were Desirous of Continuing under the protection of the British Arms, (My Informants understood this Meeting to be by Direction of Genl Clinton.) the press begun on tuesday Night was Continued on Wednesday Night with Great Warmth, a report prevails in New York that a Vessel Just Arrived had brought Account that she had Spoke a large & strong french fleet a few Days ago off the Capes of Virginia, about 20 leagues from land. In Consequence of Which, all the large ships at New York & a Number of frigates are Ordered Imediately to put to sea, Admiral Gambier has removed his flagg from the Ardent to a small frigate to remain at New York,[2] the press is said to be to Man the large Ships, the New York paper of Yesterday (which my Informants have seen) Gives the above Account & *puff* of 1300 seamen from the Transports having Entered—Volunteers, on board the large Ships In Order to Give Monsieurs a Drubing.[3] the Scarcity of bread is Confirmed not only by the Hands of the flagg sloop, But also by two Deserters Who Made their Escape from Staten Island last Night, & say they had Drawn but one lb. of flour for 4 or 5 Days, In Genl Skinners Brigade to Which they belonged, they are Men known here, had been Kidnappd & forced into their Service. All Accounts Agree that some troops are Speedily to leave this Continent.

A body of troops are lately landed at Powles hook Cannot as Yet learn any thing of their Numbers.

This Appears to me to be a Critical time with them, that they Might Easily be thrown into Great Consternation & Disorder & their plans frustrated be they what they may.

Harvest will be Generally In, in New Jersey in the Course of this Month, After Which I Can Get out 2000 or 3000 Men from My Brigade for a Short time if Wanted, Or Shall be more Mistaken than Ever I was in My life—I have the Honor to be with sincere Esteem Your Excellencys Most Obdt servt

Wm Winds

ALS, DLC:GW.

1. The previous Wednesday was 8 July.

2. Capt. John Peebles on Long Island wrote in his journal for 9 July that in consequence of the reported arrival of a French fleet in American waters, "Lord Howe is gone down himself & order'd all the large ships to the Hook" (Gruber, *Peebles' American War*, 199–200). James Gambier (1723–1789), who had served as a naval officer since 1743 and as commander in chief on the North American station from 1770 to 1773, was promoted to rear admiral in January 1778 and posted back to America. Gambier's letter of 6 July to First Lord of the Admiralty John Montagu, earl of Sandwich, confirms that Howe, having "judged fit to assemble all the ships of his Majesty's fleet of the greatest force in readiness to put to sea on the shortest notice," had directed Gambier to remove his flag from the 64-gun *Ardent*, which would join Howe

while Gambier remained at New York "to regulate the duties here and to co-operate with the commander in chief of the land forces" (*Sandwich Papers*, 2:297).

3. The New York newspaper of July 9 has not been identified. A report of news brought by Capt. George Sibbles of the armed brig *Tryon* on 9 July and the resulting voluntary enlistment of seamen appeared in Rivington's *Royal Gazette* (New York) of July 11 and the *New-York Gazette: and the Weekly Mercury* of 13 July. According to that report, the news was secondhand, having been given to Sibbles by Capt. Alan Gardner of HMS *Maidstone*.

## General Orders

Head-Quarters Peramus [N.J.] Saturday July 11th 1778.
Parole Jones—                              C. Signs Ranger. Drake.

The Commander in Chief is happy to communicate to the Army the fresh testimony of the Approbation of their Country contained in the following Resolve of Congress of 7th instant.

Resolved—That General Washington be directed to signify the thanks of Congress to the gallant Officers and men under His Command who distinguish'd themselves by their Conduct and Valor at the Battle of Monmouth.

The Left Wing will march tomorrow morning at one ôClock—Those Gentlemen belonging to it who are concerned as Witnesses in the Case of General Lee are to remain behind and attend the Court Martial.

Varick transcript, DLC:GW.

## To Major General Benedict Arnold

Dear Sir                    Head-Quarters Paramus [N.J.] 11th July 1778

Your favor of the 8th inst. affords me peculiar satisfaction by informing me that your wound begins to wear a favorable aspect, & that you are recovered from the disorder in your stomach—The left wing of the army is advanced four miles from this place, & 19 miles from Kings ferry—the other two divisions are moving on after it with proper intervals—the enemy since quitting the Jerseys have encamped in three divisions on Staten-Island, New York Island and Long Island—it does not appear to be their design or even practicable for them immediately to commence any offensive operations—this consideration added to the intense heat of the weather determines me to move very leisurely and spare the troops as much as possible—My hurry was so great when I last wrote that I omitted returng you my thanks for your obliging care in forwarding a Letter to Mrs Washington—you will be so good as to accept them now, and excuse the delinquency.[1]

The intelligence of the French fleets sailing from Toulon. gives some weight to the accounts which have been received by a Flag boat from New York of the arrival of a French Fleet off Chesapeak-bay—and induces me to congratulate you on it as matter worthy of credit—a vigorous press is said to have taken place in the harb⟨or⟩ of New York, for the purpose of manning the⟨ir⟩ large Ships which are ordered to be ready for Sea.[2] I am with great regard and es⟨teem⟩ Dr Sir &.

Df, in John Laurens's writing, DLC:GW; Varick transcript, DLC:GW.

1. GW's last letter to Arnold was apparently that of 6 July. The letter for Mrs. Washington was enclosed with a letter from GW to Arnold of 29 June (not found). In his letter to GW of 30 June, Arnold reported forwarding the letter to her.

2. For these reports, see William Winds to GW, 10 July.

## To George Clinton

Dear Sir                    Head Quarters Paramus [N.J.] 11th July 1778

The first division of the Army moved from hence this morning, about four Miles, to give room to the second. They will reach Kakiate tomorrow evening, and the North River the next day. I shall halt the remainder hereabouts a few days, to refresh the Men. I am yet undetermined as to the expediency of throwing the Army immediately over the North River. I will state my reasons for hesitating, and shall beg to hear your sentiments upon the matter.

Upon conversing with the Qr Mr and Commissary General and Commissary of Forage, upon the prospect of supplies, they all agree, that the Army can be much more easily subsisted upon the West, than upon the East side of the River. The Country on this side is more plentiful in regard to Forage: And Flour, which is the Article for which we shall be most likely to be distressed, coming from the Southward, will have a shorter transportation, and consequently the supply more easily kept up. We are besides in a Country devoted to the Enemy, and gleaning it, takes so much from them—Was this the only point to be determined, there would not remain a moments doubt; but the principal matter to be considered, is, (upon a supposition that the Enemy mean to operate up the North River) whether the Army, being all, or part upon this side the River, can afford a sufficient and timely support to the posts, should they put such a design in execution.

Upon this point then, Sir, I request your full and candid opinion. You are well acquainted with the condition of the posts, and know what opposition they are at present capable of making, when sufficiently manned, which ought in my opinion to be immediately done. After that, you will please to take into consideration, whether any, and what advantages may be derived from the Army's being upon the East side of the River, and if there, what position would be most eligible. The neighbourhood of the white plains, after leaving sufficient Garrisons in our Rear, strikes me at present. We know the strength of the Ground, and we cover a considerable extent of Country, and draw the forage which would otherwise fall into the hands of the Enemy.

In forming your opinion, be pleased to advert to the necessity of keeping our force pretty much collected, for which side soever you may determine: For should the Enemy find us disjointed, they may throw the whole of theirs upon part of ours, and, by their shipping, keep us from making a junction.

In determining the above, you are to take it for granted that we can, should it be deemed most expedient, support the Army upon the East, tho' it will be with infinitely more difficulty than upon the West side of the River.

By the latest accounts from New York, it does not seem probable that the Enemy will operate any where suddenly: They have been much harassed and deranged by their march thro' Jersey, and are at present encamped upon Long, Staten and York Islands. We have this day a rumor that a French Fleet has been seen off the Coast, and that the English is preparing to sail from New York in pursuit of them.[1] But it is but a Rumor. I have the Honor to be with the greatest Respect and Esteem Dear Sir Yr most obt and hble Servt

Go: Washington

P.S. I have just recd a letter from General Arnold at Philada in which is the following. "An Express is arrived to Congress from France by the way of Boston with intelligence, that on the 15th of April a French Fleet sailed from Toulon consisting of 12 sail of the line, 7 frigates and 4 Xbecks—which we may hourly expect to arrive in this or Chesapeak Bay—Admiral Keppel sailed the 24th April from St Helens with 11 sail of the line."[2]

The above fully corroborates the account from New York. But I do not know that it ought to be made public yet, I mean as to numbers.

LS, in Tench Tilghman's writing, NNPM; Df, DLC:GW; Varick transcript, DLC:GW. The draft and the transcript lack the postscript.
1. See William Winds to GW, 10 July.
2. GW is quoting from Maj. Gen. Benedict Arnold's letter to him of 8 July.

## From William Eden

Sir                                 New York July 11th 1778

The Book which accompanies this Letter was left at my House in London directed to your Excellency; I do not know what it is nor from whom it comes.[1]

If there is nothing improper in the inclosed Lines to Mr Smith I take the Liberty to request that they may be allowed to pass to Him.[2]

I also send in a separate Packet some Letters under flying Seals; I have not had Time to examine them, but directed none to be received except with assurances that they were solely on private Affairs.[3] I have the Honour to be with the highest personal Respect & Esteem Sir your most obedt Hbe servt

Wm Eden

ALS, DLC:GW.

    1. The book has not been identified.

    2. The enclosure, most likely to William Smith, has not been identified.

    3. These letters have not been identified. A "flying seal" was one attached but not closed, so that the letter could be read before it was delivered.

## To Major General Horatio Gates

Sir                                      Pyramus Church [N.J.] July 11th 1778

I am now as far advanced as this place from whence the left wing of the Army marched to day about Four miles. According to my present Ideas, it will move tomorrow morning, under the Baron de Kalb towards the north River, with a view of passing it, at Kings Ferry. The right wing and second line, which form the remainder, being greatly fatigued by their march and the intensely hot weather, will halt here when they arrive for a few days in order to refresh themselves; as from the latest accounts and such as seem to have come through a pretty direct channel, the Enemy are reposing themselves at new York and on long & Staten Islands, without there being any preparations like a new expedition. These are my present intentions, but I confess, that I am under some difficulty, as to what should be our movements, or what precise disposition to make of the Army, & therefore shall be exceedingly obliged by your advice as soon as possible, on the subject. It is said by the Quarter Master & Commissary General, that it will be much easier to subsist it, i.e., the Troops with me, on this side the river, both with provisions & forage, than on the other, which is a point of material importance; and besides, that we shall drain the disaffected of this Country of those supplies which the Enemy would otherwise get.[1] after considering the state of the fortifications — water defences and other matters necessary to be attended to, I request to be favored with your opinion, whether the whole or a principal part of the Army with me, can remain on this side the river and be in a condition to act properly & in time, in case the Enemy should direct their operations up the river & against those places; and if it can, what place will be most suitable for it to occupy as a Camp.

There is one circumstance, I would recommend to your particular attention, which is the care of the Boats. After Baron Kalb has passed with the wing under his Command, if not before, I think it will be more adviseable to send them up to some of the fortifications, as a place of greater security. When they are wanted, they can be easily had—but if they should be destroyed by the Enemy on any sudden enterprize, the consequences might be extremely injurious, & we should be subjected to a thousand difficulties.

We have had it reported from New York, that there is a French Fleet on the Coast. Just as I was about closing my Letter, I received one from Genl Arnold containing an account which countenances the report. You have an extract from it upon the subject.[2] I dont know whether this intelligence should be made Public for reasons which will be obvious to you. I am Sir Your Most Obet Serv⟨t⟩

Go: Washington

LS, in Richard Kidder Meade's writing, NHi: Gates Papers; Df, DLC:GW; Varick transcript, DLC:GW.

1. At this point on the draft, Robert Hanson Harrison wrote and crossed out the following text before inserting the language that finishes this paragraph in the LS: "However, essential as this is, I would not wish you to make it a governing principle in your opinion independent of all others, but you will take the matter up, upon a large and extensive scale; weighing and balancing every convenience and inconvenience, and particularising, whether the whole or only a part & what proportion of this Army should cross the river or remain on this side, and the several positions, that it should take. The state of the fortifications and the water defences on the river will be a material consideration and the number of men sufficient for their security."

2. GW is referring to Maj. Gen. Benedict Arnold's letter to him of 8 July. The extract has not been found.

## From Major General Nathanael Greene

[c.11–14 July 1778]

I would propose writing to the french Admiral that there are two objects one of the two may be improvd as a blockade or an investiture as circumstances and the practibillity of entering the Harbour of New york should be found.

The french fleet to take their station at Sandy Hook and block up the Harbour. This Army to take a position near the White Plains to cut off the Land communication and to all appearance seem to design some serious opperations against Newyork & the troops there.

General Sullivan to be wrote to, desiring to know what force he has, that may be considerd in the charactor of regular troops what force is from the neighbouring States and expected in a few days, & what Militia can be brought together in Eight days time & how the Magazines are prepard for such a consumption & whether there is Boats to make a landing upon Rhode Island to learn the Strength of the Enemy there and the number of their Ships & of what force.

In the mean time the Admiral to make himself acquainted with the depth of water into Newyork and the Ships & force there. On the return of the Express from General Sullivan the admiral to determin from the enquiry he shall make and the information General Sullivan shall give which will be the most elligible, object. But if it should be found that the fleet can come into the Harbour of Newyork, this Army will be ready to coopperate with him as far as the Nature of the Country & the situation of the Enemy will admit.

The fleet from Sandy Hook can run into Newport in three days time that, that station will be favorable for either the one or the other of the measures—as should be found hereafter to be the most certain of success.

I would inform the admiral of the difficulty of approaching Newyork by Land, of the Enemies strength there; and send a verbal account of our own strength and intended position. I would also send him a Copy of the Letter to G. Sullivan if it is not thought dangerous as it is possible it may fall into the Enemies hands.

AD, DLC:GW. This letter was probably written before GW's letter to Vice Admiral d'Estaing of 14 July. It must have been written after the army heard of the French fleet's arrival on the American coast, the news of which reached GW by 11 July.

## From Henry Laurens

Sir,                                                  Philadelphia 11th July 1778.

I beg leave to refer Your Excellency to the contents of a Letter which I had honor of writing to you last Evening by Barry.

The present Cover will convey to Your Excellency two Acts of Congress of this date.

1—Empowering Your Excellency to call in the Aid of such Militia as shall appear to be necessary from the four Eastern States, from New York & New Jersey for carrying on operations in concert with Count d'Estaing.

2—Intimating the desire of Congress that Your Excellency Cooperate with Vice Admiral Count d'Estaing in the Execution of such offensive operations against the Enemy as shall appear to be necessary.[1]

Congress have directed me to propose for Your Excellencys consideration an attack by Vice Admiral Count dEstaing upon the British Ships of War & Transports in the harbor of Rhode Island, by which possession of a safe port may be gained & the retreat of the British forces on that Island be cut off, as an alternative to a hazardous or ineligible attempt upon the British Squadron within Sandy Hook. I have the honor to be With the highest Esteem & Respect Sir Your Excellency's Most obedient & most humble servant

Henry Laurens,
President of Congress.

Sometime ago I informed Your Excellency that Congress had adopted the Stile of "North America" to these States—this day that Resolution was reconsidered & reduced to the former mode of "America."[2]

Congress Resolved on the 9th Inst. that the Committee appointed to arrange the Army do repair without delay to Head Quarters for that purpose as Your Excellency will perceive by the Inclosed Certified Order.[3]

ALS, DLC:GW; LB, DNA:PCC, item 13. A note on the letter-book copy indicates that this letter was carried "by Baldwin."

1. The enclosed copies of these resolutions are in DLC:GW (see also *JCC*, 11:684).

2. Laurens was referring to his letter to GW of 20 May 1778. For the resolution of 11 July, reconsidering a resolution of 19 May, see ibid., 11:683.

3. The enclosed copy of this resolution, certified by Laurens, is in DLC:GW (see also ibid., 11:676).

## To Elizabeth Watkins

[Paramus, N.J.] Saturday July 11th 1778.

Genl Washington presents his respectful compliments to Miss Watkins, and offers his grateful thanks for her curious present of a laurel wreath, which he shall wear, with great pleasure in remembrance of the fair giver.

The Genl was not honord with the receipt of Miss Watkinss favor till yesterday afternoon which will apologize for his delay in the acknowledgmt.

AL (facsimile), Van Rensselaer, *Annals of the Van Rensselaers*, facing p. 147. Elizabeth Watkins (d. 1846) was a daughter of John Watkins, formerly of the West Indies and then of Harlem Heights, N.Y., who was residing at Paramus, N.J., during the British occupation of New York City. In 1792 she married Robert Henry Dunkin of Philadelphia.

## General Orders

Head-Quarters Peramus [N.J.] Sabbath July 12th 1778.

Parole Bridgewater—                    C. Signs Bergen. Bristol.

At a General Court Martial in the Right Wing of the Army at Watersisson[1] July 9th 1778—Lieutt Coll Meade President, Captain Lipscomb,

Acting Quarter-Master General to the Division commanded by Majr General Baron de Steuben, tried for treating the General in a disrespectful manner.

After considering the Charge and Evidence the Court are unanimously of opinion that Captain Lipscomb is not guilty of the Charge exhibited against him and do acquit him with honor.

The General approves the sentence; He is willing to believe that Captain Lipscomb did not intend that disrespect to Baron de Steuben, which the Baron apprehended, at the same time he must observe that there was an Impropiety in Captain Lipscomb's taking quarters in a house destined for the General commanding the Division.

At the same Court Lieutt West of Coll Angell's Regiment was tried for plundering the property of Mrs Golf in the Month of December A.D. 1776. found guilty of the Charge exhibited against him and sentenced to be discharged from the service[2]—The Commander in Chief confirms the sentence, and orders it to take place immediately.

The Commander in Chief directs that no sick be left on this ground but that they be all carried to King's-Ferry—Spare Waggons are to be provided for such as cannot be conveyed on the Baggage Waggons.

The Post-Office will in future on a march move and remain with the Park.

Varick transcript, DLC:GW.

1. Wardsesson (Watsessing) in Essex County, N.J., was given its modern name of Bloomfield in 1796.

2. Ebenezer West, who was appointed as an ensign in the 11th Continental Infantry in January 1776, was commissioned a second lieutenant of the regiment, reorganized and renamed the 2d Rhode Island Regiment, on 11 Feb. 1777. Other orderly books record the victim's name as "Mrs Jeff" (orderly book of Jedediah Huntington's brigade, NHi; see also *N.C. State Records*, 12:502).

## To William Henry Drayton

Dr Sir,                              Head Quarters Paramus [N.J.] July 12. 1778

Permit me to assure you, that the cordial terms of your obliging favour of the 5th afford me the most sensible pleasure.[1] It, naturally, is my ardent wish, that my well-meant endeavours, for the prosperity of my country, may meet the approbation of my countrymen; and I cannot but be peculiarly flattered by every instance of esteem, from the discerning part of them.

The want of a longer personal acquaintance rather increases, than lessens my obligation, for your politeness on the present occasion, which certainly could need no apology on that, or on any other account. I need not say, I shall be happy in every occasion of cultivating a continuance of your friendship, and convincing you, that I am, with great regard, Dr Sir Your most Obedt serv.

Df, in Alexander Hamilton's writing, DLC:GW; Varick transcript, DLC:GW. The address to Drayton on the draft is in GW's writing.

1. Drayton had written GW from Philadelphia on 5 July: "While I am sensible that I hazard your Excellency's censure of my discretion; yet, I cannot resist the impulse I feel, to pay you my little tribute of thanks for the important Victory of Monmouth; and to express, how much I feel myself tenderly & anxiously interested in every thing respecting your safety and glory. Your Excellency's invariable conduct, naturally exposes you to such intrusions; and I rely upon it, that your good nature will pardon this.

"Personally almost unknown to you as I am, yet Sir, this obstacle is too weak to prevent a gratification on my part, which gives me the highest pleasure: Some how or other, Nature has composed me of materials, which are apt to force the bounds of common decorum, when my affections and gratitude are excited.

"That your Excellency's life may long be preserved in your glorious and disinterested defence of your country; & in the enjoyment of the fruits of your labours and victories, is my most fervent prayer" (MH: Sparks Collection).

## To Henry Laurens

Sir                Camp at pyramus [N.J.] July 12th 1778

On friday evening I had the honor to receive your Letter of the 7th Instant, with it's inclosures.[1]

The vote of approbation and thanks, which Congress have been pleased to honor me with, gives me the highest satisfaction, and, at the same time, demands a return of my sincerest acknowledgements. The other resolution, I communicated, with great pleasure, to the Army at large in Yesterday's orders.[2]

The left wing of the Army, which advanced yesterday four miles beyond this, moved this morning on the route towards King's ferry. The right and the second line, which makes the last division are now here,[3] where they will halt for a day or two or perhaps longer, if no circumstances of a pressing nature cast up, in order to refresh themselves from the great fatigues they have suffered from the intense heat of the weather.

We have had it reported for two or three days, through several channels from New-York, that there is a french fleet on the Coast; and it is added, that the Enemy have been manning with the utmost dispatch several of their Ships of war which were there, and have pushed them out to sea. How far these facts are true, I cannot determine, but I should think it of infinite importance to ascertain the first if possible, by sending out swift sailing Cruizers. The most interesting advantages might follow the information. I will try by every practicable means, that I can devise, to obtain an accurate account of the Enemy's fleet at New York. I have the Honor to be with great respect & esteem sir Yr Most Obedt sert

Go: Washington

LS, in Robert Hanson Harrison's writing, DNA:PCC, item 152; Df, DLC:GW; copy, DNA:PCC, item 169; Varick transcript, DLC:GW. The LS was docketed in part, "Read 15. 1778"; see *JCC*, 11:688–89.

1. GW was referring to Laurens's official letter to him of 8 July, enclosing resolutions of 7 July. The previous Friday was 10 July.

2. For the resolutions, see Laurens to GW, 8 July, and note 1 to that document.

3. On the draft, Harrison initially wrote, "The right is now on their ground and the second line, which makes the last division, will, I expect be here by nine or Ten oClock" before changing the text to the words of the LS.

## To Major General Alexander McDougall

Dear Sir              Camp near pyramus Church [N.J.] July 12. 1778
I am very desirous of seeing you, and request that you will be with me, as soon as you can, without injury to your health or overfatiguing yourself. I am Dr Sir with great regard & esteem Yr Most Obedt servt

Go: Washington

LS, owned (1996) by Mr. Joseph Rubinfine, West Palm Beach, Florida. GW signed the cover, which was addressed to McDougall at Peekskill, New York. McDougall's docket on the letter reads, "recd 14th at 7 A.M."

## General Orders

Head-Quarters Peramus [N.J.] Monday July 13th 1778.
Parole Courage—              C. Signs Conduct Conquest
The first Division (or Right Wing) of the Army is to march precisely at two ôClock tomorrow morning—the second Division is to be in readiness to move at three but not to march 'till further Orders—Both Divisions are to observe their late order of march and the Officers commanding them to receive their Route and have their Encampments pointed out by the Quarter Master General. The Court Martial whereof Majr General Lord Stirling is President will not adjourn from the present place of their sitting 'till further orders.

A Party of 250 men is to be ready at five ôClock this afternoon with three days provisions exclusive of the present—The Officer Commanding the detachment will receive his orders from the Adjutant General.[1]

Captain Charles Porterfield of the 11th Virginia Regiment is appointed Brigade Major in General Woodford's Brigade and is to be obeyed and respected accordingly.

The Army marching by Divisions.

Varick transcript, DLC:GW.
1. The orderly book of Jedediah Huntington's brigade specifies the adjutant general "of the Right Wing" (NHi).

## From Lieutenant Colonel Francis Barber

Sir,                                        Elisath town [N.J.] July 13th 1778

One of the persons whom you allowed me to send for Intelligence returned last night from Staten Island—He informs, that the greatest part of the British Army are encamped there, their Baggage with them—That General Grant now commands on the Island—That Generals Clinton & Cornwallis are in New York—That there appears to be no preparations for a Move either by Land or Water—That they talk of nothing else now, but the French Fleet, which some assert is near sandy-Hook [1]—That their Men of War are in readiness to sail, but have not yet moved—That all Officers on Furlough or half pay are ordered to join their respective Corps—That the Cavalry are on Long Island with some Infantry—That they confess they had more than 300 killed in the last Engagement & cannot immagine what the Devil made the Rebels fight so obstinately—That they are exceedingly alarmed at the Approach of the French fleet on account of their Provision Vessels which they are expecting daily & seem to stand in need of.

The Bearer John Hendricks brother to the Informer, who likewise was on the Island two nights ago being willing to convey this letter, I have sent to your Excellency in preference to another, that you may have an opportunity of asking him many Questions which may have escaped me—You may depend upon his & his brother Fidelity and strong Attachment to your Interest & success—They have served much in this way & suffered much with I believe, little or no reward heretofore.[2]

Gen: Maxwell, with his Brigade are in this town, I think, by advice from the Governor & Desire of the principal Inhabitants.

I hope my situation will plead an Excuse for every Inaccuracy in my Letter. I am with the highest Esteem, your Excellency's very humble Servant

F. Barber

ALS, DLC:GW.
1. British naval captain Henry Duncan, who was anchored at Staten Island, recorded in his journal that "the French fleet . . . anchored at the back of the Hook" at "2 o'clock p.m." on 11 July ("Journals of Henry Duncan," 159).
2. In 1777 Col. Elias Dayton had employed John Hendricks and Baker Hendricks (c.1756–1789) as spies. For more on their activities, see GW to John Clark, Jr.,

29 Sept. 1777; William Livingston to GW, 22 Nov. 1777 and 26 Jan. 1778; and GW to Livingston, 20 Jan. (second letter) and 2 Feb. 1778. Another informant about this time stated that the Loyalist Brig. Gen. Cortlandt Skinner had said that he knew that John Hendricks and others "had passes from the rebels and that he told them a number of Story that the[y] might communicate" (examinations of No. 1 and No. 2, n.d., FrPNA: Marine, B4, I43). In September 1780, Baker Hendricks was commissioned by New Jersey to operate two whaleboats as privateers, and in the two years following he led numerous raids against Staten Island and Bergen Neck. However, his commission was revoked in June 1782 after he was accused of using the commission to carry on "an illegal intercourse" with the enemy (Prince, *Livingston Papers*, 4:428–29).

# From Colonel George Baylor

Dear Sir                                                   Fredsburg [Va.] July 13th 1778

Since my last letter to you I have made few or no purchases of Horses.[1] having got all in this part of the country which wo'd answer as troopers, excepting the best kind; the price of which I think too extravigant, from two to three hundred pounds.

I have repeatedly spoke to Mr Hunter and his maniger at his works about the armes which I had engaged, they as often tel me that they shall be done, which has by no means been compli'd with. I have been frequently deceiv'd & much disappointed by them.[2]

Major Wash[i]ngton who could be no longer servisable here is gone to join his Regiment. A party of 36 men & 60 Horses of Colo. Blands, left this yesterday for Camp. I shall send off a party of 20 men and 40 Horses tomorrow under Lieut. Randolph. the men & Horses which I send, I think are good and pretty well Traind.

enclosd is the proceedings of a Regimental court of enquirery on Lieut. John Baylor for gameing, whome I have arrested. his plea is, a total ignorance of your ever having issued orders forbiding it. I should be glad to have your derections respecting him.[3]

As there is but little prospect of our geting many more Horses, I think it will be unnecessary to keep the recruits which I have got, here, for the purpose of taking the Horses to Camp, as I believe men may be got now, as fast as Horses.

Give me leave Sir in the most sincere manner to congratulate you on your signal suckcess in the Jearsy. I am dr Sir with the greatest Respect your most obedt and very Huml. Servant.

George Baylor

ALS, DLC:GW; ADfS, owned (1980) by Mr. David Rust, Leesburg, Virginia.

1. The most recent letter from Baylor to GW that has been identified is dated 27 May 1778.

2. For discussion of Baylor's engagement with James Hunter, Sr., see Baylor to GW, 11 May. The manager of Hunter's Iron Works was John Strode.

3. The court, held at Fredericksburg, Va., on 3 July, found John Baylor guilty (DLC:GW).

## From Vice Admiral d'Estaing

Sir                    In the Road without Sandy Hook the 13th July 1778

The desire of communicating speedily with Your Excellency determines me to make a debarkation upon the Coast of Jersey in a village which according to the Map is to the Northward of the River Shrewsbury. If our common enemy are in possession and can be driven from it, I shall fulfil the object of my descent—An instant of liberty will suffice for a good patriot to dare to show himself—Every citizen will be eager to convey my homage to the deliverer of his country. The first moments are so pretious, above all upon Sea, that it may be of the greatest importance for me to be informed four and twenty hours sooner or later of the projects of Your Excellency. I have orders to second them; I dare assure you, that I will do it to the utmost of my power. To act in concert with a great man is the first of blessings—tis one of those which flatter me the most in the commission with which I am honored. An apprehension that the letter, of which I have now the honor to send a duplicate,[1] may not come to hand 'till late, makes me hazard a step, the motive for which must be the excuse. I have the honor to be &c.

Estaing

Translation, in Alexander Hamilton's writing, DLC:GW; LS, in French, DLC:GW.

1. D'Estaing was referring to his letter to GW of 8 July.

## To David Forman

Dear Sir.                    Head Quarters Paramus [N.J.] July 13th 1778

Having received intelligence from Congress that the french fleet under the command of Admiral Count d'Estaing arrived near Chincoteague on the evening of the 5th Inst.—I have written to the Admiral in order to concert such a Plan of cooperation with him as the nature of the case will admit, and establish proper signals for reciprocal intelligence[1]—Mr Laurens is bearer of my letter to him—as it is of the utmost consequence that Count d'Estaing shd be immediately acquainted with the Strength and posture of the Enemys fleet & other matters contained in my letter, I entreat you by every means in your power to facilitate & expedite Mr Laurenss getting on board the Admirals Ship. I am with great Regard Dear Sir Yours &c.

Df, in John Laurens's writing, DLC:GW; Varick transcript, DLC:GW.

1. For the intelligence from Congress, received on the evening of 13 July, see Henry Laurens to GW, 10 July. GW's letter to Vice Admiral d'Estaing is dated 14 July.

## From Major General Horatio Gates

Sir,                                        White plains 13th July 1778.

This morning early, I was honoured by the receipt of Your Excellency's Letter of the 11th—dated from pyramus Church. In Obedience to Your Excellency's Commands, to give my Opinion of the Disposition to be immediately made, of the Troops marching with Your Excellency, I presume to say, that I perfectly approve of Your Excellency's keeping the Right Wing, & Second Line of the Grand Army, upon the West Side of Hudson's River, from Haverstraw, towards Kings Ferry; One Brigade to Occupy the post on Stoney point, and that Opposite, on the East Side of the River; as I conceive the Left Wing under Major General Baron de Kalbe, will amount to Four Thousand Men, that, in Addition to the Troops now here, will, in my humble Opinion, be Sufficient to restrain the Enemy to narrow limits on this side the River, and Guard the whole front of the Highlands. The position at Haverstraw &c., with the remaining part of the Army, will Secure more Forage, provissions, &c., than can be provided by a Junction of the whole on this peninsula: The defences on the River, and the important post of West point, will also be better Secured by this Division of the Army.

There is no Forage, Grass excepted, to be had here; and that, must soon be procured near the Enemy's Lines. I have ordered Lieut. Colonel Hay, Depy Quarter Master General, in Conjunction with General Glover, & Colonel La Radiere, (who for the present Commands at Ver plank's point,) to make the best disposition, as well for the Use, as the Security of Our Boats & Water Craft, at, and above Kings Ferry. In those Hands, I have not the Smallest doubt but Your Excellency's intentions will be fully executed.[1]

The [    ] Instant, I sent one of my Aids to Springfield, to see the Arms wanted for the Drafts brought forward; and to Order Colonel Armand's Corps to March immediately to Fish Kill, from whence, with Your Excellency's Approbation, I would post them Immediately at West point, where they may be kept in due Obedience, prevented from Deserting, and made to forward the Compleating that important Fortress: It is high time they were removed from Springfield.[2]

Inclosed are Dispatches just received from Albany, with my Answers to Brigr General Stark;[3] I wish, in Confidence, to say every thing I know, and every thing I think, to Your Excellency, upon Affairs to the Northward, and Westward: when the Troops are fixed in their proper positions, I wish to wait upon Your Excellency, for a few Hours, at Your Head Quarters. I am, Sir, Your Excellency's Most Obedt & Hume Servt

Horatio Gates

LS, DLC:GW; ADf, NHi: Gates Papers.

1. Drafts of Gates's orders of 13 July to Lt. Col. Udny Hay and Colonel La Radière are in NHi: Gates Papers. Gates directed Hay to "request General Glover, in my Name, to give you, and Col: La Radiere, every Assistance his Garrison can Afford in promoting a Service so Essentially necessary to be immediately performed."

2. When Gates wrote GW on 24 June, he asked about ordering the corps of foreign troops from Springfield, and GW's reply of 28 June agreed that the corps should be moved.

3. Gates enclosed copies of Brig. Gen. John Stark's letters to him of 7 and 9 July 1778 and his reply to Stark of 13 July. He also included a copy of a return of Col. Ichabod Alden's regiment, dated 4 July, that Stark had sent to him, and he probably enclosed a copy of Col. Peter Gansevoort's letter to George Clinton, dated 6 July, and Gansevoort's "Monthly Return of the State of the Garrison at Fort Schuyler," dated 1 July (all items, DLC:GW). Stark's 7 July letter gave his opinion that the men of Col. Timothy Bedel's regiment "were never raisd for any Service but to stay at Home" and continued: "I have wrote to Coll Beedle to march the rest agreeable to your Orders which will find out the Truth of the Matter. I desire he may have no Orders to the contrary till he Arrives. . . . I think there is Necessity of a Pay Master at this Place. part of Coll Beedles Regiment are here and they want Money. the Militia (whose times are out) Complain it will cost them more to go down to you than their Pay will come to & if they cannot be payd when their Times are out it will discourage others to turn out so readily as these have done. by that means be a detriment to the Service, I would be very sorry they should have the least reason to complain.

"I have met with some Difficulty in getting down the Gun Boats. I applyd to the Quarter Master for Pilots & withal Asked Mr Van Vachten if a number of the Assistants were not Pilots. he told me they were and he would send them, when they heard it they complain'd that it was degrading their Important Rank to take Charge of Gun Boats and Employd others by which means four of the Boats are gone And two that are Ready is left for the above Reasons. . . .

"We have had no Alarm lately but daily threatned."

Stark's 9 July letter reported that he had received a letter from Gansevoort, "who Informs me that he has got Intelligence that the Enemy are making preparations to Invest Fort Schuyler—in Consequence of which I have ordered Colonel Aldens Regiment to Reinforce him which leaves me without any troops but a few Militia and them without any Field Officers, would be glad of a few Continental Troops if not more than a Regiment it would be of Great service to us." Stark added that he had not received some promised field pieces and requested that "they might be sent as soon as possible."

Gates replied that the artillery "must be at Albany by this time" and promised that he would "immediately send a Deputy pay Master General to Albany, with 50,000 Dollars for the payment of The Troops, Continental, & Militia. . . . As to the

Sending You more Continental Troops, that, is not in my power; but General Washington, who is just at Hand, has received Your last Letter, with the Inclosures; and will himself Determine upon that Subject." Gates also wrote: "Should the Intelligence from Oswegathie, continue to Obtain Credit, and the Alarm from that Quarter increase, you will immediately Apply in my name to Hampshire, & Berkshire, for More Militia, and acquaint Colonel Ethan Allen, it is my request he immediately March with all the Militia he can without delay Collect, to Albany; it may not be amiss at the same time to intimate to the Council at Benington, that I desire their assistance, and Concurrence, in every measure you think indespensibly necessary for the public Service. Bedel's Regiment has my Orders to be at Albany the first day of Next Month, where they are to receive pay, & Cloathing."

Gansevoort's letter to Clinton of 6 July (which Clinton had sent to Gates on 10 July) reported: "A few hours ago Lieut. Gerrit Staats returned in Company with Six Oneida Indians which I had sent to obtain Intelligence from the Enemy at Oswegatie. . . . the Indians . . . Obtained Intelligence that a considerable body of british Troops and Indians was advancing up the River in order to invest this Garrison; the Circumstance in conjuction with their Intelligence they say, corroberates from the number of Indian Women they seen returning from the enemy's Encampment above Oswegatie and a report among them prevailing of an Attack being design'd against this Place, and coroberating likewise by a discharge of Artillery at the close of a Conference (as they understood) held with the Savages at the aforesaid Place. Prior to this Intelligence I have received Information from the Tuscarora Indians (a friendly Nation) that a certain Quantity of Provisions and military Stores have been forwarded to Caderaque intended for the like purpose from the above Intelligence which I have always found Authentic in the Indians I have no reason to dispute that their Designs are against this Place, the enclosed Returns will shew the State of this Garrison to which must refer for almost every Particular which is necessary for us to have, and do not Doubt but every needful Aid will be forwarded with all Dispatch: in reliance thereon and our own exertions to defend to the last extremity are the only Means we have with the favor of Heaven to save the grand Pass to the western World.

"The Indians imagine that they might have been at Oswego about three Days ago judging from the time the Warriors sent away their Women to Oswegatie from Bucks Island—if so it will afford us at least One Week to add to our preparations to give them a disagreable Wellcome and a surly Treat."

## To Major General Johann Kalb

Camp at pyramus [N.J.]
D. Sir                                    July 13 [1778] 9 oClock P.M.
I am to request that you will cross the North or Hudson's river, as soon as possible, with the Troops now under your command and take post on the other side on some good convenient grounds, where you will wait for further orders. Some advices I have received this minute require this movement to be made with every degree of dispatch. I am D. Sir with respect & esteem

Go: Washington

Df, in Robert Hanson Harrison's writing, DLC:GW; Varick transcript, DLC:GW.

## To Lieutenant Colonel Francis Barber

Sir,                          Head Quarters Paramus [N.J.] July 14th 1778

I have received your favour of yesterday, and am obliged to you for the intelligence, it contains. I beg you will continue your endeavours to procure every information, you can, concerning the enemy's situation and designs, as well with respect to their naval as to their land force, which, at this time, is peculiarly important. For this purpose, I send you a number of questions, which you will deliver to the persons you employ in the business, to direct the objects of their inquiry. If you think of any matters, not mentioned there, the knowledge of which may be useful, you will add the necessary questions for obtaining it.[1] I am at a loss what will be a reasonable compensation to Hendricks. His expectations, founded on the risk he has run, what he has suffered and what he has lost seem to be pretty high. Of these, as he was not employed under my immediate direction and I am unacquainted with the circumstances attending the execution of his trust, I cannot be a proper judge. I should be glad you would make particular inquiry, into the matter, and let me have your opinion, what may be an adequate reward. I understand he has been chiefly employed by General Wynds and Col: Dayton, who will therefore be able to inform what services he has rendered. With my best wishes for your speedy recovery and with much regard—I am Sir Your most Obedt servant

                                        Go: Washington

LS, in Alexander Hamilton's writing, DLC: Hamilton-McLane Family Papers; Df, DLC:GW; Varick transcript, DLC:GW.

1. On the draft, Hamilton wrote at this point, "I have given Hendricks a reward which I hope will be adequate to his expectations and deserts," but he crossed those words out and substituted text that essentially matches that used in the LS.

## To Vice Admiral d'Estaing

Sir.                          Camp at pyramus [N.J.] July 14th 1778

I take the earliest opportunity to advise you, that I have been informed of your arrival on this coast, with a fleet of Ships under your command, belonging to his most Christian Majesty, our Great Ally. I congratulate you, Sir, most sincerely upon this event and beg leave to assure you of my warmest wishes for your success. The intelligence of your arrival was communicated to me last night, by a Letter from the Honble Mr Laurens, president of the Congress, as you will perceive by the inclosed copy.[1]

With respect to the number or force of the British ships of War, in the port of New York, I am so unhappy, as not to be able to inform you of either, with the precision, I could wish[2] as they are constantly shifting their Stations. It is probable and I hope it is the case, that your advices on this subject from some captures you may have made, are more certain than those of Congress, or any I can offer. The number of their transports is reported to be extremely great, and I am persuaded that it is. If possible, I will obtain an accurate state of their Ships of war, which I shall do myself the honor of transmitting to you.

Before I conclude, I think it proper to acquaint you, that I am now arrived with the main body of the Army, immediately under my command, within twenty miles of the North or Hudson's river, which I mean to pass as soon as possible about fifty miles above New York. I shall then move down before the Enemy's lines, with a view of giving them every jealousy in my power. And I further think it proper to assure you, that I shall upon every occasion feel the strongest inclination to facilitate such enterprizes as you may form and are pleased to communicate to me.[3]

I would submit it to your consideration, whether it will not be expedient to establish some conventional signals, for the purpose of promoting an easier correspondence between us & mutual intelligence. If you deem it expedient, you will be so obliging as to fix upon them, with Lieut. Colo. Laurens, One of my Aids, who will have the honor of delivering you this, and of giving you satisfaction in many particulars respecting our affairs, and to whom you may safely confide any measures or information you may wish me to be acquainted with.

I have just received advice, that the Enemy are in daily expectation of a provision fleet from Cork, and that they are under great apprehensions, lest it should fall into your hands.[4] You will also permit me to notice, that there is a navigation to New-York from the sea, besides the one between Sandy Hook & Long Island. This lies between the latter and the state of Connecticut—is commonly known by the name of the sound and is capable of receiving forty Gun Ships, though the passage within seven miles of the City at a particular place is extremely narrow & difficult. I have the Honor to be with great respect Sir Yr Most Obedt sevt

G. Washington

Df, in Robert Hanson Harrison's writing, DLC:GW; copy, enclosed in GW to Henry Laurens, 22 July (second letter), DNA:PCC, item 152; copy (extract), FrPBN; copy, DNA:PCC, item 169; Varick transcript, DLC:GW. The text of the extract is the first paragraph of the draft.

1. The enclosed copy of Henry Laurens's letter to GW of 10 July has not been found.

2. The remainder of this sentence was inserted on the draft in the writing of Tench Tilghman.

3. Some of GW's thoughts about possible combined operations around this time are indicated by an undated document in his writing docketed as "Loose thoughts

upon an Attack of N. York" (DLC:GW). The document, which was written some-time after news of d'Estaing's command reached GW (10 or 11 July), reads: "An Attack, upon the enemy at New York & its dependencies, must be regulated by the posts they occupy, and the nature of their defence.

"At present they are much dispersed—Some being in the City, & some at Kings bridge—while long Island—Staten Island—Powles hook—&, (as some say) Sandy hook also have a part. a thousand remain at the points at Kings-ferry.

"If they remain thus seperated and divided when the French-fleet arrives, it ought to be the first object of Count D'Estaing to keep them so. & this is no other wise to be done than by pushing a sufficient number of Vessells by the hook—destroying all the Boats on Staten Island & by laying his ships in the Bay between New York & Staten Island prevent others getting there. Unless the Boats on Stat⟨en⟩ Island are immediately destroyed, & suc⟨h⟩ a disposition of the Ships made as will pr⟨e⟩vent others from getting there, a retreat to long Island will, & can easily be affected by the enemy. A few Ships should also be run immediately up the No. River into Haverstraw-bay. to prevent the retreat of the Garrison of Stony-point by Water & to secure the communication of the Rivr—These operations would render the reduction of those bodies of Men which occupy Staten Island & stony point certain; but the Troops on long Island—at Kings bridge—& at Powles hook may, in spite of any endeavours of the *fleet*, form a junction; & in defiance of a land force also; if it is undertaken in time.

"But to pursue the idea, & supposition, that they will continue forces on long Island and at Powles-hook (which is very probable & not less desirable) a position should be taken & inforce on the heights above Morrissena—pointing equally to Haerlam River & a passage over the East River to long Island—while it is contiguous to the North River. Every demonstration for crossing the East River should be thrown out at the sametime that real preparations are making for throwing Troops over Harlem River & possessing the heights above Harlem Plains for the purpose of cutting off the communication & retreat of the Troops from Kings bridge to the City. The demonstration is to draw the attention of the enemy to long Island & leave that of York more unguarded. feints must be practiced to give countenance to a belief that the Army is going over to long Island: but for the execution of the real design—a number of Boats must be held in readiness on the North-river (at Stony point if we are ⟨in⟩ possession of it, if not, at some other place ⟨le⟩ast liable to betray the design) ready to move ⟨d⟩own at a certain time, & to a certain place for the purpose of receiving Troops to be landed at the heights below Harlem plains. To facilitate this operation & prevent the Troops in the City from moving out, Count D'Estaing (who previous to the hour of co-operation shd also hold out every appearance of landing on long Island to form a junction with our Troops at some given point) should have his Troops Imbarked on board boats ready to land in reality, or to make a shew of it as circumstances may point out and will justify. These Troops to be covered by their own Shipping in New York bay—while those in the No. River receive protection from the French ships above spiken devil. which are to move down to prevent the retreat of the garris⟨on⟩ at and about Kings bridge & cover the flan⟨ks⟩ of our Incampment at Harlem. The Armed Vessels in the Sound should move as near Morrissena as possible to cut off all communication between Rhode Isld & New York & prevent the Troops at Kings bridge getting on to long Island by moving on the East side of Harlem river towards it.

"If this plan should Succeed—& it appears at least probable under the effect of a consternation at possessing Harlem heig. & seperating the Troops on the Island a spirited exertion with the proper means which must be previously prepared may set fire to and destroy all the Shipping in the North River provided they should be at or above Turtle-bay.

"If it shall be thought advisable after obtaining some certain knowledge of the enemy's strength on Staten Island to make an attempt upon them there, & a force in addition to that on board the fleet wanting ⟨to⟩ effect the purpose—Lord Stirlings divisio⟨n⟩ or the light infa⟨ntry⟩ & the Pensylvania Militia may be employ⟨ed⟩ on that Service with the Jersey Militia if necess⟨ary⟩.

"The foregoing operation is on the presumption that the enemy, upon the appearance of the French fleet will continue to occupy their present Posts in the manner they now hold them; but in case they should concenter themselves in, or near the City, & at Brooklyn—the plan will vary.

"It may be necessary in that cas⟨e⟩ for Count D'Estaing to Possess Staten Island with his Troops, while his Ships lay in New York bay—Lord Stirling's division or light Infan⟨try⟩ and Pensa Militia may also join them. these to be held in readiness to make a descen⟨t⟩ at long Island. at such a time & at such place as may be agreed on, in order with other Troops which may be thrown across the East River to form an Army for long Is⟨land⟩—The residue of the Troops to advance to Harlem & proceed on to York Island by w⟨ay⟩ of Kings bridge if the Garrisons are with drawn—or Harlem river if a few Troops are left in them merely to hold the Works. and take possession of the heights where the enemy had their first lines. & then Murrys Hill. The French shipping guarding the rig⟨ht⟩ Flank. good & strong pickets to secure our left & Front. a breast work of Waggons—Abbatis & Pits—or something else to guard against the effect of a sudden attack, or Night surprize.

"The rest being the work of regular approaches it must speak as circumstances direct."

A second undated document, in the hand of GW's assistant secretary James McHenry, also ruminates about the prospects for joint operations: "I admit this proposition that, In case the enemy do not mean to operate offensively their primary object will be the preservation of their fleet and army at N. York and Rhode Island—or a removal to places where they can be of more use to Great Britain.

"What are we to expect from a blockade if N. York is fixed on for such an experiment; and in case the Admiral cannot pass the bar? are we certain that the garrison want provisions or that they have not enough to hold the place till they can be relieved. To set out on such a belief is precarious. Besides the slow steps of a blockade against such a large force, is of hazardous & uncertain issue. But, are we informed that France can pursue her plans against the English dominions, and at the same time counteract such naval force as may be sent out to ruin the blockade. This supposes, at least the French naval strength equal to the British and the chances of an engagement in favor of the French.

"It may be said that the army in America is of so much importance to Englands existence as a power, that we must beleive her both blind and insane to suffer it to fall a sacrifice. The instance would be unexampelled. She will therefore it may be supposed risque every thing for the relief of N. York in case of a blockade. Of course little is to ⟨be⟩ expected from its cold operations But if any thing is to be meditated against N. York it must be sudden—While the Count d'Estaign passes the Hook (if this is practicable) we should strike some of their posts, at the same instant.

"All manouvers by land against New-York will have more of show than efficacy on our part—The most we can effect will be cutting off all supplies from the Country.

"A descent upon Rhode Island seems to promise more success, while at the same time [it] has a less hazardous complexion, both with respect to our army and the

French fleet. Both can act with more certainty at Rhode Island and co-operrate more in view of each other than at N. York. and if successful here N. York still remains.

"But An attack upon this place should be rapid and completed before they can either reinforce that post or withdraw the garrison. The present moment is precious—we should loose some blood in order to make the Count d'Estaign generous of his.

"The present moment is also precious to France. The Count d'Estaign's armament was destined to take advantage of this conjuncture. If therefore the Count does not operate *now*—his purpose and intentions may soon be counteracted by the arrival of an English squadron, or a new disposition of General Clintons force and Lord Howes fleet" (CSmH).

4. For this intelligence, see Francis Barber to GW, 13 July. The information is also reported in the examinations of No. 1 and No. 2, n.d., FrPNA: Marine, B4, I43.

## To Major General Horatio Gates

Sir                    Head Quarters Paramus [N.J.] 14th July 1778.

The report of a French Fleet's being on the Coast, as mentioned in my letter of the 11th is confirmed. I received last night advices from Congress, that a Ship of 90—2 of 80—8 of 74—1 of 64 and 4 of 36 Guns were off Chingoteague on Wednesday last, where they fell in with, and sunk the Lydia of 26 Guns on a cruise from New York.[1] The Fleet is under the command of Admiral Count D'Estaing, and was originally designed to come into the Delaware; but finding Philadelphia evacuated, and the British Ships all gone to New York, they intended to sail to Sandy Hook. After mentioning this, and congratulating you on the happy event, I must request that you will take the earliest and every possible means you can devise, to obtain an accurate account of the Ships of War at New York, or that have gone out lately, and of their respective force, which you will transmit me without a moments delay, in order that it may be put into a proper channel of conveyance to the Admiral. The importance of this will strike you at once, and therefore I will not add further upon the subject, without it is to tell you, that Admiral Keppell was to sail from Portsmouth with a Fleet in pursuit of this.

Interest and policy strongly press[2] us to cooperate with, and to give every countenance to our Friends upon this occasion; and this is the wish of Congress. I therefore think it will be material for you to circulate a report in a *proper manner*, that we are upon the point of concentering our whole force and bringing it to act against New York. This will excite the Enemy's fears, and aided by such movements and other measures as you may judge it advisable to take, may greatly facilitate the Admiral's designs, and produce the most beneficial consequences.

We should attempt to rouse their jealousy in every quarter, and in every shape. The Baron de Kalb I expect will, in the course of a day or two, cross Hudsons River with the left Wing of this Army. I am Sir Yr Most Obedt servt[3]

Go: Washington

LS, in Tench Tilghman's writing, NHi: Gates Papers; Df, DLC:GW; Varick transcript, DLC:GW.

1. See Henry Laurens to GW, 10 July.

2. Robert Hanson Harrison struck the word "invite" from the LS and substituted "press."

3. The closing is in Harrison's writing.

## To Major General Horatio Gates

Sir,                               Head Quarters Paramus [N.J.] July 14th 1778

I am just favord with your Letter of yesterday. The right wing and second line of the army marched this morning from hence and will be at Haverstraw tomorrow, where I also expect to be at the same time. I shall be glad to see you there without delay to confer on the several subjects of your letter, and on some other matters of importance. I wrote to you last night communicating the intelligence I had received from Congress of the arrival of a French fleet on our coast;[1] this morning brought me accounts, though not certain,[2] of its being arrived off the Hook.[3] This is a circumstance of serious import, and may have no small influence on our operations. I am Sir Your mo. Obet Sert

Go: Washington

LS, in Richard Kidder Meade's writing, NHi: Gates Papers; Df, DLC:GW; Varick transcript, DLC:GW.

1. GW was referring to his previous letter to Gates of this date.

2. Meade originally wrote "authentic," which was the word used in Alexander Hamilton's draft, but he replaced it with "certain."

3. GW may have been referring to the report conveyed in Lt. Col. Francis Barber's letter to him of 13 July.

## From Major General Horatio Gates

Sir,                               White plains 14th July 1778

The inclosed letter was this minute put into my Hands with a number more, and being a good deal interrupted with other Business at the time, I open'd it by mistake; for which I must entreat Your Excellency's pardon.[1] Colonel Sherburnes Report inclosed, will Satisfy You that The

Troops will pass at Kings Ferry, without the Smallest insult from the Enemy.[2] I hope my Letter to Your Excellency of Yesterday, in Answer of Your's of the 11th, has been received—it went from hence Via Kings Ferry by Express. A Variety of Deserters who have lately come to this Camp from the Enemy; All agree; that the French Fleet are Off New York, that they have taken the Rose Man of War, & Sunk a Thirty Six Gun Frigate;[3] and that all the Grenadiers, & Light Infantry, were ordered to rejoin their Corps.[4] Lord Howe sailed six days ago, with five Sail of the Line, & Seven Frigates. The Compte D'Taing, who Commands the French Fleet, has the first Character of all the Marine Officers in France. The famous Monsieur Gerrard, who concluded the Treaty with Doctor Franklin, & Mr Dean, is on board the French Admiral, coming to Congress, as plenipotentiary from His most Christian Majesty.

I beg Colonel Hay may be sent back to this post, as the Service will Suffer exceedingly without him. I am, Sir, Your Excellency's Most Obedt Hume Servt

Horatio Gates

LS, DLC:GW; ADfS, NHi: Gates Papers. Gates probably enclosed with this Brig. Gen. John Stark's letter to him of 10 July, his reply to Stark of 14 July, and a copy of James Deane's letter to Maj. Gen. Philip Schuyler of 4 July, which Gates had received from both Schuyler and Stark (all these documents are in DLC:GW; see also Gates to Schuyler, 14 July, NHi: Gates Papers). Deane wrote Schuyler that he was "very happy to have your permission to assure our Friends that effectual Measures are adopted for their Security—The six Nations seem determined upon a War with us—Forty Warriors of the Quiyoga Tribe set out last Week to attack the Frontiers of Pennsylvania, As I am informed by an oneida Indian who saw them march out of their Castle—He also informs that Ojageghte is making up another party with the same Design, and that one hundred prisoners and Scalps have already been brought into Quiyoga several of which he saw—I have also an Account which I believe may be depended upon that Mr [John] Butler has lately been joined by a considerable Body of Senecas and has marched from *Kanakalo* to *Teyoga* a place situated at the Confluence of the East and the West Branch of the Susquehannah, and that Joseph Brandt is returned to Onohoguage where he commands a party of Tories and Indians—He gives out that he is determined to attack the German Flatts—Nothing in particular transpires from the Onondagas since they turned back with the Belts, only that they have again summoned the other Tribes to a Meeting which I have not the least Expectation that they will comply with.

"The Manœuvre of sending the Belts back, I suspect was only invented to gain Time and keep the Commissioners in Suspence and so retard the Operation of any plan that might be formed to do ourselves Justice upon them for their infamous and repeated Violations of the most solemn Treaties—I am of opinion that Nothing but wholesome Severities will ever be able to recover the Friendship of the six Nations or prevent their harrassing our Frontiers. Experience has taught that they are a people not to be bound by the Faith of Treaties—Our Lenity they construe into Timidity, and our patience of their Insults into downright Cowardice. In short the only way to make them our Friends is to make them afraid to be otherwise."

Stark's letter to Gates of 10 July enclosed Deane's letter and remarked that it would "inform You the necessity there is in giving the Enemy a Check to the Westward; if some method is not taken to Carry the war into their own Country, they will Unavoidably destroy all the Frontiers to the Westward." Gates's reply assured Stark that he had taken action on the money and clothing and that "all accounts, and reports, received from you, General Schuyler & the Indian Commissioners, &c., have been regularly transmitted to Congress, & lately to His Excellency General Washington; and every means in my power constantly Supply'd for the defence both of the Northern and Western Frontiers." The letter also discussed the need for money and clothing for Stark's troops.

1. The enclosed letter has not been identified.

2. Gates evidently enclosed a copy of the letter that Col. Henry Sherburne wrote him from Tarrytown, N.Y., on 13 July: "Just before Sun Set we hove up a Small Work to the Northward of the Town, With intent to remove the Two Gallies which lay within good Shot of the 18 Pounder—But Unfortunately upon the fourth Discharge (which hull'd one of them) the Cannon Split. . . . The Gallies and Small Sloop upon our Beginning the fire Came under sail and went nearer the Jersey Shore where they have Come to Anchor—The Ship which lays above a mile to the Southward of the Town gave us one Shot only but to no Effect—I did intend this night to have hove up a Work opposite the Ship with design to try the Howitzer but I understand she is order'd to the plains. . . . If I had three peices of heavy Cannon With Travelling Carriages this passage might be soon Cleared of our Troublesome Neighbours" (NHi: Gates Papers). The actual enclosure has not been found.

3. This intelligence probably referred to the capture of the letter-of-marque ship *Rose* on 6 July off Chesapeake Bay (see *Royal Gazette* [New York], 25 July; *New-York Gazette: and the Weekly Mercury*, 27 July) and to the sinking of the *Lydia* on 5 July (see Henry Laurens to GW, 10 July, and note 2 to that document).

4. Gen. Henry Clinton's general orders of 12 July had directed, "All Officers & Soldiers belonging to Regiments upon long Island, Staten Island, &c. are to Join their Corps Immediately," and elements of the light infantry and grenadiers had "gone on board the fleet to act as Marines" (Brigade of Guards Orderly Book, DLC:GW; Gruber, *Peebles' American War*, 202).

## To Henry Laurens

sir                                         Camp Paramus [N.J.] 14 July 1778.

I had the honor yesterday evening of receiving your very important favor of the 10th instant.

Colonel Laurens, one of my aids, will set out this morning with a letter to the French Admiral the Count d'Estaing inclosing a copy of yours, and such other information as I have been able to collect. Its further purpose is for the establishing a convention of signals in case of co-operation; or to convey him such a knowledge of the enemy's naval force and position, as may from time to time come under our cognizance.

It appears by intelligence of to-day that the Count d'Estaing is off or near Sandy Hook; having already seized several fishing boats on the banks, in order to procure information and pilots.

The army is in motion and will cross the North River with all convenient dispach, where I shall pursue such measures as may appear best calculated for improving the present conjuncture. I have the honor to be with much respect sir your most obedient and very hble servt

Go: Washington

LS, in James McHenry's writing, DNA:PCC, item 152; Df, DLC:GW; copy, DNA: PCC, item 169; Varick transcript, DLC:GW. GW signed the cover of the LS, which was docketed in part, "Read 17" (see *JCC*, 11:697).

## From Brigadier General John Stark

Dear General                                   Albany 14th July 1778

I Embrace this opportunity by Colo. Lewis, to Inform your Excellency the Situation we are in at this Quarter—we are threatned on all sides—by Express from Fort Schuyler, I am Informed, that there is an Army Coming against that place—there is another Body of Indians, & Torys, Gathered at a place Called Unidillo, about Sixty Miles from Mohawk River—the Enemies Ships is at Crownpoint.[1]

this is my Situation, & not so much as a Guard to this place—there is a few (of this States) Militia, on the Frontiers—but they are only Raised for a month at a time, & then March off, often Leaving the posts they Occupy, Destitute of any Guard—I fear if there is not some Troops sent that can be Depended on—this Whole Country will be Deserted—I had but one Regiment with me and that I was oblidged to send to Fort Schuyler, to Reinforce that Garrison, so that at present there is no Guard for the Stores, nor fort, but the City Militia, & about 50 of Beedles Regiment, & neither Can much be Depended on[2]—I have Represented the Affair to General Gates, & Requested men,[3] but the Express has not yet Returned. I am Sir with Great Respect Your Obedient Humble Sert

John Stark

N.B. I am Informed by Express, that Arrived last Night, from Fort Schuyler, that all the Onandagos, & Senecas, are Gone to the Susquehannah, to Join that Body of Indians & Tories, (Mentioned in my Letter) in order to fall on the Frontiers of this State, & the Back Settlements of Pensylvania. I should Recommend Detaining those Senicas that went to you till the Event is Known.[4] as before J.S.

LS, DLC:GW.

1. For the reported threat to Fort Schuyler, see Horatio Gates to GW, 13 July, n.3. The village of Unadilla, near the confluence of the Unadilla and Susquehanna rivers, was burned by American troops in October 1778.

2. On 11 July, Lt. Col. John Wheelock wrote Col. Timothy Bedel from Albany, describing unrest in Bedel's regiment. The men had "Expected to be absent but a few weeks, but were now to be detained as unlimited Continental soldiers" and moreover had not received pay and clothing promised them. In consequence, "a considerable party determined to quit the place" until Stark ordered a regiment paraded to "secure the obstinate." While the men were "cheerfully willing to serve here during the term proposed," they had not been mustered as Continental troops (Hammond, *Rolls of Soldiers*, 4:239–40).

3. For Stark's letter to Maj. Gen. Horatio Gates of 9 July, see Gates to GW, 13 July, n.3.

4. Regarding the delegation of Seneca warriors that visited GW's camp and subsequently Congress in June 1778, see Commissioners of Indian Affairs to GW, 9 June, and GW to Benedict Arnold, 21 June (first letter).

## To John Cleves Symmes

Sir.                                    Camp Paramus [N.J.] 14 July 1778
I received your letter of the 10th Inst. dated at the Minisink.

The militia who were on service down upon the sound, have been discharged and are since ordered by the Governor to your support and assistance.

But I flatter myself from the face of intelligence that the Indians are now returning to their homes, which will render assistance from this quarter unnecessary could it be spared at present. I am Sir your obt & very hble servt.

Df, in the writing of James McHenry, DLC:GW; Varick transcript, DLC:GW.

## To Jonathan Trumbull, Sr.

Sir                        Head Quarters Paramus [N.J.] July 14th 1778
I last night recieved a Letter from Congress, informing me of the arrival of a French Fleet, on our Coast, extracts of which I have the Honor to enclose.[1] In addition to that information, I have recieved intelligence, of tolerable authenticity, to day, of its arrival off the Hook. Every thing we can do to aid and cooperate with this Fleet is of the greatest importance. Accounts from New-York speak of a Cork Fleet which is momently expected there, for the safety of which the Enemy are extremely alarmed. It is probable that this Fleet, to avoid the

French Fleet, will be directed to take its course thro' the Sound—If this should be the case, it might answer the most valuable consequences, were the eastern States to collect before hand all the Frigates and armed Vessels they can get to gether for the purpose, at some convenient place, for interrupting their passage that way. If the whole, or any considerable part of the Cork-Fleet could be taken or destroyed, it would be a fatal blow to the British Army, which, it is supposed, at this time, has but a very small stock of Provisions on hand—Should the project I have now suggested appear to you eligible, I beg the favor of you to transmit Copies of my Letter, and the enclosed extracts to the neighbouring States, and endeavour to engage their concurrence. I have the Honor to be with the greatest respect & Esteem Your Excellency's Most obedient Servant

G. Washington

P.S. From the nature of the River even small armed Boats may be useful, as the Frigates cannot protect the Transports.

LB, Ct: Trumbull Papers; Df, DLC:GW; copy, Nh-Ar: Weare Papers; copy, M-Ar: Revolution Letters, 1778; copy, R-Ar: Letters to the Governor; Varick transcript, DLC:GW. The copies were enclosed in Trumbull's letters of 18 July to Meshech Weare, to Jeremiah Dummer Powell, and to William Greene, respectively.

1. The enclosed extracts from Henry Laurens's letter to GW of 10 July have not been identified.

## From John Parke Custis

Hond Sir                                          New Kent [Va.] July 15th 78

On my Return from Mt Vernon to this Place, I found the Packet, containing your Letter and Deed.[1] I am much oblidged to you for the Trouble you have taken, to have a new Deed made out, from yourself to Me. It was the Method I proposed, but my Uncles Bassett and Dandridge thought it best, to have the Deed made from you to Henry; I shall be in no Hurry to have your Deed acknowledged, unless a good opportunity offers, as I hope, most sincerely, to see you in Virginia in Peace, long before the Time elapses.

I am happy in the thought, that my Plan of selling my Lands meets with your approbation, and I am thankful for your advice. I should most certainly have invested the Money ariseing from the Sales in the Funds, if the Purchase of Robert & Gerard Alexander's Lands in Fairfax did not point out another Way. the Particulars of the Bargains you are probably acquainted with before now. the one with Robert, Besides the extravagancy of the Price, is a very disagreable one. Nothing could have induced Me to have given such Terms, but the unconquerable Desire I had, to live in the Neighbourhood of Mt Vernon, and in the County of Fairfax. I have agreed to give Him £12 per acre, and at the Experation of twenty four years, to pay Him the Principal with compound Interest. this is a hard and disagreable Article. I shall however guard against the Evil as much as possible, by investing the Sum in the Funds, for the particular Use of dischargeing this Debt. He cannot during the twenty four years, demand of Me a Farthing, either Principal or Interest. I have agreed to give Gerard £11 per acre, the Money to be paid at Christmas. the reason that induced Me to purchase his Land, was the advantage of having my Estate under my own Eye, and the probability of getting Phil's, which I understand he wants to sell. if I should get his my Tract would be very complete, and good in Quality, Situated in a Part of the State where Lands will rise in Value, as much as in any other Part, or rather more.[2] these Purchases have induced Me to think of selling all my Lands in this Part of the State, excepting my King William and N— Kent Tracts. these Tracts are better in Quality then any of my other Lands, and from their Situation, may be overlook'd by one Manager.[3] my Estate on the Eastern Shore from Mismanagement, has not, I beleive cleared Me for the last three years £50 pr. Annum. my Hanover Land has been of no advantage to Me.[4] my Land near Willmburg has by Hill's liveing upon It, been more advantageous than any other, but that I am confident has not yeilded me the Interest of the Money it would now sell for.[5] I should be glad to dispose of this Tract, as it will be very inconvenient for Me to hold it, and I shall be under the Necessity of buying Negroes and Horses at the very extravagant Price They now sell at. Hill has drawn the likeliest Negroes I own, to this Place, and still complains of the want of Hands; if I sell this Land, I shall have Negroes, Horses, Sheep, and Cattle to stock the two Plantations I propose reserving, and my Lands in Fairfax fully. the Expense of keeping this Plantation in culture, from the great Scarsity of Timber, the number of roads running through the Land, and the amazing Deal of Ditching necessary to inclose the Feilds, besides this the Necessity of keeping a Man, above the Rank of a common Overseer, at extraordinary Wages to overlook this Plantation, will render the Income less in Proportion, with equal Management, with this or the King William Estate. Hill by confineing Himself to that Plantation, left the Management of the other Plantations entirely to the Overseers, who neglected their Business shamefully. The Land near Willmsbg will now sell very high, as Money is as plenty and of as little Value as in any Part of the Continent. I should be very glad to dispose of It. if We could settle with regard to my Mother's Dower, I shall willingly agree to any thing you shall propose, either to retain It, or dispose of it together with my Part of the Tract. My Mother says She shall willingly accede to any thing that shall be determined on between Us. I am confident that this Land will sell much higher at this Time than it will do for fifty years to come, as the Seat of Government will certainly be removed as soon as we have a Peace, and our Money will rise in Value.[6] Lots in Willmsbg and Lands adjacent must fall greatly in Value—My Intentions are, after paying for the Lands above to put the remainder of the Money in the Funds for the Purpose of Building Me a House in Fairfax whenever I can do It conveniently.

Price Posey was at Davenport's the Day before yesterday.[7] He says that their is a promiseing Crop on the Ground, but is afraid it will suffer on Account of the Sickly Situation of the Negroes, their are several of the Best Hands now sick, one has been in a very low State for Some Time. I shall take the Liberty to direct Davenport to send him to my Quarter, in hopes the change of Air will recover Him. I shall cheerfully lend Davenport every assistance in recovering his People. He attributes their Sickness to the badness of the Water.

I do with the most heartfelt Pleasure congratulate you on the Victory you obtain'd over the Enemy on the Plains of Monmouth, and do sinc[e]rely wish you a continuance of Success. I also congratulate you on the appearance of a French Fleet on our Coast. They have drove on the Eastern an English Frigate of 28 Guns. the greatest Part of the Crew are Prisoners on the Eastern Shore. They have taken or sunk two others.[8] this is the report, and I beleive it is true; I live in the most retired Part of the State, I seldom heare any thing. I did not hear of your Victory for some time after the Express went down—I have the Pleasure to inform you that my little Family are in tolerable Health. Nelly joins Me in wishing you every Blessing. I am Hond Sir yr most affecte

J.P. Custis

ALS, LNHiC: Butler Family Papers.

1. See GW to Custis, 26 May. The deed was for the Pleasant Hill plantation in King and Queen County, which Custis was selling to James Henry (see Custis to GW, 14 Jan., and note 2 to that document; see also Henry to GW, 2 June 1784).

2. For more on Custis's purchase of land belonging to Gerard and Robert Alexander that lay along the Potomac River roughly where Reagan National Airport and Arlington National Cemetery are today, see Custis to GW, 11 May, and note 5 to that document. Philip Alexander (died c.1790), another brother, owned the middle section of the tract that the three had inherited from their father. For Robert Alexander's memorandum of his agreement with Custis's agent Robert Adam, dated 1 July, see ViFaCt: Fairfax County Land Records, Liber D, no. 4 (1861–1863).

3. Custis's lands, some of which he owned outright and others of which he was renting while they were in dower to Martha Washington, derived mostly from the estate of his father, Daniel Parke Custis, who died intestate in 1757 (see Settlement of the Daniel Parke Custis Estate, 20 April 1759–5 Nov. 1761, *Papers, Colonial Series*, 6:201–315). The King William County lands were a dower plantation called Claiborne's, consisting of 2,880 acres on the Pamunkey River above Eltham, and

Romancoke, about 1,780 acres adjacent to Claiborne's. The four plantations in New Kent County, totaling 6,264 acres, were Rockahock, on the Pamunkey River about five miles west of New Kent Court House; Brick House, near where the Pamunkey enters the York River; Old Quarter, below Rockahock; and Harlow's. On 25 July, Custis advertised a New Kent plantation, probably Harlow's: "Two thousand one hundred and eighty three acres of land lying in *New Kent* county, about three miles from *Cumberland* . . . will be exposed to sale on *Thursday* the 10th of *September* . . . for ready money, or loan office certificates" (Purdie's *Virginia Gazette* [Williamsburg], 21 Aug.).

4. The Custis lands on the Eastern Shore of Virginia, totaling 4,650 acres, were Smith Island, Mockhorn Island, and Arlington, all in the southern part of Northampton County. In October, Custis advertised them for sale (Purdie's *Virginia Gazette* [Williamsburg], 16 Oct.). Custis owned about 1,000 acres in Hanover County, "twelve miles from *Richmond*, eight from *Page's*, and eleven from *Newcastle*," for which he scheduled a September auction (ibid., 21 Aug.).

5. Custis's land near Williamsburg included four plantations totaling about 3,074 acres on Queen's Creek in York County. Ship Landing, Bridge Quarter, and the Mill, or New Quarter, were dower lands that Custis was renting, while Custis owned the Great House plantation unencumbered. Another 250-acre tract called Jackson's Quarter was purchased for Custis by GW in 1771.

6. In October, GW consented to the proposed sale of the dower lands (see GW to Custis, 12 Oct.; and deed of release to Custis, 12 Oct., photocopy at ViMtV).

7. In late 1778 or early 1779 Custis placed his childhood friend John Price Posey (d. 1788), a son of GW's former neighbor Capt. John Posey, in charge of his plantations. For subsequent allegations of his mismanagement of Custis's estate, see Bartholomew Dandridge to GW, 13 March 1784, and note 3; James Hill to GW, 24 Sept. 1786; GW to Posey, 12 Jan. 1787; and Posey to GW, 27 Jan. 1787. Joseph Davenport was manager of Claiborne's.

8. The *Maryland Journal, and Baltimore Advertiser* of 21 July reported: "The Mermaid British Man of War, of 28 Guns, commanded by James Hawker, Esq: . . . was lately chased ashore by Part of Count d'Estaing's Fleet, near Chingoteague, where, it is expected, she will be entirely lost. The whole Ship's Company are Prisoners on the Eastern Shore of this State." This encounter took place on 7 July. On 5 and 6 July the *Lydia* had been sunk and the *Rose* captured.

# To William Dobbs

Sir                                                    [Haverstraw, N.Y., 15 July 1778]

A considerable fleet of french men of War, chiefly Ships of the line, has just arrived at Sandy Hook, under the command of Admiral Count D'estaing. As the Admiral is a Stranger to our Coast, and is come for the purpose of co-operating with us against the Enemy, it is absolutely necessary that he should be immediately provided with a number of skillful pilots, well acquainted with the Coast & Harbours and of firm attachment to our cause. I am assured by Govenor Clinton and Genl McDougal that you answer this description in every part, I must therefore request the favor of you to see me as early as possible, when I would flatter myself you will not have the smallest objection to going on board the fleet on so essential & interesting occasion. I will not at this time say any thing of your pay, but I doubt not we shall readily agree on a sum that will not only be just but generous and if we should not, that your services will be liberally considered & rewarded by the states. I am Sir Yr Most Obedt servt

Go: Washington

P.S. I wish you to come prepared to go as the situation of affairs will not admit of delay.

Df, in Robert Hanson Harrison's writing, DLC:GW; Varick transcript, DLC:GW. The date is taken from a docket on the draft, confirmed by Dobbs's reply of 16 July.

William Dobbs (1718–1781) was based at Fishkill. From this date until Dobbs's death, GW often called upon him to act as a pilot or to enlist other pilots for French vessels.

## From Major General William Heath

Dear General                              Head Quarters Boston 15th July 1778
    This moment Colonel Armand & a major Ottendroff called at my quarters, and being about to set out for the Army, the Major desires I would write your Excellency that he is exceeding sorry for leaving the service the last year, and wishes you would over look it; that he desires again to serve in the Army. He has made several applications to the Navy Board to serve in the navy; he is now requesting Colo. Armand to let him serve in his Corps if agreeable to you, and Colonel Armand informs me he should like him as a Major if your Excellency should approve of it, and has desired me to mention it; I know nothing of the Major's abilities, or the reasons of his leaving the Army, both of which I apprehend are fully known to your Excellency. I have the honor to be With great respect Your Excellency's Obedt Servant

W. Heath

LS, DLC:GW; ADfS, MHi: Heath Papers.

## To Jeremiah Wadsworth

Sir                                    Haverstraw [N.Y.] 15th July 1778.
    I desire you immediately to select Fifty of your best Bullocks, and give orders to have two hundred Sheep if to be procured and a parcel of poultry purchased in the most convenient part of the Country. They are intended as a present to the Count D'Estaing Admiral of the French Fleet now laying off Sandy Hook. You are to send them to the

Coast as expeditiously as possible, and upon giving notice to the Admiral he will contrive means of taking them off. A letter from me will be delivered to you for the Count which you are to forward with the provision.[1] You are to write to him in your public Character and offer him any assistance that he may want in victualling the Fleet under his command. I am Sir Yr most obt Servt

Go: Washington

LS, in Tench Tilghman's writing, Gary Hendershott Sale 34 (April 1986), item 1; Df, DLC:GW; Varick transcript, DLC:GW.

1. GW wrote to Vice Admiral d'Estaing on this date: "I take the liberty, in behalf of the United States, to present you with a small quantity of live stock, which I flatter myself, after a long sea voyage, will not be unacceptable. I have directed the commissary, who will deliver them, to execute any orders you will be pleased to give him, for procuring such further supplies as the country may afford for the accommodation of the fleet under your command" (Df, DLC:GW).

## From William Dobbs

Sir,                                          Fish Kill [N.Y.] July 16th 1778

I had the Honour of receiving your Excellency's Letter of the 15th Inst. by Express—Should have immediately complied with the Request contained therein—but that it met me on my Sick Bed, in which Situation I have lain very ill with a severe Fit of the Fever and Ague for four Days past—I have therefore recommended two Persons, every Way adapted to the Purpose of Serving their Country in so material a Point, and have sent Expresses for them to Stamford and Sawpitt, at which places they reside, with orders not to delay a Moment in repairing to Your Excellency—their names are Martin Johnson and James Howlet, Men whom your Excellency may repose a Confidence in[1]—They are well acquainted with the Coast of America, and more especially so with the Coast and Harbour of N. York—they have followed piloting for some Years and were regular Branch pilots at that place—they will present your Excellency the Letters I sent them as vouchers for their Characters.[2] I am Your Excellency's most Obedient and very Humble Servant

Willm Dobbs

ALS, DLC:GW.

1. James Howlett wrote GW on 4 Aug. 1781 from the provost at New York, asserting that he had been imprisoned for two years in consequence of his work as a pilot for d'Estaing. He was probably the "James Hallet" of Stamford, Conn., to whom GW wrote, along with Martin Johnson of Stamford and Dobbs, on 5 Oct. 1779, evidently about serving as pilots for the French fleet.

2. These letters have not been identified.

## From Major General Nathanael Greene

                    Capt. Drakes 7 miles from the [King's] ferry [N.Y.]
Sir                                                            July 16th 1778
   General Varnum is at this place and has very lately returnd from
Rhode Island, he says that there are 1500 State troops including the
Artillery Regiment. There is the Continental Battallion commanded by
Col. Greene about 130 strong. Besides these 2500 Militia are orderd
from the Massachusets, Conecticut, & New Hampshire States, part of
which are already arrivd; and the others dayly coming in. General Var-
num thinks there cannot be less than 3000 men already embodied un-
der the command of General Sullivan that can be depended upon.
   General Varnum thinks there is not above 3000 of the Enemy at
Rhode Island and only Six frigates.
   I find no place for encamping the troops short of 9 miles from the
ferry towards Crumpond. I am with great respect your Excell. Most
obedient humble Servt

                                                            Nath. Greene

ALS, DLC:GW.

*Letter not found*: from William Livingston, 16 July 1778. On 16 July, Livingston
wrote GW, "I did myself the honour this morning to acquaint your Excellency
that I had been yesterday to the Southward."


## From William Livingston

Dear Sir                              Morris Town [N.J.] 16 July 1778
   I did myself the honour this morning to acquaint your Excellency
that I had been yesterday to the Southward to forward pilots to the
hook to conduct the fleet under the Command of his Excellency
Count d'Estaing to New York[1]—As each ship ought at least to have
one, I am persuaded that it will conduce to the Service to secure some
to the Northward least we should be disappointed in the requisite
Complement in these parts—I therefore take the Liberty to mention
to your Excellency the names of some that have been recommended
to me at Peaks kill & Kings ferry, to wit Capt. William Dobbs Dennis
McQuire Isaac Symondson—Peeks kill William Sloo—Kings ferry[2]
Their political characters (a matter of the last Importance,) I know
not—I have the honour to be with the highest Esteem Dr Sir your Excellencys most humble Servt

                                                            Wil: Livingston

ALS, DLC:GW.

1. Livingston's previous letter to GW of this date has not been found. He apparently informed GW that he had recommended Patrick Dennis, "one of the Commissioners in the Marine Department in New York," to d'Estaing (see Livingston to d'Estaing, 14 July, in Prince, *Livingston Papers*, 2:391). GW's aide-de-camp Alexander Hamilton wrote Dennis on this date, asking him, "if circumstances will permit, to go on board the Admiral as early as possible. Your services may be the most important and interesting and such as will give you a just claim to the thanks and notice of your Country. If you can remain with the fleet during their operations in this Quarter it will be infinitely desireable; but if you can not, it will still be of importance for you to see the Count D'Estaing as you may inform him on several points which he may wish to know" (DLC:GW; see also Syrett, *Hamilton Papers*, 1:524).

2. A Dennis McGuire appears as a boatman in the 1797 New York City directory. Isaac Symondson had apparently moved to Elizabeth, N.J., by 4 Oct. 1779, when GW recommended him to Livingston as a good Hook pilot, suitable for assisting the French fleet. The executors of William Sloo, Sr. (d. 1798), unsuccessfully petitioned Congress in 1819 and 1821 for payment for his services "as a blacksmith and master of public vessels in the revolutionary army" (*House Journal*, 15 Cong. 2 sess., 154; ibid., 16 Cong., 1 sess., 92; *Senate Journal*, 16 Cong., 2 sess., 165).

# From Maryland Officers

Sir                                          Camp 16th July 1778

We beg leave to represent to your Excellency that our Service is rendered in some measure disagreeable by being subject to the Command of a Man who has incurred (as we presume) by his bad conduct a reputation incompatible with the Honor of the service.

Colo. Price has been branded with, and still lays under the appellation of a Coward, he has once had an examination into his Conduct, and then procured a declaration importing that nothing appeared militating against his Character as an Officer—This Decree we do Assert was procured from the humane feelings of those who were to have given evidence against him, but retired from the Court of enquiry on his promising to resign his Commission;[1] His still continuing in the Service obliges us, in duty to our Country as Officers, and ourselves as gentlemen to request of your Excellency that measures may be taken, either for his justification or removal from the Command which he now holds.[2]

We hope your Excellency will not impute this address to any disposition for Cabal, for we do assure your Excellency no such motives actuate Your Excellency's Most obedient Humble Servants

W. Richardson Colo. 5th M.R. Thos Woolford Lt Colo. 2d Maryd Regt
Jno. Gunby Coll 7th R.                    Jno. Steward Major 2 M.R.
Peter Adams L. Co. 7th M.R.        Benjamin Ford Lt Colo. 6th M. Regt
Danl J. Adams Major              Benjamin Brookes Capn Comdt 3 M.R.
Sam Smith Lt Coll 4th R.            Levin Winder Captn Comt 1st M.R.[3]

LS, in William Richardson's writing, DLC:GW.

1. For the court of inquiry into the conduct of Col. Thomas Price, see General Orders, 17 and 23 Nov. 1777.

2. GW's secretary James McHenry wrote to these officers on 11 Aug.: "That your complaint of the 16th Ulto may be properly inquired into, you will please to make out the charges against Colonel Price, and have them transmitted to Head Quarters, when a Court martial will be ordered for his tryal" (DLC:GW). After the officers submitted charges in a letter to GW of 12 Aug. that has not been found, GW's aide-de-camp Tench Tilghman wrote to Price on 13 Aug.: "Inclosed are the Charges made by Colo. Gunby and Lieus. Colo. Smith and Ford, in behalf of the Feild Officers of the Maryland line, against you. As the charges are to be materially supported by Colonels Gist and Stone and Lieut. Colo. Ramsay, His Excellency intends to postpone your trial untill their arrival, His Excellency orders me to transmit you a Copy of the Charges that you may prepare for your defence" (DLC:GW; see also McHenry to Maryland officers, 13 Aug., DLC:GW). Price apparently left camp for Philadelphia soon after to gather material for his defense (Otho Holland Williams to Elie Williams, 14 Aug., MdHi: Otho Holland Williams Papers). GW directed in the general orders of 19 Oct. that a court-martial be convened to try Price, and on 9 Nov. the colonel was acquitted of seven charges of cowardice and disgraceful behavior (see General Orders, 8 Jan. 1779).

3. Levin Winder (1757–1819) of Somerset County, Md., was commissioned a lieutenant in Smallwood's Maryland Regiment in January 1776 and a captain of the 1st Maryland Regiment in December of that year. His promotion to major of the 4th Maryland Regiment, which evidently occurred in the spring of 1779, was dated from 17 April 1777. Winder was wounded and taken prisoner at the Battle of Camden on 16 Aug. 1780, and although he was promoted to lieutenant colonel of the 2d Maryland Regiment in 1781, he remained a prisoner on parole as late as November 1782. He continued in the Continental service until April 1783. Winder was commissioned a major general of the Maryland militia in 1794. He also served in the Maryland legislature, 1789–93 and 1806–9, as governor of Maryland, 1812–16, and as a presidential elector supporting GW in 1792.

## From Major General Philip Schuyler

Dear Sir                                              Albany July 16th 1778

I do myself the Honor most sincerely to congratulate your Excellency on your late glorious Victory obtained in New Jersey—May Heaven continue its Smiles on the honest Endeavors of America and protect you from every Disaster.

On the 11th Ult. Congress determined on an Expedition to the Detroit and into the Seneca Country: and directed that such of the Commissioners of Indian Affairs as might be at Albany should co-operate with General Gates and the Officer to command in the last mentioned Expedition upon the Mode of conducting it; the Force to be employed and on all other preparations requisite for executing the Measure— These Resolutions accompanied by a Letter from the Board of War I received on the 25th Inst. and prevented me from prosecuting my

Journey to York Town on the next Day as I had intended[1]—On the 27th I wrote to General Gates on the Subject, who promised me in a Letter of the 2d Instant that he would write me on the Subject from the White plains—As I have not yet been favored with a Line from him, it is probable that he concieves himself discharged from that Business since your Arrival.

On the 14th Inst. some Chiefs of the Oneidas arrived here—They inform me that a very considerable party commanded by Butler were marched towards the Frontiers of pennsylvania that he expected to return to Tuindilla about this Time and that in about ten Days hence he with another party under the Command of Brandt intended to attack the Mohawk River and Schoharie—I have not any Reason to doubt the Truth of the Information, and I fear the Militia in that Quarter will be greatly too weak to prevent the Enemy's Depredations.

Mr President Laurens in a Letter of the 20th Ult. informs me that Charges against me and the General Officers that were in this Department when Tyonderoga was evacuated have been made out and would be transmitted to your Excellency[2]—If they are come to Hand, permit me to beg the Favor of a Copy of your orders to attend at Head Quarters for my Tryal as soon as you conveniently can order a Court Martial. I am, with the most sincere Esteem and Respect Your Excellency's obedient humble Servant.

Ph: Schuyler

LS, DLC:GW.

1. For Congress's resolutions of 11 June, see *JCC*, 11:588–90. The Board of War notified Schuyler of the resolutions in a letter signed by Timothy Pickering and dated 16 June (DNA:PCC, item 63).

2. For Henry Laurens's letter to Schuyler of 20 June, see Smith, *Letters of Delegates*, 10:150–51. For the charges, enclosed with Laurens's letter to GW of the same date, see *JCC*, 11:593–603.

## From Alexander Spotswood

Dear Sir                                    [York, Pa.] July 16 1778

My reasons for Quiting the Service at the time I did you already have[1]—two days after my arrival at home they were obviated by a letter which I receivd from Colo. Stevens informing me of my brother being Only Wounded, and likely to recover—I immediatly wrote to Our delegates informing them the Contents of Colo. Steven's letter, and my desire of reentering the service, provided I coud be reinstated in my propper place, this letter I believd reached them before my Commission—and as it was the opinion of Congress that my Case was very hard, and that I had been injured, they refused Accepting my Commission, & determind, that I shd be the next brigadier made from our State[2]—on my arrival at this place from Camp, I happen'd to be in Company with Gl Weedon who informd me he had quited the service—I immediatly waited on our delegates & expressed my desire of being reinstated according to the promise of Congress—I recd for answer that all future arangements were to be made by a Committee Which Consisted of your Excellency—Gl Read, & another Gentleman whose name I have forgot[3]—but that they woud represent my Case—I have only to beg, that, as I look on myself to be in the army my Commission not being receivd, and having the above promise from Congress, that your excellency will not forget me, I set of[f] this day for Virginia—and if Called on will be ready to set of[f] from home to the army in twelve hours—as I wish more particularly to be with it at this time, on acct of the arrival of the french fleet, which Induces me to believe, that, something great will be done in a few weeks. I am with great Esteem & respect—yr Excellencys Mt Obdt

A. Spotswood

ALS, DLC:GW.
    1. See Spotswood to GW, 9 Oct. 1777.
    2. Congress resolved on 29 Nov. 1777 "That the committee appointed to repair to the camp be instructed to intimate to General Washington that Congress are not willing to accept the resignation of Colonel Spotswood" (*JCC*, 9:981).
    3. On 4 June, Congress had resolved that the new arrangement of the army should be implemented by GW "with the advice and assistance" of Joseph Reed and Francis Dana (*JCC*, 11:570).

## From the Board of War

Sir,                        War Office [Philadelphia] July 17. 1778.
    Congress having been pleased to grant to the Marquis de Vienne (a major in the armies of his most Christian Majesty) the brevet commission of Colonel[1]—we do ourselves the honour to signify it to your Excellency; and to intimate the wishes of the Marquis to be employed in some service of utility to the states, and in which he may have an opportunity to manifest his military talents & zeal for the cause in which he is engaged. We have the honour to be your Excellency's most obedient servants. By order of the Board

Tim. Pickering.

ALS, DLC:GW; copy, MHi: Pickering Papers.
    1. Louis-Pierre, marquis de Vienne, who had arrived at the Valley Forge camp in June with letters of introduction to Lafayette, had remained with the army until

6 July, when he went on to Congress with letters of introduction from Lafayette and GW's aide-de-camp John Laurens (Laurens, *Army Correspondence*, 203; *Lafayette Papers*, 2:96, 99, 101). Congress approved Vienne's commission on 15 July (see *JCC*, 11:692–94).

## To Vice Admiral d'Estaing

Sir                    Camp at Haverstraw Bay [N.Y.] July 17: 1778.

I had the honor of receiving the night of the 14th Instant, your very obliging and interesting letter of the 13th dated off Sandy Hook, with a duplicate of another, dated the 8th at Sea.

The arrival of a fleet, belonging to his most Christian majesty on our coast, is an event that makes me truly happy; and permit me to observe, that the pleasure I feel on the occasion is greatly increased, by the command being placed in a Gentleman of such distinguished talents, experience and reputation as the Count D'Estaing. I am fully persuaded that every possible exertion will be made by you to accomplish the important purposes of your destination, and you may have the firmest reliance, that my most strenuous efforts shall accompany you in any measure, which may be found eligible.

I esteem myself highly honored by the desire you express, with a frankness which must always be pleasing, of possessing a place in my friendship; At the same time allow me to assure you, that I shall consider myself peculiarly happy, if I can but improve the prepossessions you are pleased to entertain in my favour, into a cordial and lasting amity.

On the first notice of your arrival, and previous to the receipt of your Letter, I wrote to you by Lt Colo. Laurens one of my Aides De Camp's whom I charged to explain to you such further particulars, as were not contained in my letter, which might be necessary for your information;[1] and to whom it was my wish you should confide your situation and views, so far as might be proper for my direction in any measures of concert or cooperation, which may be thought advancive of the common cause. Maj. De Chouin who arrived this day at my Quarters, has given me a very full and satisfactory explanation, on this head, and in return I have freely communicated to him my ideas of every matter interesting to our mutual operations. Those, I doubt not, he will convey to you, with that perspicuity and intelligence, which he possesses in a manner, that amply justifies the confidence you have reposed in him. You would have heard from me sooner in answer to your letter; but I have been waiting for Mr Chouins arrival to acquaint me with your circumstances and intentions, and, at the same time, have been employed in collecting information with respect to several particulars, the knowledge of which was essential to the formation of our plans. The difficulty of doing justice by letter to matters of such variety and importance as those, which now engage our deliberation, has induced me to send Lt Colo. Hamilton another of my Aids to you, in whom I place entire confidence. He will be able to make you perfectly acquainted with my sentiments, and to satisfy any inquiries you may think proper to propose; and I would wish you to consider the information he delivers as coming from my self.

Colo. Hamilton is accompanied by Lt Colo. Fleuri, a Gentleman of your nation, who has distinguished himself by his zeal and gallantry, in the present war with England. He has also with him four Captains of Vessels, whom, I hope, you will find very useful, from their knowledge of the Coast and harbours, and two persons, who have acted a considerable time in the capacity of pilots and in whose skill, expertness & fidelity from the recommendations I have had, I believe you may place great dependence.[2] I am still endeavouring to provide others of this description, who shall be dispatched to you, as fast as they can be found. With the most ardent desire for your Success and with the greatest respect & esteem I have the Honor to be Sir Yr Most Obedt & most Hble servt

Go: Washington

Df, in Robert Hanson Harrison's writing, DLC:GW; copy, DNA:PCC, item 152; copy (extract), FrPBN; copy, DNA:PCC, item 169; Varick transcript, DLC:GW. The copy in DNA:PCC, item 152, which is in Richard Kidder Meade's writing, was enclosed with GW's second letter to Henry Laurens of 22 July. The extract corresponds to the second paragraph of the draft.

1. See GW to d'Estaing, 14 July.

2. Among those accompanying Alexander Hamilton was Jonathan Lawrence, whose journal of his experiences is at RPJCB. He records that the pilots set out on 18 July, arrived at Black Point, N.J., on 19 July, and went on board d'Estaing's flagship, the *Languedoc*, on the morning of 20 July.

## From Vice Admiral d'Estaing

Sir,                    In the Rhode without SandyHook the 17th July 1778
The bar of the river Shrewsbury, the officer sailors and boats, that I have lost in the waves, have not hindered Colonel Laurens from bravg them twice to come and deliver me himself the letter, that you did me the honor to write me the 14th of this month. The desire of communicating with you alone could have induced me to hazard a descent myself the first, and with four grenadiers as my only support, in a place, the debarkation of which is as difficult as it was unknown; and where there existed not a single spot proper for embarkation. The sacrifice of several of my men appeared to me less affecting, as it was the sole mean of communication, I could have.[1]

I have occupied myself less with discovering the number of English vessels of war in the Rhode of Sandy Hook than the means of entering it. I suppose there fourteen vessels of war, a throng of frigates and a multitude of transports—This superiority of number and the goodness of the English navy will not hinder me from attacking Lord Howe in his retrenchment and under his batteries, if the depth of the water do not forbid me. I only received three pilots yesterday; they have need of recollecting their ideas, and are at this time sounding the river. The hope of giving you something positive on this head engaged me to pray your estimable, well-informed and most amiable Aide De Camp, to pass a bad night on board the Languedoc.

He will give you an account, Sir, of the regret I shall feel, if the powerful mark of friendship, which the King has given his allies, who are so dear to him, should not prove of so great utility as he might promise himself. I will not enter into any further detail in this letter. Mr Laurens will tell you more, than I can write. But it will be very important, that the arrival of so great a naval succour should produce at the same time a general effort by land. If unfortunately that should be impossible, you are too good a patriot and too great a soldier, not to feel the necessity, I shall be under, of going to seek elsewhere an opportunity of injuring our common enemy. The places, that you shall point out to me, will appear to me preferable—whenever naval circumstances and the state of my supplies will permit. 'Tis with the greatest pleasure, that I learn from Mr Gerard, the King's minister, that you are cloathed with the most ample powers, to treat with me on military operations. I cannot act, either far or near under the auspices of a greater master—You are a master; and you know, that the instant one thing becomes necessary, we ought to attempt another.

I have received a printed list of the eleven English vessels of the line, which are announced to us, on very good part. This news published by order of the Congress acquires an authenticity whi⟨ch⟩ merits the highest attention.[2]

Accept my compliment upon your last victory. Even were not the success of America become our own, by the intimate bands which bind us together; it would be impossible as a soldier and as a man not to participate in it. It is natural to love to see one laurel more adorning the brow of a great man. I have the honor to be &c.

Translation, DLC:GW; ALS, in French, DLC:GW; Df, FrPNA: Marine, B4, I46.

1. D'Estaing's report to the French marine minister indicated that the fleet's need for water as well as his desire to communicate with GW necessitated this landing, which included 400 infantry under the command of Charles-Edouard-Frédéric Henry, comte de Macdonald (Doniol, *Histoire de la Participation de la France,* 3:327).

2. Congress had ordered publication of a letter from the American commissioners in France carrying news of eleven English vessels bound for America (see Henry Laurens to GW, 10 July, n.3), but no printed list of those vessels has been identified.

## From Major General Horatio Gates

Head Quarters Havestraw [N.Y.] 17th July 1778
For the Garrison of West point, it is agreed by—Major General Gates, Major General Mac Dougall, His Excellency Govr Clinton, & Brigadier General Glover.

That, Colonel Van Schaieks, Col. James Livingstons, & Col. Armands Corps; amm[o]unting as they are Estimated, to 900 Rank, & File; be sent immediately to relieve that post; & that one Other Continental Regiment, be added to them, as His Excellency upon examination wi[t]h The Adjutun⟨t⟩ General shall please to Direct.

Horatio Gates

ADS, DLC:GW.

## From Major General William Heath

Dear Genl               Head Quarters Boston July 17th 1778
   The day before yesterday I received a letter from Peter Colt Esqr. A.C.G. of Purchases of which the enclosd is a copy[1] The provissions in our Magazines are by no means very considerable; but finding Mr Colt so pressing, and not knowing but the most fatal consequences might take place if salted provisions were not sent on, I immediately gave orders for Six Hundred Barrels of pork and four Hundred Barrels of Beef to be forwarded without delay from the Magazine at Westborough.[2] If the Enemy should not come this way we shall not feel the want of it, but if they should our Magazines will be found very scanty, If Your Excellency should be of opinion that the whole of the before mentioned Quantity will not be necessary, permit me to request that orders may be sent to Mr Colt to stop what may not be thought needful, otherwise the whole will go on—the provisions are exceedingly good; but the transporting them by land so great a distance is a disagreeable consideration.[3] I have the honor to be With great respect Your Excellency's Most Obedt Servt

W. Heath

LS, DLC:GW; ADfS, MHi: Heath Papers.
1. Colt's letter to Heath was written from Hartford on 30 June (MHi: Heath Papers), but the copy enclosed to GW is incorrectly dated "Boston July 17th." The

enclosed text reads in part: "In consequence of the Army under command of his Excellency General Washington comeing this way—I am call'd on by General Gates for more salted provissions than this State can possibly furnish.

"If we can not draw any supplies from Massachusetts the army must suffer greatly if part are not obliged to disband—I have no occassion to remin'd your honor of the ill consequence of feeding the army wholly on fresh were it in our power not to mention the absolute necessity of salted meat for scouting parties &C.—and I do assure you that the whole of our collections in this quarter are sent forward and nearly expended There is a quantity in the hands of Jos. Baker Esqr. of Westown which is the most convenient Deposit for this Post—I must request your Honor to give directions to have as much of that meat as can with safety be spared from your command to be forwarded to this place from whence we will forward it to the army" (DLC:GW).

2. See Heath to Joseph Baker, 15 July (MHi: Heath Papers).

3. Westborough, Mass., is about sixty-five miles northeast of Hartford.

## From Henry Laurens

Sir.                                      Philadelphia 17th July 1778.

Your Excellency's favor of the 14th Inst. which came to hand pretty late last Evening I shall have the honor of presenting to Congress this Morning.

At present I have no other Commands on me, but to transmit the Inclosed Act of Congress of the 15th Inst. for receiving & subsisting prisoners of War which may be taken by the Squadron under the Command of Vice Admiral Count d'Estaing to which I beg leave to refer.[1] And remain With the most sincere Regard & Respect sir Your Excellency's Most obedient & most humble servant

Henry Laurens,
President of Congress.

ALS, DLC:GW; LB, DNA:PCC, item 13. A note on the letter-book copy indicates that this letter was carried "by James Martin."

1. The enclosed resolution directed that the prisoners "be recieved by the commissary general of prisoners, and that he provide for their safe custody and subsistance in like manner as hath been usual for the prisoners of these States . . . and that the said prisoners be held at the disposition of his most Christian Majesty, and subject to the orders of his Excellency Monsr the Count D'Estaing" (DLC:GW; see also *JCC*, 11:690–91).

## To Major General John Sullivan

Dear Sir              Head Quarters Haverstraw [N.Y.] 17th July 1778

I have the pleasure to inform you, of what you have probably heard before this time, that the Admiral Count D'Estaing has arrived upon the Coast, and now lays off Sandy Hook, with a fleet of twelve Ships of the Line and four Frigates belonging to his most Christian Majesty. The design of this fleet is to co-operate with the American Armies, in the execution of any plans, which shall be deemed most advancive of our mutual interests, against the common enemy. No particular plan is yet adopted, but two seem to present themselves; either an attack upon New York, or Rhode Island. Should the first be found practicable, our forces are very well disposed for the purpose; but should the latter be deemed most eligible, some previous preparations must be made. That we may therefore be ready at all points, and for all events, I desire that you may immediately apply in the most urgent manner, in my name, to the States of Rhode Island, Massachusets and Connecticut to make up a Body of 5000 Men inclusive of what you already have—establish suitable Magazines of provision—and make a collection of Boats proper for a descent. I am empowered to call for the Militia for the purpose above mentioned, by a Resolve of Congress of the 11th instant.[1]

You will not fail to make yourself fully master of the numbers and position of the Enemy by land, and of their Strength by Sea. Should nothing come of this Matter, it will answer this valuable ⟨pur⟩pose, that the enemy will be distracted and deceived, and will probably be off their guard, in respect to the defence of New York, should that ultimately be our real design.

You should engage a number of Pilots well acquainted with the navigation of the Harbour of New port and of the adjacent Coast, and have them ready to go on board upon signals which will be thrown out by the French Admiral, and of which you will be advised. That you may have the earliest intelligence of his arrival, you should establish a Chain of Expresses from some commanding View upon the Coast to your Quarters. I need not recommend perfect secrecy to you, so far as respects any assistance from the French Fleet. Let your preparations carry all the appearance of dependance upon your own strength only. Lest you may think the Number of 5000 Men too few for the enterprise, I will just hint to you, that there are french Troops on board the Fleet, and some will be detached from this Army, should there be occasion.

I have it not in my power to be more explicit with you at present. But should the expedition against Rhode Island be finally determined upon, you may depend upon having every previous and necessary information for your Government. I am Dear Sir Yr most obt Servt

Go: Washington

P.S. As I have heard from you but once or twice since your arrival at Rhode Island, I am much at a loss for the situation of matters in that quarter.[2] Be pleased therefore to inform me in your answer to this.

LS, in Tench Tilghman's writing, NhHi: Sullivan Papers; Df, DLC:GW; Varick transcript, DLC:GW. The postscript is lacking on the draft and transcript. Sullivan submitted this letter for consideration by a council of war on 25 July (Hammond, *Sullivan Papers*, 2:113–14).

1. See Henry Laurens to GW, 11 July, and note 1.
2. Sullivan had written two letters to GW on 2 May and another letter on 26 May.

## General Orders

Head-Quarters Haverstraw [N.Y.] July 18th 1778.
Parole                                                                    C. Signs

At a Brigade General Court-Martial in General Woodford's Brigade held at Sloterdam Camp July 10th 1778—Lieutt Coll Cropper President, Ensign Cooper of the 15th Virginia Regiment tried for being drunk on the 6th instant and laying in the road in a shameful manner when he ought to have been with his Regiment, found guilty and sentenced to be cashiered.[1]

At the same Court Lieutt Burnly of the 7th Virginia Regiment tried for absenting himself from his command without leave; found guilty & sentenced to be discharged from the service.[2]

The Commander in Chief approves the sentences and orders them to take place.

Varick transcript, DLC:GW.

1. Samuel Cooper had served in the 15th Virginia Regiment since November 1776, being promoted from sergeant-major to ensign on 20 June 1777. Slotterdam referred to a region on the east side of the Passaic River including parts of what are now Fair Lawn and East Paterson, New Jersey.

2. Garland Burnley (1753–1793) was commissioned a 1st lieutenant of the 7th Virginia Regiment on 7 May 1776 and discharged on this date. In 1779 he became a captain of the Convention Army Guard Regiment in Virginia.

## From John Beatty

Sir                                           Elizth Town [N.J.] July 18th 1778

I am now to Inform you, that Yesterday I effected the Exchange, of all the Privates in the Enemy's Hands—except those in the Hospital & a few out at work—Amounting in the whole to less than a Hundred—Those Mr Loring has promised, shall be sent out in the Course of a week or ten days.

The Prisoners are in General in good Care—have therefore dispatched all the Continental Troops to Head Quarters, under the Care of Capt. Forman[1]—I must refer Your Exelly to Coll Scammel for the Number of those—the Militia—Sailors &ca—making up in the whole 647—In order to determine, among the militia, who were not in actual Service I oblidged them, before they were discharged to make exact returns to me, of their Number Regt—State—& time when taken—From this measure I find 15. men sent out here—who were taken from their own Houses & many of them out of their Beds—These I told Mr Loring I could not receive in any other Light than Citizens, nor would I return any Equivalency for them—he pretended entire Ignorance of their being so taken & said they were returned to him as Prisoners of war—after Quarreling some time—we Omitted giving Credit for them & refer'd it to a future day.

I can discover little from the Prisoners, who are come out—They seem generally to concur in saying, that they are removing—the Cannon—Stores—Baggage &ca from Staten Island—& I can not but add that from several circumstances—as that of a great Number of Small Craft plying between that & New York—a great Appearance of Tents, without men—The Crossing over a Body of Troops to Long Island—& indeed a general confusion seems to subsist among the whole—I am inclined to beleive that an Evacuation, will soon take place unless the Fleet at Sandy Hook, should remove. They hesitate no longer in saying a French war must take place—& that Brittain will now be oblidged to Exert herself.

Should Your Excelly have any Commands for me—please to direct to me at Princeton. I am Sir your most Obedt & very Hume Sert

Jno. Beatty.

ALS, DLC:GW.

1. Both Jonathan Forman (1755–1809) and Thomas Marsh Forman (1758–1845) were stationed at Elizabeth at this time. Jonathan Forman, who had served as a lieutenant of Monmouth County militia in 1775 and became a captain in Brig. Gen. Nathaniel Heard's Brigade of State Troops in June 1776, was commissioned a captain in the 4th New Jersey Regiment in November 1776 and joined the 1st New Jersey Regiment in February 1779 when the 4th Regiment was disbanded. He was promoted to major in May 1782 and became lieutenant colonel of the 2d New Jersey Regiment in February 1783. After the war, he served as lieutenant colonel commanding New Jersey troops during the Whiskey Rebellion and briefly as a brigadier general of New York militia. Thomas Marsh Forman, a nephew of Brig. Gen. David Forman, served for several months as a lieutenant in the 10th Pennsylvania Regiment before being appointed a captain in his uncle's Additional Continental Regiment in April 1777. He was made aide-de-camp to Brigadier General Stirling in January 1779 but resigned in May of that year. In the 1790s Thomas Marsh Forman represented Cecil County in the Maryland House of Delegates, and he served as a brigadier general of Maryland militia during the War of 1812.

## From Colonel Theodorick Bland

Sr                                    Petersburgh [Va.] July 18th 1778

I was yesterday favord with yr Excellency's letter of the 3d inst. dated from head Quarters Brunswic. With Respect to supplying Capt. Medici with money to proceed on his purchase and recruitg I am happy to have followed the mode you advise me to, but before the Rect of yours, I recd a letter from Govr Caswell informing me that it was impossible to advance a Shilling at present from that state, there not being one third money enough to pay the Draughts their bounty.[1] My ardent wish to reinforce the Army as speedily as possible with Cavalry induced me about a fortnight ago to send on a party of near Sixty Horses and thirty men, the latter not quite Cloathed and the former by no means equipt, except with the few articles of cloathing I could get in this part of the world; I however thought it more eligible to trust to the Chance of both than to detain them longer. I am in great expectation from present Prospects of sending on by the last of next week fifty or Sixty more horses; I have also orderd Capt. Medici to Send on fifteen of those he has purchased together with that Number of men, reserving to himself a small recruiting party; But if he cannot be supplyed with money, his stay in Carolina will be of very little service to the states, while that lasted he recruited and purchased rapidly after the enlarging his instructions. Enclosed yr Excellency will receive a return of the state and Condition of my Party and also of that of Capt. Medici.[2] Yr Commands relative to my endeavoring to procure all the accoutrements in my power shall be punctually complyed with, but I fear unless I am speedily supplyed with money it will not be in my power to comply with all the Contracts I have already made or to continue purchasing horses, having not had more than one fourth of the last remittance to Col: Baylor, sent me, That Gentn having informd me that he had made use of the rest in his department. And I find it impossible to Borrow from the state, or the paymaster here I shd therefore be happy if yr Excellency wd order me to be furnished with about forty or fifty thousand Dollars. I beg leave to Congratulate yr Excellency on the Important Victory lately obtaind over the Enemy near Monmouth; and to assure you that I am with the greatest respect yr Excys most obedt Servt

Theok Bland

ALS, DLC:GW. The cover is marked, "Ayletts Free 26th July 1778."

1. See Richard Caswell to Bland, 29 June (Campbell, *Bland Papers*, 1:89–90).

2. Bland's return, dated 17 July, records thirty officers and men and forty-five horses and also lists the numbers of arms, accoutrements, and clothing with his party at Petersburg. Capt. Cosmo de Medici's return, dated 6 July, gives the names of nineteen men in his troop of dragoons in North Carolina, records the purchase of eighteen horses, and accounts for de Medici's expenditure of funds (both returns, DLC:GW).

## From General Henry Clinton

Sir,                                        [New York, N.Y.] July 18th [1778]

Having promised my old friend Major General Phillips to ask permission for Him to pay me a Visit at New York, I have therefore to request the favor of your being so obliging to grant him a passport for that purpose, and that you will be so good to forward the Enclosed to that Gentleman.[1] I have the Honor to be, Sir your most Obedient and most humble Servant

(signed) H. Clinton.

Copy, P.R.O., 30/55, Carleton Papers. The copy is docketed in part, "sent by a Flag of Truce—the 31st July 1778."

1. A copy of the enclosure, a letter from Clinton to Maj. Gen. William Phillips of this date, is in P.R.O., 30/55, Carleton Papers. GW sent it to Phillips with his letter of 16 August.

## To Vice Admiral d'Estaing

Sir                               Haverstraw [N.Y.] July 18th 1778 8 OClock P.M.
Captain Wm Dobbs will have the honor of delivering you this. He has the character of an able experienced seaman; and, for a considerable time, has been esteemed among the first pilots, on account of his general knowledge of the Coast & Harbours, & particularly with those of New-York. Added to these considerations, he is firmly attached to the cause of America, and you may repose in him the strictest confidence. I should have prevailed on him before to wait upon you, but his indisposition prevented. I have the honor to be with the utmost esteem & respect Sir Yr Most Obedt & Most Hbl. sert

Go: Washington

Df, in Robert Hanson Harrison's writing, DLC:GW; Varick transcript, DLC:GW.

*Letter not found*: to Vice Admiral d'Estaing, c.18 July 1778. On 26 July, GW wrote d'Estaing: "I had the honor of writing you the inclosed Letter from Haverstraw Bay, which was intended to introduce Colonel Sears to your notice. This Gentlemen set out with Captain Dobbs."

## To Brigadier General John Glover

Sir                                          [Haverstraw, N.Y., 18 July 1778]
You are hereby directed to March the Brigade under your command to Fort Clinton on West Point,[1] where you are to use every Exertion for carrying on & compleating the Works—upon your arrival you are to instruct the troops now there, immediately to proceed to the Army & Join their respective Corps therein. Given at Head Quarters Haverstraw July 18th 1778.

G.W.

Df, in John Fitzgerald's writing, DLC:GW; Varick transcript, DLC:GW.
    1. GW was referring to the main bastion of the new defense works being erected
at West Point, which was known as Fort Clinton before it was renamed Fort Arnold
in May 1778.

## To William Greene

sir.                          Haverstraw [N.Y.] Head Quarters 18th July 1778
    I have the pleasure to congratulate you on the arrival of a French
fleet at Sandy Hook under the command of Admiral Count d'Estaing
for the purpose of co-operation with the American forces.
    Accounts from New-york speak of a Cork fleet which is hourly ex-
pected and for whose safety the enemy are extremely alarmed. It is
probable that this fleet, as well as other vessels, to avoid the Count
d'Estaign's will be directed to take its course thro' the sound. If this
should be the case, it might answer the most valuable intentions, were
the Eastern States to collect, immediately, all their frigates and privateers, to rendévous at some convenient place for interrupting their
passage that way. Could the whole or any considerable part of this fleet
be taken or destroyed it would be a fatal blow to the British army which
it is supposed at this time have but a small stock of provisions on hand.
I would therefore beg leave to recommend and urge the matter to your
particular consideration, as a thing of the utmost importance to our
cause at this critical conjuncture, from the proper execution of which
we may derive the most solid advantages. I am Sir with all due respect
your most obedient and very hble servt

                                                  Go: Washington

LS, in James McHenry's writing, R-Ar: Letters to the Governor; Df, DLC:GW; Varick transcript, DLC:GW. On this date GW also addressed an LS with the same text
to Massachusetts council president Jeremiah Dummer Powell, adding a postscript:
"You will be pleased to communicate this to the State of New-Hampshire" (M-Ar:
Revolution Letters, 1778).

## To Major General William Heath

Dear sir.                    Head Quarters Haverstraw [N.Y.] 18 July 1778
    I was duly favoured with yours of the 29 and 30th Ultimo with that
of the 7th Inst.
    I shall take the first opportunity of transmitting your packet to Gen-
eral Clinton.[1]
    The French fleet are now laying off Sandy Hook. I congratulate you
on this very important and fortunate event.[2]

As the Cork fleet is hourly expected with provisions for the British army; and it is probable they are directed to take their course thro' the Sound in order to avoid the Count d'Estaing; I have written to the Eastern States proposing to them, to collect and rendevous their frigates and other vessels of force to interrupt their passage that way.[3] If you can give any assistance in promoting so valuable a purpose it will be rendering the cause a very great service. I am Sir, your most obedient and very hble servt

Go: Washington

LS, in James McHenry's writing, MHi: Heath Papers; Df, DLC:GW; Varick transcript, DLC:GW.

1. GW was referring to the packet of correspondence relating to the death of a British prisoner, Lt. Richard Brown, that was sent with Heath's letter to GW of 29 June.

2. The draft initially closed at this point, but McHenry then crossed out the closing and continued the text on the back of the page.

3. See GW to William Greene, this date, and the source note to that document; see also GW to Jonathan Trumbull, Sr., 14 July and this date.

## From Henry Laurens

Dear Sir.                                 Philadelphia 18 July 1778.

Yesterday I had the honor of writing to Your Excellency a public Letter by James Martin & also of presenting to Congress Your Excellency's favor of the 14th which the House received with satisfaction.

permit me Sir, to recommend to Your Excellency's protection two packets from the Sieur Gerard to Count d'Estaing, which will accompany this. I have assured Monsr Gerard that it is altogether unnecessary to urge Your Excellency to give these dispatches the quickest safe passage to the Vice Admiral.[1]

prizes are finding the way into Delaware, one laden with Rum Limes &ca intended for the Enemy's refreshment embraced one of our Wharves the Evening before last & I learn a Rich Ship is on her way up.[2]

I have this moment Received a second Letter from the British Commissioners if I dared to venture an opinion from a very cursory reading of the performance, it would be, that this is more puerile than any thing I have seen from the other side, since the commencement of our present dispute, with a little dash of insolence, as unnecessary as it will be unavailing. If the Marquis de Vienne will indulge me till I return from Congress Your Excellency will find a Copy of that Letter within this.[3] at present he is on the Wing I must send to obtain his permission & in order to be quite ready in case he shall refuse to wait, conclude this with repeated assurances of being with the

highest Esteem & Respect Dear sir Your Excellency's Obliged & Obedient humble servant

Henry Laurens.

Private—

Returned from Congress 3 oClock—a Resolve relative to the Commissioners Letter that it ought not to be answered &c. with the Letter will
appear in print.[4]

ALS, DLC:GW; LB, ScHi: Henry Laurens Papers. The postscript is absent from the
letter-book copy.

1. Conrad-Alexandre Gérard's letter to d'Estaing of this date is in FrPNA: Ma-
rine, B4, I43. The packets contained duplicates of his dispatches of this date to the
French foreign minister Charles Gravier, comte de Vergennes (Meng, *Despatches of
Gérard*, 169–73).

2. Laurens was referring to the "schooner Lord Drummond, from Antigua . . .
taken near the Capes of the Delaware, by Captain [John] Rice" while en route to
Philadelphia "on supposition of the British forces being still in possession of it"
(*Pennsylvania Packet* [Philadelphia], 18 July).

3. A copy of the letter of 11 July from the British commissioners to Laurens and
the other members of Congress is in DLC:GW. It reads: "We received soon after our
arrival at this place your Answer to our Letter of the 10th of June and are sorry to
find on your part any difficulties raised which must prolong the Calamities of the
present War.

"You propose to us as matter of choice one or other of two alternatives which you
state as Preliminaries necessary even to the beginning of a Negociation for Peace
to this Empire.

"One is an explicit acknowledgment of the Independence of these States. We are
not inclined to dispute with you about the meaning of words: but so far as you
mean the entire privilidge of the People of North America to dispose of their property and to Govern themselves without any reference to Great Britain, beyond what
is necessary to preserve that union of force in which our mutual safety and advantage consist: we think that so far their Independency is fully acknowledged in the
terms of our Letter of the 10th June—and we are willing to enter upon a fair discussion with you of all the circumstances that may be necessary to insure or even
to enlarge that Independency.

"In the other alternative you propose that His Majesty should withdraw his Fleets
and his Army.

"Although we have no doubt of his Majesty's disposition to remove every subject
of uneasiness from the Colonies, yet there are circumstances of precaution against
our antient Enemies, which joined to the regard that must be paid to the safety of
many who from affection to Great Britain have exposed themselves to suffer ⟨in⟩ this
Contest, and to whom Great Britain owes support at every ⟨ex⟩pence of Blood and
Treasure, that will not allow us to begin with this measure. How soon it may follow
the first advances to Peace on your part will depend on the favorable prospect you
give of a Reconciliation with your fellow Citizens of this Continent and with those in
Britain. In the mean time we assure you that no circumstance will give us more satisfaction than to find that the extent of our future connection is to be determined
on principles of mere reason and the considerations of mutual interest, on which we
are willing likewise to rest the permanency of any arrangements we may form.

"In making these Declarations we do not wait for the decision of any Military
Events. Having determined our Judgment by what we believe to be the Interest of

our Country we shall abide by the Declarations we now make in every possible situation of our Affairs.

"You refer to Treaties already subsisting, but are pleased to with hold from us any particular information in respect to their nature or tendency.

"If they are in any degree to affect our Deliberations we think that you cannot refuse a full communication of the particulars in which they consist, both for our Consideration and that of your own Constituents, who are to judge between us whether any Alliance you may have contracted be a sufficient reason for continuing this unnatural War. We likewise think ourselves entitled to a full communication of the powers by which you conceive yourselves authorized to make Treaties with Foreign Nations.

"And we are led to ask satisfaction on this point because we have observed in your proposed Articles of Confederation No: 6 and 9 it is stated that you should have the power of entering into Treaties and Alliances under certain restrictions therein specified, yet we do not find promulgated any Act or Resolution of the Assembly's of particular States conferring this power on you.

"As we have communicated our powers to you, and mean to proceed without reserve in this business we will not suppose that any objection can arise on your part to our communicating to the public so much of your correspondence as may be necessary to explain our own proceedings. At the same time we assure you that in all such publications the respect which we pay to the great body of People you are supposed to represent, shall be evidenced by us in every possible mark of consideration and regard."

4. For the resolution, see *JCC*, 11:701–2. The resolution and the commissioners' letter were printed in the *Pennsylvania Packet or the General Advertiser* (Philadelphia), 21 July.

## To Brigadier General John Stark

Dear Sir                    Head quarters Haverstraw [N.Y.] July 18th 1778

I this day received your Letter of the 14th Instant, & am sorry to find you so circumstanced as to render a Reinforcment necessary which I can badly spare in the present critical & interesting State of things; I have however, order'd Colo. Butler with the 4th Pensylvania Regiment & a part of Morgan's Riffle Corps to March to the Village Wawarsink in Ulster County, from whence they may be call'd either to Albany or farther to the Westward as the Exigency of affairs will point out[1]—These, with the troops which Genl Gates informs me, are to March to your assistance,[2] will I expect prove sufficient to repell every attack which may be made upon you, & I hope in a little time to be in a Situation that I can give you every necessary support. I am Dr sir your very Hble Servt

Go: Washington

LS (photocopy), DLC:GW, series 9.

1. Letters of this date from GW's aide-de-camp Tench Tilghman to Lt. Col. William Butler and Capt. Thomas Posey (1750–1818) ordered these units to rendezvous at Smith's Clove and then march to Wawarsing, N.Y., where they would await instructions from Gov. George Clinton (both, DLC:GW). Posey was commissioned as a captain in the 7th Virginia Regiment in March 1776, and when Col.

Daniel Morgan's Rifle Regiment was organized in the summer of 1777, he became a captain in that regiment. Posey's promotion to major, dated from 30 April 1778, evidently took place during the mid-September reorganization of the Virginia line, when Posey became major of the new 7th (formerly 11th) Virginia Regiment. Posey was promoted to lieutenant colonel in September 1781 and served to March 1783. When the postwar army was expanded in 1793, Posey was commissioned as a brigadier general, a post he resigned in February 1794. His subsequent career included service in the Kentucky state legislature, as U.S. senator from Louisiana, and as governor of the Indiana Territory.

2. Gates was probably referring to the militia that his letter to Stark of 13 July had directed Stark to call out (see Gates to GW, 13 July, n.3).

## To Jonathan Trumbull, Sr.

Sir                 Head Quarters Haverstraw [N.Y.] 18th July—1778

I did myself the Honor to transmit you, a few days ago, the accounts which I had then received of the arrival of a French Fleet upon the Coast. I soon after had the pleasure of receiving a Letter from the Admiral Count D'Estaing, dated off Sandy Hook, where he now lies with twelve sail of the Line and four Frigates.[1] The British Fleet are within the Hook.

I am so fully convinced of the advantages that will result from having all our Frigates, Privateers, and armed Vessels of every kind cruising off the East end of Long Island, that I have taken the liberty of mentioning it again to you, and have wrote to the same effect to the States of Rhode Island and Massachusetts.[2] The British Fleet awed by the French, will be obliged to keep together, which will afford the noblest opportunity to our Cruisers to pick up whatever is inward bound. I have the Honor to be with great Respect and Esteem Sir your most obedient Servant

G. Washington

P.S. you will oblige me by forwarding the Letters to General Sullivan,[3] Govr Greene, and the President of Massachusetts, by a fresh Express.

LB, Ct: Trumbull Papers; Df, DLC:GW; Varick transcript, DLC:GW.

1. See GW to Trumbull, 14 July, and Vice Admiral d'Estaing to GW, 13 July.

2. For these letters, see GW to William Greene, this date, and the source note to that document.

3. GW was evidently referring to his letter to Maj. Gen. John Sullivan of 17 July.

## From Jonathan Trumbull, Sr.

Sir                 Lebanon [Conn.] 18th July 1778.

Your Letter of the 14th inst. received this moment—have sent the intelligence contained in it to New London, where are four Privates to

Middletown and Hartford where a Number of Smal Armed Boats—have prepared Letters to Govr Green, & President Powel at Massachusetts—with the Same to go by Post Monday next.[1]

hope they may be so happy as to succeed in their Attempts to intercept The Cork Fleet.

Colo. Jos. Trumbull is at my House very dangerously ill with a Relapse, look on his recovery very doubtfull. I am, with great Esteem & Regard Sir—Your most Obedt humble Servant

Jonth; Trumbull

P.S. I have no other than vague, uncertain Accounts of the Circumstances of your Success in the Jersies.

ALS, DLC:GW.

1. Trumbull's letter of this date to Massachusetts council president Jeremiah Dummer Powell transmitted a copy of GW's letter of 14 July, "In consequence of which I am sure your Hon[orabl]e Council will take such measures, as to you & them shall appear most conducive to the public Interest. I have sent & am sending advice to all armed Vessels in the eastern parts of this State, to exert themselves in looking out for & annoying the Cork Fleet" (M-Ar: Revolution Letters, 1778). He wrote the same to New Hampshire council president Meshech Weare (Nh-Ar: Weare Papers) and more briefly to Rhode Island governor William Greene (R-Ar: Letters to the Governor).

# General Orders

Head-Quarters Delavan's House[1] July 19th 1778.

The whole of the Left Wing under the Command of Major General De Kalb except Malcom's & Spencer's Regiments are to march tomorrow morning at two ôClock for the white Plains: Baron Steuben with the Right Wing, Angell's Regiment and the Regt commanded by Lieutt Coll Park excepted are to follow in an hour after; These Divisions may arive within the distance of from one to five miles of the present Camp at the Plains as Water and Ground will admit but not enter 'till a new Camp can be formed, a disposition for the whole made, and some Alteration in the present Brigades take place.

Malcom's and the Regiment commanded by Lieutenant Coll Parke are to march early tomorrow for the Fort at West-Point on Hudson's River—Spencer's will take Post at Kings-Ferry and Angell's with Glover's Brigade (when it comes up) are to wait at Croton Bridge for further orders.[2]

After the second Line of the Army under the Marquis De la Fayette have crossed the River the Quarter Master General will remove the Boats except such as are necessary for ordinary Purposes from Kings-Ferry to and above the Forts in the Highlands.

Varick transcript, DLC:GW.

Other orders adjusting troop positions on this date included letters from GW's aide-de-camp Tench Tilghman to Brig. Gen. William Maxwell and to Col. Goose Van Schaick. To the former Tilghman wrote: "His Excellency has recd some advices that induce him to beleive that the Enemy mean to evacuate Staten Island intirely. If such an event takes place, he desires you to march with your Brigade to the Neighbourhood of Hackinsack, taking such a position, that the Enemy cannot cross the North River suddenly and hem you in between Hackinsack and Pasaic Rivers. If you should move up, you are to detatch a good Officer with about 200 Men to Monmouth. They will serve to keep that part of the Country in order, and will preserve the communication between us and the French Fleet while they lay off the Hook." He informed the latter: "It is his Excellency's desire that you move with your Regiment from the Clove to the Neighbourhood of Orange Town, keeping rather farther to the Westward than the town with your main Body, to prevent you being surprised by a light Body of Troops thrown suddenly over the North River. There are already about 50 Horse under the command of Capt. Hopkins at Closter, which is about four Miles below Orange. His Excellency desires you to mix small patrols of foot with these Horse and prevent the Inhabitants from carrying supplies to New York. If you gain any material intelligence, you can send over the River at Tarry Town to the General who will be at the White plains" (both letters, DLC:GW).

1. The house of Samuel Delevan (1752–1786), a captain in the 3d Regiment of Westchester County militia, was located on present-day Hallock's Mill Road in Yorktown. Delevan's bill for £10, dated 18 July, is in DLC:GW, ser. 5, vol. 29.

2. Croton (or Pine's) Bridge crossed the Croton River near its head of navigation, about five miles east of the Hudson River.

## From Major General Benedict Arnold

Dr General,                             Philada July 19th 1778.

I beg pardon for neglecting to answer your Excellency's kind favour of the 11th Inst:—I shou'd by no means have so long omitted writing had I not known Congress had transmitted every Intelligence of Consequence.

I beg leave (tho late) to present your Excellency my congratulatory compliments on the Arrival of the French Fleet & Minister and the pleasing prospect of our Affairs.

My wounds are in a fair way & less painful than usual tho' there is little prospect of my being able to take the field for a considerable time; which consideration together with that of having been obliged entirely to neglect my private Affairs since I have been in the service has induced me to wish to retire from Public business unless an offer which my friends have mentioned should be made me of the command of the Navy to which my being wounded would not be so great an objection as it would remaining in the Army.

I must beg leave to request your Excellency's sentiments respecting a command in the Navy; I am sensible of my inabilities & the great hazard and fatigue attending the office; & that I should enjoy much greater happiness in a retired life, still my wishes to serve my Country have a greater weight with me than domestic happiness or ease.

We have just received intelligence that the French Fleet was at Anchor off the Hook the 16th—we are anxiously waiting to hear from them, & hope your Excellency in conjunction with them will soon bring the Enemy's Fleet & Army to submit. I have the honor to be with the most profound respect & esteem Dr General your Excellency's Mo: Obedt & Hble Servt

B. Arnold

ALS, DLC:GW.

## To Major General Horatio Gates

Sir                                        Drakes Farm [N.Y.] 19th July 1778.

Inclosed you have the arrangement of the Army. Be pleased to draw off Sherburns, S. Webbs and J. Livingstons Regiments to Kings Road[1] or somewhere upon your left flank with orders to hold themselves in readiness to march at a moments warning; and whenever Baron Kalb with the front division of the Army arrives near your Camp be pleased to order Enos's and McClenachans [McClellan's] Regiments to march for the Fort at West Point. If there is any conveniency for their embarkation at Tarry Town and they can do it safely it will be best. The Company of Colo. Grahams Regiment that was drawn from Tarry Town is to return thither, as the Country is not only exposed, but the people complain, as they say that Company was expressly raised for a River Guard. I would have you send out a strong party of Foot with all the Horse under a good Officer to drive off the Cattle and Sheep between you and the Bridge. If the Enemy are distressed this will add to it.[2] I am Sir Yr most obt and hble Servt

Go: Washington

LS, in Tench Tilghman's writing, NHi: Gates Papers; Df, DLC:GW; Varick transcript, DLC:GW.

1. On the draft, Tilghman wrote "Kings Bridge." The enclosure has not been identified.

2. On 22 July, Gates sent out a large detachment under the command of Brig. Gen. John Nixon, directing that, as the British were "distressed for provisions," he should "make such a Disposition . . . as will most effectually answer to the driving all the Cattle, and Stock, between their Lines & Ours, into this Camp; The Inhab-

itants fearing their Cattle may fall into the Enemys Hands, who will make them no recompense for the same, are Anxious we should take them away, & have promised to Assist You in driving them Off" (NHi: Gates Papers).

## From Brigadier General William Thompson

Sir                                                                    Philada July 19th 1778.

I expected before this time to have been made happy by the receipt of my Parole from New York, and can account for its delay upon no other Principle than the hurried and very particular situation of the British Forces at this time, which may perhaps have impeded the negotiation of that business. When it arrives at Camp I am well satisfied your Excelly will forward it to me with the necessary Expedition.[1]

The Honble the Congress having been pleased to assure me that my Rank in the Army is reserved for me, and being now just on the brink of entering into Service, I shall stand in need of two Aids de Camp. And for that purpose I have thought of appointing John Coats Esqr. who was formerly a Captain in 11th pennsylvania Regiment but who from a Wound he received, and some other Circumstances was under the necessity of resigning his Commission. When the particulars are considered that resignation I presume will be no impediment to his appointment, more especially when it is considered that the young Gentn had my Promise and was virtually in that Capacity some time previous to the resolution of Congress.[2] George Noarth Deputy Muster Mr Genl was an early and faithful Volunteer of mine at Cambridge and is entitled to every Mark of Attention that I can pay him, and as he wishes to be as actively useful as possible, and now holds the rank of a Leiut. Colo. in the line of the Army, I have no doubt but as an encouragement to merit and a reward for his long and faithful Services your Excellency will indulge him with the same rank in my family.[3]

I request a Line from your Excellency upon this Subject and am Your most Obedt Hble Servt

Wm Thompson

ALS, DLC:GW.

1. Contrary to Thompson's expectation, he was not exchanged until October 1780.

2. Thompson may be referring to the provision in the new establishment of the army, 27 May 1778, "That two aids de camp be allowed to each major general, who shall for the future appoint them out of the captains or subalterns" (*JCC*, 11:542).

3. George Noarth was appointed deputy commissary general of musters in

April 1777 and retired in September 1778. His resignation was accepted in April 1779.


# General Orders

Head-Quarters [Wright's Mills, N.Y.][1] Monday July 20th 1778.
Parole Carlisle—                         C. Signs Campton. Chester.
The Right and Left Wings are to remain on their present ground 'till further orders—The Officers will see that their men wash their Cloathes, cleanse and put their Arms in good Order as soon as possible and carefully examine their Ammunition.
The Commander in Chief directs that no drums beat after-Retreat-beating 'till Reveillee unless by a general Order—Commanding Officers of Regiments & Corps are desired to see this order punctually complied with.

Varick transcript, DLC:GW.
1. This location is taken from the orderly books of Jedediah Huntington's brigade (NHi) and the 1st North Carolina Regiment (*N.C. State Records*, 12:506).


# From George Clinton

Dr Sir                        Poughkeepsie [N.Y.] 20th July 1778
By the enclosed Copy of a Petition & Letter which I received on my arrival here; Your Excellency will observe that the usurped Government of Vermont have sentenced sundry of the Inhabitants of this State to Banishment; which Sentence General Starke has contrary to his Duty undertaken to carry into execution, by forwarding the Petitioners down the River to Genl Gates to be sent to the Enemy.[1] These unhappy People (whose pretended Crime I have some reason to believe is Attachment to this State only) before my arrival had passed this Place on their Passage down to the Enemy's Lines. I must therefore beg that your Excellency will so far interpose in this Affair as to direct the Guard who may have them in charge to return with them to this Place and deliver them to the Commissioners of this State; And I flatter myself that your Excellency will not fail calling General Starke to account for his unwarrantable Conduct in this Instance. I have the honor to be Your Excllency's Most Obedt servant

Geo: Clinton

LS, DLC:GW.

1. Clinton enclosed a copy of a letter to him of 15 July from Jeremiah Van Rens-selaer, John M. Beekman, and Isaac D. Fonda, members of the Albany County commission for conspiracies. The commissioners wrote: "In Consequence of an Application of some People from Bennington in respect to eight men that are just arrived from said Place, we waited on Genl. Starks to be informed of their Crimes, they being sent to him, with Colo. Ethan Allen; his honor informed us that it was none of our business to interfere with Tories from any other State, they were sent to him to be forwarded over the Enemy's Lines, which he was preparing to effect; as he informed us he was then writing to Genl. Gates on that head; after much altercation on the Subject he informed us that the State of Vermont by their Courts had adjudged them dangerous to the welfare of their State and he judged it expedient to comply with their Commands" (Hastings, *Clinton Papers*, 3:553). The petition to Clinton, also dated 15 July, was from five of the eight prisoners. They asserted "that your Petitioners have never in any instance acted unfriendly to the American Cause . . . that the true and real Cause of their severe and unparalleled Treatment is owing to your Petitioners acknowledging themselves to be subjects of the State of New York, and not recognizing the validity and existence of the State of Vermont" and requested that Clinton "afford us Protection and not suffer that we shall be hurried away from our families and friends before a proper enquiry be had relative to our Conduct or Crime" (ibid., 3:552). Brig. Gen. John Stark's letter to Maj. Gen. Horatio Gates of 15 July is in NHi: Gates Papers (see also Stark, *Memoir of John Stark*, 177).

*Letter not found*: from Maj. Gen. Horatio Gates, 20 July 1778. On 20 July, GW wrote Gates: "I have been favoured with your two Letters of to day, (one inclosing a return) for which I thank you." Only one letter of 20 July from Gates has been found.

# To Major General Horatio Gates

Sir                                        [Westchester County, N.Y.] July 20: 1778

I have been favoured with your two Letters of to day, (one inclosing a return) for which I thank you.[1] I am now about Six miles from where the Court House at the plains was,[2] & shall set out immediately for Reuben Rights, which will be my Quarters for the present. I am Sir Yr Most Obedt servt

Go: Washington

LS, in the writing of Robert Hanson Harrison, NHi: Gates Papers.

1. The letter enclosing a return has not been found, and the return has not been identified. Gates's other letter enclosed "Intelligence I have this moment received from Long Island; it is so very interesting, that I would not delay one minute in sending it to Your Excellency" (DLC:GW). That intelligence has not been identified.

2. The courthouse at White Plains had been burned in November 1776 (see General Orders, 6 Nov. 1776).

# From Lieutenant Colonel Alexander Hamilton

Sir,                                      Black Point [N.J.], July 20th 1778

Inclosed I transmit your Excellency a letter from the Count Destain.[1] He has had the River sounded and finds he cannot enter. He will sail for Rhode Island tomorrow evening; in the mean time he is making demonstrations to deceive the enemy and beget an opinion, that he intends to operate in this quarter. He would sail immediately but he waits the arrival, or to hear, of a frigate which carried Mr Gerard to Delaware, and which he appointed to meet him at Sandy Hook, so that he fears, his sudden and unexpected departure, before she arrives might cause her to be lost.[2] He will not however wait longer than 'till tomorrow evening. We have agreed, that five cannon fired briskly shall be a signal of his arrival by day, and the same number, with five sky rockets a signal by night. In communicat⟨ing⟩ this, to General Sullivan, the Count wishes not a moment may be lost—and that he may be directed to have persons stationed on the Coast and intermediate expresses to facilitate the Communication between them. Pilots will be a material article. He begs every thing may be forwarded as much as possible; and as many troops collected as may be. He would be glad a detachment could march from your army, or could be sent by water, for which purpose he would send covering ships, and some vessels he has taken by way of transports; but he cannot think of losing so much time as seems necessary. If the water scheme could shorten it, it would be a happy circumstance. He recommends it to your attention, and that you would take measures if the end can be better answered in this way. and meet him with information of the part he may have to act to execute the plan. I perceive he can with diff⟨iculty⟩ debark 4000 troops but he will try to do it. I am Sir Yr most Respectful & Obedt servant

Alex. Hamilton

I hope your Excellency will excuse my not being myself the bearer of these particulars the end may be answered by Letter. Mr Neville is anxious to get on—I just have heard of dispatches arrived from you; I don't know but they may contain something new which may make the Count to wish a good conveyance, to return an answer. My stay till tomorrow morning may answer that end—I shall not delay coming forward.

ALS, DLC:GW; ALS copy, DLC: Alexander Hamilton Papers. Maj. Gen. John Sullivan submitted a copy of this letter for consideration by a council of war at Providence on 25 July (Hammond, *Sullivan Papers*, 2:113–14).

1. Both the ALS and Hamilton's translation of Vice Admiral d'Estaing's letter to GW of this date are in DLC:GW. In that letter d'Estaing acknowledged receipt of

GW's letter of 17 July, carried by Hamilton, and continued: "The just desire, that this wise officer has to render you an account of our conversation, does not permit me to enter into very extensive details—Penetrated with gratitude for your favours I shall only think of deserving them—I will not answer by words—actions alone shall henceforth express my sentiments for you, for your country, for its interest and for our mutual glory.

"I thank you, Sir, for the distinguished manner in which you have received Mr Chouin. He signifies to me that you inspire equally attachment and admiration, into all those who have the happiness of a near and personal view of your character.

"It was not 'till after being authorised by Col: Hamilton, that I ventured to keep with me my countryman Lieutenant Col: Fleury. The certificate you have given him insures him my esteem and confidence. I thank you also for the Captains of vessels & pilots, acquainted with the Rhode of New York, and I will make use of them as soon as possible."

2. The frigate was the *Chimère*.

## From Major General John Sullivan

Dear General                                        Providence July 20th 1778

I beg Leave to Inform you that about four Days Since twenty one Sail of Large Transports from Newyork arrived at Rhode Island with about two Thousand troops on Board They were at first Said to be Invalids but it Now appear that they are Effectives But mostly Foreigners[1] They have Now about five Thousand Troops on the Islands & have Seven vessels of War Sloops & Small Frigates only they have in addition five Gallies They have of Late Made No Movement but it is probable they will Soon. I have the Honor to be with the Highest Respect your Excellenceys most obedt Servt

Jno. Sullivan

P.S. I most Sincerely Congratulate your Excellencey on the Late victory the Arrival of the French Fleet & the Favourable Aspect of our affairs at this time & most Earnestly wish that your Excellenceys Long Tryed Patience under The most Discouraging Misfortunes May be Rewarded with that Compleat Conquest which you have Long Sought & which Nothing but your Steady perseverance could obtain.

J: S:

ALS, DLC:GW.

1. Frederick Mackenzie, a captain of the Royal Welch Fusiliers (23d Regiment of Foot) stationed at Newport, R.I., noted in his diary entry of 15 July that "A fleet of 18 Sail came in this Evening under Convoy of The Fowey from New York, having on board The 38th Regiment, The two Battalions of Anspach, and Colonel Fanning's Regiment of Provincials, with about 50 of The Royal Artillery; amounting in the whole to about 2000 men, under the Command of Major General Prescott." The troops disembarked on 16 July (*Mackenzie Diary*, 1:309–10).

## General Orders

Head Quarters Wrights-Mill [White Plains] Tuesday July 21st 1778.
Parole Denmark—                    C. Signs Dedham. Dover.
Durkee's and late Chandler's Regiments now in Varnums are to join
Parsons's Brigade immediately.

A return of the Officers Names left in the Jersey's to superinte[n]d
the sick and now there to be made immediately.

Varick transcript, DLC:GW.

## To George Clinton

Dear Sir                    Head Quarters White plains 21st July 1778
I have been favd with yours of yesterday, and soon after, Genl Gates
transmitted me letters from Colo. Ethan Allen to Genl Stark and himself upon the same subject.[1]

I plainly perceive, that this matter is likely to be productive of a serious dispute between the State of New York and the inhabitants of Vermont, and therefore, I do not chuse to give any determination.[2] I shall
transmit the whole proceedings to Congress, and desire their decision.
In the mean time, I have ordered the prisoners to be returned to Fort
Arnold, where they are to remain, in an easy confinement under the
care of Colo. Malcom the commanding Officer.[3] I am with great Esteem Dear Sir Your most obt Servt

Go: Washington

LS, in Tench Tilghman's writing, NNU-F: Richard Maass Collection; Df, DLC:GW;
Varick transcript, DLC:GW.

1. Ethan Allen wrote Gates from Albany on 15 July: "The Court of Commissioners for the County of Bennington, and State of Vermont, Having sentenced Eight
Persons from said County, to be Banished to the Brittish lines . . . for their inimical
and Treasonable Conduct, Against the Independent states of America; This is
therefore Earnestly to Desire your Honours Interposition, so far as to send them to
the Enemies lines, agreeable to their sentance. . . . Seventeen of those Attrotious
Villains have been Thus Sentanced to Banishment, some have been sent to the
Brittish lines Thro' the State of Connecticut, the Polocy is approv'd of by Gentlemen in general, which I have Conversed with, and I hope & Expect it will meet with
your Honours approbation.

"Sure I am that it Intimidates the Tories, and their Connections, and Strength-
ens the hands of the friends of liberty, in our parts, and is Attended with the Sali-
tary Consequences which may Naturally be Supposed to result from such a procedure . . . " (NHi: Gates Papers; see also Duffy, *Ethan Allen and His Kin*, 1:83–84).
Allen's letter to Brig. Gen. John Stark has not been identified.

2. At this point on the draft, Tilghman wrote but crossed out the clause "especially as the Jurisdiction of the latter is not acknowledged."

3. See GW's letter of this date to the commanding officer at West Point.

## From George Clinton

Dear Sir.                                  Poughkeepsie [N.Y.] July 21st 1778

I have this Moment received the disagreable Account of Springfield and Andreas Town on the Western Frontier of Tryon County being destroyed by the Enemy Copies and Extracts of the several Letters forwarded to me on that Subject and the Copy of a Letter from Colo. Vroman to General Ten Broeck containing Information of the Enemy's being on their March up the west branch of Delaware River against that Place your Excellency will find enclosed.[1] I am extreamly apprehensive that notwithstanding the utmost exertions we shall be able to make with the Militia, the Enemy will lay waste that fertile Country. By General Ten Broeck's Letter your Excellency will please to observe that none of the Hampshire Militia are arrived at Albany and only about 30 of the Berkshire Militia and about 50 of Colo. Beedels Regiment are now at that Place. This unexpectedly being the Case I submit to your Excellency whether it would not be most adviseable to hasten the March of Lieut. Colo. Butlers Regiment, and instead of halting them at Wawarsink let them proceed immediately at least as far North as Schoharie as it is most probable the next attempt of the Enemy will be against that Settlement. I am with the highest Esteem Your Excellency's most Obedt Servt

Geo. Clinton

LS, DLC:GW.

1. Peter B. Vroman (Vrooman; 1736–1794), a member of the Albany County committee of correspondence from the Schoharie district in 1775, was elected a colonel of the county militia in October of that year and served in that capacity until 1781. Vroman's letter to militia Brig. Gen. Abraham Ten Broeck of 17 July asked for reinforcement "without Delay," in light of information gathered from an Indian "spy of the Enemy . . . that the Enemy are on their Way coming up the west branch of Delaware River to this place [Schoharie]" and "that they had made a wide Road . . . to bring field Pieces . . . their number is great" (DLC:GW).

Clinton also enclosed copies and extracts of letters from militia Lt. Col. Jacob Ford to Ten Broeck, 18 July; from militia Col. Jacob Klock to Ten Broeck, 19 July; from Ten Broeck to Clinton, 20 July; and from Maj. Gen. Philip Schuyler to Clinton, 20 July (all DLC:GW). Ford reported from Cherry Valley "that the Enemy Tories & Indians have made a Decent upon the Settlement called Springfield about 10 or 11 oClock this Day & have burnt & destroyed the same—The greatest Part of the Inhabitants were moved but some of them were there how many are killed & taken I cannot yet tell.

"I have about 80 Men fit for Duty besides some of the Inhabitants—The People are in the greatest Distress There is Piquets made round the Meeting House and all the Women & Children and their Household Effects are crowded into that Place for Protection so thick that it seems to me they must die there and there is so few Men here that it is not in our Power to protect them except they are together."

Klock, at Palatine in Tryon County, had "received several Expresses from Cherry Valley, Springfield and Andreastown informing that the two last mentioned Places are entirely destroyed by Indians and Tories, the Houses set on fire, several Men killed and scalped, the Fate of the Women is not known. All we could collect from Eye Witnesses agrees that the Enemy is strong This morning likewise Coll Peter Billings [Bellinger] sent several Expresses for Assistance, as the Enemy has burned Houses within four Miles from the German Flats, the continental Troops stationed amongst us are gone, the Militia under Coll Livingston is on the March for home, so that we are entirely destitute of any Assistance: I have given the necessary orders to stop the Progress of the Enemy, but the frontiers is too extensive to be guarded by the Militia alone, and if no continental Troops, or a standing force can be contin- ued, I fear the whole County by parcels may meet the fate of the above Settlements."

Ten Broeck, at Albany, enclosed those letters to Clinton, reported his actions in response, and added: "None of the Hampshire Militia are arrived here, the Berk- shire Militia are gone home, only about 30 are come to relieve those gone home, only about 50 Men of Colo. Beedells Regiment are here. Let me beseech your Ex- cellency to endeavor to get a Body of continental Troops sent to our western Fron- tiers If they do not come soon I dread the Consequences. It is now Harvest and it is with the utmost difficulty I get the Militia to turn out."

Schuyler wrote from Albany: "An hour ago I received a Message accompanied with a Belt from the Oneida's of Oriska informing me that the Enemy had de- stroyed Andersons Purchase and Springfield. that they expected the German Flatts wou'd next be attacked and when that is done they believe the Enemy will attempt Canajoharie and the other Villages in the vicinity; It is much to be lamented that the finest grain Country in this State is on the Point of being entirely ruined for want of a body of continental Troops. If any are to be sent the greatest Dispatch should be used and then perhaps they may still come in time to save part of the Settlements and numerous fine Crops of Wheat."

Springfield, in Tryon (now Otsego) County, was located at the north end of Ot- sego Lake; Andreastown (Andrus Town, Andrew's Town, Anderson's Purchase), in Tryon (now Herkimer) County, was a few miles northwest, near present-day Warren.

## To the Commanding Officer at West Point

Sir                      Head Qrs [White Plains] July 21: 1778
Captain Clark will deliver you this,[1] with Eight persons (two with families) who have been sent from Bennington under sentence of ban- ishment into the Enemys lines. There names are at the Bottom.[2] As I have received a Letter from Governor Clinton, with a Copy of a peti- tion from the prisoners and of a Letter from the Committee of Albany, all remonstrating against the proceedings had against these Men;[3] and as I am determined not to involve myself in any dispute about matters, with which I have nothing to do, I have resolved to lay the affair before Congress by the first opportunity, that they may determine upon it, as they shall think proper. In the mean time, you will take charge of the

prisoners and supply them with provisions; allowing them such indulgencies as may be reasonable. I do not wish or mean that their confinement should be close or rigorous—Yet they must not be suffered to escape. I am Sir Yr Most Hble sert

Go: Washington

Df, in Robert Hanson Harrison's writing, DLC:GW; Varick transcript, DLC:GW.

1. Capt. Isaac Clark (c.1748–1822) was assigned to guard the prisoners when they were brought downriver from Albany (see Ethan Allen to Horatio Gates, 15 July, in Duffy, *Ethan Allen and His Kin*, 1:83–84; Vt., *Rolls of Soldiers*, 797). Clark, who served in 1777 as a lieutenant in Col. Samuel Herrick's Regiment of Rangers, was promoted to major in January 1781 and to lieutenant colonel by 1782. He subsequently served as a state legislator, as a county judge, and from 1812 to 1815 as a colonel in the U.S. infantry.

2. The list of "prisoners names" at the bottom of the page reads: "John Phillips—with a family[,] Saml Phillips[,] Oliver Colvin[,] Wm Jones—with a family[,] Stephen Fairfield[,] Burges Hall[,] Timothy Bull." The eighth prisoner was apparently John Phillips, Jr.

3. See George Clinton to GW, 20 July, and note 1 to that document.

*Letter not found*: from Maj. Gen. Horatio Gates, 21 July 1778. On 21 July, GW wrote Gates: "I have been favoured with yours of this date."

## To Major General Horatio Gates

Sir                                  Head Qrs [White Plains] July the 21st 1778

I have been favoured with yours of this date with the Inclosures, respecting the prisoners sent from Bennington.[1] previous to it's coming to hand, I received a Letter from Governor Clinton, with a Copy of an Address from the prisoners to him & of a Letter from the Committee of Albany; all remonstrating against the proceedings had against these men.[2] Under these circumstances, as I am determined not to involve myself in any dispute, not coming properly within my cognisance, I shall order the men to West point, there to remain under the care of the Commanding Officer at that post, till the pleasure of Congress is known upon the subject, to whom I shall transmit all the papers, which I have received relating to it, by the first opportunity. I am Sir Yr Most Obedt servt

Go: Washington

LS, in Robert Hanson Harrison's writing, NHi: Gates Papers; Df, DLC:GW; Varick transcript, DLC:GW.

1. Gates's letter to GW of this date has not been found. For the enclosures, see GW to George Clinton, this date, n.1. Also on this date, GW's aide Tench Tilghman wrote Gates, "His Excellency has not yet returned from his Ride, the moment he does yours shall be delivered to him" (NHi: Gates Papers).

2. See Clinton to GW, 20 July, and note 1 to that document.

# From Major General Nathanael Greene

Sir                                    Camp at the [White] Plains July 21. 1778

Your Excellency has made me very unhappy. I can submit very patiently to deserved censure; but it wounds my feelings exceedingly to meet with a rebuke, for doing what I conceivd to be a proper part of my duty; and in the order of things.

When I left your Excellency at Haverstraw you desird me to go forward and reconnoiter the Country, and fix upon some proper position to draw the troops together at.[1] I was a stranger to all this part of the Country and could form no judgment of a proper place until I had thoroughly examined the ground.

Croten River was the only place that I could find suitable for the purpose all circumstances being taken into consideration. I wrote your Excellency what I had done, and where I was, that if you had any thing in charge I might receive your orders. I wrote you the reasons for my not waiting upon you in person were I had many Letters to answer and many matters to regulate in my department which prevented me from returning.[2] Besides which it was almost half a days ride the Weather exceeding hot and my self not a little fatigued. And here I must observe that neither my constitution or strength are equal to constant exercise.

As I was a stranger to all the lower Country I thought it absolutely necessary for me to come forward. A thorough knowledge of a Country is not easily obtaind. such a one at least as is necessary to fix upon the most elligible position for forming a Camp.

The security of the Army, the ease and convenience of the troops as well as a desire to perform the duties of my office with a degree of reputation all conspird to make me wish to fix upon the properest ground for the purpose. This it was impossible for me to do unless I came on before the Troops. And I must confess I saw no objection, as your Excellency had wrote me nothing to the contrary, and what I wrote naturally led to such a measure.

I expected you on every hour and was impatient to get forward, that I might be able to give some account of the Country when you came up. Before I left Crumpond I desird Mr Pettit to wait upon you at your arrival and take your orders; and if there was any thing special to forward it by express.

If I had neglected my duty in pursuit of pleasure or if I had been wanting in respect to your Excellency I would have put my hand upon my mouth and been silent upon the ocasion but as I am not conscious of being chargeable with either the one or the other, I cannot help thinking I have been treated with a degree of severity, that I am in no respect deserveing of.

And I would just observe here that it is impossible for me to do my duty if I am always at Head quarters. I have ever given my attendance there as much as possible both from a sense of duty and from inclination; but constant attendance is out of my power unless I neglect all other matters. The propriety of which, and the consequences that will follow I submit to your Excellencys consideration.

Your Excellency well knows how I came into this department. It was by your special request; and you must be sensible there is no other man upon Earth could have brought me into the business but you. The distress the department was in the disgrace that must accompany your operations without a change; and the difficulty of engageing a person capable of conducting the business, together with the hopes of meeting your approbation and haveing your full aid and assistance reconcild me to the undertakeing.

I flatter my self when your Excellency takes a view of the state ⟨*mutilated*⟩ things were in when I first engagd; and consider the short ⟨time⟩ we had to make the preparations for the opening Campaign and reflect with what ease and facillity you began your march from Valley Forge; and continued it all through the Country. Notwithstanding we went great part of the way entirely out of the line of preparations. You will do me the justice to say I have not been negligent or inattentive to my duty.

I have in every respect since I had my appointment strove to accomodate the business of the department to the plan of your Excellencys opperations. And I can say with great truth that ever since I had the honour to serve under you, I have been more attentive to the public interest and more engagd in the support of your Excellencys charactor, than ever I was to my own ease interest or Reputation.

I have never solicited you for a furlough to go home to indulge in pleasure or to improve my interest which by the by, I have neglected going on four Years. I have never confind my self to my particular line of duty only. Neither Have I ever spard my self either by Night or Day, where it has been necessary to promote the public service under your direction. I have never been troublesome to your Excellency to publish any thing to my advantage. Altho I think my self as justly entitled as some others who have been much more fortunate. Particularly in the action of Brandywine.[3]

I have never sufferd my pleasures to interfere with my duty; and I am perswaded I have given too many unequivocal proofs of my attachment to your person and interest to leave a doubt upon your mind to the contrary. I have always given you my opinion with great candour and executed your orders with equal fidelity. I do not mean to arrogate to

my self more merit than I deserve or wish to exculpate myself from being cha[r]geable with error and in some instances negligence⟨.⟩ However I can speak with a becoming pride, that I have always endeavord
to deserve the public esteem and your Excellencys approbation.

As I came into the quarter masters department with reluctance so I
shall leave it with pleasure. Your influence brought me in and the want
of your approbation will induce me to go out.

I am very sensible of many deficiencies; but this is not so justly
chargeable to my intentions as to the difficult circumstances attending
the business. It is almost impossible to get good men for the conducting all parts of so complex a business. It may therefore naturally be expected that many things will wear an unfavorable complexion; but let
who will under take the business they will find it very difficult not to say
impossible to regulate it in such a manner as not to leave a door open
for censure and furnish a handle for reproach. I am with all due respect your Excellencys most Obedient humble Servt

Nath. Greene

ALS, DLC:GW.

1. GW maintained his headquarters at Haverstraw, N.Y., 14–18 July. His orders
to Greene were probably given verbally.

2. The letter that Greene describes here has not been found.

3. For a more detailed exposition of Greene's view that his contributions at
Brandywine had been slighted, see his letter to Henry Marchant, 25 July 1778
(*Greene Papers*, 2:471).

## To Major General Nathanael Greene

Dear Sir,                                    [White Plains, 21 July 1778]

I cannot at this time ⟨(h)aving many People round me, & ⟨Lett⟩ers by
the Southern Post to read) go fully in⟨to⟩ the cont⟨ents⟩ of yours of this
date, ⟨but⟩ with ⟨the⟩ same truth I have ever done, I still ass⟨ur⟩e you, that
you retain the same hold of my affections that I have professed to allow
you—With equal truth I can, and do assure you⟨,⟩ that I have ever been
happy in your friendship, & have no scruples in declar⟨ing⟩, that I think
myself indebted to your Abilities, honour, and candor—to your attachment to me, and your faithf⟨ul⟩ Services to the Public, in every capacity
you have served it since we have been together in the army—But my
dear Sir, these must not debar me the priviledges of a friend (for it was
the voice of friendship that spoke to you) when I complained of Neglect—I was four or five days without seeing a single person in your department, and at a time when I wished for you in two capacities, having

business of the utmost importance to settle wi⟨th⟩ th⟨e⟩ Count de Estaign (which made it ⟨neces⟩sary for me to see you as Qr Mr Genl &) wch kept me closely engaged at Have⟨r⟩straw till the mom⟨ent⟩ I crossed the No. ⟨R.⟩—But let me beseech you my dear Sir—not to harbor any distrusts of my friendship, or conceive that I meant to wound the feelings of a Person who⟨m⟩ I greatly este⟨em⟩ & regard—I speak to you freely— I speak the language of sincerety, & should be sorry if any Jealousy should be entertained, as I shall ever say more (in matters of this kind) to you, than to others of you, being very truely Yr Obedt & Affecte

Go: Washington

ALS (photocopy), NjP: Armstrong Collection. The document is badly deteriorated. Characters in angle brackets have been supplied with the assistance of the text given in Fitzpatrick, *Writings*, 12:199–200, which was transcribed from a photostat made at a time when the document's deterioration was probably less severe.

## To Colonel William Malcom

Sir                                                [White Plains, 21 July 1778]

You are immediately to repair to Fort Arnold at West Point and take upon you the command of that post. You are to use your utmost diligince in carrying on and compleating the necessary Works, and when the Regiments, destined for the Garrison of the Fort, arrive, you are to send down all the new Levies that they may join their respective Regiments. Given at Head Quarters near White plains the 21st July 1778.

G.W.

Df, in Tench Tilghman's writing, DLC:GW; Varick transcript, DLC:GW.

## To Lieutenant Colonel Jeremiah Olney

Sir                              Head Quarters White plains 21st July 1778

You are immediately to march with Colo. Angells Regt to Providence by the Rout above mentioned.[1] The Regt is still to be annexed to a Brigade which will be formed under the command of Genl Varnum, under whose command you are to put yourself if you meet with him upon the march.[2] You are to use every possible endeavour to prevent your men from stragling or committing any kind of hurt or waste to the persons or properties of the Inhabitants. I am &c.

Df, in Tench Tilghman's writing, DLC:GW; Varick transcript, DLC:GW. The itinerary and note at the top of the draft are in a different, unidentified writing.

1. The route suggested at the top of the draft ran from Croton to North Salem, N.Y., Danbury, Newtown, Woodbury, Waterbury, Southington, Farmington, Hartford, Bolton, Windham, Canterbury, Plainfield, Voluntown (now Sterling Hill), Conn., Coventry, and Providence, R.I., with the distances for each leg adding to a total of 160 miles. A note also advised, "It will be Necessary to draw Provision to last danbury—from danbury draw to last to Hartford—from Hartford to Windham from Windham to Providence It will be best to have the Q. Mr go forward to the different Places where You are to draw Provision—before the Regiment as the March is—unknown at those places they may not be so well prepared."

2. On this date GW wrote Brig. Gen. James Mitchell Varnum: "You are to take the command of Colo. James Livingstons Regt Colo. Sherberns & Colo. Saml Webbs, & proceed agreeable to the rout as given you below. It will be necessary as you approach these places to send your Qr Mr forward, that you may meet with no delay in furnishing your men with provision. . . . When you arrive at Providence you are to put yourself under the command of major General Sullivan or any other superior Officer Commanding at that Post or follow such further orders as you may hereafter receive from me." Varnum's route was to Stamford, Norwalk, Fairfield, Stratford, Milford, New Haven, Branford, Guilford, Killingworth, Saybrook, Lyme, New London, Groton, Preston, Voluntown, Conn., Coventry, and Providence, Rhode Island. Voluntown at this time included both present-day Voluntown and the communities of present-day Sterling. Unlike Olney, Varnum was probably routed through present-day Voluntown.

## To Charles Young

Sir                              Head Quarters White plains 21 July 1778.
Being informed that you have applied for teams to transport cloathing to Philadelphia, I would be glad to know for what purpose it is to be sent away when it is so much wanted here, or the propriety of doubling the course of carriage, and burthening the Continent with an unnecessary expence.

Mr Kemper has a large quantity of Shoes at Morris Town, you will be pleased to direct him to have them brought forward to the army immediately.[1] He has also some shirts and over alls which he will send with the Shoe⟨s⟩. I am &.

Go: Washington

Df, in James McHenry's writing, DLC:GW; Varick transcript, DLC:GW.
1. Daniel Kemper (1749–1847), who attended King's College, 1766–68, was appointed an assistant clothier general by spring 1777. After the war he was a weigher at the New York City customs house, 1792–1806.

## From Charles Young

Sir,                              FishKill [N.Y.] 21 July 1778
I have your Excellencys favour of this morning, and am to acquaint you, that on my coming here last Thursday,[1] I found in different places

at this post, 94 Hogsheads of Clothing. My Instructions on my leaving
Mr Mease were, to forward all stores on to philada I thought necessary,
that I might meet on the road or find h⟨ere⟩. On Examing these, I
found 85 packages were Appropriated to particular regiments, &
markd or Addressd to the Commanding Officers of such, This Occa-
siond my concluding to continue them here, & Immediately wrote Mr
Mease what I had done: The Teams I applyed for, were to remove the
remaining 9 Hhds to fishKill Landing, 5 of which I wrote the Qtmr on
the other side[2] to prepare teams for, to send to phila., The other 4,
were to have been sent from the Landing to Tarry town by Water, Addressd to Mr Kemper. The Invoice of the 9 Hhds is herewith enclosed,
that your Excellency can Judge the propriety of my proceedings.[3] How
such a representation could have been made your Excellency, I cannot
conceive, It was really far from my design to Execute. Your Excellencys
favour will procure me the Teams so long applied for, in the Morng, so
that some good is like to arise from this misinformation.

A Mr Measam has come to this post from Albany, by order Genl
Gates, at a time Mr Mease's Assistant was acting here, on which account
the latter resign⟨d.⟩[4] Mr Measam is a Gent:, who does not View himself
accountable to Mr Mease for his proceedings. Three Hogsheads of
Blanketts came this day from Boston to him, Tho' I did not Expect attention would be paid to my request, I thought it my duty to require his
Assistant (he being ⟨mutilated⟩) to send them on with the 4 hogsheads
to Tarry town, His reply was, Mr Measams orders to him were, on their
coming to receive them, & Immediately acquaint Genl Gates, who
would direct their distribution, & from which he could not alter.[5]

Your Excellency may be Assured that during my Stay here, I shall forward all on to the Army of Cloathing Kind, that comes to my Knowledge. I have the honour to be Your Excellencys most Obt hble Servt

Cha. Young D.C.G.

ALS, DLC:GW.

    1. The previous Thursday was 16 July.

    2. The quartermaster at Newburgh, N.Y., was Andrew Taylor.

    3. The invoice includes a note: "47 Hhds of the 85. are for Genl Knoxs Artillery,
The rest for diff. regts of the Eastern troops" (DLC:GW). GW's assistant secretary
James McHenry replied to Young on 23 July: "The General is surprised, that you
did not, on finding the 85 packages marked for particular Regiments give immediate notice to the commanding officers. This ought to have been done with the
smallest loss of time as the Regiments were at hand to receive them which a day
might alter by their being ordered on detachments.

    "It is not his intention that any thing should be sent to Philadelphia that can be
made up as conveniently in the neighbourhood of the army. The General directs
that all possible industry may be used in collecting and forwarding Shoes—Shirts
and all such light articles as the army more immediately wants He cannot but

blame the great inattention which has uniformly marked the Clothiers department. He is assured that to this cause is to be attributed, why the soldiery have been so ill supplied, while the goods they were suffering for lay in the places where landed when they were bought—or in different parts along the road, without the necessary exertion to have them brought on to Camp And he expect in future more attention and regard will be paid to your department" (DLC:GW).

4. George Measam (died c.1782), a Montreal merchant who acted as commissary of stores for the Continental army during the 1775–76 Canadian campaign, was appointed commissary of clothing for the northern army in October 1776. In June 1780 Congress appointed Measam to be a commissioner of the Chamber of Accounts. Clothier General James Mease had appointed Peter Hughes as the assistant clothier at Fishkill, N.Y., in October 1777, and he served until June 1778. Measam arrived at Fishkill between June 11 and 18.

5. Measam was en route to Boston to expedite the shipment of clothing. Measam's assistant, the clothier at Fishkill at this time, was Peter Hansen. His letter to Gates requesting orders about issuing 176 blankets is dated 27 July (NHi: Gates Papers). For more of Measam's activities, see his letter to Gates of 28 July (DLC:GW).

## General Orders

Head Qrs Wrights-Mills [N.Y.] Wednesday July 22nd 78
Parole Exeter                                    C.S. Egypt Elk.

The Troops will be brigaded as follow and the necessary changes are to be made accordingly

No. Carolina–Clarke
    Patton [1]
Woodford ——Heth
    Cropper
    Mason
    Febiger
Muhlenberg –Parker
    Davies
    G. Gibson
    Smith
Scott————Wood
    Green } joined
    Gibson}
    Hall—Delaware
    Grayson.
Smallwood —Stone
    Gist
    Richardson
    Gunby.
2d Maryld ——Price

Glover ———Shepherd
    Wigglesworth
    Bigelow
    Vose
Patterson——Brewer
    Marshall
    Bradford
    Tupper
late Learned–Bailey
    Jackson
    Wesson
    Mead—Militia
Poor————Cilly
    Hale
    Scammell
    Hazen.
Wayne ———Chambers
    Steward
    Irvine
    Humpton

Hall
Williams
German-Battn
Varnum ——Angell
Sherburn
S.B. Webb
J. Livingston
Nixon ——Greaton
Nixon
Putnam
Wood's—Militia[2]

2d Pensa ——Craig
Johnson
Magaw
R. Butler
Clinton ——Vanscoick
Courtlandt
Livingston
Dubois
Parsons ——Meigs
Wyllys
Durkee
Chandler
Huntington –Prentice
C. Webb
Bradley
Swift

Woodford's, Muhlenberg's, Scotts, Smallwoods & the 2d Ma[ryland] Brigades are to compose the right wing of the first line—No. Carolina, Nixon's, Patterson's, Learneds, & Poors Brigades, are to compose the left wing of the same line—And Waynes, Second Pensylvania, Clintons, Parsonss & Huntingtons are to form the Second line.

Poors Regiment of Militia, and Moseleys a⟨re⟩ to march at Four Oclock tomorrow morning for West Point & put themselves under the Command of Colo. Malcom or the Officer Commanding at that Post.[3]

The detachment under the Command of Colo. Henry Jackson is to be[4] in readiness to march at a moments warning with their Baggage.

The Quarter Master Genl so soon as he has marked the ground for a Camp is to direct the march of the Troops to it. They are to be Incampd in the Order just mentioned, beginning upon the right of each line.

The three Senr Majr Genls present, will command the right & left wing, and second line of the army according to their Rank.[5]

When the Troops arrive at their next Camp, Baron Steuben will please to resume his office of Inspector Genl and make his arrangements accordingly—He will please also to accept the thanks of the Commander in chief for his extra Services in conducting the right wing of the army from Brunswick to its present ground, and for his care and attention to the Troops during their march.

The Brigade Majors will in future attend at the Orderly Office daily precisely at—twelve oClock.

AD, in GW's writing, NHi: George and Martha Washington Papers; Varick transcript, DLC:GW. The dateline and parole and countersigns, which were written at the end of the document, are not in GW's writing, nor is the last sentence of the orders.

1. John Patten (1733–1787), who served as a captain at the Battle of Alamance in May 1771, was commissioned a major of the 2d North Carolina Regiment in September 1775. Promoted to lieutenant colonel in April 1776 and to colonel in November 1777, he was taken prisoner at the fall of Charleston, S.C., on 12 May 1780, and although paroled, he had not been exchanged by November 1782. He remained on the army rolls until January 1783.

2. Ezra Wood (1726–1815) of Worcester County, Mass., served as a colonel of the Massachusetts militia from 1775 to 1779. At this time he was acting as colonel of a regiment raised for eight months, which served from May 1778 to February 1779.

3. Thomas Poor (1732–1804) of Andover, Mass., was a brother of Brig. Gen. Enoch Poor. He served in 1775 as a captain and major in Col. James Frye's Essex County regiment and was commissioned in May 1778 to be colonel of a regiment raised for service at Peekskill. Poor's regiment was discharged in February 1779. Increase Moseley, Jr. (1740–1811), of Woodbury, Conn., was commissioned lieutenant colonel of the 13th Regiment of Connecticut militia in March 1775 and promoted to colonel in October 1776. On 24 July, GW's secretary Robert Hanson Harrison wrote Col. William Malcom at West Point that Moseley had "represented to his Excellency, that the number of men in it is too small and inconsiderable for the proportion of Officers which is all but complete, supposing that the Regiment was full in point of privates; and has also intimated that under these circumstances, he thought many or at least some of them might be permitted to return Home without injury to the service. His Excellency desires that you will inquire into the matter and if an arrangement can be made, which will justify the return of a part of the Officers, without detriment to the service, he will have no objection to the measure, if it is their choice" (DLC:GW). Malcom's return of the West Point garrison, dated 25 July, shows Moseley's regiment with 14 officers and 277 rank and file, only 147 of whom were "Present fit for Duty" (DNA:PCC, item 78).

4. At this point on the manuscript, GW wrote but struck out the words "attached to the Park of Artillery till further Orders."

5. On 23 July, Maj. Gen. Alexander McDougall addressed Major General Kalb in regard to this order, confessing that "I have not the pleasure of being informed whether you or I is Senior" and asking for the date of Kalb's commission. Kalb replied on the same day that his commission dated from 31 July 1777, prior to McDougall's (both documents NHi: Alexander McDougall Papers).

## From Major General Benedict Arnold

Dear General                           Philadelphia July 22d 1778
    I have the honor to Inclose to your Excellency Two Letters which I received last evening from Mrs Washington, who was well when the Express came from Virginia.[1]
    There is no news here of any Importance, We have not heard from Count D'Estaing these Two days, when He wrote last his Pilots had Just returned from Sounding the Hook, & reported there was not water Sufficient to Carry over his Ships, He had then thoughts of going to Rhode Island, the French Minister has wrote him requesting his Stay at the Hook, the express is expected back every minute, I hope the Admi-

ral will Continue in his Station, and your Excellency soon have it in your power of bringing the British Army to Terms. I have the Honor to be with the most perfect respect & Esteem Your Excellencys most Obedt Hble Servt

B. Arnold

ALS, DLC:GW.
    1. The letters have not been found.

## To Colonel Theodorick Bland

Dear Sir                    Head Quarters White plains 22d July 1778
    I have yours of the 27th ulto. I am exceedingly mortified at hearing, that after Colol Temple has been so many months ⟨in⟩ Virginia employed solely in procuring cloathing for the Regiment, that the greatest part of what he had engaged should have been applied to other purposes, by Mr Finnie. The Men of your Regiment now here are in a manner destitute ⟨o⟩f cloathing, and having still depended upon receiving a supply from Virginia every day, have made no provision.[1] The Officers who had the charge of procuring necessaries for Moylans and Sheldons Regiments have long since compleated the Business and the men are well equipped. Matters being thus circumstanced with you, I see nothing better to be done than for Lt Colo. Temple to come immediately forward with what Cloathing he has, and to call upon the Cloathier Genl in Philada and leave an order for what is deficient.
    I cannot give any direction about the disposal of the Money sent to Colo. Baylor and yourself, that is a matter which you must settle between yourselves. He undoubtedly, if it comes first to his hands, should give you your share, and not suffer you to be embarrassed on acct of your public engagements.
    If you think that the eight or ten Men, mentioned by you, cannot come forward without danger of taking the small Pox upon the Road, you had better innoculate them; but I had rather they should have it done after they join the Regt. I am &c.

Df, in Tench Tilghman's writing, DLC:GW; Varick transcript, DLC:GW.
    1. On 30 July, GW's aide-de-camp Alexander Hamilton wrote to the Virginia commissary of clothing: "His Excellency is informed, that there is a quantity of state-cloathing coming on under your direction for the use of the Virginia troops. It has been hinted to him, that measures are taking to get particular regiments fully supplied to the disadvantage of others, which certainly would be altogether inequitable and improper. He desires you will make a point whatever partial applications may be made, to observe one general equal rule in distributing the

Cloathing—that every regiment may have a due proportion according to its numbers and wants. This, with proper care you will have it in your power to effect and justice and the good of the service essentially demand the most exact adherence to it" (DLC:GW).

## To Vice Admiral d'Estaing

Head Quarters near White plains
July 22. 1778. 1 oClock P.M.

Sir

I this moment received the Letter which you did me the honor of writing by Lt Colo. Hamilton.[1] I cannot forbear regretting that the brilliant enterprize which you at first meditated, was frustrated by Physical imposibilities—but hope that something equally worthy of the greatness of your sentiments is still in reserve for you. Upon the report made me by Lt Colo. Laurens of the depth of Water at Sandy hook, and the draught of your Ships of the line, I thought that no time was to be lost in marching a reinforcement to Genl Sullivan, that he might be in a situation for a vigorous co-operation—I am happy to find that we co-incided so exactly in the importance of this expedition. Mr Laurens, who will have the honor of delivering you this, will inform you of my opinion relative to the stationing a ship of the line in the sound—as well as of other particulars, which I have communicated to him[2]—I shall not therefore employ your attention farther than to assure you, that you have inspired me with the same sentiments for you, which you are so good as to entertain for me; and that it will be my greatest happiness to contribute to the service of our Great ally, in pursuing our common enemy—and to the glory of an officer, who has on every account so just a claim to it, as the Count d'Estaing.

The amiable manners and agreable conversation of Major Chouin, would of themselves, entitle him to my esteem—if he had not the best of titles in your recommendation and I beg you to be assured, that nothing on my part shall be wanting to render his stay in Camp agreable. At the same time permit me to add, that your great civilities and politeness to my aids cannot but increase my regard while they serve to give me additional ideas of your worth.

I have now only to offer my sincerest wishes for your success in this and every enterprize; and the assurances of the perfect respect and esteem, with which I have the honor to be Sir Yr Most Obedt & Most Hle servt

Go: Washington

LS, in Robert Hanson Harrison's writing, FrPNA: Marine, B4, I46; Df, DLC:GW; Varick transcript, DLC:GW.

1. For d'Estaing's letter to GW of 20 July, see Alexander Hamilton to GW, 20 July, n.1.

2. GW's undated memorandum to Lt. Col. John Laurens reads: "Colo. Laurens will suggest to his Excellency Count de Estaign the advantages which would more than probably result from a French Ship of sufficient force getting into the Sound, as far up as the lyons tongue, or somewhere thereabouts—A Measure of this kind would clear that channel of the British armd Vesls which now infest it, and cover the Passage, & landing of a party of Men which might be sent to long Island for the purposes of removing the Cattle out of the way of the enemy, destroying their Horses &ca—& would afford supplies of Fresh Provisions to the Fleet, vegetables & other comforts.

"The Vessels belonging to the Harbours of Connecticut, would presently take off the fat Cattle & other stock⟨, if⟩ the British Cruizers were driven from the communication between the Island and the Main.

"How far the enterprize upon Rhode Island is compatible with a watch of the Fleet in the Harbour of New York is left to the Admirals superier judgment—But, as an imbarkation of the Army at that place cannot happen without notice being had of it, nor an evacuation of the harbour after it is begun in less than 48 hours, it is submitted whether a capitol stroke might not be aimed at that Fleet upon its departure from the hook.

"The enterprize upon Rhode Island might be followed by an attempt upon Hallifax; which, if fortunate, would be a deadly stroke to G. Britain; as it is the only Dock on the Continent in which Ships of large Force can Careen. and Moreover abounds in Naval & Military Stores of all kinds" (ADS, DLC:GW).

## To Colonel Roswell Hopkins

Sir                          Head Quarters White plains 22d July 1778.

I recd yours of yesterday informing me of your having been stationed at King's Ferry before Colonel Spencers arrival there.[1] Be pleased to send for the Cloathes and Tents of the Men under your command, to Fort Arnold, and after they have recd them, let them march to Camp under the care of proper Officers that they may join the Regiments of the State to which they belong. When they arrive, the commanding Officer must report them to me. I am Sir Yr &c.

Df, in Tench Tilghman's writing, DLC:GW; Varick transcript, DLC:GW. Roswell Hopkins (1733–1827), a justice of the peace from Amenia, N.Y., was appointed lieutenant colonel of the 6th Regiment of Dutchess County militia in October 1775 and was promoted to colonel in March 1778. He moved to Vermont in 1784.

1. Hopkins had written GW from King's Ferry on 21 July: "I was ordered here with 300 men the 12th Instant only for 2 or 3 Days to Cover Some Cannon until the Grand Army had Crossed the ferry which is now Done.

"And Colonel Spencer arrived Yesterday with his Battalion of N. Jersey troops with orders to Encamp at this plaice without orders to Relive me, and as my men are without tents or Cloathes which are at Fort Arnold and they a Detachment of nine months men, and I was out with a Regt of N. York Militia who are all Discharged.

"Desire your Excellency would give orders that Colo. Spencer or Some others may Relive us" (ALS, PHi: Gratz Collection).

## To Major General Lafayette

Sir                                    Head Qrs White plains 22d July 1778

You are to have the immediate command of that detatchment from this Army which consists of Glovers and Varnums Brigades and the detatchment under the command of Colo. Henry Jackson.[1]

You are to march them with all convenient expedition and by the best Routs to Providence in the State of Rhode Island—When there, you are to subject yourself to the orders of Major Genl Sullivan who will have the command of the expedition against Newport and the British and other troops in their pay on that and the Islands adjacent.

If on your march you should receive certain intelligence of the evacuation of Rhode Island by the enemy, you are immediately to countermarch for this place, giving me the earliest advice thereof.

Having the most perfect reliance on your activity and Zeal and wishing you all the success—honor and glory that your heart can wish—I am with the most perfect Regard Yrs

G.W:

Df, in Tench Tilghman's writing, DLC:GW; Varick transcript, DLC:GW.

1. On this date GW sent letters to Brig. Gen. James Mitchell Varnum, Col. Henry Jackson, and the officer commanding Glover's brigade (Col. Joseph Vose): "The Marquiss de la Fayette will command under the orders of Major General Sullivan, the detachment from this army consisting of Glovers & Varnums Brigades, and the detachment under the care of Colonel Henry Jackson—You are, consequently, to obey his orders" (LS, addressed to Jackson, MH: Dearborn Collection; ADfS, DLC:GW).

## To Henry Laurens

Sir                                    Camp near White plains July 22d 1778

Since I had the honor of addressing you on the 14th, I have been favoured with your Letters of the 11th and 17th, with their respective inclosures.

The next morning after the receipt of the former, which came to hand on the 17th, I dispatched Lt Colo. Hamilton another of my Aides, with the best pilots and the most skilful masters of ships, I could procure, to Admiral Count D'Estaing, to converse with him more fully on the subject of his operations, than I was able to direct Lt Colo. Laurens to do, for want of the information which I afterwards obtained from Major Chouin, and a knowledge in several other points besides. On sunday night[1] Mr Laurens returned and I found by him, that it was the Count's first wish to enter at Sandy hook in order to possess himself of, or to destroy, if possible, the whole of the British fleet, lying in the Bay of New York; and that for this purpose he had been much engaged in his inquiries about the depth of water, and in sounding the channel to ascertain it. The result of which was, that the water from the experiments made, was too shallow at the entrance to admit his large Ships— or if they could be got in, it appeared that it would not be without a great deal of difficulty and risk. After this disappointment, the next important object which seemed to present itself was an attempt against Rhode Island, which the Count inclined to make, unless I should advise the contrary, as soon as the Chimere frigate, which had carried his Excellency, Monsieur Girard, into the Delaware, should rejoin him. Lt Colo. Hamilton, who was well informed of our situation and of my sentiments on every point, was instructed to give the Admiral a full and accurate state of facts, and to acquaint him, what aid and how far we could co-operate with him, in case of an attempt, either against New York or Rhode Island; and also to obtain his ideas of the plan and system, which, he might think, ought to be pursued, and to agree with him on certain Signals.

Previous to my dispatching Mr Hamilton, from the information I received on my inquiries respecting the navigation at the Hook, I was led to suspect, however interesting and desireable the destruction or capture of the British fleet might be, that it was not sufficient to introduce the Count's Ships. Under this apprehension, I wrote General Sullivan on the 17th by Express, that an Expedition might take place in a short time against Rhode Island, and urged him, at the same time, to apply to the States of Massachussets—Rhode Island & Connecticut for as many men, as would augment his force to Five thousand, and also to make every possible preparation of boats—provision—pilots &c., as if the event was fixed and certain.

From this time till about Twelve OClock on Sunday the Troops continued passing the River, when I crossed with the last division. On Monday afternoon I arrived at this place, in the neighbourhood of which the right and left wing encamped that night, with the second line a few miles in their rear. And here I am happy to add, that their passage across the river was effected without any accident, or without any more delay than necessarily attended the work.

Being persuaded now from the conversation which I had had, with several pilots and Masters of Vessels of character, as well as from the accounts of other Gentlemen and Colonel Laurens's report on his return, that the passing of the Count's Ships by the Hook would be extremely precarious—if not impracticable, I determined yesterday, which was as soon as it could be done, without waiting for further intelligence upon the subject, to put Two Brigades under marching orders.[2] They accordingly marched this morning at Two OClock for

Rhode Island, under the particular command of Generals Varnum and Glover respectively—and both under the direction, for the present, of the Marquiss de la Fayette. A Water conveyance was thought of, and wished for the ease of the Troops, but on consideration of all circumstances, such as the difficulty of providing vessels—the change and precariousness of the winds—The risk from the Enemy's Ships &c., their route by land was deemed by far the more eligible. The force with General Sullivan from the best and latest advice, I have been able to obtain is about Three thousand. A Detachment under Colo. Jackson will follow Varnums & Glovers brigades.

The inclosed papers No. 1, respecting Eight persons sent from Bennington and ordered into the Enemy's lines came to hand yesterday.[3] About the same time, I received a Letter from Governor Clinton, containing a petition by the prisoners and a Letter from the Committee of Albany; all remonstrating against the proceeding.[4] As this is a matter, in which I have no authority to act, nor in which I would wish to intermeddle, I take the liberty of referring it to Congress, that they may decide upon it. The prisoners are at West point and ordered to be detained there for the present.

I would also take the liberty of transmitting to Congress a Letter from Capn Gibbs, and of recommending him to their consideration.[5] His Letter was to have been sent by the Baron Steuben, before we marched from Valley forge, but his declining to go to York town, at that time, and our move through the Jersey's delayed it's being done. The Captain has been in the Army from the commencement of the War, and in the capacities, which he mentions. When Congress were pleased to honor me with the appointment of Officers for the Sixteen additional Batallions, I offered to make some provision for him, but this he declined; preferring to remain in my family.[6] The Guard he originally commanded, consisted of Fifty men, but since the arrival of Baron Steuben, it has been augmented to a hundred and fifty. The Baron advised that there should be a select corps of this number to receive the manœuvres in the first instance and to act as a model to the Army; and proposed that it should be formed of the old guard company and drafts from the line. I presume, if it should be Congress's pleasure, a Majority would be highly agreable to the Captain, and that it is as much as he expects.

1 OClock. P.M. I this minute received a Letter from Colo. Hamilton, who is on his return to the Army, dated the 20th at Black point. He informs that the Count D'Estaing would sail the next Evening for Rhode Island, being convinced from actual soundings that he could not enter his Ships. He was anxiously waiting the arrival of the Chimere, but at all events, meant to sail at the time he mentions. The Admiral has agreed

on Signals with Mr Hamilton. Immediately after this Letter came to hand, My Aid Mr Laurens set out for Providence, having many things to communicate to General Sullivan upon the subject of his co-operation, which neither time nor propriety would suffer me to commit to paper. Genl Sullivan is directed not to confine the number of his Troops to Five thousand, but to augment it, if he shall judge it necessary to ensure his success.[7]

I was informed by Mr Laurens that the Count D'Estaings magazine of bread is not so large as we could wish, and that in the course of a few weeks he will be in want. This circumstance I thought it right to mention, and I should suppose, that any quantity of Biscuit may be provided in a little time at philadelphia.

The Inclosures No. 2, are Copies of three Letters from myself to the Admiral.[8] I flatter myself the present of stock, which I directed for him, on his first arrival, in behalf of the States, will be approved by Congress.[9]

The accounts from the Western frontiers of Tryon County are distressing. The spirit of the Savages seems to be roused, and they appear determined on mischeif and havoc, in every Quarter. By a letter from Governor Clinton of the 21st, they have destroyed Springfield and Andreas Town, and are marching towards the settlements on the West branch of the Delaware. These incursions are extremely embarrassing to our other affairs,[10] and, I think, will justify a conclusion that Sr Henry Clinton's intention was to operate up the North River. Whether it may have changed with circumstances, cannot be determined. I have detached the 4th pensylvania Regiment and the remains of Morgan's corps under Lt Colo. Butler, and also Colo. Graham with a York State regiment, to co-operate with the Militia and to check the Indians if possible. Colo. Butler is an enterprizing—good Officer and well acquainted with the savage mode of warfare; and I am persuaded, whatever comes within the compass of his force and abilities, will be done. I have the Honor to be with great esteem & respect Sir Yr Most Obedt sert

Go: Washington

LS, in Robert Hanson Harrison's writing, DNA:PCC, item 152; Df, DLC:GW; copy, DNA:PCC, item 169; Varick transcript, DLC:GW. The LS is docketed in part "Read 27 referred to the board of war, in what respects cpn Gibbes"; see *JCC*, 11:722. GW wrote another letter to Laurens on this date: "Baron d'Arendt Colonel of the German Batallion, who will have the honor of delivering you this, waits on Congress to make application for leave to retire from the service—the reasons he urges to me are—irreconcileable disputes between him and his officers, which make it impossible for him to join his regiment—and the great uncertainty of his being elsewhere employed in a military line—As he requests that this letter may be a certificate to Congress of his past conduct—and assures me that he does not mean to use it as a foundation for solliciting higher command—I very readily assure them that as far as his conduct has come under my cognizance, and his infirm health has permitted him to act—it has ever been that of an intelligent, experienced officer" (LS, ScU).

1. The previous Sunday was July 19.

2. For GW's orders to Brig. Gen. James Mitchell Varnum, see GW to Jeremiah Olney, 21 July, n.2. The orders to the commander of John Glover's brigade have not been found.

3. The enclosures have not been identified.

4. See George Clinton to GW, 20 July, and note 1 to that document.

5. The letter from Caleb Gibbs to Laurens, dated 14 June, has not been identified.

6. For Congress's resolution of 27 Dec. 1776 authorizing GW to raise sixteen additional Continental regiments and appoint their officers, see *JCC*, 6:1045–46. No written offer to Gibbs has been identified.

7. See GW to Maj. Gen. John Sullivan, this date.

8. The enclosed copies of GW's letters to Vice Admiral d'Estaing of 14, 15, and 17 July are in DNA:PCC, item 152.

9. On the draft, the preceding text is in Harrison's writing, but the remaining paragraph, on a separate page, is in James McHenry's writing.

10. On the draft the preceding four words are in GW's writing.

## To Brigadier General Thomas Nelson, Jr.

My dear sir.      Head Quarters White Plains 22 July 1778

I had the pleasure of your favor of the 30th Ultimo by the last post.

I am sorry to find such a backwardness in Virginia in the service of the army. Perhaps it is fortunate for the cause, that our circumstances stand in less need of the great exertions of patriotism than heretofore, from the changes in foreign councils, and the open interposition of the French in our favor. But I am convinced you have left nothing undone, of encouragement, for the increase of your corps, or that could be of advantage to the service; and shall be happy to see you with such a number as you have collected as soon as their condition will admit of their joining the army. I would not advise you however to waste any time in waiting for the accoutrements you mention, as there is a pretty large supply of pistols and carbines coming on from the Eastward with which they may be furnished. In much esteem, I am Dear sir, your most obt and very hble servt.

Df, in James McHenry's writing, DLC:GW; Varick transcript, DLC:GW.

## To Major General Philip Schuyler

Dear Sir      Head Quarters White plains 22d July 1778

I have your favor of the 16th instant, and thank you for your congratulations on the success of our Arms on the 28th ulto and for your kind wishes on my personal account.

I am in a great measure a stranger to the expedition against Detroit, and intirely so, to that against the Seneca's. Agreeable to the Direction of Congress, I sent General McIntosh and two Regiments to Fort Pitt, but whether an expedition is immediately intended against Detroit, or whether those Troops are to remain as a defence for the Western frontier, I do not know.[1] The parties of Indians and others, under Butler and Brandt, have already done considerable mischief on the North East corner of Pennsylvania; having cut off the inhabitants; and destroyed the Settlement of Wyoming. Upon a representation from Govr Clinton, I have sent up Lieut. Colo. Butler with the 4th Penna Regt and Capt. Posey with a detachment of Morgans Rifle Corps to assist the Militia of New Jersey and New York in repelling their farther incursions.[2] If the expedition agt the Seneca Country is to be prosecuted, I imagine you and the Gentlemen joined with you in the commission for Indian Affairs will hear more of it from Congress and those who at first had the management of it.

As it does not appear clear to me, from your letter, whether you have ever been furnished with a copy of the charge against you, I now enclose it.[3] But it is impossible to determine at what exact time your trial can be brought on. General Lee's Court Martial will yet take up a considerable ti⟨me⟩ and when that is finished General St Clairs is to come on. The Committee of Congress appointed to State the Charges, having first taken up Genl St Clair's matter, it seemed proper to bri⟨ng⟩ on his trial first in conformity thereto: But as you may p⟨er⟩haps be in some measure involved, I shall give you notice, th⟨at⟩ you may attend if you please. Your trial may immediately follow.

Df, in Tench Tilghman's writing, DLC:GW; Varick transcript, DLC:GW.

1. In a resolution of 2 May, Congress ordered two regiments raised in Virginia and Pennsylvania "for the protection of, and operations on the western frontiers" and "desired" that GW appoint a new commander for Fort Pitt (*JCC*, 11:416–17). GW's letter to Brig. Gen. Lachlan McIntosh of 26 May assigned him that post. Henry Laurens's letter to GW of 14 June had enclosed Congress's resolutions of 11 June directing expeditions against Detroit and into the Seneca country.

2. While George Clinton was visiting GW's headquarters (sometime between 13 and 17 July), he received a letter of 11 July from Brig. Gen. Abraham Ten Broeck, enclosing an affidavit of James Armitage, 6 July, reporting that a force of "15,000 Indians and Government men" under the command of John Butler were preparing to attack the New York frontier, and he "immediately" communicated that information to GW (see Armitage affidavit and Clinton to Ten Broeck, 21 July, in Hastings, *Clinton Papers*, 3:525–28, 573–75). For the orders to Thomas Posey and William Butler, see GW to John Stark, 18 July, n.1.

3. For the charge of "neglect of duty" against Schuyler, recommended by a committee of Congress on 12 June and forwarded to GW on 20 June, see *JCC*, 11:602.

## To Major General John Sullivan

Dear Sir                    Head Quarters [White Plains] 22d July 1778

When I had the pleasure of writing to you on the 17th Inst.—I mentioned the probability of an enterprize being meditated against Rhode Island, as the next capital object, in case the shallow entrance at Sandy Hook, should frustrate admiral d'Estaings first design of an attack, upon the Enemys Fleet, in new York Harbour, The most experienced Pilots have been employed in sounding, and after the deepest consideration of what might be effected by lightening the Ships and the like, the attempt has been determined unadvisable—nothing detained the admiral from sailing immediately to Newport, but the absence of a Frigate which he was daily expecting from the Delaware. But as she has probably joined him by this time—I think it proper to apprise you, that the instructions which were given in my last, relative to collecting a proper force &ca, are to be regarded as having an immediate object,[1] I have this morning detached two Brigades to reinforce your strength, and am this moment instructed of the sailing of the fleet for Rhode Island. You will, I am well assured, pursue every measure in your power that can render the enterprize happy and fortunate, and as its success will depend in a great degree on the promptness & energy of its execution, I trust the conduct will answer the spirit & hopes of the expedition.[2]

The inclosure will shew you the demonstrations of the admirals arrival on the coast, and point out to you what is to be done on your part.[3]

This Letter is entrusted to one of my aids Lt Colo. Laurens, he has had an interview with the Count D'Estaing, and is fully possessed of all such information, as concerns the present enterprize. I am Dr Sir Yr Most Obet Servt

Go: Washington

P.s. In my letter of the 17th I mentioned the drawing together as many men as would make up 5,000 including your present force—I do not mean to restrict you to that number—but wish you to get as many as will insure your success. I should suppose there will be many Volunteers on this occasion.

I opened the letter after it was sealed to subjoin this Postscript.

Go: Washingto⟨n⟩

LS (photocopy), in Richard Kidder Meade's writing, DLC:GW, series 9; Df, DLC:GW; Varick transcript, DLC:GW. GW signed the cover of the LS. Sullivan submitted this letter for consideration by a council of war on 25 July (Hammond, *Sullivan Papers*, 2:113–14).

1. On the draft, the preceding text was written by John Laurens, who continued: "and that your exertions should be the more vigorous, as the success of the Enterprise in great measure depends upon the promptness and energy of the execution." That text was struck out, and the remainder of the draft is in James McHenry's writing.

2. On the draft, McHenry initially closed the letter at this point.

3. GW likely enclosed an extract of Alexander Hamilton's letter to him of 20 July, describing the signals agreed upon.

## From Major General John Sullivan

Dear General                                        Providence July the 22d 1778

I have the Honor to Inclose you the Intelligence reced from Rhode Island Last night which is not only from Good Authority but is Corroborated by Intelligence Received from various other Quarters.[1] Three Regiments of the Enemy Encamped yesterday on Connannicut Island Three more came out & Encamped in the North part of Rhode Island next Bristol: They may have Some Design upon us but I Rather Suppose they are preparing to guard agt the French Fleet.[2] I think it necessary to keep you advised of their movements here that you may the better know how to Regulate your opperations—twenty one Sail of Square Riggd vessels (mostly Ships) went up the Sound Day before yesterday for newyork. I cant Learn what was in them. I am pretty Certain they had no troops on Board. I cannot help Supposing that the Enemy will Soon bring the principal part if not the whole of their Army this way Either for the purpose of operating in the Quarter, or to make their Retreat in this way to Hallifax: most probably the Latter. If they Intended to Act offensively in the York Department they would not have Sent off Such a [number] of Troops from their Main Army So Soon after a Defeat—which Convinced them of your Exelys Superiority in the Field: to Suffer their whole Army to Lay in newyork inactive is what they Cannot afford & what in my opinion they will never attempt[.] to Leave a Garrison there while there is a Superiour Army in the Field & a greater Naval Force at the Entrance of the Harbor would (at Least) be Hazarding the Loss of the whole as Their Supplies would Effectually be Cut off both by Sea & Land unless The British Fleet from England Should Arrive and oblidge The French Fleet to remove for I can by no means think They would Leave their Garrison trusting to Supplies by way of the Sound as a Superiour Army might possess itself of Such posts in the Neighbourhood of Hell gate as would Effectually Cut off all Supplies through that Channel it Therefore follows of Course that unless they are Certain of the Speedy arrival of a British Fleet to assist them they must Remove & Even then Should the French

Fleet which Laid at Brest follow their Situation would not be much mended: nor Can I See any Solid Advantage Arising from their Coming to Act offensively in this Quarter as they must Labor under the Same naval Disadvantages and in a Short time if not at once be Checked in their operations by Land. for these & many other Reasons (among which is that of their having Sent two Foreign Regiment with a Considerable part of their Heavy Cannon from Philadelphia to Hallifax)[3] I am of opinion that they will Try to make their Retreat to Hallifax but that at all Events they will Quit New york your Excellencey will pardon this Trouble & believe me to be with Every Sentiment of Respect & Esteem your Excellenceys most obedt Humble Servant

Jno: Sullivan

P.S. Since writing the above I Recd the Inclosed Intelligence from Colo. Williams have also Examined the Deserter & find he adds that he Saw the Enemy Embarking their Light Brass pieces in order to Come & attack this place[4] I have in Consequence called in the militia to oppose any Design they may have formed against this place & to keep them within proper Bounds.[5]

J: S:

ALS, DLC:GW.

1. Rhode or Aquidneck Island is the name given to the large island upon which Newport, R.I., is located. Sullivan probably enclosed the following undated and unsigned letter: "The Boat is returned this Moment, about Midnight. Tis generally beleived there, that the Reinforcement they have lately had exceeds 3000 effective Men. They are very Busy in fortifying Brenton's Neck and the Island of Conanicut; and have removed all their heavy cannon there; in Expectation of the French Fleet, which they have Intelligence of. I shall remain here, in order to make further Tryal to Morrow Night, in Hopes of fuller Intelligence . . . " (DLC:GW). Similar information was given by exchanged prisoners who arrived at New London, Conn., on 21 July (*Connecticut Gazette; and the Universal Intelligencer* [New London], 24 July).

2. The diary of Capt. Frederick Mackenzie of the Royal Welch Fusiliers indicates that this movement took place on 20 July. He noted on that date that "The 38th Regt marched from Newport this morning, and encamped on Windmill [Butts] hill, a short distance from the right of the 22d; and fronting Howland's ferry" and that "two Battalions of Anspach embarked at 9 o'Clock in flat boats, and encamped on that part of Connonicut called Beaver's tail." The purpose, Mackenzie said, was "to possess the Island, and cover the Batteries at Fox-hill, (which fires on the Narraganset passage) and the Dumplins; (which fires on the entrance of the harbour)" (*Mackenzie Diary*, 2:315; see also Döhla, *Hessian Diary*, 80).

3. This information had been reported in the *Independent Chronicle. And the Universal Advertiser* (Boston), 9 July, citing "a Gentleman late from Halifax."

4. Lt. Col. James Williams wrote Sullivan on this date: "I herewith send you a Deserter from the Island of Conanicut, He informs Me that the Fleet which came in to Rhode Island, which you have had information of, brought three thousand effective Men, and that another Fleet went out yesterday, Containing twenty two sail mostly Ships and was followed by two or three others which went out in the Eve-

ning the Deserter informs that another reinforcement is expected in Consisting of four thousand Men, And that the Light House is ordered to be lighted for them to Come in by; The Light House was certainly lighted last night, I saw it myself, which was the first time it has been lighted, since the British Army has been in this State— The Deserter says, their design is to burn Providence which is to be done next thursday Night. A Number of Tents were Sprung yesterday on Conanicut, they are fortifying on the Island, with a considerable Party, the Fleet mentioned by the Deserter was seen from our Shore" (DLC:GW). James Williams of Scituate, R.I., was appointed a lieutenant in the Rhode Island Army of Observation in June 1775 and a captain in the Rhode Island militia in 1776. Appointed a captain of the 2d Rhode Island Regiment in February 1777, he became a major in the Rhode Island state brigade in June of that year and was promoted to lieutenant colonel in February 1778.

5. After receiving the first intelligence, Sullivan had written New Hampshire governor Meshech Weare and Massachusetts council president Jeremiah Dummer Powell, reporting British strength and adding, "Pray will it not be necessary to reinforce this Post with some Militia." The second intelligence roused him to send out more forceful letters, asking the governors to "forward immediately to Rhode Island such numbers of Militia, as can possibly be spared." Sullivan also called out Rhode Island militia and requested assistance from Connecticut (Sullivan to Weare, to Powell, to William Greene, and to Jonathan Trumbull, Sr., all 22 July, in Hammond, *Sullivan Papers*, 2:96–99).

## To Jonathan Trumbull, Sr.

Sir                               Head Quarters White Plains 22nd July—1778
I was yesterday honored with your's of the 18th and thank you for the Steps you have taken to carry my requests into execution. I must make an apology for not informing you in particular, of our Success at Monmouth, on the 28th last month. The multiplicity of affairs, then upon my hands, prevented me from writing but to the Congress and General Gates, and I expected, that the intelligence would have reached you through the latter Channel. You must, before this time, have seen my public Letter, which contains a full account of the action.[1]

The intention of the Count D'Estaing, was to have entered the Harbour of New York, but, unluckily, there is not sufficient Draught of water to admit Vessels of the rate of his Line of Battle Ships. He has therefore determined to operate against Rhode Island, to which place he has sailed ere this. I have made a large Detachment from this Army, as circumstances would admit of, to cooperate with him. The Admiral will, probably, be able to land some force, but our principal dependence must be on our own Troops, and the rapidity with which they are collected and operate.

I had, upon presumption that this expedition would take place, desired General Sullivan to draw together five thousand men, from the States of Connecticut, Rhode Island, and Massachusetts, in consequence of a Resolve of Congress of the 11th instant.[2]

I am convinced that you will be so well satisfied of the importance of the subject in view, as to exert yourself, to turn out the force of your State upon the occasion—I would go more longly into the Matter, had I not an opportunity of referring you to Lieut. Colo. Laurens one of my Aids, who I am sending express to General Sullivan.

I am exceedingly sorry to hear of the illness of your Son Colo. Joseph Trumbull, whose recovery I hope is not so much despaired of as you seem to apprehend. I have the Honor to be with great Regard and Esteem Sir your most Obedient Servant

Go: Washington

LB, Ct: Trumbull Papers; Df, DLC:GW; Varick transcript, DLC:GW.

1. See GW to Henry Laurens and to Horatio Gates, 29 June. The "public letter" was GW to Laurens, 1 July.

2. See GW to Maj. Gen. John Sullivan, 17 July. For the resolution, see *JCC*, 11:684.

## General Orders

Head-Quarters Wrights Mills [N.Y.] Thursday July 23rd 1778.
Parole Farmington—                C. Signs Freehold France.

John Ternant and Robert Forsythe Esquires are appointed Deputy Quarter Masters General and are to be respected and obeyed accordingly.[1]

At a Division General Court-Martial held at Kakeat Camp July 16th 1778—Coll Gibson President Lieutenant Deavors and Ensign Gassaway of the 3rd Maryland Regiment tried for disobedience of Orders and neglect of duty in absenting themselves from their Regiment without leave, found guilty of a breach of the 2nd Article of 13th section of the Articles of War and the Court considering the evil tendency of such Conduct which has been too generally practiced by the Officers throughout the line & which Lieutt Deavor and Ensign Gassaway have offered in mitigation of their Offence, are unanimously of Opinion they be severely reprimanded in General Orders and beg leave to observe that nothing but a tacit Consent of the Commanding Officer of the Regiment prevents the Court from being much more severe in their sentence.[2]

It gives the Commander in Chief most sensible Pain to find any Officers Conduct so very blameable as that of Lieutenant Deavor and

Ensn Gassaway—The striking Propriety and Necessity of Officers staying in Camp with their Corps is well known to every Private—The
General is therefore sorry that he is obliged to reprimand Lieutt
Deavor and Ensn Gassaway or that an Example of so pernicious & fatal
a tendency should be seen in the records of the Army.[3]

Varick transcript, DLC:GW.

GW's aide-de-camp Tench Tilghman wrote to Assistant Commissary General of
Purchases John Chaloner at Philadelphia on this date, "None of the Stores which I
bespoke for his Excellency have yet arrived. We are out of Tea and Sugar and if they
are not already sent on, be pleased to send a pound of the former and half a dozen
loaves of the latter by the very first conveyance. The other things to follow as quick
as possible." GW signed the cover of that letter (PWacD: Sol Feinstone Collection,
on deposit PPAmP).

Col. Jeduthan Baldwin of the artillery artificers recorded in his journal for this
date: "I rode with Genl. Washington thro King street, took a View of the sound, &
round Camp & dind with him" (Baldwin, *Revolutionary Journal*, 130).

1. Robert Forsyth (c.1754–1794) of Virginia had been acting as an aide-de-
camp for Maj. Gen. Nathanael Greene. He left the quartermaster department in
early 1779 and became deputy commissary of purchases in Virginia, later serving
as commissary of purchases for the southern department. In September 1789 GW
appointed Forsyth to be federal marshal for Georgia, where he was killed while
serving court papers in January 1794.

2. John Deaver (1758–1813) of Baltimore was commissioned a lieutenant in the
3d Maryland Regiment in December 1776. He resigned his Continental commission in April 1779 and became a captain in the Baltimore militia a month later.
Nicholas Gassaway (1757–1806), who enlisted as a sergeant in the 1st Maryland
Regiment in December 1776, was appointed an ensign in the 3d Maryland Regiment by 17 April 1777. By 1780 he was serving as a lieutenant with a commission
dated from 17 April 1777. In January 1781 he transferred to the 2d Maryland Regiment, and he served to the end of the war. For the cited article of war, see *JCC*,
5:797.

3. Maj. Gen. Benjamin Lincoln's orderly book for this date adds: "The Auditor's
office is kept at one Mr Martins a mile in front of General Gates's Quarters on the
right of the Village at White Plains" (MHi: Lincoln Papers; see also orderly book of
Jedediah Huntington's brigade, NHi).

# From James Caldwell

Sir                                    Springfield [N.J.] July 23. 1778.

The Comy General having requested me to convey to the Count
D'Estaing Your Excellencys present, I hurried the Cattle down & got
them on board in time. For fear of some delay I went down myself and
the Count in politest terms desired me to return his thanks to your Excellency for the seasonable Present, and told me that as he had a supply of sheep & Poultry in another way, he woud not have those sent on

Board directd by your excellency, till I shoud receive further orders from him. The next morning, Yesterday, the fleet got under way.

By faithful men from New York, I am informed the Transports are watering, & the common report is that they woud get home if they could, The inhabitants suffer for Provetions & only hope for relief by a superior fleet from England. Officers openly curse the Ministry, & the noise increases.

The report at the Hook is that part of your Army is to return & the Troops from the fleet to land & join them—That the fleet sail out for a blind & decoy. Howe will probably be perplexed—Although he well knows that large ships cannot come in to disturb him, & he has nothing to fear from small ones. With kindest wishes & all due respect, Your Excellencys most obedt and very huml. sert

James Caldwell

ALS, DLC:GW.


## To George Clinton

Dear Sir                    Head Quarters White plains 23d July 1778.

I was last Night favd with yours, communicating the distressing accounts of the Ravages of the Indians upon the frontier of this State.[1] I wish it were in my power to afford an adequate Releif, but as you are well acquainted with our force, and with what we have to oppose, I am certain you will think that I have done every thing possible. Colo. Butler having shifted his ground before my orders got to his hands, has been the occasion of some delay, he is however to go this day up to New Windsor by water, where he will meet Capt. Posey. They will take their orders from you, and march from thence where ever you may direct. Immediately upon the Rect of yours, I gave orders to Colo. Grahams State Regt to march to New Windsor, there to take orders from you. But they were unluckily, with other troops, covering a large forage in the lower part of the County.[2] However that no time may be lost, I have directed the Qr Mr Genl to send for Craft to Tarry town to be ready to take them in when they return from the foraging party.

Be pleased to forward the enclosed for General Schuyler[3] and oblige Dear Sir Your most obt and humble Servt

Go: Washington

LS, in Tench Tilghman's writing, CtY: U.S. Presidents Collection; Df, DLC:GW; Varick transcript, DLC:GW.

1. See Clinton to GW, 21 July, and note 1.

2. For discussion of the foraging expedition, see Brig. Gen. John Nixon to GW, 24 July, and notes.

3. GW probably enclosed his letter to Maj. Gen. Philip Schuyler of 22 July.

## From Thomas Conway

sir,                                    Philadelphia the 23d july 1778

I find my self just able to hold the penn During a few Minutes, and take this opportunity of expressing my sincere grief for having Done, Written, or said any thing Disagreeable to your excellency. my carreer will soon be over, therefore justice and truth prompt me to Declare my Last sentiments. you are in my eyes the great and the good Man. May you Long enjoy the Love, Veneration and Esteem of these states whose Libertys you have asserted by your Virtues. I am With the greatest respect sir your Excellency's Most obedt humble Servant

Ths Conway

ALS, DLC:GW. The docket on the back of the letter erroneously reads, "July 22d 1778."

## To Brigadier General John Glover

Sir                          Head Quarters White plains 23d July 1778

Upon Colo. Malcoms arrival at West Point, you are to join your Brigade, now upon its march to Providence. As the Colo. Commandant has his orders you need not come down here, but go directly across the Country. There is the greatest necessity for the Speedy arrival of these Troops at Providince and therefore, if you find your Baggage any incumbrance, leave it to come on under a small Guard of Men who may perhaps be fatigued by the march. I am Sir Yr most obt Servt

Go: Washington

LS (photocopy), in Tench Tilghman's writing, CSmH; Df, DLC:GW; Varick transcript, DLC:GW.

Glover received this letter on 25 July (see Glover to Horatio Gates, that date, NHI: Gates Papers).

## From William Gordon

My dear Sir                          Jamaica Plain [Mass.] July 23. 1778

It's with great pleasure I congratulate you upon our late success, on a double account—the advantage it is of to the Continent—& the honour it reflects upon your Excellency. I hope this happy beginning will, thro' the blessing of heaven, be productive of so glorious a campaign as to admit your changing the toils & hazards of the field for the repose & safety of domestic happiness. I shall rejoice to have the war terminated, & a stop put to the effusion of human blood, & I pray God to crown you with the glory of finishing the great work of securing those American liberties for the defence of which you offered yourself so willingly, & have so perseveringly exposed your life, I may add also your reputation, when the country hath failed in affording you the promised & necessary support. In this world character depends more upon success than any thing beside: And how often doth the want of success flow from the neglects & carelessness of others? By fixing yourself in the winter as you did, you gave the united States an opportunity of enabling you to have demolished the British army before the arrival of spring, but they were too languid to embrace it. Thro' the like languor we have lost many a golden opportunity, the war hath been prolonged, & we had nearly lost our cause; but the timely interposition of France hath changed the face of our affairs, & filled me with the pleasing expectation, that the British troops will quit our shores or have their weapons taken away from them before the setting in of winter.

I should with the highest satisfaction pay your Excellency a visit this fall, but apprehend my affairs will not admit of it: but notwithstanding personal absence am ever mindful of you. When your Excellency can retire to y⟨our ha⟩bitation, & have your papers about you, must then apply for the honour of being admitted ⟨*mutilated*⟩ for a few weeks, that I may collect the proper materials for my intended history, which I propose shall be a narrative of facts & not merely an entertaining tale.[1] Mrs Gordon joins me in tendering you our best wishes, & in desiring to be respectfully remembered to your Lady. With great esteem I continue your Excellency's most affectionate friend & very humble servant

William Gordon

ALS, DLC:GW. The docket on this letter is in GW's writing.

1. For discussion of Gordon's history, see Gordon to GW, 19 Dec. 1776, and the source note to that document.

## From Lieutenant Colonel Alexander Hamilton

Sir, Newark [N.J.] July 23d [1778] One OClock
I wrote to Your Excellency the evening of the 20th by Major Neville. I remained in the neighbourhood of Black Point 'till the afternoon following. The Count had received his expected dispatches from Congress and was to sail, as I mentioned before, the first fair wind. At

Brunswick yesterday, Mr Caldwell joined me. He was immediately from the Point and brought intelligence that the fleet got under way yesterday morning. The wind unfortunately has been much against them, which is so much the more to be regretted, as they are rather in want of water.[1] I need not suggest to your Excellency that an essential part of the Rhode Island plan, is to take every possible measure to watch the enemys motions and to establish expresses from place to place to give the Count instant information of any movement among their fleet. This will enable him to be in time to intercept them should they attempt to evacuate New York, while he is at Rhode Island, and will in general facilitate the intercourse and cooperation between him and your Excellency.

I have nothing new to communicate; besides what was sent by Major Newille and what I now send. All the ideas interchanged between the Count and myself were such as were familiar before I left Head Quarters. He was to go to Rhode Island and in conjunction with General Sullivan endeavour to possess himself of the enemy ships and troops there; if on his arrival he had good reason to think it could be effected without further assistan⟨ce.⟩ If not he will be glad of a reinforcemt from you in the most expeditious manner possible. What manner you think will be most expeditious you will adopt and if his aid may be useful he will afford it, as soon as he is informed of it.

This being the case my immediate presence at Head Quarters is the less necessary as to this business; and I hope your Excellency will indulge me, if do not make all the dispatch back, which a case of emergency would require; though I do not mean to delay more than a moderate attention to my frail constitution may make not improper. ⟨I am Yr Excellencys Most Respectful & Affect. Sevt

Alex. Hamilton⟩

AL, DLC:GW; copy, DLC: Alexander Hamilton Papers. Where the closing and signature were removed from the AL, the text has been supplied from the copy.

1. British naval captain Henry Duncan recorded in his journal for 22 July that "At 9 a.m. the French fleet got under way, and stood off and on until 4 p.m., when they all stood to the seaward" ("Journals of Henry Duncan," 160).

## From Louis-Pierre Penot Lombart, Chevalier de La Neuville

Excellencÿ,                                                   White Plain [N.Y.] this 23 julÿ 1778
    the reunion of the both armÿ in one depriving me of the place of inspector Général of the northern armÿ, being verÿ Sensible that the good of the service requires that a man onlÿ maÿ have the care of the

discipline, I résign mÿ commission as inspector, and will continüe to Serve the allÿ's of mÿ King as a Volunteer, mÿ rank in france, the Senioritÿ of mÿ Services allowing not me to be assimilated to Some Gentlemen who have never been in the Service in mÿ countrÿ.

I have been happÿ enough to obtain some honourable certificates of mÿ zeal from the Générals Gates and Parson.[1] I beg your goodness for mÿ brother captain in france, and to grant him the leave to continüe the functions of an inspector as he has been appointed bÿ the Général Gates, if ÿou consent to See the Général's Parson brigade, it will be the proof of his zeal and understanding. I can not help me to make the greatest encomium of the talents, and of the zeal of major Read.[2] he, my brother, and me we have made all our endeavours to contribute to the improvment of the armÿ, and we have found in the Officers a Such good will as the Success has passed our hopes.

I will present ÿou the plates of the maneuvres we have executed, with the manners explained to perform them and which are certainlÿ the same that ÿou have adopted the mine coming of the King of Pruss. I am with great respect, Excellencÿ Your most obedient Servant

Laneuville

ALS, DLC:GW.

1. Copies of the certificates of Brig. Gen. Samuel Holden Parsons, dated 28 June, and of Maj. Gen. Horatio Gates, dated 24 July 1778, are in DNA:PCC, item 41.

2. La Neuville may be referring to Maj. James Randolph Reid of the 2d Canadian Regiment, which was transferred back to the northern department in January 1778.

## From Lieutenant Colonel John Laurens

Sir.                                              Lebanon [Conn.] 23d July 1778.

I delivered Your Excellencys letter to Governor Trumbull this evening[1]—his deep affliction on account of his sons death seems to incapacitate him for public business—his council is to be convened to morrow and he desires me to assure you that the militia will be collected and marched with the greatest expedition—Pilots he thinks will be found in great abundance at Providence—As there is a deposit of continental horses at Colchester, it will be very easy to establish a proper chain of stationary expresses, for the speedy communication of intelligence, and the Governor has undertaken to give immediate orders for the purpose.

General Sullivan has written in the most pressing terms to the Governor for a reinforcement of Militia, in consequence of intelligence which he has received from Rhode Island, and which no doubt is contained in his letter to you[2]—the account I received of the Fleet & Troops which he alludes to, was totally different—it was that only four hundred effective men were on board—the rest were sick and wounded, sent to Hospital at Rhode Island—and that the fleet returned after having landed them—Genl Greenes brother gave me this information & said it came from one of four Seamen who deserted & brought off a captain of a transport with them. I have the honor to be with the greatest respect Your Excellencys most obedt Servt

John Laurens.

ALS, DLC:GW.
    1. See GW to Jonathan Trumbull, Sr., 22 July.
    2. Laurens was alluding to Maj. Gen. John Sullivan's letter to Trumbull of 22 July (Hammond, *Sullivan Papers*, 2:102) and Sullivan's letter to GW of the same date.

# From Colonel Stephen Moylan

Sir                                    Topan [Tappan, N.Y.] 23d July 1778
    your orders of the 16th reachd me the 19th instant, and agreeable thereto I have Marchd the three Regiments of horse to this place.[1]

I have seen your Excellencys instructions to Captain Hopkins, to which I will pay due attention,[2] the English Neighborhood, woud be a good place for the Cavalry, if they are to stay any time on this Side the River, I shall expect further orders from your Excellency by the bearer[3] and I am with truth Sir your most obligd H. St

Stephen Moylan

P.S. I am Engagd to Miss Vanhorne.[4]

ALS, DLC:GW.
    1. On 16 July, GW's secretary James McHenry wrote Moylan at Bound Brook, N.J.: "It is his Excellency's desire that you proceed immediately with the horse under your command to Orange Town where you will find Captn Hopkins who has instructions for the Cavalry—You will be pleased to advise the General of your arrival and wait his further orders" (DLC:GW).
    2. On 16 July, GW's aide Tench Tilghman wrote Capt. David Hopkins: "It is His Excellency's desire that you fall down with the detatchment of Horse under your command to Closter, which is about four Miles below Orange Town. You are to keep Scouts down towards the English Neighbourhood, with orders to watch the River, and if they perceive any Ships or Vessels moving up to give you immediate Notice. If these Vessels are of any considerable Number you are to send an Express to the commanding Officer at Kings Ferry, desiring him to forward the intelligence to His Excelly whereever he may be; but if only a single Vessel or a few Boats goes up, you are to take it for granted that they are after Supplies of some kind, and are there fore to send a party to keep pace with them and prevent their landing upon this Shore" (DLC:GW).
    3. This letter was carried by Maj. William Washington.

4. Moylan married Mary Ricketts Van Horne (born c.1754), daughter of Philip Van Horne, in the fall of 1778.

## From Brigadier General John Stark

Dear General—                    Head Quarters Albany 23d July 1778

I yesterday Received your favour of the 18th Instant—some part of the Troops that was Expected here, I fear will be of Little, or no Benefit to me, or any other part of the United States, that is, Colo. Beedles Regiment, about forty of them is now on the Ground, out of one Hundred that was sent for, the Remainder are ordered Positively, to be here by the first of August, but I put no dependence on them, as I am very sure, that they will not come.

some part of the Militia, from Hampshire, & Berkshire, Counties, have already Arri⟨ve⟩d & the Remainder, to make up Two Hundred, is daily Expected—the Enemy has Burnt up the Towns of Springfield, & Andrews Town, near the Mohawk River, the particulars of the Affair, has not yet come to hand.

I think we never Shall be safe, in this Country, till an Expedition is Carried into the Indians Country, & Effectually, Root out those nefarious Wretches, from the face of the Earth.

However Readily submitting to your Better Judgement—I am with Great Respect Your obedient Very Humble Sert

John Stark

N.B. the Militia from this State seems very Negligent, out of Six Hundred that was Called for Last month they did not Turn out 200. as above J.S.

LS, DLC:GW.

## To Brigadier General William Thompson

Dr Sir                    Head Quarters White plains 23 July 1778

Your favor of the 19th Inst. was duly received.

I have not as yet had the least intimation of your parole; but should it come into my hands I shall take a pleasure in its early transmission, and be happy to see you again with the army.

It is entirely out of my power to do any thing either in the case of Mr Coats or Mr Noarth, as all aides agreeable to a late resolve of congress are to be taken from the line.[1] The matter therefore only lays with Congress. I am Sir &c.

Df, in James McHenry's writing, DLC:GW; Varick transcript, DLC:GW.

1. GW may be referring to the army establishment resolution of 27 May, which specified that the major generals should appoint their aides "out of the captains or subalterns" (*JCC*, 11:542).

## General Orders

Head-Quarters Wrights-Mills [N.Y.] Friday July 24th 1778.
Parole Hackensack— C. Signs Holland. Hull.

The Commanding Officers of Corps will take particular Care that their Men are made acquainted with all such Orders which are necessary for their Government, as the plea of Ignorance will not be admitted in Excuse.

The Rolls are to be called regularly twice a day (at troop and retreat beating) and every possible means used to keep the soldiers within the limits of the Camp—Those who disobey are to be severely punished.

Pay-Abstracts to the 1st of June are immediately to be made and examined by the Pay-Master General and Auditors for all the Continental Troops, that Warrants may issue for Payment to that date.

Accurate Lists of all the Field Officers belonging to the Brigades now on the Ground according to the present disposition are to be made out and brought to the Orderly-Office tomorrow morning nine ôClock, at which time the Brigade Majors will bring in a morning Report of the several Brigades.

Varick transcript, DLC:GW.

## From Lieutenant Colonel Robert Ballard

Sir Williamsburg [Va.] July 24th 1778

Agreeable to your instructions I waited on Governor Henry, on Monday the 20th Inst., expecting to receive from him an Order for recruiting Money &c.,[1] The Governor inform'd me he did not know at that time what to do in the matter, as 10 Gentlemen were already employed for to recruit men to fill up the Virginia Regts, but he woud consult the Council on the Occasion; the result of which, was, that the whole of us (meaning the Officers of Gl Muhlenbergs Brigade) was immediately to set out in search of Security for the Money intended to be given us. I was to provide Security for the whole of the Money, & take Security of each Officer for the respective sums given them, at my risque.

I convened the Officers and inform'd them of the Governor & Councils Instructions. They (for very cogent reasons in my Opinion) unanimously objected to the instructions, alledging that after marching 3 or 4 hundred Miles on foot, and having met me agreeable to my Appointment, and then, to set out again in persuit of Security on foot, was an obligation too hard to comply with, and what was not expected by you, nor was it a practice in your Army to go after Security when Ordered on the like business. besides the Officers say they do not know where to provide security, and it is unnecessarily drawing reflections on them; for, if they cannot procure security, the publick is directly aquainted thereof.

As to my part, I conceive it totally out of my power to obtain security for 20 or 30 thousand pounds on the principal of runing the risque of the Money given to each Officer, especially as the Council refus'd to undertake to refund their expences; indeed I thought it unjust to ask a friend to become my security on those terms. I acquainted the Governor & Council of the mode adopted in your Army when Officers were sent out to recruit: And if they chose to Issue Money to me and wou'd receive each Officers rect to whom I delivered money, & place to my Credit I wou'd undertake it with all my heart, but they possitively refused; on which I altogether refus'd to attempt Security.

The Governor and Council affected much Surprize when inform'd of the Number of Officers Sent to Virginia to recruit, and pretended that *those 10 Gentn* which they had employed was Sufficient for the undertaking.[2] Those employed were Gentn who had been living at home enjoying themselves in peace and plenty, taking the advantage of the times to accumulate wealth, to whom very considerably Wages was given; when your Officers who had experienced every hardship at the risque of Life & fortune, for the protection and ease of those in private life, was refus'd any extra pay for their necessary expences. I fear we have an ungrateful publick.

The Officers who march'd under my Command to this place ⟨are⟩ much distressed for want of Money, several of whom I was oblig'd to advance Money, to get them home, I made the Governor & Council acquainted thereof, & beg'd they wou'd Order two or three Months pay to each, 'till I cou'd acquaint you, but I was put off with a kind of a recommendation to any Continental Pay Master I might meet with; at the same time they knew there was no Money in the Military Chest here. I never was so trifled with, by Gentn, in all my life. The Officers beg'd me to request your Excellencys favor in Ordering them pay here, if to remain any time.

I flatter myself my conduct will meet with your Excellencys Approbation. Any Commands Your Excellency may please to communicate shall to the utmost of my power be attended to. I have the Honor to be Your Excellencys Most Obt Sevt

                                                          Robt Ballard

P. S. Colo. H. Recheson is here, & meets with the Same fate with me.[3]

ALS, DLC:GW.

1. For Ballard's instructions, see GW's letter to him of 18 June.

2. "An act for recruiting the continental army" passed at the May 1778 session of the Virginia legislature authorized the governor "with the advice of the council . . . to appoint from time to time such and so many recruiting officers in this state as in their judgment shall be requisite" (Hening, 9:454). On 10 July the Virginia council appointed "Francis Smith & Alexander Baugh of Chesterfield; John Lewis of Pittsylvania; Elisha White & Thomas Richardson of Hanover; John White of Louisa; Daniel Barksdale of Caroline; John Holcombe of Prince Edward; William Allen of James City; and Alexander Cummins of Bedford" to fill the positions (*Va. State Council Journals*, 2:164).

3. The journals of the Virginia council do not record decisions about recruiting for Muhlenberg's and Woodford's brigades by Ballard and Lt. Col. Holt Richeson, but on 24 July the council considered a request by recruiters from Scott's brigade and decided "that the recruiting Officers already appointed under the late Act of the Assembly would probably succeed better than any of the said Officers—it is judged unnecessary to issue the Warrants they desired" (ibid., 2:172).

## To John Beatty

Sir                                    Head Quarters White plains 24 July 1778

I recd yours of the 18th by Capt. Forman, who delivered most of the exchanged men committed to his care. Those who stragled have, I beleive, generally come in and joined their Regiments.

Inclosed you will find a Copy of a resolution of Congress directing you to take charge of the prisoners that may be taken by Admiral Count D'Estaing.[1] You will be pleased to transmit it to your Deputies and give them orders to pay a proper attention to it. I am &c.

Df, in Tench Tilghman's writing, DLC:GW; Varick transcript, DLC:GW.

1. For the resolution of 15 July, see Henry Laurens to GW, 17 July, n.1.

## From George Clinton

Dear Sir                              Poughkeepsie [N.Y.] July 24th 1778

I have received your Letter of the 23d instt inclosing one to General Schuyler which I immediatly forwarded to him—I am sensible, that however distressing the Situation of our Western Frontier may be, that your Excellency has taken every Method to Afford it Security that is in your Power consistant with the general good of the Service—I wou'd not wish therefore that any Representation of mine shoud occasion a Demunition of your present Force, And as Colo. Grahams's Regiment is composed of Men who are intimately acquainted with every part of the Country between the Enemies Lines and yours, and may be of peculiar Service where they now are—I beg leave to Submit to your Excellency's farther consideration whether it would not be most Adviseable to continue it with you at present in which Case I will endeavour to call out a larger proportion of the Militia for the Defence of the Frontiers. This I think the Militia ought chearfully to submit to, as, if they were not required for that Service it would be but reasonable that they should March to Reinforce the Army under your Excellency's immidiate Command—I have already Ordered out one fourth part of the Militia of Orange and Ulster to the Western Frontier of those Counties who will Amount to near 600 Men, and have directed them to take their Stations so as to secure the most important Passes leading into the Settlements—If they do this and are vigilant I trust that Part of the Country will experience a Degree of Safety—In Addition to this I have Issued positive Orders to Brigadier General Ten Broeck and the Commanding Officers of the several Regiments in Tryon County to Detach one fourth of their Militia (such Regiments as may be necessary for the safety of the Northern Frontier excepted) for the Protection of the Western Frontier in that Quarter, and to Act under and Assist Colo. Butler in any Offensive Operations which may be thought necessary to be carried on by him against the Enemy—Colo. Butler (whose March on receiving the Intelligence I lately transmitted to your Excellency I wished to be hastened,)[1] was this Morning at New Windsor and will proceed directly to Albany, and from thence to Schohary or Cherry Valley as General Starke (whose Department he will then be in) shall direct,[2] and if Joind by Aldons Regiment and the Detachment of Militia which I have Ordered out, will form a pretty respectable Force in that Quarter—In the mean time If I should receive any new Intelligence that may render its Augmentation necessary, It shall immidiatly be communicated to your Excellency[3]—I propose if nothing extraordinary happens to prevent it, to do myself the pleasure of waiting on your Excellency next week. I am with the highest Esteem & Respect Your Excellencys Most Obedt Servt

Geo: Clinton

LS, DLC:GW; copy, CtY: U.S. Presidents Collection. Clinton's signed note on the cover indicates that this letter was sent "favoured by Colo: Willit."

1. See Clinton to GW, 21 July.

2. The community of Cherry Valley in Otsego County, N.Y., about seven miles east of Lake Otsego and about fifty miles west of Albany, had a small garrison at the newly constructed Fort Alden. The settlement was burned by a mixed Tory and Indian force on 11 Nov. 1778.

3. Some additional intelligence is given in a letter of this date from Col. Peter B. Vroman at Schoharie to Brig. Gen. Abraham Ten Broeck: "Capt. Harper a Gentleman of varicity gives me Intelligence that the Enemy are at Unidilla, very Strong

amounting to nigh Three Thousand, and by one of my Scouts which arrived this afternoon brings Intelligence, that they saw four Indians within fourteen miles of this place, going from this which they supposed to be a Scout, and I believe it is very Likely, the Scout also Informs me that they staid last night in sight of one Services, a great Enemy to the Country upon the Susquahanna where they heard frequent Yellings of the savages" (DLC:GW). How and when that letter was transmitted to GW has not been determined, but another copy is in Clinton's papers (Hastings, *Clinton Papers*, 3:538–84).

## From Thomas Johnson

*24 July 1778*. Encloses a letter that "may occasion a comfortable Supply if not intire Relief to two worthy Men"[1] and requests "that it may be sent the first favourable Opportunity."

ALS, DLC:GW.
  1. Neither the enclosure nor the men have been identified.

## To Henry Laurens

⟨Dr Sir                                    Camp near White plains July the 24th 1778
    I had yesterday the pleasure to receive your favor of the 18th Instant with the inclosure and packets, which you mentioned.
    I should have been sorry, if you or Monsieur Gerard had found the smallest difficulty in recommending the packets for the Count D'Estaing to my care; and I am happy to inform you, that they will meet with a speedy and safe conveyance to him by an Officer, who has set off for Rhode Island.
    It is very pleasing as well as interesting, to hear that prizes are already finding the way into the Delaware. The event seems the more agreable, as that Navigation but yesterday as it were, could scarcely contain the Enemy's fleet and their numerous captures, which were constantly crouding in. Happy change! and I should hope, that the Two prizes which have entered will be succeeded by many more. The want of information on the one hand of philadelphia's being evacuated, and the countenance which our Armed Vessels will derive from the French Squadron on our Coast, must throw several into our possession.
    The second Epistle from the Commissioners, of which you have so obligingly favoured me with a Copy, strikes me in the same point of view that it did you.[1] It is certainly puerile—and does not border a little on indecorum, nothwithstanding their professions of the regard they wish to pay to decency. It is difficult to determine, on an extensive scale, though part of their design is tolerably obvious, what the Gentlemen

would be at. Had I the honor of being a Member of Congress, I do not know how I might feel upon the occasion; but it appears to me, the performance must be received with a sort of indignant pleasantry, on account of it's manner on the one hand, and on the other as being truly typical of that confusion, in which their prince and nation are.

By the time this reaches you, I expect the Messieurs Nevilles will be in philadelphia. From the Certificates these Gentlemen have provided, if I may hazard a conjecture, they are in quest of promotion, particularly the Elder. How far their views may extend, I cannot determine; but I dare predict they will be sufficiently high. My present intention is to tell you, and with freedom I do it, that Congress can not be well too cautious on this head. I do not mean or wish, to derogate from the merit of Messieurs Nevilles. The opportunities I have had, will not permit me to speak decisively for, or against it. However, I may observe from a certificate, which I have seen, written by themselves, or at least by one of them & signed by Genl parsons probably through surprize or irresolution, that they are not bad, at giving themselves a good character;[2] and I will further add, if they meet with any great promotion, I am fully convinced it will be illy borne by our own Officers; and that it will be the cause of infinite discontent. The ambition of these men (I do not mean of the Messieurs Nevilles in particular, but of the Natives of their Country and *Foreigners* in general) is unlimited & unbounded; and the singular in[s]tances of rank, which have been conferred upon them in but too many cases, have occasioned general disatisfaction and general complaint. The feelings of our own Officers have been much hurt by it, and their ardor and love for the service greatly damped. Should a like proceeding still be practised, it is not easy to say, what extensive murmurings and consequences may ensue. I will further add, that we have already a full proportion of Foreign Officers in our General Councils, and should their number be encreased, it may happen upon many occasions, that their voices may equal if not exceed the rest. I trust you think me so much a Citizen of the World, as to beleive that I am not easily warped or led away, by attachments merely local or American; Yet I confess, I am not entirely without 'em, nor does it appear to me that they are unwarrantable, if confined within proper limits. Fewer promotions in the foreign line, would have been productive of more harmony, and made our warfare more agreable to all parties. The frequency of them, is the source of jealousy and of disunion. We have many—very many deserving Officers, who are⟩ not opposed to merit wheresoever it is found, nor insensible of the advantages derived from a long Service in an experienced Army—nor to the principles of policy. Where any of these principles mark the way to Rank, I am perswaded, they yield a becoming and willing acquiescence; but where

they are not the basis, they feel severely. I will dismiss the subject, knowing with you, I need not labour, either a case of justice or of policy. I
am Dr Sir With sentiments of very warm regard & esteem Yr much
obliged & Obedt Servt

Go: Washington

P.S. The Baron Steuben will also be in Phila. in a day or two. The os-
tensable cause for his going is to fix more certainly with Congress his
duties, as Inspector General, which is necessary;[3] However, I am disposed to beleive, the real one is, to obtain an actual command in the
line as a Majr Genl; and he may urge a competition set up by Messr
Neville for the Inspectors place, on this side the Hudson, and a denial
by him of his the Baron's authority, as an argument to effect it, and the
granting him the Post as a mean of satisfying both.

I regard & esteem the Baron, as an assiduous—Intelligent & experienced Officer; but you may rely on it, if such is his view & he should accomplish it, we shall have the whole line of Brigadiers in confusion.
They have said but little about his Rank as Majr General as he has not
had an actual command over 'em; But when we marched from Brunswick, as there were but few Majr Generals & almost the whole of the
Brigadiers engaged at the Court Martial either as Members or Witnesses, I appointed him protempore and so expressed it in orders, to
conduct a Wing to the North River.[4] This measure tho founded in evident necessity & not designed to produce to the Brigadiers the least
possible injury, excited great uneasiness & has been the source of complaint. The truth is, we have been very unhappy in a variety of appointments, and our own ⟨Officers much injured. Their feelings from
this cause have become extremely sensible, and the most delicate
touch gives them pain. I write as a Friend, and therefore with freedom.
The Baron's services in the line he is in, can be singular, and the Testimonials he has already received are honorable. It will also be material
to have the point of the Inspector Generalship, now in question, between him & Monsr Neville adjusted. The appointment of the latter it
is said, calls him Inspector General in the Army commanded by Genl
Gates, and under this, as I am informed, he denies any Subordination
to the Baron and will not know him in his *Official capacity*. There can be
but one head. Yrs

G.W.⟩

ALS, Parke-Bernet Galleries, Inc., sale 2134, *Manuscripts, etc., from the Collection of
the Late Philip G. Straus*, 23 Oct. 1962; Df, DLC:GW; Varick transcript, DLC:GW.
The sale catalog published only one page of the ALS; the text in angle brackets has
been taken from the draft, which is in Robert Hanson Harrison's writing.

1. For the letter from the British commissioners to Congress, 11 July, see Laurens
to GW, 18 July, n.3.

2. A copy of the certificate of Brig. Gen. Samuel Holden Parsons, dated 28 June, is in DNA:PCC, item 41.

3. See Steuben to GW, this date.

4. See General Orders, 2 and 5 July.

## From Massachusetts Legislature

                                        State of Massachusetts Bay
Sir                      Council Chamber [Boston] July 24. 1778.

Capt. John Blunt the Bearer hereof who has been a long time in Captivity on Long Island and has suffered much from the Ill treatment of the Enemy, yet nevertheless he is very desireous of continuing in the Service of the United States.[1] And he having Sustained a good Character as an officer as appears by Sundry Brigadiers in the Continental Army, the Council have taken the liberty to recommend the said Blunt to your Excellency for some Office in the Army, Provided there is any Vacancy which he is capeable of filling with advantage to himself and the Publick. Your complyance herewith will greatly oblige an old Officer who is ever ready to render all the service to the Publick that is in his power. I am Sir with all due Respect Your Excellencys Obedient Humble Servant

                                        President[2]

Copy, M-Ar: Revolution Letters, 1778; LB, M-Ar: Secretary's Letterbooks, vol. 7.

1. The legislature was apparently referring to John Blunt (1736–1804) of Winthrop, Mass., who was commissioned a lieutenant in the 11th Continental Infantry in January 1776. Captured at Long Island on 27 Aug. 1776, he was exchanged on 20 April 1778. For short periods in 1779 and 1780 Blunt served as a captain in the Massachusetts militia.

2. The council president at this time was Jeremiah Dummer Powell.

## To Gouverneur Morris

Dear Sir,                              White plains July 24th 1778.

Whether you are indebted to me, or I to you a Letter I know not, nor is it a matter of much moment—The design of this is to touch, cursorily, upon a Subject of very great importance to the well being of these States; much more so than will appear at first view—I mean the appointment of so many foreigners to Offices of high rank & trust in our Service.

The lavish manner in which Rank has hitherto been bestowed on these Gentlemen, will certainly be productive of one, or the other of these two evils, either, to make it despicable in the eyes of Europe, or, become a mean of pouring them in upon you like a torrent, and adding to your present burthen—but it is neither the expence nor trouble of them I most dread—there is an evil more extensive in its nature, and fatal in its consequences to be apprehended and that is, the driving all your own Officers out of Service, and throwing not only your Arms, but your Military Councils, entirely in the hands of Foreigners.

The Officers my dear Sir on whom you must depend for defence of this cause, and who from length of Service—their Connexions—property—and (in behalf of many) I may add, military merit, will not submit much, if any longer, to the unnatural promotion of men over them, who have nothing more than a little plausability—unbounded pride and ambition—and a perseverence in application, which is not to be resi[s]ted but by uncommmon firmness, to support their pretensions—Men, who in the first instance tell you, that they wish for nothing more than the honour of serving in so glorious a cause, as Volunteers—The next day sollicit rank without pay—the day following want money advanced them—and in the course of a Week want further promotion, and are not satisfied with any thing you can do for them.

When I speak of Officers not submitting to these appointments, let me be understood to mean, that they have no more doubt of their right to resign (when they think themselves aggrieved) than they have of a power in Congress to appoint—both being granted then, the expediency, & the policy of the measure remain to be considered; & whether, it is consistent with justice, or prudence, to promote these military fortune hunters at the hazard of your Army. especially as I think they may be denominated into three classes—to wit mere adventurers without recommendation, or recommended by persons who do not know how else to dispose of, or provide for them. Men of great ambition, who would sacrafice every thing to promote their own personal glory—or, mere spies, who are sent here to obtain a thorough knowledge of our situation, circumstances &ca; in the execution of which, I am perswaded, some of them are faithful emissaries, as I do not believe a single matter escapes unnoticed, or unadvised, at a foreign Court.

I could say a great deal on this subject, but will add no more at present; I am led to give you this trouble, at this time, by a *very handsome* certificate shewed me yesterday in favour of Monsr Neville written (I believe) by himself, and subscribed by General Parsons. designed, as I am informed, for the foundation of the superstructure of a Brigadier-ship.[1]

Baron Steuben I now find is also wanting to quit his Inspectorship for a command in the line, this will also be productive of much discontent to the Brigadiers. In a word, altho I think the Baron an excellent Officer, I do most devoutly wish that we had not a single Foreigner among us, except the Marquis de la Fayette, who acts upon very different principles than those which govern the rest. adieu. I am most sincerely Yrs

Go: Washington

P.S. This Letter as you will perceive, is written with the freedom of a friend do not therefore make me enemys by publishing what is intended for your own information & that of particular friends.

ALS, NNC.
    1. A copy of the certificate of Brig. Gen. Samuel Holden Parsons, dated 28 June, is in DNA:PCC, item 41.


## From Brigadier General John Nixon

Sir,                                    Camp White plains July [24][1] 1778
    On the 22d Instt I marched the Party under my Command (consisting of about 2000 Foot & 200 Cavalry) in the following Order.[2]
    I detached Genl Parsons with Colo. Wylly's Meiggs, Hazens & Grahams Regts together with One half the Cavalry under the Command of Lt Colo. Blagdon, to proceed on the East Side the Brunks down to East & West Chester, with Orders to make the best Disposition of his party, which would most effectually Answer to the driving in to our Camp all the Stock from that Quarter, ⟨w⟩hile I marched with Colo. Greatons, Putnam & Nixons ⟨Re⟩gts down on the West Side the Brunks to Mile Square, ⟨t⟩ogether with the remainder of the Cavalry under the Command of Colo. Shelden; and One peice of Artillery. And when Arrived I made a Disposition of the Troops under my immediate Command as follows—Ordered Colo. Greaton with his Regt & a party of Cavalry to Occupy the Road leading from Kings-Bridge to Phillips's and to send off Partys on the Roads leading from thence to Dobbs's Ferry and Saw Mill River Bridge,[3] in order to collect all the Stock on the Roads. Colo. Putnam with his Regt & a party of Cavalry Occupyed the Road leading from Kings Bridge to Mile Square & to send a party on the Road leading to this place on the West Side the Brunks. I remained on Vollentines Hill with Colo. Nixons Regt; the Remainder of the Cavalry & the Artillery, after Detaching a party from that Regt on the middle Road to collect the Stock—Remained on the Ground till about Sun-rise at which time, I ordered the several Regts to take the same Routs on which they had detached their respective partys, in order to collect such Stock as might escape them.[4]
    As to the particulars of Genl Parsons's progress, I shall refer your Excellency to his Return to me, which I have enclosed.[5]

Seven Deserters from the Queens Rangers with their Arms and Accoutrements, joined me in the course of the Night, which I sent to Head Quar⟨ters⟩ the 23d Instt.

I send You by the Bearer John Johnston, James Pell, David Bonnet & Ned Pell a Negro, mentioned in Genl Parsons's Return.[6] Sir I am with great Esteem Your Excellencys most Obedt Humbl. Servt

Jno. Nixon B.G.

LS, DLC:GW.

1. Nixon left a blank space after "July," but the letter is docketed 24 July, and his enclosures are dated 24 July.

2. For Nixon's orders, see GW to Horatio Gates, 19 July, n.2.

3. The Saw Mill River enters the Hudson River about six miles below Dobbs Ferry and runs northward to pass about one mile east of that crossing.

4. For a description of this expedition from the viewpoint of a private in the 5th Massachusetts Regiment, see "Vaughan Journal," 109.

5. Brig. Gen. Samuel Holden Parsons's report of his command, dated 24 July, reads: "On the 22d Wyllys, Meigs, Hazen's & Graham's Regiments with Two Peices of Artillery proceeded to Ward's House, I then detachd 100 Men under the Command of Capt. Leavensworth to Weschester to remove the Stock from thence; with the other Troops I marchd toward Williams's Bridge; posted Hazen's Regt at the School House on the Road from East Chester to Mile Square; and Detachd Majr Taylor with 150 foot & 12 Dragoons to Williams's and the main Body with the Artillery halted one Mile in the Rear on an advantageous Height back of Briggs's— Patroles were kept constantly to the advancd Guard & to every Ford over the Bruns in the Vicinity of the Troops—The Enemy's Advancd Post was discoverd to be near [Isaac] Voluntine's about one Mile from our advancd Picket. Two Light Dragoons deserted from the Enemy; who are sent to Head Quarters. in order to execute the orders I receivd in the most effectual Manner I orderd Cols. Wyllys & Hazen's Regiments with one Peice of artillery on the Road by Ward's with the other Regiments I returnd by New Rochel We marchd from Williams's a little before Sunrising having first beat the Troop & mounted Guard. The Enemy made no Movement from their Camp, not advancing a Patrole towards Us.

"We took from the Inhabitants 188 Head of Cattle 60 Horses 55 Hogs & 13 Sheep—By order of the General the Cattle Horses &c. have been deliverd to the Owners to drive in the Country & some few for the present Subsistance of their Families except 52 horned Cattle 19 Horses & 5 Hogs which Still remain in the Custedy of my Brigade Quarter Master.

"We took Prisoners of the Inhabitants [—] Nat. Underhill and Three Negro Men of Weschester accusd of incouraging Horse Thieves[,] one Johnson & Pell Accusd of taking up Deserters & returning them to the Enemy[,] one Bonnet who has once been Committed for Misdemeanors & broke Goal at Marbel Town[,] a negro Accusd of Stealing Cattle[—]which are orderd to your Honor for your Direction" (DLC:GW).

Nixon apparently also enclosed his own return, dated 24 July, "of the Horses, Cattle &ca collected and brought into Camp agreeable to Genl Gates's Orders to me of 22d Inst.," which reported the stock gathered by Parsons and an additional 48 horses, 153 cattle, 27 sheep, and 145 swine "Collected on the West Side the Brunks" (DLC:GW).

6. A James Pell, most likely of Pelham Manor, was among those who assembled at White Plains in April 1775 to declare their "detestation of all unlawful commit-

tees and congresses" and their support for the king (*Rivington's New-York Gazetteer*, 20 April 1775). A David Bonnet of New Rochelle claimed that he fled to New York City in September 1776 because of persecution and that he was later involved in gathering forage for the British magazines (Coldham, *American Loyalist Claims*, 43–44).

## From Captain Thomas Posey

Sir                                          New Winsor [N.Y.] 24th July 1778
   Agreable to your Orders of the 20th Inst. I have Joind Lieut. Colo. Butler at this place where we have Embarkt for Albany.[1]
   Upon the Rect of your Orders, I sent the Paymaster acting to my Party, to draw there Pay. youl much Oblidge in leting him Know our distanation as the men are in Extream need. I am sir Yr Obt sert
                                                              Thomas Posey

ALS, DLC:GW.
   1. No orders to Posey of 20 July have been identified, but see the orders of 18 July (GW to John Stark, 18 July, n.1).

## From Major General Steuben

Sir                                  Camp Wrights Mills [N.Y.] July 24 1778.
   Your Excellency having been pleased to order me in the General Orders of 22d Instant to resume my Office of Inspector General & make my Arrangements accordingly, I beg leave to refer you to my letter of 17th June on the subject of the Inspection & to your kind Answer of 18th in which you granted me permission to go to York Town & desired me to lay before Congress such a Plan as would be most likely to obviate all the difficulties I was acquainted with & comprehend all the essential duties of my Office. The final determination of Congress which appeared to me at that time highly necessary seems at present indispensable before I can resume with satisfaction to myself & benefit to the Army the functions of my Office I foresee some difficulties in the way particularly with regard to the Inspector appointed by Congress to General Gates Army; that Gentleman declared to me long since, that he was by no means subject to my Orders or controul in the exercise of his Office;[1] In short as I am willing to avoid every difficulty & to labour unmolested for the good of the Service; I beg your Excellency to postpone my entering into the Office of Inspector General untill Congress have after your Opinion & directions about the matter finally pronounced. In the mean time with your Excellen⟨cys⟩ permission I will take this Opportunity of making a tour to Philadelphia to see my Friends—I shall have the honour of wait-

ing on you tomorrow morning to receive your Commands & remain with the greatest respect Your Excellencys most Obedient humble servant

Steuben

LS, DLC:GW.

1. Steuben was referring to Louis-Pierre Penot Lombart, chevalier de La Neuville. For the resolution of 14 May appointing him "inspector of the army under the command of Major General Gates," see *JCC*, 11:498–99.

## From Major General John Sullivan

My Dear General                                                          Providence July 24th 1778

I had Last Evening the honor of Receiving your Excellencys favor of the 17th Instant & Shall immediately make Every preparation mentioned.[1] I had previous to the Receipt Sent two Expresses Informing your Excy of the Reinforcements Sent by the Enemy to Rhode Island & Inclosed you the Intelligence I had obtained Those Letters must Reach Yr Excy before this.[2] by the Last of which you will find that the Militia are already Called for the Reasons therein mentioned; which Steps I hope will meet your Excys approbation. So that the Number of troops your Excy mentions will be on the Ground the magazines were forming & I hope will Soon be adequate to the purpose the Pilots will be Ingaged & Every thing Shall be in perfect Readiness. I Inclose your Excellencey The Intelligence Received from the Island Since the Last Express was Sent off.[3] I Should more frequently have informed Your Excellencey of my Situation but nothing material had Turned up on Either Side from the time I gave Information to the time I Sent the Two Last mentioned Expresses. & as I Sensibly felt for your Excellecy ⟨in⟩ y⟨o⟩ur perplexed Situation I did not wish to Deprive you of a Single moment That might offer itself to Releve you from your weight of Business By any Relation from this Quarter which was not material your Excellencey will therefore please to attribute my Silence to the Cause above mentioned which will be Sufficiently Evident from the Letters Sent upon the first Change of affairs in this Quarter & which you must be possessed of before this Reaches you My own Interest & Inclinations would Induce me in Every Instance to write your Excellencey & Claim a Share of that advice which you are Ever Ready to give & of which I have So often Availed myself. But I cannot add to the weight on your Excellencys mind Except when it becomes absolutely necessary. In Every Such Case your Excy will hear from me Let my Situation be in whatever Quarter of America it may. My other two Letters & the Inclosed papers will Enable Your Excy to form as Just an opinion

of the Enemys & my Situation as can be come at. They had on the Island before General Browns arrival 3717 his & the arrivals Since have
Increased them to near 7000. Should the French Fleet arrive here I
can Soon have a Sufficient number of troops to Coopperate with them
& I trust to give a Decisive Blow to our Enemies I have the Honor to be
Dear General with the most perfect Sentiment of Esteem & Respect
your Excys most obedt Servant

Jno. Sullivan

E⟨v⟩ery movement of the Enemy in this Quarter Shall be immediately
Communicated.

   I Inclose the Last New port paper.[4]

ALS, DLC:GW.
   1. Elsewhere Sullivan wrote that he received GW's letter of 17 July "the 22d Inst.
after Noon" (Sullivan to Vice Admiral d'Estaing, 25 July, DLC:GW). On 24 July, Sullivan wrote to Massachusetts council president Jeremiah Dummer Powell and to
Connecticut governor Jonathan Trumbull, Sr., citing GW's letter as authority to call
out 1,000 militia from Massachusetts and 500 from Connecticut. He also wrote a
second letter to each, adding a request for volunteers (Hammond, *Sullivan Papers*,
2:107–8, 110–11).
   2. See Sullivan to GW, 20 and 22 July.
   3. Sullivan enclosed an unsigned letter from Little Compton, R.I., dated 23 July:
"We have at last obtained a Memorial from the Island, our Correspondent has endeavour'd to take a Plan, but was fustrated by the Enemy who are excessive zealous, and watchful, the Bearer was both Nights on with my Sns and has taken the
greatest pains imaginable to procure all possible intelligence—The last Paper will
accompany the Memorial, which contains a just account of their last Reinforcement, tho the Inhabitants in general don't believe it—The Officers in the Army
Declare publicly the superiorety of the Frence fleet, which they Say is now at Sandy
Hook, and has effectually Blocked up Lord Howe, which from their own account
must be the Case the rest the Bearer will communicate" (DLC:GW). The "Memorial" may have been the following undated intelligence, which was probably enclosed as well: "It is impossible, on Account of the distracted Condition of the Enemy, to obtain anny correct Account of their Situation in Force; because what may
hold good for to Day, may be useless to Morrow; they being under dreadful apprehensions of a French Fleet here, are making Preparations accordingly. they are fortifying Brenton's Point and Rose Island, strenghtening Fort Island, and repairing
the North Battery. their Transports have fallen down Town, within the Fort, and
have moved their Provisions up the Hill. they are bringing heavy Cannon into
Town, and the same Day carrying them out. In short all is confusion.
   "The Number of their Troops they say is 6000, which is not true, nor can I say
with certainty what their Numbers are But exclusive of the Troops that were here
before suppose to be about 3000 effective Men there have arrived Colonel Brown's
Regiment of Rebel⟨s⟩ consisting of 344 Men; and since have arrived 2 Regiments
of Anspach, the 38th of British, and Colonel Fanning's Regiment of Rebels, the
four Regments making about 1400.
   "I have made several Attem⟨pts⟩ to discover what Works they have, where they
a⟨re⟩ and what Guns are in them; but in Vain they have so increased their Number
of Forts and Redoubts, and grown so suspicious and watchful, and I having twice

narrowly escaped being taken, that I despair of being able to accomplish that Matter. I shall therefore only men⟨ti⟩on what comes within my Knowledge; which is that 2 Regiments are at connanicut, one at G. Irish's, one Company of Hessians in the Fort at yaminy [Miantonomi] Hill, one Regiment down Neck, at Harris's Mill, one Company of Hessians near the Road, half way between the Town and and James Coggeshal's, where they have a Breast Work, with two Field Pieces mounted pointing West. they have a Guard at Codington's Cove and Point, and Centinels placed down the Neck near the Road, within Call of each other, as far as Churches, also on the Hill at Brenton's Wood, so as to overlook the Beach.

"N.B. This is wrote by a Person that cannot read a word of English. If my Name is not mentioned no Accident can discover me. It is as unsafe for my Name to be spoke of there, as it would be here" (DLC:GW).

4. Sullivan was probably referring to the *Newport Gazette*, published from January 1777 until October 1779.

## General Orders

Head-Quarters White Plains Saturday July 25th 1778.
Parole Kilkenny—                    C. Signs Keen. Kensington—

All Officers who have received public Monies, which are yet unaccounted for will prepare and settle their Accompts immediately with the Auditors.

The troop will beat at six ôClock in the morning—the guards to be on the Parade at seven precisely; The Brigade Majors are reminded to bring on the Super-numeraries, one to every twelve men.

The Grand Parade is assigned on the Main-Road near the Park in Rear of the Old Lines.

A large Cut and thrust sword silver mounted left at General Poor's quarters—Inquire of Majr McClintock.[1]

Varick transcript, DLC:GW.

1. Nathaniel McClintock (1757–1780), who graduated from Harvard University in 1775 and was commissioned a second lieutenant of the 8th Continental Regiment in January 1776, was appointed adjutant to the 2d New Hampshire Regiment in November 1776 and brigade major in April 1777. He resigned his commission in 1779 and was later killed in a naval engagement while commanding marines aboard the privateer *General Sullivan*.

## Council of War

[White Plains, 25 July 1778]
At a Board of General Officers, assembled at Head-Quarters at Reuben Wright's, in the Neighbourhood of White Plains, on saturday the 25 day of July 1778.

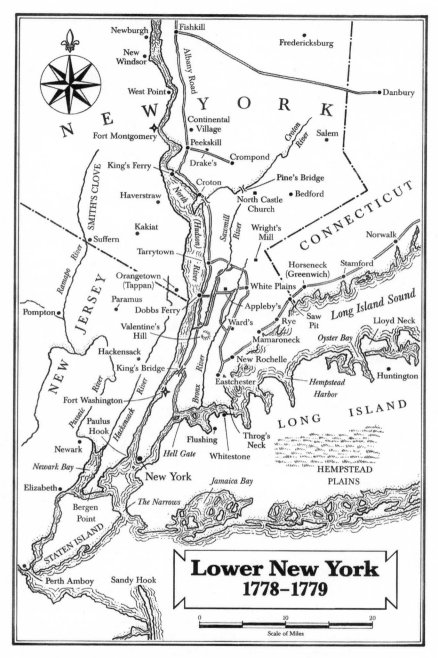

*Lower New York, 1778–1779. (Illustrated by Rick Britton. Copyright Rick Britton 2005)*

Present

His Excellency, the Commander in Chief.

| Major Genls | | Brigadrs | |
|---|---|---|---|
| | Putnam | | Nixon |
| | Gates | | Parsons |
| | Greene | | James Clinton |
| | Lord Stirling | | Smallwood |
| | Kalb | | Knox |
| | McDougal | | Poor |
| | Steuben | | Glover |
| | | | Patterson |
| | | | Wayne |
| | | | Woodford |
| | | | Muhlenburg |
| | | | Scott |
| | | | Huntington |
| | | | Portail |
| | | | Lewis Morris |

The Commander in Chief stated to the Board, that the Two Armies, which had heretofore acted in different Quarters, had formed a junction. That the whole was composed of Troops from the several States from New Hampshire to North Carolina inclusive. That the Army was about to take a Camp, which might possibly be of some permancy. That for it's regularity and more effectual operation; as well as to prevent every possible ground of jealousy, and to preserve harmony through all it's parts, it was necessary to adopt some mode of arrangement and a certain disposition.

Having stated these several matters to the Board, the Commander in chief requested them to take them into consideration, and propounded the following Questions for their advice.

1st    Will it be best for the Troops of each State to encam⟨p⟩ together?

Ansr    It will be best that they should encamp together.

2d—    What will be the best mode of arranging and disposing of the Troops throughout the line, upon the present or a future occasion?

Answr    It will be best, that they should be arranged Geographically as far as circumstances will permit for the present Campaign, agreable to the position of their respective States and their relative front to the Ocean and that they do parade accordingly; and that this disposition and arrangement shall not fix or give any post of Honor between them.

The Board having given their advice upon the foregoing points, the Commander in Chief proceeded to state,

That the proposed Camp at White plains was about 15 miles from York Island. That the Enemy from the information he had received, were in possession of Fort Independance &c. on the Heights this side King's bridge [1]—and also of Fort Washington and the strong grounds at the North entrance of York Island.[2] That from the advices he had been able to obtain, they had Two Camps on Long and Staten Islands; but as to the precise number of men in each or either he was uninformed. That he could not ascertain the Enemy's present force on York Island and the Heights this side King's bridge—nor what their whole strength would be, if the Troops were drawn from Long and Staten Islands; However, that he should suppose it would amount to about 14,000—rank and file, fit for duty; and that from his latest and best accounts, they had Several ships of War between New York and Sandy Hook.

That by the last return we had 16782 rank and file fit for duty. That out of this number, a detachment of about 2000 had marched to the Eastward. That another detachment of about 400 had moved towards the Western frontiers of this State. That Maxwells Brigade consisting of 1100 were at Elizabeth Town in Jersey. That Vanschaicks Regiment of about 400 was in the Neighourhood of Hackensack. That about 900 fit for duty were at the posts in the Highlands and at Kings ferry, besides the New levies which are ordered down. That the remainder of the Army amounting to between 11 & 12,000 were at the White plains and in their vicinity.[3] That the French Squadron, under Admiral, Count D'Estaing had left Sandy Hook and put to Sea.

The Several matters above, being before the Board, the Commander in Chief requested, that after their consideration of the same, they would deliver their Opinions, upon the following Questions.

1st Whether we can make an attack upon the Enemy's posts, either on the Heights on this side King's bridge, or on those on York Island, with a probability of success?

Answer We cannot make an Attack with any probability of success.

2d If an Attack cannot be made, in the opinion of the Board, with a probability of success, should the Army advance and take post nearer the Enemy, or continue on the Grounds it now occupies, at or about the White plains?

Answer The Army should not advance.

| | | |
|---|---|---|
| Israel Putnam | Jno. Nixon | J. Huntington B. Genl |
| Horatio Gates | Saml H. Parsons | duportail |
| Nathanael Greene | James Clinton | |
| Stirling | W. Smallwood | |
| The B[ar]on de Kalb | H. Knox | |
| Alexr McDougall | Enoch Poor | |
| Steuben | Jno. Paterson | |

Anty Wayne
Wm Woodford
P. Muhlenberg
Chs Scott

DS, in Robert Hanson Harrison's writing, DLC:GW; Varick transcript, DLC:GW.

1. Fort Independence was located on the heights between the Boston and Albany post roads at what is now Fort Independence Park, south of the Jerome Park Reservoir in Bronx County.

2. An undated report of a Loyalist deserter, recorded in GW's writing and apparently gathered about this time, gives information about enemy positions in this area: "Philip Miller. Belonging to D'Lanceys Regt Incamped on spiten devil hill on the Island of New York. where are the 2d Battn of D'Lanceys Regt upon the Hill. near the Mouth of the creek. the strength of this Battalion does not exceed (fit for duty) one hundred men. No other Troops upon that Hill but this Battalion. The 71st Regiment la⟨y⟩ below in the Fork of the Road leading to the top of it, and the other to the Bridge & about 300 yds from the No. River. a guard (Sergeant Corporal & 12 Men) kept at the point of the spiten devil hill (next fort Washington hill)—On spiten devil hill near the point at the Mouth a redout with two Ambraza opened towards the Bridge & No. River at the No. F⟨ork⟩—the Gate next the No. River—to get to which y⟨ou⟩ must pass through the Incampment of the abov⟨e⟩ Battalion—the Qr Guard of wch consists of a Serg. Corporal & 9 Men & is on the No. of the Redoubt & between that & the Mouth of the Creek.

"Two Armed Vessels to wit a 12 & a 6 Gun lay opposite the Redoubt. near the East or Enemys shore keep no Guard boats out. there were also two Row Galleys but believes there is but one there now.

"The 45th & 52 Regiments (he thinks, but is sure that they are two British Regiments lays) lays on th⟨e⟩ hill just above the Bridge on the Island side of New York. & keep out only Qr Guards. A Regiment (the 49th) lays at a block House on the Hill above Hærlam River near to where we threw up a breast work in the year 1776.

"At Fort Washington are only Hessians. they are Incamped from (within a Stones thro⟨w⟩ of the Fort) towards New York back of the orchar⟨d⟩ which adjoins the Tavern—does not think to⟨o⟩ strong—& believes they only keep a Guard (except what may be in the Fort) at the Battery which we erected in 1776 on the point opposite Fort Lee.

"Near Morriss House on the Right hand side ⟨o⟩f the road as you go to New York lays the 4th Regiment. he thinks there is no other Troops there Nor any between that & New York.

"There are two redoubts on the Hill on the No. of spiten devil where the Yaugers are. does not know what Troops are on the heights No. of Hærlam but thinks they are strong—In Fort Independance he Judges, from appearances, that there are a Captn 2 Saps & abt 40 Men Mount Guard—the next Fort to this towards Moriss ⟨now⟩ is called No. 4. No lines of Communication between the Redoubts nor no abbettees but ⟨aro⟩und the Forts & these old & rotten.

"General Vaughan Commands at Kings Bridge & its dependances—does not know ⟨w⟩here Genl Kniphausen is" (DLC:GW).

3. The previous return has not been identified. Adj. Gen. Alexander Scammell's "Weekly Return of the Continental Army under the immediate Command of His Excellency George Washington . . . " for this date shows 12,360 rank and file fit for duty, not including artillery, which was not reported (DNA: RG 93, Revolutionary War Rolls, 1775–1783).

## To Silas Deane

Dear Sir                                    White Plains July 25th 1778.

With very great pleasure I heard of your safe arrival at Philadelphia.[1] with still greater, that you were speedily to re-imbark for France—The reasons which produced the one, or may have induced the other, I have not heard, nor have I a desire to know; sufficient it is to be informed, that you are again called upon for a further exertion (at a foreign Court) of those abilities, and that integrity, which you have already displayed so successfully for your Country, and with so much honor to yourself.

As an individual who wishes well to the rights of Mankind, and who hopes to see the liberty of America established upon firm & independant principles, your zeal & labour to obtain them have my sincere and grateful thanks.

During your residence at Paris I was honoured with several Letters from you, but as they were merely introductory of others, I never gave you the trouble of an acknowledgment of them, from a perswation that you had other matters of greater importance to engage your attention than reading Letters of mere ceremony.

I beg you may be perswaded, that no Man wishes you greater success in your embassy—or more prosperity in your public, or private character, than Dr Sir, Yr Most Obedt and Most Humble Servant

Go: Washington

ALS, MBU: Irving P. and Helen J. Fox Collection.
1. Deane, who had returned from France with the French fleet, arrived at Philadelphia on 12 July.

## From Major General William Heath

Dear General                          Head Quarters Boston 25 July 1778

I have been honored with yours of the 18th Instant. The greatest expectations are formed of the most singular and important advantages to the American Cause from the seasonable arrival of the French Squadron, it is to be hoped that the most sanguine will not be disappointed.

I immediately communicated that part of your Excellency's Letter to the Navy Board which respected the rendezvousing the Frigates near the East end of the Sound, and proffered them any aid that might be in my power. the Warren has sailed—the Rawleigh & Dean are not yet manned; every exertion is in exercise to effect it.[1]

Since my last mentioning the forwarding of the 1000 Barrels of wet provisions, I have had the most pressing applications from Major General Sullivan for provisions &c. I have ordered on (which is now for-warding) 800 Barrels of Flour, 500 Barrels of Beef & pork, 150 Tierces of Rice, 5 Tons of hard Bread, 500 Quintals of Salt Fish & 100 Barrels of Salmon, Mackrel &c.—shall continue to afford every assistance that our Magazines will admit of.[2]

I do myself the honor to enclose a request of Major Lithgow's, for leave to resign his Commission in the Army.[3] He is a Gentleman that would do honor to the Service, but his wound and the injury his Con-stitution has received make him apprehensive that he shall not be able to endure the fatigues of the Camp.

While I wish your Excellency the Laurels of Victory & every falicity, I cannot but lament that my situation will not allow me to participate of those active Scenes which are my ardent wish. I have the honor to be with the greatest respect Your Excellency's Most Obedt Servant

W. Heath

LS, DLC:GW; ADfS, MHi: Heath Papers.

1. The *Warren, Raleigh*, and *Deane* were Continental frigates. The *Warren*, built at Providence in 1776, had remained penned at that port until March 1778. She had put in at Boston on 23 March. The *Warren* apparently sailed on 20 July, but whether she succeeded in leaving the harbor is unclear—she had failed in several attempts by 23 July (see James Warren to William Vernon, 20 and 23 July, "Vernon Papers," 251–54). The ship was burned at Penobscot Bay in August 1779. The *Raleigh*, built at Portsmouth, N.H., in 1776, had undergone refitting in France in late 1777 and arrived back in the United States in early April 1778. She sailed from Boston in September and was captured by British ships off Penobscot Bay shortly thereafter. The *Deane* was built at Nantes, France, in late 1777 as the *Lion* (*Lyon*) and renamed. She arrived at Boston in May 1778 and did not leave the port until January 1779. The *Deane* was decommissioned in 1783.

2. See Heath to GW, 17 July. By this time Heath had received Maj. Gen. John Sul-livan's two letters of 24 July, requesting flat-bottomed boats, artillery, and flints, and the first of Sullivan's two letters of 25 July, which requested provisions (see Sulli-van's letters and Heath's two replies of 25 July, in Hammond, *Sullivan Papers*, 2:105–6, 115–19).

3. William Lithgow, Jr. (1750–1796), served in 1776 as a lieutenant and captain of various Massachusetts militia detachments stationed at Falmouth in the District of Maine. Chosen in November 1776 to be major of a regiment raised in Maine, he became major of the 11th Massachusetts Regiment in January 1777. In the enclo-sure, a letter to Heath of 24 July, Lithgow asked to resign because "a Musket Shot in my right arm, which penetrated and very much fractured the joint of the Elbow," had left him with "a very partial and imperfect use of" his hand; "this unhappy Cir-cumstance co-opperating with an inveterate dysentery, which originated in the hardships to which (from the peculiar circumstances of that part of the army that retreated from Ticonderoga) I was necessarily exposed during the Campaign . . . deeply impresses me with a sense of my inability to endure the fatigues of a Camp, or to discharge the important and active duties of my station" (DLC:GW). Lith-gow's discharge, authorized by GW's letter to Heath of 14 Aug., was dated 5 No-vember. In 1789 GW appointed Lithgow U.S. attorney for the District of Maine.

# From Major General Lafayette

Stratfort [Conn.]

dear General 25 july at seven o'clock in the morning

inclos'd I have the honor to send you a letter from General Sullivan which I took the liberty to oppen[1]—if the suppos'd expedition against providence has taken place we can not Come up time enough as to prevent it—but I am Rather inclin'd to believe we wi'll find the ennemy fortifying themselves, and therefore the Sooner we may begin our visit the better it will be.

I have found general Varnum yesterday at this place, who Says we could march much faster than we will do, was it not on account of provisions which ca'nt come up with us—there were no Magazines prepar'd principally for the article of flour—the provisions must follow upon oxen-teams—however general Varnum has sent a head to take every precaution in his power, for facilitating our journey—if the baggage embarass us we'll leave it behind—we are much Retard'd by the ferrys, and the best way will be to separate the brigades—with the highest respect I have the honor to be dear General Your most obedient Servant

the Marquis de lafayette

ALS, PEL. After the war, Lafayette edited this and other letters he wrote to GW during the war, sometimes altering, inserting, or omitting words to clarify meaning and sometimes obliterating entire passages. The original text has been restored where possible.

1. See Maj. Gen. John Sullivan to GW, 22 July.

# From Lieutenant Colonel John Laurens

Point Judith 40 Miles from Providence

Sir. 25th July 1778.

I had the honor of writing to your Excellency from Lebanon—the 23d inst.—the day following at 3 oClock in the afternoon I arrived at Providence—as soon as I had delivered Genl Sullivan Your Excellencys dispatches and instructions[1]—I set out for this place with Col. Wall and an ample number of Pilots whom General Sullivan had provided and put under his command—Col. Wall is a man of Character and property perfectly acquainted with the coast &ca[2]—those under him are experienced Pilots and men of responsibility—We arrived here at nine oClock this morning—having been detained till that time in procuring a party of militia—and making arrangements both for securing such boats as we shall want for our own immediate use—and such as without this precaution might be employed in communicating intelligence to the enemy—We have agreed with four whale-boat privateers belonging to Connecticut manned with enterprising experienced mariners—and pressed four belonging to this state—we have given them to understand that the Frigate lying at Connecticut River is to push out of the sound—and that we are to meet her with hands to enable her to go round and join the french fleet[3]—for which purpose their boats are necessary—the number that we have is amply sufficient for our business—and now we are in readiness—two Sentinels will be posted in an advantageous place, whose business will be to attend to whatever Signals may be given from the Sea-bord—besides which Col. Wall the Master-pilots and myself will alternately hold watch and keep our attention awake—'till last night 12 oClock unfavorable winds have prevailed—if the Gale which we have at present does not prove inconstant, it will not be long before we are called upon— Our Situation commands a view of the several entrances to New-port—and block island is directly opposite to us—so that nothing can pass to or from New-port unnoticed— Genl Sullivan estimates the enemys land force here at 7000—the State of their Shipping he informs me is as follows—in the E. Channel, (or that between Seconet Point and Rhode Island) 2 Galleys and 1 Small frigate—in the West Channel (or that between Boston neck[4] and Connanicut Island) 2 Small frigates—In the Middle or main Channel 2 Frigates—at New-port 2 or 3 Frigates As Genl Sullivan will probably write to Your Excellency—I forbear descending to farther particulars—he has been indefatigable and nothing on his part will be wanting. I have the honor to be with the greatest respect Your Excellencys most obedt Servt

John Laurens Aide de Camp

ALS, DLC:GW.
    1. See GW to Maj. Gen. John Sullivan, 22 July.
    2. William Wall (d. 1803?) of Providence was appointed a lieutenant colonel of the Rhode Island artillery regiment in December 1776. According to a letter from Providence published in the *Continental Journal, and Weekly Advertiser* (Boston), 30 July, on the evening of 24 July "thirty pilots were dispatched for Point-Judith, to go on board the fleet."
    3. Laurens was evidently referring to the Continental frigate *Trumbull*, which was launched in September 1776 but remained in the Connecticut River until 1779 because its deep draft created difficulty in crossing the bar at the river's mouth into Long Island Sound.
    4. Boston Neck is on the Rhode Island mainland, north of Narragansett and west of Conanicut Island.

## To Colonel Stephen Moylan

Dear Sir                    Head Quarters White plains 25th July 1778
    I recd yours of the 23d by Major Washington. I think the best position for the Cavalry, to answer the purposes of foraging and covering

the Country, will be about Hackensaik New Bridge. You then have an oppertunity of drawing supplies from the Country between the North River and Hackensaik and Hackensaik and Pasaic as your Station will be central. You also hinder the inhabitants from carrying provision to New York, either by the way of Bergen, or Barbadoes Neck.

As soon as the Forage master has got matters in his department fixed, I shall order all, but abt 50 Horse, over to this side. You will therefore be ready to move at a moments warning.[1] I am &c.

Df, in Tench Tilghman's writing, DLC:GW; Varick transcript, DLC:GW.
    1. Moylan replied to GW from Orangetown, N.Y., on 26 July: "Major Washington deliverd me your Excellencys Letter of Yesterday, I propose to move what horse are fit for duty to the Newbridge to morrow, agreeable to your orders and shall endeavor to fulfill the duty reccommended therein.
    "Whenever your Excellency will order us over, you will find the Cavalry ready to obey your Commands" (ALS, DLC:GW).

*Letter not found*: from Brig. Gen. Thomas Nelson, Jr., 25 July 1778. On 20 Aug., GW wrote Nelson: "Since writing the foregoing, I have been favoured with your Letter of the 25th Ulto from Baltimore."

## To Major General Stirling

My Lord        Head Quarters Wrights Mills [N.Y.] 25th July 1778
    I desire that you and the General Officers upon the Court Martial would meet here at five OClock this Afternoon, when the other General Officers will be assembled, to consider of some measures that respect the Army at large.[1]
    I would submit it to the Court, whether it would not be more convenient to adjourn to the plains, where the Witnesses may be attending their respective duties, and be at hand when called for. I am my Lord Your most obt Servt

Go: Washington

LS, in Tench Tilghman's writing, PPRF; Df, DLC:GW; Varick transcript, DLC:GW.
    1. The court-martial for the trial of Maj. Gen. Charles Lee was meeting at North Castle, N.Y., at this time. For the measures to be considered, see Council of War, this date.

## From Jonathan Trumbull, Sr.

Sir,        Lebanon [Conn.] 25th July—1778
    I recieved a Letter from Majr General Sullivan of the 22nd advising that he expects the Enemy will make a Descent on Providence in a very short time—that they are now 7,000 Strong, and in a day or two will be eleven, requesting aid from this State[1]—Although we are exceedingly

exhausted of Men &c.—and this critical moment for securing the Labours of the last and the produce of this year, which is of essential consequence, rendered it additionally distressing to take off more of our Militia—yet, I doubt not, we should have made an effort to support them—But before we had come to a full determination, Your Excellency's Favor of the 22nd from White Plains came to hand, advising of Admiral D. Estaing's Design at Rhode Island which has greatly relieved our anxiety for the Fate of Providence. I was this Day with my Council considering how and in what manner to raise or furnish aid &c. agreeable to your Excellency's Requisition when I just recieved another Letter from Majr Genl Sullivan of yesterday requesting, from authority derived from you, five hundred Militia from this State, to act under his command at Providence[2]—So exceedingly difficult was it to take off any more from the pressing Labours in the Field, that, instead of it, we have thought it necessary to call these Companies from our Sea Coasts, which strips them from Fairfield to New-London, and leaves us none of four Regiments raised heretofore by enlistment and detachment for our own Defence, in addition to all in the various Continental Services in which so many of our Inhabitants are engaged.[3]

If a larger number of the Enemy's Troops should be drawn from New-York to New-Port than Your Excellency was aware of, perhaps you may be able to spare a further Detachment from Your Army, so as to release our Men who will leave our Sea Coasts exposed.

Agreeable to your desire signified by Lieut. Colonel Laurens, I yesterday gave orders for a suitable number of Skilful Pilots to be sent out from New London in quest of the French-Fleet whose seasonable aid appears probable to be of very great importance, and with whom this State will be forward to cooperate to the utmost of our power.

I very sincerely thank Your Excellency for your friendly and affectionate good will and wishes towards my late Dear Son whom it pleased the Sovereign Arbiter of Life and Death to remove from this World about Sunrising of the 23d instant—This is a heavy and sore breach upon me and my Family, but it is my duty to be still and know that God has done it, who has a right to dispose of all his Creatures as he pleaseth, and ever exercises that Right in perfect consistence with Holiness, Justice and Goodness. I am, with great Esteem & Regard Your Excellency's Afflicted—Obedient humble Servant

Jonth. Trumbull

ALS, DLC:GW; LB, Ct: Trumbull Papers. Trumbull's note on the cover of the ALS indicates that it was sent "⅌ M. Genl Sullivan's Express." Tench Tilghman's docket, which misdates the letter 26 July, reports that it was "Ansd 28th."

1. For Maj. Gen. John Sullivan's letter to Trumbull of 22 July, see Hammond, *Sullivan Papers*, 2:102.

2. See Sullivan to Trumbull, 24 July (ibid., 2:110). The letter-book copy continues here with a sentence omitted from the ALS: "In consequence of which we have given Orders for eight Companies of Militia-men to be marched immediately to Providence."

3. The Connecticut council of safety began consideration of GW's letter on 24 July and on 25 July resolved "that Col. Oliver Smith with the two companies of draughted militia, except the guard stationed at Lyme, and Lt. Col. Gallop with one company of the six battalions now at New London, Major Backus with the two companies of draughted militia at Newhaven, Capt. [    ] Pitkin with his company at Fairfield, and Capt. [    ] with his company at Fairfield, and Capt. Tyler with his company of matrosses, be ordered by the Capt. General forthwith to march to Providence and join the forces there under command of Major Genl Sullivan" (*Conn. Public Records*, 2:100–101).

## General Orders

Head-Quarters White-Plains Sunday July 26th 1778.
Parole Moravia—                    C. Signs Minden. Manchester.
Colonel Wood's Regiment of Militia is to be employ'd in collecting forage 'till further orders. Coll Wood will receive directions where and how to employ his men from the Forage-Master General—Additional Pay will be allowed them whilst on that duty.

One man from each Brigade who is acquainted with burning Coal to be paraded on the Grand Parade tomorrow morning at Guard mounting.

The General Court Martial whereof Coll Putnam is President is dissolved and another General Court-Martial of the Lines to assemble tomorrow morning nine ôClock at the New dining Room on the Left of the Park nigh General Morris's Quarters to try all such Persons as shall be brought before them—Coll Stewart will preside. Lieutt Coll Ball Major Furnald and a Captain from each of the following Brigades No. Carolina, Woodford's Scott's, 1st and 2nd Maryland, 2nd Pennsylvania, Clinton's, Parsons's, Huntington's, Nixon's, Paterson's, Late Larned's and Poor's.

As it is necessary for the sake of regularity that there should be some fixed general Rule for arranging and disposing in the Line of the Army the Troops of the different States during the present Campaign; They are to take post so far as Circumstances will permit according to the relative Geographical Position of the States to each other, supposing their front to the Ocean; This Arrangment is not to establish any Post of honor or Precedency between the Troops.

All Guards and detachments are to parade agreeable to this rule.

Varick transcript, DLC:GW.

## To Vice Admiral d'Estaing

Sir                                      Head Qrs White plains July 26th 1778.

Major General Greene, who is now Quarter Master General of our Army, will have the honor of delivering you this. Besides the military abilities of this Gentleman, he is a Native of the state of Rhode Island, and having always resided there till the commencement of the war, he is intimately acquainted with every part of it and with its navigation. From These circumstances, added to his weight & influence in that Country I have thought that his services might be of material importance in the intended enterprize against our Common Enemy. I recommend him to your notice and attention as a brave Intelligent Worthy Officer, and in whom you may place the utmost confidence. I have the Honor to be with the most perfect considn & respect Sr Yr Most Obedt & Most Hbl. se[rvan]t

Go: Washington

Df, in Robert Hanson Harrison's writing, DLC:GW; Varick transcript, DLC:GW.

## To Vice Admiral d'Estaing

Sir                                      Head Qrs White plains July 26th 1778

I had the honor of writing you the inclosed Letter from Haverstraw Bay, which was intended to introduce Colonel Sears to your notice.[1] This Gentlemen set out with Captain Dobbs, a pilot, of the first established reputation, to offer their services to the Squadron under your command. Before they had an opportunity of reaching the Fleet, they sailed from the Road off Sandy Hook. Colo. Sears is still desirous of manifesting his zeal in this our common cause and will be happy if he can contribute in the smallest degree to the success of the Enterprize, which you have formed against Rhode Island. I have the Honor to be with every sentiment of respect & esteem Sir Yr Most Obedt sert

Go: Washington

Df, in Robert Hanson Harrison's writing, DLC:GW; Varick transcript, DLC:GW.
    1. The enclosed letter has not been found.

## To Henry Laurens

Sir                                      Head Quarters White plains 26 July 1778

The Baron De Steuben will have the honor of delivering you this. I am extremely sorry, that this Gentlemans situation and views seem to have determined him to quit the service, in which he has been heretofore and is capable still of being extensively useful. Some discontents which arose among the Officers on account of the powers with which the Office was at first vested, induced me to arrange the duties of it upon a plan, different from that in which it began.[1] The moving state of the Army has for some time past, in a great degree, suspended the exercise of the Inspectorate. When the Troops marched from Brunswic, the scarcity of General Officers, most of them being engaged with the Court Martial either as Members or Witnesses, occasioned my giving the Baron a temporary command of a Division, during the March. On our arrival near our present incampment, I intended he should relinquish this charge and resume his former Office, for which purpose a General Order was accordingly issued.[2] But I find that he is intirely disinclined to the measure, and resolves not to continue in the Service unless he can hold an actual command in the line. Justice, concurring with inclination, constrains me to testify, that the Baron has in every instance discharged the several trusts reposed in him with great Zeal and Ability, so as to give him the fullest title to my esteem, as a brave indefatigable, judicious and experienced Officer.

I regret there should be a necessity that his Services should be lost to the Army: At the same time I think it my duty explicitly to observe to Congress, that his desire of having an actual and permanent command in the line cannot be complied with, without wounding the feelings of a number of Officers, whose rank and merits give them every claim to attention, and that the doing it would be productive of much dissatisfaction and extensive ill consequences. This does not proceed from any personal objections on the part of those Officers against the Baron: on the contrary, most of them whom I have heard speak of him, express a high sense of his military worth. It proceeds from motives of another nature, which are too obvious to need particular explanation, or may be summed up in this, that they conceive such a step would be injurious to their essential rights and just expectations. That this would be their way of thinking upon the subject I am fully convinced, from the effect which the temporary command given him, even under circumstances so peculiar as those I have mentioned, produced.[3] The strongest symptoms of discontent appeared upon the occasion. I have the Honor to be with great Respect and Esteem Sir Your most obt and humble Servt

Go: Washington

LS, in Tench Tilghman's writing, DNA:PCC, item 152; Df, DLC:GW; copy, DNA:PCC, item 169; Varick transcript, DLC:GW. The LS is docketed in part: "Read August 1st Referred to Mr Reed Mr Boudinot Mr Chase"; see *JCC*, 11:737, where it is erroneously called a letter of 25 July.

1. See GW's general orders of 15 June, an extract of which he enclosed with this letter. At this point on the draft, Alexander Hamilton wrote, "This arrangement

did not prove to be so satisfactory to the Baron as might be wished, which together with," but those words were struck out.

2. See General Orders, 22 July.

3. At this point on the draft, Hamilton wrote and struck out the sentence "It was generally the object of much complaint and inquietude."

*Letter not found*: from Richard Henry Lee, 26 July 1778. On 10 Aug., GW wrote Lee: "A few days ago I received your favor of the 26th Ulto."

## From Colonel William Malcom

Sir                                     West point [N.Y.] July 26 1778

I have taken the Command, according to your Excellencys orders,[1] and General Glover is gone on to his Brigade—It may be that this post is in good order—but not in my opinion—I can find but very few that know what they are here for[2]—I expected to have sent your Excellency A perfect State of every department by this Oppty but altho' I called for returns three days ago I have got none yet but such as might have been expected about the 19th of Aprill 75.[3]

As Provissions is a Capital Article I enclose the Commissarys return.[4]

In about a week I hope to furnish a Compleat State of every thing— but an *Engineer* is necessary—The Militia orderd from Camp are Straggling in—I have however ordered off the detatchments of Levy called Nixons & Putnams, (about 500) because I apprehend they ought to be arranged as soon as possible—and Greatons shall follow the day after tomorrow.

I am posting the Militia Regts on the Out Works and assigning particular duty to each—Mr Kosiesko tells me that—

| | | |
|---|---|---|
| 300 men will finish Putnams Redt in | | 3 weeks |
| 200 | Webbs | 3 |
| 300 | wyllys, Meigs & shereburns | 2 |
| 300 | Chain battery | 3 |
| 1100 —[5] | | |

But I beg leave to remark, That The Fort is in a very unfinish'd State— a Vast deal of work to do on the aproaches—not a little Occassional fatigue & Also the Garrison duty, which requires 80 men dayly—There is also a Block house proposed to be built on a Hill West of Putnams Redt which, commands the whole.

From this Estimate your Excellency will be able to determine what the strength of the Garrison ought to be making allowa⟨nce⟩ for Reliefs— and the estimate is moderat⟨e.⟩

The Two Small Continental Regts are absolutely in Rags[6]—no Shirts—Shoes or Overhalls—There are some of those Articles in Store at Fish Kill—I Pray your Excellency will indulge me with an order for about 320 pair of each, & Some Blankitts. The Regts have a Number of Waggons—we want but few here and its difficult to provide forrage—i.e. it takes too many men from more importent duty to assisst the F. Master in bringing it over the River—Shall they be discharged & return'd to Conecticut, or will the Q. M. General employ them untill the expiration of the time of Service of the Regiments they came with expire (about two Mos.).

A Garrison C: Martial is often Necessary—Will your Excellency Authorise me to Constitute one Occessionely?

There are Three articles of Expence which I beg leave to propose to your Excellency—viz. The Young Gentleman who Acted as M. of Brigade wt. Spencer, to do duty something in that way[7]—to assisst in training the Troops & conducting the duty—And another in the Style of an asst A. Genl to the Garrison to make returns &c.—There is abundance of employment for both nor can the duty be carried on without them—with any degree of regularity—and if I do that myself—more capital Servi[c]e must be neglected—They will both only cost the public abt the triffling Sum of forty dollars ⅌ Mo.

The other Article, I do not urge—it is some extra allowance as Subsistance for myself—There are a world of people resort here, on bussiness-who must eat, & drink and as Commanding Officer, they expect it from me—I am content to give the Q. Mr my pay & Subsistance if he shall be orderd to supply me—I do not mean to be extravagant—nor wou'd I be hired to live in dessipation—Your Excellency may pronounce on these matters as they appear reasonable.

at General Warners request & from my own Knowledge of its propriety I have sent a Capt. Santford of my Regt to take the Command at Fish Kill, & have orderd him to send the Levys on to Camp except a few for Guards & fatigue in the D. Q. M. Dept and to report to your Excellency every material circumstance that Occurs—I hope this will meet with approbation—I have the Honor to be with great respect May it please Your Exclly Your Excellencys mo. obt & very Hbl. Sert

W. Malcom

does the German Regt now at F. Kill come here[8]—Grahames woud be usefull in fatigue also if they can be Shared.

ALS, DLC:GW.

1. See GW to Malcom, 21 July.

2. In a letter to Col. John Lamb of 2 Aug., Malcom confided that he found his new command "in just as bad order as even your Imagination can conceive—will you believe that there was not 1 lb of meat in the Garrison of any Kind—and but 200 barrells of flour.... If the Enemy do come I shall fight them in the field, which is my only chance—the works are not worth a farthing" (NHi: John Lamb Papers; see also Malcom to Horatio Gates, 28 July, NHi: Gates Papers).

3. The battles at Lexington and Concord took place on 19 April 1775.

4. For the enclosed return, made on this date by Assistant Commissary of Issues John Elderkin, see DLC:GW.

5. The redoubts at West Point were named after the colonels commanding the regiments that commenced their construction. Fort Putnam was on Crown Hill, about two-thirds of a mile southwest of Fort Arnold. Fort Webb was about a fifth of a mile east of Fort Putnam. Fort Wyllys was about a fifth of a mile south of Fort Webb, with Fort Meigs, closer to the river, just southeast of Fort Wyllys. Sherburne Redoubt was about an eighth of a mile northwest of Fort Arnold. When Malcom sent the same information to Henry Laurens, "chain battery" was replaced by "Constitution (East side the River)" (Malcom to Laurens, 1 Aug., DNA:PCC, item 78).

6. Patton's and Malcom's Additional Continental Regiments stationed at West Point together totaled about 150 rank and file fit for duty (Lesser, *Sinews of Independence*, 77).

7. Malcom may have been referring to William Peck, who served as brigade major for Joseph Spencer's brigade in 1776.

8. Malcom was referring to Armand's corps.

## From Brigadier General William Maxwell

Sir                                    Elizth Town [N.J.] 26th July 1778

I take this opertunity by Mr Furman[1] to in form Your Excellency of what I know respecting the Enemy. Viz. the night before last a Deserter came in from the Island to Amboy seem'd to be verry intiligent; says, he is shure that the 5th Regt—10th 15th 27th 40th 55th Regts lyeth on Statten Island, besides some of the new Leveys; that the 15th came there the day before he Deserted. There is two Redoubts on the High grounds & two Batterys at the narrows on Statten Island.

At the narrows on long Island, the 17th 33d and 46th Regts is supposed to be erecting, or going to erect Batterys. The 23d Regt and 17th Dragoons lyeth at Jamaica Long Island. The 35th Regt & a number of Hessians ly's on the outside of New York; the others gone to Kings Bridge &Ca the general talk of the Armey is that a large part of the Armey is to go to the West Indias as soon as the French Fleet is gone; supposed to be 20 Regiments for that service.[2] The 38th Regiment gone to Rhode Island.

Mr Furman & Mr Caldwell have been with me and informed that they are going to forward large quantitys of Provissons from Trenton by way of Paramus & on to the Armey, they are very desirous if consistant with my orders I would keep a Guard below Paramus for the security of the Teams passing I informed them that as the Enemy now lay I did not think I could with safety extend my Troops any further they are about to apply to You for some Troops and I will wait Your Excellencys Iinstructions and am Your Most Obedient Humble Servant

Wm Maxwell

ALS, DLC:GW. Tench Tilghman docketed this letter in part, "not ansd."

1. Moore Furman (1728–1808), a former postmaster of Trenton and merchant of Trenton and Philadelphia, was a deputy quartermaster general of the Continental army. He also served as a judge in New Jersey, 1777–86, and was appointed mayor of Trenton in 1792.

2. Secret instructions sent to British general Henry Clinton on 21 March directed that he detach 5,000 troops for an immediate attack on the island of Saint Lucia in the West Indies and an additional 3,000 men to reinforce British positions in the Floridas (George Germain to Clinton, 21 March, P.R.O., Colonial Office, 5/95, Military Correspondence of the British Generals; see also Davies, *Documents of the American Revolution*, 15:74–76). On 11 July and again on 27 July, however, Clinton wrote British secretary of state for the colonies George Germain that the arrival of the French fleet had led to a postponement of the expedition, although the troops would remain ready to embark whenever Admiral Richard Howe judged that a convoy was safe (both letters, P.R.O., Colonial Office, 5/96, Military Correspondence of the British Generals). The troops were not finally dispatched until November.

*Letter not found*: from Juan de Miralles, c.26 July 1778. On 26 July, Henry Laurens wrote John Laurens: "I send in the Packet with this, four Letters for yourself and sundry for Head Quarters. . . . There is a Letter in the Packet for his Excellency the General from Don Juan De Miralis" (*Laurens Papers*, 14:80–81).

## From Major General John Sullivan

My Dear General                 Providence July 26 1778 8 oC. A:M.

By a former Letter Sent by Express[1] I acknowledged the Rect of your Excellenceys favor of the 17th Instant which arrived only the Evening of the 22d & Colo. Laurens arrived with your Excys favor of the 22d on the 24th Inst. two of Clock afternoon—This gave me but Little time to prepare I however Endeavoured to improve it in the Best Manner & have the pleasure to Inform your Excy that Every Effort of mine to prepare for Executing your Excys orders has Succeeded beyond my most Sanguine Expectations & Every thing now promises Success. The French Fleet has not yet arrived Colo. Laurens with the Best of Pilots & a Sufficient number of them are waiting at Point Judith—I have the honor to Inclose your Excy a Letter from Colo. Laurens in which I Suppose he gives your Excy an Account of appearences in this Quarter[2]—I find I Shall have a Sufficiency of Stores of Every kind & I hope Boats & troops Enough to make the attempt with a moral Certainty of Success the moment the Marquis & Admiral Arrive. I Inclose your Excellency Copy of my Letter to the Count now in the hand of Colo. Laurens to be Delivered him on his arrival[3] wish it may meet your Excellenceys approbation & have the Honor to be with the most profound Respect your Excellys most obedt Servant

Jno. Sullivan

ALS, DLC:GW.
    1. See Sullivan to GW, 24 July.
    2. See John Laurens to GW, 25 July.
    3. In Sullivan's letter to Vice Admiral d'Estaing, dated 25 July, he pointed out that when he received GW's instruction on 24 July, "I had sixteen Hundred standing Forces, & scarcely a Sufficiency of Provisions for them & was under no Apprehension of such an Attempt in this Quarter. Added to all this the Enemy in their Descent on the 25th of May last had burned almost all the Boats prepared for a Descent—But as this short Notice arose from natural & necessary Causes which could not have been foreseen I have used every Endeavor to prevent Your Excellys being delayed in Your Design—I have forwarded the Pilots who will wait Your Signal at Point Judith: I have also collected a considerable Number of Boats sufficient I hope to make good our Landing under the Fire of Your Ships; I have established a Chain of Expresses on both Sides Rhode Island upon the Main for the Purpose of receiving from & carrying to Your Excelly every Kind of Intelligence that may be thought necessary I will also have Boats plying in the Bay round Your Fleet for the same Purpose when it arrives—I have called upon the Country for Troops & have taken every Step to procure Provisions & other Necessaries that the Time would permit & I flatter myself we shall not be disappointed. I am exceeding sorry that our Situation renders it uncertain whether we can co-operate the Moment of Your Arrival—The Marquis La Fayette is on his March with a Division of the main Army; I trust he will be here in four Days—As his Troops may be depended on & mine are principally Militia I think the Attempt even if we were ready in other Respects would be hazardous before his Arrival: But as Your Fleet is superior to every Thing on the Sea I think no great Difficulty can arise from a Delay of one or two Days after Your Arrival should that from the above Circumstances happen. There are three Entrances to the Harbor viz. one on the East of Rhode Island at Seconnet Point, one on the West called the middle Channel which runs between Rhode Island & Conannicut which Island of Conanicut lies to the westward of Rhode Island, to the westward of which there is still another Channel called the West Channel—This will at once appear to Your Excelly on View of the Map which I sent You by Lieut. Colo. Laurens & will be sufficiently explained to You by the Pilots sent onboard."
    Sullivan continued with "Hints" for d'Estaing's naval operations: "I think the Mouth of the East Channel should be blocked up immediately on Your Arrival by three Frigates or by two Frigates and a small Ship of the Line: The Enemy have in that Channel a small Sloop of War with two large Gallies they cannot remove as our Batteries above will prevent their going up & Your Ships below will prevent their going out—These Frigates will be ready to move up when notified that we are ready to go on, can soon silence the Enemy's Vessels & cover our Landing from Tiverton—I would also place four of the next smaller Vessells that can be spared at the Mouth of the west Channel three of which should be sent up to capture two small Frigates which lay in that Channel—These Ships may turn Conannicut Island on the North, fall into the Bay above Rhode Island & lay out of Shot from any Part of the Shore with their Prizes & remain there till they are notified to fall down to cover the Landing of the Troops or assist in such other Operations as Your Excellency shall order—The Rest of Your Fleet should in my Opinion take Possession of the Middle Channel leading between Conannicut & Rhode Island and commonly called Newport Harbour & lay there out of Reach of their Forts till we are ready to co-operate with You—This Disposition will in my Opinion cut off all Possibility of Retreat from the Enemy prevent their receiving Reinforcements & enable Your Excelly to co-operate with us whenever we are ready to act of which Your

Excellency shall be timely advised—There are not in this Department more than seven or eight small Frigates unless lately arrived & cannot at any Event be sufficient to injure You in this Disposition.

"I shall notify Your Excelly when we are ready and of the Place of Landing that You may order such Ships as You think proper to cover our Landing—The Enemy have a Number of Redoubts scattered through the Island upon commanding Eminences all of which I mean to pass after my Landing & proceed to the Town of Newport which is defended on the Land Side by a Chain of Redoubts on an Eminence which runs nearly across the Island & commands the Town: These must be stormed & I doubt not will be carried without much Difficulty if attacked in the Manner hereafter mentioned—I wish at the Time of our Landing Your Excelly would make a Show of landing Your Troops at or near Newport to deceive and amuse the Enemy & to give us an Opportunity of getting possessed of the Island—When we are ready to storm the Redoubts we will fix upon a Signal to notify Your Excelly & then if it appears adviseable You will move up Your Ships to cannonade the Town of Newport which must soon be abandoned and then land all the Troops You can possibly spare under Fire of Your Cannon to co-operate with us in our Attempt upon the Redoubts above the Town—The Reason of my passing the Redoubts on the north Part of the Island is because we can pass clear of their Fire & as no Possibility of Retreat or Escape will remain we can reduce them at our Leisure after having made ourselves Masters of the Town—I shall leave a sufficient Number of Troops to watch their Motions & keep them within Bounds—The Reason of my wishing the larger Part of Your Force being destined to block up the Middle Channel is to prevent a Reinforcements being thrown upon the Island from New York, to render Your Fleet so strong as to prevent any Attempt of the Enemys Fleet from New York & to co-operate with those Ships which pass up the west Channel & turn Conannicut in preventing three British Regts now encamped on that Island from passing over in their Boats to reinforce the Troops on Rhode Island who after that is carried must all become Prisoners of Course." He went on to ask d'Estaing "to pardon my Freedom in giving these Hints" and promised to "chearfully co-operate" with d'Estaing in executing whatever measures he thought "most adviseable" (DLC:GW).

## To Thomas Tillotson

Sir,                                              [White Plains, 26 July 1778]

You are to proceed, immediately, with two assistants to Doctor Isaac Foster D. Director in the Eastern department, and take his instructions for the procuring of hospital furniture, medicines instruments, and such things as may be thought necessary in the formation of a military & flying hospital for the use and benefit of the troops under the command of Major General Sullivan, at Providence, Rhode Island, in case or provided a proper hospital arrangement has not already taken place in that quarter either by the orders of Major General Sullivan or Doctor Foster. But should there be as yet no establishment of this kind you will repair to and continue with Major General Sulliva[n] [1] in the faithful exercise of the several functions of your profession till dismissed by General Sullivan, the commander in that quarter, or the commander in chief of the army of the United States. Given at Head Quarters this 26th day of July 1778.

G. W——n

Df, in James McHenry's writing, DLC:GW; Varick transcript, DLC:GW. Thomas Tillotson (1751–1832), who was appointed a senior surgeon in June 1776, had been serving as physician and surgeon general for the northern army at least since October 1777. He served to the close of the war. After the war, Tillotson was elected to Congress in 1801 but did not serve, and he was New York secretary of state, 1801–8.
    1. The draft reads, "Sullival."

## General Orders

Head-Quarters White-Plains Monday July 27th 1778.

Parole Lexington                            C. Signs London. Lebanon.

The Gentlemen who have offered themselves as Candidates for Commissions in the Companies of Sappers & Miners are requested to wait upon General Du Portail, Chief Engineer who will examine their respective Pretensions & Qualifications & make a report to Head-Quarters accordingly.

A Hogshead of Rice will be delivered to each Brigade for the use of the sick.

At a General Court-Martial July 17th 1778—Coll Putnam President, Mr James Davidson, Quarter Master of Coll James Livingston's Regiment tried for defrauding the soldiers of their Provisions, embezzling Continental Property and disposing of several Articles belonging to the United States, found guilty and sentenced to be cashiered.[1]

The Commander in Chief approves the sentence and orders it to take place immediately.

At the same Court Henry Scott a soldier in Colonel Sherburne's Regiment was tried for desertion, found guilty and sentenced to receive fifty lashes on his bare back and be confined in some Gaol 'till he can be put on board the Continental Navy there to remain during the War.[2]

The Commander in Chief orders him to receive his lashes on the Grand-Parade tomorrow morning at Guard-mounting and then to return to his Regiment.

Likewise Alexander Graham *alias* Smith a soldier in Coll Meigs's Regiment tried for desertion unanimously found guilty and sentenced to be shot to death.[3]

John Craige of 4th Maryland Regiment, at a Brigade General Court Martial July 10th 1778—was tried for deserting to the Enemy—found guilty and unanimously sentenced to suffer death.[4]

His Excellency the Commander in Chief approves the two last mentioned sentences.

Varick transcript, DLC:GW.

On this date Reuben Wright gave a receipt for £28.18.10, received in full payment of his account for GW's "family Expence," 20–27 July (DLC:GW, ser. 5,
vol. 29).

1. James Davidson had been appointed quartermaster of the 1st Canadian Regiment in March 1777.

2. Henry Scott enlisted in Col. Henry Sherburne's Additional Continental Regiment in September 1777 and deserted in December of that year. After he rejoined
the regiment in April 1778, he was reported as confined until he was transferred
to a Continental ship in 1779.

3. Sgt. Maj. Benjamin Gilbert of the 5th Massachusetts Regiment identified this
man as "one Smith formally Belonging to Colo. Greatons Regt" (Symmes, *Gilbert
Diary*, 35). An Alexander Smith of Col. John Greaton's 3d Massachusetts Regiment
enlisted for the war in February 1777 and deserted in July of that year. He, or another man of the same name, was convicted of desertion and sentenced to lashes
earlier in July 1778 (see Horatio Gates general orders, 15 July, NN: Emmet Collection).

4. John Craig, who had enlisted as a private for three years' service in May 1778,
was pardoned (see General Orders, 21 Aug.), and he later reenlisted for the war.

*Letter not found*: to Colonel Armand, c.27 July 1778. On 27 July, GW wrote Col.
William Malcom: "I now inclose a letter to Colo. Armand or the commanding
Officer [of his corps]."

## To Major General Benedict Arnold

Dear sir                               Head Qrs Whe Plains 27th July 1778
This will be deliver'd to you by Majr Cabell who goes to Philadelphia in order to Collect & bring forward all the soldiers belonging to this Army who may have gone back to, or remain'd in the City,
or its Neighbourhood—You will please give him every Necessary assistance in the Execution of this duty I expect you will find Colo.
Heartly's Regiment with Colo. Proctors sufficient for Garrison duty, &
you know how injurious it is to Soldiers, both in their Military & Moral
Line, to be seperated from their Regiments, without proper officers to
inspect their Conduct add to this that our Situation renders it highly
proper that our Regiments should be as complete as we can possibly
make them.

As Major Cabell belongs to Virginia he goes more particularly to
bring on the soldiers of that State—but any Others that can be collected he will take charge of it will be highly necessary to order all
officers to Camp who are not on immediate duty with you or have not
regular leave of Absence. I am &C.

G.W.

Df, in John Fitzgerald's writing, DLC:GW; Varick transcript, DLC:GW.

## To John Beatty

Sir                                    Head Quarters White plains 27 July 1778

I would recommend the laying a copy of the inclosed letter to you from Mr Pintard, dated the 21st Instt before congress for their consideration.[1]

you will take their judgement on the exchange of our mariners, and those of the French now in their hands for a like number of British seamen as proposed by admiral Gambier.

The supplying our prisoners in New-York with provisions is another matter that demands particular attention. I do not wish them to suffer for want of what may be thought necessary for their suport; but at the same time we should carefully guard against throwing flour into the hands of the enemy. If we are to credit the different accounts from New-York the army there is much straitened in this material article. This should lead us, therefore, to devise if possible a plan for liquidating our debts in such a manner as would not administer to their wants, and teach us the expediency and propriety of only sending in to our people a supply adequate to their subsistence, without paying any attention to the requests of individual officers. This is a subject at present of too much importance to be overlooked. I am Sir &c. &.

Df, in James McHenry's writing, DLC:GW; Varick transcript, DLC:GW.
1. The enclosed letter has not been identified.

## From the Board of War

Sir                                    War Office [Philadelphia] July 27th 1778

I have the Honour to enclose several Resolutions of Congress relative to two Expeditions intended to be undertaken against the Indians.[1] Had our Affairs permitted an earlier Attention to this Business or our Abilities in the Articles of supply enabled us sooner to proceed in it much Distress to the Inhabitants of the Frontiers would have been avoided. But as the principal Armies were our primary Objects it was impossible to procure the Means of prosecuting these Expeditions without interfering too much with more important Concerns. Your Excellency will percieve that the Views of Congress in one of the Enterprizes are narrowed by the present Plan, Detroit being originally in Contemplation but from our exhausted Situation in the Articles of Provisions Horses & other Necessaries & the Lateness of the Season the Attempt against this Place is laid aside. The Supplies however for the intended Expedition against that Place were in some Forwardness & will afford us an Oppertunity on the present smaller Scale to strike the Savages with Terror & overawe them into present Submission at least if not to prevent them by Destruction of the hostile Towns from doing us farther Mischief Every necessary Measure is taken for the forwarding the western Expedition & General McIntosh has Orders to march from Fort Pitt the first of September by which Time we have not the least Doubt all Things will be in Readiness.

As your Excellency now immediately commands the Northern Department it is necessary for the Board to correspond with you on the Subject of the Expedition into the Seneca Country which I am to desire in Persuance of the Resolutions of Congress may be forwarded with all possible Disspatch. This Expedition is not merely intended against the Senecas but against all such of the six Nations as are hostile. General Gates will inform you in what Forwardness the Bussiness of this Expedition now is. In his Letter to Congress of the 28th of June he mentions that he had "ordered Col. Bedel's Regiment to assemble at Albany the 1st of August & should have every thing there prepared to invade this Country" In his Letter of the 2d July he confirms the Idea of the Men being ready on the Day first mentioned but says that a Supply of Provisions depended upon Mr Commissary Cuyler suggesting too that the Expedition against the Senecas had better have been undertaken from Wioming,[2] but however proper this might have been, it is now impossible for a Variety of Reasons. General Gates had fixed upon Lieut. Col. Willett of Gaansevorts Regiment to command the Expedition. The Board concieve the highest Opinion of Col: Willetts Abilities but are of Opinion much Inconvenience & Disgust will arise from giving so extensive a Command to an Officer of his Rank: But leave this & all other Matters relative to this Expedition to your Excellency's Determination. General Schuyler is of Opinion that the Place of Rendezvous should be Fort Schuyler & thinks that the greater Part of Gaansevorts Regiment might go on the Expedition leaving Militia to garrison the Fort; if you should be of this Opinion & should order the Regiment Col. Willet will go with it & his Knowledge of the Country & military Talents would then be made use of altho he had not the superior Command. As your Excellency must have your Hands full of Bussiness the Board beg Leave to suggest to you the Propriety of appointing some active Officer to take the whole Management of all Things relating to the forwarding the Expedition as well in Ease of yourself as the more readily to facilitate the Wishes of Congress who are anxious that their Plan may be perfectly executed by the Proceedure of both Expeditions about the same Time which will effectually chastize distract & terrify the Savages. The Person you appoint may consult your Excellency on important Points & manage all lesser Concerns himself. I have the Honour to be with great Respect your very obed. Servt

> Richard Peters
> By Order of the Board

By the latest Advices from the Frontiers of this State we have the greatest Reason to believe the main Body under Butler after breaking up the Wioming Settlement are on their Way towards the Frontiers of New York carrying off their Prisoners & Plunder but they have left a Number of small Parties who are committing daily Ravages & the most savage Barbarities. Col. Brodhead is now at Munsey on the West Branch of Susquahanna protecting the Inhabitants in getting in their Harvest. Col. Hartley it is hoped is near him & will take his Place as Col. Brodhead must march to Fort Pitt & compose Part of the Troops under General McIntosh.[3] The enclosed Letter from Genl Schuyler contains a disagreeable Piece of Information unless Matters are in greater Forwardness than he seems to be acquainted with.[4]

ALS, DLC:GW.

1. Peters enclosed copies of resolutions of 11 June and 25 July. The former proposed an expedition "to reduce if practicable, the garrison of Detroit" and another "from the Mohock river to the Seneca Country in order to chastise that insolent & revengefull Nation." The latter "deferred" the expedition against Detroit in favor of the destruction of "such Towns of the Hostile tribes of Indians as . . . will most effectually tend to chastise & terrify the savages & to check their Ravages on the frontiers of these states" and directed that the Seneca expedition "be forwarded with all possible dispatch" (DLC:GW; see also *JCC*, 11:587–90, 720–22).

2. These letters are in DNA:PCC, item 154.

3. Col. Daniel Brodhead arrived in the township of Muncy in Northumberland (now Lycoming) County, Pennsylvania, by 20 July and remained there until early August. In August and September, Col. Thomas Hartley had Fort Muncy constructed in that area, north of the Muncy Hills near a sharp bend in the West Branch of the Susquehanna River, about three and a half miles north of the modern town of Muncy.

4. In the enclosed letter to Henry Laurens, dated 19 July, Maj. Gen. Philip Schuyler reported from Albany: "I believe it will be labour lost to hold any more Conferences with the Senecas, Cayngas And Onandagers until an Army is marched into their Country, the necessaty of which becomes daily more evident, and I was in hopes that preperations for the Enterprize, which Congress directed on the 11th ult. to be prosecuted from the Mohawks River would have been in considerable Forwardness by this time *but I cannot learn that any orders have been received in this quarter for the purpose, nor have I been favoured with a line from Genl Gates on the Subject.*

"I am very Sorry to find that the Indians who returned from Philadelphia were informed that Expeditions were to be carryed on from Fort Pitt & the Mohawk River, because if it is still the intention of Congress to prosecute them, some disadvantage may arise from the objects being known, & because as soon as Butler knows of it, he will hasten his march to Schoharie & the German Flatts, and destroy those places before any Troops can arive, and because if the Expedition should be laid aside it will induce the Indians to believe that we cannot spare any Men from the Sea-Coast and they will be the more encouraged to continue their Barbarous incursions on the destressed Frontier Inhabitants.

"On Wednesday last four Chiefs of the Oneidas and Tuscaroras arived here— They inform me that as all hopes of bringing the Cayngas & Senecas to peacable Sentiments are lost they are now ready to join our Arms & Assist us in punishing

them—I have sent a small Party of Oneidas by the Way of Schoharie to watch Butlers motions and directed others to remain in the neighbourhood of the German
Flatts and keep out Scouts from thence" (DLC:GW).

## To Captain Bartholomew von Heer

Sir.                                    Head Quarters White plains 27 July 1778
    Upon receiving this letter you are immediately to repair to camp to
the exercise of the duties of your office[1]—There is no useful purpose
answered that I know of by your absence, while the advantages of the
institution are in a great measure lost to the army.
    If you have procured cloathing for your corps, it may be directed to
be sent on after you. I am Sir your obt hble servt.

Df, in James McHenry's writing, DLC:GW; Varick transcript, DLC:GW.
    1. Heer had been appointed in June 1778 to command the new Marechaussée
Corps. He was apparently at Philadelphia making a representation to the Board of
War about difficulties in recruiting for the corps (see *JCC*, 11:729). A copy of the
resolution passed in response on 29 July is in DLC:GW.

## To Major General Lafayette

Dear Marquis.                        Head Quarters White plains 27th July 1778
    This will be delivered you by Major General Greene, whose thor-
ough knowlege of Rhode Island, of which he is a native, and the
influence he will have with the people, put it in his power to be particularly useful in the expedition against that place; as well in providing
necessaries for carrying it on, as in assisting to form and execute a plan
of operations proper for the occasion. The honor and interest of the
common cause are so deeply concerned in the success of this enterprise, that it appears to me of the greatest importance to omit no step
which may conduce to it, and General Greene on several accounts will
be able to render very essential services in the affair. These considerations have determined me to send him on the expedition, in which as
he could not with propriety act, nor be equally useful merely on his
official capacity of Quarter Master General, I have concluded to give
him a command in the troops to be employed in the descent. I have
therefore directed General Sullivan, to throw all the American troops
both Continental State and Militia into two divisions making an equal
distribution of each, to be under the immediate command of General
Greene and yourself.[1] The Continental troops being divided in this
manner to the Militia, will serve to give them confidence, and probably make them act better than they would alone. Though this arrange-

ment will diminish the number of Continental troops under you, yet this diminution will be more than compensated by the addition of militia; and I persu[a]de myself your command will not be less agreeable or less honorable, from this change in the disposition. I am with great esteem & affection Dear Marquis Your most Obedt servt.

Df, in Alexander Hamilton's writing, DLC:GW; Varick transcript, DLC:GW.
    1. See GW to John Sullivan, this date.

## To Colonel William Malcom

Sir                          Head Quarters [White Plains] [1] 27 July 1778
    I this morning recd yours of the 26th by Capt. Bicker.[2] I shall be glad to receive a perfect Return of the State of the Works, and what will be necessary for their completion, as soon as possible. In the mean time I shall lay the Commissary's return of provision before the Commy General and desire him to lay in what further supply may be necessary. The Qr Mr Genl has given orders to Colo. Hay respectg the supernumerary Waggons.[3] If the commanding Officers of the two Continental Regiments will make out Returns of the Cloathing wanting and will apply to the Cloathier at Fishkill, he will supply them, if he has the Articles. If he has not, he must immediately order them from Boston or from Philada.

    Colo. Kosciusko was left at the Fort as acting Engineer and I have always understood is fully competent to the Business, I do not therefore see why another is necessary.

    By the 12th Article of the 14th section of the Articles of War you are empowered to hold Garrison Courts Martial.[4] If any case occurs which affects life or the trial of a Commd Officer, I will, upon application, order a general Court Martial.

    I have no objection to the person you mention doing the duty of Major of Brigade. But I think the same person may very well perform both duties of Brigade Major and Adjt General, as the whole Garrison may be thrown into one Brigade.

    There certainly is reason in your demand of some thing extra for your Expences as Commandant of the Posts. I am therefore willing to allow you double your stated subsista⟨nce,⟩ but as this, if known, may be drawn into precedent where there is no right or real occasion, I would wish you to say nothing about the matter.

    I some time ago directed the German or Armands Regiment to be sent to Fort Arnold as the most proper place of security, they being chiefly deserters. But as the order has been neglected I now inclose a letter to Colo. Armand or the commanding Officer directing him to repair thither.[5] I cannot at present spare Grahams Regiment. A few days ago I sent up eight persons to Fort Arnold who were sent from Vermont.[6] If they could be confined in any other place, I think it would be more proper, as, if they are really inimical, they may make themselves masters of the state of the Garrison, Works &ca. If you can see Govr Clinton, you may consult him upon a proper place. I am &ca.

Df, in Tench Tilghman's writing, DLC:GW; Varick transcript, DLC:GW.

    1. Tilghman wrote, "Valley Forge."

    2. Walter Bicker (1747–1821), a son of Col. Henry Bicker, was appointed as a lieutenant and adjutant of the 3d Pennsylvania Regiment in January 1776. Captured at Fort Washington on 16 Nov. 1776, he was apparently exchanged by January 1777, when he was commissioned a captain in Col. John Patton's Additional Continental Regiment. Bicker was left out of the new arrangement when Patton's regiment was consolidated with Col. Thomas Hartley's Additional Continental Regiment in January 1779, but he was paid as a captain until April of that year.

    3. Tilghman inserted this sentence on the draft in place of his original sentence, which read: "I shall lay that part of your letter which respects the Waggons before the Qr Mr General and he may either discharge them or bring them down to the Army, as he thinks proper."

    4. For this article, see *JCC*, 5:802.

    5. The enclosed letter has not been found, and the previous order has not been identified.

    6. See GW to the commanding officer at West Point, 21 July.

## To Major General John Sullivan

Dr Sir                    Head Qrs white plains July 27th 1778

I have thought it expedient to permit General Greene to go to Rhode Island, to take a part in the Enterprize, intended against the Enemy in that Quarter. You know his merit and his services, as well as I do, and therefore I need not add on that head. When the Marquiss Fayette set out, I put Varnums & Glover's Brigades under his command, and, according to his instructions, they were to act in this manner. Upon a more mature consideration of the matter, I am convinced the success of the Enterprize will be more advanced, by disposing of the Continental Troops among the Militia. You will therefore make your arrangement in this way, and forming the whole of *our* force into Two Divisions, General Greene will take the direction of one—the Marquiss of the other—You yourself the general command of course. I have written to the Marquiss upon the subject.[1] Besides the service, which General Greene will be of, both in Council and in the Field, upon this very interesting and important occasion, his presence will contribute greatly to expedite your Operations by an earlier provision, it is probable, of many matters in the line of his Department.

There is one thing more, which I would mention. Most likely, there will be a debarkation of Troops from the Count D'Estaing's fleet, to assist in reducing the Island and the Enemy's force. These Troops, the Admiral may place under your general direction. His wish should be complied with, as to the particular command of them. I should suppose the Marquiss would be his choice. Success and Laurels attend you. I am Dr Sir with great regard & esteem Yr Most Obedt sert

Go: Washington

P.S. What I have said, respecting the command of the Count D'Estaings Troops is intirely a matter of incertainty. I do not know that he will in case of a debarkation, choose that they should be with our's—or under any Other than their Own Officers. Harmony & the best understanding between us, should be a Capital & first Object. The Count himself is a Land Officer and of the high rank of Lt General in the French Army.

Your Letters of the 20th & 22d were received on Saturday Evening.[2]

G. W——n.

LS, in Robert Hanson Harrison's writing, NNU-F: Richard Maass Collection; Df, DLC:GW; Varick transcript, DLC:GW.

1. See GW to Lafayette, this date.
2. Saturday fell on 25 July.

## From Major General John Sullivan

My Dear General                    Providence July 27 1778 10 of C. A:M:
    I have the pleasure to Inform you that we have already Collected a Magazine amply Sufficient for all possible Demands. The French Fleet has not yet arrived the Marquis will be in on the 29 as he writes me and we Shall be in perfect Readiness My numbers I trust will be Sufficient for the purpose if a few more old troops had been Sent on it might have been Better but Even as it is I have not a Doubt of Success I have now & I trust Shall have as many Boats as I could wish—your Excey Doubtless will among other Defects in my plan of operations Inclosed you perceive that I have Said nothing in case we find it impraticable to Carry the Redoubts by Storm[1] I beg Leave now to mention to your Excy That I had Thought of it from the beginning & have Gabions Faschines & Every thing in preparation for Establishing a post on the Island I have plenty of heavy artillery & Every kind of ammunition for them—I had also Collected all the Intrenching tools in this Quarter previous to my Receiving your Excy order of yesterday through Colo. Tilman immediately upon which I Sent off to Boston after more[2] your

Excellencey Shall be advised from time to time of Every proceedure here. And it will (if possible) Increase the obligations I already feel myself under to your Excellencey if you will be kind Enough to give me your Advice & Direction in the Several Situations I may possibly be in in the Course of the attempt I have the Honor to be Dear General your most Devoted Servant

Jno. Sullivan

ALS, DLC:GW.

1. Sullivan was referring to the plan of operations suggested in his letter to Vice Admiral d'Estaing of 25 July, enclosed in his letter to GW of 26 July (see note 3 to that letter).

2. The order has not been found. On 26 July, Sullivan sent Maj. Gen. William Heath a copy of "Genl Washington's Letter recommending to me the Necessity of collecting" entrenching tools and requested that Heath "forward a very considerable Number with all possible Despatch" (MHi: Heath Papers; see also Hammond, *Sullivan Papers*, 2:126).

## General Orders

Head-Quarters White Plains Tuesday July 28th 1778.
Parole Gerrard—                    C. Signs Great—Good.

The Commander in Chief desires that the Officers who did not compose part of the Grand Army last Winter and Spring and who may be unacquainted with the General Order relative to the duties of the Officers of the day as there pointed out will have recourse to one issued on the ninth day of June last at Valley-Forge and govern themselves thereby.

The Commander in Chief also begs leave to inform such Officers as may be unacquainted therewith that it is His Wish and Desire that the Field Officers of the day when they are relieved from their tour of duty would dine with him at Head-Quarters, and where there is no particular Reason to prevent it he would take it as a favor from them to be punctual, as it enables him to invite Company accordingly.

The Inspector and Brigade Major of the day are meant to be included in this Invitation, and the General further requests that the Chaplains would also dine with him in turn each coming with his Brigadier when of the day.

Varick transcript, DLC:GW. Maj. Gen. Benjamin Lincoln's orderly book for this date includes additional orders: "Major [Peter] Fell [of the Dutchess County militia] to take command of the three days-detachment," and "The men ordered to go in detachment tomorrow are to be furnished with three days provisions this afternoon; one half salt if it can be procured" (MHi: Lincoln Papers; see also "Chambers Orderly Book," 289).

## To John Brown

Sir                    Head Quarters White plains 28 July 1778

I had, a few days ago, the pleasure of receiving yours of the 9th instant. The Butt of Wine has not yet arrived, but I doubt not, when it does, that it will answer your recommendation. Permit me to return you my thanks for the generosity of your present, and to express my wishes, that Fortune may continue to be as indulgent to you as she has hitherto been. I am &c.

Df, in Tench Tilghman's writing, DLC:GW; Varick transcript, DLC:GW.

## From Major General Lafayette

                                        lime over Say brook ferry [Conn.]
dear General                                   the 28 july 1778

I take the opportunity of an express going from General Sullivan to your Excellency for to let you know how far we are advanc'd and in which situation is the detachement you have intrusted to my Care—I am here with General glover's brigade, and we have all cross'd the River—I hope we schall be at coventry the 31st of the present—General Varnum and his officers having Represented to me that on account of the Scarcity of flour, but principally on account of the ferrys which are very frequent and troublesome, it was much better to take the upper Road, I have had no objection to his going that way because he knows the Roads and theyr advantages much better than I do in this part of the Continent—it is true to Say that had we been together, we would have lost at least two days—our men are in good spirits, not much tired for making Such a march, and will not want a long Rest to be fit for action. if the men were too much fatigu'd to morrow I could halt one day at new london, because I do'nt believe General Varnum may be at *Coventry* before the 1st of next month—I have Sent to day to General Sullivan in order of knowing his directions when I'll arrive at Coventry which is 18 miles from providence.[1]

I am very uneasy on account of Clel hamilton as I understand he was not yet arriv'd a few days ago—I hope some of the gentlemen of your family will be so kind as to let me know if they have heard from him.[2]

it Seems to me that the british have a good mind to defend theyr ground, and I hope we will have a very interesting work to perform—with the highest respect, and most tender affection I have the honor to be My dear General Your most obedient Servant

                                        the Marquis de lafayette

I beg leave to present my compliments to your *family*.

ALS, MWA: U.S. Revolution Collection. Where Lafayette edited this letter after the war, the original has been restored as much as possible.

1. For Lafayette's letter of this date to Maj. Gen. John Sullivan, see *Lafayette Papers*, 2:119–20.

2. Col. Alexander Hamilton had returned to GW's headquarters from his mission to Vice Admiral d'Estaing by 26 July.

## To Henry Laurens

Sir                                    Head Qrs White plains July 28: 1778

This will be presented to Congress by Genl Putnam. He arrived from Connecticut the day after I came into the Neighbourhood of this Camp. As I have not received any Resolution of Congress, respecting the Court of Inquiry, which they directed and which was transmitted them, on the subject of the posts in the Highlands, taken last year, I am at a loss in what point of view to consider him. He wishes some decision in this instance, and his journey to philadelphia is for the purpose.[1] I have the Honor to be with great respect & esteem Sir Your Most Obedt servt

Go: Washington

LS, in Robert Hanson Harrison's writing, DNA:PCC, item 152; Df, DLC:GW; copy, DNA:PCC, item 169; Varick transcript, DLC:GW. The LS is docketed in part: "Read 4 Aug. 1778 Referred to Mr Hosmer Mr R. H. Lee Mr Scudder"; see *JCC*, 11:743.

1. For GW's transmission of the court of inquiry proceedings, see his third letter to Laurens of 18 June. For Congress's action, see Laurens to GW, 20 August.

## To Lieutenant Colonel John Laurens

My dear Sir                    Head Quarters White plains 28th July 1778

I recd yours from Lebanon and that from Point Judith.[1] You have my warmest thanks for the great expedition of your Journey and for your exertions since your arrival at Rhode Island. I anxiously wait an account of the Admirals arrival, and of the effect which the appearance of the Fleet had. I wish you success and safety as I am My dear Sir sincerely and Affecty Yrs

Go: Washington

LS (photocopy), in Tench Tilghman's writing, DLC:GW, series 9. GW signed the cover of the LS.

1. See Laurens to GW, 23 and 25 July.

## From Richard Peters

Sir                              War Office [Philadelphia] July 28th 1778
    Col. Nicola complains that altho' his Corps might be exceedingly
useful in Garrison were he enabled by its Numbers to turn out sufficient Guards yet from the great Inattention of the Officers commanding Regiments or Corps in Camp who repeatedly give Discharges from
the Service to Men very capable of Duty in the Invalid Regiment his
Number is now very small. I am therefore to request your Excellency
will be pleased to remind the Officers under your Command of the
Regulations on which Col. Nicola's Corps is established[1] & to direct
them to assist in encreasing its Numbers not only by not discharging
Men fit for Garrison Duty but by taking proper Measures to have them
conveyed to Philada there to join the invalid Regiment.[2] Officers at
Hospitals should be particularly attentive to this Matter. I have the Honour to be with great Respect Your very obedt Servt

                                                    Richard Peters

If Col. Nicola's Regiment was full there would be no Necessity of detaining Troops in this Town for Garrison Duty who are capable of doing Service in the Field.

ALS, DLC:GW.
    1. Peters was probably referring to Congress's resolution of 26 Aug. 1776 (*JCC*,
5:705).
    2. GW addressed this issue in the general orders of 4 August.

## From Major General Philip Schuyler

Dear Sir                              Albany July 28th 1778
    On the 26th I was honored with your Excellency's Favor of the 22d
Instant. When I did myself the Honor to write you last[1] I beleived that
you might have been informed of the Resolutions of Congress of the
11th Ultimo directing an Expedition to be prosecuted against the
Senecas—As you was not advised of it when your Letter was written I
take the Liberty to inclose you Copy of the Resolution.[2] But as it seems
impracticable, at this important Crisis to carry it on I shall embrace the
Opportunity of going to Peek's Kill to take my Trial and propose to
render myself there in the Course of next Week. Be pleased to accept
my best Wishes & Assurances that I am with the greatest Respect and
Esteem Your Excellency's most obedient humble Servt

                                                    Ph: Schuyler

LS, in the writing of John Lansing, Jr., DLC:GW. Tench Tilghman docketed the letter in part, "Recd 9th Augt."

1. See Schuyler to GW, 16 July.

2. The enclosed copy of the resolutions of 11 June, signed by Schuyler's secretary John Lansing, Jr., is in DLC:GW (see also *JCC*, 11:588–90).


## To Major General John Sullivan

Dr Sir                                        Head Qrs White plains July 28th 177⟨8⟩

I was this morning favoured with your Two Letters of the 24 & 26th Instant with the papers to which they referred.

I am exceedingly happy to find, that your efforts to prepare for the intended enterprize ag⟨ai⟩nst the Enemy, had succeeded so well—and that ⟨things in⟩ general were in so promising a train.

With respect to the Enemy's force in y⟨our⟩ Quarter, I think your Estimate must be far too large. In your Letter of the 24th you say it amounts to 3717 before General Brown's arriv⟨al.⟩ Supposing this to have been the case, which is ma⟨king⟩ it as great, as I conceive it could be, the only reinf⟨orce⟩ment, which I have been able to learn, has go⟨ne⟩ from New York did not exceed 14 or 1500 at the ⟨outside⟩, upon a very liberal allowance for the strength ⟨of⟩ the Corps. It is a good and a safe way to coun⟨t⟩ sufficiently upon the Enemy's force, because, acc⟨ording⟩ to this we should always provide and act; howev⟨er,⟩ by fixing it too high, it may injure, by exciting ⟨in⟩ the Troops if it should come to their knowledge, a spirit of diffidence & distrust—the contrary of whic⟨h⟩, you know, is essential to success. By a Letter fr⟨om⟩ Govr Trumbull of the 25th he mentions, you had sta⟨ted⟩ it at 7000 & that in a day or two, it would be 11,000. This, perhaps, you might immagine would give your requisition for men a more vigorous & successful efficacy.

With regard to the plan of operation, whi⟨ch⟩ you submitted to the Admiral, my want of a more precise knowledge, than what I have, in a variety o⟨f⟩ facts and circu⟨ms⟩t⟨an⟩ces⟨,⟩ will not permit me to deci⟨de⟩ upon it; but it appears to me, there are many useful and interesting hints in it, and such as I hope and am persuaded, are founded in consideration and an investigation of the matter. The cutting off the three Regiments on Connanicut & preventing further Reinforcements are great and important Objects, if they can be effected. General Greene set ⟨out this⟩ morning in order to join you and will arrive, I expect, by the time this reaches you. The fleet sailed from the Road off Sandy Hook, on Tuesday morning,[1] and I should suppose are now with you. I have only to repeat my warmest wishes for your success, and assurances that I am, with great esteem & regard Dr Sir Your Most Obedt servt

Go: Washington

⟨P.⟩S. From very good ⟨inf⟩ormation I have reason ⟨to⟩ believe that the late Re-in⟨forc⟩ement sent to Rhode Island ⟨does⟩ not exceed 1200 Men.

Go: W——n

LS, in Robert Hanson Harrison's writing, NhHi: Sullivan Papers; Df, DLC:GW; Varick transcript, DLC:GW. The postscript of the LS is in GW's writing, and the draft and transcript lack the postscript. Where the LS is damaged, the characters in angle brackets have been supplied after consulting the draft.

1. The previous Tuesday was 21 July.


## To Jonathan Trumbull, Sr.

Sir            Head Quarters White Plains 28th July 1778

I was this morning honored with yours of the 25th. I think you need be under no apprehensions for the safety of your Coast, while the Count D'Estaings Squadron lays off the harbour of New port, as the Enemy will have sufficient upon their hands to prevent their carrying on a predatory War—I took the Liberty of suggesting to the Count, the advantage of sending a Ship of force down the Sound, to prevent the Enemy from reinforcing thro' Hell-Gate;[1] but whether he will incline to divide his Fleet in that manner, I cannot say.

I am well aware of the inconveniency of drawing out the Militia at this time, but I am in hopes that the importance of the object, and I think I may say, the moral certainty of Success, if the enterprize is supported with spirit, will outweigh every other consideration. Besides, the time of service will probably be but short, as the expedition will either be immediately determined in our favour, or must be laid aside.[2]

It is impossible for me to spare larger detachments from this Army, than I have already done, as the Enemy in and about New-York are superior in force to our main Body. Should they reinforce Rhode Island, I shall do so of course.

I sincerely condole with you on the death of your worthy Son Colo. Joseph Trumbull, whose exertions in the Cause of his Country, while he continued in a public character, will reflect honor upon his memory; and for whom, when living, I entertained a most cordial regard. I am, with the greatest Esteem Sir your most Obedient hble Servt

Go. Washington

LB, Ct: Trumbull Papers; Df, DLC:GW; Varick transcript, DLC:GW.

1. See GW to Vice Admiral d'Estaing, 22 July, and note 2 to that document.

2. This letter was among several considered by the Connecticut council of safety on 1 Aug., when they approved a proclamation calling out additional troops for the Rhode Island expedition (see *Conn. Public Records*, 2:104–6).

## General Orders

Head-Quarters White-Plains Wednesday July 29th 78.
Parole Netherlands—                           C. Signs Nantz Natick.

The Regimental Quarter Masters are to be pointedly exact in having Vaults sunk for necessaries and see that they are regularly covered every morning; They are also to pay strict attention to the Cleanliness of the Camp, seeing that all Offal, putrid flesh and bones are buried. Altho' this is the particular duty of the Quarter Masters it is expected that the Commanding Officers of Corps will know that the duty is performed, as the sweetness of a Camp and the health of the men depend upon it.

Particular attention agreeable to former orders[1] is to be paid to the slaughtering Pens that no offensive smell may proceed from them.

Coll Baldwin is appointed by the Quarter Mastr General to the command and superintendency of the Artificers belonging to the Army.

All Officers commanding Companies of Artificers are therefore to make return to him forthwith of the number of men in their respective Companies, and for the future to make such weekly and other returns to him as he shall direct.

In the monthly returns which are to be brought in to the Orderly-Office next saturday (and hereafter the last saturday of every month) particular attention must be paid to insert the monthly Alterations regimentally, distinguishing between those discharged by the Muster Master General or Surgeons and those whose terms of service are expired.

Varick transcript, DLC:GW.
1. See General Orders, 3 July.


## From Colonel Stephen Moylan

Dear Sir                              Hackensac [N.J.] 29th July 1778

I had the honor to inform your Excellency by Mr Lott, that I intended coming with the Cavalry to this neighborhood,[1] on my arrival I reconoitred the country and found a great majority disaffected, and taking every oppertunity of Supplying the enemy, yesterday I Sent a party of 80 horse to Bergen, with orders to drive up what Catle they Coud Collect, from that town, to the point,[2] which they have effected by bringing with them near 300 head of horned Cattle 60 sheep Some horses mares & Colts, many of the first are milck Cows, and tho its certain that the milck & butter is for the chief part Sent to Newyork from that Quarter, there appears a great degree of cruelty in taking from a number of famillys, perhaps their only Support, I am teased by the women, and with difficulty can prevail on my feelings, to Suspend my giving to them their Cows, until I have your Excellencys opinion and orders on this Subject—this manœvre has alarmed the City, Powles Hook & the encampment on Staten Island the Fort was mand, So was the Redout at Powleshook, and the army at Staten Island turned out, to the amount, as near as Coud be judged by Major Clough (who Commanded the party) of 3000, tho their encampment woud promise 5000.

I have just Come in from Fort Lee, the heights from Harlem up to Kingsbridge are interspersd with Tents the chief encampment on york Island Seems to me to be at Fort Washington, those immediatly about the Fort are Hessians, there is a pretty large encampment on your Side of Spiten Devil Creek—and a redout with a magazine in its center— one ship pretty near on a line with Col. Morris⟨s⟩ house, another with three small craft near the entrance of the abovementiond Creek, are all the vessels in the North river that I Coud discover At 12 ôClock this day—a report prevails of a French & Spanish fleet being at the Hook, it is believd at Bergen, which your Excellency knows is but four Miles from Newyork. I have the honor to be with great affection Dear Sir Your most obligd H. St

Stephen Moylan

a party Supposed to be of Horse past Fort Washington towards Kingsbridge yesterday morning from Newyork—our Horses fare well, and will I hope be in good order, when your Excellency will please to Command us, I think one weekes rest, will make them fit for any thing—the Sooner I have your Excellencys orders, the more pleasure it will give Your assd H. St

S. M.

ALS, DLC:GW. Moylan's signed note on the cover of this letter reads: "Let the Dragoon who is bearer hereof pass the ferry."

1. Moylan was referring to his letter to GW of 26 July (see GW to Moylan, 25 July, n.1).

2. Bergen Point, at the tip of the peninsula south of Bergen, N.J., is north of Staten Island. British engineer James Montresor noted in his journal for 28 July: "About 100 Rebel Light Horse drove off Cattle from Bergen Neck" (Scull, *Montresor Journals*, 507).

# From Brigadier General John Stark

Dear Sir                          Head Quarters Albany July 29th 1778
the fourth Pensylvenia Regt and a Detatchm. of the Rifle Corps Arrived here 27th Inst. but in a very deplorable Condition for want of Cloaths—I Inclose you a Return of what is Wanted by them for the

present and without which they will not be fit for Scouting which seems to be the duty they were sent for—[1] Nevertheless I shall send them to the Frontiers Immediately to protect the Affrigted Inhabitants and whose fears are too well Grounded.

I think we Never shall have peace in the Western Frontiers untill we march an Army into the Indian Country and drive those Nefarious Wretches from their Habitations Burn their Towns and Destroy their Crops & make proclemation that if Ever they Return they shall be serverd in Like manner.

I have nothing from Fort Schuyler of Late from that I Judge they are in peace—I send this by Lieut. Randolph an officer from Colo. Butlers Regt who will wait for the Cloathing and Answer. I am Sir with Great Respect your Hunbl. Serv.

John Stark

LS, DLC:GW.
 1. The enclosed return has not been identified.

*Letter not found*: from Lund Washington, 29 July 1778. On 15 Aug., GW wrote Lund Washington: "Your Letter of the 29th Ulto, Inclosing a line from Captn Marshall to you came to my hands yesterday."

## General Orders

Head-Quarters W. Plains Thursday July 30th 1778.
Parole Palmyra—                                    C. Signs Pitt Plymouth.
The Guard at Terrytown is to be reinforced with a Captain 2 Subalterns, 3 Serjeants 3 Corporals a Drummer and Fifer and fifty five Privates and to be commanded by a Field officer.

The Guard at Burtisses[1] is to be reinforced by a Serjeant, Corporal Drum and Fife and thirteen Privates and to be commanded by a Captain; and the Guard at Saw-Mill River Bridge is to be reinforced by a Captain 2 Subalterns—3 Serjeants 3 Corporals and 40 Privates and be commanded by a Field Officer; From this Guard a Subaltern Serjeant and twenty Rank & File is to be detached to Pugsley's[2]—A detachment of Artillery to be sent to Terry-town.

The Field Officers in performing their rounds are to examine whether the Guards upon the Communication between Dobbs's-Ferry and Maroneck can afford a Chain of Centinels; if not they are to direct the Patroles to pass at such times and in such a manner as to secure the communication perfectly.

One Light Dragoon is to be at each of the following Guards 'till Coll Moylan arrives, after which two are to be placed to each; namely Terrytown, Dobbs's-Ferry, Saw-Mill River Bridge, Pugsley's, Appleby's,[3] Burtiss's, Tomkins's 2 Miles, Cornell's and Maroneck; The horse guard at Pugsley's may be withdrawn and aid in this service.

The Dragoons attending these Piquets are to keep their horses constantly saddled by night and ready to mount at a moments warning; In the day they may graze.

After Orders July 30th—

Captain Smith late Inspector in Genl Varnum's Brigade is appointed to do that duty in General Parson's Brigade and is to be respected accordingly.[4]

Varick transcript, DLC:GW.

1. The orders are probably referring to the estate of William Burtis, Sr. (died c.1778), a Loyalist who lived near the junction of the Tuckahoe Road and the road from White Plains to Dobbs Ferry. After his death, his family fled to the British lines in 1778, and his son William Burtis, Jr. (1760–1835), became active as a British spy.

2. The orders are probably referring to the house of David Pugsley (1737–1805), who lived west of Sprain Brook on the road between White Plains and Dobbs Ferry, about two and a half miles east of the ferry.

3. This probably refers to the house of Joseph Appleby (1732–1791), about three and a half miles from Dobbs Ferry on the road from the ferry to White Plains. GW used the house as a headquarters in July 1781.

4. In Maj. Gen. Benjamin Lincoln's orderly book, an additional order appears at this point: "Major General Gates will take command of a detachment which is to be paraded at 5 o'clock tomorrow P.M., furnished with three days provisions, & 40 rounds pr man. Brigr Genls for the detachment—Clinton & Wayne—Field Officers Col. Meiggs, Col. Patton, Col. Gibson, Lieut. Col. Symes, Lieut. Col. Reid, Lieut. Col. Hay, Lieut. Col. Mead, Majors Oliver, Talbot, Johnson, & Merryweather" (MHi: Lincoln Papers; see also orderly book of Jedediah Huntington's brigade, NHi, and Artillery Brigade orderly book, NHi).

## From Major General Benedict Arnold

Dear General                                   Philada July 30th 1778

I have this minute the honor receiving your Excellencys favour of 27th Inst. Colonel Hartleys Regt was ordered by Congress from this City the 14th Inst. to the Frontiers of this State,[1] except a Party of Sixty Men who, Guarded a Number Prisoners to Elizabeth Town, & were afterwards Ordered to East Town—Inclosed is a return of the Troops in Town who are barely sufficient to do the Garrison Duty, & most of them sickly & in want of Arms, & Cloathg.[2] a Detacht of Twenty Men of Glovers Brigade, March to'morrow Morning with a Number Prisoners to Elisabeth Town, & are ordered to Join their Brigade as soon as posible. Inclosed is a List of Officers who were in Town the 25th Also, a General Order of the 22th & 25th Inst.[3] no Officers are remaining in Town except the Supernumeries, respecting whom I wish to know your Excellencys pleasure—None of the Virginia Troops have ben detained here a moment—and all who Arive shall be Sent on with the greatest Expedition.

I heartily wish your Excellency a succesfull Campaign, and am with great Respect & Esteem Your Excellencys most Obedt Humble Servt

B. Arnold

ALS, DLC:GW.

1. On 14 July, Congress directed the Board of War, "in conjunction with the supreme executive council of Pensylvania, to take the most speedy and practicable measures for repelling the present irruption of the Indians, and for protecting the continental magazine at Carlisle" (*JCC*, 11:688). The board and the council met at Arnold's quarters, and by 15 July, Hartley's Regiment had been made a part of the council's arrangement for frontier defense (*Pa. Archives*, 6:643–45).

2. Lewis Nicola's return of the troops quartered at Philadelphia, dated 29 July, accounted for 420 men, 318 of whom were rank and file (DLC:GW).

3. On 22 July, Arnold had directed: "The Town Major is Ordered to make particular Inquirry for all Officers of the Army who Arive in Town, & those whose Furloughs are Out or who have absented themselves from the Army without leave are to be reported to Head Quarters." On 25 July, Town Major Nicola listed the twenty-three officers who had reported to him, with the regiments and justifications for each, and Arnold issued an additional order: "The General is much surprised to find so great a Number of Officers in Town at a time when their Services are so essential in the Army, and when a General Action with the Enemy may be daily Expected—Those Officers who do not belong to the Garrison, supernumeries, and such as have leave of Absence from his Excellency G. Washington excepted, Are Ordered immediately to Join the respective Corps to which they belong" (all documents, DLC:GW).

## From Henry Laurens

Sir,                                                        Philadelphia 30th July 1778.

I have had the honor since my last under the [     ] Inst.[1] of presenting Your Excellency's Letter of 22d to Congress, whence it was committed to the Board of War & I received no order except to Issue a Commission for Capt. Caleb Gibbes to rank Major in the service of the United States. I shall transmit the Act of Congress upon that occasion to Major Gibbs & under the present Cover Your Excellency will receive the Commission.[2]

the 15th Inst. I signed by order a Brevet to the Marquis de Vienne Certifying his Rank, Colonel in the Army. Another Brevet is ordered for Monsr Noirmont Lanuville to Rank Major from the date of his appointment as Aid de Camp to Gen. Conway 28th Jany 1778—and another the 29th Inst. to Monsr Francis Joseph Smith to rank Ensign.[3] I have the honor to be with the highest Esteem & Regard Sir Your Excellency's Most Obedient & humble servant

Henry Laurens.
President of Congress.

ALS, DLC:GW; LB, DNA:PCC, item 13. A note on the letter-book copy indicates that this letter was carried "by [Richard] Ross."

1. Laurens's most recent letter to GW was dated 18 July.

2. For the resolution of 29 July, promoting Gibbs to major, see *JCC*, 11:730. The enclosed commission has not been identified.

3. For discussion of the brevet given to Louis-Pierre, marquis de Vienne, see Board of War to GW, 17 July, and note 1 to that document. The Board of War had agreed on 18 May to recommend to Congress that René-Hippolyte Penot Lombart de Noirmont de La Neuville be appointed a brevet major, but action was postponed at that time. The resolution giving him that rank was passed on 29 July (ibid., 11:508, 729). Smith had "requested a commission to be made use of in case of his being made prisoner while serving as a volunteer in the American army," and on 29 July, Congress resolved to give him the brevet commission (ibid., 11:730). He settled in Pennsylvania after the war.

## To Ensign James Lovell, Jr.

Sir                                          [White Plains, 30 July 1778]

The recruits under your command belonging to Colo. Lee's Regiment, who were either Prisoners or Deserters from the Enemy, you will immediately deliver to Colo. Malcom at West Point, who will until further orders put them to such employment as he thinks fit. Given &c. 30 July 78.

Copy                                                        G.W.

Df, in Richard Kidder Meade's writing, DLC:GW; Varick transcript, DLC:GW. James Lovell, Jr. (1758–1850), a son of Massachusetts delegate to Congress James Lovell, Sr., was commissioned an ensign in Col. William Raymond Lee's Additional Continental Regiment in May 1777 and became the regimental adjutant in May 1778. He remained with the regiment, which was consolidated into Col. Henry Jackson's Additional Continental Regiment in April 1779, until March 1780, when he joined Maj. Henry Lee's Legionary Corps, serving there as cornet and adjutant to the end of the war.

## From Colonel William Malcom

Sir                                      Westpoint [N.Y.]. July 30 1778

I have the Honor to Inclose herewith the Returns of this Garrison.[1]

your Excellency will perceive that when we add to the detail of Batterys & redoubts, those on the East side of the River, where there are six Cannon already mounted, that I have but one Artillerst to a Gun.

Capt. Brown's Company, and the detatchments of Bay dfts, called greaton's are Station'd at Fort Constitution—When Armant's Regt arrives, McLelan shall relieve the latter, and they shall be sent to Camp.[2]

The Estimate contain'd in my last will turn out vastly short, I have examined the different Works Since I had the Honor to write to your Excellency and find that there are several very important ones omitted in that Calculation.[3]

There are Two brass cannon (one a 12 pd) in Putnams Redoubt, I propoze to Substitute an Iron Gun. of the same Size, and if your Excellency pleases it may be orderd to Your park or FishKill as in our present condition I really think it too Valuable to risque in an out work.

Your Excellency may depend that the Troops shall be Kept to duty and every thing done to put the post in a respectable State.

The Out works are so many distinct Forts—they may support each other but in case of an attack—cannot reinforce—I remark this that your Excellency may callculate the Garrison Accordingly.

I presume again to request the Service of Mr Lawren[c]e, every day convinces me of the necessity of such an appointment[4]—and when I inform Your Excellency, that the Troops are encamp'd on the Groun[d][5] where they work—remote from each other—one party aCross the River—that we are oblidg'd to parade them ourselves every morning when they turn out to Work—& to be about amongst them through the day—besides a Variety of [Revu] & other bussiness. I hope your Excellency will consent.

The Tory prisoners appear to be decent people—I have them and some others of the same Kind at Work by themselves—& think there is no danger—I shall consult the Governor about them as your Excelly directs.[6]

Inclosed is the proceedings of a Garrison Court Martial[7]—I wish Mr Tilghman woud Send me a Copy of the Articles of war, and the Late Act of Congress concerning Rations—I give 1¼ lb. of beef & the same Quantity of flour.[8]

There are a World of Artifficers employd from New Windsor to Kings ferry—I believe to little Account—unless to the projectors—I cou'd Wish your Excellency would be pleased to order proper Engineers and Mr Erskine, to View their work & to report to your Excellency—I imagine thereby the public money would be saved & we shoud get 150 good men at this far more important Service. I Have the Honor to be with great Respect May it please your Excellency Your Excellencys Most obedient and very Humble Servt

W. Malcom

ALS, DLC:GW.

1. GW's secretary Robert Hanson Harrison wrote on the last page of this letter, "return delivd Colo. Scammell," and the enclosure has not been identified. However, it was apparently a duplicate of the "Return of the Garrison at West Point, Commanded by Col. William Malcom," dated 25 July, that Malcom transmitted to Congress on 1 Aug. (DNA:PCC, item 78).

2. Jonathan Brown of Connecticut was commissioned a captain of the 1st Continental Artillery in January 1777 and resigned in September 1779. Samuel McClellan (1730–1807) of Woodstock, Conn., who had been a lieutenant in the French and Indian War and a captain in the Lexington Alarm, was appointed a major in the 11th Regiment of Connecticut militia in October 1775 and promoted to lieutenant colonel in December 1776. On 13 Aug. 1777, the general assembly appointed him colonel of a volunteer regiment being raised to serve in the northern department. McClellan was promoted to colonel of the 11th Regiment in January 1779 and was appointed a brigadier general of militia in May 1784. McClellan also represented Woodstock in the Connecticut general assembly, 1776–78.

3. See Malcom to GW, 26 July.

4. Malcom was referring to Jonathan Lawrence, Jr. (1759–1802), who had been commissioned a second lieutenant in Malcom's Additional Continental Regiment in March 1777. He was appointed an assistant adjutant general at West Point in August 1778 and served in that capacity to the end of the year. Lawrence, who was promoted to first lieutenant in October 1778, became a supernumerary officer in April 1779. In January 1780 he was commissioned a captain of the miners and sappers, a position he held until resigning from the army for reasons of health in November 1782.

5. Malcom wrote "Groung."

6. See GW to Malcom, 27 July.

7. The enclosed proceedings of a court-martial held on "Tuesday Morning" [28 July] recorded the trials for desertion of privates Christopher Springsteel of Malcom's Additional Continental Regiment and Michael Camel of Patton's Additional Continental Regiment (DLC:GW).

8. Congress had not revised the ration it specified in a resolution of 4 Nov. 1775, which included one pound of beef and one pound of flour per day (*JCC*, 3:322). However, GW's general orders of 16 April 1778 had directed a ration of a pound and a half of flour and a pound of beef.

## To Colonel Stephen Moylan

Dear Sir          Head Quarters White plains 30th July 1778

I recd yours of Yesterday by your Dragoon. I approve of the step you took to drive off the Stock from Bergen, but if it appears to you that the families will be distressed by keeping their milch Cattle, you have liberty to restore them to such persons and in such numbers as you think proper.

I desire you will, upon the rect of this, come over with all the Cavalry except about twenty four, who are to act in concert with the detatchment of foot. If that number appears too few, you may increase it to any as far as fifty. Colo. Sincoe told Capt. Sargent (who went down with a flag yesterday) that Admiral Byron was arrived.[1] Be pleased to endeavour to find out the truth of this. I am &c.

P.S. leave orders with your Officer to keep a good look out from Fort Lee and if he perceives any extraordinary Movement to make report to me.

Df, in Tench Tilghman's writing, DLC:GW; Varick transcript, DLC:GW.

1. John Graves Simcoe (1752–1806) entered the British army as an ensign in 1771 and had risen to captain by 1777, when he was nominated a major commanding a new provincial corps, the Queen's Rangers. He received a local rank of lieutenant colonel in June 1778. He served in America until December 1781, by which time he had become a colonel in the army. Simcoe, who was appointed lieutenant governor of Upper Canada in 1791, subsequently rose to major general in 1794 and lieutenant general in 1798. John Byron (1723–1786), who was appointed a midshipman in 1740, became a captain in 1746, a rear admiral in 1775, and a vice admiral on 29 Jan. 1778. His fleet sailed from England on 9 June but had been scattered by storms. On this date the *Cornwall* became the first of the fleet to arrive off New York (see "Journals of Henry Duncan," 160; Scull, *Montresor Journals*, 507; *Kemble Papers*, 1:158; Gruber, *Peebles' American War*, 205). Byron himself landed at Halifax, Nova Scotia, and the fleet was not collected at New York until late September.

## General Orders

Head-Quarters White-Plains Friday July 31st 1778.
Parole Ringwood—                    C.Signs Rye Raymond—
At a General Court Martial of the 2nd Line July 22nd 1778—Coll George Gibson President, John Jenkins Zechariah Ward, Richard Burk, Michael Carmer William McConklin of the 6th Maryland Regiment and Nicholas Fitzgerald of the 7th Maryland Regiment were tried for desertion and attempting to get to the Enemy, all found guilty and unanimously sentenced to suffer Death.[1]

Also John Daily of the 7th Maryland Regiment tried for desertion, found guilty and sentenced to receive one hundred lashes on his bare back well laid on.[2]

At the same Court July 23rd Solomon Lyons of the 2nd Virginia Regiment was tried for desertion, found guilty and unanimously sentenced to suffer Death—Likewise David McClemens of the Delaware Regiment was tried for the same Crime and acquitted.[3]

His Excellency the Commander in Chief approves the aforegoing sentences; The Sentence against John Dailey to be put in Execution tomorrow morning 6 ôClock at the head of the Regiment to which he belongs—David McClemens to be immediately released from confinement.

Varick transcript, DLC:GW.

GW's aide-de-camp Tench Tilghman wrote Col. Peter Gansevoort on this date: "By order of His Excellency I am to desire you will furnish the Wife and four Children of Nicholas Jordan employed as an interpreter to the Indians with one Ration each for two Months from the time this reaches you. It will be afterwards continued if Jordan is detained from his family. The enclosed Bill of thirty dollars is sent by him to his Wife, to whom be pleased to have it delivered" (ADf, DLC:GW).

1. John Jenkins was a private in Lt. Nathan Williams's company of the 6th Maryland Regiment. Zachariah Ward, who enlisted in the 6th Maryland Regiment in May 1778, was discharged in January 1779 with a notation that he had deserted, and Richard Birk, who likewise enlisted in May 1778, was discharged in December 1779, deserted. "Carmer," who appears as "Carmen" or "Corman" in subsequent orders of 14 and 21 Aug. and on this date in other orderly books (Christopher Meng orderly book, NN; *N.C. State Records*, 12:518; *Pa. Archives*, 2d ser., 11:293), may have been Michael Kernan, a private who enlisted in May 1778 and was discharged in August 1780 with the notation "missing." "McConklin" was probably William McLaughlin (McGloughlan), a private who enlisted in May 1778 and was discharged in June 1779 with a note that he had deserted. The orders of 14 and 21 Aug. refer to William McLaughlin, and some orderly books use that name on this date. Nicholas Fitzgerald (c.1757–1821) enlisted in the 7th Maryland Regiment in May 1778 and served until May 1781, when his term expired. In 1820 he resided in Washington County, Maryland.

2. The muster rolls of the 7th Maryland Regiment list two privates named John Dailey, both whom were recorded as deserters. One enlisted in September 1777 and was discharged in July 1780; the other enlisted in May 1778 and was discharged in May 1780.

3. David McClemmons, a private in Capt. John Patten's company of the Delaware Regiment, was recorded as having deserted in the first half of 1777. Solomon Lynes, who enlisted as a private in the 2d Virginia Regiment in September 1777, deserted on 31 Nov. 1777 and was retaken on 30 June 1778. He was pardoned and served with the regiment until at least March 1779.

## From John Beatty

Sir                                Prince Town [N.J.] July 31st 1778

I am now to acknowledge the receipt of your Favor of the 27th Instant which has just come to hand and am to Inform you, that I have already complied with part of the Instructions therein contained: In a Letter from the Marine Committe of Congress, I was Authorized to Inform Admiral Gambier that his proposition relative to the Exchange of Marine Prisoners was Acceeded to by Congress—binding themselves to return a like number in our possession with as little delay as possible—I have wrote to Admiral Gambier Yesterday acquainting him that I shall attend at Elizabeth-Town Tomorrow there to receive and give him Credit for whatever number of Prisoners he shall deliver over—Pledging the Public Faith of these States for an equal return.[1] in my Answer to the Committe I informed them of my having no particular instructions respecting Marines, mentioning particularly the case of the French men. I now wait their Orders on that head.[2]

I am just returned from Philadelphia where I have in as pointed a manner as I was capable of laid before Congress the distressed Situation of their Prisoners, representing at the same time the Accounts al-

ready contracted and the Impractibility as well as Impropriety of discharging those debts in the Manner heretofore adopted, begging they
would furnish me only with as much Hard Money as would answer the
present demand and put Mr Pintard upon a more reputable Footing
whose private Credit is already engaged for more than he can ever pay
and who is in danger of being throw'd into a Provost unless some measures are speedily taken to relieve him. Congress have not paid that attention to it I thought the Urgency of the Case Demanded and after
waiting a number of Days for an Answer, was dismised without any
other, then that they would resume the Consideration of it.[3]

I shall endeavour always to administer a sufficient supply of Provision to the Prisoners in New York and shall strictly comply with your orders with regard to Individuals.

I fear I shall be detained longer from Head Quarters than I at first
immagined Occasioned by the very slow returns of the Prisoners from
the different places they have been confined in As well as this last order from Congress respecting the Exchange of Marines.

I shall however at all times wait your Excellencys Commands and will
be found by Directing your letters to me at Prince Town, if not there
they always know where to send to me I am Your Excellencys Most Obedient and Very Humble Servant

Jno. Beatty.
Com: Gen: Prisr

LS, DLC:GW. Beatty signed the cover of the LS.

1. Neither Beatty's correspondence with British admiral James Gambier nor the
letter from the Marine Committee has been identified, but the committee had evidently authorized an exchange of "an equal number of Prisoners of the same rank
and condition—making a distinction betwixt men and Boys, Sick and well" (see
Marine Committee to Beatty, 12 Aug., DNA:PCC, Miscellaneous Papers, Marine
Committee Letter Book; see also Smith, *Letters of Delegates*, 10:433–34).

2. Beatty's "answer" to the Marine Committee of 29 July has not been identified,
but the committee replied on 30 July that instructions relating to the French seamen would come "from the French Minister through Colo. Boudinot" (DNA:PCC,
Miscellaneous Papers, Marine Committee Letter Book; see also ibid., 10:373).

3. Beatty raised this issue in a letter to Congress of 24 July (DNA:PCC, item 78).
Congress read Beatty's "representation" on 28 July and laid it on the table (*JCC*,
11:725).

## To Brigadier General James Clinton

Sir,                                           [White Plains, 31 July 1778]

With the Detachment under your command, which is to comprehend the Corps now advanced with Colo. Morgan, you are to move towards Kings Bridge & the Enemys lines thereabouts.[1]

The principal objects in view are, to cover the Engineers & Surveyors, while they reconnoitre & as far as time will permit, survey the Ground & roads in *your* rear, & in front of this Camp—to countenance and encourage that spirit of desertion which seems so prevalent at present—to discover, if possible, those unfriendly, and ill disposed Inhabitants who make a practice of apprehending, & conveying within the Enemy's line such deserters from their Army as happen to fall into their hands[2] & with such witnesses as are necessary to ilucidate the facts send them to the Head Quarters of this Army—And lastly to try what effect this detachment's approach may have upon the Enemy.

I do not mean, or wish, that you should Incamp very near the Enemy of nights; but wherever you do Incamp, that you do it in proper order of Battle, so that your officers & men may rise at once upon the Ground they are to defend. Your flanks & front should be well secured by Patroles of Horse & foot, sufficiently advanced upon every possible approach; always remembering how disgraceful a thing it is for an officer to be surprized, & believing, that if the Enemy are in force at the Bridge, they will certainly attempt it.

When I speak of your flanks, I have an Eye particularly to the North river, as the Enemy can, with facility move with both secrecy & dispatch by water, if they are provided with Boats at, or near the Bridge, or even at the City, so as to be upon your right flank & even rear, without much difficulty, or notice.

Have your Evening's position well reconnoitred before hand, & unless there are good reasons to the contrary, I would advise against kindling fires at Night, as the weather is warm, & your position woul⟨d⟩ be discovered, & advantages taken from the knowledge of it.

You may continue out with this detachment two, or three days, & nights, according to the state of your provisions & other circumstances, & when you return, leave an officer & sixteen Dragoons of Colo. Sheldons Regiment, with Colo. Morgan who with the Detachment under his immediate command is to remain till further orders.[3]

As the Grounds on the West side of the Brunx River are much stronger, than those, on the East, it may possibly be more eligible to go down on that side, & return on the other, in case any attempts should be made to harrass your rear.

You will give me the earliest, and fullest intelligence of all occurrences worthy notice. Given at Head Quarters at the White Plains this 31st day of July 1778.

Go: Washington

LS, in Richard Kidder Meade's writing, NNPM; ADf, DLC:GW; Varick transcript, DLC:GW. Alexander Hamilton made several minor revisions to the ADf. Identical instructions were given to Brig. Gen. Peter Muhlenberg on 4 Aug. (DLC:GW).

1. For more on this detachment, see General Orders, 30 July, n.4.

2. At this point on the draft, GW wrote "and are desirous of leaving their Service," but those words were crossed out.

3. On 1 Aug., GW's aides Tench Tilghman and Alexander Hamilton each wrote to Clinton regarding the detachment. Tilghman wrote: "In addition to what I wrote to you last Night His Excellency desires that you would not advance your main Body farther down than prudence will dictate, or in other words, he would not have you put it to the least risque. small parties of Horse and foot well advanced as Colo. Morgan advises will answer the purpose. As the day is like to be hazy, His Excellency desires you to keep a very good look out towards the North River lest the Enemy should endeavour, under the cover of the Fog, to throw a party up the River and into your Rear." Apparently later, Hamilton wrote: "The General has received a Letter written by Mr Erskine by your desire at half past Nine oClock this morning; by which he perceives there are parties of the Enemy hovering about you. He desires you will take the most effectual measures to ascertain what force they are in; and be particularly watchful, that while they may be amusing you in front, they may not throw a force superior to yours on your right flank & rear, and perhaps cut off your detachment. You will remember that it is not the object of it, to effect any thing material against the Enemy; and therefore you will be pleased carefully to avoid any untoward accident happening to it. If the Enemy should be near you, in any considerable force, you will fall back upon the Army" (both drafts, DLC:GW).

## From Captain Lieutenant Abraham Hargis

[White Plains]
May it Please your Excellency                     [c.31 July 1778]

Having suffered greatly by the Enemy in Philadelphia and am informed the Savages are Murdering &Ca and destroying my Property in the Back parts of Pennsylvania—I am Anxious and desirous to engage in the *Expedition* now carrying on against them it being my Natural Home.

I therefore beg leave to resign my Commission of Captain Lieutenant in the Tenth Pennsylvania Regiment—And Pray your Excellency will accept of this as my Resignation. I am with the greatest respect your Excellencies most obedient Humble Servant

Abraham Hargis
Capt. Lieut. 10th Pennsylvania Regiment

ALS, DNA: RG 93, manuscript file no. 31435. Hargis did not date the letter, but Col. Richard Humpton's note on it, certifying that Hargis was not indebted to his regiment, is dated 31 July 1778, and the docket also uses that date. Abraham Hargis was appointed a second lieutenant in Col. Samuel Miles's Rifle Regiment in September 1776 and became a lieutenant in the 10th Pennsylvania Regiment in December 1776. His resignation was accepted as of 1 August.

## To Major General Lafayette

Dear Marquis                    Head Quarters White plains 31st July 1778

I had, last Night, the pleasure of receiving yours of the 28th dated at saybrook. I hope your next will inform me of your arrival at Providence, and of your having seen the Count D'Estaings Fleet off the Harbour of Newport, an event, of which I am most anxious to hear. The inclosed letters were recd from Philada by Express.[1] I am Dear Marquis with the greatest Regard Yr most obt & humble Servt.

Df, in Tench Tilghman's writing, DLC:GW; Varick transcript, DLC:GW.
 1. The enclosures have not been identified.

## From Henry Laurens

[Philadelphia] 31st July [1778]

I Am this minute favor'd with Your Excellency's very obliging Letter of the 24th.

The British Commissioners, for, in the Act of one, there is good ground for charging the whole, having by various means attempted to bribe Congress[1] and thereby offer'd the highest possible affront to the Representatives of a virtuous, Independent People, are in my humble opinion rendered wholly unworthy of the further regard of Congress in their Ambassadorial character.

Viewing them in this light I have been from the first reading of their last Address[2] under that kind of anxiety which had possessed my Mind when there was some cause for apprehending that General Burgoyne and his Troops would have slipt thro' our fingers into New York or Philadelphia, an anxiety to which I am a stranger, except in such momentous concerns.

I have for several days past urged my friends to move Congress for a Resolve that they will hold no conference with *such Men*, assigning reasons in ample, decent terms—to transmit the Act by a flag to the Commissioners, and make them the bearers of their own indictment; they will not dare to withhold the Resolve of Congress from their Court. Thence it will soon descend to the Public at large, and expose themselves and their Prompters to the just resentment of a deluded and much injured Nation, whose deplorable circumstances I must confess deeply affects my heart. These Commissioners will be also held up in scorn at every Court in Europe, and finally be transmitted to Posterity in Characters which will mark their Memory with Infamy.

An immediate display of the intended bargain and sale will discourage the impudent, polemic Writers on American Affairs in London, or, invalidate their bold assertions and give force to the declarations of Congress.

If we leave the story to be related after Governor Johnstone's departure from this Continent, he will confidently deny the fact and how few in the World will be thenceforward well informed? Attack him Letters in hand upon the spot, his guilt will be fix'd from his own confession, for he cannot deny.[3]

I am not commonly tenacious of my own Ideas, but in the present, as in the former case, I feel as if I clearly perceived many good effects which will be produced by a proper Act on our part—justice is due to our own Characters, to the present age of America and future Generations will with much satisfaction dwell in history upon the transactions of Congress with these corrupt insidious Emissaries.

If a predilection to my fellow Citizens when standing in competition with strangers, of no more than equal merit, be criminal, I must own myself not free from guilt.

From habit I am disposed to give countenance to strangers, and I have besides, endeavoured, for obvious reasons, to be civil to such French Gentlemen as have called upon me, hence my conduct had been mistaken, and I discover'd at a certain time that my friends had expressed doubts whether my courtesy had not been carried to excess—I had the happiness soon to convince them that good manners and plain dealing were not incompatible—upon this occasion I intreat Your Excellency will excuse the freedom which I take of sending with this, extracts of Letters written by me in answer to applications from foreign Gentlemen for employment and promotion in the Army;[4] the same sentiments have always governed my replies in private oral importunities, I have carefully avoided amusing or flattering any of them.

I have often regretted the hesitation and indecision of our Representatives; on some occasions, and perhaps as often, their precipitancy on others respecting foreign Officers—as a free Citizen I hold myself warranted to speak with decent freedom of the conduct of those whom I have appointed my Attornies, respectful animadversion tends to produce reformation.

From the fluctuations which I allude to, have sprung, to speak in the mildest terms, many inconveniencies, Your Excellency's experience may call them Evils. The dilemma to which we are now reduced in the case of the elder Lanuville, is one instance; if encouragements, tantamount to promises are of any weight, this Gentleman must receive a Brevet to rank Brigadier General the middle of next Month—at his first arrival he presented a Memorial in which was set forth the vast expence which had attended his voyage and journey to York Town. He solicited the grade above mentioned or an immediate negative; intimating that in the latter case he would return to his own Country—a direct Answer was not return'd, he was amused from time to time: an increase of expence and the plea of flattering hopes strengthned his claim. At length he was put into a state of probation.[5] Certificates which he produced of his abilities and assiduities in the character of "*Inspector of the Northern Army*" were expressed in terms somewhat higher than merely favorable—I eyed the paper signed by General Parsons with some degree of jealousy as I read it, but it did not become me to paraphrase, and it passed unnoticed by every body else. On this ground I have said, he must obtain the Brevet in a few days;[6] you would smile Sir, if I were to repeat the principle upon which the delay is founded. This Gentleman is now gone with an intention to act as a Volunteer in the suite of Marquis de la Fayette, and if I understand him, he means soon to return to France.

The Younger de Ianuville your Excellency is informed has obtained a Brevet to rank Major, what title had he to this promotion? Were I to draw the Gentleman into comparison with Major Gibbs and many other worthy Officers, I should answer, none. But he has only a Brevet. Your Excellency is appriz'd of the restrictions on that kind of Commission by an Act of Congress of the 30th of April and I trust the good sense of my Countrymen will lead them to reflect and distinguish properly, and to make some allowances.[7]

Your Excellency will discover in one or more of the extracts the strong desire of French Gentlemen for printed Commissions. I dont know what peculiar advantage they might have had in view, but in opposition to them and even to some attempts here, I have always confin'd myself to the mode of a simple Certificate in pursuance of the Resolve of Congress referr'd to in each case.

In the first conversation I had the honor of holding with Monsr Girard; with a view of learning what reception those French Gentlemen had met, who had return'd some 8 or 9 months ago, murmuring and dissatisfied to France; I took occasion to signify my concern for the disappointment which some of them had suffer'd, and in honor of Congress made brief recitals of Commissions granted to many French Officers now in the Army, observing that it had been impossible to gratify the wishes of every one for promotion. Mr Girard reply'd, His Court had seen with pain so many Frenchmen applying for permission to resort to the American Army, and that very few had receiv'd encouragements; the Court were sensible that crowds of foreigners pressing for Commissions would tend to embarrass Congress, that since his arrival at Philada he had been solicited in many instances for recommendations, every one of which, he had refused to listen to, and added, I might rest satisfied, Congress would never be troubled with Petitions under his auspices.[8] In this sensible declaration methinks I discern sound Policy, be that as it may it will in some measure relieve Congress—I most earnestly wish our noble friend the Marquis could be persuaded to adopt the determinations of Monsr Girard.

Very soon after I shall have the pleasure of conversing with Baron Stüben, his pursuits in the journey to Court will be known to me. I shall be equally explicit on my part, and your Excellency shall be as candidly informed, if it shall appear to be necessary.

On Thursday the sixth of August Congress will receive Monsr Girard in his public character. Your Excellency will find within, copies of the intended Address of the Minister and Answer of the Representatives of the thirteen United States of America—speaking as a Citizen I cannot forbear disclosing to you, Sir, that there is a reluctance in my Mind to acknowledgments of obligation or of generosity where benefits have been, to say the least, reciprocal—this opinion has not been form'd since I read the Address and Answer, as I am warranted to say from the Extract of a Letter to Monsr Du Portail.[9]

After hours of disputation shall be exausted the point will remain moot.

Among other papers I take the liberty of inclosing copy of a curious performance of Mr Maduit which is believed to be genuine.[10] If he is not delirious in the present time, his friends must conclude that he was raving from 1774 to the commencment of the present Year, time employed by him in dinning the Coffee houses with his cries against the Inhabitants of these States and against their Claims, down with America! I will not further presume on Your Excellency's moments but to repeat that I continue with the most sincere and respectful attachment and the highest Esteem. Sir Your Excellency's &c.

LB, ScHi: Henry Laurens Papers. A note on the letter-book copy indicates that this letter was carried "by Ross."

1. For the charge that British commissioner George Johnstone had attempted to bribe congressmen Joseph Reed and Robert Morris to support the British peace proposals, see Laurens to GW, 13 Aug., n.6.

2. For the British commissioners' letter to Laurens of 11 July, see Laurens to GW, 18 July, n.3.

3. The preceding two paragraphs were written at the end of the letter-book copy and marked by Laurens for placement here.

4. The enclosed extracts have not been identified.

5. Louis-Pierre Penot Lombart, chevalier de La Neuville, had requested a commission from Congress in late January 1778, but Congress did not act until 14 May, when they resolved to employ him as inspector general for the northern army, with a promise "that Congress will be disposed, after an experience of his services . . . for the space of three months, to confer on him such rank as his merits may justly entitle him to" (*JCC*, 11:498–500).

6. A copy of the certificate of Brig. Gen. Samuel Holden Parsons, dated 21 June, is in DNA:PCC, item 41. The Board of War reported to Congress on 29 July that La Neuville should receive a brevet commission as brigadier general, but consideration was postponed. It was not until 14 Oct. that Congress voted to give him the commission, dated 14 Aug. (see ibid., 11:728, 12:1010).

7. Congress voted on 29 July to give René-Hippolyte Penot Lombart de Noirmont de La Neuville a brevet commission as major (ibid., 11:728–29). Congress's resolution of 30 April specified that a brevet commission gave rank "only upon detachments from the line, and in general courts martial," conveying neither extra pay nor any higher rank in the unit to which the breveted officer belonged (ibid., 10:410).

8. At about this time Gérard wrote to the French foreign minister that he saw a spirit of pretension and discontent in almost all the French officers that he had occasion to see. He added, "J'ai beaucoup à travailler pour persuader à quelques uns de ces M[essieu]rs que l'objet principal de ma mission n'est pas de solliciter des grades pour eux" (Gérard to Vergennes, 3 Aug., in Meng, *Despatches of Gérard*, 197).

9. The enclosed copies have not been identified. Gérard sent a copy of his address to Congress on 16 July, and Congress approved a draft for the reply on 30 July (*JCC*, 11:695, 730, 733). For the texts delivered on 6 Aug., see ibid., 11:754–57. Laurens had expressed in a letter to Duportail of 20 May his objection "to the stress which you seem to lay on the sense of *obligation* which ought to be acknowledged by these States" to France (*Laurens Papers*, 13:334–36).

10. Israel Mauduit (1708–1787), a London businessman and political pamphleteer known in part for his support of parliamentary authority and rejection of colonial claims to charter rights, had published anonymously in March 1778 a handbill that argued that French support of the American cause meant "All hope of conquest is therefore over. . . . We have no possible chance of making peace with her, but by an immediate act of parliament, giving her perfect independence." Mauduit contended that "If we pretend to retain any authority over them, we immediately throw them into the arms of France," while by granting American independence, England could prevent America's "close alliance" with France and might avoid war with France altogether. Immediate independence would leave England with a "full share" of the American trade, while in a long war the Americans would "be totally Gallicized, and estranged from us." A copy of the handbill sent by Arthur Lee, who stated that it was "written by Mr. Mauduit, under the direction of Lord North, and circulated through England by order of Administration," was printed in the *Pennsylvania Packet or the General Advertiser* (Philadelphia), 22 August.

# From Colonel David Mason

Sir                                                                 Wburg [Va.] July 31st 1778

It's with the Greatest unease I am now Reduced to the Necessity of Accepting of Your Excellencys Permission to resign [1] & imbrace this Oppertunity by Mr Thompson to Inclose You my Commission; [2] I have Deferred this Until this Oppertunity, as well to collect all the draughts I ⟨p⟩ossably coud get as to Transact other Continental Matters within this State, by d[e]sire of the Govr and Council, By Mr Thompson I send to Head Quarters Eight or Ten Men which are all I can Collect, nor can I give You the most Distant hope's of those Yet Behind ever coming in as they Meet with every indulgence they can wish for Amongst the Inhabitants of this State, And am Sorry to Say the Militia Officers (a few only Excepted) are Exceedingly Remiss, Permit me Sir, to Suggest a Method ⟨t⟩o your Excellency, which Probably may Induce those Unhappy Men to Join their Regements, which is that if You were to Offer them Pardon & that they Shoud only Serve the time they originally were inlisted for or Draughted, this might Influence Many to give themselves up His Excellency the Govr & the Council with myself have conferrd on Something Proper to be done but we coud not Devise any Method that we thought Elligible as I had no Power from Your Excellency to make any Special Offer's to the Deserters, I Shall be Exceedingly Happy When Hond with Your Excellencys Command in anything that I may be Able to Serve my Country in, in my Retirement I have only to Add My Sincere Wishes for Your Health & ⟨prosperity⟩ And have the Honr to be with the Greatest Regard Your Excellencys Mot Obedt Servt

David Mason

ALS, DNA: RG 93, manuscript file no. 31304.
  1. See GW to Mason, 19 May.
  2. The enclosed commission has not been identified.

## To Jeremiah Dummer Powell

Sir                                  Head Quarters White plains 31st July 1778
  About Nine hundred of the Nine Months Men[1] from the State of Massachusets have joined the Army, and have been attatched to Nixon's, Pattersons, and late Learneds Brigades. As Glovers has yet had no proportion, I desire that three hundred of those yet to come on, may be ordered to stop at Providence and join that Brigade, which will make it equal to the others.
  It is my intention to proportion all these Recruits among the Brigades of your State, that they may be upon a level, but they claim a right of choice to join which they please, which right they say is founded upon the law for raising them. As I have not a Copy of this law, I shall be glad to be furnished with one, that I may regulate myself according to the Terms of it.[2] I am &c.

Df, in Tench Tilghman's writing, DLC:GW; Varick transcript, DLC:GW.
  1. GW was referring to the troops raised in accordance with Congress's resolution of 26 Feb., directing the states to complete their Continental regiments by drafting troops for nine months' service (*JCC*, 10:199–203).
  2. The troops raised by the resolution of 20 April 1778 "for filling up and compleating the fifteen battalions of Continental troops" were to be delivered "to such

Continental officers as may be appointed by the Commander in Chief there, to receive them" (*Mass. Resolves*, May 1777–April 1778 [1 April–1 May 1778], 16–21).

## From Brigadier General John Stark

Dear General                          Head Quarters Albany 31st July 1778
    I Received orders last Jany to Raise a Number of Voluntiers to Burn
the Shipping at St Johns a Copy of which I Inclose[1]—I proceeded to
Raise a Number of men for that purpose and had them Ready to march
when the Expedition fell Through which put me and the officers to A
good deale of Expence and the men I Raised are daily Haunting me for
their pay—would be glad if your Excellency would put me in a way to
get some Recompence for my Extra Expences and the pay of the
Officers & Soldiers Engaged for that Service.
    there is a number of State Prisoners in this Goal which draw provi-
sion out of the Continental Store which I look upon to be very wrong
your orders on this Head I should be Very glad off—besides them,
there is a Number of Soldiers Wifes, in this City, in almost a Starving
Condition, and no person to give them any Relief, I have applyed to
the Corporation but they Refuse to take any care of them I would be
glad of your Instructions on that Matter. I am Sir with Great Respect
your Very Humbl. Servt

                                                          John Stark

N.B. I have been oblidged to purchase fifty Pairs of Shoes for the Rifle
Detatchment before they could be fit for a march. as before

                                                          J.S.

LS, DLC:GW.
    1. The enclosed copy of Congress's resolutions of 3 Dec. 1777 is in DLC:GW (see
also *JCC*, 9:999-1001).

## To Major General John Sullivan

Dear Sir                    Head Quarters White plains 31st July 1778
    I have been favd with yours of the 27th 10 Oclock A. M. Upon open-
ing of it, I was much disappointed at not hearing of the Count D'Estaing's arrival, who I hope will have made his appearance off the Harbour of Newport before this time, as a Reinforcement passed
Maroneck the day before Yesterday Morning. I wish it had been in my
power to have spared a larger detatchment of Continental Troops, but
remember, I am left very near the Enemy, with a Force inferior to theirs
upon New York and the adjacent Islands. I am much pleased with the

account of the readiness which you were in, to begin your operations, as soon as the Count, and the Marquis should arrive, and I flatter myself, that you will receive no small assistance from Genl Greene, in the department of Qr Mr Genl, as well as in the military line.

As you have mentioned the matter of carrying the Enemy's works by storm, and have submitted it to my consideration and advice, I will only say, that as I would not, on the one hand, wish to check the Ardor of our Troops, so I would not, upon the other, put them upon attempting what I thought they could not carry but with a moral certainty of success. You know the discipline of our Men and Officers very well, and I hope you, and the General Officers under your command, will weigh every desperate matter well before it is carried into execution A severe check may ruin the expedition, while regular and determined approaches may effect the work, tho' perhaps they may take something longer time. Upon the whole, I will not undertake, at this distance, to give orders, I submit every thing to your prudence, and to the good advice of those about you. You have my sincere wishes for your success, as I am Yrs &c.

P.S. By a letter from the Officer of the Maroneck Guard, he does not seem certain that the Vessels which went thro' the sound the day before yesterday had troops on Board at least any considerable number.[1]

Df, in Tench Tilghman's writing, DLC:GW; Varick transcript, DLC:GW.
  1. This letter has not been identified.

*Document not found*: Speech to Oneida Indians [July–August 1778]. This document, in James McHenry's writing, was offered for sale in *The Frank T. Siebert Library of the North American Indian and the American Frontier*, Sotheby's sale 7315, 21 May 1999, item 189. It is dated by the abstractor's assertion that the speech mentions "the British evacuation of Philadelphia, the British defeat at Monmouth, and a French fleet at Rhode Island assisting Boston warriors." One page reproduced in the catalog reads: "Brothers—We are going to take leave of each other. You have been with us a long time and behaved faithfully. But Before you go I have several things to say—I would confirm to you the good will of my heart towards all of your nation, the good Oneidas. And I would intrust you with a message to the Sachems and warriors of the Senecas who do not mind what is just nor do what is right—The Senecas have long done wrong—The have not acted like the Oneidas who are a brave and wise people.

"Brothers—You have fought along with our warriors—you have helped them to take one large army and to recover two of our great Towns Boston and Philadelphia—you are now to go home—You will take the news to your nation that the swarms of warriors which the King of Engl⟨and⟩ (who keeps himself beyond the great water) are almost all cut off—They are now weak as little children—They fled from one of our great Towns that they boasted to keep as long as trees grow, leaving behind them very rich goods—you."

The abstractor quotes a later portion, which reads: "The Senecas are not like the Oneidas, but have lifted up the hatchet with our enemies, and destroyed our corn, and burned our houses, and drunk the blood of our harmless wives and little children. They have been very wicked and very cruel—and this has made our wise men angry, and kindled the fire of our warriors against them. . . . if they do not immediately bury the bloody hatchet under a big mountain, this army and all the great warriors in America will come up against them."

## General Orders

Head-Quarters White Plains saturday Augt 1st 1778.
Parole Tuscany—                                    C. Signs Truro—Tartary.

At a Division General Court-Martial held at Peek's-Kill July 16th 1778—Lieutenant Coll Hay President Lieutenant James Armstrong of the 3rd Pennsylvania Regiment was tried for behaving in a scandalous manner, beating a number of Persons, breaking Windows, and being guilty of other abusive treatment—After due consideration the Court are of opinion that Lieutenant Armstrong was guilty of beating Quarter Master Bradford but think the Provocation was in some degree equal to the Offence; that he was guilty of breaking Cellar Windows and of other abusive treatment—but upon the whole cannot pronounce his behaviour scandalous, tho' unjustifiable and notwithstanding his good Character as an Officer and soldier do sentence him to be reprimanded in General Orders.[1]

At the same Court Captns Thomas Moore and James Christe of said Regiment were tried for the same Crime.[2]

The Court are of Opinion that they are not guilty of behaving in a scandalous manner, beating a number of Persons or of breaking Windows, but find them guilty of abusive treatment and sentence them to be reprimanded by the Commanding Officer of the Brigade.

The Commander in Chief is sorry that he has Occasion to declare that Captains Christe and Moore and Lieutenant Armstrong were, thro' the whole of this affair in Circumstances that did them very little Honor—He laments they should suffer themselves so far to deviate from that line of delicacy and decorum which they owe to their own Characters as to engage in a Riot and Tumult of so singular a Complexion, especially as it rather appears by their own defence that they left their Regiment without leave—Captns Moore & Christe and Lieutenant Armstrong are released from their Arrests.

The Brigade Major and Adjutants of the day are to be very alert in telling off the guards so soon as they are assembled on Parade, that the men may not be fatigued by long standing—They are also to see that the men stand firm with their heads erect and observe the strictest Silence while this is doing.

A Chain of Centries is to be posted along the Front of the Parade at forty yards distance within which none but the General, Field and other Officers of the day are to be admitted.

As there is something extremely awkward and unmilitary in Officers saluting at different times and in different manners the following general Direction is to be observed; The saluting Officer is to look full in the Face of the Officer saluted, his body upright and his step firm and to begin at such a distance as to finish the salute when opposite the Person for whom it is intended—The Motions of the Sword or Fusil & the Feet ought to be exactly in Concert; in order to which and for the graceful Performance of salutes it is expected Officers will spare no Trouble or Pains to perfect themselves and arrive at Dexterity and Uniformity as it is a matter which forms no unessential Part of their duty and will be highly ornamental to their military Appearance and Character.

When the guards are ordered to march off the Brigade Major is to see that they all step off at the same instant with their left feet and the Officers of Platoons will be particularly attentive that the step is afterwards preserved: As the Platoons pass in Review before the Major General or Officer Commanding the Parade the men are to hold up their heads and look full in their Face.

No Officer who has Regimentals is to mount guard in any other dress, and when men are warned for guard they are to be directed to come on with clean hands and faces hairs combed and powdered, and are to appear in all respects as decent and solderlike as circumstances will permit.

Brigade Majors and Adjutants will recollect that it is an indispensible part of their duty to attend to this and see that the mens Arms Ammunition and Accoutrements are continually in the best order.

The Major General of the day thro' the Field Officers will have a careful Inspection made into these several matters and where there appears to be any deficiency will call the Brigade-Majors and Adjutants to account on the spot, and either reprimand arrest or acquit as circumstances shall warrant; These are to be considered as standing orders which it is expected all officers and soldiers will be made acquainted with & punctually observe.

The whole Army to be under Arms tomorrow morning at five ôClock precisely with their Tents struck and rolled up and their Packs slung; further orders will then be given by the Adjutant General.[3]

The Troops of the whole line will exercise and manœuvre on the Principles heretofore established for the Main Army twice a day from

five to seven in the morning and from five to seven in the Evening—
The Brigade Inspectors will perform the duties of their Office as
heretofore directed by the order of the 15th of June last.

Coll Davies will superintend the Right Wing and three Brigades on
the Right of the second line. Lieutenant Colonel Brooks will superintend the Left Wing and two Brigades on the left of the second Line—
conformable to the spirit of the same order.

The Brigadiers and Commanding Officers of those Brigades who
have no Brigade Inspectors appointed, will recommend to Head-
Quarters proper Officers for that Purpose.

Varick transcript, DLC:GW.

1. James Armstrong (d. 1800), who was appointed regimental quartermaster for
the 2d Pennsylvania Regiment in February 1776, became an ensign of that regiment in May 1776 and a second lieutenant in November 1776. Commissioned a
first lieutenant of the 3d Pennsylvania Regiment in April 1777, he subsequently
joined Lee's Legion, where he was promoted to captain by early 1780. He was captured at Dorchester, S.C., on 13 Dec. 1781 and remained a prisoner until December 1782. After the war, Armstrong moved to Georgia, where he represented Camden County in the legislature and on the executive council. When the army was
briefly augmented during the Quasi-War, Armstrong served as a major of the 5th
U.S. Infantry Regiment from July 1799 to July 1800. Robert Bradford (1750–
1823), who was commissioned an ensign of the 23d Continental Regiment in January 1776, was promoted to lieutenant and regimental quartermaster of the 2d
Massachusetts Regiment in January 1777 and became brigade quartermaster in
January 1778. He was promoted to captain of the 2d Massachusetts Regiment in
June 1779 and served to the end of the war.

2. Thomas Lloyd Moore (1756–1813) was a son of Philadelphia merchant William Moore (c.1735–1793), who was on the Pennsylvania board of war and later
became president of the Pennsylvania supreme executive council. The younger
Moore was commissioned a lieutenant in the 2d Pennsylvania Regiment on 5 Jan.
1776 and promoted to captain on 21 May 1776, joining the 3d Pennsylvania Regiment in early 1777. Moore, who was promoted to major of the 9th Pennsylvania
Regiment in May 1779, transferred to the 5th Pennsylvania Regiment in January 1781 and served until January 1783. During the Quasi-War, Moore was commissioned in January 1799 as lieutenant colonel commandant of the 10th U.S. Infantry Regiment and served until June 1800.

3. Private Zebulon Vaughan of the 5th Massachusetts Regiment recorded in his
diary for 2 Aug.: "we all Struck tents the holl armey under ae noshon of a march
But it turned out to Bee a Sarch thro the holl armey." Capt. Paul Brigham's entry
in his diary for the date suggests a cause: "had a Sarch [Search] Throughout the
Army for to find Some Stolen Goods" ("Vaughan Journal," 109; "Brigham Diary,"
29; see also Symmes, *Gilbert Diary*, 34).

*Letter not found*: from Robert Erskine, 1 Aug. 1778. On 1 Aug., GW's aide-de-
camp Alexander Hamilton wrote Brig. Gen. James Clinton: "The General has
received a Letter written by Mr Erskine by your desire at half past Nine oClock
this morning" (DLC:GW).

*Letter not found*: from Col. William Malcom, 1 Aug. 1778. On 4 Aug., GW wrote Malcom: "Yours of the 1st instant inclosing the weekly return ⟨has⟩ been received."

## From Major General Steuben

Sir                                                    Philadelphia [c.1] Augt 1778

I cannot any longer defer acknowledging the many favors I have received from you & expressing my desire of your Excellencys continuing the same favorable sentiments towards me.

Immediately after my arrival here Congress were pleased to appoint a Committee to hear my Proposals—the Committee consists of Gen. Reed Mrss. Boudinot & Chace, & meet for the first time on saturday 8th Inst.;[1] in the mean time, I am preparing a plan for the establishment of an Inspection, & as it is my wish, it shall be my endeavour, to form it on such principles, as may be agreable to your Excellency & the Army in general, and at the same time comprehend all the essential duties of the Office.

In preparing this Plan, the good of the Service is my only motive, all personal views will be laid aside, & the duties of Inspector General laid down & defined, not for myself, but for any person the Congress may think proper to appoint to that Office.

The Plan being fixed & approved by Congress—I shall, before it receives their final ratification insist on its being sent to your Excellency for your opinion thereon, & I beg my dear General that laying aside any partiality in my favor you will freely make any observations on it you may think proper.

Whatever may be the result of this Affair I beg you will believe me with the greatest respect & esteem Sir Your Excellencys most Obedt hum. Servt

                                                                    Steuben

LS, DLC:GW.

1. Steuben carried GW's letters to Henry Laurens of 18 June and 26 July, which were referred to the indicated committee on 1 Aug. (see *JCC*, 11:737).

## From Major General John Sullivan

Dear General                          Head Qrs Providence August 1st 1778

It is with pleasure I inform your Excellency that our preparations in this Department are as forward as Circumstances will admit, or Industry and application could make them.

I submitt'd the Plan of Operations (sometime since communicated to your Excellency) to Admiral Count D. Estaign & was happy in its receiving his approbation & concurrence.[1]

Upon his proceeding to put part of them in Execution the greatest Consternation apparently prevail'd on the part of the Enemy—The Crews of the Kings Fisher & two of their Gallies (at the appearance of the French fleet) abandon'd & sat them on fire, after Charging their Cannon with Grape to prevent their being Extinguish'd—they were entirely consum'd.[2]

I wait with Impatience the arrival of the Marquiss & the different Corps order'd to this Station. Their Motions are by no means so rapid as I could wish, but your Excellency may rely that when collected I shall proceed without delay to put them into immediate Action.

My Acknowledgments are due for your kind attention in sending Genl Green to my assistance & Council—I have the Honor likewise to acknowledge the receipt of your Commands of 27th & 28th last Month & promise your Excellency that I shall religiously observe the Recommendations they contain.

From what past in my late Interview with Count D. Estaign I think I can venture to assure your Excellency that the greatest Harmony will subsist between us, with respect to command. I have the Honor to be with the utmost Attachment & respect Your Excellency's Oblig'd & very Hble Servant

                                        sign'd Jno. Sullivan

P.s. The Regiments on Conanecut abandon'd it on the coming up of the french ships & retir'd to Rhode Island My best accounts of the Enemy's strength makes them not more than 5.200 which are better warrant'd than my former Accounts.[3]

Copy                                                        J.S.

Copy, DNA:PCC, item 152; copy, DNA:PCC, item 169. The copy in item 152 was enclosed with GW's letter to Henry Laurens of 3–4 August.

    1. Sullivan was referring to the plan of operations suggested in his letter to Vice Admiral d'Estaing of 25 July, enclosed in Sullivan's letter to GW of 26 July (see note 3 to that letter). For d'Estaing's reply to Sullivan's plan, dated 30 July, see Hammond, *Sullivan Papers*, 2:151–53.

    2. D'Estaing wrote to Sullivan on 31 July that "The frigate [sloop] Kingfisher, having 18 nine-pounders, and 2 three-pounders, as well as the galley Spitfire, carrying two eighteens, two twelves, and six sixes, with the galley Lamb, carrying two eighteens, two nines and two sixes, were burned under an English battery at the approach of my frigates, which were . . . infinitely weaker, owing to the enormous difference in the calibre of the guns" (ibid., 2:154; see also *Mackenzie Diary*, 2:321; Robert Pigot to Henry Clinton, 31 July–1 Aug., P.R.O., Colonial Office, 5/96, Military Correspondence of the British Generals).

3. According to the diary of Capt. Frederick Mackenzie of the Royal Welch Fusiliers, after the French fleet appeared off Rhode Island on 29 July, "Boats were immediately sent over to Connonicut, from whence the Two Battalions of Anspach and Brown's Regiment of Provincials were withdrawn, leaving small detachments only in the Batteries on Fox-hill and The Dumplins." Private Johann Conrad Döhla of the Anspach Regiment recorded that those detachments evacuated the island on 30 July after the French ships fired on the batteries (ibid., 2:319; Döhla, *Hessian Diary*, 81; see also Prechtel, *Diary*, 22, 143; "Newport in the Hands of the British," 72).

## General Orders

Head-Quarters White-Plains Sabbath Augt 2nd 1778.
Parole Ulster—　　　　　　　　　　　C. Signs Virginia Wenham.
A Return as usual of the sick in Camp to be made to the surgeon General tomorrow morning 9 ôClock and every succeding Monday at the Post-Office near the Artillery-Park, where attendance will be given to receive them—When the Surgeon is absent the Surgeon attending the Regiment will make the Return.[1]

Return of Arms, Ammunition and Accoutrements good bad and wanting in the several Brigades to be made and delivered to the Orderly-Office by the Brigade Quarter-Master, tomorrow morning at Guard mounting.

A like Return of Cloathing and Necessaries to be delivered in at the same time by the Majors of Brigade.

Varick transcript, DLC:GW. On this date GW's aide Tench Tilghman wrote Commissary of Prisoners John Beatty, apparently enclosing a copy of a letter of 20 July written by William Cleveland to Ezekiel Williams. Cleveland, a lieutenant of the 10th Continental Infantry who had been captured in the retreat from New York, 15 Sept. 1776, complained: "The circumstances attending my Confinement, are no less singular than cruel, it is almost two years since I was made prisoner, have received but very little supplies from the Public; have had the mortification to se a considerable number of my Rank taken some two, Some four, Some Seven, some twelve, and Some fifteen Months after me, Exchanged whilst I am left, but for what reason I know not" (DLC:GW). Tilghman told Beatty, "By the inclosed letter it appears that Mr Cleveland has great reason to complain; but I am certain that it has not been owing to any wilfull neglect in either Mr Boudinott or yourself. I am apt to beleive that the Gentlemans name has been omitted in the Return of prisoners. His Excellency desires that you would make enquiry as soon as possible, and if his Case is such as he represents, that immediate means may be fallen upon to procure his Exchange" (DLC:GW). Cleveland, who died in 1778, was still a prisoner on Long Island when a return of American officers and other prisoners was compiled on 15 Aug. (DNA: RG 93, Revolutionary War Rolls, 1775–1783), but his service records indicate that he was eventually exchanged.

1. Weekly returns of the sick and wounded at White Plains for 24 Aug. and 7 Sept., compiled by Surgeon General William Burnet, Sr., are in DNA: RG 93, Revolutionary War Rolls, 1775–1783.

## To Major General Horatio Gates

sir                          Head Quarters White plains 2d August 1778

I have just received the inclosed from the board of war[1]—I beg of you to inform me what steps have been taken in consequence of the resolves of the 11th of June last—What troops you had in contemplation for the expedition into the country of the Senecas—What number you conceive adequate to the service—What were your prospects of supplying them with provisions—stores and other necessaries—And with what convenience and readiness the means of transportation can be provided—In a word, I wish for every information that can enlighten my own judgement and enable me to carry the views of Congress into execution, with all possible and practicable dispatch, as the time appointed for the co-operation of General McIntosh is near at hand.[2]

When you have read the inclosed papers you will please to return them under cover, with your sentiments on the above matters. I am Sir yr most Obt hble servt

Go: Washington

LS, in James McHenry's writing, NHi: Gates Papers; ADfS, DLC:GW; Varick transcript, DLC:GW.

1. See the Board of War to GW, 27 July. On the draft, GW began the next sentence with the clause "As the subject is new to me, and unexpected," but those words were struck out.

2. GW also sought information about the preparations for the expedition from Commissary General of Purchases Jeremiah Wadsworth. His aide Tench Tilghman wrote Wadsworth on this date: "I am commanded by His Excellency to inform you that an Expedition against the Indians is in Agitation. The place of rendezvous will probably be at Albany and from thence up the Mohawk River to Fort schuyler from whence they will proceed to such places as may be deemed most expedient. His Excellency desires to know what Magazines you have already formed, or what you have a certain prospect of forming upon the above communication. What Number of Men are to be employed upon the expedition is not yet determined but they will not be very great. Be pleased to give an answer in writing as soon as you can inform yourself" (DLC:GW).

*Letter not found*: from Brig. Gen. William Maxwell, 2 Aug. 1778. On 4 Aug., GW wrote Maxwell: "I was last Night favd with yours of the 2d with a York paper."

## From Gouverneur Morris

Dear General                          Philadelphia 2 Augt 1778.

I was in your Debt. It is my Fate always to be so with my Friends. But beleive me my Heart owes Nothing. Let me add that you can do me no Favor so great as to comply with your Wishes except an Opportunity to serve the Public which indeed is your highest Wish as you have evidenced fully to all the World & particularly to your Friends. I feel the full Force of your Reasoning.[1] The Faith of Congress is in some Measure plighted to Mr De la Neuville but it is not their Intent that his Brevet shall give Command. I will take Care to get this expressed by a particular Resolution. The Baron has a Claim from his Merit to be noticed but I never will consent to grant what I am told he requests & I think Congres will not. At least they wont if I can help it. I this Instant was informed of the Opportunity for Camp which goes immediately— Let me however congratulate you on the Affair at Monmouth On the *whole* Affair. It might have been better it is said. I think not for you have even from your Enemies the Honor of that Day. You have Enemies. It is happy for you that you have. A Man of Sentiment has not so much Honor as the Vulgar suppose in risquing Life & Fortune for the Service of his Country. He does not Value them as highly as the Vulgar do. Would he give the highest Evidence let him sacrifice his Feelings. In the History of last Winter Posterity will do you Justice. Adieu. Beleive me sincerely yours

Gouvr Morris

ALS, DLC:GW.

1. Morris was referring to the ideas contained in GW's letter to him of 24 July.

## To Jeremiah Dummer Powell

Sir                                     Head Qrs [White Plains] Augt 2d 1778

As General Glover's brigade has been detached to Rhode Island— and is intended to form a part of the Troops—which are to operate in that Quarter, I take the liberty to request, that such of the recruits of your State as have not actually marched, may proceed and join him. This will not only place them in a way of rendering immediate service; but will prevent them the trouble of a long and fatiguing march at this season. Your recruits now here will join the Massachussets Brigades— which compose a part of this Army. I have the Honor to be with the greatest respect & esteem Sir Yr Most Obedt sert

Go: Washington

LS (photocopy), in Robert Hanson Harrison's writing, M-Ar: Revolution Letters, 1778; Df, DLC:GW; Varick transcript, DLC:GW.

## General Orders

Head-Quarters White-Plains Monday Augt 3rd 1778.
Parole Alexandria—                    C. Signs Boxford. Cambridge.

The Connecticutt Militia Light-Horse commanded by Captain Skinner are discharged and have his Excellency's thanks for their good Services.

At a General Court Martial whereof Coll Stewart was President July 29th 1778—Lieutenant Coll Regnier tried 1st—For leaving his Regiment when alarmed by the firing of the Patroles upon the lines on the morning of the 29th of June last and not joining it again 'till the Alarm was over—2ndly For purchasing a horse from a soldier which properly belonged to the Continent—3rd for treating Adjt Sackett in an unofficer and ungentlemanlike manner.[1] The Court having considered the Charges and the Evidence are unanimously of opinion that Lieutt Coll Regnier is not guilty of either of the Charges exhibited against him, and are farther of opinion, that they are groundless, vexatious and dictated by private Pique & Malice; They do acquit him with honor.

At the same Court Martial July 31st Captn Silleron acting as a Volunteer in the 4th New-York Regiment was tried 1st—For calling Adjutant Sackett a Liar and drawing his sword on him when unarmed—2ndly for insinuating that he was a Coward and challenging him to fight a Duel—The Court having considered the first Charge and Evidence are of Opinion that Captn Silleron is guilty thereof, but as the Abuse was reciprocal and as Captain Silleron could not mean by drawing his sword to take Advantage of Mr Sackett's being unarmed—The Court think the Punishment of lying in Arrest (a punishment pointed out in the Articles of War of which his Crime is a breach and which Captn Silleron has already suffered) is adequate to the fault he has committed; They are likewise of opinion that Captain Silleron is guilty of the second Charge exhibited against him, but as the Challenge was given by him immediately, as it proceeded from the instantaneous Resentment of an incensed Gentleman and was not sent on cool reflection; the Court are of opinion that Captain Silleron has not been guilty of a breach of the Article of War which prohibits sending challenges and do determine that he does not merit Censure.[2]

Likewise Lieutenant Norton of the 2nd Pennsylvania Regiment tried for entering the Encampment of the 3rd Pennsylvania Regiment in Company with several others in a riotous and mutinous manner and for attempting to enter Coll Craige's house between the hours of twelve and one in the morning of the 4th of June with a drawn sword & unanimously acquitted of the Charge exhibited against him.[3]

His Excellency the Commander in Chief approves the sentences. Coll David Hall is appointed President of the Court-Martial now sitting, *vice*, Coll Stewart.

Major Oliver is appointed Inspector in General Nixon's Brigade & is to be respected accordingly.

Varick transcript, DLC:GW.

1. Peter Sackett (b. 1757) of Long Island was appointed adjutant of the 4th New York Regiment in November 1776 and resigned in late August or early September 1778.

2. Article 2, section 7 of the articles of war prohibited officers or soldiers from sending challenges (*JCC*, 5:793).

3. Thomas Norton, who had served as a sergeant in the 2d Pennsylvania Regiment, was promoted to ensign in March 1777 and commissioned a second lieutenant in April of that year. Norton was appointed regimental quartermaster on 5 Sept. 1778 and continued in that post until August 1779, meanwhile being promoted to first lieutenant in March 1779. He resigned on 3 Sept. 1779.

## To Major General Benedict Arnold

Dear sir.                    Head Quarters White plains 3 August 1778

Your two agreeable favors of the 19 and 22 Ulto came to hand, which I now have to acknowledge.

I am very happy to learn that your wounds are less painful and in so fair a way of doing well—the only drawback in the pleasure [I] [1] receive is that the condition of your wounds is ⟨s⟩till such as not to admit of your active services this campaign.

You will rest assured that I wish to see you in a situation where you can be of the greatest advantage, and where abilities like yours may not be lost to the public; but I confess myself no competent judge in marine matters to offer advice on a subject so far out of my line—beleive me tho' that it is my desire that you may determine, in this case, in a manner most conducive to your health honor and Interest. I am Dr Sir &c. &c. &c.

Df, in the writing of James McHenry, DLC:GW; Varick transcript, DLC:GW.

1. The word on the draft is "the," which was not crossed out when McHenry substituted "receive" for "account gives me."

## To Colonel George Baylor

Dear Sir                    Head Quarters White plains 3d Augt 1778

I am favd with yours of the 13th ulto. As you seem to have proceeded as far as you can in the purchase of Horses without indulging the exorbitant demands of the holders, I would have you desist, and come immediately to Camp with all the Officers, Men and Horses. If you have any Arms or Accoutrements unfinished, or any Men and Horses unfit to come forward when this order reaches you, I would have you leave an Officer, upon whose diligence you can depend, to bring them on when they are ready.

Lieut. Baylor under arrest for gaming, is to come on with you.

I have written to Colo. Bland and desired him to give over purchasing, and to come on to Camp also, as it is my intent to draw as strong a Body of Cavalry as possible together, that we may keep the Enemy from foraging or drawing other supplies from this part of the Country.[1] I am Dear Sir Your most obt Servt

Go: Washington

LS, in Tench Tilghman's writing, NNU-F: Richard Maass Collection; Df, DLC:GW; Varick transcript, DLC:GW. GW signed the cover of the LS, which was offered for sale in 1988 (Robert F. Batchelder catalog 64, item 16).

1. GW's letter to Col. Theodorick Bland of this date informed him that Baylor's letter of 13 July had led GW to conclude that "Horses had got to such ⟨e⟩xtravagant prices that it was in vain to think of procuring but very few more for Dragoon Service." GW informed Bland of the instructions given to Baylor and told him: "I desire you may do the same" (LS, ViW: Charles Campbell Papers; see also DLC:GW).

## To the Board of War

Gentlemen,                    Head Quarters White Plains Aug. 3d 1778

I had the honor of receiving your favour of the 27th Ulto on the 1st instant, inclosing sundry resolves of Congress and other papers respecting two expeditions meditated into the Indian Country one from the Southward and the other from the Northward. I have since the receipt of it[1] been endeavouring to collect the necessary information concerning the means already provided, or to be provided towards prosecuting the latter; and I sincerely wish our prospects were more agreeable to the views of Congress than they are; but after examining the matter [from][2] every point of light, I am sorry to say an entreprise of this nature at the present time under our present circumstances appears to me liable to obstacles not easily to be surmounted.

On receiving your letter I wrote to General Gates, copies of mine to him and of his answer to me are inclosed.[3] I do not find that any preparations have been made for the intended expedition; If the project should be continued almost every thing is still to be done. The Board will perceive that General Gates imagined it was laid aside.

Govr Clinton happening to be in Camp, I took occasion to consult him and General Gates jointly on the affair. They both concurred fully in opinion, that a serious attempt to penetrate the seneca settlements at this advanced season & under present appearances[4] was by no means adviseable—would be attended with many certain difficulties and inconveniences, and must be of precarious success. The reasons for this opinion are in my judgment conclusive.

Supposing enemys force is fifteen or sixteen hundred men according to the estimate made by the Board[5] (Accts make it larger)[6]—to carry the war into the interior part of their country, with that probability of succeeding, which woud justify the undertaking would require not less than three thousand men. And if the attempt is made it ought to be made with Such a force as will in a manner insure the event; for a failure could not but have the most pernicious tendency. From inquiries I have made, not more than about twelve hundred militia from the frontier counties could be seasonably engaged for a sufficient length of time to answer the purpose of the expedition; little or no assistance can be looked for from the people of the Grants, who are said to be under great alarm for their own security, which they think is every moment in danger of being disturbed by way of Choas.[7] The deficiency must be made u⟨p in⟩ Continental troops; and as there are only four or five hundred already in that quarter who might be made use of on the occasion, the residue must go immediately from this army. The making so considerable a detachment at this time, is I conceive a measure that could not be hazarded, without doing essential injury to our affairs here.

Of this the Board will be fully sensible, when they are informed, that the enemy's strength at New York and its dependencies is at a moderate computation 14000 men [and our][8] strength on the present ground less than 13,000[9] Besides this number only a bare sufficiency has been left in the Highlands to garrison the forts there. We have been lately reduced by a large detachment to Rhode Island, and it is possible a further detachmt may become necessary. Should we weaken ourselves still more by an entreprise against the Indians, we leave ourselves in some degree at the mercy of the enemy, and should either choice or necessity induce them to move against us, the consequences may be disagreeable. Though there is great reason to suppose the enemy may wish to withdraw their force from these states, if they can do it with safety; yet if they find their departure obstructed by a superior maritime force, it may become a matter of necessity to take the field, and endeavour at all hazards, to open a communication with the country in order to draw supplies from it and protract their ruin; this they will of course effect, if we have not an equal or superior army in the field to oppose them with— We should endeavour to keep ourselves so respectable as to be proof against contingencies.

The event of the Rhode Island expedition is still depending; if it should fail we shall probably lose a number of men in the attempt—To renew it, if practicable, we should be obliged to send reinforcements from this army, which could very ill be spared with its present strength; but would be impossible, if it were diminished by a detachment for the Indian expedition. And then should the enemy unite their force, they would possess so decisive a superiority as might involve us in very embarrasing circumstances. If on the contrary we succeed at Rhode Island a variety of probable cases may be supposed with reference to Europ: affairs which may make it extremely interesting to the common cause, that we should have it in our power to operate with vigor against the enemy in this quarter; to do which, if it can be done at all will at least require our whole force.

These considerations sufficient[l]y evince, that we cannot detach from this army the force requisite for the expedition proposed, without material detriment to our affairs here. And comparing the importance of the objects here with the importance of the objects of that expedition, it can hardly be thought eligible to persue the latter at the expence of the former. The depredations of the savages on our frontiers and the cruelties exercised on the defenceless inhabitants are certainly evils much to be deplored, and ought to be guarded against, as far as may be done consistent with proper attention to matters of higher moment; but they are evils of a partial nature which do not directly affect the general security, & consequently can only claim a secondary attention. It would be impolitic to weaken[10] our operations here, or hazard the success of them to prevent temporary inconveniences elsewhere.

But there are other objections to the measure of almost equal weigh—The season is too far advanced for the entreprise—To raise and collect the troops to lay up competent magazines, and to make the needful preparations and then to march to the Seneca settlements and back again would exhaust at least five months from this time; and the rivers would be impract⟨icable⟩ before it could be effected. This time will not be thought too long, if it is considered, that the preparations of every kind are yet to be begun; and that when completed an extent of more than three hundred miles, is to be traversed, through a country wild and unexplored, the greater part hostile and full of natural impediments—The rivers too at this time of the year are more shallow than at others, which would be an additional source of difficulty and delay. I shall say little on the subject of pr[o]visions, though it is a serious question, whether our resources are so far equal to our demands, that we can well spare so extensive supplies, as this expedition will consume—Besides feeding our own troops, we shall probably soon have to victual the French fleet which is said to have twelve thousand men on board.

Notwithstanding the opinion I entertain of this matter founded upon a knowlege of many circumstances which Congress could not be fully apprized of—in obedience to their orders, I shall without delay take measures for forming magazines at Albany & upon the Mohawk River[11] and for preparing every thing else for the expedition, except calling out the Militia; and shall be glad of the further directions of Congress, as speedily as possible. If it is their pleasure that it should still go on, I shall apply for an aid of Militia and can soon march the detachment of troops which must be sent from this army.

I take the liberty however to offer it as my opinion, that the plan for subduing the unfriendly indians ought to be deferred till a moment of greater leisure. We have a prospect that the British army will ere long be necessit⟨ated⟩ either to abandon the possessions they now hold and quit these states, or perhaps to do something still more disgraceful— If either these should arrive, the most effectual way to chastise the Indians, and disarm them for future mischief, will be to make an expedition into Canada. By penetratring as far as Mo[nt]real, they fall of course, destitute of supplies for continuing their hostilities, and of support to stimulate their enmity.[12] This would strike at once at the root, the other would only lop off a few branches, which would soon spead out anew nourished and sustained by the remaining trunk.

Instead of the expedition resolved upon, it might be adviseable to establish a well furnished Garrison of about three hundred continental troops some where near the head of the Susquehanna, at Unidilla, or in the vicinity of that place. And at the same time to establish a good post at Wyoming, with some small intermediate post. These posts would be a great security to the frontiers; and would not only serve as barriers against the irruptions of the savages, but with the occasional aid of the militia would be convenient for making little inroads upon their nearest settlements; and might facilitate a more serious entreprise, when it shall be judged expedient. I shall be glad of the sentiments of Congress on this proposition.

Df, in Alexander Hamilton's writing, DLC:GW; Varick transcript, DLC:GW. This letter was laid before Congress on 10 Aug., at which time it was returned to the Board of War for a "report thereon" (*JCC*, 11:768).

1. On the draft, GW inserted the words "in the receipt of them," and Hamilton changed "them" to "it."

2. This word was crossed out, apparently in error.

3. See GW's letter to Maj. Gen. Horatio Gates of 2 Aug.; Gates's reply has not been found.

4. GW inserted "& under our present circumstances" on the draft, but Hamilton crossed out "our" and changed "circumstances" to "appearances."

5. This estimate appeared in the resolutions of 11 June, enclosed to GW with the board's letter to him of 27 July (see *JCC*, 11:587).

6. GW inserted "and much larger by their accts," which Hamilton altered to make the parenthetical phrase.

7. GW was referring to the New Hampshire Grants, as Vermont was called. The upper Connecticut River valley, especially the area around current Newbury, Vt., and Haverhill, N.H., was called the Coos (or Cohos) country.

8. The bracketed words were crossed out on the draft; the Varick transcript reads, "Men. our strength," at this point.

9. Hamilton originally wrote "not more than 12 or 13,000," which GW altered to read "under 13,000" and Hamilton revised to the present phrasing.

10. The word "of," which was inadvertently left in the text when the word "weaken" replaced the phrase "hazard the success of" at this point, is omitted here.

11. The preceding five words were inserted on the draft by GW.

12. At this point on the draft, GW wrote a sentence that was subsequently crossed out: "A measure of this sort would strike at the root, the other is only checking a few sprouts which will soon grow again."

*Letter not found*: from Maj. John Clark, Jr., 3 Aug. 1778. On 14 Aug., GW's secretary Robert Hanson Harrison wrote Clark: "The multiplicity of business in which his Excellency has been engaged, would not permit him to take the subject of your Letter of the 3d Inst. into consideration before to day. It seems but reasonable that the public should have the emoluments arising from desertion or the death of Soldiers in preference to Officers; yet there is no Article of War or Resolution of Congress known here that will directly authorize the order you request. The General is desirous to give the Auditors every countenance in his power to promote the purposes of their appointment & when Opportunity will admit of your absence, he requests you to call at Head Qrs, that you & I may talk more fully upon the matter you have in view" (DLC:GW).

## To John Parke Custis

Dear Custis,                                    White plains Augt 3d 1778.

Your Letter of the 15th Ulto from New Kent came to my hands by the last Post, and gave me the pleasure of hearing that you, Nelly, & the little ones were well.

You should not delay recording my Deed to you, because you cannot, I am told, make a proper conveyance to Henry till this happens the postponing of it therefore may not be a pleasing circumstance to him. As you seemed so desirous of living in Fairfax—as I know it will be an agreeble measure to your Mother—and a pleasing one to me, I am very glad to find that you have purchased Robt & Gerrd Alexanders Lands as they are pleasantly situated, and capable of great improvement—These two Gentn not only knew how to take advantage of the times but resolved to profit by them and here, early, & in time—as a friend & one who has your welfare at heart—let me entreat you to consider the consequences of paying compound Interest—Your having 24 Yrs to pay Mr Robt Alexander, without his having it in his power to call upon you for any part of the principal or Interest is in my judgment an unfortunate circumstance for you—a Dun, now and then might serve as a Monitor, to remind you of the evil tendency of paying compound Interest, and the fatal consequence which may result from letting a matter of this sort Sleep without it, you may be plunged into a most enormous debt without thinking of it, or giving that timely attention, which the importance of is requisite I presume you are not unacquainted with the fact of £12,000 at compound Interest amounting to upwards of £48,000 in twenty four years— Reason therefore must convince you that unless you avert the evil by a deposit of the like Sum in the loan Office—and there hold it sacred to the purpose of accumulating Interest in the proportion you pay, that you will have abundant cause to repent it—No Virginia Estate (except a very few under the best of management) can stand simple Interest how then can they bear compound Interest—You may be led away with Ideal profits—you may figure great matters to yourself to arise from this, that, or t'other Scheme, but depend upon it they will only exist in the imagination, and that year after year will produce nothing but disappointment and new hopes—these will waste time, whilst your Interest is accumg and the period approaches when you will be called upon unprepared perhaps to advance 4 times the original purchase money— Remember therefore, that as a friend, I call upon you with my advice to shun this rock by depositing the Sum you are to pay Alexander, in the loan Officer—let it be considered as alexanders money, & sacred to that use and that only. for if you shd be of opinion that pay day being a great way off will give you time enough to provide for it & consequently to apply your present Cash to other uses it does not require the gift of prophecy to predict the Sale of the purchased Estate or some other to pay for it.

After this dissertation upon a subject which perhaps you may think I have no business *now* to intermeddle in I shall approve your proposal for selling the Lands mentioned in your Letter to me provided you can get an adequate price but one circumstance should not be forgotten by you in these transactions and that is that *your* Lands will go but a little way in the purchase of *others* if you sell at three or four pounds an Acre and give twelve after this remark I shall only add that if Mrs Washington has no objections to you selling *her thirds* in *your Lands* about Williamsburg, *or else where* I have not—The loan Office Interest, of whatever Sum they fetch, I shall be content to receive whilst I have any concern in it and your Mother, if she should be the Survivor, consenting to do the same removes every impediment & difficulty to yr selling and places the matter in my opinion upon a fair, just, and equitable footing as you will have the principal if you choose it paying the Interest or may deposit it in the loan Office to raise the Interest there (if more desirable) during her life when the whole will revert to you as the Land would do.

As you seem so well disposed to live in Fairfax and have now fixed the matter by your late purchases of the Alexanders, I should, were I in your place, extend my Ideas & views further than you have done. that is over & above the Sale of the Eastern shore, Williamsburg & Hanover Lands with the Lotts in the City[1] I would sell, or exchange, the whole below— for depend upon it, that whilst you live in Fairfax you will get very little benefit from an Estate in New Kent or King William, unless you have much better luck than most who have Plantations at a distance.

When I advise selling, I would no⟨t⟩ be understood to mean at all hazards—I would try in the first place, what I could get for my own Lands without bargaining for them unless it was conditionally. I would then see whether some large Tracts of Land (not leased out) could not be had in Fairfax, Loudoun, Fauquier, Berkeley, or Frederick—or, on the Maryland side of the Potomack and upon what terms they could be purchased you will then from a comparative view be a judge of the propriety of selling your own & buying others or holding fast what you have—among those who hold large Tracts in Fairfax are the Fitzhughs, Mr B. Fairfax, &ca—In Loudoun & Fauquier The Carters (who probably would be glad to exchange) the Lees, Turbervilles, Pag⟨es,⟩ Burwells, &ca—Most of these being low landers, I think it not improbable but that bargains may be had of them, either by purchase or exchange.

With candour I have given you my opinion upon the several matters contained in your Letter. If it is faulty, it proceeds from error in judgment, not from the want of Attachment—Affection to you—or honest sincerety—and is open to correction.

Go: W——n.

ADfS, DLC:GW; Varick transcript, DLC:GW. GW made numerous revisions on the draft, but the original language, which is retrievable only in part, seems to have offered the same advice to Custis.

1. The Custis house in Williamsburg on a four-acre tract on Francis Street or the back street had been assigned to Martha Washington's dower, but Custis was renting it. After GW consented in October to Custis's sale of dower lands, Custis advertised the house and lot for sale (GW to Custis, 12 Oct.; Dixon and Hunter's *Virginia Gazette* [Williamsburg], 27 Nov.). The Custis estate also included three or more lots on the south side of Duke of Gloucester Street between Palace and Nassau Streets.

# From Vice Admiral d'Estaing

At sea the 3. of August 1778.

It is difficult to console ones self for the obstacles as numerous as insurmountable which stopped me at Sandy-Hook. The importance of

New York, the happiness of fighting the English fleet and the extreme satisfaction of acting directly with you made me desire with the greatest ardor the possibility of entring. I offered, to too little purpose, in an Assembly of your experienced pilots a recompense of fifty thousand crowns, to him who should find us a sufficiency of water. Tis only by action, that my regret can be diminished, and as yet we do nothing—your foresight and your orders have nevertheless, anticipated my wants and rendered my delays less long. The reinforcement you have so properly sent, will, as I am informed, arrive this evening; and it will most assuredly be on the part you have so wisely and expeditiously taken, that our success will depend.

General Sullivan has done me the honor to come and see me and to communicate his views; I will second them with all my power. He is full of that spirit of activity and combination, with which you inspire all those, who have served under your orders—I believe him as fully persuaded as I am of the necessity of acting: The intrenchments that are visible above Conanicut increase dayly; they are numerous. The time I have been at sea begins to make me lose a number of men with the scurvy. The extreme difficulty of procuring water at Shrewsbury, and the tardiness with which it is collected here from different places, have long since obliged me to retrench our allowance The officers and men support this terrible privation with courage and patience; and we have acquired a virtue which has been hitherto refused us—the virtue of perseverance. We doub[t]less owe it to the flattering hope of being useful to allies whom our national taste had itself given us; before the orders of the king had prescribed it.

The Gentlemen, your Generals, will acquit themselves better than I, of the duty, of rendering you an account of the certain state of the preparations going on, and of the small burning of three English vessels, which guarded the Eastern channel.[1] I will confine myself to repeating to you, what I cannot well describe, the zeal and the infinite pains of Lieutenant Colonel Laurens. He is on the wing the four and twenty hours round, to procure us refreshments; and when this is done, remains on board during very long days with all the patience of an old sailor. We are indebted to him for a hospital established on shore and for disembarrasing us of our prisonners; which in our situation form two important articles.

I desire much that the present expedition may be speedily terminated, to give me leisure to employ myself with purging the Sound of the English Vessels which now infest the navigation. I have received Col: Sears, with all the consideration and all the confidence, which those merit, whom you are pleased to send me, and when it shall be time for it, I will consult him with the greatest eagerness.

Accept the homage of the attachment & respect with which I have the honor to be—Sir.

P.S: Since writing my letter, I received that which you had the goodness to address me the 26 of July, by Major General Greene—I am going to look for him on shore, that he may not lose any of the present precious moments. The reputation of this General Officer made his arrival to be wished. His influence on his countrymen and his knowledge of the country will render him formidable to our common enemy. You know how to divine whatever we stand in need of; and from what I have seen, the discerning and employing men proper to the business in hand, seem to be one of the qualities which compose the illustrious character you bear. This is perhaps the most important part of the Great General.

Translation, DLC:GW; LS (in French), DLC:GW; Df (in French), FrPNA: Marine, B4, I46; copy (in French), FrPNA: Marine, B4, I46; copy (in French), DNA:PCC, item 152; translation, DNA:PCC, item 59; copy (of DNA translation), ScHi: Henry Laurens Papers; copy (in French), DNA:PCC, item 169; copy (extract in French), FrPBN. The copy in DNA:PCC, item 152, was enclosed with GW's second letter to Henry Laurens of 7 August. The extract omits the discussion of Colonel Sears and the complimentary closing.
    1. For discussion of the burning, see John Sullivan to GW, 1 Aug., and note 2.

# From George William Fairfax

(Copy)
My Dear Sir                           Bath [England] Augt 3d 1778
    By Genl Burgoynes great Politeness & kindness, I am not only made happy, by the fullest, and most Satisfactory Account I have had in three Years, of the Health and Situation of my Friends in Virginia, but also am enabled to make my acknowledgements for your kind Attention, under the apparent neglect of four years silence on my part.[1] I recived your Letter informing me of your appointment,[2] and as I know that it was impossible for you to attend to your own extensive affairs, I immediately wrote, to beg you would empower Mr R:C: Nicholas, or some other Person of integrity to transact my business, I also wrote to Mr Lund Washington in answer to one from him, covering some Bills of Exch.[3] As the communication was then in some degree open, I am much surprized that those Letters should have miscarried, as I was careful not to touch upon any improper subject. I am sorry to hear that Belvoir is going to decay, but hope if the House is kept light and dry, it cant suffer much. I wish the few Pictures left in it had been removed to Mount Vernon. I am apprehensive my Interest has suffered greatly, and tho' tis late, must now

intreat, that you'l do me the favor to Depute Mr Nicholas, Colo. Lewis of Fredericksburg, or some Gentn of Character to inspect the Manager & Stewards Accot and proceedings. your power is full & adiquate to what I desire, you know the impossibility of my appointing an Attorney, as Witnesses are always required to prove the Execution here to make it valid, this I hope will be my excuse for giving you the trouble of Deligating the Power you have.[4] My situation here is truely pitiable, as the Chancery Suit that brought me over, is as far from a conclusion as ever, owing to the Villainy of my Sollicitor, who had taken up several thousands pounds, upon one of my Estates in Yorkshire while I was in America, which He had Mortgaged for Money applyed to his own use, while my Cause was suffered to be dismiss'd for want of proceeding in, the knowledge of this transaction is but lately discoverd, so that I've only just now obtained an Order from the Court of Chancery, to have my Papers, Title Deeds &c. deliverd up to me, in order to my renewing the Suit, which tis incumbent upon me to do, ⟨Or⟩ I shall not only loose one Moiety of my recoverd Estate at Reedness, but ⟨be⟩ Saddled with the whole Costs of a Chancery Suit of twenty Years standing.[5]

Pardon my good Sir, my troubling you with the Minutie of my Affairs, it may be a matter of consequence, that my Friends should be informed, that I have good reason for my Stay in England, & this opportun⟨ity⟩ through the Channel of a Gentn of honor is not to be missed, & as a proff that tis' not, be assured, that I've wrote more than ten Letters to You & Mr Nicholas relative to my business, and with all necessary caution, it was therefore wanton cruelty only, that could have occasioned their being stoped.[6]

Upon our finding ourselves absolutely Cut off from a remittance from V——a we thought it necessary to retrench Expences greatly; I was ordered, at the same time to drink these Waters, heither we came, without any intention of ⟨*illegible*⟩ here, but finding the Place beautiful & convenient, we were induced to take and Furnish a small House in which we have resided since May was two years. This Spaw has contributed greatly to my Health, my poor Wives is so dreadfully bad that She has little enjoyment of life.

Genl Burgoyne was so obliging as to find Us out in my Cott[age], and to deliver your favor into my hand. accept my hearty thanks for it, and the pleasing information it contained of Lord Fx Mr Carys and other Friends health. When opportunity offers, be pleas'd to present my Affect: respects to his Lordship, and all other Friends, as if I had named every individual, Mrs Fx joins me in Affect: regards to you, and amiable Lady, Mr & Mrs Custis, We lament their loss of Children.[7] I am Dear Sir Your Affect: and Most Obedt Humble Servt.

AL (copy), DLC:GW.

1. Lt. Gen. John Burgoyne had carried GW's letter to Fairfax of 11 March.

2. Fairfax was referring to GW's letter of 26 July 1775.

3. None of these letters have been identified.

4. For GW's account of his attempts to delegate the power of attorney that Fairfax had given him in 1773, as well as a general review of his management of Fairfax's affairs, see GW to Fairfax, 30 June 1786 (*Papers, Confederation Series*, 4:135–41).

5. Reedness is a town about twenty miles south-southeast of York in what was formerly the West Riding, but is currently the Goole district of the East Riding, of Yorkshire, England.

6. The most recent letter from Fairfax to GW that has been found is dated 2 March 1775.

7. The first child of John Parke Custis and Eleanor Calvert Custis, a daughter, was born in 1775 and died in infancy. Their other daughters, born in 1776 and 1777, had, however, survived.

*Letter not found*: from Maj. Gen. Horatio Gates, c.3 Aug. 1778. On 3 Aug., GW wrote the Board of War: "On receiving your letter I wrote to General Gates [2 Aug.], copies of mine to him and of his answer to me are inclosed"; the answer has not been found.

## To Henry Laurens

Sir                              Head qrs White plains August the 3d[–4] 1778

I do myself the honor of transmitting to Congress a copy of a Letter from General Knox, and of sundry observations and remarks on the Ordnance establishment of the 11th of February, which I received about the time we marched from Valley Forge.[1] These would have been transmitted before, had it not been for the moving state of the Army and a variety of other Objects which engrossed my attention. We have found by experience, that some inconveniences have resulted from the Establishment, which I conceive, have proceeded principally from the total independence of the Commissary General of Military stores, on the Commanding Officer of Artillery. It seems some alterations are necessary and what they shall be, Congress will be pleased to determine.

It is not without reluctance that I am constrained, to renew my importunities on the subject of the Committee of Arrangement.[2] The present unsettled state of the Army is productive of so much disatisfaction and confusion—and of such a variety of disputes, that almost the whole of my time is now employed, in finding temporary and inadequate expedients to quiet the minds of the Officers and keep business on a tolerable sort of footing. Not an hour passes without New applications and New complaints about rank—and for want of a proper adjustment of this and many other essential points—our Affairs are in a most irksome and injurious train. We can scarcely form a Court Martial—or parade a Detachment in any instance, without a warm discussion on the subject of precedence—and there are several Good Officers now, who are forced to decline duty, to prevent disputes and their being commanded by Others, who upon every principle are their Inferiors; unless their having obtained Commissions before them, from the opportunities they had of making earlier applications from local circumstances, should be considered sufficient to give them a superior claim. There are many other causes of disatisfaction on this head, but I will not enter into a minute relation of them. I sincerely wish, that the Gentlemen appointed or such Others as Congress may think proper to nominate for the occasion, would immediately repair to Camp. The present opportunity is favourable for reducing matters to System and order—and from painful experience I know, there is an absolute necessity for it.

I should also hope, that Congress will excuse me, for mentioning again the necessity there is for appointing some Brigadiers. The Massachussets, by the resignation of General Learned wants One—Pensylvania as General Hand is not here, has but One with the Army—Maryland, which has Two large Brigades in the field, has only General Smallwood and the North Carolina Troops, since the departure of Genl McIntosh, have been without any. As I had taken the liberty upon a former occasion, to offer my sentiments to Congress and their Committees upon this subject, I should not trouble them now, if I was not more & more convinced that the service required promotions in this line.[3] The frequent changes which take place among the Officers, where there are no Brigadiers, are attended with great inconvenience and detriment; and they are an effectual bar to the introduction of discipline. In such cases, the Officers know, that their command is but temporary—always liable to cease—and therefore they do not find themselves sufficiently interested to promote order and subordination; nor will the rest look up to them with that respect and deference which are essential. Every day's experience proves this—and shews beyond question, that the Affairs of a Brigade can never be in a right train without a Brigadier—or some General to direct them. It is certain, these appointments at the first view will add a little to the list of expence, but in the end they will be a great saving—and produce many important advantages.[4] We are also a good deal distressed at this time for Major Generals; however, as this arises more from the peculiar circumstances and situation of many, which prevent them from duty in the line, than from a deficiency in the number appointed, I shall not add upon the occasion.

There is another branch of the Army, which in my opinion calls loudly for the appointment of a General Officer—and this is the Cavalry. For want of a proper regulating Head in this Corps, the whole has been in confusion, and of but very little service; whereas, under a right management, it might be most useful. The principal Officers in it do not harmonise, which circumstance with their disputes about rank would, were there no other Objections, effectually prevent the Corps from rendering the Public the services they have a right to expect— and of which it should be capable. To promote any Gentleman now in it to a general command, would not be acquiesced in by the rest—(nor do I know that any of them wish it) and it would encrease their misunderstanding and of course disorder. I mean to draw all the Horse immediately together, when I trust they will be under the direction of a General Officer, appointed by Congress for the purpose. Who he shall be, will remain solely with them to determine. However, I will take the liberty to add, that he should be intelligent—active—attentive; and as far as I can judge, General Cadwalader or General Reed would fill the post with great honor and advantage—tho it would seem from the seat the latter has taken in Congress and from his late appointment to the Council of pensylvania, as if he had declined every military view. The abilities of these Gentlemen, as well as their Attachment are generally known—and I am led to beleive that either would be as acceptable to the Corps, as any person that can be found;[5] indeed, I have learnt as much from two of the Colonels.

I have been waiting with the most impatient anxiety to hear of Count D'Estaing's arrival at Rhode Island, but as yet I have not been so happy. My last intelligence from thence is a Letter from Genl Sullivan dated at 10 OClock in the forenoon of the 27th; when he had no advice of the Fleet. He was in high spirits and from the preparation in which matters were, he entertained the most flattering hopes of success in the intended Enterprize. The Brigades of Varnum and Glover, with Jackson's detachment would arrive, I expect on the 2d Instant.

As the Army was encamped and there was no good prospect of a sudden removal, I judged it adviseable to send Genl Greene to the Eastward on Wednesday last;[6] being fully persuaded his services, as well in the Quartermaster line as in the field, would be of material importance in the expedition against the Enemy in that Quarter. He is intimately acquainted with the whole of that Country—and besides he has an extensive interest and influence in it. And in justice to General Greene, I take occasion to observe, that the public is much indebted to him for his judicious management and active exertions in his present department. When he entered upon it, he found it in a most confused—distracted and destitute state. This by his conduct and industry has undergone a very happy change—and such as enabled us with great facility, to make a sudden move with the whole Army & baggage from Valley forge in pursuit of the Enemy—and to perform a march to this place. In a word he has given the most general satisfaction and his affairs carry much the face of method and System. I also consider it as an act of justice, to speak of the conduct of Colo. Wadsworth, Commissary General. He has been indefatigable in his exertions to provide for the Army and since his appointment our supplies of provision have been good and ample.

August 4th. At 7 OClock in the Evening yesterday, I received the inclosed Letter from Genl Sullivan, with one addressed to myself, a Copy of which I do myself the pleasure of forwarding.[7] I am exceedingly happy in the Count's arrival—and that things wear so pleasing an aspect.

There is another subject, on which I must take the liberty of addressing Congress, which is that of the Cloathier's department. I am perfectly satisfied, that unless this very important and interesting Office is put under better regulations—and under a different Head, than it now is, the Army will never be cloathed. Mr Mease is by no means fit for the business. It is a work of immense difficulty to get him to Camp upon any occasion—and no order can retain him there sufficiently long—either to answer the demands of the Troops, or to acquire more than a very slight and imperfect knowledge of them. This of itself according to my ideas, would make him highly culpable—but there are other circumstances. He is charged with inactivity, in not pursuing the best and all the means that present themselves, to provide Cloathing. His Agents too, who have been with the Army—from inability or a want of industry—or proper instructions from their principal, have been very incompetent to the purposes of their appointment. Besides these objections, Mr Mease unhappily is represented to be of a very unaccomodating cast of temper, and his general deportment towards the Officers who have had to transact business with him, has rendered him exceedingly obnoxious. The constant and daily complaints against him, make it my indispensible duty to mention these points—and it is the more so, as I believe both Officers and Men, particularly the latter, have suffered greater inconveniences and distresses, than Soldiers ever did before for want of Cloathing; and that this has not flowed more from a real scarcity of Articles—than a want of proper exertion and provident management to procure them. It is essential that something should be done and immediately, to place the department on a better footing. We have now a great many men entirely destitute of Shirts and Breeches and I suppose not less than a fourth or fifth of the whole here, who are without Shoes. From the deficiences in this line numbers of desertions have proceeded—not to mention deaths, and what is still worse, the Troops which remain and see themselves in rags want that spirit and pride necessary to constitute the Soldier.[8]

I have been informed by Several Officers and by such as I can depend on, that many of the late Draughts are willing and desirous of enlisting during the War.[9] I do not conceive myself at liberty to give direction on the point and therefore submit it to Congress to decide. However, if they can be engaged for the usual bounties allowed by the Continent, after proper precautions are taken to prevent fraud, I think the measure will be expedient. It is true our Affairs have an agreable aspect at present—but the War may continue and we want men. A third of the time of some them, and a half in the case of others, is already expired; and as they will rise in their views and become more difficult in proportion as their service draws to a conclusion, if the step is considered adviseable, the sooner we attempt to enlist—the better in all probability will the work succeed. I have the Honor to be with great respect & esteem Sir Your Most Obedt servant

Go: Washington

LS, in Robert Hanson Harrison's writing, DNA:PCC, item 152; Df, DLC:GW; copy, ScHi: Henry Laurens Papers; copy, DNA:PCC, item 169; copy (extract), CtHi: Jeremiah Wadsworth Papers; Varick transcript, DLC:GW. The LS is docketed in part, "read 10"; see *JCC*, 11:767–68. The extract, which is composed of the sentences praising Nathanael Greene and Jeremiah Wadsworth, was sent by Roger Alden to Wadsworth, 28 July 1789 (CtHi).

1. See Henry Knox to GW, 15 June, and note 2 to that document. For the ordnance establishment of 11 Feb., see *JCC*, 10:144–50.

2. For GW's earlier request that the committee of arrangement repair to camp, see his letter to Laurens of 7 July.

3. GW had previously urged the prompt appointment of general officers in his letter to Laurens of 24 March.

4. The remainder of this paragraph is not on the draft, although the draft seems to be marked for text to be inserted.

5. On the draft, the remainder of this paragraph is in GW's writing.

6. The previous Wednesday was 29 July.

7. GW enclosed Maj. Gen. John Sullivan's letter to Laurens of 1 Aug. (DNA:PCC, item 160; see also Hammond, *Sullivan Papers*, 2:165–67) and a copy of Sullivan's letter to himself of the same date.

8. On Clothier General James Mease's absence from camp, see GW to Mease, 17 April, 16 May, and 18 June, n.2; and Mease to GW, 23 May. The congressional committee to which this paragraph was referred reported on 19 Aug., proposing resolutions that would have returned responsibility for clothing supply to the states and suspended Mease pending a court of inquiry. Consideration of the report was postponed. Another committee was created in October, but no final action was taken until 23 March 1779 when Congress restructured the clothier's department (*JCC*, 11:812–13, 12:983, 996–97, 14:353–60).

9. GW was referring to the troops raised in accordance with Congress's resolution of 26 Feb., directing the states to draft troops for nine months' service to complete their Continental regiments (*JCC*, 10:199–203).

## To Colonel William Malcom

Sir                              Head Quarters [White Plains] 3d Augt 1778
    At the earnest intercession of Colo. Armand I have consented to ad-
vance his Corps, consisting of Horse and Foot, near the Enemy's lines.
You will therefore permit Lieut. Colo. Vrigny to march with the Foot of
that Corps to Camp. I am Sir Your most obt Servt.

Df, in Tench Tilghman's writing, DLC:GW; Varick transcript, DLC:GW.

## General Orders

                    Head-Quarters White-Plains Tuesday Augt 4th 78.
Parole Bloomendale—                        C. Signs Andover. Croten.
    The sixth Virginia Regiment being ordered to join the Tenth in the
Arrangement of the Brigades was a Mistake—it is to continue with the
second as usual.[1]

All Officers commanding Regiments having men who from their
state of health will not be fit for active service in a short time are desired to make a return of them to the Orderly-Office that those proper
for the Purpose may be draughted to join the Invalid Corps under Colonel Nichola in Philadelphia.[2]

    The several Regimental Pay-Masters are requested to make out a list
of the Prisoners, Deserters and dead men belonging to their respective
Regiments immediately, together with the sums that are due each, &
file the same with the Auditors, who will give them directions in what
manner their Accompts are to be made out, in order that the same may
be adjusted and settled without delay.[3]

Varick transcript, DLC:GW. Maj. Gen. Benjamin Lincoln's orderly book for this
date records: "For Detachment General Muhlenburgh[,] Colonels Humpton Van
Schaick[,] Lt Colonels Allison Russel[,] Majors Adams Torrey" (MHi: Lincoln Papers). The instructions that were issued to Brig. Gen. Peter Muhlenberg on this
date (DLC:GW) are identical in content to those issued to Brig. Gen. James Clinton on 31 July. The detachment left White Plains about five P.M. and returned on
7 August. For a brief record of their movements, see "Beatty Journal," 83.
    1. GW's general orders of 22 July listed Col. John Gibson's 6th Virginia Regiment
and Col. John Green's 10th Virginia Regiment as "joined."
    2. In a letter of 28 July, Richard Peters of the Board of War had requested that
GW issue such an order.
    3. An additional paragraph appears at this point in the orderly book of Maj. Gen.
Benjamin Lincoln: "Wanted for the auditors office in the grand army two persons
who can write a good hand and are well acquainted with Ac[coun]ts—None need
apply but such as can be well recommended for their honesty, Industry, and So-
briety—a handsome salary will be given" (MHi: Lincoln Papers).

## To John Parke Custis

[White Plains, c.4–8 August 1778]

I thank you for your cordial and affectionate congratulations on our late success at Monmouth, and the arrival of the French Fleet at the hook[1]—the first might, I think, have been a glorious day, if matters had begun well in the Morning; but as the Court Martial which has been setting upwards of a Month for the tryal of Genl Lee, is not yet over, I do not choose to say any thing on the subject, further, than that there evidently appeared a capitol blunder, or something else, somewhere. the truth, it is to be hoped, will come out, after so long an investigation of it. If it had not been for the long passage of the French Fleet, which prevented their arrival till after the evacuation of Philadelphia—or the shallowness of the Water at the entrance of the Harbour at New York, which prevented their getting in their, one of the greatest strokes might have been aimed, that ever was; and, if successful, wch I think, would have been reduced to moral certainty, the ruin of great Britain must have followed; as both army & Fleet must, undoubtedly, have fallen. Count D. Estaign with his Squadron are now at Rhode Island to which place I have detached Troops, and hope soon to hear of some favourable Adventure there as an attempt will be made upon the Enemy at that place.

After the Battle of Monmouth I Marched for this place, where I have been Incamped more than a fortnight. We cut off by the present position of the Army, all Land supply's to the City of New York; and had the best reasons to beleive that the Troops there were suffering greatly for want of Provisions, but the French Fleet leaving the Hook, opens a door to the Sea, through which no doubt they will endeavour to avail themselves.

Give my love to Nelly Colo. Bassett and the rest of our friends & be assured that I am with sincere regards & affectn Yrs

Go: Washington

ALS (fragment), ViHi. GW learned of the French fleet's arrival at Rhode Island on the evening of 3 Aug., on which date he completed a fortnight at the White Plains camp, so this letter could not have been written before 4 August. It could not have been written later than 12 Aug., when Maj. Gen. Charles Lee's court-martial was completed, and it was almost certainly written before GW learned, on 8 Aug., that a British fleet had sailed from Sandy Hook. As both this text and GW's draft letter to Custis of 3 Aug. (above) respond to Custis's letter of 15 July, it is possible that the two texts were joined to form a single ALS, which might have been dated on the third and continued or redated to reflect the date that it was completed and sent.

1. See Custis to GW, 15 July.

## To Major Caleb Gibbs

WHITE PLAINS, Aug. 4th, 1778.

*Dear Gibbs:*—If your attempt upon Rhode Island should prove [fortunate],[1] and I think there is scarce a possibility of its failure, unless a superior Fleet should compel Count d'Estaing to quit his station; you will have it much in your power to provide for the use of this family, many articles of which you know we stand in much need—as also some things which I should be glad to procure for my own use—among which I find myself in want of a genteel cutting sword.—I do not mean a true horseman's sword; and yet one fit for riding. Many things among the officer's baggage, if it should happen to fall into the hands of our troops, or should be sold by themselves, might be convenient for me; such as table and other camp equipage, properly assorted and contrived for stowage.

To be particular in the recital of my wants I cannot, not having time for recollection.—Your knowledge of them, reminded by what you may see, will prove more adequate than vague directions. Tea equippage, plates and dishes, bowls, basins, camp stools, are essentially necessary;—such of them as can be procured, of materials not liable to break, should be preferred.

The money necessary for the purchase of these things will be advanced by General Greene, upon showing him this letter. I most sincerely wish success to the enterprize, and much honor and reputation to yourself, being with great truth and sincerity Your affectionate,

GEO. WASHINGTON.

*United States Gazette* [Philadelphia], 25 Oct. 1826.

1. The newspaper text reads, "unfortunate," which is most likely a printer's error, as GW clearly meant "fortunate."

*Letter not found*: from Maj. Gen. Nathanael Greene, 4 Aug. 1778. On 8 Aug., GW wrote Greene: "I received your favor dated the 4th Inst."

## From Lieutenant Colonel John Laurens

Sir,                    Providence 4th August 1778

I had the honor of receiving your Excellencys letter of the 28 Ulto the day before yesterday. The following is a short journal of what has passed since the date of the letter which I wrote from point Judith.[1]

July 25. Our situation at the point being dangerous from the facility with which the enemy might land a party in our rear and cut off our retreat, I sent the greater part of our pilots to quarter three or four miles out of the cul de Sac—and reserved only a sufficient number for

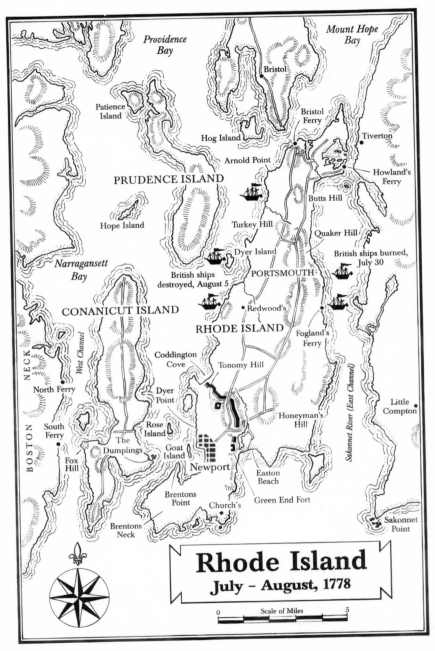

*Rhode Island, July-August 1778. (Illustrated by Rick Britton. Copyright Rick Britton 2005)*

attending to the signals which we expected—their safety was provided for by a horse patrole of militia. A twenty gun Sloop went into Newport harbour.[2]

26—Recd an open letter from General Sullivan for the Admiral containing his plan of operations.[3]

He informs Count d'Estaign that three entrances to Rhode Island— one East of the Island called Seakonnet or the Eastern passage in which there are 2 gallies and one small frigate. Another on the west of the Island between it & Connanicut I.—called the main channel, in which there are 2 frigates—besides 3 gallies and 2 or 3 frigates at New-Port. a third on the west of Connanicut Island—called the west passage in which there are 3 Frigates That the enemys land force amount to 7000 men including three regiments on Connanicut. He proposes that the Admiral should detach a proper force up the east and west channels to take the frigates & galleys stationed there which force might afterwards serve to cover the passage of the American troops— from Bristol and Tiverton—And that the main body of the Squadron shd block up the principal or middle Channel—so as to prevent the escape of the enemys ships—and the arrival of succours.

his design is to pass all the enemys works on the north part of the Island—leaving a sufficient detachment to observe the troops stationed in them—and to advance rapidly to the attack of the redoubts which immediately environ the Town—at the moment of this attack he wishes the Count to begin his upon the batteries which defend the harbour to cannonade the Town—and land his troops in the most favourable place for seconding the American attack.

He refers the Count to a sketch of the country sent by me—as this did not appear to be sufficiently accurate and detailed to be satisfactory I wrote to the general entreating him if possible to inform the Admiral as nearly as he could—the strength of the profiles in each battery—height of parapet—height of the ground above the surface of the water—distance to which they might be approached—number of guns and their callibers—observing that tho' from the sketch both the entrance and bason of New-port harbour appeared to be subject to a dangerous cross-fire—yet upon a more minute investigation they might be found contemptible compared with the force to be employed against them—I likewise enquired whether the right and left flank of the enemy's chain of redoubts were not so situated—as to admit of vessels anchoring near enough to fire ricochet along the line.

27th. Two deserters crossed from Rhode Island—they say that the scarcity of provision occasions murmuring among the troops—that the new levies are employed in mowing—that the French fleet is expected—and the troops are busily employed in raising new works.[4]

28—A Ship and sloop appear off block Island—two british Frigates beat out of the harbour at New-port—but returned towards evening—thick hazy weather.

29—The Fog cleared away and the appearance of the French Squadron was as sudden, as if they had been brought to view by raising a curtain—The gentleman who had the superintendence of the pilots did not choose to venture them till the signal agreed upon should be given—I went on board the admiral with my dispatches—He informed me that his intention was to have gone into New-port harbour and fired the signal there—the receipt of Genl Sullivans letter—the expediency of distributing pilots among the ships—and the advanced hour of the day—induced the admiral to anchor his squadron off the main channel and order two frigates with a tender up the Eastern Channel and the Sagittaire a Ship of the line up the west.[5]

30—The orders relative to the ships and frigates could not be executed till the morning—the Sagittaire was fired upon from a two gun battery of twenty four pounders on the west side of Connanicut—she returned a broad side and passed it—from an explosion which we discovered immediately after we judged that the enemy had blown up their magazine and evacuated the battery—the Sagittaire received two slight scratches in her hull—Upon the approach of the Aimable and Alcmene frigates in the East channel—the enemy set fire to the King Fisher 20 gun sloop—The lamb galley mounting 2 eighteen—2 nine and 2 six pounders—and sent the spit-fire galley mounting 2 eighteens—2 twelves & six six pounders—in form of a fire-ship.

The latter blew up, soon after the Count de Grasse had caused a grapnel to be fixed in her—and while his crew were in the act of towing her off—but neither they nor their gallant commander received the least injury—Mr Dorset who boarded the King Fisher with a party, with a view of saving her from total destruction—had an escape equally providential—the remains of her powder blew up while they were on board—without doing them any hurt[6]—Previous to making the gran[d][7] attack on the batteries in the harbour—the Admiral judged it of the greatest importance to make himself master of connanicut Island—The difficulties in the way were these—If he were to attack them only on one side—viz.—the western—the enemy would have nothing to hinder them from empowering our attack with reinforcements to station some ships on the E. side of Connanicut would effectually cut off the communication and the admiral would have ordered the ships to run the gauntlet thro' the entrance of the harbour—if they could afterwards have anchored out of the reach of the batteries within, but this was pronounced impossible—And to expose them both to the fire of the passage, and the more deliberate cannonade from the batteries would be exposing them too much in a preliminary operation—It was determined therefore to call upon General Sullivan for a proper number of militia to oppose such reinforcements as it was judged the enemy could spare—By the admirals desire Col. Fleury and myself set out to represent the importance of the object and ask his assistance. In our way we met Genl Sullivan—he informed us that he had several new matters to propose to the admiral and judged a conference with him necessary—he was received on board with proper military honors—and at his departure the admirals ship was manned, and fired fifteen cannon—Gen. Sullivan brought a draught on a larger scale—but a draught which the admiral had was infinitely more correct and minute—The Genl informed the Count that the enemy's principal work was on domine hill[8]—that this was the highest point in that part of the Island and commanded both the redoubts and the Town—that this carried either by storm—or if that were found impracticable, by heavy artillery and mortars all the rest would follow of course—here consequently he intended to bend his strength, he proposed that the American troops should land on the east side of the Island and the French on the west—each to support the other in case of attack—he still judged it unnecessary for the Count to make his attack on the batteries—till the moment in which the attack on the enemys works should take place.

This evening some of the outermost ships made signals of the appearance of a fleet the squadron was ordered under sail to be in the greater readiness either for chace or fight—the vessels from the E. & W. channels ordered out.[9]

31st   The Squadron returned to their Station. The Fleet announced by the signals proved to be eight transports convoyed by a Frigate. Some say they were loaded with wood from Long Island for New port. It is generally beleived they were loaded with Beef and Flour. They put about as soon as they discovered the French Ships and escaped under the Veil of Night.

American privateers men who had landed upon Connanicut and several of the inhabitants asserted that the Enemy had evacuated that Island. The Count determined to send a party towards Evening to ascertain the facts. Among other plans, it was once proposed that the whole fleet should proceed up the West Channel, turn the North end of Conanicut, and descend the main Channel, till it should arrive at a proper place for operating. This it was urged would avoid the Cross fire at the entrance, and put the ships in a position from whence they would be less exposed to the fire of the interior Batteries—But upon further examination it was found, that to effect this detour, the ships must either have a Wind which would answer both to go up the West and come down the middle passage—or, that after going up with a fair wind they must wait at the North end of Conanicut for a favorable change to come down or lastly that they must beat down the main Channel. The uncertainty and delay incident to the two first were discouraging—The last was declared by the most experienced pilots to be impracticable for ships of the line—As the narrow limits of the Channel would not allow sufficient scope for working, and missing stays in such circumstances would be fatal.

By the Admirals desire I went on shore to make some arrangement for the reception of the sick and prisoners—and for establishing Signals at point Judith, that he might have the earliest intelligence of the approach of any of the enemy's ships.

The Admiral sent a party to Conanicut for the purpose beforementioned, their report confirmed the accounts of the privateers men &ca.

1st Augt   As soon as the morning Fog which generally prevails at this season, was dissipated—The Count landed with a detatchment on Conanicut, in order to reconnoitre the Harbour and Batteries of New port. In the Battery on the West side of Conanicut which had fired upon the Sagittaire, we found two twenty four pounders spiked up, their carriages intire and their heavy ammunition. From thence we proceeded through the incampment of the three Regiments, which appeared to have been precipitately abandonned, to the Battery on the East side called Dumplins Rocks Battery. The two 24 pounders belonging to this, the Enemy had thrown down the precipice on which the Battery stood. We discovered them with their carriages at the waters edge below. in both Batteries the platforms appeared to have been newly laid.

From the Heights on the East side of Conanicut we had a very distinct View of the Battery on Brenton's point—the Cannon appeared to be 24 pounders—two fire obliquely on the entrance of the harbour—and two directly across.[10]

The Battery on Goat Island is partly of Earth and partly of Masonry—It has a great many embrasures—but we could not discover any Cannon in it—besides it appears to be in a ruinous condition and its low situation must make it yield at the first salute from the lower tear & Top, as it may be approached to a very convenient distance. The Battery on Dyers point appears to be most respectable and has this advantage over us—that the Ships of the line cannot approach any nearer than half a mile—but this circumstance will only retard our success a little—The Work on Domini Hill appears considerable—but the face presented to us is not flanked—we discover Two frigates at the upper end of the main passage—some distance beyond the town, An East Indiamen armed as a Ship of war (which appears the most respectable Ship of War they have) and a Frigate between Goat Island and the Town in front of the Town—along the Kuays a number of merchantmen and Transports—within Brenton point One Vessel which is said to be a fire Ship—We discovered an Encampment just above the Town—Brenton point Battery is guarded by a Detachment of Hessians.

2d—The Admiral disembarrassed his Squadron of the Sick—prisoners & prizes. The Two last are ordered to providence. The Sick are in Houses near the North & South ferry, up the West passage. Genl Sullivan has appointed a Commissary to supply them with necessaries. In this neighbourhood is the watering place for the fleet—the daily consumption is so great, that they supply themselves slowly.

3d By the Admirals desire Col. Fleury & myself set out for providence to know in what forwardness matters are for the land attack.

4 Early in the morning we arrived at providence.

what I have gathered concerning the Enemy's force—and our own is as follows.

| | |
|---|---:|
| Strength of the enemy previous to reinforcements | 3000 |
| 1st Reinforcement under Genl Brown | |
| 1st Batallion of his Brigade | 344 |
| 2d Reinforcement under Genl Prescott | 1200 |
| Total | 4544 |
| Marines and Sailors | 1000 |
| | 5544 |

The British Regiments are the 38—43—54—22d—there are Six foreign Regiments & 2 American Corps.

| | |
|---|---:|
| General Sullivan has in this State | |
| Continentals | 2000 |
| Militia | 3000 |
| He expects from Massachussets Militia | 3000 |
| Connecticut | 1000 |
| New Hampshire | 600 |
| | 9,600 |

Besides this the Division under the Marquiss de la Fayette, part of which arrived yesterday—and part the day before—Several Corps of Volunteers—inclusive of a Regiment of Artillery from Boston.

We shall labour under a great disadvantage in having no brass field pieces of large Calibers—The Iron ordnance that we must from necessity use will be very unweildy—From the tardiness of the Militia and the necessity of constructing transport Boats, I have no hopes of our being ready for action before monday next.[11] General Sullivan exerts himself as much as possible, but he cannot hasten the wished for day. The Count D'Estaing's case is cruel when I consider what a noble Squadron he commands—That by a long voyage he missed meeting the British Fleet at Sea—that by a physical impossibility he was obliged to renounce the Splendid enterprize at Sandy Hook—That by new misfortunes he is losing the most precious moments—at a time when the Eyes of all Europe are upon him—As I think him a great Officer and most respectable man, I cannot but most sincerely feel for him.

In obedience to your Excellency's command I represented to Count D'Estaing the advantages that would result from stationing a Ship of the line in the sound—and the practicability of his overtaking the British fleet in such a situation as we would wish should the evacuation of New York take place.[12] He was perfectly of your Excellency's opinion in both points—but he seemed to think that the attack of Rhode Island would require all his force—and besides it seems to be his principle to keep his Squadron together—and not to weaken it by Detachment. As soon as the present expedition is over he will be ready to bend his course either to Hallifax or Sandy Hook, as the General good may require—If Hallifax should be the next Object, will not a co-operation on our parts by land, be necessary, and in that case, will it not be advisable to make some timely arrangements.

Inclosed I transmit your Excellency a Map, which may be useful in illustrating the proposed plan of Operations.[13] The french Troops are to land on the west side of Rhode Island above Dyers Island. The Americans on the East side nearly opposite. We have reason to beleive that the Enemy have abandoned their works on the North part of the Island—and have centered themselves within their lines at new port.[14] I omitted to mention to your Excellency that when the Sagittaire was detached up the west passage—it was represented to the Admiral that she was out of supporting distance and was exposed to an Attack from the Enemy's whole naval force. He therefore ordered the Fantasque another Ship of the line to take same Station.

I fear I have tired your Excellency with detail—and hope my next will contain more important matter in fewer words. I am with the most inviolable attachment & sincere respect Your Excellency's dutiful Aid

John Laurens

P.S. The Admiral has sent a Ship and frigate to take one of the Enemy's frigate's that is stationed near block Island and gives intelligence of the french fleet to every British Vessel that appears.

Copy, in James McHenry's, Tench Tilghman's, and Robert Hanson Harrison's writings, DNA:PCC, item 152; copy, ScHi: Henry Laurens Papers; copy DNA:PCC, item 169. The transcribed copy was enclosed with GW's second letter to Henry Laurens of 7 August.

1. John Laurens's letter from Point Judith was dated 25 July.
2. Laurens was probably referring to HMS *Sphynx*, which returned from a cruise on 25 July (*Mackenzie Diary*, 2:317).

3. For Maj. Gen. John Sullivan's letter of 25 July to Vice Admiral d'Estaing, see Sullivan to GW, 26 July, n.3.

4. The deserters were a black man employed as a groom and a member of the "New Levies"; for more on their intelligence, see Laurens to Sullivan, 27 July (Hammond, *Sullivan Papers*, 2:128–29).

5. The *New-York Journal and the General Advertiser* (Poughkeepsie) of 3 Aug. reported, on the authority of "a gentleman whose veracity may be depended upon," that on 29 July "the French fleet . . . was off Point-Judah, where Capt. Nathaniel Shaw of New-London, went on board, with a number of pilots, to pilot them to Newport."

6. Etienne, comte de Grasse de Limermont (1725–1790), commanded the *Guerrier* in d'Estaing's fleet. D'Orset was an ensign on the *Alcmene*. He may possibly have been François-Joseph d'Orset (b. 1743). D'Orset came to America as a volunteer in 1777 but failed to obtain an army office and was sent back to France in November of that year. By November 1778 he was sous-lieutenant in the voluntaires étrangers de la marine, and he served in the Grenada combat under d'Estaing's overall command in 1779. He rose to the rank of captain in the regiment by 1781. He later served in the Guadeloupe regiment, 1783–93, and was named chevalier de Saint-Louis à la Martinique in 1798.

7. McHenry wrote "grant."

8. Laurens was referring to the fortification on Miantonomi (Tonomy) Hill, then north of Newport.

9. At this point McHenry ceased and Tilghman began writing the copy.

10. At this point in the copy, Tilghman's writing ceases; the text following is in the writing of Harrison. References to Brenton's Point designated the spit of land just west of Brenton's Cove (now the site of Fort Adams), which should not be confused with the modern Brenton Point on the southwest edge of Rhode Island.

11. The next Monday was 10 August.

12. For the undated memorandum giving this command, see GW to Vice Admiral d'Estaing, 22 July, n.2.

13. The enclosed map has not been identified.

14. The diary entry of British officer Frederick Mackenzie for 4 Aug. indicates that the British forces on the northern parts of the island had sent their baggage and tents to Newport but had not yet abandoned their positions (*Mackenzie Diary*, 2:328).

## To Colonel William Malcom

Sir                                    Head Quarters White plains 4 Augt 1778

I recd yours of the 30th with the Returns of the Garrison, I should have answered you by the same person who brought it, but he did not call upon me.

It is not in my power at present to add to the Strength of the Garrison, the detatchment to Rhode Island having taken every Man that can be possibly spared from this Army.

I think you will do well to send down the Brass 12 pounder to this park.

If Mr Laurence's service as a deputy Adjutant General is indispensably necessary, you may take him into employ as such, but I should have thought that your Brigade Major with the assistance of the Regimental Adjutants might have done the duty.[1] Rations have varied at different times according to the scarcity or plenty of Meat and Flour. The Ration at present delivered out by you is much the same as the Commissary General proposes at this time, and therefore you may continue it. In future direct your Commy of Issues to take his orders from the Commy General of Issues.

It falls into the Qr Master Generals department to see that the Artificers are properly employed, and therefore if you think those upon the North River are idling away their time, you should apply to Colo. Hay, who will order them to repair to West point or any other place where they are wanted.

I cannot approve of the sentence of the Court against Springsteel, because the Court Martial w⟨as⟩ illegally constituted as being held without my order. But that he, or capital Offenders may be brought to justice in due form in future, I inclose you a power to hold General Courts Martial when necessary.[2]

Yours of the 1st instant inclosing the weekly return ⟨has⟩ been received.[3] I am Sir Yr &c.

Df, in Tench Tilghman's writing, DLC:GW; Varick transcript, DLC:GW.

1. Malcom's general orders of 7 Aug. announced: "His Excellency General Washington hath appointed Lieut. Jonathan Lawrence to do Duty as Assistant adjutant General in this Garrison" (Aaron Burr's orderly book, NHi).

2. The enclosure has not been identified, but on 10 Aug., Malcom dissolved his garrison court-martial and formed a new one "by Virtue of authority from his Excellency the Commander in Chief." Christopher Springsteel, who had enlisted in Malcom's regiment in March 1777 and deserted in September of that year, was captured and confined at Goshen in February 1778. He broke jail in April but was recaptured by July and confined at Fort Arnold. According to Malcom's general orders of 18 Aug., Springsteel was retried and sentenced to receive "one Hundred Lashes and be sent on board the Galleys during the war." GW confirmed the lashes but ruled that he should "be kept at hard Labour in the Garrison instead of Gowing on board the fleet" (Aaron Burr's orderly book, NHi). Apparently returned to normal service in October 1778, Springsteel deserted again in May 1779.

3. This letter has not been found.


## To Brigadier General William Maxwell

Sir                              Head Quarters White plains 4 Augt 1778

I was last Night favd with yours of the 2d with a York paper for which I am obliged to you.[1] I have only to recommend to you, to keep a vigilant watch upon the motions of the Enemy upon Staten Island, and upon their fleet in the Bay. If you procure any certain intelligence that any considerable number of ships are preparing for sea, let me know it immediately, that I may communicate it to Count D'Estaing who has arrived at Rhode Island. I am &c.

P.S. direct your spies to be very inquisitive whether they are embarking Baggage and Stores and if any troops move from Staten Island whether they go on board Ships or up to N⟨ew⟩ York.

Df, in Tench Tilghman's writing, DLC:GW; Varick transcript, DLC:GW.
  1. Maxwell's letter to GW of 2 Aug. has not been found.

## To Major General John Sullivan

Dear Sir                    Head Quarters White plains 4th Augt 1778
  I was, last Evening, favd with yours of the 1st instant, which releived me from the greatest anxiety, as so much longer than the usual time of passage had elapsed, since the Count D'Estaing left the Hook. I am very happy to hear your presages of a good understanding between the Count and yourself in respect to command. I wish you had mentioned how many of the Enemy's ships of War were in the harbour, and what stations they took upon the arrival of the French Fleet. If their situation should be such, that there is no possibility of their escape, I would have you inquire of the Count, whether it would be improper, or inconsistent with the Rules of War, to warn them not to destroy them upon their peril. You will just suggest this matter, in a transient way, and let the Count act as he thinks prudent.
  You must suppose that I shall be most anxious to hear as often as possible from you, and I therefore beg you will keep me constantly advised of your operations. Even if nothing material should happen in the course of a day or two, just to hear that all is well will be a relief to me.
  If you gain any more certain accounts of the strength of the Enemy, than what were mentioned in your last, be pleased to transmit them to me. If we can come at an exact knowledge of the detachment at Rhode Island, we can form a truer judgment of the numbers remaining at New York.
  I must beg your care of the inclosed for the Count D'Estaing, to whom be pleased to present my most respectful Compliments and good Wishes. Be pleased also to deliver the letters inclosed for Colo. Laurens and Capt. Gibbs.[1] I am Dear Sir Your most obt & humble Servt
                              Go: Washington

P.S. The most certain way of calculating the Enemy's strength, is first to ascertain the number of Regiments, and then endeavour to find out the number of M⟨en⟩ in them by examin⟨ing⟩ deserters and oth⟨ers.⟩

LS, in Tench Tilghman's writing, NhHi: Sullivan Papers; Df, DLC:GW; Varick transcript, DLC:GW. The characters in angle brackets are supplied from the draft.
  1. See GW to Maj. Caleb Gibbs, this date. GW called Gibbs a captain because he had not yet received notice of Gibbs's promotion on 29 July. The enclosures for Lt. Col. John Laurens and Vice Admiral d'Estaing have not been identified.

## From Jonathan Trumbull, Sr.

Sir—                          State of Connecticut—Lebanon 4th Augt 1778
  Enclosed is a resolution of the Governor and Council of Safety of this State—It is hoped that your Excellency will make no hesitation to grant a Warrant for the amount of the enclosed Account.[1]
  It appears reasonable that payment be made to B. General Saltonstal from the Chest of the United States of America, rather than from this State—to whom he will look, when he fails from your Excellency. I am, with great Esteem & Regard Your Excellency's most Obedient humble Servant

                                                   Jonth. Trumbull

ALS, DLC:GW; LB, Ct: Trumbull Papers.
  1. Trumbull may have enclosed the vote of the Connecticut council of safety, 30 May 1778, "That his Excellency the Governor be desired to write to his Excellency General Washington and request him to examine and liquidate Brigadier General Saltonstall's abstract while in service of the United States and draw on &c. in his favour" (*Conn. Public Records*, 2:88). The enclosed account has not been identified.

## General Orders

                      Head-Quarters W. Plains Wednesday Aug't 5th 1778.
Parole Cromwell—                          C. Signs Bronx—Ashford.
  The Commander in Chief in very express and positive Terms forbids soldiers to remove, burn or otherwise destroy the Rails belonging to the Inclosures in and about Camp and expects that Officers of all Ranks will use their utmost Exertions to prevent this wanton & injurious Abuse of Private Property, or bring to severe Punishment the Offenders.
  The Adjutant General in ordering a detachment for Guards or Scouts is always to mention the number of days for which they are to draw Provisions—Notice of which being communicated to the Regimental Quarter Masters (thro' the proper Channel) makes them responsible for the men of their respective Regiments that they bring the Provision ordered.
  The Commanding Officer of every detachment for more than a day is, before he marches from the Parade to inquire if the men are pro-

vided agreeable to order and if they are not to lodge the names of the deficient men and the Regiment they belong to, with the Adjutant General, who is positively directed to arrest and bring to trial the delinquent Quarter-Masters; and if the Commanding Officer of the Party neglects to make this Inquiry before he leaves the Parade, he makes himself responsible and must answer accordingly. This is to be considered as a standing Order, and all Officers are to pay strict obedience thereto, as it hath been found in some Instances that a neglect has defeated the End of detachments and in others that the Country People have suffered greatly in having their Provisions forced from them to support these Parties.

Major Fish, late Inspector in General Poor's Brigade is appointed to do that duty in General Clinton's and is to be respected accordingly.

A Return of Drums, Fifes, Drum heads &c. wanting in the respective Brigades to be made immediately.

Varick transcript, DLC:GW.

## To Colonel Morgan Lewis

Sir                                        Head Quarters White plains 5th Augt 1778

As an expedition against the Indians to the Westward is in contemplation, I desire you will give orders to have the Batteaus in the Mohock River put in order and kept ready for such an event. Some Waggons and Horses will likewise be wanting should the expedition take place, but I would not have you either hire or purchase immediately upon an uncertainty, only be making such arrangements, that you can command them suddenly if called for. You need not be cautioned to keep the reason of these preparations secret. All other matters in your department should also be put into a proper train, to forward the expedition should it take place. Genl Schuyler is particularly well acquainted with what preparations will be necessary upon such an occasion and I would therefore have you consult him. I am &ca.

Df, in Tench Tilghman's writing, DLC:GW; Varick transcript, DLC:GW.

## To Captain Thomas Posey

Sir                                        Head Qrs White plains Aug. 5: 1778

A few days ago I received your favor dated at New Windsor on the 24th Ulto, but how or by whom I do not recollect—As the person, acting as paymaster to your detachment, has not applied for their pay; and as the Officers and Men may have occasion for Money, I have drawn a Warrant on the Pay Master at Albany, payable to you or *your Order* for Two thousand five Hundred Dollars, which you will find inclosed. I have also written him a Letter of advice upon the subject, which you will send with the Warrant when it is presented for payment.[1] You will have to account for this Money & therefore you will be careful in taking receipts or proper Vouchers for the disbursement of it among the Officers & Men—that you may meet with no difficulty in settling with the Auditors. I wish you success—and am Sir Yr Most Obt st

G.W.

Df, in Robert Hanson Harrison's writing, DLC:GW; Varick transcript, DLC:GW.

1. On this date GW wrote to Assistant Paymaster General Jonathan Burrall: "Captain Thomas posey was detached a few days ago from this Army, with a party of Riflemen to act on the Frontiers of this State. At the time they marched, they had not an opportunity of receiving their pay—I have therefore drawn a Warrant on you for Two Thousand five Hundred dollars which I request you to pay to the Captain or any person he may authorise to receive it" (Df, DLC:GW). Burrall (1753–1834), who had acted as an assistant paymaster general since October 1776, served 1780–89 as a Treasury Department commissioner for settling various accounts. He served as assistant postmaster general, 1789–91, and after leaving government service, he became a banker in New York, commencing as cashier of the Bank of the United States at New York City.

## To Brigadier General John Stark

Sir　　　　　　　　　　　Head Quarters White plains 5th Augt 1778

I recd yours of the 29 July by Lieut. Randolph and of 31st inclosing the order of Congress for raising those Men who are now demanding pay. As this is a matter of a particular nature, I cannot undertake to settle it. I think the charges, whatever they may be, ought to [be] drawn out and submitted to Congress—I cannot determine what is to be done respecting the State prisoners at Albany who draw continental provision. Govr Clinton says those at Pougkepsie are furnished with provision by the state. I would have you enquire of the Magistrates of Albany and know of them how it first happened that those prisoners drew from the continental store. The Commy should keep an exact Acct of what he issues.

I cannot see why the Soldiers Wives in Albany should be supported at public expence. They may get most extravagant wages for any kind of work in the Country and to feed them, when that is the case, would be robbing the public and encouraging idleness. If they would come down and attend as Nurses to the Hospitals they would find immediate employ. When I sent up Lieut. Colo. Butler with his own Regiment and a detatchment from Morgans, I intended he should have taken the command of all the troops employed upon that service, provided it did not require a Genl officer He is not only a very brave but an experienced Officer especially for such an expedition. If Colo. Alden is with his Regiment, and forms a junction with Lt Colonel Butler, he must command him of course, except Colo. Alden could by any means be put upon some other service. If the thing could be so managed it would be very agreeable to me, as I place great dependance upon Colo. Butlers Abilities as a Woodsman.[1]

I will send up as many of the Articles as can be procured for Butlers and Morgans Regt by Lieut. Randolph. I am &c.

Df, in Tench Tilghman's writing, DLC:GW; Varick transcript, DLC:GW.

1. Shortly after his arrival at Albany, Lt. Col. William Butler had written New York governor George Clinton on 29 July with a string of complaints about Stark, including that, by ordering Col. Ichabod Alden to join his regiment, Stark had deprived Butler "of the Honor your Excellency intended me in the Command of the whole." On 4 Aug., Clinton wrote Butler from GW's camp at White Plains, reporting that he had "communicated the Contents" of Butler's letter to GW and "that if it can be done without giving just Cause of Offence to Officers of Supperior Rank he wishes you may have the Command of the Detachments allotted for" offensive operations against the Indians (Hastings, *Clinton Papers*, 3:595–96, 605–6).

## General Orders

Head-Quarters White-Plains Thursday Augt 6th [1778]
Parole Delaware—                    C. Signs Eden. Franklin—

The Officers commanding the several Guards are to be pointedly exact in reporting in time the Occurrences of the day; at any rate they are not to delay doing this beyond 12 ôClock, that the whole may be drawn into one view and presented by the Majr Genl before 3 P.M.

That the whole Army may be served with the same Ration, the Commissary General is 'till further orders to issue as follows, one pound and a quarter of flour or soft bread or one pound of hard bread, eighteen ounces of beef, fresh or salt or a pound of Pork or a pound of fish and two ounces of butter, a Gill of Rum or Whiskey when to be had; The usual allowance of soap and Candles.[1]

The Major Generals with the Brigadiers and Officers commanding Brigades under them are to examine the ground well in front and round about their respective Encampments and assign each Brigade it's Alarm-Post; In doing this, after the Ground hath been previously examined, they are to cause the Brigades to be drawn up on such as shall be respectively intended for them, that the space required for each may be ascertained.

A Discharge of three Pieces of Cannon as usual from the Park is to be the signal for an Alarm.

At a General Court-Martial July 27th 1778 — Coll Stewart President Doctor Brown of the 14th Virginia Regiment tried 1st — For going home, not only without the leave but against the express Consent of the Commanding Officer, and that at a time too when the distressed situation of the Regiment required the Doctor's particular Attention — 2ndly — For neglecting to have a furlow, which he said he obtained from Doctor Cochran registered as is positively directed in general Orders of the 22nd of December last.[2]

The Court having considered the Charges and the Evidence are unanimously of opinion that Doctor Brown is guilty of the Charges exhibited against him, being breaches of 5th Article 18th section of the Articles of War and of a General order issued the 22nd of December A.D. 1777 — but in Consideration of his very bad State of health at the time he left his Regiment and his conceiving that a furlow from Doctor Cochran was intirely sufficient, the Court only sentence him to be reprimanded in General orders.

Tho' the fact stated in the first charge is proved, yet the Commander in Chief cannot think that it contains any Imputation of guilt, because by the Establishment of the Medical Department, the Surgeon General had a Right to give Doctor Brown a furlow in the manner he did, and it appears besides that the Doctors State of health did not permit his attendance on the Regiment, his Conduct was certainly blameable in not having the Furlow registered as directed by General Orders, an Ignorance of which is the worst of all possible Excuses.[3]

Varick transcript, DLC:GW.

1. On 3 Aug. generals Horatio Gates, Stirling, Alexander McDougall, Samuel Holden Parsons, Anthony Wayne, Charles Scott, Arthur St. Clair, Enoch Poor, William Woodford, Jedediah Huntington, William Smallwood, James Clinton, Henry Knox, and John Nixon had reported to GW that this ration, with twenty rather than eighteen ounces of beef, was "a sufficient allowance for the Troops of the United States" and recommended "the inserting the same in General Orders when His Excellency Genl Washington Commander in Chief shall think proper" (DLC:GW). Knox wrote with his signature, "I think 18 ounces beef sufficient," and McDougall and Nixon stated that the soap ration was insufficient.

2. Daniel Brown (1753–1795), appointed surgeon of the 14th Virginia Regiment in early 1777, was reported absent without leave in May 1778 and resigned on 26 Sept. 1778.

3. The following additional orders appear in Maj. Gen. Benjamin Lincoln's orderly book for this date: "A noncomissiond Officer and seven Dragoons, from each of the following regts, viz. Bland, Sheldons, and Moylands to be paraded on the grand parade tomorrow morning, furnished with two days provision.

"For three days detachment to be furnished with two days provision ready cooked and 40 rounds ℔ man — Lt Colonels Reynier and Starr, Majors Ledyard and Winslow.

"For two days guard, to be furnished with two days provision and 40 Round pr man: Lt Colo. Smith & Majr Sumner" (MHi: Lincoln Papers).

## From Major General William Heath

Dear General                          Head Quarters Boston Augst 6th 1778
    Some Time in the month of april last Capt. Willoe of the Troops of the Convention, went to Canada by the way of Hallifax in order to forward to this Place the Baggage Belonging to those Troops—to which by the Convention they had a Right if it was found necessary, nothing has been heard of Capt. Willoe Since, General Phillips applies for leave for an other Officer to go to Canada by the way of the Lakes—not knowing the Condition of our Posts on that rout or whether it would be Prudent to let an Officer go that way. I am led to request your Excellencys Opinion & Direction.[1]
    Every Exertion is in Exercise Here for the reduction of Rhode Island The Roads are filled with Companies of Militia and volluntiers Three Thousand Militia have been ordered to be Drafted, The State Regt of artillery under Colo. Crafts marched Some Days Since, as did an artillery Company Commanded by Major Bumstead of this Town, The Independent and Light Companies march this Day & to morrow[.] a Large Company from Salem and another from Newbury Port Composed of Gentlemen of the first Families & Fortunes marched through this Place yesterday and the Day before for Providence[2]—General Sullivan has a Train of Field artillery Consisting of Thirty Brass 6 and 4 pdrs, Four Brass Howitz Eight or nine Brass Mortars—and a Marine one of 13 Inches this latter I have Sent from this Place—Genl Hancock Sets out to morrow or Next Day—Brigadiers Lovell and Titcomb are gone with the militia[3]—I have the Honor to be with the greatest respect your Excellencys most obt Servt

                                                         W. Heath

ADfS, MHi: Heath Papers; copy (extract), DNA:PCC, item 152; copy (extract), DNA:PCC, item 169. The extract in item 152 was enclosed with GW's first letter to Henry Laurens of 16 August. Both extracts consist of the first paragraph of the letter.
    1. Heath enclosed Maj. Gen. William Phillips's letter to him of 29 July, in which Phillips requested that if Heath was disinclined to grant his request, "an Officer may go to General Washington for his directions" (DLC:GW).
    2. Thomas Bumstead was commissioned a captain in the Massachusetts militia in November 1776. Thomas Crafts, Jr., was commissioned as colonel of a Masssachusetts artillery regiment in November 1776 and resigned in February 1779. According to the *Continental Journal, and Weekly Advertiser* (Boston), 6 Aug., Crafts's regiment marched on 31 July and Bumstead's company marched on 3 August. One hundred and eight volunteers from Salem left Boston on the morning of 4 Aug.,

while the Newburyport company arrived on 5 Aug. and left on the morning of 6 August. The Boston light infantry company was to march on the afternoon of 6 Aug., and John Hancock's independent company on 7 August (see also "Price Diary," 334).

3. Solomon Lovell (1732–1801) of Weymouth, Mass., was commissioned as colonel of a Suffolk County regiment of militia in February 1776 and as brigadier general of the Suffolk County militia in June 1777. His service on this Rhode Island expedition ran from 1 Aug. to 14 Sept. 1778. He subsequently served on the Penobscot expedition from July to October 1779 before resigning his commission in August 1780. Jonathan Titcomb (1727–1817), who represented Newburyport in the Massachusetts General Court at this time, was commissioned as colonel of an Essex County militia regiment in February 1776 and as brigadier general of the Essex County militia in October 1777. He served on the Rhode Island expedition from 28 July to 11 Sept. 1778. Appointed a major general of militia in June 1781, Titcomb served at that rank at least until 1787. In 1789 GW appointed him to be naval officer at Newburyport, Mass., a post he filled until 1812.

# From Captain John Paul Jones

Honored Sir                                    Passy near Paris August 6th 1778

As the Scene of War by Sea is now Changing from America to Europe I have been induced to give up the Command of the American Ship of War Ranger and to continue for some time in Europe in compliance with the request of the Minister of the French Marine in a letter to our Ministers Plenipotentiary at the Court of Versailles.[1]

I will not intrude on your Excellencies time even by attempting to pay you the respect wh⟨ich⟩ you so Justly Command: the intention of this letter is o⟨nl⟩y ⟨to⟩ beg your acceptance of two Epaulettes with which it i⟨s acco⟩mpanied, and which my Freind Mr Williams of Nantes has undertaken to forward.[2] I expected to have had the honor of delivering this little present into your own Hands—but not having that satisfaction If in the meantime I can render you any acceptable Services in France I hope you will Command me without reserve being with Sentiments of pe⟨r⟩fect Esteem Honored Sir Your very Obedient and Very humble Servant.

ADf, DLC: Peter Force Papers, John Paul Jones Collection; LB, MdAN; copy, DLC: Peter Force Papers, John Paul Jones Collection.

1. See the letter from the French minister of marine and the colonies, Antoine-Raymond-Gualbert-Gabriel de Sartine, to the American commissioners, 5 July 1778, in *Papers of John Adams*, 6:265; see also the commissioners' reply to Sartine, 11 July, in Butterfield, *Adams Diary and Autobiography*, 4:158.

2. Jonathan Williams, Jr. (1750–1815), Benjamin Franklin's grandnephew, was the commercial agent for the United States at Nantes, France.

# From Major General Lafayette

dear General                                           providence 6th august 1778
I have receiv'd your Excellency's favor by general greene,[1] and have been much pleas'd with the arrival of a gentleman who not only on account of his merit, and the justness of his wiews, but also by his knowledge of the country and his popularity in this state may be very serviceable to the Expedition—I willingly part with the half of my detachement tho' I had a great dependance upon them, as you find it convenient to the good of the service—any thing, my dear general, you will order or even wish, schall alwaïs be infinitely agreable to me, and I will alwaïs feel happy in doing any thing which may please you or forward the public good—I am of the same opinion as your Excellency that dividing our Continental troops among the militia will have a better effect than if we were to keep them together in one wing.

You will receive by general Sullivan an account of his dispositions, preparations &c. I therefore have nothing to add but that I have been on board of the admiral the day before yesterday—I saw among the fleet an ardor, and a desire of doing some thing which would soon turn into impatience if we do'nt give them a speedy occasion of fighting—the officers ca'nt contain theyr soldiers and saylors, who are complaining that they are since four month running after the british without getting at them—but I hope they will be soon satisfied.

the count d'estaing was very glad of my arrival as he could oppen freely his mind to me—he express'd the greatest anxiety on account of his wants of every kind, provisions, water &c. he hopes the taking of Rhode island will enable him to get some of the two above mentionn'd articles. the admiral wants me to join the french troops to these I Command as soon as possible—I Confess I feel very happy to think of my Cooperating with them, and had I Contriv'd in my mind an agreable dream, I Could not have wish'd a more pleasing Event than my joining my Countrymen with my brothers of America under my Command and the same standards—when I left Europe I was very far from hoping such an agreable turn of our business in the American glorious revolution.

tho' I have no account neither reflexions to Give to your excellency as I Am here *a man of war of the third rate*, I will after the expedition scribble some lines to you, and join to the account of general Sullivan the assurance that I have all my limbs and that I am with the most tender affection, entire confidence in yours, and high respect Your excellency's Most obedient humble servant

                                           the Marquis de lafayette

I beg leave to present my compliments to the family and Monsieur de chouïn.

ALS, PEL. Where Lafayette edited this letter after the war, the original has been restored as much as possible.

1. See GW to Lafayette, 27 July.

*Letter not found*: from Lt. Col. John Laurens, 6 Aug. 1778. On 10 Aug., GW wrote Laurens: "I have only to acknowledge the receipt of your letter of the 6th Inst. and to wish that this may find you in the full possession of the object of the enterprize" (Df, DLC:GW).

*Letter not found*: from New Jersey field officers, 6 Aug. 1778. On 9 Aug., GW wrote Col. Israel Shreve: "I have been favd with a letter of the 6th signed by yourself and other Feild Officers of the Jersey Brigade."

## From Major General John Sullivan

Dear General.                          Head Qrs Providence Augt 6 1778.

I have the honor to inform your Excellency that some time since three of the enemy's frigates quited their former stations—sailed to the North end of Rhode-Island and anchored between Dyers Island and Bristal ferry—Count d'Estaign on the 4 Inst. meditated an attack upon them, and on the 5th issued orders that two of his ships should turn the North end of Connanicut Island and give them battle. These orders they proceeded to comply with, but on their approach, the English frigates were set fire to, abandoned, and entirely consumed, without making use of any means of defence, or shewing the least appearance of resistance. Their names & force have not yet been ascertained, but when known, shall be transmitted to your Excellency.[1]

I am sorry to inform your Excelly that the motions of the militia are excedingly tardy—I have been but inconsiderably reinforced by the militia of Connecticut—nor do I expect much from them—Those of New Hampshire & Massachusetts I am informed are on their march and have reason to expect them by saturday next.[2] Your Excy may rest assured that I shall make every previously necessary preparation for their reception, so that no time be lost between their arrival and the immediate execution of our intended invasion. I have the honor to be &c. &c.

John Sullivan

P.S. I have this moment learned from certain intelligence that four frigates and one tender were destroyed.

Copy, DNA:PCC, item 152; copy, DNA:PCC, item 169. The transcribed copy was enclosed with GW's second letter to Henry Laurens of 9 August.

1. Four English frigates had initially left Newport harbor on 29 July, and after moving back toward the town on 2 Aug., had, along with the *Pigot* galley, on 3 Aug. again anchored north of the town: the *Lark* and *Pigot* "off Freeborn's Creek"; the *Orpheus* and *Cerberus* above and below Dyer's Island, respectively; and the *Juno* "near Codrington's Cove." When the two French ships began moving at around five o'clock on the morning of 5 Aug., the captain of the *Cerberus* attempted to retreat to Newport but "was obliged to run her on shore behind Redwood's, and set her on fire. . . . The ship blew up about 8 o'Clock." Not long after that the *Juno* was set afire when one of the French ships "tacked, as if intending to run down towards the town," and that ship also soon exploded. The other three English ships observed "other French ships coming up between Prudence and [Rhode] Island" and "were immediately run on shore; the Orpheus at Almy's point [modern Coggeshall Point], and the Lark and Pigot at Freeborn's Creek." All were set afire. "The Orpheus blew up about 7 o'Clock; the others not till near 12." The French ships returned to anchor off the north point of Conanicut Island. According to Capt. Frederick Mackenzie of the Royal Welch Fusiliers, the British captains had been under orders since 21 July to burn the frigates before letting them fall to the French, and preparations for the burning had begun on 29 July (*Mackenzie Diary*, 2:316, 319, 321, 327–28, 329–30; see also Döhla, *Hessian Diary*, 82; "Newport in the Hands of the British," 105; *Providence Gazette; and Country Journal*, 5 Sept.).

2. The next Saturday was 8 August.

## General Orders

Head-Quarters White-Plains August 7th 1778.
Parole Flanders—                                  C. Signs Epping Dobbs.
All returns for Arms, Ammunition, Accoutrements &c. are first to be made out by the Regimental Quarter Masters, which after examined and signed by the Commanding Officers of Regiments are to be given to the Brigade Quarter-Masters who are to digest them into Brigade Returns, get them examined and signed by the Brigadiers or Commandants of Brigades, then present them to the Adjutant General for an Order upon the Commissary of Military Stores, taking receipts from the Regimental Quarter Masters for such Articles as shall be delivered them which they are to charge to the several Companies—The Commanding officers of Companies are again to charge their men with such Arms &c. as shall be delivered them respectively and severely punish any non commissioned Officer or soldier who shall carelessly or willfully waste or destroy them besides making them pay the full value thereof: And as there has been in many Instances a wanton waste of Arms Accoutrements and Ammunition, the Commander in Chief enjoins it upon the Commanding Officers of Regiments to see this order pun[c]tually executed, and as it is of the highest Importance that strict Œconomy should be observed with respect to those essential Articles he desires the Brigadiers to pay particular attention to the observance of the same.

The Commander in Chief directs that Doctor Cochran and Doctor Burnet in conjunction with the officers of their departments take the immediate Charge of the Flying-Hospital.

The Muster-Rolls of the Army to be drawn agreeable to the directions and forms prescribed by the Commissary or Deputy Commissary General of Musters—The absent Officers to be accounted for by the Commanding Officers of Corps—the dates of Inlistments and different terms of service for which the troops are engaged to be continued on the Rolls—The strictest attention will be expected to this order.

A return of the State of the Arms Accoutrements and Cloathing of the Regiments to be made to the Officers of Musters on the day of every Muster—The Rank of the Field Officers of the four Regiments of Light Dragoons having been settled by a board of General Officers at White-Marsh on the 24th day of November last, the Officers are to rank in the following manner—

| Colonels— | L. Colonels | Majors. |
|---|---|---|
| Moylan. | White. | Washington. |
| Baylor. | Bird. | Jameson. |
| Bland. | Temple. | Clough. |
| Sheldon— | Blackden. | Talmadge. |

The Quarter Master General is authorized to direct the Waggon Master General or his Deputies to use their best endeavours to enlist Waggoners out of the Militia now in service, and if a sufficient number cannot be procured in that way, they are to engage such as may be deficient out of the draughts or levies from the several States—In the latter Case they are not to take on any Account more than four men out of a Company.

Lieutenant Jones of the 15th Virginia Regiment is appointed Pay-Master to the same.

Varick transcript, DLC:GW; copy (extract certified by Col. Stephen Moylan), DNA:PCC, item 152; copy (extract), DNA:PCC, item 169. The extracts consist of the order about the ranks of dragoon officers. A note on the item 152 extract reads, "to follow letter to Maj. Washington 5th Novr."

*Letter not found*: from Lt. Caleb Brewster, 7 Aug. 1778. On 8 Aug., GW wrote Brewster: "I have received your Letter of yesterday from Norwalk."

## To Henry Laurens

Sir                                     White plains August 7th 1778

Yesterday afternoon I had the Honor to receive your favor of the 30th Ulto.

Major Gibbs is now at Rhode Island. I shall embrace the first safe opportunity to transmit him your Letter and the Commission, with which Congress have been pleased to honor him.[1]

Since my Letter of the 3d & 4th Instant, I have received no advices from General Sullivan, so that I can give no information of our operations against the Enemy in the Eastern Quarter. I am told the Militia of Massachussets & Connecticut were collecting fast—and proceeding to reinforce him.[2]

I have the pleasure to acquaint Congress, that Major General Lincoln arrived here yesterday—and that he is happily so far recovered from his wound, as to be able to take his command in the line.

The inclosed paper from NewYork came to hand last night. It contains an account of the fire, which unfortunately broke out in the City on Sunday night—and of the damage which was occasioned by it.[3] It also contains the latest advices that I have seen from Britain—and such as appear to be interesting.[4] I have the Honor to be with great respect & esteem sir Yr Most Obedt servt

Go: Washington

LS, in Robert Hanson Harrison's writing, DNA:PCC, item 152; Df, DLC:GW; copy, DNA:PCC, item 169; Varick transcript, DLC:GW. The LS is docketed in part, "Read 10"; see *JCC*, 11:770.

1. For Laurens's letter to Caleb Gibbs of 30 July, announcing Gibbs's promotion to major, see DNA:PCC, item 13.

2. At 10 P.M. on this date, GW wrote a second letter to Laurens that read: "Since I had the honor of addressing you to day, I received Letters from the Count D'Estaing & My Aid Lt Colo. Laurens. These contain the latest advices I have from Rhode Island, & of which I do myself the pleasure of transmitting Copies by this Conveyance" (LS, DNA:PCC, item 152). He enclosed Vice Admiral d'Estaing's letter to him of 3 Aug. and John Laurens's letter to him of 4 August.

3. The previous Sunday was 2 August. GW probably enclosed Rivington's *Royal Gazette* of 5 Aug., which reported that "On Monday morning about one o'clock the city was alarmed by a tremendous fire, which broke out at the House of Mr. Stewart, at Cruger's dock, and notwithstanding the utmost efforts of the navy, army, and inhabitants, soon consumed all the buildings on the east, south, and west end of said wharf, with every house on the south side of Little Dock Street. . . . the flames soon communicated to the north side of Little Dock Street, and consumed the whole (five houses excepted) at the west end. The fire . . . burnt every house to the east of Mr. Isaac Low's, as far as the old slip, and three opposite the slip. . . .

"The loss on this melancholy occasion is great, there being no less than 64 dwelling houses, besides stores, consumed.

"There were two small vessels burnt, but we hear of no lives being lost."

4. The *Royal Gazette* of 5 Aug. printed news brought by the *Earl of Sandwich* packet, which left Falmouth on 9 June and arrived at New York on 2 August. The reports included an account of General Burgoyne's appearance before the House of Commons on 26 May, rumors of a "new arrangement in administration," questions in the House of Lords about the detention of the Convention army in America, and the king's speech to Parliament on 3 June. On the draft, an additional

paragraph followed this, which read: "On my arrival at this Camp, the paper In-dorsed No. 2 was put into my Hands by a Mr Wheelock. The Gentleman informed me he was Lieutenant Colo. of a Regiment, ordered to be raised last Winter by the Marquiss Fayette for the intended Canada expedition, and on the terms of double pay." At this point on the LS, Harrison began a new paragraph with the words "On my arrival at this Camp," but that text was erased.

*Letter not found*: from William Livingston, 7 Aug. 1778. On 11 Aug., GW wrote Livingston: "I was favor'd with yours of the 7th in[stant] this morning."

*Letter not found*: from Col. William Malcom, 7 Aug. 1778. On 9 Aug., GW wrote Malcom: "I recd yours of the 7th with the weekly returns enclosed."

*Letter not found*: from Brig. Gen. William Maxwell, 7 Aug. 1778. On 8 Aug., GW wrote Vice Admiral d'Estaing: "I have just received a letter from Brigadier General Maxwell . . . dated yesterday at nine oClock in the forenoon"; GW also wrote Maxwell on 8 Aug.: "I just now rec'd your favor of yesterday." For quota-tions from Maxwell's letter, see GW to John Laurens, 8 August.

## General Orders

Head-Quarters W. Plains Saturday Augt 8th 78.
Parole Europe—                                    C. Signs Finland. Durham.
The Regimental Pay-Masters are to apply to the Pay-Master General for Pay for the Months of April and May[1]—Those who have not received their Ration money since the first day of January last are to apply imme-diately as the Pay Master General is ordered to forward the Accounts to Congress.

Right Wing to be paid on Monday next Second Line and Artillery on Tuesday and Left Wing on Wednesday.[2]

At a General Court Martial August 4th 78 Coll Hall President, An-thony Matica an Inhabitant of this State was tried for supplying the En-emy with Fuel and acquitted.

Also William Cole on Suspicion of being a Spy and acquitted of the Charge exhibited against him; Both are to be released from their con-finement.

At the same Court John Armstrong a Private in Captain Pollard's Company of Artificers was tried 1st "For stealing a Key["]—2nd For striking and giving abusive language to Lieutenant Parker—found guilty and sentenc'd to receive one hundred lashes.[3]

Also John Duffey a soldier in the Delaware Regiment tried for de-sertion to the Enemy, found guilty and sentenced to receive one hun-dred lashes.[4]

The Commander in Chief approves the sentences and orders them to be put in Execution tomorrow morning at Guard mounting at the head of the Troops to which they respectively belong.

Lieutt Herbert of the 6th Pennsylvania Regiment is appointed to do the duty of Brigade Major in the 2nd Pennsylvania Brigade 'till further Orders and is to be respected accordingly.[5]

After Orders August 8th 1778.

For the Safety and Ease of the Army and to be in greater readiness to attack or repel the Enemy, The Commander in Chief for these and many other Reasons orders and directs that a Corps of Light-Infantry composed of the best, most hardy and active Marksmen and commanded by good Partizan officers be draughted from the several Brigades to be commanded by Brigadier General Scott, 'till the Committee of Arrangement shall have established the Light-Infantry of the Army agreeable to a late Resolve of Congress.[6]

Field Officers for the Corps.

| Colonels— | Lieut. Colls | Majors. |
|---|---|---|
| Parker | Harmer. | J. Stewart |
| Gist | Simms | Taylor[7] |
| Butler | Shearman. | Ledyard. |
| Henly— | | |

Coll Graham's Regiment to be added to this Corps.

The details of the several Brigades are to be draughted and got in readiness as soon as possible.

Varick transcript, DLC:GW. Maj. Gen. Benjamin Lincoln's orderly book for this date begins with an additional order: "For two days guards—to be furnished with two days provisions and 40 rounds pr man—Lieut. Col. Hubley—Major Thompson" (MHi: Lincoln Papers). Additional routine orders regarding the two days guards, which appear frequently in Lincoln's and other orderly books for August and September 1778, will not ordinarily be noted.

1. GW's Revolutionary War warrant book lists four pages of disbursements to paymasters on this date (DLC:GW, ser. 5, vol. 19).

2. An additional order appears at this point in Maj. Gen. Benjamin Lincoln's orderly book: "Twenty four light Dragoons, properly officered to attend the grand parade tomorrow morning at guard mounting furnished with two days provision" (MHi: Lincoln Papers). Additional routine orders regarding the appearance of dragoons at guard mounting, which appear frequently in Lincoln's and other orderly books for August and September 1778, will not ordinarily be noted.

3. John Armstrong served from January 1777 to November 1779 as a private in one of the companies of quartermaster's artificers that were organized under Col. Jeduthan Baldwin's command in July 1778. Phineas Parker of Andover, Mass., who was commissioned an ensign in an artificer company in January 1777, was promoted to lieutenant in March 1778 and to captain in January 1779. He served at least until the end of 1780, by which time the Quartermaster Artificer Regiment had been formally created.

4. John Duffey, a private in Capt. Robert Kirkwood's company of the Delaware Regiment, reportedly deserted on 1 May 1777 and returned on 3 Aug. 1778 (*Delaware Archives*, 1:203, 227).

5. Stewart Herbert, Jr. (1754–1795), a printer from Lancaster County, Pa., enlisted in the German Regiment as a sergeant in July 1776 and became an ensign of the 12th Pennsylvania Regiment in October of that year. Promoted to second lieutenant in May 1777 and to first lieutenant in January 1778, he transferred to the 6th Pennsylvania Regiment on 1 July 1778. Herbert, who had been wounded in a battle at Short Hills, N.J., in June 1777, was again wounded, and this time captured, at Green Spring, Va., on 6 July 1781. Although paroled, he was not exchanged as late as November 1782. He was assigned to the 1st Pennsylvania Regiment in the January 1783 reorganization of the Pennsylvania line and may have subsequently moved to the 3d Pennsylvania Regiment, serving out the war. After the war, Herbert served from August 1784 to September 1785 as a lieutenant and adjutant for a U. S. infantry regiment formed to defend the northwest frontier, and from 1790 until his death he printed a newspaper at Hagerstown, Maryland.

6. GW was referring to the first of Congress's resolutions of 27 May on the establishment of the army (*JCC*, 11:538–39).

7. This officer was probably Maj. Richard Taylor (1744–1829). Taylor, who was commissioned a lieutenant in the 1st Virginia Regiment in September 1775 and promoted to captain in March 1776, became major of the 13th Virginia Regiment in February 1778. He became lieutenant colonel of the 2d Virginia Regiment in December 1779 and retired from the army in February 1781. After the war Taylor moved to Kentucky, where, in 1790, GW appointed him collector of customs at Louisville. Taylor was the father of President Zachary Taylor.

# To Lieutenant Caleb Brewster

Sir,                                        White plains Augt 8th 1778.

I have received your Letter of yesterday from Norwalk.[1] Let me entreat that you will continue to use every possible means to obtain intelligence of the Enemys motions—not only of those which are marching Eastward, upon Long Island, but others—In a more especial manner, I have to request, that you will, by every devise you can think of, have a strict watch kept upon the Enemy's ships of war, and give me the earliest notice of their Sailing from the hook—To obtain speedy & certain intelligence of this matter may be of great Importance to the French Fleet at, & the enterprize on, Rhode Island; for which reason, do not spare any reasonable expence to come at early & true information; always recollecting, & bearing in mind, that vague, & uncertain accts of things, on which any plan is to be formed or executed is more distressing & dangerous than receiving none at all—Let an eye also be had to the Transports, whether they are preparing for the reception of Troops &ca—Know what number of men are upon long Island—whether they are moving or stationary—what is become of their draft Horses—whether they appear to be collecting of them for a move—How they are supplied with Provisions—what arrivals—whether with Men, or Provisions—and whether any Troops have Imbarked for Rhode Island or else where within these few days. I am Sir Yr Most Obedt Servt

G. W——n.

ADfS, DLC:GW; Varick transcript, DLC:GW. Caleb Brewster (1747–1827) had been commissioned an ensign in the 4th New York Regiment in November 1776 and a lieutenant of the 2d Continental Artillery Regiment on 1 Jan. 1777. From this time until he left the service in July 1783, Brewster was stationed "on the Sound to keep open a communication with the City of New York by the way of Long Island, for the purpose of [GW's] secret corrispondence" (GW's certificate of 10 July 1784, DLC:GW). He was promoted to captain lieutenant in June 1780.

1. This letter has not been found.

## To Vice Admiral d'Estaing

Sir,                                    Head Quarters White plains 8 Augt 1778[1]
    I had the honor last night of receiving your favour of the 3d instant. I most sincerely sympathize with you in the regret you feel at the obstacles and difficulties you have heretofore encountered—Your case has certainly been a case of peculiar hardship; but you justly have the consolation which arises from a reflection that no exertions possible have been wanting in you to insure success, the most ample and adequate to your wishes and to the important expectations from your command—The disappointments you have experienced proceed from circumstances which no human foresight or activity can controul. None can desire more ardently than I do, that the future may compensate for the past and that your efforts may be crowned with the full success they deserve.
    I have just received a letter from Brigadier General Maxwell who is stationed in the Jerseies near Staten Island dated yesterday at nine oClock in the forenoon. Inclosed are extracts from it, which contain very interesting information.[2] The terms made use of are so positive and express, that it is natural to conclude the intelligence is well founded. Its importance induces me to lose no time in communicating it. What may be the real design of this movement can only be the subject of conjecture. Unless the fleet may have received advice of a reinfor[ce]ment on the coast, which it is gone to join, with intention to bend their united force against you, it can scarcely be supposed that Lord Howe will be hardy enough to make any serious attempt with his present inferiority of strength. If he should it can only be accounted for on the principle of desperation stimulated by a hope of finding you divided, in your operations against Rhode Island. this however is a very

probable supposition—It is more likely, he may hope by making demonstrations toward you to divert your attention from Rhode Island and afford an opportunity to withdraw their troops and frustrate the expedition we are carrying on. I shall not trouble you with any further conjectures, as I am persuaded you will be able to form a better judgment than I can, of his intentions and of the conduct it will be proper to persue in consequence.[3]

In order to aid in removing the inconveniences you sustain in the article of water, and relieve the sufferings of the brave officers and men under your command, whose patience and perseverance cannot be too highly commended, I have w[r]itten to Governor Trumball of the state of Connecticut, requesting his endeavours, to collect vessels and load them with water at New London for the use of your Fleet[4]—I shall be happy if this application is productive ⟨of the desired effect.⟩[5]

I send you a New York paper of the 5th, which is not unworthy of attention.[6]

Allow me to assure you of the warm respect and regard with which I have the honor to be—Sir Your most Obedt servt.

Df, in Alexander Hamilton's writing, DLC:GW; copy (extract), FrPBN; Varick transcript, DLC:GW. The extract consists of the first paragraph of the letter.

GW sent this letter to Maj. Gen. John Sullivan with the following cover letter of this date: "The inclosed for Count D Estaing is of the utmost importance and must be forwarded instantly. It announces to him the sailing of the British fleet from the Hook, which according to intelligence received happened the day before yesterday" (Df, DLC:GW). According to Johann Kalb, the courier was dispatched at two in the afternoon, as soon as the departure of the British fleet was known (Kalb to the comte de Broglie, 10–15 August, in Stevens, *Facsimiles*, vol. 8, no. 845).

1. The dateline is in Tench Tilghman's writing.

2. Maxwell's letter to GW of 7 Aug. has not been found. For the text of the enclosed extracts, see GW to John Laurens, 8 August. GW also may have enclosed a list of the British fleet that sailed from Sandy Hook (see John Hancock to Jeremiah Dummer Powell, 11 Aug., *Continental Journal, and Weekly Advertiser* [Boston], 13 Aug.).

3. At this point the draft is marked with an asterisk, but no corresponding mark appears. The paragraph that follows appears after the closing on the draft but was moved to this point in the Varick transcript, a reasonable interpretation of the asterisk's meaning.

4. GW's letter of this date to Jonathan Trumbull, Sr., reads: "The Fleet at Rhode Island under the Count D'Estaing suffers many inconveniences in the procuring of Water. I could wish, in case you think it practicable, in case it can be any ways effected, that Vessels may be sent forward immediately from New-London with a proper supply. From the situation of his Squadron with respect to water it is a measure, which, if undertaken, and executed with alacrity, cannot fail of being of the utmost consequence to the Count—It may prevent also accidents of a very alarming nature—should he be obliged to put to Sea—You will, therefore, I hope, take the matter into consideration, and give it that attention which its importance demands" (LB, Ct: Trumbull Papers).

5. The words in angle brackets are taken from the Varick transcript.
6. GW probably enclosed a copy of Rivington's *Royal Gazette* of 5 August.

## To Major General Nathanael Greene

Sir.                                    Head Quarters White plains 8th Augt 1778.

I received your favor dated the 4th Inst. informing me of your arrival at Providence, and the flattering disposition of things in that quarter.[1]

We have just received an account from Genl Maxwell of Lord Howes sailing from the Hook with his fleet of armed vessels early on Thursday morning last.[2] Whether it is to make demonstrations of fighting the Count d'Estaign, in order to favor the withdrawing or reinforceing of the troops on Rhode Island is not easy to determine. I would hope however that it is not to join a squadron from England, or if it is that your operations will be determined before they can act.

Wishing you all manner of success and glory, I am Sir your obt & very hbl. servt.

P.S. you have referred me for particulars to a letter from Genl Sullivan—no such letter came to hand.

Df, in James McHenry's writing, DLC:GW; Varick transcript, DLC:GW.
1. Greene's letter of 4 Aug. has not been found.
2. The preceding Thursday was 6 August.

## To Lieutenant Colonel John Laurens

⟨My dear Sir                          Head Quarters White plains 8 Augt 1778

Yesterday Afternoon I recd your favr of the 4th inst. You have my warmest thanks for your indefatigable exertions to promote the intended enterprise agt the Enemy, and my sincerest wishes that you may see them crowned with the fullest success. I shall be happy if things are in a proper train at the time you mention to begin our operation.

About an hour ago I recd a letter from General Maxwell, dated at Elizabeth Town the 7th at 9 oClock A.M. which contains the following paragraphs "I have to inform your Excellency that early yesterday Morning Lord Howe sailed out of the Hook, with his whole Fleet of armed Vessels. They were out of sight in the Afternoon and supposed to be going to Rhode Island. No troops nor transports were thought to be with them."

"some transports are drawn up between Governors Island and Yellow Hook, supplied with wood, water and provisions. their Number sufficient to carry three Regiments to the West Indies. The Regiments supposed to be going are the 7th 29th and 71st but they were not embarking." He adds a Nota bene "No British Fleet is arrived yet, that we can hear of."[1]

I have written to Count D'Estaing by this Conveyance and⟩ communicated the above advices. I have also transmitted him a York paper of the 5th Instant containing British intelligence to the 4th of June, from which it would appear that Adml Keppel was then watching the Brest fleet.[2]

Your Journal & Map were very satisfactory and as I am deeply interested in the success of our Operations, I need not urge to you my wishes for constant information respecting them. What is & what is not are both very material.

I shall not write to Genl Sullivan by this opportunity. You will be pleased to remember me to him. I am Dr Sir with great regard & esteem Yr Most Obt servant

Go: Washington

P.S. In a Letter from Genl Greene which came when yours did,[3] he mentions one from Genl Sullivan. If he wrote his Letter miscarried.

I dare say the Count DEstaing has taken the wisest precautions in his power to obtain information of any Sea-movements of the Enemy on our Coast—& particularly of the approach of any fleet towards him. I hint however to *you*—that if he has not already done it, I think he might employ light Cruizers off Rhode Island & the South side of Long Island to answer important purposes.

LS, in Robert Hanson Harrison's writing, Sotheby, Parke-Bernet, sale no. 4184, *Printed Books and Autograph Letters*, 28–29 Nov. 1978, item 93; Df, DLC:GW; Varick transcript, DLC:GW. Because only a portion of the LS was reproduced in the sale catalog, the text in angle brackets is taken from the draft, which is in Tench Tilghman's writing.

1. Brig. Gen. William Maxwell's letter to GW of 7 Aug. has not been found.

2. See GW to Vice Admiral d'Estaing, this date. Rivington's *Royal Gazette* of 5 Aug. printed "A LIST of Admiral KEPPEL'S FLEET, which has blocked up the principal part of the French Navy assembled at Brest."

3. Maj. Gen. Nathanael Greene's letter to GW of 4 Aug. has not been found.

## From Andrew Lewis

Dear General　　　　　　　　　　　　　　Fort Pitt August 8th 1778

I have been asked in such a Manner by the Board of this State to attend as a Commissioner in this quarter that I knew not how to refuse tho I had but little hopes of having it in my power to be of real Service, as a Treaty with the Indians I believed to be what was principally in View.[1] I arrived at this place on the 1st Instant but found neither Indians, Agent, or Commissioner, from the State of Pennsylvania nor the Instructions which I was told would be found on my Arrival at this place, I shall wait an Answer to a letter sent on this Occasion to Congress that I may know the Cause of all the Disappointments and Embarrasments that seems unhappily to attend what was had in prospect.[2]

I am confident that your Excellency will think with me that at a Time when our extensive Frontiers in every Settlement of this State as well as Pennsylvania are dayly ravaged by the depredations of a combination of all the Savage Tribes (except a few of the Delawares who seem to be friendly disposed) nothing can be expected by a Treaty before they are heartyly drubbed into a peacifick dispositition. And this leads me to mention something of the present embarrassing Circumstances of General McIntosh who is crossed in all his expectations, disappointed in the Levies that were to join his few Regulars, the Provisions of Flesh laid in last Winter damaged, unacquainted with what further Supplys he may be furnished with or when it may be expected, the Savages frequently Murdering & Scalping without having it in his power to afford protection even in the defensive way, the Season of the year far advanced, and in every respect without having the least prospect of effecting any thing that can redound to his credit or the safety of the Inhabitants, and tho he has had no regular Notice that Congress has laid aside the Scheme of attacking Detroit this Year, yet from the backwardness above mentioned as well as from a representation & Opinion of the Board of this State to Congress, he has reason to believe it will be the case;[3] but however that may be the Attacking of that Post this Year however Necessary is altogether out of the Question. this being the case I hope your Excellency will pardon the freedom I take when I say that unless General McIntosh be enabled to carry the War into the Indian Countrys this Year the Savages will become more and more Insolent, and the back Settlements depopulated, in short nothing but Murder, Burning, Devestations, and wretched Captivity can be expected. I hope in god that matters has or will take such a turn in your favour that your Excellen[c]y will be able to reinforce the General so that a check may be given the Indians in the Offensive way and in the mean Time preperations effectually made for the Reduction of Detroit next Year.

Were it not that I am apprehensive for the safety of my Family as well as the back Inhabitants in general I could be happy in my retirement, And I hope Congress are happy in the proofs they have given of their Infallibility in giving promotion out of the line of Seniority, tho some think that suspension & the proceedings of a General Court Martial are against it⁴—I am Your Excellency Most obedt and very Humble servt

Andw Lewis

LS, DLC:GW.

1. On 4 June, Congress resolved that three commissioners should be appointed, two by Virginia and one by Pennsylvania, "for the purpose of holding a treaty with the Delawares, Shawnees, and other Indians who may assemble at Fort Pitt, on the twenty third of July next" (*JCC*, 11:568). On 18 June the Virginia council of state appointed Lewis as one of the commissioners authorized by that resolution (*Va. State Council Journals*, 2:150).

2. A letter of 6 Aug. "from Andrew Lewis and Thomas Lewis, commissioners at Pittsburg, with sundry papers enclosed" was read in Congress on 18 Aug. (*JCC*, 11:810), but it has not been identified.

3. For Congress's resolutions of 11 June, directing an expedition against Detroit, see *JCC*, 11:588–90. The Virginia council of state on 7 July voted that the proposed expedition was "utterly impracticable within the present Campaign" and directed Gov. Patrick Henry to submit their opinion to Congress (*Va. State Council Journals*, 2:161–62). For Henry's letter of 8 July, in DNA:PCC, item 71, see *Laurens Papers*, 14:7–10.

4. Congress had passed over the more senior Lewis when they appointed five major generals, including Arthur St. Clair and Adam Stephen, on 19 Feb. 1777 (*JCC*, 7:133). Subsequently Congress had resolved on 14 Nov. 1777 that St. Clair "be at liberty to attend his private affairs" until ordered to headquarters for a still-pending inquiry into his conduct while commanding at Fort Ticonderoga (ibid., 9:901), and Stephen had been dismissed from the army after a court-martial on his conduct at the battles of Brandywine and Germantown (see General Orders, 20 Nov. 1777).

# To Brigadier General William Maxwell

Sir,                                    Hd Qrs [White Plains] 8th Augst 1778

I am uncertain whether you may not already have a party somewhere in Monmouth County but however this may be, it is my wish you should without delay have one of 50 Men stationd under a very vigilant and intelligent Officer, at some place in that County most convenient for commanding a view of the Hook & its environs; in order to watch the motions of the Enemy's Fleet and to advise me from time to time of every thing that passes. of all Vessels that arrive to them, or go out from them. Lt Colo. Brearly, Ray or Major Howel would either of them be very proper for this business. I would wish the officer who is to have the charge of the party to go instantly on & his party to follow as soon as possible. If you have any Militia Horse it would be desireable to send a few with him, & to remain with the party.

For conveying any important intelligence with dispatch, I inclose you a letter to Mr Caldwell directing him to station expresses at proper distances between the party you send and Elizabeth Town;[1] & I shall expect whenever it comes to you, you will not lose a moment in forwarding it to me, by a trusty hand, on whose activity & care you can depend; and when there is any thing particularly interesting you will send duplicates for fear of accidents. as the obtaining good & certain intelligence is a matter of great importance to us, I must intreat you to continue you[r] other exertions for procuring such as may be depended on—I am &c.

G. W——n

P.s. I just now rec'd your favor of yesterday & the intelligence it contains respecting the Fleet seems so certain that it cannot well admit of a doubt[2]—Yet should it be otherwise, I must request you to give me the very earliest information of it. The importance of such a circumstance you must be fully sensible of, & therefore I make no doubt you will upon similar occasions have the fullest proof before you hand it to me as fact—I have transmitted a Copy of that part of your letter which Count D'Estaign is so materially interested in, to him.[3] You will be pleased to Seal the inclosed before you forward it.
Copy

G. W——n

Copy, in Richard Kidder Meade's writing, DLC:GW; Varick transcript, DLC:GW.

1. GW's letter of this date to Assistant Deputy Quartermaster James Caldwell reads: "To-day I have directed Genl Maxwell to station a party of men in Monmouth for the purpose of watching the motions of the enemy. for the better facilitating their discoveries to head Quarters you will be pleased instantly on receipt of this to establish a train of expresses between the situation of this party and Elizabeth Town, that there may be the least possible delay in the communication of intelligence" (Df, DLC:GW).

2. Maxwell's letter to GW of 7 Aug. has not been found, but for the intelligence, see GW to Lt. Col. John Laurens, this date.

3. See GW to Vice Admiral d'Estaing, this date.

## From Brigadier General John Stark

Dear Sir                           Head Quarters Albany 8th August 1778
since my last[1] nothing Extraordinary has Turned up, in this Department, Except Seven Deserters from Canada, who shall be sent to you as soon as possible—Colo. Butler has sent four Torys from the frontiers—I Inclose you a Letter found with one of them, & am in hopes by this time that the Writer is a Prisoner Likewise.[2]

I am Informed that forty Indians, from the Enemitical Tribes, are on their way to this place, to make a Treaty with us, while their young men are Cutting our throats[3]—I think untill their Insolence, is Chastised in a Severe Manner, we never can Expect peace in this Quarter.

the Bearer hereof Majr Quackingbush,[4] h⟨as⟩ found 55 Shells, 12 Boxes Musquet Balls, one Vice, & one pair Handscrews, in the River, near Saratoga, it is Reported that the Enemy Sunk some Cannon in the River, before their Surrender last year, should think a further Search would be Necessary, but by Reason of the Scarcity of men, in this Department, it has been Neglected. I am Sir with Great Respect Your Humble Sevt

John Stark

LS, DLC:GW.

1. See Stark to GW, 31 July.

2. In the enclosed letter from Charles Smith to Joseph Brant, written from Harper's Patent, N.Y., on 27 July, Smith explained that the harvest had retarded his efforts to raise troops for Brant: "But know as Most of them has got thare grane Taken Care of I Expect Maney To Cum With Me But hare is one thing that hinders tha are a frade that the Reabels Will Ruen them Before We Cum to thare Asistence and tha are a frade to Leave home But I gives them the gratest of Incuragements as I Think it My Duty So to Do But them Men that Left younedelle [Unadilla] has Discuraged the pepel and Sayd that We Sufferd for preavisons and that the Indens Took thare plunder from them and for that Reason hinderd Maney from Cumming to Joyn Us But it Being My Duty I Told them it Was fals and No Truth in it But that We had the Best of yousege givin and grate Plenty of preavisons and What We Wanted Was that the frinds of goverment Might Cum and Show thare Selve that tha Might Not Suffer With tha Reabels I Was a Cumming out to Se you But Meting Archabl Tomson I have Now Reaturned to Bring out My Men and Joyn as Soon as posabl I Bring them from Basick and from the Bever Dam and from the Healeaborake [Helderberg] and them parts But I am Oblidged To Say More then tha Truth to Incurage them to Cum out I Shall give you to Under Stand that tha Expect you at Schoharra and Makes all the preaprarasons tha Can But the Cuntry is in grate Confuson and But few Men to Be had for tha are all Struck With Tarrow and Tha Expect the Shipping Up the River Soon and the Nothern Armey I Under Stand has gaven them a Sad Stroke and tha Sent Word to albany for More Men or Elce Tha Must Surander I Shall See you Soon I hope and I Shall March in the frunt of My Men panted and Sum or all of My Men So ples to give Notice To My Breathern of it" (DLC:GW; see also *New-York Journal, and the General Advertiser* [Poughkeepsie], 17 Aug. 1778, and other newspapers). Lt. Col. William Butler's troops "Kill'd Smith & Brought in his Scalp" (Butler to George Clinton, 13 Aug. 1778, in Hastings, *Clinton Papers*, 3:631). The prisoner with the letter was Archibald Thompson, who settled in Niagara after the war and was awarded a small sum by the Loyalist claims commission for lost property. For more about the deserters, see John Taylor to Clinton, 9 Aug., ibid., 3:616–17.

3. A letter from Albany dated 9 Aug., published in the *Connecticut Courant, and the Weekly Intelligencer* (Hartford), 25 Aug., stated that "Forty Indians came in here yesterday, under the conduct of Mr. Deane, (the Agent and interpreter appointed by Congress for the Indian department) to sue for peace, some Oneida's, who are true hearts, some Onondoga's, and some Tuscurora's, whose designs are suspicious. These treaties serve only for a decoy, whilst some of their tribes are executing the most diabolical designs. They will meet with a very cold reception." At the Indians' meeting with the commissioners on 15 Aug., the Onondaga delegation reported that they had been unable to get other tribes to come to a treaty meeting

but pledged that they would maintain peace, although they acknowledged that fifteen of their warriors had joined the enemy (DNA:PCC, item 166).

4. Stark may have been referring to Nicholas Quackenbush (1734–1813), an assistant deputy quartermaster general with the rank of major.

## From Lieutenant Colonel Benjamin Temple

sir                                               [Virginia] August 8th 1778.

I am exceedly unhappy to find in your's to Colo. Bland of July 22d, after all the pains and fatigue I have taken to be censured about the clothing of the Regt; I do not know what Colo. Bland has inform'd your Excelly nor do I know what is meant, by the greatest part of the clothing, I have engaged should have been apply'd for other purposes, by Mr Finne, he only made use of one hundred & thirty four Shirts, after I had given him a receipt for them, I can with truth, assure yr Excelly that altho I lost many articles, that I had engaged, when I first came in, for the want of money, I have long since compleated that business, with a sufficient quantity of every article to compleatly cloath every man, in the Regt except Boots, they may want a few pair, which I inform'd your Excelly were not be had,[1] and I doubt not but they will be as well equipt as Colo. Moylands, or Colo. Sheldens Regts, and might been at Camp two months ago, if I had not received orders from Colo. Mead and Colo. Bland to remain in Virga to assist him in purchasing accoutrements, which was by no means agreeable, as the Tradsmen expect ready money, for every thing they do, and I have not yet been furnish'd with money to comply with my engagments for the clothing, and not one shilling till the month of June, I got Ten thousand Dollars of Mr Finne, I have engaged Sixty setts of accoutrements, which will be compleat in ten days, and have promised the tradsmen, they shall have the money as soon as the work is finished, On application to Colo. Bland, who promised to pay the money when done, he informs me he is quite out, and has sent me an order on Colo. Baylor which he refuses to pay, in this disagreeable situation have I been ever since I have been in Virga the inclos'd letter will show that my long stay in Virga was by no means my wish, and that I have not been imploy'd solly in procuring clothing,[2] I am with great respect Yr Excelly Mo. Obt Hhble Servt

Benja. Temple

ALS, DLC:GW. Temple apparently enclosed with this letter an undated "Memd. of goods sent to Camp by Benja. Temple" (DLC:GW).

1. Temple had reported his inability to purchase sufficient boots in his letter to GW of 20 Feb. 1778.

2. Temple enclosed Col. Theodorick Bland's letter to him of 27 June, which read in part: "As to your Going to Camp it is what I can by no means consent to at pres-

ent. as it is not only inconsistent with the Genls orders but wd leave me altogether destitute of that aid in the Cloathing and accoutring department without which it will be utterly impracticable for me to forward the parties as required of me. if the Cloaths for the Soldiers accordg to the memorandum I gave you do not arrive at this Place before wednesday eveng I shall send off from hence a party of between fifty and Sixty Horses an⟨d⟩ 25 or 26 Men. You will be pleased to see them as well equipt as our situation will permit and forwarded to Camp. Cornet [Griffin] Fauntleroy will command the Party and they will Serve as a Guard for the Cloathg &c. As Mr [Baylor] Hill has hitherto been of little service in Recruiting or purchasing you will please to order him on here to Releive Cornt Fauntleroy. I have inclosed you [Edward] Simpsons offer; and as the engaging and seeing to the making of accoutrements will be wholly entrusted to your Care in that district shd be glad you wd immediately agree with him for the number he proposes or any greater Number if he can make them" (DLC:GW).

## General Orders

Head-Quarters W. Plains Sabbath Augt 9th 1778.
Parole Gadsden—                              C. Signs Hatfield Ipswich.
Lieutenant Coll Russell will take Command of the 10th Virginia Regt until further orders.[1]

Varick transcript, DLC:GW. The orderly book of Maj. Gen. Benjamin Lincoln includes the following additional orders for this date: "For detachment to parade tomorrow 5 oClock P.M. furnished with 40 rounds p. man and two days provisions ready cooked—Colonel Courtlandt Lt Colonels Mebbin and Millen Majors Buchert and Hait—Sixteen light Dragoons properly officered are to parade at the same time, furnished with the like quantity of Provisions—A non commissiond officer with 6 light Dragoons are to attend the parade tomorrow Morning at guard mounting" (MHi: Lincoln Papers).
1. Lincoln's orderly book has "Colo. Russell"; the order refers to Col. William Russell of the 13th Virginia Regiment.

## To Major General Benedict Arnold

Dear Sir                      Head Quarters White plains 9th Augt 1778
I have been favd with yours of the 30th ulto inclosing a return of the Troops in the City and of the Officers. All those of Pennsylvania had leave of Absence for a particular reason, and may therefore remain untill further orders. Those from other States, (Lt Colo. parke in particular) should be ordered to join their Corps, except they can make it appear that they are upon Business. I would wish that all the effective Continental troops may be sent forward to the Army. I should think that the few men necessary for Town Guards might, upon application, be furnished from the City Militia.

I have regularly furnished Congress with all my intelligence from Rhode Island, you will therefore, through the members, receive a state of matters in that quarter, which hitherto wear a favorable aspect. Dear Sir Sincerely Yours.

Df, in Tench Tilghman's writing, DLC:GW; Varick transcript, DLC:GW.

## To Henry Laurens

Sir                                    White plains August 9th 1778
At 10 OClock last night the Inclosed Letter came to hand from General Sullivan with one addressed to myself, a Copy of which I do myself the honor of transmitting.[1] The Enemy seem determined that none of their Ships of War shall fall into the Count D'Estaings hands.

Yesterday I received a Letter from Genl Maxwell dated at 9 OClock A.M. on the 7th at Elizabeth Town, containing the following paragraph. "I have to inform your Excellency that early yesterday morning Lord Howe sailed out of the Hook with his whole fleet of Armed Vessels. They were out of sight in the afternoon and were supposed to be going for Rhode Island—No troops or Transports supposed to be with them." His Letter also had the following Nota bene—"no British fleet arrived yet that we can hear of."[2] General Maxwell's information respecting Lord Howe's sailing from the Hook was stated in such pointed and positive terms, that I thought it my duty to communicate it to Count D'Estaing, and accordingly I dispatched an Express with it, in a very little time after I was advised on the subject, subjoining a copy of this Nota bene.[3] I have the Honor to be &c.

Go: Washington

Df, in Robert Hanson Harrison's writing, DLC:GW; Varick transcript, DLC:GW. Congress read this letter on 14 Aug. (*JCC*, 11:787).
1. GW sent a copy of Maj. Gen. John Sullivan's letter to him of 6 August. No manuscript of the enclosed letter from Sullivan, presumably to Laurens and of 6 Aug., has been identified. The text of Sullivan to Laurens, 6 Aug., printed in Moore, *Materials for History*, 116, is identical to Sullivan's letter to GW of that date.
2. The quoted letter has not been found.
3. See GW to Vice Admiral d'Estaing, 8 August.

## To Henry Laurens

Sir                                    [White Plains, 9 August 1778][1]
Mr Fuhrer & Mr Kleinsmit[2] have lately left the British lines and come in to us. The account they give of themselves is this—That they had been first lieutenants in the Hessian Corps—were taken prisoners at

Trenton, resided during their captivity at Dumfries in Virginia—were lately exchanged and have since resigned their commissions—That having solicited permission to come out from the enemy and being refused, they determined to leave them at all hazards, and have now put their design in execution. The circumstances of their captivity are known to several Officers in our army.

They are desirous of entering into our service, observing that there are a number of German Officers in the same disposition with themselves, who will resign and join us, if they find that these meet with proper countenance. It appears to me, that important advantages may attend the encouraging a disposition of this nature, if it really exists, which is far from being impossible; from the influence it will necessarily have upon the soldiery, by increasing that spirit of desertion and discontent, which already prevails among them.

Congress will best judge of the propriety of employing these Gentlemen.[3] I have been thinking in what manner it might be done; and the mode least exceptionable, which at present occurs to me, is to authorise them to raise a Corps for themselves, by inlisting such German inhabitants, and such of the prisoners and deserters from the foreign troops, as may be willing to engage. The Corps at first as it is only by way of experiment need not be large; but may be afterwards encreased, as circumstances shall point out. This measure, I apprehend, cannot be attended with any material inconvenience and may be productive of utility. If the Gentlemen are employed at all it must be in a new Corps, as they could not be introduced into any of those already formed, without injuring the Officers in them, and producing dissatisfaction, murmurs and resignations.

I have sounded them on the plan here suggested and they seem to be very sanguine in it's success and anxious to undertake it. They expect some augmentation in ra⟨nk⟩ and indeed it seems necessary in order the more effectually to interest others to follow their example; but caution should be used not to carry the idea too far, because besides other weighty considerations, the higher the rank conferred on them, the more difficult it will be to provide for those, who may hereafter come to us and who will of course frame their expectations by comparison. I have the honor to be With the greatest respect, Sir Your most Obedt Servt

Go: Washington

P.S. An additional grade to the rank they held in the corps they come from will in my opinion be sufficient.[4]

LS, DNA:PCC, item 152; Df, DLC:GW; copy, DNA:PCC, item 169; Varick transcript, DLC:GW. Dockets on the cover of the LS read in part: "Recd & Read in Congress 18 Augt 1778" and "Referred to the board of war" (see *JCC*, 11:809).

1. The LS is undated, but the draft is dated "Aug. 9th 1778."

2. The preceding five words were written in different ink, apparently after the rest of the letter was completed. On the draft and the Varick transcript, the text reads, "Two persons." Carl Friedrich Führer (1756–1794) from Felsberg, an ensign in Knyphausen's regiment, and Carl Wilhelm Kleinschmit (born c.1755) from Landau, an ensign in what was formerly Rall's regiment, deserted to the American lines on 7 August. On 3 Sept., Congress resolved to grant them captains' commissions, provided that they each enlisted at least thirty men to serve in a new corps of troops to be raised from German deserters. According to the Hessian major Carl Leopold Baurmeister, the two had some success in persuading those captured at Trenton to take service in the American army. However, after the Board of War questioned their characters, Congress voted on 5 Dec. to cancel the project and pay them off. By October 1780, according to Baurmeister, they were making "very humble requests to be pardoned and received" within the British lines (Baurmeister, *Revolution in America*, 228, 390; *JCC*, 12:866–67, 1192–93). No pardons were forthcoming; indeed, on 2 Oct. 1781 the British advocate general announced that the landgrave of Hesse had approved sentences of death for their "Treason and Desertion" and ordered that they be hanged in effigy "till their Persons (now absent) shall fall within the reach of Justice" (*Royal Gazette* [New York], 3 Oct. 1781). Führer, at least, remained in America. He unsuccessfully petitioned Congress for a pension on 15 Nov. 1781, asserting that his property in Germany had been confiscated and claiming, in addition to his service with the stillborn German volunteer corps, that he had commanded some Virginia state troops sent to the Carolinas in 1779 but not "Established" (DNA:PCC, item 42). When Führer, who had taken the name Charles Fierer, made the same claim to the Virginia legislature in 1793, he was given compensation for his service (*Va. House of Delegates Journal 1793*, 15–16, 97–98; Shepherd, *Va. Statutes at Large*, 1:282; see also Charles Fierer to GW, 10 July 1793, DNA: RG 59, Miscellaneous Letters, which requests a copy of this letter to support the Virginia claim). As Fierer, he printed newspapers in Georgetown, D.C., 1789–91, and in Dumfries, Va., 1791–93.

3. On the draft, Alexander Hamilton wrote the preceding sentence to replace text that he had previously written and struck out: "I submit to Congress whether it may not be proper to give them some suitable employment and."

4. The postscript does not appear on the draft or Varick transcript.

## To Colonel William Malcom

Sir               Head Quarters White plains 9 Augt 1778

I recd yours of the 7th with the weekly returns enclosed. I have not the least objection to making Robinsons House an Hospital if it is convenient. Doctor Treat must apply to the director General for the necessary Stores.[1]

I desire you will immediately order a sufficient number of Artificers from Windsor to Fort Arnold to build a Bomb proof Magazine and such other works as may be necessary.

If you can contrive to man the Gun Boats when they are fitted, I am very willing that they should be kept at the Fort: I cannot spare a sufficient number of men from the line for that service. the Regiments are already too much reduced by the draughts for Waggoners &ca. One of the purposes, for which Colo. Warner wanted an officer stationed at Fishkill, was, to receive the draughts coming from Massachusetts;[2] but as the remainder of the draughts are ordered to join Genl Glover at Rhode Island, he will not have that duty to attend to. An Officer will notwithstanding be wanting there and the one, you had sent, may remain. I mean that that post and Windsor should be included in your command.

Last winter, owing to the necessity of the case, the commanding Officers of Corps drew Hydes to exchange for shoes, but as much inconveniency has arisen from that mode, a stop has been put to it. If the Officers know of any persons who have shoes to dispose of, they must direct them to the Cloathier who will purchase them, and they must then draw them from him. This is putting the Business in its regular line. I am &c.

Df, in Tench Tilghman's writing, DLC:GW; Varick transcript, DLC:GW.

1. Malcom's letter to GW of 7 Aug. has not been found. Malachi Treat (c.1735–1795), who was elected physician general of the hospital in the northern department in April 1777 and was appointed a chief hospital physician in the medical department reorganization of October 1780, served to the end of the war. He died in 1795 of yellow fever contracted while acting as physician for the port of New York.

2. GW probably meant Brig. Gen. Jonathan Warner, rather than Col. Seth Warner. Jonathan Warner was the commissioner appointed to receive at Fishkill the Massachusetts troops raised in accordance with the resolution of 20 April (*Boston-Gazette, and Country Journal*, 15 June; compare also Malcom to GW, 26 July).

## To James Mease

Sir,                              Head Qrs [White Plains] Augst 9th 177[8][1]

Major Clough has informed me thro Capt. Smith that he has lately received a letter from Colo. Baylor by which he is made acquainted that he has not been able to procure any Cloathing for the use of his Regt.[2] As it is represented to me that they are much in want, you will deliver to Major Clough's order such articles as he may demand or you be able to supply him with.[3] I am &c.

G. W——n

Df, in Richard Kidder Meade's writing, DLC:GW; Varick transcript, DLC:GW.

Also on this date GW's aide Robert Hanson Harrison wrote Lt. Col. Samuel Smith of the 4th Maryland Regiment about clothing: "It being His Excellency's wish & intention that all the Maryland Troops should stand upon an equal footing in point of cloathing; and he having been informed that the 2nd & 4th Regiments in the 2d Brigade had lately received pretty large supplies from the public Stores;

I am to request by his command that you will make him a return as soon as you can of the cloathing with which these Two Regiments have been lately furnished, that a proper distribution may be directed of that which is to be now drawn from the Cloathier here, in consequence of his Order last night delivered to Genl Smallwood" (DLC:GW).

1. The draft is dated "1777" but docketed "1778," which from context is correct.
2. The letter from Col. George Baylor has not been identified.
3. GW's aide-de-camp Richard Kidder Meade wrote Maj. Alexander Clough on this date: "As His Excellency could not ascertain the quantity or articles of Cloathing that Colo. Baylors Regt is in need of; He was obliged to give you an unlimited order on Mr Mease, desiring from the scarcity of Cloathing in his hands that you will be as sparing as possible, demanding only of him, what the Regt cannot do without" (DLC:GW). Mease apparently did not satisfy Baylor, for the Board of War on 9 Sept. issued orders to Otis & Andrews in Boston for clothing the regiment, after Baylor "represented to the board the ill condition of his regiment, in point of clothing, & the impossibility of getting it elsewhere" (Board of War report to Congress on clothing, 5 Oct., DNA:PCC, item 147).

*Letter not found*: from Brig. Gen. Thomas Nelson, Jr., 9 Aug. 1778. On 20 Aug., GW wrote Nelson: "Since writing the foregoing, I have been favoured with your Letter of the 25th Ulto from Baltimore, and 9th Instt from Philadelphia."

## To Colonel Israel Shreve

Sir                    Head Quarters White plains 9th Augt 1778
    I have been favd with a letter of the 6th signed by yourself and other Feild Officers of the Jersey Brigade.[1] You cannot feel, more sensibly than I do, the inconveniencies that arise from a delay of the new arrangement of the Army. Just as the Committee had made a beginning of that business at the Valley Forge, the removal of the Enemy from Philada obliged them to desist. Congress have since directed them to repair to the Army and proceed in the Business.[2] As some time has elapsed since the Resolve was passed, and the Gentlemen have not arrived; I took a few days ago, the liberty to mention to Congress the total derangement of the Army for want of their presence, and my wish that they should come immediately forward.[3] I therefore am in hopes that we shall see them soon, or that some other mode will be pointed out to compleat the Work. I am sir Your most obt Servt

                                          Go: Washington

LS, in Tench Tilghman's writing, NjP: GW Misc. Mss; Df, DLC:GW; Varick transcript, DLC:GW. GW signed the cover of the LS.
1. The letter of 6 Aug. has not been found.
2. Congress passed a resolution to this effect on 9 July (*JCC*, 11:676).
3. See GW to Henry Laurens, 3–4 August.

# General Orders

Head-Quarters W. Plains Monday Augt 10th 1778.
Parole Killingsly—                           C. Signs Lynch. Munster.
Lieutenant Colonel Carlton is appointed to take command of the Post at Terrytown.

Ensign Alexander Benstead of the 10th Pennsylvania Regiment is appointed Pay-Master to the same.

Varick transcript, DLC:GW.

# To Major General Lafayette

My dear Marqs,                           White plains Augt 10th 1778
Your favor of the 6th Instt which came to my hands yesterday, afforded a fresh proof of the noble principles on which you act, and has a just claim to my sincere & hearty thanks.

The common cause, of which you have been a Zealous supporter would I know, be benefitted by Genl Greene's presence at Rhode Island, as he is a native of that State—has an interest with the People—and a thorough knowledge of the Country—and therefore I accepted his proffered Services[1]—but was a little uneasy lest you should conceive that, it was intended to lessen your Command. Merely as Qr Master Genl, Genl Greene did not incline to act in a detached part of the Army; nor was it to be expected; It became necessary therefore to give him a Command, and consequently, to divide the Continental Troops. Your chearful acquiescence to the Measure, after being appointed to the command of the Brigades that Marched from this Army, obviated every difficulty, and gave me singular pleasure.

I am very happy to find that the Standards of France & America are likely to be united under your Commd at Rhode Island—I am perswaded that the supporters of each will be emulous to acquire honor, & promote your glory upon this occasion.[2]

The Courier to Count D'Estaing is waiting, I have only time therefore to assure you, that with the most perfect esteem, & exalted regard, I have the honor to be My dear Marqs Yr Obedt & Affecte Servt

Go: Washington

ADfS, DLC:GW; LB, DLC:GW; Varick transcript, DLC:GW.
    1. The letter-book copy adds the words "with pleasure" at this point.
    2. At this point the letter-book copy continues with two paragraphs that are not in the draft or Varick transcript: "Apropos, can you, my Dear Marquis, through the medium of your lovely lady (if she is at the Court of Versailles) or by any other in-

direct means, discover whether there is any truth in the information given to me at Paramous by Mrs Watkins & other ladies, that your amiable Queen had honored Mrs Washington with an elegant testimonial of her approbation of my conduct. These Ladies asserted, so confidently, that a present from her Most Christian Majesty, to Mrs Washington had been taken by the Enemy, carried into New-York, & there sold at public auction for the benefit of the Captors; that altho' it was too great an honor to be expected, I could not forbear giving credence to the report; and am anxious to know the truth, that if I am indebted to her Majesty for such distinguished honor, I may get some friend of yours to lay my thanks at her feet, with an assurance of such perfect respect & attachment as *you know* I have always professed & felt for your Queen, on account of her virtues—her sentiments in favour of America and the general rights & liberties of Mankind.

"The reason, my Dear Marquis, for wishing that this enquiry may be carried on in an indirect way, is obvious; for altho' I should prize such a testimonial (if it has really happened) above rubies, and would prostrate my grateful thanks at the Queens feet for the honour intended; yet, I would not, if the case is otherwise, invite by the most distant hint, nor even accept, from the Empress of the universe, a present, if I should conceive that it was not prompted by an Act of the Will."

## To Richard Henry Lee

Dear Sir,                                              White plains Augt 10th 1778.

A few days ago I received your favor of the 26th Ulto, inclosing one from Colo. Spotswood, for which I thank you.[1] The reputation which this Gentn had acquired, of being an attentive Officer and good disciplinarian, was justly founded; and I considered his leaving the Army a loss to the Service. The supposed death of his Brother, it is natural to believe, had a painful influence upon his mind—but he had long before been very uneasy in his situation, on acct of the determination in the case between him and Colo. McLanahan (and I am perswaded was only prevented from quitting the line in consequence, thro^ my means).[2]

My regard for Colo. Spotswood, and the opinion I entertain of him as an Officer, would induce me to interest myself in his favor, whereever I could with propriety—In the present instance however I cannot, because I think I shd do an injury to the Officers of the Virga line (if not to those of the line at large) and because I am convinced his promotion would excite infinite discontents and produce many resignations.

When he left Camp in the Month of October, he made a surrender of his Commission to me according to the then prevailing custom. This was accepted—and a new arrangement took place among the field Officers. After this I could not suppose him to continue in the line—and to attempt to recall the rise of the Officers, to give him a place again, would be to attempt an impossibility. No reasoning upon the subject would be sufficient to get them to consent to it.

With respect to the report of the Board of General Officers to which you allude you will excuse me when I say, in my opinion, it will not apply. The case there was, that sundry inferior Officers, or juniors of the same rank, from local circumstances, and the oppertunities of application, obtained from the Committees, or Councils of the States in whom the power of appointing Officers to the Army for 1777 was vested, new Commissions prior in date to those granted afterwards to their Seniors—and in consequence claimed a right to rank before them. The Board determined their claims unjust and, that the rank which the Officers immediately held before their new Commissions should govern, as it did not appear that the Councils intended to supercede the Senior Officers[3]—But here, there had been no interruption or relinquishment of the right to rank by resignation—surrender of Commission—or any other act of the Parties. Nor could I ever think, that Colo. Spotswood had cause to complain of the decision on the point in question between him and Colo. McClanahan. It was founded on the practice, which had commonly prevailed—I believe universally, in like cases—viz.—that when state Officers became Continental they should rank, with respect to each other, according to their state precedence. This principle appeared to be just, and I am certain, was the only one that could be adopted to give general satisfaction. As many of our Regiments in the first instance, and particularly those from virginia, were raised by the States without any order by Congress, a contrary rule would have involved great inconveniencies—& would have proved an effectual bar to many valuable Officers coming into Service.

I have not the most distant suspicion that Colo. Spotswood is influenced in his wishes, upon the present occasion, in the smallest degree by any considerations arising from the half pay establishment—I am convinced that he is not—Nor do I believe that any Officer will impute a matter of the sort to him—or object to his being reintroduced into the line from motives of personal dislike—they will oppose it as an injury to their rights.

I thank you much for your congratulations. The prospect we have before us is certainly pleasing, and such as promises a glorious and happy issue to all our struggles. Success in the intended enterprize against Rhode Island, wd operate powerfully, I should suppose, upon the minds of the British Nation, and bring matters to a speedy conclusion.[4] I wait impatiently to hear from thence. I am Dr Sir Yr most Obedt H. Ser.

Go: Washington

ALS, PPAmP: Correspondence of Richard Henry Lee and Arthur Lee; DfS, DLC: GW; Varick transcript, DLC:GW. The draft and the Varick transcript are dated 9 Aug., but a docket on the draft reads, "10th Augt 1778."

1. Lee's letter of 26 July has not been found; for the enclosure, see Alexander Spotswood to GW, 16 July.

2. The decision that Col. Alexander McClanachan outranked Spotswood was made by a board of general officers on 9 July 1777. For GW's response to Spotswood's request for a reconsideration, see his letter to Spotswood of 13 Aug. 1777.

3. GW was evidently referring to the report of 19 Aug. 1777 by a board of general officers appointed to settle the ranks of the Continental officers of the Pennsylvania line (see General Orders, 17 Aug. 1777, n.4).

4. On the draft, which is otherwise in Robert Hanson Harrison's writing, the remaining text is in GW's writing.

# From Brigadier General John Stark

*Albany, August* 10, 1778.

*Dear General*—Your letter of the 5th instant has come to hand by express. I am very happy to hear that the disposition of the troops in this department will so well agree with your sentiments.

The posts of Schoharie and Cherry Valley I look upon as exposed to equal danger. For that reason I have stationed Colonel Butler at one, and Colonel Alden at the other.

By the inclosed letters, you will perceive the progress Colonel Butler has made, since he took the command at Schoharie;[1] and if he should be removed, and form a junction with Colonel Alden's regiment, I shall find some method to remove Colonel Alden, so that Butler may have the command, and Alden be satisfied. Concerning the provisions, that have been issued to the State prisoners, upon inquiry, I find it to be by some general order a year ago; but I shall stop it until farther orders. We are in daily expectation of some important news from you. I am, sir, Your humble servant,

JOHN STARK.

Stark, *Memoir of John Stark,* 184.

1. These enclosures have not been identified. One was, according to GW's reply, a letter from Lt. Col. William Butler.

# To Major General John Sullivan

Dear Sir,                          Head Quarters White Plains Aug. 10th 1778
I have been duly favoured with yours of the 6th.

I regret much the tardiness of the militia, as every moment is infinitely precious, and the delay, it produces, may not only frustrate the expedition, which is a matter of the greatest importance in itself;

but may expose the French fleet to some fatal disaster. I have no doubt of your utmost exertions to forward the business with all dispatch.

I have received advice from Long Island, that a party of the enemy, from twelve to fifteen hundred men were marching under General Tryon, towards the East End of the Island, collecting all the waggons, they can find, in their way. They were at *Setacket* the 6th, and were to continue their march early the next morning. I have had information of another party more considerable being at Jamaica plains; but this fact is not so well ascertained as the former. I conclude the design of these parties is to sweep the Island of all the stock and grain upon it, particularly the cattle collected upon the neck, at the East-end; which will be an immense acquisition to them, in their present circumstances.[1]

While the navigation of the Sound is open to the enemy, it would be too perilous an attempt, to throw a body of troops from this army upon the Island; not withstanding it is a very desireable object to intercept the enemy and disappoint their intended forage. Could the Count with propriety have sent a ship or two down the Sound, agreeable to a proposal made him, through Colonel Laurens,[2] the enterprise might have been effected without difficulty; and I had resolved upon sending troops to collect the cattle on the neck;[3] at the same time, I am fully sensible of the weight of the reasons which prevented his doing it. It has occurred to me, that there is a possibility it may be in your power[4] to throw a part of the troops, under your command, upon the Island, for the purpose here mentioned; though from your last accounts, it is to be apprehended the expedition against Rhode Island will not be completed in time to admit of a measure of this kind. If it should be, this will be an object well-worth your attention. A sufficient body of troops, under the protection of some ships of war, thrown across, so as to take post just within the neck, might cut off the enemy's detachment without great risk, and collect all the cattle there for our own use. A stroke of this kind would be attended with several obvious advantages. Besides the loss of their troops to the enemy, the disappointment in supplies, of which they stand in great need, would be severely felt; and we should gain a quantity of good cattle, which would afford extensive refreshment to the French fleet.

How far it may be convenient to the Count to assist in an operation of this kind, I cannot perfectly judge. I know he will want to repose and refresh his men, and repair the injuries, which a fleet necessarily suffers, from being a long time at sea. If circumstances make the project suggested in other respects practicable, which I very much question, you will consult the Count; but it is not my wish, he should be, in any instance, pressed to engage in a thing, to which he discovers

the least reluctance. I am with great regard, Dr Sir, Your most Obedt
Serv.

Go: Washington

LS, in Alexander Hamilton's writing, NhHi: Sullivan Papers; Df, DLC:GW; Varick
transcript, DLC:GW.

1. British officer Francis Downman noted in his journal for 7 Aug., "General
Tryon with some provincial corps has gone to the east end of Long Island" (Whinyates, *Services of Francis Downman*, 72). William Tryon remained out "with a detachment of near one thousand provincials" until 4 Sept. "to secure the peaceable behaviour of the disaffected inhabitants in that quarter and assist the commissary in
obtaining about one thousand fat cattle for the army" (Tryon to George Germain,
5 Sept., in Davies, *Documents of the American Revolution*, 15:198).

2. See GW to Vice Admiral d'Estaing, 22 July, and note 2.

3. On the draft, which is mainly in Hamilton's writing, GW added the words "&
I had resolved upon the attempt," which Hamilton revised to reach the preceding
text.

4. At this point on the draft GW added the clause "if your operations are not
much delayed," but the words were struck out.

## From Major General John Sullivan

Dear General                    Portsmouth Rhode Island 10 Aug. 1778
    The Count De-Estaing and myself were by Agreement to land our
Forc[e]s here this Morning but I having received Intelligence early
Yesterday Morning that the Enemy had abandoned the north End of
the Island entirely in Consequence of the French Fleets coming up the
River thought it best to push over without Loss of Time the whole of
my Troops which accordingly was done [1]—immediately after our landing a Fleet of 29 Sail, 8 or 10 of which appeared to be Vessells of Force
were discovered standing into Newport under Eng. Colours [2]—As the
Wind was small & unfavourable the Count kept his Position but this
Morning he got under Way with a fine Breeze, passed the Batteries at
Newport and those which are below with all his Ships of the Line &
went in Chace of the English Fleet—At 11 oClock I had the Pleasure
of seeing them fly before him.

    The Count has left three Frigates in the East Passage—It is out of my
Power to inform You when we shall make the Attack on the Enemy as
it is uncertain when the French Fleet will return and I think it necessary to wait their Arrival as their Troops are on b[o]ard. I have the
Honor to be with much Respect, dear General, Your most obedt & very
hble Servt

Jno. Sullivan

LS, DLC:GW; copy, DNA:PCC, item 160. The copy was enclosed in GW's letter to
Henry Laurens of 13 August.

1. Manasseh Cutler, chaplain for Brig. Gen. Jonathan Titcomb's brigade of Massachusetts militia, recorded in his journal for 9 Aug.: "This morning the army was ordered to parade near Howland's Ferry, in order to embark and re-embark in the boats, that they might better understand such a maneuver; but a reconnoitering party having discovered that the enemy had left the upper end of the Island, and retreated into Newport, the troops embarked and proceeded over, formed on the opposite beach, and marched up and took possession of their works, which were not at all damaged" (Cutler, *Rev. Manasseh Cutler*, 1 :65–66).

2. The British fleet consisted of the *Cornwall*, mounting 74 guns; the *Eagle, Trident, Nonsuch, Raisonable, Somerset, St. Albans*, and *Ardent* of 64 guns; the *Preston, Centurion, Experiment, Isis*, and *Renown* of 50 guns; the *Phoenix* and *Roebuck* of 44 guns; the 36-gun *Venus*; the *Richmond, Pearl*, and *Apollo* of 32 guns; the *Sphynx* and *Vigilant* of 20 guns; the sloop *Nautilus*; and three fireships, two bombs, two tenders, and four galleys ("List of the Squadron of His Majesties Ships which Sailed from Sandy Hook under the Command of the Vice Admiral the Viscount Howe, August the 6th 1778," P.R.O., Adm. 1/488, fol. 319).

# General Orders

Head-Quarters W. Plains Tuesday Augt 11th[–12] 78.
Parole New-Windsor—                                    C. Signs Orange. Peru.

A sufficient number of Officers having not yet presented themselves as Candidates for Commissions in the Companies of Sappers and Miners—The General requests all those who may be disposed to enter into this service immediately to give in their names and wait upon General Du Portail as he is desirous of having the Companies established without delay—This being a species of service well worthy the Ambition of Gentlemen of Zeal and Talents who wish to advance themselves in military knowledge and Distinction and being held in the highest Estimation in every Army—it will be expected as heretofore that those who apply should be well recommended for their good Character and liberal qualifications.

The Field Officers in the Maryland Line are desired to assemble and either collectively or by a Committee state the Pretensions of Rank claimed by the Officers of that Line; together with the reasons or grounds upon which those Pretensions are founded and report as soon as may be.

The Issuing Commissaries are carefully to preserve the Provision Barrels or Casks after the Meat or Flour is taken out of them 'till the Coopers have repaired them, when they are to be returned to the Commissary General of Issues.

At a General Court Martial whereof Coll David Hall was President August [4]th[1] 1778—Captn Seely of the 5th Pennsylvania Regiment tried for leaving his guard before he was regularly relieved found guilty of the Charge exhibited against him, being a breach of the 4th Article,

12 Section of the Articles of War and sentenced to be reprimanded in General Orders.[2]

The Commander in Chief confirms the sentence tho' he could wish a severer punishment had been decreed to an offence which is of the highest military Criminality and of the most dangerous tendency; the safety of the Army altogether depending on the strict discipline & unremiting Vigilance observed by Officers on Guard particularly at the out Posts.

At the same Court Neil Megonigle a soldier in the 7th Pennsylvania Regiment tried first, for threatning Captain Scott's Life, 2ndly drawing his Bayonet and stabbing him repeatedly while in the Execution of his Office, found guilty of the Charges exhibited against him, being breaches of the 5th Article 2nd section of the Articles of War and sentenced by a Majority of more than two thirds to be shot to Death.[3]

His Excellency the Commander in Chief confirms the sentence.

Wednesday Morn Augt 12th 1778.

The Light Troops are to be paraded this afternoon at two ôClock on Chatterton's Hill—A number of Tents and Camp Kettles proportionate to the number of men from each Regiment are to be sent with them.

The Brigade Quarter Masters will see that those tents are brought on the ground in Waggons at the time fixed.

The Commissary General of Issues will immediately appoint an issuing Commissary to the Light Corps.

Varick transcript, DLC:GW.

1. The transcriber wrote "14th," but the correct date of 4 Aug. appears in other orderly books (*N.C. State Records*, 12:532).

2. The general orders should have cited article 4 of section 13 for this offense (*JCC*, 5:797).

3. Neal McGonagle had enlisted as a private in the 6th Pennsylvania Regiment in 1776 and remained with the regiment after its redesignation as the 7th Pennsylvania Regiment in January 1777. Pardoned for this offense, he was again in trouble in May 1779, when he was found guilty of being absent without leave (General Orders, 14 May 1779). Captain Scott was most likely Joseph Scott of the 1st Virginia Regiment. The cited article prescribes death or other punishment for any officer or soldier who shall "offer any violence" against a superior officer (*JCC*, 5:790).

## To Lieutenant Caleb Brewster

Sir                         Head Quarters White plains 11th Augt 1778

I perceive by a letter of yours to Genl Parsons that Genl Silliman had granted liberty to Lieut. French to return to Long Island upon parole.[1] Genl Parsons tells me that upon rect of your letter he directed Mr French to be detained untill he consulted me upon the propriety of the Measure. I desire that he may be immediately sent back to the place from whence he came, and inclosed is a letter for Genl Silliman informing him of my reasons for as doing.[2] I am &c.

Df, in Tench Tilghman's writing, DLC:GW; Varick transcript, DLC:GW.
1. Brewster's letter to Brig. Gen. Samuel Holden Parsons has not been identified. Lieutenant French may have been Arthur French of the 47th Regiment, who had surrendered with Lt. Gen. John Burgoyne at Saratoga, or perhaps the Loyalist James French (c.1745–1820), who was commissioned a lieutenant in Delancey's Brigade in August 1777.
2. The enclosed letter to Brig. Gen. Gold Selleck Silliman of the Connecticut militia reads: "By a letter from Lieut. Brewster who is stationed at Norwalk, I am informed that you had granted permission to Lieut. French a prisoner of War to return to Long Island upon parole. There are very particular reasons for putting a stop to this matter at present, and I have therefore ordered Mr French back to the place from whence he came.
"As many inconveniencies arise from a variety of persons undertaking to negotiate exchanges, I must desire that neither Mr French or any other prisoner may be sent out of the State, except by order of the Commander in Chief, The officer commanding in a separate department, or the Commy General of prisoners" (Df, DLC:GW).

## To Henry Laurens

sir                         White plains August 11th 1778
I take the liberty of transmitting to Congress the Inclosed Letter, which I just now received from the pay Master General.[1] They will perceive by it, that the Military Chest is entirely exhausted, and, that a third of the Army remains unpaid for the Months of April and May. The importance & necessity of an immediate and large supply will at once appear—and I am persuaded it will be ordered and forwarded with all possible expedition.

Since I had the honor of writing by Colo. Heth on Sunday last,[2] I have not received any advices from Rhode Island. I have the Honor to be with great respect & esteem sir Your Most Obedt sert

Go: Washington

LS, in Robert Hanson Harrison's writing, DNA:PCC, item 152; Df, DLC:GC; copy, DNA:PCC, item 169; Varick transcript, DLC:GW. GW signed the cover of the LS, which is docketed in part, "Received 15th P.M." Congress read this letter on 17 Aug., when the enclosure was referred to the Board of Treasury; see *JCC*, 11:802.
1. William Palfrey's letter of this date has not been found.
2. GW was probably referring to his first letter to Laurens of 9 August.

## To William Livingston

Dear Sir,                    Head Quarters White Plains 11 Augst 1778.
I was favor'd with yours of the 7th in[stant] this morning.[1]

You will perceive by the enclosure from Colo. Biddle the Forage Master General to the Army the prices that have been given for hay in the different States and that the proper measures will be used to exempt Somerset County from her proportion of Forage.[2]

The last accounts from Rhode Island was of the 6th with the news of the Enemy's destroying several of their Frigates upon the approach of two of the Count D'Estaings Ships to give them battle. I am dear Sir &c.

Go: Washington.

Copy, MHi: William Livingston Papers; Df, DLC:GW; Varick transcript, DLC:GW.
1. Livingston's letter of 7 Aug. has not been found.
2. This enclosure has not been identified. On this date GW's secretary James McHenry had written to Clement Biddle: "The inclosed letter from Governr Livingston came to Head Quarters this morning—The General desires to know the reasons why a greater price is given in Pennsylvania than the State of Jersey for hay—He also wishes that attention may be paid to the County of Sommerset as circumstanced it should if possible be exempted from its proportion of forage." McHenry asked that Biddle return Livingston's letter (DLC:GW).

## To Colonel William Malcom

Sir,                    Head Quarters [White Plains] 11th Augst 1778
Captain John Stevens who will deliver you this, I find was properly authorized to project a Machine in the river, at West Point, for the purpose of setting fire to any of the Enemy's Shipping that might attempt a passage up it. He represents that, for the want of hands, he is unable to carry it on—being totally unacquainted with the circumstance, I have taken the opinion of some Gentlemen who have long commanded in this department, & they advise that as the principal Labor & expence has been already used that the Captain should be enabled to compleat it—I have therefore to request that unless it very materially interferes with your operations, that you will furnish him with such a number of hands as may be necessary to accomplish the work. I am &c.
Copy                                      G. W——n

Df, in Richard Kidder Meade's writing, DLC:GW; Varick transcript, DLC:GW.

## From Brigadier General Thomas Nelson, Jr.

My Dear sir                        Philada Aug: 11 1778
Will you pardon a liberty I am about to take with you. I have been inform'd that you have had the misfortune to lose your favorite Horse & that you are not mounted at present as you ought to be. The Liberty I am about to take with you, is that of sending you a Horse that will suit

you better than any one in Am[e]rica. But then I must insist that he be accepted as a present, for his value cannot be ascertain'd. He is now nine years old and of most excellent qualities. He is not quite reconcild to the beat of Drums, but that he will soon be familiariz'd.[1] I must again apologize for this liberty and beg that you will believe me with the greatest sincerity Your Obedt Servt

Thos Nelson Jr

ALS, DLC:GW. The cover indicates the letter was sent "By favor of Mr Randolph."
   1. The horse was probably the chestnut with white face and legs called Nelson that, according to George Washington Parke Custis, GW rode when receiving the surrender at Yorktown (Custis, *Recollections*, 166).

*Letter not found*: from William Palfrey, 11 Aug. 1778. On 17 Aug., Congress read GW's letter of 11 Aug., "enclosing one, of the same date, to him from William Palfrey, Esq. pay master general" (*JCC*, 11:802).

## To Alexander Spotswood

Dear sir                              White plains August 11th 1778
   A few days ago I received your favor of the 16th Ulto, which Colonel Lee was so obliging as to transmit.
   From the regard I had for you and the estimation in which I held you, as an Officer, I wished your continuance in the Army; and considered your departure from it a loss to the service. This you will readily believe, as you well know my persuasions had been used to prevent it's taking place before it did. At this time, I can neither interest myself to introduce you into the line again—nor advise you to persevere in your application for the purpose. I am convinced, if the measure were to take place, it would excite infinite discontents—and produce a variety of resignations. When you left the Army, you made a surrender of your Commission, according to the usual and then prevailing custom. This,[1] tho very reluctantly (but indeed you left me no choice) was accepted by me and in consequence, many Officers were promoted. To attempt to recall their rise, would be to attempt an impossibility—and no reasonings on the subject would be sufficient to obtain their consent to it. Their objection, I am persuaded, would not proceed from any motives of personal dislike—but from an opinion, that your being introduced again would be an essential injury to their rights. I have every reason to believe, that this is the light in which the matter would be viewed by the Virginia Officers—and I am by no means clear, that the disgust would be confined to them. Whether you were injured or not in the question determined between you and Colo. McClenachan, is a point I shall not undertake to discuss. However, the decision given upon the occasion, was agreable I am certain, to the common, & I be-

lieve, universal practice in like cases,[2] Viz. that state Officers should rank according to their State precedence when incorporated into the Continental Army. This appears to me to have been a Rule, strongly founded in principles of justice and policy—& to have been calculated to promote a more general harmony than any other that could have been devised. Indeed, in the more early period of the War, there was an absolute necessity for it, as most of the Troops raised in the first instance were State and not Continental; and as a different principle would have been an effectual bar to a large proportion of Officers coming, or at least continuing in service. Nor would policy or the public interest, suffer a discrimination to be made—though the Officers did not all come into the line at one & the same instant.

I have written to you with freedom and as a Friend. I wish you had continued in the Army—but you did not, a regard to the rights of Others and the tranquility of the Virginia line—& perhaps that of the Army at large are opposed to my interesting myself in the smallest degree, to promote your present views. I am Dr sir with great esteem & regard Yr Most Obd. sert

G.W.

Df, in Robert Hanson Harrison's writing, DLC:GW; Varick transcript, DLC:GW. A purported ALS was offered for sale in Stan. V. Henkels's catalog, *Autograph Letters and Documents, being the papers of Cæsar Rodney, Signer of the Declaration of Independence, Thomas Rodney, Member of the Continental Congress, and Cæsar Rodney, Attorney General of the United States*, 13 June 1919, item 241, described as "To Isaiah G. Park?" The transcription printed there shows no significant variation from the draft.

1. The words from this point to the end of the parenthesis following were added to the draft in GW's writing.

2. For the decision on the relative ranks of Spotswood and Col. Alexander McClanachan, see Proceedings of a Board of General Officers, 9 July 1777.

## General Orders

Head-Quarters W. Plains Wednesday Augt 12th 1778.
Parole Quercy—                    C. Signs Rutland. Sidney.
The Brigade Commissaries are daily to deliver the hides and tallow at the Magazines of Provisions.

Varick transcript, DLC:GW.

## From Silas Deane

Dear sir                    Philadelphia August 12th 1778
I had the pleasure of receiving your polite & Freindly Letter of the 25th Ulto but Three days ago, and Col. Bannister informing me, he

should set out in a Day, or Two, for the Army,[1] prevented my instantly writing to tell you, how happy I am to find that my Conduct has met your Approbation, & how much I consider myself honored by it. next to the satisfaction which rises from a consciousness, of having faithfully and successfully served one's Country, a Satisfaction, which no one in the world can enjoy to a greater degree than Yourself, a generous mind must ever esteem that, which flows from the approbation of Persons, of your distinguished character, and merit. my design is to reimbark for France in a few Months, but whither in a public Character, or not, is uncertain. I have not as yet learned, except from The information of my Freinds in private, what were the reasons for my being recalled, and though I have understood by their and by the general Conversation of others that it is expected, that I return to France in a public Character yet as the Affairs I was engaged in, for the public, which I was obliged to leave unsettled, oblige me to return, though it should be in a private Character, I have not been sollicitous about the resolutions that may be taken on the Subject. The reception of the French Minister and other affairs, which have engaged the Attention of Congress since my return has prevented my having a public Audience, but I expect One in a few Days,[2] after which I shall do myself the honor, of paying you a Visit at Head Quarters, and am in hopes that his Excellency Mr Gerard will visit you at the same Time; he is very desirous of an Opportunity of paying personally his respects to one, for whom he, as well as his Nation, & I may add, all the brave and generous in Europe have the highest Esteem. I promise myself the pleasure of communicating many things in a personal Conversation which may be agreeable and entertaining to You, but which cannot so well be put into a Letter; meantime I have taken the Liberty of enclosing the Copies, of a Letter from Mr De Vergennes to the President of Congress, of one from him to Me, & of one from Docr Franklin to the President.[3] I send them because I think it will be agreeable to You to find that the Sentiments entertained of Me by his Majesty & the Court of France, & by Our mutual Freind have been similar to those which you have honored Me with. I most sincerely congratulate You on the favorable prospects before Us, happily oweing to the perseverance, and bravery of your Army, in a principal degree, and though I have not had the honor of sharing with You the dangers & the honors of the Feild; yet no one has, or can ever be more sensibly affected, & interested by both the one, & The other, in hopes that I shall soon have the honor of waiting on You in person, I am with the most sincere respect & Esteem Your Excellencys most Obedt & Very humle servt

Silas Deane

ALS, DLC:GW.

1. Congress added John Banister to the committee of arrangement on 10 Aug., and he wrote St. George Tucker on 11 Aug. that he intended to leave for camp the next day. However, he apparently did not leave until after 15 Aug., as he was recorded in a number of votes on that date (*JCC*, 11:769, 794–97, 800; Smith, *Letters of Delegates*, 10:422).

2. Deane was introduced at Congress on 15 Aug. and was then requested to appear again on 17 Aug. "to give, from his memory, a general account of his whole transactions in France, from the time of his first arrival, as well as a particular state of the funds of Congress, and the commercial transactions in Europe, especially with Mr. Beaumarchais" (*JCC*, 11:799, 801).

3. Charles Gravier, comte de Vergennes (1717–1787), was the French secretary of state for foreign affairs, 1774–86. Translations of his letters of 26 Mar. to Deane and to Henry Laurens are in DLC:GW, as is a copy of Benjamin Franklin's letter to Laurens of 31 March. Both of the letters from Vergennes expressed the French king's "satisfaction" with Deane's conduct. Franklin testified "that I esteem him a faithful active & able Minister who to my knowledge has done in various ways great & important Services to his Country."

## To Vice Admiral d'Estaing

Head Quarters White Plains
Sir,                         Augt 12th 1778 [    ] OClock P.M.

I have just received a second letter dated the 10th from General Maxwell, confirming the intelligence of the departure of the British fleet from the Hook, with some further particulars, which it may not be useless or unsatisfactory to you to know—an extract from which I do myself the honor to inclose.[1] The state of the winds for two or three days past makes me hope this communication may not arrive too late. With the most ardent wishes for your success and the sincerest respect I have the honor to be Sir Most Obedt servt

G.W.

Df, in Alexander Hamilton's writing, DLC:GW; Varick transcript, DLC:GW. GW enclosed this letter in one to Lt. Col. John Laurens of 9 P.M. on this date that directed: "The inclosed letter, for Count D'Estaing, is to be delivered to him, provided the British Fleet should not have been arrived, or being arrived, he should not have come to an engagement with them: For, if the Count should have come to an engagement with the British Admiral before this reaches you, the intelligence, which the letter contains, will be useless to him, and therefore need not be communicated" (LS, ScHi: Henry Laurens Papers).

1. The enclosed extract reads: "There is no doubt of the Fleet's being gone, as I mentioned before. Captain [Thomas] Randal from Chatham, came up from the Shore yesterday and confirms the same; Colo. Beatty also returned from Staten Island and brought with him the inclosed List of the Fleet which was gone; but as it was their account (the Enemy's) he does not believe it to be so strong. No body allows there are above Two men of War lately come from England, and most say there is but One" (ScHi: Henry Laurens Papers). GW had sent extracts of a previous let-

ter from Brig. Gen. William Maxwell, dated 7 Aug., in his letter to d'Estaing of 8 August.

*Letter not found*: from Maj. Gen. Nathanael Greene, 12–13 Aug. 1778. On 21 Aug., GW wrote Greene: "On Wednesday afternoon I re⟨ce⟩ived your favor of the 12th & 13th Inst."

## From Major General William Heath

Dear General                    Head Quarters Boston Augst 12th 1778
Yours of the 24th June and 3rd July Came to hand by this Days Post. where they have been so long detained I cannot Conceive, as they Contain Several Peices of Intelligence of the then motions of the Enemy—had they Come to hand in the Usual Time would have gratifyed the Publick exceedingly; be pleased Sir to accept my warmest acknowledgements of Gratitude and Thanks for the Honor Done me in writing of them.
I some time Since received a resolve of Congress accepting the resignations of Colo. Lee & Major Swaseys Commissions—the latter I do my Self the Honor to enclose⟨.⟩[1] Colo. Lee is Gone a voluntier on the Expedition to Rhode Island—and I beleive Commands the Boats.
I am happy in having your Excellency's approbation of my Conduct respecting the Unfortunate Death of Lt Brown of the Troops of the Convention.
all the Military Stores which Some time Since arrived at Portsmouth to which your Excellency is pleased to allude in yours of the 3rd July have been Sent on to Springfield, and had I received the Signification of your Pleasure those for the Horse should have been Sent Immediately to the North River.
The whole attention of the Publick is turned to the Rhode Island Expeditio⟨n.⟩ as I apprehend your Excellency has every intelligence directly from that place it will be needless for me to make mention of any from that Quarte⟨r.⟩ I have the Honor to be with the greatest respect your Excellencys most Obt Hbble Servt

W. Heath

N.B. Capt. Sewall's Commission goes wth this.[2]

ADfS, MHi: Heath Papers.
    1. Congress had accepted the resignations of Col. William Raymond Lee and Maj. Joseph Swasey on 24 June (*JCC*, 11:640). The enclosed commission of Swasey has not been identified.
    2. GW's letter to Heath of 29 April had authorized him to accept Capt. Stephen Sewall's resignation. Sewall's commission has not been identified.

# From Colonel John Lamb

Sir                                     Park of Artillery [12 August][1] 1778

I am extremely sorry to inform your Excellency, that, a dispute has arisen between Colo. Harrisson of the Artillery, and myself, respecting Seniority; As I came into the Service, a Capt. in the Artillery, on 30th June 1775, and had the honor of being appointed (by Congress) to the sole Command of the Artillery in the Northern Department, with the Rank, and Pay of Major 1st Janry 1776 (at the first of which periods, I am informed Colo. Harrisson was not in the Service) I conceive myself possessed of the right of Seniority; And cannot possibly submit to be commanded by him, 'till his right is properly ascertain'd.

And as disputes of this nature, destroy that harmony which ought to prevail among Officers, who are embarked in the same Common Cause, & may have a tendency (if not settled soon) to injure the Service,[2] I must intreat your Excellency, to Order a Board of Genl Officers, for that purpose, as soon as may be convenient. I have the honour to be, with the greatest Respect, your Excellency's most Obedient Servant.

Copy, in Lamb's writing, NHi: Lamb Papers.

1. Lamb wrote "Sepr" on the copy, but GW's reply of 13 Aug. makes it clear that this letter was dated 12 August.

2. On the preceding day, 11 Aug., Capt. Gershom Mott of Lamb's regiment wrote him to complain of directions about the regiment that Mott had received from Col. Charles Harrison (NHi: Lamb Papers).

# From the Council of Maryland

Sir.                                     In Council 12th Augt 1778.

Lieut. Colo. Smith by his Letter of the 26th last, informs us that he is desired by the Officers of the second Maryland Brigade to apply to us for Money to inlist the nine Months Men, many of whom they have inlisted for three Years and the greatest Number of whom may be before their Time has expired; that the Money, which they will frequently want, will induce them and, he conceives an Order through your Excellency to the Paymaster General would be the most convenient Method.[1] We very much wish to prevent, as far as possible, the like Inconveniencies again occurring in reinlisting and recruiting as we have too often experienced and, if it can be done with Propriety, hope you will give the necessary Orders for the Advance of the forty Dollars Bounty allowed by this State for such of the nine Months Men as may inlist in our Regiments. If this Mode of Advance on Account of the State cannot be effected, we shall endeavour to furnish the Officers in some other Method, though none offers itself at present. We are Sir with the greatest Respect &ca.

LB, MdAA: Council Letterbook, 1777–1779.
    1. The council was referring to Lt. Col. Samuel Smith's letter of 26 July to Gov. Thomas Johnson (MdAA). The troops were those raised in accordance with Congress's resolution of 26 Feb. 1778, directing the states to draft troops for nine months' service to complete their Continental regiments (*JCC*, 10:199–203).

*Letter not found*: from Maryland officers, 12 Aug. 1778. On 13 Aug., GW's secretary James McHenry wrote to Col. John Gunby and other Maryland officers: "Colonel Price has been transmitted a copy of the charges against him in your letter to his Excellency of yesterday that he may prepare for tryal. When the evidence you think necessary to carry on the prosecution are collected, you will be pleased to signify it in order that this affair may be finally determined" (DLC:GW).

## General Orders

                Head-Quarters W. Plains Thursday August 13th 1778.
Parole Worcester—                              C. Signs Upton Tweed.
    Two Colliers from each Brigade are to be constantly employed under direction of Colonel Baldwin in burning Coal for the use of the Army.
    All the Teams attached to the different Brigades fit for service are to be turned out daily by the Waggon Master General to be employed by the Commissary General of Provisions and Forage in the Invirons of Camp except so many as may be necessary for Camp duty, which the Waggon Master General will allot.

Varick transcript, DLC:GW.

*Letter not found*: from Lt. Col. William Butler, 13 Aug. 1778. On 24 Aug., GW wrote Butler: "I recd yours of the 13th instant dated at Schohary." Butler wrote New York governor George Clinton on 13 Aug.: "I have wrote to his Excellency Genl. Washington informing him of my situation &c. of the same date" (Hastings, *Clinton Papers*, 3:632).

## To Colonel Peter Gansevoort

Sir,                              Head Quarters, White Plains Aug. 13th 1778
    I have received the proceedings of a Court Martial held by your order respecting Samuel Gake.[1] As neither the articles of war, nor any resolves of Congress authorise the constituting General Courts Martial by any others, than the commander in chief, the commanding officer in

a separate department, or a General-Officer commanding in a particular state, I should have been under the necessity of ordering a second trial, and appointing a Court for the purpose, if it had been judged expedient to bring Gakes to punishment. But as his confession contains information very pointedly against Major Hammel, which concurs with other accounts I have received, I think it of more importance to the public to save Gakes as a Witness against Hammel, than to make an example of him.[2] You will therefore keep him in such a kind of confinement, as will effectually prevent his escape 'till matters are ripe for the prosecution of Major Hammel, and at the same time, will be as little rigorous as the nature of the case will admit. He need however know nothing of my intention. I am Sir Your most Obedt servt

Go: Washington

LS, in Alexander Hamilton's writing, NN: Gansevoort-Lansing Collection; Df, DLC:GW; copy, NN: Gansevoort-Lansing Collection; Varick transcript, DLC:GW. The copy was enclosed in GW's letter to Gansevoort of 29 August. GW signed the cover of the LS.

1. At the court-martial on 1 July, Samuel Gake (Geake), a private in the 3d New York Regiment, was tried on "Susspicion of being a Spy from the Enemy." The chief witness testified that when he and another sergeant made pretense "of being dissatisfied with the service," Gake "told them That he came out of New York as a Spy on the same boat with Major Hammell and that it was agreed between the Prisoner & said Major Hammell to pretend that they had made their Escape from the Enemy and that Hammell Charged him to be faithfull and not devulge his mind to any one and to entice as many men as he could to join him and That Lord Rodnam [Rawdon] had promised him the said Hammill a Colonel's Commission in his Brigade and That he the prisoner was to be a Lieutenant in the same Regiment with Hammell. That the Prisoner told the deponent that he should have as good a Commiss⟨ion⟩ as him the said Prisoner if he would join him. That he intended to go to the Southard and then to Philadelphia That the Prisoner spoke highly in favor of Lord Rodnam and said he was an Irishman (One of their Country Men)" and drew up a paper for them to sign promising to desert to the British. Gake was found guilty and sentenced to death by hanging (DLC:GW). He remained in custody and under sentence until 1779, when he was allowed to rejoin his regiment. Gake served until November 1780, when he deserted.

2. For an earlier report on Brigade Major Daniel Hammill, see Samuel Holden Parsons to GW, 22 May 1778, and note 1 to that document.

## To Colonel John Lamb

sir Head Qrs [White Plains] August the 13th 1778
I have been favoured with your Letter of ⟨yes⟩terday.
A Board of Officers cannot sit at this time upon the point in question between you and Colo. Harrison; but you may be assured, that as soon as circumstances will permit, I will order One, as there is nothing that

I wish for more than an adjustment of disputes about rank. In the mean while I request, that you will transmit me a full state of your claim, that I may lay it before the Board when they meet, with such other papers as may be nec⟨e⟩ssary upon the occasion.[1] I am sir Your Most Obedt servant

Go. Washington

LS, in Robert Hanson Harrison's writing, NHi: Lamb Papers; DF, DLC:GW; Varick transcript, DLC:GW.

1. On 15 Aug., Lamb wrote New York delegate to Congress Francis Lewis for "a Copy of the Resolve of Congress, in regard to the raising Colonel [Charles] Harrisson's Regiment; and also the Resolve, respecting the raising the Continental Artillery; and whether Colo. Harrison's Regiment, was at first ordered to be raised as a State Regiment . . . or for the Continental Service" (NHi: Lamb Papers). When GW's aide-de-camp Robert Hanson Harrison wrote Lamb on 27 Aug., "His Excellency desires to know whether you are ready to lay your claim before a Board of Officers, The situation of the Army will allow one to sit at this time," Lamb evidently replied that he had not obtained the resolutions, for Harrison wrote Lamb again on 28 Aug. to inform him that he could see the relevant resolutions at headquarters (both letters, NHi: Lamb Papers). The board of officers, which GW instructed on 11 Sept. and which met on 15 Sept., ranked Lamb above Harrison but Harrison's regiment above Lamb's (see General Orders, 15 Sept.).

## To Henry Laurens

Sir,                    Head Quarters White Plains Aug. 13th 1778

I have the honor to transmit you a letter from General Sullivan, which, from the tardiness of the expresses, is but just come to hand— I suppose it gives Congress the same information communicated to me; but lest there should be any particulars mentioned in his letter to me, which may not be contained in the one to you, I am induced to accompany the latter with a copy of the former.[1]

The papers sent from Congress to Head Quarters and returned, respecting the case of Major General St Clair, will be wanted immediately, as it is probable his trial will now very speedily come on.[2]

I beg you will excuse the trouble, I give you, in requesting you will favour me, in your next with copies of the resolve of Congress, for raising the regiment of Artillery in Virginia, and appointing Col: Harrison to the command of it, and of another passed the latter end of 76, for raising three batalions of Continental Artillery.[3] Some disputes about rank have arisen which make these resolutions necessary; and it happens, that my papers of that period are absent. With the utmost respect I have the honor to be Sir Your most Obedt servt

Go: Washington

P.S. I request you will be pleased to forward the inclosed to Mr Serjeant without delay.[4]

LS, in Alexander Hamilton's writing, DNA:PCC, item 152; Df, DLC:GW; copy, DNA:PCC, item 169; Varick transcript, DLC:GW. Congress read this letter on 15 Aug.; see *JCC*, 11:801.

1. GW enclosed Maj. Gen. John Sullivan's letters to him and to Laurens of 10 August. Sullivan's letter to Laurens contains much the same information as his letter to GW, but it adds the detail that the French fleet "came through Newport Harbor on Saturday night [8 Aug.] & Silenced two of their Batteries" (DNA:PCC, item 160; see also *Laurens Papers*, 14:145–46).

2. On 7 Feb. the Continental Congress evacuation committee had sent to GW the evidence that they had collected against major generals Arthur St. Clair and Philip Schuyler, but GW wrote Henry Laurens on 27 Feb. to request that Congress "state explicitly the charges they wish to have exhibited against the Officers." On 29 April, Congress appointed a new committee to examine the evidence and state charges, and on the following day, Laurens wrote GW to request the return of the papers. GW returned them to Congress on 1 May.

3. For the three resolutions, of 26 Nov., 30 Nov., and 27 Dec. 1776, see *JCC*, 6:981, 995, and 1045–46.

4. For GW's letter to Jonathan Dickson Sergeant, see GW to William Paterson, this date, source note.

## From Henry Laurens

Sir                                     [Philadelphia] 13th August [1778]

Since my last of the 30th July I have had the honor of presenting to Congress Your Excellency's several favors of the 3d, 4th and 7th Inst.[1]

The transcript from the journal of Congress dated the 10th Inst. and here inclosed will shew Your Excellency how those of the 3d and 4th were dispos'd of.[2]

I likewise inclose with this, an Act of Congress dated the 10th, and three dated the 12th Inst. together with the declaration of the last mention'd date.

1. for adding two Members to the Committee of Arrangement[3]
2. for permitting Colonel Knobeloch to act as a Volunteer in the Army, and for allowing him 125 Dollars per Month[4]
3. for allowing a compensation for horses kill'd in battle[5]
4. a Declaration That Congress hold it incompatible with their honor in any manner to correspond or have intercourse with George Johnstone Esquire one of the British Commissioners[6]
5. An Act of Congress of the 12th for sending the said Declaration to the Commissioners by a Flag.[7]

Congress request Your Excellency will give directions for carrying this immediately into execution.

Yesterday I presented to Congress a letter from Mr Ferguson, Secretary to the Commissioners of the 7th Inst. and the Paper referred to in that letter. Copies of these I take the liberty of transmitting herewith, merely for your Excellency's information.[8] I have the honor to be With the highest Esteem and Regard.

LB, DNA:PCC, item 13. A note on the letter-book copy indicates that this was sent "by a Messenger from Monsr Gerard."

1. Although Laurens had written to GW on 31 July, he is evidently referring to his letter of 30 July as his last official letter. Laurens is also referring to GW's letter of 3–4 Aug. and two letters of 7 Aug.; there is no indication that GW wrote any separate letter of 4 Aug. to Laurens.

2. The enclosed transcript has not been identified. Congress referred GW's comments on the artillery and the enlistment of drafts to the Board of War and his comments on the clothier general's office to a committee of Samuel Adams, Roger Sherman, and Nathaniel Scudder. They also resolved "That a commander of the horse be appointed to morrow" (*JCC*, 11:767–68).

3. For this resolution of 10 Aug., adding Roger Sherman and John Banister to the committee, see ibid., 11:769.

4. The extract from the minutes on this subject in DLC:GW differs somewhat from what appears ibid., 11:778–79, but the resolutions in the two sources are the same. According to his letter to Congress of 27 July 1778, the baron de Knobelauch was "a Nobleman of an ancient Family in the Electorate of Brandenbourg" and a veteran of the Seven Years' War who had thirty years of service in the Prussian, Russian, and Danish armies (DNA:PCC, item 78). On 24 Aug. 1777 Benjamin Franklin had written a letter for Knobelauch to deliver to GW, stating that he "is recommended to me as an Officer of much Experience, and capable of rendring good Service in our Armies if employ'd" (DLC:GW; see also *Franklin Papers*, 24:459). Knobelauch apparently served as a volunteer until December 1778 and remained in the United States until June 1780 without obtaining employment that he found satisfactory (see Knobelauch to Congress, 5 June 1780, DNA:PCC, item 78).

5. For this resolution of 12 Aug., see General Orders, 19 Aug. (see also *JCC*, 11:777–78).

6. The declaration passed on 11 Aug. quoted Johnstone's letter of 11 April to Joseph Reed, stating that "The man who can be instrumental in bringing us all to act once more in harmony . . . will deserve more from the king and the people . . . than ever was yet bestowed on human kind," and Johnstone's letter of 16 June to Robert Morris, suggesting "that honor and emolument should naturally follow the fortune of those who have steered the vessel in the storm and brought her safely to port. I think Washington and the president have a right to every favor that grateful nations can bestow, if they could once more unite our interest and spare the miseries and devastations of war." Congress claimed that the letters, in conjunction with a late June conversation in which "a married lady of character" told Reed that Johnstone was prepared to offer him "£10,000 sterling, and any office in the colonies . . . in his majesty's gift" if he would "promote . . . a re-union between the two countries," must "be considered as direct attempts to corrupt and bribe the Congress." The resolution of nonintercourse with Johnstone expressed "the highest and most pointed indignation against such daring and atrocious attempts to corrupt their integrity" (ibid., 11:770–75).

7. For this resolution, see ibid., 11:776.

8. The enclosed copies have not been identified; for Adam Ferguson's letter to Laurens of 7 Aug. and the remonstrance of the British commissioners of the same date, see DNA:PCC, item 57 (see also *Laurens Papers*, 14:139–40). The remonstrance protested the "unjust Detention" of the troops of Gen. John Burgoyne's army who had surrendered at Saratoga.

*Letter not found*: from Col. William Malcom, 13 Aug. 1778. On 17 Aug., GW wrote Malcom: "I rec'd your favor of the 13th inst."

## To Brigadier General William Maxwell

Sir                            Head Quarters White plains 13th Augt 1778
I have your favr of the 10th inclosing a list of the French Fleet.[1] I am informed that Lieut. Lane of your Brigade, who was the Officer that recd the Flag at second River, opened the packet from the British Commissioners to Congress—read the Contents and made them known to several persons; one of whom is ready to prove the fact. I therefore desire that Mr Lane may be arrested and sent up here, to be tried for so unofficer a like a procedure.[2]

There are not at present either Cartouch Boxes or Tin Cannisters in the hands of the Commy of Military Stores. I will direct him to send to the Magazines and Manufactories and endeavour to obtain a supply. I am Sir Yrs &c.

Df, in Tench Tilghman's writing, DLC:GW; Varick transcript, DLC:GW.

1. Only an extract of Maxwell's letter that GW sent to Vice Admiral d'Estaing with his letter of 12 Aug. has been found. The enclosed list has not been identified, but the extract indicates that it was of the British, not the French, fleet.

2. Aaron Lane, who was commissioned an ensign in the 2d New Jersey Regiment in 1775, was promoted to second lieutenant in November 1776 and to first lieutenant in July 1777. He was cashiered on 25 Aug. 1778 (see General Orders of that date). The packet contained the British peace commissioners' letter to Henry Laurens of 7 August. Maxwell sent the packet to Laurens on 8 Aug., along with a letter noting that it had been opened (both items, DNA:PCC, item 57).

## From Officers of the 3d New York Regiment

*13 Aug. 1778*. "Petition" for relief from duty at Fort Schuyler, where the officers have served "Seventeen Months" with "not the least Prospect of our being called to any other Employ than Hard Labour, which has been our Constant Exercise, since we arrived." Request "an Opportunity of serving with the Grand Army, or taking the Feild in some other Place," as they are "Anxious to have an equal opportunity with our Bretheren, to Improve in Knowledge & acquire Honor."

DS, DLC:GW. A note on the cover of the document reads: "favoured by Lieut. [Thomas] McClellan." The petition is signed by six captains, one captain lieutenant, eight lieutenants, eight ensigns, a surgeon, and a surgeon's mate.

## To William Paterson

sir                                   York State, White plains August the 13th 1778
   You will perceive by the Inclosed Copy of the proceedings of Congress, that they have appointed you, to assist and co-operate with the Judge Advocate in conducting the Trial of the General Officers, who were in the Northern Department, when Tyconderoga and Mount Independence were evacuated.[1] I think it proper to inform you, that a General Court Martial will sit at this place on Monday the 24th Instant, to try Major General St Clair, who is one of the Officers under this description. I am sir Your Most Obedt servant

Go: Washington

LS, in Robert Hanson Harrison's writing, NNU-F: Richard Maass Collection; Df, DLC:GW; Varick transcript, DLC:GW. GW signed the cover of the LS. A note on the draft reads: "the same to Jonathan D. Sergeant, Esqr. Attorney Genl of pensylvania," and there is a similar notation on the Varick transcript.
   William Paterson (1745–1806), a graduate of the College of New Jersey at Princeton who represented Somerset County in the New Jersey provincial congress of 1775–76, was chosen to be attorney general of New Jersey in September 1776. Although elected to the Continental Congress in November 1780, he declined to serve, remaining as attorney general until 1783. He later served as a New Jersey delegate to the Constitutional Convention of 1787; U.S. senator, 1789–90; New Jersey governor, 1790–93; and justice of the Supreme Court, 1793–1806.
   1. For the resolution of 5 Feb. appointing Paterson and Jonathan Dickson Sergeant to assist in the trial, see *JCC*, 10:125.

## To Brigadier General John Stark

Sir                                   Head Quarters White plains 13 Augt 1778
   I am favd with yours of the 10th inclosing a letter from Colo. Butler, whose presence I hope will curb the disaffected and stop the Ravages upon your frontier. If an expedition of any consequence should be carried on, a proper supply of light Artillery shall be furnished; in the mean time let me know whether you want Ball for any Artillery that you already have.
   I think you had better inform the Civil Authority that they must in fu-

ture supply their State prisoners with provision—Be pleased to forward the inclosed to Colo. Gansevoort by the first opportunity.[1] I am &c.

Df, in Tench Tilghman's writing, DLC:GW; Varick transcript, DLC:GW.
    1. See GW to Peter Gansevoort, this date.

## From Major General John Sullivan

Dear General.                    Head Quarters Rhode Island Augt 13th 1778.
    In my last I had the honor to inform your Excellency of my being in possession of the enemies works on the North end of this Island, and of the arrival of a British fleet the moment we had landed, with the addition of Count d'Estain's sailing in pursuit of them.[1] As this last unfortunate circumstance deprived me of the assistance I had reason to expect from the French troops, I found it absolutely necessary to remain inactive until my numbers were sufficiently encreased, to warrant my advanceing without them.[2] But fortune (determined to shew us the extent of his power[)] brought on a storm so violent that it last night blew down tore, and almost irreparably ruined the few tents my troops had in their possession. The arms of course were rendered unfit for immediate use and almost the whole of the amunition damaged. My men have suffered much, the greater part of them have had no kind of covering, nor would tents if they had them prove a sufficient security against the severity of the storm.[3] Our communication with the main is intirely cut off by the violence of the winds which will scarcely permit the passage of a whale boat. Should the enemy move out to take advantage of our situation, our dependence must rest on the superiority of our numbers and the length of our Bayonets. How our Militia would behave on such an occasion I am unable to determine—*they may be desperate* when they find it impossible to retreat, and that their only alternative is to conquer and die....[4] Many men have perished already, and I wish the mortality may end with the storm.[5] I despair of deriving any immediate advantage from our allies, as they must have been driven to a distance, far from affording us any, if not entirely from our coasts.
    To combat all those difficulties and to surmount all those obstacles, require a degree of temper and a persevering fortitude which I could never boast of, and which few possess in so ample a manner as your Excellency. I will however endeavour by emulating the excellence of your example, to rise superior to the malevolence of fortune, and flatter myself, that if heaven will deign once more to smile upon me, I may yet answer in some measure, the expectations your Excellency may have conceived of the enterprize.[6]

I am sorry your Excellency's letter respecting the enemy's burning their shipping did not come to hand until they had burned every vessel of force and sunk almost all their vessels of whatever denomination to block up the channel.[7] The letter you inclosed to Count d'Estaign did not arrive till after he had sailed,[8] nor did I receive the intelligence from the council of Massachusetts informing that Admiral Byron appeared off the Western Islands, till a day after his departure. The account says that Byron was spoke with the 29th of June,[9] and had thirteen sail of the line under his command. The fleet to which the Count gave chace consisted of five sail of the line, some frigates & transports under the direction of Lord Howe. They landed no men here. An apprehension that some such event as this might take place to deprive me of the Counts assistance induced me to call out more men than I otherwise would have done. The number of the enemy are nearly thus.

| | | |
|---|---|---|
| 2 Hessian Regiments | 600 each | 1200 |
| 2 Anspach Do | 500 each | 1000 |
| Brown & Fanning | | 600 |
| 22d 38th 43d & 54th British Regiments | 400 each | 1600 |
| 2 Hessian Regiments | 500 each | 1000 |
| Whitmans Regiment | | 100 |
| To these we may add of seamen | | <u>1000</u> |
| | | 6500[10] |

My numbers on the Island are about nine thousand rank and file. I am Sir with the greatest respect your Excellys most obt very hble servt

Jno. Sullivan

P.S. Deserters come out in great numbers.

Copy, in James McHenry's writing, DLC:GW; ADfS, NhHi: Sullivan Papers; copy (extract), DNA:PCC, item 160; copy (extract), ScHi: Henry Laurens Papers. The extract in PCC was enclosed in GW to Henry Laurens, 16 August. For discussion of the text omitted from the extracts, see note 6. A purported ALS of this letter was offered for sale by Parke-Bernet Galleries, Inc., catalog 596, *The James McHenry Papers*, 30–31 Oct., 1944, item 189. The ADfS shows many variations from the copy, most of which do not alter the meaning. The most significant are indicated in notes 2, 3, 4, 5, and 9.

1. See Sullivan to GW, 10 August.

2. On the ADfS the passage corresponding to the preceding sentence reads: "as this unfortunate Circumstan[ce] deprivd us of the assistance we promisd ourselves from the French Troops I found it necessary to wait on the Ground till the tenth at night; when finding my o[w]n Troops numbers had Increased Sufficiently to warrant my advancing to the Town without waiting the Return of the Fleet: I Issued orders for the Army to march the 11th at Six in the morning."

3. Private Stephen Popp of the Bayreuth Regiment wrote in his journal for 14 Aug.: "Had a violent storm of rain and wind for forty-eight hours, the worst in all my campaigns" ("Popp's Journal," 32; see also Prechtel, *Diary*, 145; *Mackenzie Diary*,

349–51; Cutler, *Rev. Manasseh Cutler*, 1:66–67; Gibbs diary, 5–30 Aug., *Pa. Archives*, 1st ser., 6:734–35). At this point, the draft continues with a sentence omitted from McHenry's copy: "my men are mostly Lying under the Fences half Covered with water without Ammunition & with Arms Rendered useless."

4. Whether the apparent ellipsis indicates text omitted from the copy cannot be determined in the absence of the LS. The ADfS includes at this point a sentence reading: "perhaps under these Circumstances an Attack upon us might be of great advantage."

5. On the ADfS the passage corresponding to the preceding sentence reads: "Several men have perished with the Severity of the weather & I Expect more will as I See no probability of the Storm Ceasing."

6. The preceding paragraph was not included in the copy of this letter that GW sent to Congress.

7. Sullivan was evidently referring to GW's letter to him of 4 August.

8. Sullivan was apparently referring to GW's letter to Vice Admiral d'Estaing of 8 August.

9. On the draft the date is "24th of June."

10. For a British report of the strength of their army, 10 Aug., showing that Sullivan's estimation of the total was not far off, see *Mackenzie Diary*, 2:346.

## General Orders

Head-Quarters W. Plains Friday Augt 14th 1778.
Parole Almanza—                    C. Signs Atlas. Albany.

A Detachment of Light Dragoons commanded by a Field Officer to join the Light Infantry this afternoon and to be relieved Weekly.

The General Court-Martial whereof Majr General Lord-Stirling is President is dissolved—Also that whereof Colonel Hall is President; and another order'd to sit at the usual place tomorrow morning nine ôClock to try all such Persons as shall be bro't before them—Coll Hazen will preside. Members—Lieutt Colonel Russell,[1] Major Haws and a Captain from each Brigade except Scott's, Parsons's & Poor's.

The Regimental Pay-Masters are to prepare the Pay-Rolls for the Months of June & July and deliver the same to the Pay-Master General for examination; They are to be careful to make them up agreeable to the Resolves of Congress of May 27th—and June 2nd[2]—a Column is to be added for subsistence of the officers which is to be charged at the following Rates.

| | | |
|---|---|---|
| Coll | pr month | 50 Dol. |
| Lieut. Colonel | | 40. |
| Major | | 30. |
| Captain | | 20. |
| Regil Surgeon | | 30 Doll. |
| Lieutt & Ensign | | 10. |
| Surgeon's Mate | | 10. |

The Pay of the Infantry remains as before except as follows—

| | Doll. |
|---|---|
| Lieutenant | 26⅔ pr Mo. |
| Serjt Majr Qr Mastr | |
| Serjt & Serjeants | 10— |
| Dr. & Fife Majors | 9— |
| Surgeon pr Mo. | 60. |
| Surgeon's Mate | 40. |

The following Officers if taken from the line to be allowed in addition to their Pay in the line—

| | |
|---|---|
| Aide-de Camp | 24 Dol. pr Mo. |
| Brigade Major | 24. |
| Quartr Master | 13. |
| Adjutant | 13. |
| Pay-Master | 20. |

The Officers of the Staff taken from the line are not to be made up in the Pay-Rolls of their respective Companies, but to receive their Pay in the manner heretofore practiced by the Staff.

The Pay-Masters of the Artillery and Cavalry may receive the Establishment of their respective Corps by applying to the Pay-Master General.

Next monday nine ôClock in the morning is appointed for the Execution of David Potter, Solomon Lynes, Alexander Graham, Nicholas Fitzgerald, Zechariah Ward, Richard Burk, Michael Carmen, William McLaughlin, John Jenkins, John Craige & Neil Megonigle now under sentence of Death, the ten first for desertion &c. and the last for wounding an Officer in the Execution of his office.[3]

Varick transcript, DLC:GW.

1. The orders apparently refer to Lt. Col. Giles Russell of the 4th Connecticut Regiment. Although Russell's subsequent promotion to colonel of the 8th Connecticut Regiment was backdated to 5 March 1778, he did not assume command of the regiment until December 1778.

2. For these resolutions, see *JCC*, 11:538–43, 560–61.

3. The next Monday was 17 August. In his journal entry for that date, Col. Jeduthan Baldwin wrote: "11 Prisoners brought out for Execution, one Shot the others Reprieved untill Friday [21 Aug.], a Vast Concorse of People" (Baldwin, *Revolutionary Journal*, 132). The man "shot Near Head Quarters" was Alexander Graham, who, Pvt. Elijah Fisher recorded, was executed "for Enlisting seven times and taken bountys" (Godfrey, *Commander-in-Chief's Guard*, 281; see also "Beatty Journal," 83; Symmes, *Gilbert Diary*, 35). David Potter of Holden, Mass., had been a private in Col. Thomas Nixon's Regiment (later the 6th Massachusetts Regiment) since March 1777 but was reported as absent without leave or deserted from June 1777 to April 1778. Pardoned with the other prisoners on 21 Aug., he continued to serve in the regiment, rising briefly to corporal in June 1780, but in November 1780 he was again reported as a deserter.

*Letter not found*: from the Board of War, 14 Aug. 1778. On 28 Aug., GW wrote the board: "Your favor of the 14th Instant has been duly received."

## To Major General William Heath

Dear sir.                          Head Quarters White plains Augt 14th 1778
Within a few days past I have been favoured with your several letters of the 15. 17 & 25 Ulto and of the 6th Inst.

Mr Attendorff shall never act as a Major or in any capacity as an officer in the army with my consent; and I am much surprised that he should entertain the most distant idea that he would be received. His conduct deserves a very different notice.

With respect to the salt provisions which you mention, Col. Wadsworth, the Commissary general had given directions about them before your letter came to hand, and matters of this nature are principally left to his management.

I have no objection to your receiving Major Lithgows resignation, as he appears unfit for service and to be very desirous of a discharge. you will use the proper and accustomary precautions in like cases respecting a settlement of his accounts.

I thank you much for your kind wishes. It is natural for you to desire to be in a more active scene; but the important objects of your present command, requiring an intelligent and attentive officer I do not see how your services can be dispensed with.

I have transmitted a copy of General Phillips's letter to Congress on the subject of an officers going to Canada.[1] This I have never thought regular, or given direction in any matter respecting the Convention troops of my own accord.[2] Indeed I wish that when there are any points in which they are concerned, and which you cannot determine yourself you would make your application immediately to them.

The zeal of the gentlemen volunteers deserves great commendation. I hope their exertions will be crowned with success and with all the honor they desire. I am dr Sir with great regard & Esteem Your most obt servt

Go: Washington

LS, in James McHenry's writing, MHi: Heath Papers; Df, DLC:GW; Varick transcript, DLC:GW.

1. GW was referring to Maj. Gen. William Phillips's letter to Heath of 29 July, which Heath had sent in the letter of 6 Aug. for GW's "Opinion & Direction." GW enclosed a copy of Phillips's letter in his to Henry Laurens of 16 August.

2. On Robert Hanson Harrison's draft the preceding sentence reads: "This I thought regular, as I have never given direction in any matter, respecting the Convention Troops of my own accord."

# From Major General William Heath

Dear General,                    Head Quarters Boston Augst 14th 1778

The Express who came from Congress being taken Sick here, prevents his returning at Present I am therefore to request the favor that your Excellency would be pleased to Send on the Packet addressed to the Hon. President by the First Express that goes from your Quarters—which will lay me under great obligation.[1] I have the Honor to be with the greatest respect your Excellencys most Obt Hbble Servt

W. Heath

ADfS, MHi: Heath Papers. GW apparently acknowledged this letter as one of 13 Aug.; whether GW erred or Heath wrote a different date on the letter sent has not been determined.

1. At this place on the draft, Heath crossed out all of the remaining text except for the closing. The deleted text reads: "as the Papers contain matters of Importance in particular respecting Ensign John Brown of Colonel Greaton Regt who was Some Time Since Tryed at a General Court Martial Here—and Sentenced to be shot, for leaving his Regiment without permision, after his return home presenting for Muster by rong names Seven or Eight men part of whom were before inlisted & part not inlisted at all, Except by feigned names—and for entering himself as a Private Marine on Board a Continental vessel to all which He plead Guilty and received Sentence as above—I approved the Sentence and ordered Execution—the Culprit beged leave to Petition Congress for a Pardon which I granted—Congress denied the Prayer of the Petition, and wrote me to have him executed, upon receiving the order of Congress, a number of Inhabitants Petitioned the Council to Desire me to Stay Execution untill another Petition was prefered to Congress, I did it and forwarded the Petition." The packet probably included Heath's letter to Roger Sherman, Henry Marchant, and William Henry Drayton of 10 Aug., as well as his letter to Laurens of 11 Aug. (both DNA:PCC, item 157).

*Letter not found*: from Brig. Gen. John Paterson, 14 Aug. 1778. On 15 Aug., Richard Kidder Meade wrote Paterson: "His Excy rec'd your favor of Yesterday" (DLC:GW).

# To Major General Philip Schuyler

Dr Sir                    Head Quarters White plains 14 Augt 1778

I had not the pleasure of receiving your letter of the 28 ulto till the other day. It was found by a soldier in a tavern, and delivered to Colonel Hay who immediately sent it forward.

I have now to inform you that the Court martial for the tryal of General St Clair sits the 24th Inst. I am Sir &[ca]

G.W.

Df, in James McHenry's writing, DLC:GW; Varick transcript, DLC:GW.

## To Brigadier General Charles Scott

sir.                                              [White Plains, 14 August 1778]

With the detachment of light troops under your command you are to take post in front of our camp and in such a position as may appear best calculated to preserve the security of your own corps and cover this army from surprise.

For the better execution of these purposes you will make yourself master of all the roads leading to the enemies lines.

You will keep up a constant succession of scouting parties as large as can possibly be spared from the detachment without harrassing it by too severe duty.

These parties are to penetrate as near the enemy's lines as possible, and to continue within observing distance at all times. In order that these parties may avoid all surprise, they will have their evenings position well reconnoitred and choose it at a greater distance than the ground wch they occupied during the day—They will mov⟨e⟩ to it under circumstances the least liable to excite attention, and be careful not to kindl⟨e⟩ fires in the knight as these might betray their situation.

These parties will make you constant reports of their discoveries, and you will give me the earliest and fullest intelligence of all occurrences worthy of notice. Given at Head Quarters &c. this 14 August 1778.

G.W.

Df, in James McHenry's writing, DLC:GW; Varick transcript, DLC:GW.

## General Orders

Head-Quarters W. Plains Saturday Augt 15th 1778.

Parole Williamsburgh—                          C. Signs Wells. Waldo

Varick transcript, DLC:GW. On this date GW's aide-de-camp Richard Kidder Meade wrote Brig. Gen. John Paterson: "His Excy rec'd your favor of Yesterday, inclosing a copy of Division orders issued by Major Genl De Kalb, & directs me to inform you, that he shall take the necessary steps in the matter—The Baron He is sensible was actuated by some good motive, & that he did not at the time of issuing the order advert to his not having the power of determining on capital Points" (DLC:GW).

*Letter not found*: from William Smith, 15 Aug. 1778. On 21 Aug., GW wrote Smith: "I received your letter of the 15th Inst. by Lieut. Colonel Burr."

## From Brigadier General John Stark

*Albany, August 15, 1778.*

*Dear General*—The deputy paymaster of this department informs me that he is recalled, and that your excellency is of opinion that we have no occasion for one. Your excellency must be deceived as to the distances of our detachments from head quarters.

One body is stationed at Otter creek, one hundred and thirty miles north-east of this place; one at Fort Edward, fifty miles; one at Fort Schuyler, one hundred and twenty miles; and Alden's and Butler's regiments are posted on two other stations.[1] Beside these, the militia are employed for short terms, and the wages they earn will not justify the expense of sending to you. Under these circumstances, a deputy paymaster is often of the greatest importance at this place. I leave the matter, however, for your judgment.

As Congress has been pleased to make provision for the battalion officers,[2] but not any as I have heard for the generals or staff, I should be glad of your opinion in what manner I shall make up my accounts, as I am in a separate command, which makes my expenses much greater than if I acted with the army. I wish to be able to live up to my station, which can not be done by the bare allowance of a brigadier, as I am obliged to purchase everything at a high price: for instance, for a gallon of rum, $14; a pound of sugar, $2.50; and every thing in proportion.

Capt. McKean is with me, and informs that he can raise a company of good rangers to scour the woods on the western frontier, if he can have proper encouragement. He served with me in the ranging service during most of the last war.[3]

I have ordered him to raise them, which I hope you will approve, as I think one company of such men can do more than a regiment of militia. I am, sir, your ob't serv't,

                                              JOHN STARK.

Stark, *Memoir of John Stark*, 217. In GW's letter to John Stark of 29 Aug., this is acknowledged as a letter of 13 August. Whether Tench Tilghman miswrote on that draft or Caleb Stark mistranscribed the date of this letter has not been determined.

1. Fort Edward was located on the Hudson River north of Albany at what is now Rogers Island. Col. Ichabod Alden's regiment was stationed at Cherry Valley, N.Y., and Lt. Col. William Butler was at Schoharie, New York. Otter Creek, which runs through Vergennes, Middlebury, and Rutland, Vt., is nowhere as far as 130 miles from Albany. The main post on the creek at this time was Fort Ranger at Rutland.

2. Stark was probably referring to Congress's resolution of 2 June 1778, which set provision allowances for officers below the rank of general (*JCC*, 11:560–61).

3. Robert McKeen (McKean; d. 1781) was commissioned a captain in the 1st New York Regiment in November 1776 to date from March 1776, when he was appointed a captain in the New York militia. He resigned his Continental commission in January 1778 but subsequently served as a captain of New York levies. On 10 July 1781 he was mortally wounded in an engagement with Indian and Loyalist troops at present-day Sharon Springs, New York. Stark had served as a lieutenant and later as a captain with Robert Rogers's Rangers during the French and Indian War.

# To Lund Washington

Dear Lund,                                          White plains Augt 15th 1778.

Your Letter of the 29th Ulto, Inclosing a line from Captn Marshall to you came to my hands yesterday—I have no reason to doubt the truth of your observation, that this Gentleman's Land, & others equally well situated, & under like circumstances, will sell very high [1]—The depreciation of our money—the high prices of every article of produce, & the redundancy of circulating paper, will, I am perswaded, have an effect upon the price of land—nor is it to be wondered at, when a Barrl of Corn which used to sell for 10/. will now fetch 40—when a Barl of Porke that formerly could be had for £3. sells for £15. & so with respect to other Articles which serves to enable the Man who has been fortunate enough to succeed in raising these things to pay accordingly; but, unfortunately for me, this is not my case; as, my Estate in Virginia is scarce able to support itself whilst it is not possible for it to derive any benefit from my labors here.

I have premised these things to shew my inability, not my unwillingness, to purchase the Lands in my own Neck at (almost) any price. & this I am yet very desirous of doing if it could be accomplished by any means in my power, in the way of Barter for other Land—for Negroes (of whom I every day long more & more to get clear of)—or in short for any thing else (except Breeding Mares and Stock of other kinds) which I have in my possession—but for money I cannot, I want the means. Marshalls Land alone, at the rate he talks of, would amount to (if my memory of the quantity he holds is right) upwards of £3000. a sum I have little chance, if I had much inclination, to pay; & therefore would not engage for it, as I am resolved not to incumber my self with Debt.

Marshall is not a necessitous Man—is only induced to offer his Land for Sale in expectation of a high price—& knowing perhaps but too well my wish to become possessed of the Land in that Neck will practice every deception in his power to work me (or you in my behalf) up to his price, or he will not sell. this should be well looked into, and guarded against—If, as you think, & as I believe, there is little chance of getting more (at any rate) than the reversion of French's Land, I have no objection to the Land on which Morris lives going in exchange for Marshalls, or its being sold for the purpose of paying for it, but remember, it will not do to contract at a high price for the one, before you can be assured of an adequate Sum for the other—without this, by means of the arts which may be practiced, you may give much and receive little, which is neither my Inclination nor intention to do. If Negroes could be given in Exchange for this Land of Marshalls, or sold at a proportionable price, I should prefer it to the sale of Morriss Land as

I still have some latent hope that Frenchs Lands may be had of D——
for it. but either I wd part with.[2]

Having so fully expressed my Sentiments concerning this matter, I
shall only add a word or two respecting Barry's Land.[3] The same motives which induce a purchase in the one case prevail in the other, and
how ever unwilling I may be to part with that small tract I hold on
difficult Run (containing by Deed, if I recollect right 275 acres, but by
measurement upwards of 300) on acct of the valuable Mill Seat
Meadow Grds &ca[4] yet I will do it for the sake of the other but if the
matter is not managed with some degree of address you will not be able
to effect an exchange without giving instead of receiving, Boot—For
this Land also I had rather give Negroes—if Negroes would do. for to
be plain I wish to get quit of Negroes.

I find by a Letter from Mr Jones that he has bought the Phæton
which you sold Mr Geo: Lewis and given him £300 for it—I mention
this, with no other view than to remind you of the necessity of getting
the Money for wch you sold it, of Lewis (if you have not already done
it)[5]—He, probably, will prepose to settle the matter with me, but this,
for a reason I could mention, I desire may be avoided.

In your Letter of the 29th you say you do not suppose I would choose
to cut down my best Land, & build Tobo Houses, but what Am I to do—
or—how am I to live—I cannt Support myself if I make nothing—& it
is evident from yr acct that I cannot raise Wheat if this Crop is likely to
share the fate of the three last. I should have less reluctance to clear-
ing my richest Lands (for I think the Swamps are these & would afterwards do for meadow) than building Houses.

I should not incline to sell the Land I had of Adams[6] unless it should
be for a price proportioned to what I must give for others. I could wish
you to press my Tenants to be punctual in the payment of their Rents—
right & Justice with respect to my self requires it—& no injury on the
contrary a real service to themselves as the Man who finds it difficult to
pay one rent will find it infinitely more so to pay two, & his distresses
multiply as the rents increase. I am &ca

G. W——n

ADfS, DLC:GW; Varick transcript, DLC:GW.

1. Lund Washington's letter to GW of 29 July has not been found. Thomas Hanson Marshall, who had become a captain in the Charles County militia by 1776,
owned a tract of almost 500 acres bordering the Mount Vernon plantation on the
west. GW had been attempting to buy that land since 1760, and Lund Washington
purchased it for him in 1779 (see Marshall to GW, 18 June 1769, and note 1, *Papers, Colonial Series*, 8:217–20).

2. Daniel French's widow, Penelope Manley French (born c.1739), owned life-
time rights in two parcels of land totaling over 500 acres, one on Dogue Run and

the other south of Marshall's tract. On her death the land would belong to Benjamin Tasker Dulany (c.1752–1816), whose wife, Elizabeth French Dulany (born c.1756), had reversionary rights to the land. GW tried for a number of years to buy the land, but Mrs. French refused to sell. Finally, however, Dulany signed his and his wife's rights over to GW in 1785, and in 1786 Mrs. French relinquished her ownership to GW in exchange for land that GW had bought on Hunting Creek (see *Diaries*, 4:84–85, and Fairfax County Deed Book P [1784-85], 311–21, and Deed Book Q [1785-86], 392–96, ViFaCt). The dower slave Morris, who was overseer at the Dogue Run farm, may have been residing on one of the several Dogue Run tracts that were largely cut off from the rest of the Mount Vernon lands to the south. Some of those tracts were transferred to Lund Washington in 1785 as payment for Lund's 1779 purchase of Marshall's land (see n.1 and Fairfax County Deed Book P [1784-85], 415–17, ViFaCt).

3. GW had been trying since 1770 to buy a tract of about 193 acres adjoining his mill property. Although GW acquired about 75 acres in December 1770 from Valinda Wade, the remainder of the land was controlled by John Barry (d. 1775), widower of Valinda's sister Eleanor Wade Barry, for his son William, and he refused to sell. GW eventually acquired the remaining 118 acres from William Barry in 1783 (see Deed from Valinda Wade, 18 Dec. 1770, *Papers, Colonial Series*, 8:417–18, and deed from William and Sarah Barry to GW, 16 June 1783, ViMtV).

4. The tract on Difficult Run, between the Great and Little Falls of the Potomac in Loudoun County (now in Fairfax County), Va., was acquired from Bryan Fairfax in 1763 (see Ledger A, 49; Loudoun County Deed Book C [1761-63], 458–63, ViLoCt). GW still owned the land at his death.

5. The letter from Joseph Jones has not been found. George Lewis paid Lund Washington £200 "for a Phaeton" on 12 June 1778 (Ledger B, 153).

6. GW was referring to the approximately 550 acres of land in Charles County, Md., that he acquired in December 1775 as payment of a debt from Daniel Jenifer Adams (see GW to Lund Washington, 20 Aug. 1775, and note 4, and Lund Washington to GW, 10 Dec. 1775, and note 1).

## General Orders

Head-Quarters W. Plains Sunday Augt 16th 1778.
Parole                                                              C. Signs

Return to be made immediately of the Carbines and Pistols, Good, Bad and Wanting in the several Regiments of Horse.

The Brigade Quarter Masters are to apply to the Deputy Commissary General of Military Stores tomorrow for their proportion of tin Cannisters, Wires and Brushes, Fifes, Drum-heads, Snares, Sticks &c.—and proportion them to the several Regiments agreeable to a late order[1]— The tin Cannisters are to be put into the hands of those men who are in the Light Infantry[2].

Varick transcript, DLC:GW.

1. This is probably a reference to GW's general orders of 17 June 1778.
2. The words "with General Scott" appear at this point in Maj. Gen. Benjamin Lincoln's orderly book (MHi: Lincoln Papers).

## From Elias Boudinot

Dear Sir,                          Baskinridge [N.J.] Augt 16. 177[8] [1]
Since my recovery from my late Indisposition so far as to attend to any Business, I have been looking over the Papers relating to my late Office of Commy Genl of Prisoners, and among them I find the report of my transactions at German Town just before and at the time of the Enemies evacuating of Philadelphia, which was designed for your Excy but prevented from being sent by my sudden illness. [2]
Knowing how little Time your Excy has to spare to any unnecessary avocation, I should not now trouble you with a report of so old a date, did I did not think it might by accident so turn up, that a Knowledge of that transaction may become essentially necessary—At least I think the evidence of such an equivocal piece of Conduct in Persons of so high rank with the Enemy, ought to be preserved. I hope this will excuse my troubling your Excy with these Papers now enclosed. I also add Mr Loring's Justification of himself from the Complaints of Prisoners, which I promised him to deliver to your Excy, but which has been delayed in the like manner. [3] Am &c.

Copy, Elias Boudinot Papers, DLC: Peter Force Collection.
  1. The copy reads "1777."
  2. Boudinot is apparently referring to his letter to GW of 28 June–6 July 1778.
  3. This enclosure has not been identified.

*Letter not found*: from Lt. Gen. Wilhelm von Knyphausen, 16 Aug. 1778. On 23 Aug., GW wrote Knyphausen: "I had the honor to receive your letter of the 16th Instant."

## To Henry Laurens

Sir                          Head quarters White plains August 16th: 1778
I take the liberty, by the conveyance now offered me by Captain Riley, to transmit to Congress the proceedings of the Court Martial in the case of Major General Lee. [1]
The Inclosed papers comprehend a request by General phillips, for an Officer to go to Canada by way of the Lakes, on the subject of Cloathing for the Convention Troops. I do not conceive myself at liberty to answer General Heath upon the point, who referred it to me, and request that Congress will favor me with their direction as soon as they conveniently can, that I may enable him to satisfye General phillips respecting it. [2]

I have not received a single tittle of Intelligence from Rhode Island, since General Sullivan's Letter of the 10th, a Copy of which I transmitted in mine of the 13th. I am extremely anxious to hear from thence—and of Count D'Estaing's safe arrival in port. The moment I do, I shall do my self the honor to advise Congress. I have the Honor to be with the greatest respect & esteem sir Yr Most Obedt servant

Go: Washington

LS, in Robert Hanson Harrison's writing, DNA:PCC, item 152; Df, DLC:GW; copy, DNA:PCC, item 169; Varick transcript, DLC:GW. Congress read this letter on 21 Aug. and referred the second paragraph to a committee of Samuel Chase, William Duer, and Richard Henry Lee. The enclosed court-martial proceedings were laid on the table to be considered on 26 August. See *JCC*, 11:824–25.

1. GW may have been referring to Capt. John Reily (1752–1810) of the 3d Pennsylvania Regiment. Reily, a lawyer who was commissioned a lieutenant of the 12th Pennsylvania Regiment in October 1776, was severely wounded during a skirmish at Bonhamtown, N.J., on 15 April 1777, and although he was promoted to captain in May of that year, he evidently was not completely fit for active duty thereafter. Reily became a captain of the 3d Pennsylvania Regiment in July 1778, but he seems not to have performed any duties at this time. In July 1780 Reily's commander brought him up on charges for failure to join the regiment, and shortly thereafter, in August 1780, Reily was transferred to the Invalid Regiment, where he served as captain until the end of the war. The enclosed court-martial proceedings have not been identified, but the full proceedings were published at Philadelphia (see *Lee Papers*, 3:1–208). An undated retained document in GW's writing lists the charges and sentence of the court: "Charges agt Majr Genl Lee. First, For disobedience of Orders in not attacking the Enemy on the 28th of June agreeable to repeated Instructions.

"Secondly—For misbehaviour before the Enemy on the same day, by making an *unnecessary, disorderly & shameful Retreat.*

"Thirdly—For disrespect to the commander in chief in two Letters dated the 1st of July & the 28th of June.

"Judgement of the Court. The Court having considered the first charge against Majr Genl Lee the evidence and his defence, are of opinion that he is guilty of disobedience of Orders, in not attacking the enemy on the 28th of June agreeable to repeated Instructions, being a breach of the latter part of Article 5th Section 2d of the Articles of War.

"The Court having considered the second charge against Major Genl Lee the evidence and his defence are of opinion he is guilty of misbehaviour before the enemy on the 28th of June by making an unnecessary, and in some few instances a disorderly retreat being a breach of the 13th Article of the 13th Section of the Articles War.

"The Court having considered the third charge against Majr Genl Lee are of opinion that he is guilty of disrespect to the Commander in chief in two Letters dated the 1st of July & 28th of June being a breach of the 2d Article Sectn 2d of the Articles of War.

"The Court do sentence Majr Genl Lee to be suspended from any Command in the Armies of the united States of North America for the Term of Twelve Months" (DLC:GW).

2. GW enclosed an extract of Maj. Gen. William Heath's letter to him of 6 Aug. and a copy of British major general William Phillips's letter to Heath of 29 July (both DNA:PCC, item 152).

## To Henry Laurens

Sir                                                  Head Qrs White plains Augt 16: 1778

Since I had the honor of addressing you to day by Captain Riley, I received a Letter from General Sullivan, a Copy of which you have inclosed.[1] From this it appears the Count D'Estaing had not returned with his Squadron on the 13th Inst.—and there is reason to fear from the violence of the Weather ever since, that he has not yet got in. This accident has much deranged our views—and I shall be happy if it does not totally defeat our Enterprize against Rhode Island. I feel much for the Count. He has been peculiarly unfortunate in the combination of several untoward circumstances to frustrate his plans.

The Letter addressed to you accompanied mine from General Sullivan.[2] They were both delivered at the same instant and through inadvertency, I broke the seal of yours. Before I had opened it I discovered the mistake, and the contents have not been seen. This relation I trust will apologize for the measure. I have the Honor to be with the greatest respect & esteem Sir Your Most Obedt servant

Go: Washington

P.S. Your favor of the 13th has come to hand.

LS, in Robert Hanson Harrison's writing, DNA:PCC, item 152; Df, DLC:GW; copy, ScHi: Henry Laurens Papers; copy, DNA:PCC, item 169; Varick transcript, DLC:GW. Congress read this letter on 19 Aug.; see *JCC*, 11:812.
    1. See John Sullivan to GW, 13 August.
    2. GW is referring to Sullivan's letter to Laurens of 14 Aug. (DNA:PCC, item 160).

## From Henry Laurens

Sir.                                            [Philadelphia] 16th August [1778]

I had the honor of writing to Your Excellency the 13th by a Messenger from Monsr Girard, since which Your Excellency's several favors of the 9th, 11th, and 13th, together with the several papers refer'd to have reached me.[1] The latter I receiv'd Yesterday at half past four P.M. in Congress, and immediately presented that and General Sullivan's of the 10th to the House.

By the Messenger abovemention'd I forwarded a Packet from the Secretary of Congress directed to Major General St Clair, and I shall transmit another directed to Your Excellency by the present conveyance, these I am informed contain all the documents relative to the charge against the General. They had been long out of my custody.[2]

Your Excellency will find inclosed with this duplicates of the Acts of Congress of the 26th and 30th of November and 27th of December 1776 for raising the regiment of Artillery in Virginia and appointing Colonel Harrison to the command, and for raising three Battalions of Continental Artillery.[3]

Also an Act of Congress of the 13th Inst. for correcting abuses and granting passes to persons to go into New York.[4]

Your Excellency's letter of the 11th I received late last Evening, it shall be laid before Congress with Colonel Palfrey's tomorrow Morning and I trust the application of that Gentleman will be immediately attended to. I have the honor to be With the utmost Respect & Esteem &c.

LB, DNA:PCC, item 13. A note on the letter-book copy indicates that this letter was sent "by Dunn."

1. Laurens apparently had not yet received GW's second letter of 9 August.

2. The packets probably contained both the materials specifically requested by GW's letter to Laurens of 13 Aug. and the charges that were reported by the committee created on 29 April to state charges in the case. St. Clair was charged on five counts—four, involving "neglect of duty . . . cowardice . . . treachery . . . incapacity as a General . . . inattention to the progress of the enemy," under the article 5 of section 18 of the articles of war and the fifth, of "shamefully abandoning the posts of Ticonderoga and Mount Independence," under article 12 of section 13. For the charges, seven "remarks" made by the congressional committee, and documents introduced into evidence (which may have been in the packets), see *St. Clair Court Martial.*

3. The enclosed copies have not been identified; for the resolutions, see *JCC,* 6:981, 995, and 1045–46.

4. This resolution directed that only Congress or GW should issue passes to New York and that Maj. Gen. Benedict Arnold should recall any passes he had issued for travel from Philadelphia to New York (ibid., 11:779).

## To Major General William Phillips

Sir                                    Head Quarters White plains 16 Augt 1778

The inclosed packet was sent to me a few days ago by Sr Henry Clinton. I should be happy to oblige Sir Henry or yourself in any thing I could do with propriety; but it is not in my power to grant the request made by him in this instance, as all matters respecting the officers and troops of the Convention are under the immediate direction and controul of Congress.[1] I am with due Respect Sir Yr most obt & hble servt.

Df, in Tench Tilghman's writing, DLC:GW; copy, P.R.O., 30/55, Carleton Papers; Varick transcript, DLC:GW. The copy was enclosed with Phillips's letter to Gen. Henry Clinton of 27 Aug. (P.R.O., 30/55, Carleton Papers).

1. GW enclosed the packet sent with Gen. Henry Clinton's letter to him of 18 July, which also requested a passport for Phillips to visit New York.

## To Major General John Sullivan

dear sir                                   Head Qrs White plains August 16th 1778

On Thursday[1] I received your favor of the 10th Instant, advising of your descent on Rhode-Island—of the arrival of the British fleet & of Count D'Estaing's pursuing them. Since this I have not had a single tittle of intelligence on the subject of your operations—and of course I have been in a disagreable state of suspence and anxiety. I must earnestly request that you will be more frequent in your advices. It is material for me to know and extremely satisfactory what you are doing or not doing. I trust Count D'Estaing has got into port again—and unless he was fortunate enough to overhaul Admiral Howe's Squadron and give them a drubbing, I consider their appearance as a very unlucky event. I am Dr sir with great regard & esteem Your Most Obedt servant

Go: Washington

P.S. The Letters which accompany this, you will dispose of agreable to their addresses. Those for Count D'Estaing you will forward to him immediately.[2]

Df, in Robert Hanson Harrison's writing, DLC:GW; Varick transcript, DLC:GW.
    1. The preceding Thursday was 13 August.
    2. These letters have not been identified.

## General Orders

Head-Quarters W. Plains Monday Augt 17th 1778.

Parole Thessaly—                           C. Signs Thames. Taunton.

The Sub-Inspectors are to receive thirty dollars pr Month in addition to the Pay which they derive from their Rank in the Line; and Brigade Inspectors twenty dollars pr Month in addition &c. This Pay to commence from the time of their respective appointments.

The Execution of the ten remaining Criminals who were to have suffered death this day is postponed to next friday morning nine ôClock.[1]

Major Cabbell is appointed Inspector in Genl Muhlenberg's Brigade, vice, Captn Lewis & is to be accordingly respected and obeyed.

Varick transcript, DLC:GW.

1. The next Friday was 21 August. The executions had been scheduled by the general orders of 14 August.


## To George Clinton

Sir,                                    Head Quarters White Plains Aug. 17th 1778
    Mr Benson having signified to me, that you would stand in need of a flag to conduct some persons to the enemy's lines on the 19th instant;[1] I am to inform Your Excellency, that an officer will attend at Fish Kill on the day appointed to receive and execute the orders, which shall be given him for that purpose.[2] I have the honor to be With the greatest respect Sir, Your most Obedt servt

                                                    Go: Washington

LS, in Alexander Hamilton's writing, PWacD: Sol Feinstone Collection, on deposit PPAmP; Df, DLC:GW; Varick transcript, DLC:GW.
    1. Robert Benson, secretary of the New York provincial congress in 1775 and 1776 and secretary of the New York senate, 1777–84, reputedly also acted as Clinton's private secretary. The persons in question were "Mr. Saml. Bayard & family & a second Cargo of banished Tories" (Clinton to William Malcom, 18 Aug., in Hastings, *Clinton Papers*, 3:657).
    2. GW's aide-de-camp Alexander Hamilton wrote to Col. William Malcom on this date: "You will appoint a genteel sensible officer to go to Fish Kill the 19th instant, where he will receive orders from the Governor or the Commissioners for conducting in character of a flag some inhabitants who are to [be] sent to New York. You will caution him to treat the persons in his charge with decency and politeness. It will be necessary to be very exact as to the time; and so to order it that the officer may be at Fish Kill the night before or early in the morning" (DLC:GW).


## To Colonel William Malcom

Sir,                                    Hd Qrs [White Plains] Augst 17th 1778
    I rec'd your favor of the 13th inst. & can not determine the question you put respecting adjutants on the establishment of 1777, for want of the resolves.[1]
    with respect to that part of your Memorandum given to Mr Oliver concerning the exchange of Hides for Shoes, I must beg to decline giving the permission, as it makes the business of the commissary in that department too complicated—He has the power of making all such contracts, & it would be well if you'd direct the Shoemakers you mention to see him—& make their bargains with him—the Shoes may be deliverd to you after being in the hands of the Clothr Genl.
    Inclosed is a letter to the Clothier at Fish Kills, to furnish you with such necessaries as he may have, for the use of the men you mention[2]—you

will be pleasd to inform him for what Corps they are intended that he may charge them properly—this you can do by giving a particular return. I am &c.

Copy                                                  G. W——n

Df, in Richard Kidder Meade's writing, DLC:GW; Varick transcript, DLC:GW.

1. Malcom's letter to GW of 13 Aug. has not been found.
2. On this date GW wrote Peter Hansen, the clothier at Fishkill: "You will recieve a return from Colo. Malcom at West Point for some articles of cloathing for a few Men under his command, who stand much in need of them, these you will please to deliver & charge to the several Corps Agreeable to the return—you will get from him" (Df, DLC:GW).

## From Major General John Sullivan

Head Quarters Rhode Island
Dear General.                                    August 17th 1778.

Notwithstanding the train of misfortunes (mentioned in my letter of the 14th Inst.)[1] sufficient in number and aggravation to drepress even the spirits of fortitude and damp the ardor of enterprise, I have by the interposition of heaven and unabated industry nearly recovered from the deplorable situation of which my last contained but an imperfect description—I have by sending for supplies to different quarters replenished my magazine with Amunition, and my stores with provision, and by timely addresses to my men have exhilerated their spirits & reconciled them in a great measure to the vicissitudes of war. Having not heard any thing from Count d'Estain and apprehensive of the bad consequences of delay, I on the 15th Ulto marched down in columns (so disposed) as to render forming the lines as familiar and as easy as possible; and I am happy in informing your Excellency that the regularity and good order observed by the different corps on their march excited admiration in every beholder, & infinitely exceeded my most sanguine expectations[2]—I halted the army in full sight of and within long shot of the enemy (in hopes) that they would be thereby tempted to meet us in the plain and become an easy conquest. But the event convinces me, that how contrary soever they may act to the dictates of nature in other instances, they implicitly obey her commands so far as they respect self-preservation—After disposing my army in such a manner as to effectually invest their works I began my approaches (under cover of night) within two hundred and fifty yards of their lines. This days fog favors my operations, and I promise your Excellency that by to-morrow noon, I shall be able to keep up so warm a fire upon them as to render the properties of a salamander essentially necessary to their existence. And I think I may venture to assure your Excellency, that I shall have it shortly in my power either to force them to an action, upon disadvantagious destructive principles, or reduce them to honourable terms of capitulation.[3] I have the honor to remain (in expectation of this agreeable event) your Excellency's obliged

(a copy)                                                    John Sullivan

Copy, enclosed with GW to Henry Laurens, 19 Aug., DNA:PCC, item 160. A purported ALS of this letter was offered for sale by Parke-Bernet Galleries, Inc., catalog 596, *The James McHenry Papers*, 30–31 Oct. 1944, item 300.

1. Sullivan was referring to his letter to GW of 13 Aug., which was evidently not sent until 14 Aug., as it enclosed a letter to Henry Laurens of that date.

2. For other glowing reports of the march, see Thomas Crafts to William Heath, 15 Aug., and Daniel Lyman to Heath, 16 Aug., MHi, Heath Papers; see also Cutler, *Rev. Manasseh Cutler*, 1:67–68.

3. Capt. Frederick Mackenzie of the Royal Welch Fusiliers described the American operations in his diary entry for this date: "The fog did not clear up until 11 this day, when we perceived the Rebels had broke ground during the night, and had thrown up part of a small Redoubt on Honeyman's-hill, about 150 yards to their right of the Orchard. It appears a very trifling work, ill constructed and injudicially placed. . . . They also began a trench from their left of No I, to the high road from Honeyman's hill to Green-end, and continued to work at it all day. Some other works appear in front of thier Camp, but they are only works of defence." By 18 Aug., Sullivan's troops had begun work on a second battery "on their left of the road, in a line with Honeyman's Orchard" and a third "about 100 yards N.E. of No I" (*Mackenzie Diary*, 2:357–58; see also Lyman to Heath, 17 and 18 Aug., "Heath Papers," 4:255–56).

## General Orders

Head-Quarters W. Plains Tuesday August 18th 1778.
Parole Cadwallader—                         C. Signs Concord Crosswicks.

A board of General Officers to consist of Majr General McDougall, Brigadiers General Parsons and Knox to sit tomorrow morning at ten ôClock at Genl Smallwood's large Marquee to hear the Claims of the Officers in the Maryland Line respecting their Rank and to make such Arrangement of the same as they shall think right which they are to report to the Commander in Chief—In order to facilitate the business, three officers are to be chosen by that line out of those who were in the Regiment formerly commanded by General Smallwood, the Independent Companies and Flying Camp, to attend the board and represent the Claims and Pretensions of the Rest who have been respectively promoted from those Corps into the present Battalions from that State.[1]

The Commander in Chief will also lay such Papers before the board as have been transmitted to him by the State upon the subject; and they will besides call upon such Persons as they may judge necessary to give Information on the Points in question.

Lieutenant John Potter is appointed Pay-Master in Colonel Wood's Regiment of Militia.[2]

Varick transcript, DLC:GW.

1. The board of general officers reported on 7 Sept., ranking seven colonels, five lieutenant colonels, five majors, thirty-two captains, forty-one first lieutenants, thirty-two second lieutenants, and thirty-eight ensigns (DNA: RG 93, War Department Collection of Revolutionary War Records, Revolutionary War Rolls, Maryland).

2. John Potter (1746–1818), who was commissioned as a first lieutenant of the 4th Worcester County Regiment of Massachusetts militia in 1777, served as a lieutenant in Col. Ezra Wood's regiment of militia from June 1778 to January 1779.

## From Colonel Peter Gansevoort

[Fort Schuyler, N.Y., 18 August 1778][1]

I have the unhappiness to inform your Excellency that desertion has lately been very frequent from this Garrison—since the 26t of last March we have had 3 Serjts 2 Corpls & 20 Privates desert from this Battn besides 1 bumdr 1 Gunr & 1 Matrs from the Arttillery before the date above mentioned several soldiers had been tryed by a General Court Martial at this Garrison, for de[se]rtion, but never recieved the Punishment due their Crimes, the Sentences of these different Court Martials were carefully sent to Commanding General of this Department but no returns have been ever recievd some time in June last Colonel Varick informd me a Recruit who had just joined our Battn was susspected of being a Confederate with Major Hammill. I orderd his Conduct to be narrowly inspected—he was detected in the fact of Corrupting & enticing the Soldiers to desert upon being apprehended, he confessed that he came upon such desings, & was sent by Lord Aid du Camp to Genl Sir Harry Clinton as a spy to endeavour to enlist what Irish men he could from the American Army[2]—there was every Appearance of his being a spy. he was immediately tryed by a General Court Martial the sentence was directly sent down for Approbation, but no Answer has been recieved—& the Man Still lays confined in Irons—finding the Spirit of desertion to increase, & the Men in General to be exceeding uneasy—probably arising from their being so long stationed on this Frontier Post—they have been frequently heard in thier private Conversations to say—that they woul'd sooner die, tha[n][3] stay here the ensuing winter, My Officers as well as myself was

Convinced that—unless some Example was made, we shoul'd not be able to check this growing Evil—A party of five Men deserted on the 10 of August. they were taken by the Tuscarora Indians, on their way to Canada fifty Miles from this Fort—they were brought in on the 13th— a General Court Martial was convened on the 15th—they were sentenced—to die, the Officers in a body, desired their Immediate Execution, as the only way effectually to stop the increasing spirit of desertion[4]—whilst these Men were under sentence of death, a party returned from the German flatts, who been on Command to drive Cattle to this Garrison, they had lost Six Men by desertion, who were pursued, but without effect—this together with the above Reasons & being apprehensive of some design of the Enemy, & a Report that they had carefully spread among the Savages of having upwards of seventy Men enlisted in this Garrison, who woul'd rise upon their appearance—Convinced me of the Necessity of a Rigid Example, & resolved me to take the advice of my Officers, by Ordering the prisoners to be Executed, & they were accordingly shott at the Head of the Regiment on the 17th—In doing of which altho, I coul'd not find the Articles of warr gave me the fullest Authority yet as Commanding Officer of a frontier Post, & far distant from the Commander in Chief, & having a seperate Commission from Congress as Commandant of this Post, I concieved, myself fully impowered, in a Case of such great Necessity[5] unprecedented to me—I hope Your Excellency will be convinced of the Necessity, & approve of the Justness of the Execution—Inclosed your Excellency has a Copy of the Proceedings of the Court Martial.[6]

ADf, NN: Gansevoort-Lansing Collection.

1. The date and location are taken from the docket on the draft.

2. Gansevoort was referring to the case of Samuel Gake, for which, see GW to Gansevoort, 13 Aug., and note 1 to that document. Gake's court-martial referred to "Lord Rodnam," evidently a reference to Francis Rawdon (later Rawdon-Hastings; 1754–1826). Lord Rawdon had come to America in 1774 as a lieutenant in the 5th Regiment of Foot and had risen to captain of the 63d Regiment by January 1778, when he was appointed a supernumerary aide-de-camp to then Maj. Gen. Henry Clinton. By May of 1778 Rawdon was recruiting "ALL Gentlemen, Natives of Ireland, who are zealous for the Honour and Prosperity of their Country" to form a Loyalist regiment to be called the Volunteers of Ireland, and Clinton again appointed Rawdon as an aide-de-camp in his general orders of 30 May 1778 (*Royal Gazette* [New York], 9 May 1778; *Kemble Papers*, 1:586–87). Rawdon was appointed adjutant general with the rank of lieutenant colonel in June 1778 but resigned that post in September 1779. In the spring of 1780 Rawdon was posted to the southern theater, where he took part in the capture of Charleston and the Carolina campaigns, before leaving America in July 1781. Subsequently Rawdon rose to the rank of general in the British army, and as Lord Moira, he served as governor-general and commander in chief in India, 1813–21, and at Malta, 1824–26.

3. Gansevoort wrote "that."

4. A petition to this effect, dated 15 Aug. and signed by twenty officers of the 3d New York Regiment, is in NN: Gansevoort-Lansing Collection.

5. The words from "Congress" to this point were written at the end of the text and marked for insertion at this point.

6. A copy of the court-martial proceedings of 15 Aug. is in NN: Gansevoort-Lansing Collection.

*Letter not found*: from Brig. Gen. William Maxwell, c.18 Aug. 1778. On 21 Aug., GW wrote Maj. Gen. Nathanael Greene: "By a Letter which I received yesterday from Genl Maxwell, inclosing one from Major Howell . . . it appears certain, that Sixteen of Lord Howes fleet entered the Hook on the 17th." GW's other correspondence with Maxwell around this time suggests that the travel time for letters from Richard Howell to Maxwell was about one day and for letters from Maxwell to GW about two days.

*Letter not found*: from Brig. Gen. John Stark, 18 Aug. 1778. On 19 Aug., Stark wrote GW: "I yesterday wrote you concerning clothing," and on 29 Aug., GW wrote Stark: "I have duly recd yours of the 13th 18th 19th and 21st instants."

*Letter not found*: from Joseph de Valnais, 18 Aug. 1778. On 30 Aug., GW wrote Valnais: "I recd yours of the 18th."

## General Orders

Head-Quarters W. Plains Wednesday Augt 19th 78.
Parole Sardinia—                              C. Signs Sharon. Saw-Pitts.

The Commander in Chief is informed that many Corps which have had Cloathing sent to them from their respective States continue nevertheless to make returns and draw from the Continental Stores in the same manner as if no such Provision had ever been made for them— This Practice he does in express and positive terms forbid, unless the Officers commanding such Corps will evince beyond a doubt that the Cloathing from their respective states is not and never will be made a Continental Charge.

The honorable the Congress were pleased to pass on the 12th instant the following Resolution—Resolved, That every Officer in the Army of the United States whose duty requires his being on horseback in time of Action be allowed a sum not exceeding five hundred dollars as a compensation for any horse he shall have killed in battle; This resolution to have retrospect as far as the 1st of May 1777—and that the Quarter Master General be and he is hereby authorized to pay the Value of such horses not exceeding the said sum to the respective sufferers on the Facts being properly authenticated.[1]

Lieutenant Hiwill of Colonel Cranes Regiment of Artillery is appointed Inspector and Superintendent of Music in the Army and is to be respected accordingly[2]—His Pay and Rations to be made equal to a Captains in the Train.

Varick transcript, DLC:GW.

1. For this resolution, see *JCC*, 11:777–78.

2. John Hiwell (d. 1788) had been a lieutenant in Col. John Crane's Continental Artillery Regiment (later the 3d Continental Artillery Regiment) since its organization in early 1777. He continued to serve in the regiment and as inspector of music until June 1783, being promoted to first lieutenant in February 1780. After the war he settled in Savannah, Ga., where he taught music.

## To Major General Lafayette

My dear Marquis,                                   White-plains Augt 19th 78
This Letter will be delivered to you by Monsr Laneville, to whom, I have no doubt, you will shew civility, as he appears to me to be a Gentn of sense & science.[1] I hope, however, he will come too late to afford you any aid—I say so, because I could wish he may find the work already done, of which, I have some hope from Genl Sullivans last Letter.[2]

I have lately received a horse for you from Colo. Bland, so exceedingly poor that he can scarce walk—I have put him into the care of my Groom and have ordered him to use his utmost exertions to get him in order for you, but it will be many Months before he can be fit for any kind of Service.

Adieu my dear Marqs may honr & glory attend you—this is the sincere wish of your affecte friend

Go: Washington

ALS, Czartoryski Library, Cracow, Poland.

1. On this date GW wrote to Maj. Gen. John Sullivan: "Mr La Neuville, who will have the honor to deliver you this, being desirous, if he can arrive in time, to serve with you, in the expedition you are carrying on, in character of volunteer, I take occasion to introduce him to your acquaintance and civilities, and to recommend, that you will give him every opportunity of being useful, which his situation and other circumstances will permit. I have not the happiness to have had personal experience of this Gentleman's military accomplis[h]ments—He is a Major in the French service and brought from Europe very handsome and ample testimonials of his merit; In America he has served in the Northern army in character of Inspector General, and as I am informed with ability and in a manner that gave general satisfaction" (Df, DLC:GW; the Varick transcript is misdated 17 Aug.).

2. GW is referring to Maj. Gen. John Sullivan's letter to him of 17 August.

## To Henry Laurens

sir                                   Head Qrs White plains August 19th 1778
I do myself the honor to transmit you a Copy of a Letter from General Sullivan, dated the 17th Instant, which I just now received with the Letter Inclosed.[1] It appears that Count D'Estaing was still out with his fleet—but yet that the General was in high spirits and entertained the strongest hopes of success. I flatter myself they are well grounded—

and that in the course of a few days he will announce the entire reduction of the Enemy's force on the Island.

The Declaration respecting Governr Johnstone has been sent by a Flag to the British Commissioners.[2] I have the Honor to be with great respect & esteem sir Your Most Obedt servant

Go: Washington

P.S. I send three York papers.[3]

LS, in Robert Hanson Harrison's writing, DNA:PCC, item 152; Df, DLC:GW; copy, DNA:PCC, item 169; Varick transcript, DLC:GW. Congress read this letter on 21 Aug.; see *JCC*, 11:825.

1. The "Letter Inclosed" was probably Sullivan's letter to Laurens of 17 Aug., which text was the same as Sullivan's letter to GW of that date (see *Laurens Papers*, 14:184–85).

2. Regarding this declaration, see Laurens to GW, 13 Aug., and notes 6 and 7. At this point on the draft, Harrison wrote and deleted a paragraph that reads: "I could wish the earliest decision of Congress on the subject of reenlisting the Troops whose time of service will shortly expire. There are several in the Virginia line who have been long in the army & who have but a little time to stay. I am informed by the Officers that most of these, as well as many of the Drafts can be reingaged, if the present opportunity is embraced."

3. The postscript is lacking on the draft and the Varick transcript.

*Letter not found*: from Col. William Malcom, 19 Aug. 1778. On 24 Aug., GW wrote Malcom: "I recd yours of the 19th inclosing the weekly Return of the Garrison."

## From Brigadier General John Stark

*Albany, 19th August, 1778.*

*Dear Sir*—I yesterday wrote you concerning clothing for Major Whitcomb's corps of rangers, and sent a return of the said corps.[1] The bearer hereof waits on you for clothing, and can inform you of the sad condition of the men.

I understand that Colonel Winship, deputy commissary general, has resigned. I know of no person so attentive to his business as Bethuel Washburn, assistant deputy commissary general at this place.[2] I hope he may be appointed, as his fidelity may be relied on.

Inclosed is the report of Lieutenant Colonel Wheelock, who has been upon a scout to Unadilla, which will inform you of the situation of the enemy.[3] If an expedition should be made to that quarter, a number of pack-saddles will be necessary. Colonel Wheelock's information may be depended on, as he is a gentleman of undoubted character. I am, sir, your ob't serv't,

JOHN STARK.

Stark, *Memoir of John Stark,* 187–88.

1. The letter has not been found. An undated "State of Three Independent Companies of Rangers under the Command of Major Benjamin Whitcomb" from about this time is in DLC:GW. It records twenty commissioned and noncommissioned officers, fifty-four rank and file, and six deserters. The companies were at Rutland, Vermont. Whitcomb (1737–1828), who had been promoted to major in November 1777, continued to command troops on the New Hampshire frontier until January 1781, when the independent companies were disbanded and he retired on half pay.

2. Bethuel Washburn, an Albany merchant, remained the assistant commissary of issues at that city at least until 1780.

3. The enclosed report of Lt. Col. John Wheelock has not been identified, but his expedition was summarized in a letter from Albany of 22 Aug. published in the *Connecticut Courant, and the Weekly Intelligencer* (Hartford), 8 Sept.: "Col John Wheelock, accompanied by Major Clyde, and a small number of men, as a reconnoitring party, at the request of General Stark has penetrated the Indian country to the enemy's lines at Tunadilla, above fifty miles south west of Cherry Valley. His business was to view the nature and situation of the country, and, if possible, the strength and designs of the enemy. . . . He is now returned and brings the following intelligence, viz. That the number of the enemy Indians and Tories is about 1000 men, under the independent command of Capt. Joseph Brant: That they expect us to attack them; but if not, are determined on a vigorous and fatal attack upon some part of the frontiers of Mohawk River; That there are from two to three hundred men about the mouth of Tunadilla River; but their chief place of rendezvous is at Onoughquago; That the Indians are now disaffected to [John] Butler and that he is not at Tunadilla, but in some part of the western country; That some of Butler's party have joined Capt. Brant; That Brant's party are in high spirits, eager for action, and that he conducts his affairs with as much secrecy as possible; That scouting parties from the enemy are continually out, especially up the Susquehannah; and a rambling guard from Flax Island in the Susquehannah River, over the barren mountains to Tunadilla River, by which means the inhabitants and refugees are environed, and think themselves entirely secure." Wheelock (1754–1817), a son of Dartmouth College president Eleazer Wheelock, was commissioned in November 1777 as lieutenant colonel of the regiment of volunteers raised for the proposed invasion of Canada and commanded by Col. Timothy Bedel. John Wheelock became president of Dartmouth College in 1779.

## To Major General John Sullivan

Dr Sir,

Head Quarters White Plains
Aug. 19th 1778 ¼ past 9 A.M.

Your favour of the 17th came to hand an hour and a half ago; and at the same time, that I regret extremely the Count not being arrived, for whose fate, I feel the greatest anxiety, I am happy to learn, that you had been able to extricate yourself from the difficulties you laboured under, and that you had so favourable a prospect before you—I shall wait the issue with the most anxious expectation; and earnestly hope both for your own sake and that of the public, the success may answer your warmest wishes.

If your next does not announce the return of the French fleet, I shall be glad to know how they were provided with water and other necessaries when they sailed: my apprehensions on this score, are very great.[1]

I observe letters, for Congress, generally accompany those you send to me—I presume they contain the same information you give me, yet as I was not certain of it, I have hitherto made a point of transmitting copies of those I received—You will please to advise me on this head that I may know whether it is necessary to continue this practice, or not.

I have discovered that the expresses stationed between us are sometimes employed in sending private letters; the impropriety and inconvenience of this are obvious—you will give the strictest orders to prevent it, in future. I am, with great regard Dr Sir Your most Obedt.

Df, in Alexander Hamilton's writing, DLC:GW; Varick transcript, DLC:GW. GW also wrote two letters of introduction to Sullivan on this date. For one, see GW to Maj. Gen. Lafayette, 19 Aug., n.1. The other reads: "This will be delivered you by Col. De la Radiere, a Gentleman of the corps of Engineers. The nature of your operations, if they are not completed before he arrives, may make the addition of a Gentleman in this capacity useful, which is my inducement for sending Mr De la Radiere. He is superior in commission to Mr Gouvion; but there are certain punctilios of service observed among these Gentlemen, which I have left to be arranged by General Du Portail, Chief Engineer. I wish you to let them operate as far as may be consistent with the good of the service.

"If the Count should return before the expedition is accomplished, and there still should be a land co-operation between you, agreeable to the original plan, which may make an Engineer necessary to him, and he should be unprovided, it will be well to accommodate him in this particular with the services of one of the Gentleman, I have sent you" (LS, NhHi: Sullivan Papers).

1. The preceding paragraph was written fourth on the draft, but the paragraphs were numbered to place it second.

## From Major General John Sullivan

Dear General          Rhode Island Head Qrs Augt 19th 1778

I am honored this day by the receipt of your favor of the 16th Inst.[1] Wherein you complain of my want of attention in giving you more frequently an acct of my situation and progress of my operations and in answer can assure your Excellency that want of interesting matter not of inclination has given rise to the suspicion—I can recieve no greater satisfaction than what arises from contributing to yours. and the most exquisite pleasure that I shall taste from the success of this or any future operation will result from your approbation, and be regulated in degree by the satisfaction you express. . . . I cannot learn a single sylla-ble from Count d'Estain, & consider his absence in the same point of view with your Excellency. . . . I have raised several batteries one of them within half musquet shot of their outworks, in defiance of an in-cessant tho ineffectual[2] fire from their redoubts—They have not in-jured any of my works—lessened my number a single man, or pre-vented me a moment from making my approaches, in advancing of which I have been greatly favoured by a fog. I could have opened upon them from a battery or two some time since, but was determined to wait until my preparations would enable me to speak with decision—I shall this day give them a lecture on the force of gunpowder and make them feel my weight of metal and resentment. The consequence shall be the subject of my next. I have the honor to be Dear General with the greatest respect & regard your very hble Servt

John Sullivan

Copy (extract?), in James McHenry's writing, PWacD: Sol Feinstone Collection, on deposit PPAmP; copy (extract), DNA:PCC, item 160. The extract in DNA:PCC, which is in Tench Tilghman's writing, was enclosed in GW's letter to Henry Laurens of 21 August. A purported ALS was offered for sale by Parke-Bernet Galleries, Inc., catalog 596, *The James McHenry Papers*, 30–31 Oct. 1944, item 301.

1. The text from this point to the ellipses was omitted from the copy GW sent to Laurens.

2. The preceding two words were omitted from the copy GW sent to Laurens.

## From Lund Washington

Dr Sir                                          Mount Vernon Augst 19th 1778.

Two Posts have past and no letters from you unless they have been sent on to newcastle where mrs Washington directed when she left home, hers shoud go[1]—when I was below I see Mr Hill who Askd me whether you had given any orders about your Estate in his Hands—his meang I suppose was, as Custis and he are about to part, who was to take Charge of the Estate and further said, he wishd he had known I was down, he woud have provided money which he had of yours, I told him to give it to Mrs Washington.[2] I recieved £50 of one Wms who formerly lived in Norfol⟨k⟩ and Bought Flour of Newton, it was in part of £180.[3]

I was at your Plantation under Davenport, He told me there was 200 Barrels of Corn to sell which he had long expected Mr Hill wou'd have sold, but did not believe it was yet agreed for, the price now giveg for Corn is 30/ I advised, it to be immediately sold, and not keep it longer in expectation of a Higher price, He likewise said 40. Cattle fit for Beef might be sold—I see the Cattle they are small, but in good order, they will never be larger as they are of Full age—I advised they shoud be immediately sold for two reason, one is the price is high & they perhaps can never be disposed of to better Advantage, the Other that the Destemper is in the Neighbourhood all round the Plantation & may by some means or other get there & destroy the whole Stock. Davenport says he Uses every precaution to prevent its getg Among your Stock he never suffers either his to go out or any other to come on the place—He has about 40 that decended from Custis's Bull, 3 of which he has turn'd out for Bulls they are more than years old, & very likely he keeps them seperate from the Stock, & puts his Cows that are Bullg to them, he haveg Killd [h]is old Bulls that he might immediately get into the English Breed.

Never was there more rain of a Summer than this we have more wet Days than Fair, No such thing as plowg, nor is it in the power of people to keep their corn Fields in proper order for sewg Wheat, with Hoes, for the grass can only be stinted in it is growth, to kill it is impossible Frequently we have with the rain Violent winds which Break the Corn off below the Ear, which is totally lost, & most of it Blown down in such a manner that it will be impossible to plow in wheat before the Fodder is got—for set it up right one day, & it is down the next, the ground being so soft. I am determined to make Morris & Davy[4] prepare for makeg Tobacco next year, & do not mean to make Morris sew more than 40. Acres of Land in wheat, so very wet is the mill swamp that I fear I shall not be able to sew the ground I had prepared, and which was in very fine order before Harvest, in Timothy, I meant within this month to have given it two good workgs by which I expected to have destroyd all roots &c.—but if the weather keeps on as it now is raing every Day that cannot be done, the ground I sewed last Fall is well taken with Timothy but there are many Briers & Bushes come up in it, we are now cleang it, of all such growth—As yet I have no other worckmen but Lanphier & his man[5] nor can I get a Possitive promise of any some there are who say they will come if Possible soon, I have made a mill for the purpose of pressg Corn stalks, and am putg up Kettles to Boil the juice in, this Day I expect to have all ready & shall begin to morrow about makeg Mollasses—our Family are pretty well as is all other things with us—am Dr Sir your affectionate Servt &c.

Lund Washington

Old Billy Harding wants to Rent part of the Land you Bought of Mercer on four mile Run & desired me to ask you to Rent it.[6]

ALS, ViMtV.

1. Martha Washington visited GW's King William County plantation called Claiborne's in August (see GW to James Hill, 27 Oct.).

2. GW had hired James Hill in 1772 to manage John Parke Custis's plantations "together with his other business—As also of my Plantation in King William, Lotts in Williamsburg &ca" (Memorandum of Agreement with James Hill, 17 Mar. 1772, MH). Hill discusses GW's money and the parting with Custis in his letter to GW of 5 September.

3. An entry for 12 Aug. in GW's accounts lists the receipt of £50 from "Jacob Williams in part of a Debt contracted by Mr Thos Newton for Flour Sold at Norfolk & left with Mr Hill to Collect" (Ledger B, f. 154, DLC:GW). Newton had acted as GW's agent for the sale of flour at Norfolk since 1773.

4. The dower slaves Morris and Davy were overseers at GW's Dogue Run farm and Mill farm, respectively.

5. Lund Washington paid the carpenter and joiner Going Lanphier for forty-four days' work by his man Joe and thirty-five days' work by Lanphier himself in July and August (Lund Washington's Mount Vernon account book, f. 65, ViMtV).

6. Lund Washington may have been referring to William Harden (d. 1781), whose will lists a Fairfax County plantation and several leased lands in Fairfax and Loudoun counties (Fairfax County Will Book D-1 [1776-82], 236–37, ViFaCt). For discussion of GW's acquisition of approximately 1,200 acres on Four Mile Run in Fairfax County from James Mercer in December 1774, see GW to Mercer, 12 Dec. 1774, and note 3 to that document, *Papers, Colonial Series*, 10:201–5 (see also GW to Mercer, 26 Dec. 1774, ibid., 10:211–14).

## General Orders

Head-Quarters W. Plains August 20th 1778.
Parole Dunstable                                 C. Signs Dublin. Deal.
The Tents of the whole Army are to be struck three times a week on Mondays, Wednesdays & Fridays from ten in the morning 'till two in the afternoon when the weather will permit; The Officers will be careful to have the ground between and where the tents stood well cleansed.

No Persons whatever whether belonging to the Army or not are to pass beyond the advanced Corps without Permits from Head-Quarters—The Commanding Officer of that Corps is directed not only to stop all Persons who shall hereafter attempt to pass without such Permits but to report their names and take away any other Passes they may have and send them to the Adjutant General—The General also reminds the Officers of a former order, forbiding any under the degree of commanding Officer of a Brigade from giving Passes to soldiers and expects a strict observance.[1]

Lieutenant George Purvis is appointed Adjutant of the Delaware Regiment.[2]

Returns of Medicines, Instruments, Bandages &c. now in the several Regiments to be made out by the Regimental Surgeons and delivered to the Physician and Surgeon General next Monday.[3]

Returns of all the Negroes in the several Regi. to be made out immediately Regimentally, digested into Brigade Returns and brought into the Orderly-Office next saturday[4] specifying those present and the particular Places where the absent or on command are.

Varick transcript, DLC:GW.
    1. GW was referring to his general orders of 17 April 1778.
    2. George Purvis (1750–1801) served as a quartermaster for the Delaware Battalion at the Flying Camp in 1776, then became a second lieutenant of the Delaware Regiment in December of that year. He was promoted to first lieutenant in October 1777. Purvis was captured at the Battle of Camden, 16 Aug. 1780, and he remained a prisoner in November 1782, but he had evidently been exchanged by March 1783, when he was continued in service as adjutant of the Delaware Regiment. GW then referred to him as a captain, but the date of that promotion, if indeed it occurred, has not been determined.
    3. The following Monday was 24 August.
    4. The next Saturday following these orders was 22 August. Adj. Gen. Alexander Scammell compiled the results on 24 Aug. into a "Return of the Negroes in the Army" that showed 586 "Present," 98 "Sick absent," and 71 "On Command" (DLC:GW).

# Proceedings of a Council of General Officers

[White Plains, 20–24 August 1778]
At a meeting of the General Officers at Head Quarters White plains Augt 20th 1778

Present

The Commander in Chief

| Major Generals. | Brigadier Generals |
| --- | --- |
| Gates | Knox. Smallwood |
| Sterling | Woodford. Muhlenberg |
| Lincoln. | Wayne. Clinton |
| McDoughal | Huntington. Parsons |
| Baron D'Kalb. | Poor—Patterson |
|  | Portail |

The commander in chief states to the council, that, by the articles of war, the highest corporal punishment allowed to be inflicted on offenders, by sentence of Courts martial is one hundred lashes—That there are no gradations of intermediate punishment between this and death[1]—That, in consequence, courts martial are obliged to adopt either the one, or the other, with respect to all crimes of a higher nature, from whence these inconveniences result, that they have it not in their power to distribute a proper proportion of punishment to the different degrees of guilt, which occur; and deeming a hundred lashes inadequate to a variety of cases, that come before them, think themselves bound in duty to decree the only greater penalty, they have in their choice, which being that of death, capital sentences become so numerous, that it is impossible to execute them, without degenerating into cruelty, and destroying in a great measure the effect, by the too great frequency of the example; that to avoid these disagreeable consequences a necessity too often arises of granting pardons, which not only occasions many atrocious criminals to escape, with impunity; but affords a strong encouragement to a repetition of crimes.

Having stated these things, his Excellency requests the sentiments of the Council on the expediency of punishment by hard and severe labor, instead of death, with such circumstances of rigor as may tend to make the terror and influence of the example the greater; and on the particular modes and degrees, they would think adviseable; in order, that, if any system of this kind can be devised, which promises to be effectual, for preventing crimes and obviating the necessity of capital punishments, it may be finally submitted to the consideration of Congress.[2]

At a Meeting of General Officers, held at White Plains, by Order of His Excellency The Commander in Chief, August 24th 1778. It was unanimously decided by them, that Severe hard Labour be recommended to The Honorable The Congress, to be the intermediate punishment between One Hundred Lashes, and Death: The Board also unanimously resolved, that repairs of The Roads, Fortifications, and such necessary public works, as The Commander in Chief— Quarter Master General, or Chief Engineer, think proper to direct, Shall be the Duty to be performed by such delinquents, and in such proportion, as either a General, or Regimental Court Martial, shall decide. The Board advise, that in the framing this Addition to the penalties inflicted by the present Articles of War, The Courts Martial, General, and Regimental, may have power to Order Severe hard labour, as a punishment in all cases whatsoever.

The Board further take the Liberty to recommend, that a prison be established in each Division, where all NonCommissioned Officers, & Soldiers, guilty of Drunkeness, and such enormities as frequently proceeds from Drunkeness, are to be confined for such a Term, as a General, or Regimental Court Martial shall decree; and for, & during that Term, suffered to receive no other sustenance, than Bread & Water.

Horatio Gates
Stirling,
The Baron deKalb—
Alexr McDougall
Saml H: Parsons
W. Smallwood
Henry Knox
Enoch Poor
Jno. Paterson
J. Huntington

DS, in James McHenry's and Horatio Gates's writings, DLC:GW; copy, DNA:PCC, item 152; copy, DNA:PCC, item 169. The copy in item 152 was enclosed in GW's letter to Henry Laurens of 31 August.

1. GW is referring to article 3, section 18, of the articles of war (see *JCC*, 5:806).
2. On the DS, McHenry's writing stops at this point.

## To Henry Laurens

Dear Sir                    Head Quarters [White Plains] Augt 20th 1778

I am now to acknowledge my obligations for your favor of the 31st Ulto & for its several Inclosures.

The conduct of Governor Johnstone has been certainly reprehensible—to say no worse of it—and so I think the world will determine. His Letters to Messrs Morris and Reed are very significant and the points to which they conclude quite evident. They are, if I may be allowed so to express myself, of a pulse-feeling cast, and the offer to the latter thro the Lady, a direct attempt upon his integrity.[1] When these things are known, he must share largely in public contempt—and the more so from the opposite parts he has taken.

I am sorry you troubled yourself with transmitting me copies & extracts of your Letters to the French Officers, in answer to their applications for Rank. Your word, Sir, will always have the fullest credit with me whenever you shall be pleased to give it upon any occasion; and I have only to regret that there has not been the same degree of decision and resolution in every Gentleman, as you have used in these instances. If there had, it would not only have contributed much to the tranquility of the Army—but preserved the rights of our own Officers. With respect to Brevet Commissions, I know many of the French Gentlemen have obtained nothing more. That these were intended as merely honorary—and that they are not so objectionable as the other sort; however these are attended with great inconveniencies, for the instant they gain a point upon you, no matter what their primary professions and engagements were, they extend their views and are incessant in teasing for actual command. The reason for their pressing for printed Commissions in the usual form, in preference to the Brevits you give them is obvious. The former are better calculated to favor their Schemes as they import an idea of real command—and of consequence afford them grounds for their future sollicitations for the purpose. I am well pleased with Monsr Girards declaration—and if he adheres to it, he will prevent many frivolous & unwarrantable applications; for finding their pursuits not seconded by his interest, many of the Gentlemen will be discouraged, and relinquish every hope of success. Nor am I insensible of the propriety of your wish respecting our friend the Marquis. His Countrymen soon find access to his heart and he is but too apt afterwards to interest himself in their behalf, without having a sufficient knowledge of their Merit—or a proper regard to their extravagent views. I will be done upon the Subject. I am sure you have been severely punished by their importunities as well as myself.

The performance ascribd to Mr Mauduit is really curious as coming from him, when we consider his past conduct. He is a sensible writer— and his conversion at an earlier day, with many others that have lately happened, might have availed his Country much. His reasoning is plain & forcible and within the compass of every understanding.

I have nothing new to inform you of. My public Letter to Congress yesterday contained my last advices from Rhode Island. I hope in a few days from the high spirits and expectations of General Sullivan, that I shall have the happiness to congratulate you on our success in that Quarter. I am Dr Sir With the most perfect esteem & regard Yr Most Obedt & Obliged Sert

Go: Washington

ALS, NNPM; Df, DLC:GW; Varick transcript, DLC:GW. The letter is docketed in part, "Rec'd 25th."

1. The lady was Elizabeth Graeme Ferguson, wife of the British commissary of prisoners Henry Hugh Ferguson. For Joseph Reed's account of her involvement with this controversy, see Reed, *Joseph Reed*, 1:381–87. For discussion of the letters from George Johnstone to Reed and to Robert Morris, see Laurens to GW, 13 Aug., n.6.

## From Henry Laurens

Sir                               [Philadelphia] 20th Augt [1778]
My last to Your Excellency went by Dunn dated the 13th since which I have had the honor of receiving and presenting to Congress Your Excellency's second of the 13th and one of the 16th Inst.[1] I have at present nothing to trouble Your Excellency with but an Act of Congress of the 17th for exonerating the Commanding Officers on Hudsons' river from any censure for the loss of the Posts in the Highlands.[2] I have the Honor to be With great Esteem and Respect &c.

LB, DNA:PCC, item 13. A note on the letter-book copy indicates that this letter was carried "by [Joseph] Burwell," perhaps the Joseph Burwell, of Quakertown, N.J., who had advertised as a post rider between New Jersey and Philadelphia in 1768 (*Pennsylvania Gazette*, 22 Dec. 1768).

1. Laurens is evidently referring to his letter to GW of 16 Aug. rather than 13 August. The letter that Laurens calls GW's "second of the 13th" is apparently his second letter of 9 Aug., the LS of which is undated and was received by Congress on 18 August. Laurens is referring to GW's second letter of 16 August.

2. For this act, see *JCC*, 11:803–4.

# From Henry Laurens

Sir					[Philadelphia] 20th Augt [1778]

I had the honor of writing to Your Excellency this Morning by Burwell and late the present Evening of receiving Your Excellency's dispatches by Captain Riley.[1] These shall be presented to Congress tomorrow. Inclosed with this will be found a Report of a Committee on Your Excellency's letter, relative to Baron Steuben, which Congress request Your Excellency will take under consideration, and return it as speedily as the case will admit of, together with Your Excellency's opinion on the several parts, and any amendments or additions which shall appear to be necessary.[2] I am with great Respect &c.

P.S. Baron Arndt has obtain'd from Congress leave of absence for twelve months.

LB, DNA:PCC, item 13. A note on the letter-book copy indicates that this letter was carried "by Colo. Boudinot."
1. See GW's first letter to Laurens of 16 August.
2. For the report of 20 Aug., which resolved that Steuben should be appointed "Inspector General of the Armies of the United States" with the rank of major general and described his duties and subordinate officers, see *JCC*, 11:819–23. GW's official letter to Laurens regarding Steuben was dated 26 July.

# To Brigadier General Thomas Nelson, Jr.

My dear Sir,			Camp at the White-plains Augt 20th 1778

In what terms can I sufficiently thank you for your polite attention to me, and agreeable present? and, which is still more to the purpose, with what propriety can I deprive you of a valuable, and favourite Horse? You have pressed me once, nay twice, to accept him as a gift;[1] as a proof of my sincere attachment to, and friendship for you, I obey, with this assurance, that from none but a Gentn for whom I have the highest regard, would I do this, notwithstanding the distressed situation I have been in for want of one.

I am heartily disappointed at a late resolution of Congress for the discontinuance of your Corps,[2] because I pleased my self with the prospect of seeing you, and many other Gentn of my acquaintance from Virginia, in Camp—As you had got to Philadelphia, I do not think the saving, or difference of expence (taking up the matter even upon that ground, which under present circumstances I think a very erroneous one) was by any means an object suited to the occasion.

The arrival of the French Fleet upon the Coast of America is a great, & striking event; but the operations of it have been injured by a number of unforeseen & unfavourable cercumstances—which, tho they ought not to detract from the merit, and good intention of our great Ally, has nevertheless lessened the importance of their Services in a great degree—The length of the passage in the first instance was a capitol misfortune, for had even one of common length taken place, Lord Howe with the British Ships of War and all the Transports in the River Delaware must, inevitably, have fallen; and Sir Harry must have had better luck than is commonly dispensed to Men of his profession, under such circumstances, if he and his Troops had not shared (at least) the fate of Burgoyne—The long passage of Count D'Estaign was succeeded by an unfavourable discovery at the hook, which hurt us in two respects; first in a defeat of the enterprize upon New York—the Shipping—& Troops at that place; and next, in the delay that was used in ascertaining the depth of Water over the Bar; which was essential to their entrance into the Harbour of New York—And lastly after the enterprize upon Rhode Island had been planned, and was in the moment of execution, that Lord Howe with the British Ships should interpose, merely to create a diversion, and draw the French fleet from the Island was again unlucky, as the Count had not return'd on the 17th to the Island tho drawn off from it the 10th; by which means the Land operations were retarded, and the whole subject to a miscarriage in case of the arrival of Byrons Squadron.

I do not know what to make of the enemy at New York; whether their stay at that place is the result of choice, or the effect of necessity, proceeding from an inferiority in their Fleet—want of Provisions—or other causes, I know not, but certain it is that if it is not an act of necessity it is profoundly misterious unless they look for considerable reinforcements and are waiting the arrival of them to commence their operations. time will shew.

It is not a little pleasing, nor less wonderful to contemplate, that after two years Manœuvering and undergoing the strangest vicissitudes that perhaps ever attended any one contest since the creation both Armies are brought back to the very point they set out from and, that that, which was the offending party in the beginning is now reduced to the use of the spade and pick axe for defence. The hand of Providence has been so conspicuous in all this, that he must be worse than an infidel that lacks faith, and more than wicked, that has not gratitude enough to acknowledge his obligations—but—it will be time enough for me to turn preacher, when my present appointment ceases; and therefore, I shall add no more on the Doctrine of Providence; but make a tender of my best respects to your good Lady—the Secretary[3] & other friends and assure you that with the most perfect regard I am Dr Sir Yr Most Affecte & Obliged Hble Ser.

Go: Washington

P.S. Since writing the foregoing, I have been favoured with your Letter of the 25th Ulto from Baltimore, and 9th Instt from Philadelphia[4]— The method you propose to take with the Public Horses in your volunteer Corps will be very proper & agreeable to me.

G. W——n

ADfS, DLC:GW; Varick transcript, DLC:GW.

1. See Nelson to GW, 11 August.
2. For this resolution of 8 Aug., see *JCC*, 11:766.
3. GW is referring to Nelson's uncle, Thomas Nelson, Sr.
4. These letters have not been found.

## General Orders

Head-Quarters W. Plains Friday Augt 21st 1778.
Parole Rotterdam—                    C. Signs Rumney—Riswick—

The Commander in Chief has tho't proper to pardon the following Criminals who were under sentence of Death and to have been executed this day—Solomon Lynes, John Craige, Zechariah Ward Richard Burk, Michaël Carmen, William McLaughlin, John Jenkins, Nicholas Fitzgerald David Potter and Neil Megonigle.[1]

Notwithstanding the general good Character of the Criminal as a soldier, the Wounds he has received in fighting for his Country; the warm Solicitation of several respectable Officers and even the special Intercession of Captain Scott himself to whom the Injury was offered, it was with extreme difficulty the Commander in Chief could prevail with himself to pardon an Offence so attrocious as that committed by Megonigle; The least disrespect from a soldier to an Officer is criminal in an high degree & deserves severe Punishment; when it proceeds to any kind of personal Violence the offender justly merits death, but when it extends to an attempt upon the Officers life as was the Case in the present instance it, assumes a Complexon so enormous and aggravated that it wants a name, and puts the Criminal almost beyond the reach of Mercy itself—The General is happy to reflect that this is the first time an Instance of this nature has come before him—He thinks it necessary to warn every soldier that a similar one will never hereafter be forgiven, whatever may be the Character of the Offender or the Intercessions of the Officers.

Several Deserters from the Army to the Enemy who have since returned having been permitted with Impunity to join their Regiments— The General to prevent an Abuse of his Lenity by its being drawn into Precedent and made an Encouragement to others to commit the same Crime, takes occasion to declare in explicit terms that no man who shall desert to the Enemy after the Publication of this order will ever be allowed to enjoy the like Indulgence, but whether he return voluntarily himself or fall into our hands by any other means will infalliably suffer the Punishment decreed to his Crime.

Captn Lieutt Ambrose Buchanan is appointed Pay-Master to Coll Harrison's Regiment of Artillery.[2]

Varick transcript, DLC:GW.

1. A draft of the pardon, in the writings of Alexander Hamilton and Robert Hanson Harrison, is in DLC:GW. Col. Jeduthan Baldwin recorded in his journal that the prisoners were "brought out to the place of Execution" before receiving the pardon (Baldwin, *Revolutionary Journal*, 132).

2. Ambrose Bohannon (Buchanan) was a captain lieutenant in the 1st Artillery Regiment (Harrison's) with a commission dated from 13 Jan. 1777. He served as paymaster at least into 1780 and as captain lieutenant to the end of the war.

## To John Beatty

sir                    Head Quarters [White Plains] 21 Augt 1778

Lewis Johnson Costagan a Lieut. in the 1st Jersey Regt was taken prisoner early in 1777.[1] I would wish that the speediest means may be used for the obtaining his Exchange, at the same time you will observe such caution in conducting the affair as not to alarm the enemy or induce them to detain him. You will not seem over anxious, and yet take such measures as cannot fail to procure his liberty.

As soon as he comes out you will be pleased to direct him to repair immediately to the Head Quarters of the army. I am Sir &c.

G.[W.]

Df, in James McHenry's writing, DLC:GW; Varick transcript, DLC:GW.

1. Lewis Johnston Costigin (c.1744–1822) was commissioned a first lieutenant of the 1st New Jersey Regiment in November 1775. According to his memorial to GW of 4 April 1782 (DLC:GW), he was taken prisoner in January 1777 and remained in captivity until September 1778. At that time he was paroled to New Brunswick, and he apparently was exchanged in December 1778. Costigin supplied intelligence from New York over the signature "Z" from the time of his parole or before until late December 1778, but he had come out of the city by March 1779.

## To Major General Nathanael Greene

Dear Sir                    White-plains Augt 21st 1778.

On Wednesday afternoon I re⟨ce⟩ived your favor of the 12th & 13th Inst. by Mr Hulet the Pilot, who did not arrive in Camp till then.[1] I am much obliged by your particular relation of matters, and request that you will continue it from time to time whenever oppertunity will permit.

There was one circumstance in your relation, of which I was exceedingly sorry to hear. You will readily know which it is. I wish the utmost harmony to prevail, as it is essential to success—and that no occasions be omitted on our part to cultivate it.

Your operations have been greatly retarded by the late violent storm, but as it is now over, I trust things will go on prosperously, & that you will be rejoined by Count D'Estaign who has been kept out so long by it. Indeed, from General Sullivans Letter of the 17th, I flatter myself you will have made a compleat reduction of the Enemy's force before this reaches you, & that the next advices I receive, will announce it.[2] If the fact is otherwise, let me beseech you to guard against Sortees & surprizes—The Enemy, depend, will fall like a strong Man—will make many Sallies, & endea⟨v⟩our to possess themselves of, or de⟨s⟩troy your Artillery—and in one of these, should they put the Militia into confusion, the consequences may be fatal.

By a Letter which I received yesterday from Genl Maxwell, inclosing one from Major Howell (whom I have stationed at black point for the purpose of observation) [3] it appears certain, that Sixteen of Lord Howes fleet entered the Hook on the 17th—That on that, and the preceeding day, there had been heard severe Canonades at Sea—& that it was reported in New York that a 64 Gun Ship and several Transports had been taken by the French Squadron.[4] I wish the fact may be so as to the capture, and that the Count may be with you to give a narrative of it himself.

I cannot learn that Admiral Byron is arrived—nor do I believe that he is. It is said that one Ship only of the Corke Fleet is yet arrived. I have not time to add more, as Majr Blodget is in a hurry to proceed, than to assure you, that I am, with the most perfect esteem & regard Dr Sir Yr Obliged & Affecte Frd

Go: Washington

ALS, DLC: Nathanael Greene Papers; Df, DLC:GW; Varick transcript, DLC:GW.

1. Greene's letter of 12–13 Aug. has not been found. The previous Wednesday was 19 August. "Mr Hulet" was probably James Howlett.

2. On the draft, which is in Robert Hanson Harrison's writing, the remainder of this paragraph, with slight variations in wording, was added by GW.

3. GW added the parenthetical clause to the draft.

4. Neither Brig. Gen. William Maxwell's letter to GW nor its enclosure has been found. British captain John Peebles noted in his diary for 16 Aug., "hear'd firing in the afternoon," and for 17 Aug., "a fleet arrived at the Hook of between 20 & 30 Sail supposed to be Lord Howe" (Gruber, *Peebles' American War*, 209).

*Letter not found*: from Patrick Henry, 21 Aug. 1778. GW wrote Henry on 13 Sept.: "I have been honored with yours of the 21st Augt."

## To Henry Laurens

sir                                   Head Qrs White plains August 21st 1778
    Your Favor of the 16th, with the several papers to which it referred, came duly to hand on Wednesday Afternoon.[1]
    I this minute received from General Sullivan the Letter I have now the honor of forwarding you, with One addressed to myself. A copy of the latter is also inclosed.[2] The General seems to have been very near the Enemy's lines—& on the point of opening all his Batteries. Things appear to be in a promising train.
    By advices from an Officer of rank and intelligence, who is stationed with a party in Monmouth County,[3] I am informed, that sixteen Ships entered the Hook on the 17th, one having a Flag, & that on that & the proceding day a Heavy Canonade was heard at Sea. I have the Honor to be with the greatest respect & esteem sir Your Most Obedt servt
                                                    Go: Washington

LS, in Robert Hanson Harrison's writing, DNA:PCC, item 152; Df, DLC:GW; copy, ScHi: Henry Laurens Papers; copy, DNA:PCC, item 169; Varick transcript, DLC:GW. Congress read this letter on 25 Aug.; see *JCC*, 11:836.
    1. The previous Wednesday was 19 August.
    2. GW enclosed Maj. Gen. John Sullivan's letter to Laurens of 19 Aug. (DNA:PCC, item 160) and an extract of Sullivan's letter to GW of the same date.
    3. GW was referring to Maj. Richard Howell.

## To Henry Laurens

sir                                   Head Qrs White plains Augt 21: 1778
    I do myself the honor of transmitting to Congress the inclosed Memorial of Colo. Rawlings, presented in behalf of himself and the Maryland Officers, who were under his command in the year 1776.[1] The facts which are stated in it, are generally true—and I can not but feel myself exceedingly interested in favor of these Gentlemen. The conduct of this whole Corps, when Fort Washington was attacked is so generally known and approved, that it is almost unnecessary to add upon the subject. However, I think it but justice to observe, that every representation of that day's transaction gave them the highest credit. They fought with a degree of veteran bravery—and though but a handful, they maintained their ground a considerable time, notwithstanding the most vigorous efforts to force them. All who were spectators upon the occasion have declared this—and the Enemy themselves have not refused 'em applause. It seems hard that Officers of their merit should be overlooked—and a loss to the service, that they should remain unemployed. But the consequences that would attend their incorporation with any of

the Corps now existing, appear too disagreable to try the experiment. Colo. Rawlings himself from the information I have had, does not incline to give any uneasiness to the line of the Army—and would rather make a distant part of it against the Indians, in case he could be provided for in that way. Captain Beal who is charged with this, will be able to inform Congress more fully than I can of the wishes of the Colonel and the rest of his Officers; and his account may lead perhaps to some suitable and practicable provision for them.[2] As I have observed before they are men who deserve well of their Country. I only mention the Maryland Officers upon this occasion, because that part of the Corps which came from Virginia, was provided for by the state in their present arrangement, as I have been credibly advised.

Mr Rawlings was never in the compleat and actual command of the Regiment under his direction, as Colonel, because he never obtained a Commission; but he became intitled to it, according to the then common rule of promotion, by the death of Colo. Stephenson and the Nonacceptance of Colo. Morgan who was appointed to it. With the latter circumstance Mr Rawlings I am persuaded, was never apprised, as it was kept a secret, from an apprehension that the Enemy might claim an Officer of the rank of Colo. in exchange for Morgan who was then a prisoner on parole, if his promotion came to their knowledge. Major Williams of the Maryland part of the Corps, was appointed by the State to one of her regiments now in the field, and is the only Officer in his predicament I know of, that they arranged. I have the honor to be with great respect & esteem sir Your Most Obedt servant

Go: Washington

LS, in Robert Hanson Harrison's writing, DNA:PCC, item 152; Df, DLC:GW; copy, DNA:PCC, item 169; Varick transcript, DLC:GW. Congress read this letter on 25 Aug. and referred it to the Board of War (see *JCC,* 11:836).

1. The undated memorial to GW from Lt. Col. Moses Rawlings states "That sometime after his entering into the Army (by the usual gradation thereof) he obtained the Command of a Regiment composed of five Companies from Virginia, and four from Maryland. That on the 16th of November 1776, your Memorialist together with all the officers and privates under his Command were either Killed wounded or taken Prisoners at Fort Washington; that during his confinement with the Enemy the States Adopted the method of Alloting to each Colony or Province the number of Regiments they were deemed Capable of raising towards filling up the Continental Army, in complying with which allottment your Memorialist & his Regiment have been totally Overlooked, neglected, or forgot, by the State of Maryland, so that he and the officers under his command are quite out of the Line of Promotion by the new Arrangement of the Army. Your Memorialist has hereto Subjoined a List of the Officers belonging to his Regiment at the Battle of Fort Washington together with the number of Privates fifty of which were killed & wounded in the field & most of those that survived the Battle died Prisoners with the Enemy. If your Excellency thinks the Peculiar Situation of your Memorialist, & his officers, Merits and admits

any Relief and your Excellency will take the same under consideration your Memorialist as in duty bound shall pray &c." The subjoined list includes 16 Maryland officers and 9 Virginia officers and states that 214 privates were made prisoner (DNA:PCC, item 41).

2. Thomas Beall (1744–1823) of Frederick County, Md., a captain in Rawlings's regiment, was listed by Rawlings as exchanged. By 1780 he was stationed at Fort Pitt as captain commandant of the remnants of Rawlings's regiment, but in August of that year he was sentenced to dismissal by a court-martial, a sentence that GW confirmed in general orders of 13 Oct. 1780. After the war, Beall founded what became the town of Cumberland in Allegheny County, Maryland.

## From Major General William Phillips

Sir                                Cambridge [Mass.] August 21st 1778
The situation of the Troops of the Convention of Saratoga being such as calls upon my earnest attention, will, I hope, plead for me in apology for giving you, Sir, the trouble of this Letter.

By an Article of the Treaty made at Saratoga with Major General Gates it was to be allow'd that an Officer might be sent to Canada for the Cloathing for the Troops of the Convention[1]—By application thereupon to Major General Heath he consented that an Officer might go by way of Halifax but did not allow any one to go by Land and the Lakes; I was obliged to accept this only alternative of procuring the cloathing; and Captain Willoe went with proper passports to Halifax and sailed from thence in April for Quebec; but he has not since been heard of, nor have I received any accounts what ever from Canada: under this description of the matter, and being in much anxiety for the welfare of the Troops I wrote a request to Major General Heath in the last month, which I repeated a few days since for permission to send an Officer by Land to Canada—Copies of my Letters and the Answers of Major General Heath I enclose to you, Sir, as fully explanatory on the Subject and will serve to offer as a reason for this direct application to you which Brigadier General Wilkinson going to your Army Affords me.[2]

I will take the liberty to most seriously request you will, Sir, have the goodness to allow of my sending an Officer by the Lakes to Canada, with permission that he may return the same way with accounts of the Cloathing for the Troops which is at present much wanted but in a short time will prove of the utmost consequence to men who are Almost naked.

I will not intrude longer on your time but leave my request to the decision of your good Sense and humanity.

I have a Pay Master and a Secretary in Canada to whom I writ by way of Halifax to Come here, the one to settle some public Accounts, the other to remain Some time with me in his way to Europe—May I offer my desire that should those two Officers be Still in Canada they may have leave to join me by way of Lake Champlain.

I do protest, Sir, that if it did not appear to me that an Officer going by Land to Canada would be attended with no consequences either political or military I would not give you the trouble of my request, and my Parole however strict, shall be subscribed to.

Should the Letters to New York contain no thing improper I will hope you may allow of their passing to that place.[3] I am Sir, with great personal respect your most Obedient most humble Servant

W. Phillips

LS, DLC:GW.

1. Article 12 of the 17 Oct. 1777 Convention of Saratoga provided that the British army should be able to send for their clothing and baggage "in the most convenient manner and the necessary passports granted for that purpose" (DNA:PCC, item 57).

2. The enclosed copies of Phillips's letters to William Heath of 29 July and 17 Aug. and Heath's replies of 1 (an extract) and 20 Aug. are in DLC:GW. On 1 Aug., Heath had promised, "I will write His Excellency General Washington by the first opportunity, and request to be informed whether he has any objection to your Sending to Canada by the way of the Lakes." To Phillips's renewed application, he responded that he had not yet received GW's reply, and "As His Excellency is now within the limits of the Northern Department it would be very improper for me to permit an Officer to pass that way without his knowledge and Consent."

3. An undated note from Phillips to GW may have accompanied this letter. It reads: "Major General Phillips requests of Genl Washington if he is so good to permit these letters to go into New York that he will be pleased to Seal them first— That enclos'd in the Cover directed to Thos Forsyth particularly" (PPRF). Phillips probably enclosed his letter to Henry Clinton of this date (P.R.O., 30/55, Carleton Papers).

## To William Smith

Sir.                    Head Quarters [White Plains] August 21st 1778
I received your letter of the 15th Inst. by Lieut. Colonel Burr.[1]

It gives me pleasure to find that the conduct of the flag was such as contributed to your ease; and I am much obliged to you for the attention shewn to the convenience of my officers.

It was really altogether out of my power to take any concern, (without interfering with the civil authority) in the matter of your request, but I have transmitted the letter to Governor Clinton who I doubt not will do every thing proper on the occasion.[2] I am Sir your Most Obt Servt.

Df, in James McHenry's writing, DLC:GW; Varick transcript, DLC:GW.

William Smith (1728–1793), a New York lawyer and historian, had served from 1763 to the outbreak of the Revolution as chief justice of the Province of New York and since 1767 as a member of the provincial council. Having twice refused to take an oath of allegiance to the state, he was among those ordered banished within enemy lines by the state commissioners for detecting and defeating conspiracies. Smith left New York with the British troops in 1783, and in 1785 he was appointed chief justice of Canada, where he served until his death.

1. Smith's letter of 15 Aug. has not been found, but according to Smith's memoirs, he wrote GW "to thank him for the Civilities of his Officers and to solicit his Permission to my Servants to follow me with the Horses" (Sabine, *Smith's Historical Memoirs, 1778–1783,* 4). According to Lt. Col. Aaron Burr, Smith's letter "requested his Negroe Slaves, his Coach Horses, and the Remainder of his Moveables now at Haverstraw" (Burr to George Clinton, 19 Aug. 1778, NHi). GW had appointed Burr on 1 Aug. to conduct Smith and other Loyalists to New York City (see Robert Hanson Harrison to Burr, 1 Aug., NjMoNP, and Clinton to the Commissioners for Conspiracies, 2 Aug., in Hastings, *Clinton Papers,* 3:601–2).

2. GW wrote George Clinton on this date: "The inclosed was received by Colo. Burr, who conducted the Flag which was sent in with Mr Smith and his family. As I did not conceive myself authorised to interfere or give any orders respecting the matter referred to me, I barely acknowledged the Receipt of it, and informed Mr Smith that I had forwarded it to you" (LS, CSmH).

## From Brigadier General John Stark

Dear Sir,               Head Quarters [Albany] 21st August 1778.

I am under the disagreeable Necessity of complaining of the Qr Mr General, of this Department,[1] altho I could Cincerely wish, never to be under such Necessity, it is not only myself but almost Every Person, that has Business with him has Reason to Complain, as he seems very unwilling [to] oblige any Person whatever, he has no Tents, neither can I learn as he tries to provide any, by which means Colo. Aldens Regiment is in a suffering Condition, not having above Seven Tents in the Regiment, and no probability of their wants being supplyed, the Militia at this Place has not half Camp Kettles enough for their use, and Informed by the Qr Mr that he has none for them.

The Troops at Otter Creek (our most Northern Frontier) has never been supplyed with Provisions, for more than five days before hand, and several times intirely out, and obliged to borrow Flour from the Inhabitants for their subsistance by the Negligence of the Qr Mr General.

I have (after several Applications for some kind of Grain for my Horses,) been informed that I can have none unless I advance hard Money for the same, and you are very Sensible that I receive no such Payment which renders me unable to support them, & I think it a very surprising affair, if the Continental Money will not purchase a Little

Grain for some Horses, but I am fully of opinion that such like Gentle-man, by offering hard Money, has been very Instrumental, in Reduc-ing the Continental Money, to its present low State.

I must beg that if he cannot be removed or Reformed, that I may be recalled, and some other Officer sent (if any such there be) who can bear such Repeated insults. I am this Moment informed that part of the Troops has come from Otter Creek, for want of Provisions and Ar-rived at Bennington. I am Sir with great Respect—Your Most Obedient Very Humble Servt

John Stark.

Copy, NHi: James Duane Papers.
    1. Stark was referring to Morgan Lewis.


## From Major General John Sullivan

Dear General.

Head Quarters before Newport [R.I.]
Augt 21st P.M. [1778]

I have within this hour had the honor of receiving your favor and am happy in having it in my power to relieve your Excellency from the state of anxiety you are in for the Counts safety.[1] He last evening ap-peared of this harbour & I was soon after surprised with the inclosed letter from Count d'Cambis who was dispatched in a frigate by the Ad-miral for the purpose of more speedily conveying the intelligence it contains.[2] From it your excellency will learn, the situation of the languedoc & another ship of the line—the former having lost all her masts, the latter her fore-mast in the late storm—as also the seperation of a 74 gun ship during the gale, which has not joined the squdron as yet. Thier success was by no means adequate to our expectations—The Senegal of eighteen Guns and a bomb-Ketch are the only prizes they have taken[3]—In consideration (I suppose) of his loss Count d'Estain had almost determined to sail for Boston and refit without touching upon this Island & it is manifest from the letter I have the honor to transmit your excellency that to co-operate with us was not his motive for, or intention in calling—As soon as I discovered this, I detached General Greene & the Marquiss and Colonel Langden one of the Con-tinental ship agents to confirm him in the validity of the following as-surance—viz. That it was as practicable and more convenient to repair his ships in this harbor than in that of Boston—That the danger of be-ing blocked up in either was the same, as a superior fleet could as eas-ily effect it in the latter as they could in the former. That there was a certainty in our being able to reduce the Island in a few days with his assistance—In short I made use of every argument that could incline him to desist from his purpose and partake of our glory and our danger—concluding with a request that should he notwithstanding what was offered persist in his resolution of sailing he would at least leave the land forces he had on board. I would feign hope my arguments have had the desired weight with him as he has since stood in and anchored near the Town. General Greene and the Marquiss have not yet returned—nor have I heard from them, but shall communicate the Counts answer as soon as it comes to hand—He could not have wanted water in his cruize as I had taken every possible method of supplying him with it. And I shall continue to furnish him with every necessary that he may want or I can procure. In order to do this I beg your Excellency would give orders that provisions should be forwarded as expeditiously as possible for their use, as it may not be in my power to supply them with such quantities as he may require.

The enemy soon after we had opened a four gun battery (18 pounders) evacuated a redoubt that was most exposed to its fire[4]—I have since raised batteries far advanced of this, and shall to-morrow morning have twenty eight pieces of heavy cannon playing at an inconsiderable distance, upon their works—These well served will (I doubt not) with what mortars I have at hand oblige them to retire from all their advanced redoubts and leave their lines open to o⟨ur⟩ future operations which will be greatly accelerated should Count d'Estain conclude to divert them in another quarter. I am &c. &c.

(a copy)                                              Jno. Sullivan

Copy, DNA:PCC, item 160. The copy was enclosed in GW to Henry Laurens, 24 August.

1. Sullivan was probably referring to GW's first letter of 19 August.

2. According to GW's letter to Laurens of 24 Aug., Sullivan failed to send the enclosure. Cambis's letter to Sullivan, dated 20 Aug., reported the damage to the *Languedoc* and the *Marseillais* and stated that, in consequence of the need for repairs, "the French fleet will approach no nearer to Rhode Island but will go to Boston." Comte d'Estaing asked Sullivan to order the French ships "in the East Channel" to rejoin the fleet "promptly" (Hammond, *Sullivan Papers*, 2:237–38). Charles-François, comte de Cambis-Lézan (1747–1825), was a lieutenant de vaisseau aboard the *Languedoc* and at this time in command of the captured sloop *Senegal*.

3. The separated French ship was the *César*. The captured British ketch was the *Thunderer*.

4. Lt. Johann Ernst Prechtel of the 1st Anspach Regiment wrote in his diary for 19 Aug.: "the enemy, for the first time today, fired on our defenses and camp from the new fort. Only 18-pound cannonballs were fired. A private in the English camp had his foot shot off, and a horse was killed. A cannonball fell in a tent hitting eight musketeers. Our camp therefore was changed and we moved closer to Newport, behind the great defensive position of Tominy Hill" (Prechtel, *Diary*, 25; see also ibid., 146–47; Döhla, *Hessian Diary*, 85; and Cutler, *Rev. Manasseh Cutler*, 70).

## General Orders

Head-Quarters W. Plains saturday Augt 22nd 78.

Parole Experience—                     C. Signs Enjoy—Esteem.

Varick transcript, DLC:GW. Maj. Gen. Benjamin Lincoln's orderly book for this date records the following orders: "Major Holdridge for two days guard, furnished with two days provision ready cooked & 40 rounds ⅌ Man—Twenty two light Dragoons to attend parade at guard mounting tomorrow Morning with a like quantity of Provisions—Southern, Northern & Eastern posts to set out on Monday" (MHi: Lincoln Papers; see also Alexander McDougall orderly book, NHi).

## To James Caldwell

Sir                        Head Quarters White plains 22d Augt 1778
   A few days ago I recd yours inclosing sundry papers relating to Capt. Randolph.[1] I think him justly intitled to the pay of a Captain (in which rank he acted when taken) from the time Genl Sullivan took him into employ, untill he was released. When he returns, I will, upon application, give him a Warrant for the Amount of his pay.
   I would not have you employ the stationary Expresses upon common occasions, because, as you observe, they may be out of the way when dispatches of consequence are going on. Whenever you are under the necessity of using them, some persons should be engaged to remain at the stages till they return, lest it should occasion the delay of an important dispatch. I am &c.

Df, in Tench Tilghman's writing, DLC:GW; Varick transcript, DLC:GW.
   1. Caldwell's letter and its enclosures have not been identified. GW may be referring to Capt. Nathaniel FitzRandolph (1748–1780) of the Middlesex County, N.J., militia. FitzRandolph was captured on Long Island, 27 Aug. 1776, and exchanged in April 1778. By June 1778 he had resumed military activity—the results of a raid on Staten Island were reported in the *New-Jersey Gazette* (Trenton) of 10 June. Though elected a naval officer by the New Jersey council and assembly in December 1778, FitzRandolph evidently continued his raids on Staten Island, so in February 1779 a Loyalist raiding party crossed over from the island and seized FitzRandolph at his Woodbridge, N.J., home. FitzRandolph was again exchanged in May 1780, and he died in July 1780 of wounds received in a battle at Springfield, N.J., on 23 June 1780.

## From Silas Deane

Dear sir                        Philadelphia Augst 22d 1778.
   I wrote you by Col. Bannister, which Letter You will have received before this;[1] I now write by Capt. Webb, just to ask if any thing can be done

for the Exchange of Col. Webb Prisoner as I learn on Long Island, I am
very desirous of seeing him before I leave Philadelphia not only on Account of the Affection I bear him, but on Business of some Consequence
to Us both, if an exchange cannot be effected at present, can he by no
means obtain Liberty, to come out for a few Weeks, on his Parole? I am
extremely sorry to Trouble You on the Subject, but I know your Freind-
ship to both of Us, and I know not where else to apply. We are here in a
kind of dead Calm, as to News, and very impatient for something favorable from NewPort. every thing that meets the least Opposition in Congress is subject to such delay that I really dare not hazard a Conjecture
as to The Time I shall be detained here, I promise myself however To
have the honor of waiting on You in about a Fortnight from This, in the
meantime I am as ever Dear sir with the most sincere respect Your Excellencys most Obedt and Very humble Servt

Silas Deane

ALS, DLC:GW.
  1. See Deane to GW, 12 August.

*Letter not found*: from Maj. Gen. Nathanael Greene, 22 Aug. 1778. On 1 Sept.,
GW wrote Greene: "I have had the pleasure of receiving your several letters,
the last of which was of the 22d Augt."

## From Brigadier General William Maxwell

Sir                                    Elizth Town [N.J.] 22d August 1778
  I have little to inform your Excellency of but even that will be more
agreeable to you, I emajin than not to hear from us at all. I have intiligence almost dayly from the likelyest places for news. The Troops lyeth
mostly as they did when I wrote you of the partys going to Cow neck
which is still confirmed, & that a party had gone to Joyn Governor
Tryon on the East of the Island.[1] besides the Artillery that went to him,
the rest was mostly Greens or New Levys. my informant says there is
4 or 5 Vessels has come up to New York (the Smallest of which is
40 Guns) to be repaired, they are much shattered Masts and riging tore
to pieces. They try to brag of having done great things with the French
Fleet but the Feathers have carryed away the Birds. Their rapid retreat
from before the Harbour of New Port on the Counts steering for them,
will not suffer their friends to believe they intended to fight.
  No news from black Point. We had a small alarm from Major Clow, that
he had great reason to think the Enemy was to come two nights ago to take
or destroy the Provisions at Acquackinac. they did not come, and upon
examination I found there was two much provisions there, well worthy
their notice, Viz. 1200 Barrels, my sittuation being such that I can give it

little or no support; I ordered the Provisions to be forwarded as soon as possable, and not to leave Such a temptation in their way again. I am Your Excellencys Most Obedint Humble Servant

Wm Maxwell

N.B. I had intiligence last night that confirms 3 or 4 Vessels coming up for repair some reports that the French Fleet lyeth off the Hook some says that Byrons is there, but I believe neither. no news from Black Point.

W.M.

ALS, DLC:GW.
1. This previous letter from Maxwell to GW has not been found.

## From Brigadier General Charles Scott

Sir                    [Westchester County, N.Y.] 22d of Augt 1778
    Previous to the rect of Your orders through Colo. Tilghman I had sent Colos. Butler and parker with an Escort of 12 D[r]agoons To the Neighbourhood of Frogs point, with orders To take every possable Means in their power To git the Very best Intelegence from thence,[1] I mentioned to them, giting some inhabitant Who they Could confide in. I also desierd them to Make enquiery whether there was any troops on Board and from where, in short to leave nothing ondon that might Leade to infermation I have again Sent to Colo. Gist to do every thing in his power to git intelegence on the Land side, I have Detached a Capt. with forty men who is well Acquainted with all that Country to do every thing in His power also. I think if there be a Possability of Coming at their designs I Shall Shortly git it. I am Yr Excellencys Obt Servt

Chs Scott

ALS, DLC:GW.
1. These orders through GW's aide-de-camp Tench Tilghman to Scott have not been identified. Throg's Point is the tip of Throg's Neck, New York.

## To Major General John Sullivan

Dear Sir,                Head Quarters White Plains Aug. 22nd 1778
    I have received information, which has the appearance of authenticity, that the enemy have from an hundred to an hundred and fifty vessels in the sound near Frog's point. This intelligence, I think it necessary to communicate to you that you may be upon your guard.[1] What may be the purpose of these vessels can only be matter of conjecture. On the supposition, that the enemy have reason to believe the French

fleet so remote, either in consequence of the storm or other circumstances as to afford them an opportunity to operate by way of the sound, it is perhaps most probable, these vessels are designed to transport a body of troops for the relief of those on the Island.

On another hand, the enemy may think the present moment favourable for evacuating New York; concluding the French fleet may be so much in want of necessaries; as to oblige them when they get into port again, to remain there awhile for fresh supplies; and, at the same time, so much injured, by being several months at sea, and by the late storm, as to stand in need both of rest and repairs. In this case, they might deem it expedient to conceal their real aim, by creating a jealousy of the sound; while the ships sent there may also serve to facilitate their embarkation.

They may perhaps meditate som incursions along the coast by way of diversion; or they may possibly have it in view to operate against this army, by way of the Sound, which however appears to me the least likely supposition.

Whatever may be the meaning of it, the fact itself deserves attention; and I dare say, you will use every precaution in your power to obtain the earliest discovery of the approach of these vessels, if they should be destined your way; and to secure the troops under your command from any untoward accident. And I am equally persuaded, that you will not suffer any ill-founded or premature alarm to produce any change in your disposition, which may injure or frustrate the enterprise, you are carrying on. The present state of the wind makes me hope, that if Rhode Island is the enemy's object, this letter will get to you before they can accomplish it. I am Dr Sir Yr Most Obedt servt

Go: Washington

P.S. I doubt not you have taken every measure in your power to secure the passage across to the Main on any emergency.[2] If the expresses stationd between this place and you, go by way of providence as this route is productive of delay, you will give directions to have it changed.

Your letter of the 19th was received yesterday.

LS, in Alexander Hamilton's writing, NhHi: Sullivan Papers; Df, DLC:GW; Varick transcript, DLC:GW. In addition to the changes indicated in notes below, there are many small differences in wording between the draft and the LS, none of which alter the meaning. A note with the LS, signed by Hamilton, reads: "The expresses are positively ordered to ride day & night without fail."

1. On the draft, Hamilton continued this sentence: "against any attempts which may be intended to relieve Rhode Island."

2. On the draft, Hamilton wrote, instead of the preceding three words: "in case it should become necessary." The remainder of the postscript does not appear on the draft.

## General Orders

Head-Quarters White-Plains sunday Augt 23rd 1778.
Parole Pensacola—                    C. Signs Potts-dam. Plymouth—

A General Court-Martial whereof Majr General Lincoln is appointed President will sit tomorrow morning nine ôClock at the new dining Room near Baron De Kalb's quarters for the trial of Major General St Clair—Brigadiers General Nixon, Clinton, Wayne and Muhlenberg—Colonels Grayson, Russell, M. Gist, Greaton, Putnam, Meigs, Stewart and Cortlandt are to attend as Members—All Evidences and Persons concern'd will attend.[1]

The General Court-Martial whereof Coll Hazen is President will assemble at the President's Marquee at the time to which it stands adjourned.

Varick transcript, DLC:GW.

1. The proceedings of this court-martial, which continued until 29 Sept., were published in 1778 (*St. Clair Court Martial*; see also *Collections of the New-York Historical Society*, vol. 13 [New York, 1880], 1–172).

*Letter not found*: from Maj. Alexander Clough, 23 Aug. 1778. On 24 Aug., GW's aide-de-camp Richard Kidder Meade wrote Clough: "His Excellency commands me to acknowledge the receipt of your favor of Yesterdays date—& thank you for the intelligence it contain'd—He wishes you to continue your endeavours to collect the most perfect accots possible; the circumstance in particular which you mention is of no small importance & it cou'd be wished that you wou'd examine strictly evry person on that Head, when by comparing the whole together, you may pretty well determine on the truth—This or any other matter of consequence you will be pleased to transmit to His Excy" (DLC:GW).

## To Lieutenant General Wilhelm von Knyphausen

sir.                    Head Quarters White plains 23d August 1778
I had the honor to receive your letter of the 16th Instant.[1]

Altho' it is not my business to inquire into those private motives which may induce officers to leave your service, yet I cannot but be sensible of the consideration that could give me notice of their characters.

The officers I can assure you brought no horses to this army, or any of its posts that I know of. I am Sir, with great personal respect your most obedient and very humble servant.

Df, in James McHenry's writing, DLC:GW; Varick transcript, DLC:GW.

1. This letter has not been found, but Knyphausen described it in his report to the Prussian Landgrave of 23 Aug. 1778: "Under a flag of truce I informed General Washington of the character of these two men, that they had deserted because they had contracted so many debts and had rendered themselves liable to be cashiered from their conduct, and at the same time requested that he should be so good as to

have the two horses returned which they had taken away with them, as they belonged to residents here" (NjMoNP: William Van Vleek Lidgerwood Collection of Hessian Transcripts, Correspondence of General von Knyphausen). Knyphausen was probably referring to ensigns Carl F. Führer and Carl W. Kleinschmit (GW to Henry Laurens, 9 Aug. [second letter], and n.2).

## From Lieutenant Colonel John Laurens

Sir.                            Camp before Newport [R.I.] 23d August 1778.
    I am just returned from a fruitless pursuit of the french Squadron—General Sullivan will inform Your Excellency of the fatal determination of the counts officers in a Council of War—as well as of the several Remonstrances and final solemn protest made by the American Generals[1]—The Admirals Ship being dismasted fore and aft, at the moment that he had overtaken the british fleet and was promising himself an important victory—another Ship Of the line being in like manner dismantled and a seventy four gun Ship being separated from the Squadron[2]—all the effects of a most dreadful Storm which Suddenly arose—were regarded as sufficient reasons added to the expectation of Admiral Byrons Arrival—for abandoning the American troops in the midst of a very important expedition—and reducing them to the necessity of making a desperate attack, or a precipitate Retreat—The honor of the french Nation, the honor of the Admiral, the safety of his fleet, and a regard for the new alliance required a different conduct—but the Counts hands were tied—the Cabal of marine officers who wish his destruction because he was introduced from the land Service into their Corps left him it is said, no choice—I cannot however but be of opinion that a solemn protest might by affording a justification for his acting in direct contradiction to the unanimous voice of his officers—have induced him to remain here—he might have been furnished at this place with all the means of refitting which he can expect at Boston—he might have been as well secured against a superior force—and in case he had chosen to fight he wd have been in better condition in still water with dismantled Vessels—where every one knows that with springs upon his cables, he might fight his Artillery as well as if he had masts and Sails—whereas at Sea, in case of a separation from his fleet, the Languedoc may fall a prey to a Vessel of half her force.
    As I find that I am detaining the express—and I am sure General Sullivan will have written your Excellency more fully than my present hurry, and confusion of ideas for want of Sleep will permit me to do—I must entreat your Excellencys excuse for closing my letter abruptly. I have the honor to be with the greatest r⟨espect⟩ Your Excellen⟨cy's⟩ most obedt S⟨ervt⟩

                                                    John La⟨urens⟩

ALS, DLC:GW.

1. See Maj. Gen. John Sullivan to GW, this date. For a French report of the council of naval captains on 21 Aug., see Doniol, *Histoire de la participation de la France*, 3:346.

2. Vice Admiral d'Estaing's flagship was the *Languedoc*, the other dismasted ship was the *Marseillais*, and the separated ship was the *César*.

## From Alexander Spotswood

Fredericksburg [Va.] Augt 23d 1778

Your Excellencys Favour of the 11th Came to hand this day.

I ever thought, from the small Connection betwen us by marraige, that I had a share in your regard, and am happy to find, that, as an Officer, I was not low in your Esteem.[1]

To enter into a detail of what has past, woud b⟨e⟩ only Takeing up your Excellencys time, and now, woud answer no purpose; I shall only add, that, as events have turned out, I have been unfortunate in quiting a life that I was fond of—which I find to my sorrow has put it out of my power of ever distinguishing myself in a millitary Character—indeed it was a subject I shd not have revived, had I not have had repeated assureances from members of Congress—that my Commission was refused, and that ere long I shd be ranked as the next Brigadier from Virginia, which I now find will not be the Case. wishing your excellency a Glorious & happy Campaign—I remain with great Respect & regard yr Excellencys mt Obt St

Alexr Spotswood

ALS, DLC:GW.

1. In 1769 Spotswood had married Elizabeth Washington (1749–1814), eldest daughter of GW's half brother Augustine Washington (c.1720–1762).

## From Major General John Sullivan

My Dear General          Camp before Newport [R.I.] Augt 23d 1778

The Fates have Decreed that you Shall receive nothing but Disagreable Intelligence from this Quarter. Major General Green & the Marquis Returned the night before Last from the French Admiral. my Letter their Intreaties & General Greens written Remonstrance Drawn up on Board the Languedoc have only produced the Letter which I Inclose.[1] it Seems That the Captains of the French Fleet are So Incensed at the Count Destaings being put over them he being but a Land officer that they are Determined to prevent his Doing any thing that may Redound to his Credit or our advantage—The Count himself wished to

Come in but his Captains were to a man for Leaving us I then Drew up a Letter in behalf of all the officers of the Army & Sent on Board but he Though the wind was not fair for Boston put off to Sea night before Last this Letter was followed by the Inclosed protest both of which I have ordered after him in a Fast Sailing Privatier[2]—I am however well perswaded that nothing will alter the Determination of the Captains & that he will follow their Councill though he knows they wish his Ruin. This Sudden & unexampled proceedure Renders my Situation Exeeding Delicate The Enemy have twice attempted to Relieve the place by Reinforcements the Last Fleet had 4000 Troops on Board Should they make another attempt They must Succeed They will then have Near Ten thousand Troops on the Island & the Command of the water on Every Side of us as we have been oblidged to Dismantle our Forts at Bristol & Tivertown to forward our opperations against the Town I Inclose your Excy Copy of the Questions proposed by me to the General officers & Commandants of Brigades this Day[3]—I also Inclose your Exccellencey Copy of the protest Sent after the Count D Estaing. As my Situation at present can promise nothing to advantage Except from a Sudden Attack I wish the opinions of the officers may Justify me in making this Last Effort. I have the Honor to be my Dear General yours most affectionately

Jno. Sullivan

I offered the Count in My Letter to make the Attack The moment he would Land his Troops & put them in the Boats I had prepared for them General Green & the Marquiss assured him that we would not request the Stay of his Fleet & Troops more than 48 Hours But nothing could Induce him to assist us with Either a Single moment.

J:S:

ALS, DLC:GW; copy, DLC:GW; copy, DNA:PCC, item 152; copy, DNA:PCC, item 169. The copy in PCC, item 152, was enclosed with GW's official letter to Henry Laurens of 25 August.

1. The LS (in French) of Vice Admiral d'Estaing's letter to Sullivan of 21 Aug. is in DLC:GW. A translation is in DNA:PCC, item 152, with the copy that GW sent with his letter to Laurens of 25 August. D'Estaing, who initially wrote to inform Sullivan of his intent to go to Boston, opened his letter to add a long postscript acknowledging Sullivan's letter of 20 Aug. (not identified) but refusing to alter his decision. "Admiral Howe," he explained, "came to attack us when he thought us divided and in a position which he knew was disadvantageous and which rendered us weaker than him," and if the weakened French fleet again entered the harbor, Howe might again appear to engage them. News of the arrival of Admiral John Byron's fleet reinforced d'Estaing's decision: "The express orders I have from the King direct me in case of a superior force to retire to Boston."

An ALS copy of Maj. Gen. Nathanael Greene's letter to d'Estaing of 21 Aug. is also in DLC:GW. It may have been enclosed by Greene in his letter to GW of

22 Aug. (not found). Greene urged: "The expedition against Rhode Island was undertaken upon no other consideration than that of the French fleet & Troops acting in conjunction with the American Troops.

"There has been a great expence and much distress brought upon the Country in calling the Militia together at this busy season of the Year. A force nearly sufficient for the reduction of the place is now collected and all the necessary aparatus provided for subdueing the Garrison. If the expedition fails for want of the countenance of the Fleet and the Troops on Board. It will produce great discontent and murmuring among the People."

Acknowledging the damage done to the French fleet, Greene observed "that it is the general opinion of those best acquainted with the Coast, that the Fleet runs a much greater risque in attempting to go round to Boston, in the present shatterd state they are in, than they possibly can by staying here." Pointing out that a failure of this first effort at cooperation would "produce a disagreeable impression respecting the Alliance; and leave a door open for our Internal enemies as well as the common enemy to annimadvert upon the conduct of our allies in leaving us at such a critical period," Greene promised "every assistance in repairing your Fleet, you can wish or desire, as far as the resources of the Country will admit," and gave his opinion "that with the Assistance of the Fleet & French forces, we can get possession of Newport in two Days."

2. There are three copies of the protest of Sullivan's general officers, 22 Aug., in DLC:GW. One was sent by d'Estaing with his letter to GW of 5 Sept.; a second was made by GW's assistant secretary James McHenry; the third was probably this enclosure. The officers, who protested against d'Estaing's decision "as derogatory to the Honor of France, contrary to the Intentions of his Most Christian Majesty & the Interest of his Nation & destructive in the highest Degree to the Welfare of the United States of America & highly injurious to the Alliance formed between the two Nations," gave nine reasons for the protest. "1st Because the Expedition against Rhode Island was undertaken by Agreement with the Count De-Estaing. An Army has been collected & immense Stores brought together for the Reduction of the Garrison all of which be liable to be lost should he depart with his Fleet leave open the Harbour to receive Reinforcements from New York & Ships of War to cut off the Communication with the Main & totally prevent the Retreat of the Army.

"2dly Because the Proceeding of the Fleet to Boston can answer no valuable Purpose as the Injury it has received can be repaired much sooner here than at Boston & the Vessels secured against a superior Naval Force much better here than there.

"3dly Because there is the most apparent Hazard in attempting to carry round Nantucket Shoals those Ships which are disabled & will in all Probability end in the total Loss of two of his most Christian Majesty's Ships of War.

"4thly Because the Taking of dismasted Ships out of Port to carry them to another Port to receive their Masts instead of having their Masts brought to them is unwarranted by Precedent & unsupported by Reason.

"5thly Because the Honor of the French Nation must be injured by their Fleet abandoning their Allies upon an Island in the Midst of an Expedition agreed to by the Count himself. This must make such unfavorable Impressions on the Minds of Americans at large & create such Jealousies between them and their hitherto esteemed Allies as will in great measure frustrate the good Intentions of his most Christian Majesty & the American Congress who have mutually endeavoured to promote the greatest harmony & Confidence between the French People and the Americans.

"6thly Because the Apprehension of Admiral Byron's being upon the Coast with a superior Fleet is not well founded as it wholly arises from the Report of a Master of a British Merchantman who says he was told by the Greyhound Frigate that Admiral Byron was spoke with on the 24th of June off the Western Islands & Accounts from England up to the 24th of June mention Nothing of his having sailed & more than eight Weeks having elapsed since this Fleet was said to be near the Western Islands & no Account having been had of their Arrival in any Part of America it is evident that this Relation must be false. As to the Captains of two of the French Ships supposing that they had discovered a three Decker it is possible that in the thick Weather they may have been deceived but even if they are not it is by no Means evident that this Ship belonged to Byron's Fleet & even if it did it only proves that his Fleet has been seperated & must rendezvouz in some Place before they can act of which the French Fleet cannot fail to have timely Notice & before it is probable they can act the Garrison may be easily reduced.

"7thly Even if a superior Fleet should arrive the French Fleet can be in no greater Safety at Boston than Rhode Island: It can as easily be blocked up in the former as the latter Place & can be much easier defended in the latter than the former.

"8thly The Order said to be received from the King of France for his Fleet to retire to Boston in Case of Misfortune cannot without doing Injustice to that wise & good Monarch be supposed to extend to the Removal of his whole Fleet in the Midst of an Expedition on Account of an Injury having happened to two or three of his Ships.

"9thly Because even though the Facts pretended were fully proved & it became necessary for the Fleet to proceed to Boston yet no possible reason can be assigned for the Count De-Estaings taking with him the Land Forces which he has on board & which might be of great Advantage in the Expedition & of no possible Use to him in Boston."

3. Sullivan's communication to the officers, dated 23 Aug., reads: "The Count De Estang having abandoned us, in the Present Enterprize, And opened the Harbour for the Reception of Reinforsements from New York, It becomes my part, to inform the General Officers, And Officers commanding Brigades of my present force, And that of the Enemy, As Nearly as can be collected, And at the same time to request Their Oppinion upon Several Questions, The Number of Our army amounts to Eight Thousd one hundred & 74 Rank & file Exclusive of Eight Hundred Artillery men, The whole exceedingly well Officer'd, And a Reinforsement of three thousand men will probably be here in a few days—The Number of the Enemy from the best Calculation amounts to about Six thousand Including Artillery men, Sea men &c. In Our present Situation, One of three things only can remain to be done, Vizt To Continue the Seige by Regular Approaches, And Hazard the Arrival of a Reinforsement—To make an emmeadiate attack on their Lines, Or to Retreat from the Island, with the Stores &c. which have been collected—Your Oppinion upon which of these three is most advisiable in our present Situation is Requested, Should you be for continuing the Siege you will mention your Oppinion Respecting the Securing a Retreat, in case a British Fleet should arrive with a Reinforsement—Should you be of oppinion that an Attack Should be made, You will please to point out the manner in which you would wish it to be carried into Execution—Should your Oppinion be in favour of a Retreat you will please to Signify whether you think it Should take place immediately And your Reasons for its taking place at all—Your Oppinion in writing upon these Questions, is expected without Loss of Time" (DLC:GW). For the officers' replies, see Hammond, *Sullivan Papers*, 2: 248–63.

# General Orders

Head-Quarters W. Plains Monday Augt 24th 1778.
Parole Framingham—                    C. Signs Fez—France.

Brigade returns of all the horses in each Regiment and by whom kept to be made out immediately and delivered in to the orderly Office by 12 ôClock tomorrow.

The honorable the Congress have been pleased to agree to the following Report of their Committee and to pass the resolution annexed to it.

In Congress August 17th 1778.

The Committee to whom was referred a letter from General Washington of the 28th of July respecting Genl Putnam and the report of the Court of Enquiry on the subject of the Posts in the Highlands of Hudson's River taken last year which was transmitted to Congress, report, That upon a careful examination of the Facts stated by the Court of Enquiry & consideration of the Evidence taken and transmitted, it appears that those Posts were lost not from any fault, misconduct or negligence of the Commanding Officers but solely thro' the want of an adequate Force under their command to maintain & defend them. Resolved, that Congress agree to the said Report.[1]

At a Brigade Court-Martial in the Corps of Artillery Augt 14th 1778 — Lieutt Coll Popkin President, Lieutenant Waters and McNamara were tried for speaking disrespectfully of the Commander in Chief treating Lieutt Hill in a scandalous manner unbecoming the Characters of Gentlemen & raising a Riot, and contemptuous treatment of Coll Harrison after being arrested[2]—After mature deliberation the Court are of opinion that Lieutenant Waters is guilty of treating Mr Hill in a scandalous manner, unbecoming the Character of a Gentleman, but as the provocation from Mr Hill was so considerable and so very apt to produce in Mr Waters the forgetfulness of his Character as a Gentleman and Officer, they view the Crime in some measure palliated & therefore only sentence him to be reprimanded by the Commanding Officer of Artillery in Presence of all the Officers of the Corps—The General approves the sentence & orders it to take place tomorrow morning at Roll-Call.[3]

The Court find Lieutt McNamara of Colonel Harrison's Regiment of Artillery guilty of speaking disrespectfully of His Excellency General Washington, treating Lieutt Hill in a scandalous manner, unbecoming the Character of a Gentleman & contemptuous treatment of Coll Harrison after being arrested and unanimously adjudged that he shall be cashiered.

The Commander in Chief is sorry to be under the Necessity of Deciding in a Case of this Nature & would readily remit the sentence against Lieutt McNamara if his behaviour to Colonel Harrison, his Commanding Officer had not been so gross and disorderly as to compel the General to confirm it.

The General Court-Martial whereof Major General Lincoln is President will sit tomorrow at the time and Place mentioned in yesterdays orders—Members the same, except Coll Wyllys *vice* Coll Cortland who is absent on Command.

Varick transcript, DLC:GW.

Maj. Gen. Benjamin Lincoln's orderly book for this date begins with the following orders: "Major Merriweather for two days guard, supplyed with two days provisions & 40 rounds pr man—The Detachments for a weeks & fortnights command to be supplyed with the like quantity of provision & also 22 light dragoons, who are to parade to morrow morning" (MHi: Lincoln Papers; see also *N.C. State Records*, 12:542).

On this date GW's aide-de-camp Alexander Hamilton wrote to Brig. Gen. Anthony Wayne to convey GW's request that Wayne look into Capt. John Nelson's complaint about his arrest and detention (PHi: Wayne Papers; see also *Hamilton Papers*, 1:536). Also, a council of general officers replied to the question posed to them by GW on 20 Aug. (see Proceedings of a Council of General Officers, 20–24 Aug.).

1. For this report, see *JCC*, 11:803–4.

2. All three lieutenants were in Col. Charles Harrison's 1st Continental Artillery Regiment. Richard Waters had been commissioned a first lieutenant in January 1777. He was appointed regimental adjutant in September 1778 and promoted to captain lieutenant in August 1779. Taken prisoner at Camden, S.C., on 16 Aug. 1780, he was on parole at the end of the war. Michael McNamara was commissioned a second lieutenant in January 1777 and promoted to first lieutenant in January 1778. He had been serving as regimental adjutant since 1 July 1778. Richard Hill was commissioned a second lieutenant in January 1777 and promoted to first lieutenant in October of that year. He resigned in April 1779.

3. The artillery brigade orders for 25 Aug. reported that "Upon a representation made to his Excellency the Commander in chief, he has been pleased, to remit the Sentence of reprimand ordered Lt. Waters; who is hereby released from his arrest" (Artillery Brigade orderly book, NHi).

# To Lieutenant Colonel William Butler

Sir                                   Head Quarters White plains 24 Augt 1778

I recd yours of the 13th instant dated at Schohary, giving me an account of events in that quarter since your arrival there.[1] I am very glad to hear of the success of your two scouting parties, and I hope that these checks, tho' small, and the appearance of a force upon the Frontier, will give spirit to our friends, discourage the disaffected, and establish the confidence and friendship of those who have been frightened or deluded. I have desired General Stark not to send any Officer of superior Rank to interfere with you in command, as I have great reliance upon your activity and skill in conducting such an expedition as that which you are now upon. The inclosed were sent here by some of your friends to be forwarded.[2] I am Sir Yr most obt Servt.

Df, in Tench Tilghman's writing, DLC:GW; Varick transcript, DLC:GW.

1. Butler's letter to GW of 13 Aug. has not been found, but Butler probably conveyed the same information as in his letter to George Clinton of that date. There Butler wrote: "On my Arrival here I found three Forts erected by the Inhabitants for their Protection within 4 Miles of each other. I took Post at one I thought most liable to be Attacked & immediately sent out a Subaltern with a small Scout to reconnoitre the Country, & to make what discoveries he cou'd of the Enemy." This party shot "one Services [Christopher Servos], a Noted Villain who had Constantly supply'd the Enemy," and took four prisoners. Having received intelligence "of one Smith who had raised a Number of Tories and was Marching to Join the Enemy," Butler "immediately detached Capt. Long of the Rifle Choir [corps] with a party to intercept their March." Long's detachment killed Smith, took one prisoner, and captured documents indicating that the Tories intended to meet at Servos's "& there divide one party to Attack Cherry Valley & the other" Schoharie. Butler "detached Major Church with 120 Men . . . to lay in Ambuscade" for the Tories, who did not come. "The Major then drove off all the Cattle in that Neighbourhood as their principal supplies was from that Quarter." Butler added that "Except in these Instances I have been Obliged to Act totally on the Defensive" and that the most recent intelligence reported the enemy "about 1500 in Number at Unindilla about 80 or 90 Miles distance from" Schoharie (Hastings, *Clinton Papers*, 3:630–32).

2. The enclosures have not been identified.

*Letter not found*: from Maj. Alexander Clough, 24 Aug. 1778. On 25 Aug., GW wrote Clough: "I recd yours of yesterday late last Night."

# From John Laurance

SIR,                                                    *White Plains, August 24, 1778.*

AS the Congress have resolved that two Counsellors learned in the law should assist and co-operate with me in the prosecution of the General Officers respecting the evacuation of Ticonderoga, I am under the necessity, previous to my proceeding to the trial of Major General St. Clair, of requesting your Excellency to inform me whether those gentlemen have been desired to attend agreeable to the Resolution of Congress.[1] *I am, with much respect, Your Excellency's obedient Servant,*

JOHN LAURANCE, Judge Advocate.

*St. Clair Court Martial*, 5.
1. For the resolution of 5 Feb., see *JCC*, 10:125.

## To John Laurance

sir                                        Camp [White Plains] Augt 24th 1778
    On the 13 Instant I wrote to Wm Patterson and Jonathan D. Sargeant Esquires, Attorney Generals for Jersey & pensylvania by Express & transmitted a Copy of the Resolution, which you mention; notifying them at the same time, that Genl St Clair's trial would come on to day. I have received an Answer from Mr Patterson, by which he declines attending.[1] From Mr Sergeant I have not heard. The Letter to him, I inclosed to the care of Mr Laurens, president of Congress, with a request that it might be forwarded to him, as I did not know in what part of pensylvania he then was. I am Sir &c.

                                                                    G.W.

P.S. The president received my Letter of the 13th, which inclosed Mr Sergeant's—& I am informed dispatched to him by Express.

Df, in Robert Hanson Harrison's writing, DLC:GW; Varick transcript, DLC:GW.
    Harrison also wrote Laurance on this date: "In consequence of your request and his Excellency's permission I send you the Resolution which you want. You will be pleased to take care of it" (DLC:GW).
    1. William Paterson's answer has not been found.

## To Henry Laurens

sir                                        Head Qrs White plains Aug. 24: 1778
    I had yesterday the honor to receive your favor of the 20th Instant.[1]
    I take the liberty of transmitting you a Copy of a Letter, which this minute came to hand from Genl Sullivan, advising of the Count D'Estaing's arrival. He omitted to inclose the Admirals Letter to which he refers and therefore, I can give no further intelligence than what the Copy contains.[2] From the suffering of the fleet the Storm must have been exceedingly severe at Sea. I also inclose Two york papers of the 19th & 20th. These mention an engagement off Sandy Hook on the 16th. It could only have been partial on the side of the French Squadron at any rate, as the Languedoc & the Seventy four Gun ship must have lost their Masts before that time. It would seem by the account given in the papers—that the Isis & some other ships on the part of the Enemy had been damaged.[3] I have the Honor to be with the greatest respect sir yr Most Obedt st

                                                                    Go: Washington

LS, in Robert Hanson Harrison's writing, DNA:PCC, item 152; Df, DLC:GW; copy, DNA:PCC, item 169; Varick transcript, DLC:GW. Congress read this letter on 27 Aug. (see *JCC*, 11:843).

1. GW is apparently referring to Laurens's first letter to him of 20 August.
2. See John Sullivan to GW, 21 Aug., and note 2 to that document.
3. James Rivington's *Royal Gazette* (New York) of 19 Aug. printed an "Extract from the Journal of Mr. Alexander McPherson, Commander of the ship *Elderslie*, of Glasgow," which described an encounter between HMS *Isis* and a French ship mounting "at least 80 guns" on the afternoon of 16 August. The *Isis* reportedly gave the larger French ship several broadsides and forced her to flee, but "The situation of the Isis, having her masts rigging and sails shattered to pieces, particularly her yards, having neither lifts nor braces standing, and her foremast without a shroud, prevented her giving chace." The *Royal American Gazette* (New York) of 20 Aug. reported that "the Zele [actually the *César*], of 74 guns, a French Rear-Admiral's ship, bore down upon his Majesty's ship Isis of 50 guns," but she was driven off and "would have struck" had the *Isis* been able to pursue. That paper also described an engagement of 15 Aug. in which the British ship *Renown* attacked the French *Languedoc*, "which had been dismasted in the late storm." Darkness intervened, and the appearance of "six large French ships" the next morning at "day-break" caused the *Renown* to bear off.

## To Colonel William Malcom

Sir                                    Head Quarters White plains 24 Augt 1778
    I recd yours of the 19th inclosing the weekly Return of the Garrison.[1] If you cannot spare workmen to assist Capt. Stephens in the construction of his Machine it must be laid aside for the present. I will not undertake to say how far the Gentlemen, who have given their opinions of the Machine, may be right, but some others who have seen and considered the plan, view it in a different light from them. If it will be a work of much expence, the probability of its answering the end proposed shall be well considered before it is carried into execution.
    Genl Knox informs me that altho' he has sent but two Companies to relieve Colo. Lambs three, yet they consist of a greater number of Men, consequently you are better off in respect to Artillery Men than you were before. I am &c.

Df, in the writing of Tench Tilghman, DLC:GW; Varick transcript, DLC:GW.
    1. Malcom's letter to GW of 19 Aug. and the enclosed return have not been found.

## General Orders

                    Head-Quarters White-Plains Tuesday Augt 25th 1778.
Parole Oronoko—                                    C. Signs Orr. Otway.
    The whole Army to have their tents struck & loaded into Waggons, their Packs slung and to be in every respect ready for marching tomorrow morning at six ôClock[1]—The Quarter Master General, Commis-

saries Clothier &c. will in like manner be ready to move with the affairs of their respective departments.

At a General Court Martial August 15th 1778—Coll Hazen President Lieutt Lewis of the 9th Virginia Regimt tried for disobedience of orders on the 27th of last June—found guilty of the Charge exhibited against him and sentenced to be reprimanded in General Orders; The good Character given Lieutenant Lewis by his Commanding Officer, has prevented the Court from being more severe in their sentence.[2]

The Commander in Chief looks upon Lieutt Lewis's Conduct as an inexcusable breach of military discipline—The Plea of not knowing Coll Swift under whose immediate Command he then was, cannot be admitted, as Lieutt Lewis, if he was in any doubt, might very easily, and very naturally ought to, have asked from whom the order came.

At the same Court Joseph Cooler of the 3rd Maryland Regiment & John Fowler of Coll Nixon's Regiment were tried for desertion found guilty and sentenced to receive one hundred lashes each—The Commander in Chief approves the sentences and orders them put in Execution tomorrow morning at guard mounting at the head of the Regiments to which they respectively belong.[3]

At the same Court Augt 20th Lieutt Lane of the 2nd Jersey Battalion was tried for unofficerlike Procedure in opening a Packet from the British Commissioners to Congress, while on Command at second River, unanimously found guilty of the Charge exhibited against him, being a breach of the 5th Article of 18th section of the Articles of War & sentenced to be cashiered.

At a Brigade General Court Martial Augt 22nd 1778. Coll Patten President, Lieutt Levi Gatlin of the 2nd North Carolina Battalion, was tried for neglect of duty and disobedience of orders, unanimously found guilty of the Charges exhibited against him & sentenced to be dismissed the service.[4]

The Commander in Chief approves the two last mentioned sentences and orders them to take place immediately.

At another Brigade General Court Martial August 21st—Colonel Chambers President, Francis Murray a soldier in the 1st Pennsylvania Regiment was tried for desertion to the Enemy—The Court duly considering the Evidence, the Prisoner's defence and the aggravating Circumstances, are unanimously of opinion that he is guilty of desertion to the Enemy and do therefore sentence him to suffer Death.[5]

His Excellency the Commander in Chief approves the sentence.

Varick transcript, DLC:GW. The entry for this date in Maj. Gen. Benjamin Lincoln's orderly book begins with the following additional order: "A Court of enquiry to sit tomorrow morning 9 oClock at Colo. Marshals Marque or Quarters who is appointed President, upon a complaint exhibited by Dr Brown against Colonel Davi[e]s—Members Lt Cl Woolford Major Reed & a Capt. from the 1st Pennsya & Clinton's Brigades" (MHi: Lincoln Papers; see also Alexander McDougall orderly book, NHi; *N.C. State Records*, 12:544).

1. Sgt. Maj. Benjamin Gilbert of the 5th Massachusetts Regiment recorded in his diary for 26 Aug.: "Wee Struck all our Tents and Loaded our Bagage. Swept the peraide and then pitch our tents again by 12 oClock" (Symmes, *Gilbert Diary*, 36; see also "Beatty Journal," 83).

2. John Lewis (c.1755–1823) was commissioned an ensign in the 9th Virginia Regiment in March 1776 and promoted to second lieutenant in November of that year. Promoted to first lieutenant in May 1778, he resigned his commission on 15 Sept. 1778. Lewis served as a captain in the Virginia militia, 1780–81, and later became proprietor of the Sweet Springs spa.

3. The orders were probably referring to Joseph Cooley, who had enlisted as a private in the 3d Maryland Regiment on 16 April 1778 and had been absent fifteen days as a deserter. Cooley deserted again, apparently in November 1778, and was discharged. John Fowler (born c.1759) of Marblehead, Mass., enlisted in November 1776 and served in Capt. Adam Wheeler's company of Col. Thomas Nixon's 6th Massachusetts Regiment. He had deserted in 1777 and was later recorded as having deserted in January 1779.

4. Levi Gatlin was commissioned an ensign in the 10th North Carolina Regiment in 1777 and was promoted to lieutenant in February 1778.

5. Pennsylvania records suggest that Murray was not executed at this time but died later in the war.

## To Major Alexander Clough

Sir                                    Head Quarters White plains 25 Augt 1778

I recd yours of yesterday late last Night.[1] I am very anxious to obtain a true account of what is passing in New York, and am therefore endeavouring to send in a variety of persons from different quarters who have no connexion or communication with each other. By comparing their accounts, I shall be able to form a pretty good judgment. I have desired them to attend particularly to some matters of which the inclosed are the Heads.[2] I shall be obliged to you to procure some intelligent person to go into the City, and as it will be unsafe to give him a written paper, I desire you to impress the inclosed upon his memory by repeating them to him; when he returns, let me know his Answer to each head. If the person, who goes in, cannot make an excuse of Business, he must be allowed to carry a small matter of provision in, and bring something out, by way of pretext. I am &c.

Df, in Tench Tilghman's writing, DLC:GW; Varick transcript, DLC:GW.

1. Clough's letter to GW of 24 Aug. has not been found.

2. The enclosure was evidently a version of the "particular observations to be made by persons going into N——Y——" that GW sent out about this time. The draft of that document, in GW's writing with the last paragraph in Tench Tilghman's writing, reads: "Get into the City.

"There, in the best manner possible, learn the designs of the Enemy.

"Whether they mean to evacuate New York wholly—in part—or continue the Army there. A discovery of this kind will be best made by attending a little to the conduct of Delancy, Bayard, Matthews &ca—as they, more than probably, will be preparing for a removal if the City is to be left, wholly, or in any considerable degree.

"Or secondly, whether they have any views of Operating against this Army—which will be best known by their preparations of Waggons, Horses &ca—these will want Shoeing, repairing, & Collecting together.

"Enquire whether the Transports are Wooding & Watering—Whether the Stores are removing from the City into them—& whether any Regimental Baggage is Imbarked.

"Enquire also, how the Enemy are off for Provisions—whether the Cork Fleet is arrived. & the number of Provisions ships it consists of.

"Enquire also if Admiral Byrons Fleet is arrived—where Lord Howe & the New York Fleet is—whether within Sandy hook, or gone out to Sea, & for what purpose.

"Whether any Troops have been Imbarked lately & for what place. Whether any have arrived from England lately, or are expected.

"Whether the Merchants who came from Europe and those who have been attached to Government are packing up or selling off their goods. Attend particularly to Coffin and Anderson who keep a large dry goods Store and supply the Officers and Army" (DLC:GW).

## From Brigadier General Edward Hand

Sir                                         Lancaster [Pa.] 25th Augt 1778.

I have the Honour to inform your Excellency that I last Evening arrived here from Fort Pitt & in a very few days intend to wait on the board of war to give that Honorable Body a State of Affairs on the Western frontiers & settle the Accounts of that Departmt during my Command there, in the mean Time shall be happy to receive your Excellency's orders & am Sir with the greatest respect Yr Excellencys most obedt & most Humble servant

Edwd Hand

LB, DNA: RG 93, vol. 156, Letters Sent and Orderly Book, Brig. Gen. Edward Hand, Oct. 1776 and Apr.–Aug. 1778.

## From Major General Lafayette

Camp before Newport [R.I.]
My dear general                             25[–26] august 1778

I had expected for answering to your first letter that Some thing interesting would have happened that I might Communicate to your Excellency—every day was going to terminate our uncertainties—nay, every day was going to bring the hope of a succés which I did promise myself to acquaint you off—such was the Reason of my differing[1] what my duty and inclination did urge me to do much sooner—I am now indebted for two favors of yours which I beg leave to offer here my thanks for[2]—the first letter Reach'd me in the time we expected to hear again from the french fleet—the second I have just Receiv'd—my Reason for not writing the same day the french fleet went to boston, was that I did not choose to trouble your friendship with the sentiments of an afflicted, injur'd heart, and injur'd by that very people I came from so far to love and support. do'nt be Surpris'd, my dear general, the generosity of your honest mind would be offended at the schoking light I have under my eyes.

So far I am from a critical disposition that I will not give you the journal of our operations, neither of several instances during our staying here which however might occupy some room in this letter—I will not even say to you how contract'd was the french fleet when they wanted to come in at theyr arrival which according to the rapport of the desertors would have had the greatest effect, how surpris'd was the admiral—when after a made and agreed Convention, one hour after the American general had given a new writen assurance, our troops made the landing a day before it was expected—how mortified the french officers were to find out that there was not a gun left in these very forts to whose protection they were recommanded—all those things and many others I would not take notice of, if they were not in this moment the suppos'd ground upon which it is said that the count d'estaing is gone on to boston—believe me, my dear sir, upon my honor—the admiral tho' a little astonish'd by some instances of Conduct on our part, did Consider them in the same light as you and myself would have done, and if he is gone off it is because he thought himself oblig'd by necessity.

let us consider, my dear general, the motions of that fleet since it was propos'd by the count d'estaing himself and granted by the king in behalf of the united states—I wo'nt go so far up as to remember other instances of the affection the french nation have for the Americans—the news of that fleet has occasion'd the evacuation of philadelphia—its arrival has oppened all the harbours, secur'd all the coasts, oblig'd the british Navy to be together—six of those frigattes, two of them I have seen sufficient for terrifying all the trading people of the two Carolinas, are or taken or burnt—the Count d'estaing went to offer the battle and be a check to the british Navy for a long time at new york—it was agreed he schould go to Rhode island an[d] there he went—they prevented him from going in at first—afterwards he was desired to come in, and so he did—The same day we land'd without his knowledge, an english fleet appears in sight—

his being divided in three parts by *our directions* for tho' he is a *lieutenant general* he never avail'd himself of that title—did make him uneasy about his situation—but finding the next morning that the wind was northerly, being also convinc'd that it was his duty to prevent any Reinforcement At newport, he goes out under the hottest fire of the british land batteries, he puts the british Navy to flight, pursues them, and they were all in his hands when that horrid storm arrives to Ruin all our hopes—both fleets are divided, scattered—the Cæsar a 74 guns schip is lost—the Marseïllois of the same size looses her masts, and after that accident is oblig'd to send back a ennemy's schip of 64—the languedoc having lost her masts, unable to be govern'd, and make any motions, separated from the others, is attaqu'd by a schip of the line against which sche could only bring six guns.

when the storm was over, they met again in a schattered Condition, and the Cæsar was not to be found—all the Captains Represented to theyr general that after a so long navigation—in such a want of victuals, water, &c. which they had not been yet supplied with—after the intelligences given by General Sullivan that there was a british fleet coming they schould go to boston—but the count d'estaing had promis'd to come here again, and so he did at all events—the news of his arrival and situation came by the *Senegal* a frigatte taken from the ennemy—general greene and myself went on board—the count express'd to me not so much as to the envoy from general Sullivan, than as to his friend, the unhappy circumstances he was in—bound by express orders from the king to go to boston in case of an Accident or a superior fleet, engag'd by the common sentiment of all the officers *Even of some American pilots* that he would ruin all his Squadron in differing his going to boston, he call'd a new council of war, and finding every body of the same opinion, he did not think himself justifiable in staying here any more, and took leave of me with that true affliction of not being able to assist America for some days, which has been Rewarded with the most horrid ungratefulness—but no matter—I am only speacking of facts—the count said to me these last words—after many months of sufferings, my men may rest some days, I will mann my schips, and if I am assisted in getting masts &c. three weeks after my arrival, I schall go out again, and then we schall fight for the glory of the french name and the interests of America.

the day *the Count* went off the general american officers draw a protestation, which as *I had been very strangely call'd there*, I Refus'd to sign, but I wrote a letter to the admiral—the protestation and the letter did not arrive at time.[3]

Now, my dear general, I am going to hurt your generous feelings by an imperfect picture of what I am forc'd to see—forgive me for it—it is not to the Commander in chief, it is to my most dearest friend General Washington that I am speacking—I want to lament with him the ungenerous sentiments I have been forc'd to see in Many American breasts.

Could you believe that forgetting any national obligation, forgetting what they were owing to that same fleet, what they were yet to expect from them, and instead of Resenting theyrs accidents as these of allies and brothers, the people turn'd mad at theyr departure, and wishing them all the evils in the world did treat them as a generous one would be asham'd to treat the most inveterate ennemys—you ca'nt have any idea of the horrors which were to be heard in that occasion—many leaders themselves finding they were disapointed abandonn'd theyr minds to illiberality, and ungratefulness—frenchmen of the highest characters have been expos'd to the most disagreable Circumstances, and me, yes, myself the friend of America, the friend of General Washington, I am more upon a warlike footing in the American lines, than when I come near the british lines at newport—nay, many worthy characters, gentlemen to be entirely depended upon, assure me that the french hospital was abandonn'd as soon as the fleet went off, and that they could not find any body who would give them what they wanted—however they have been now sent to boston, and by a french man who met them I am inclin'd to think they will be very unhappy all the Rout.

Such is, my dear general, the true state of matters—I am sure it will infinetlly displease and hurt your feelings—I am also sure you will approuve the part I have taken in it, which was to stay much at home with all the french gentlemen who are here, and declare in the same time that anything thrown before me against my nation I would take as the most particular affront.

inclos'd I send you the general orders of the 24th upon which I thaught I was oblig'd to pay a visit to general Sullivan who has agreed to alter them in the following manner[4]—Remember, My dear general, that I do'nt speack to the Commander in chief, but to my friend, that I am far from Complaining of any body—I have no Complaints at all to make you against any one—but I lament with you that I have had a occasion of seeing so ungenerous sentiments in American hearts.

I will tell you the true Reason—the leaders of the expedition are most of them asham'd to Return after having spoken of theyr Rhode island succés in proud terms, before theyr family, theyr friends, theyr internal ennemies—The others Regardless of the expense france has been brought in by that fleet, of the tedious, tiresome voyage so many men have had for theyr service, tho' theyr Angry that the fleet takes three weeks upon the whole Campaign to Refitt themselves, Can not bear the idea of being brought to a small expense, to the loss of a little time, to the fatigue of staying some few days more in a camp, at some few miles from theyr houses—for I am very far to look upon the Expedition as miscarried, and there I see even a Certainty of succés.

if as soon as the fleet will be Repair'd which (in case they are treated as one is in a country one is not in war with) schall be done in three weeks from this time, the count d'estaing was to come arround, the expedition seems to offer a very good prospect—if the ennemy evacuates New york, we have the whole Continental army—if not we might perhaps have some more men, what however I ca'nt pretend to judge—all What I know is that I will be very happy to see the fleet Cooperating with general washington himself.

I think I will be forc'd by the board of general officers to go soon to boston—that I will do as soon as Requir'd tho' with Reluctance for I do'nt believe that *our position on this part of the island is without danger*—but my principle is to do every thing which is thaught good for the service—I very often have Rode express to the fleet, to the frigattes, and that I assure you with the greatest pleasure—on the other hand I may perhaps be useful to the fleet—perhaps too it will be in the power of the count to do something which might satisfy them—I wish, my dear general, you would know as well as myself how desirous is the Count d'estaing to forward the public good, to help to your Succés, and to serve the Cause of America!

I instantly beg you would Reccommend to the several chief persons of boston to do any thing they Can to put the french fleet in situation of sailing soon—give me leave to add that I wish many people by the declaration of your sentiments in that affair, could learn how to Regulate theyrs and blush at the sight of your generosity.

You will find my letter immense—I begun it one day and did finish the next as my time was swallow'd up, by those eternal Councils of war—I schall have the pleasure of writing you from boston—I am affraid the count d'estaing will have felt to the quick the behaviour of the people on this occasion—you Ca'nt Conceive how distress'd he was to be prevented from serving this country for some time—I do assure you his circumstances were very narrow and distressing.

for my part my sentiments are known to the world—my tender affection for general washington has yet added to them—therefore I do'nt want apologies for writing what has afflicted me as an american, and as a frenchman together.

I am much oblig'd to you for the Care you are so kind as to take of that poor horse of mine—had he not find such a good stable as this of head quarters he would have cut a pitiful figure at the end of his travels, and I would have been very happy if there had Remain'd so much of the horse as the bones, the skin, and the four schoes.

farewell, my dear general; when ever I quit you I meet with some disappointement and misfortune—I did not want it to desire seeing you as much as possible—with the most tender affection, and high Regard I have the honor to be your Excellency's the most obedient humble Servant

the Mis de lafayette

dear general

I must add to my letter that I have Receiv'd one from general greene very different from the expressions I have Right to complain of, and that he seems there very sensible of what I feel[5]—I am very happy when in situation of doing justice to any body.

ALS, PEL.

1. When Lafayette wrote "differing" here and later in this letter, he meant "deferring."

2. Lafayette is apparently referring to GW's letters of 10 and 19 August.

3. For the American officers' protest to Vice Admiral d'Estaing, 22 Aug., see John Sullivan to GW, 23 Aug., n.2. Lafayette's letter to d'Estaing of that date expressed his disapproval of the protest and sympathy for the admiral (see *Lafayette Papers*, 2:139).

4. The enclosed extract from Sullivan's general orders reads: "The General cannot help lamenting the sudden & unexpected departure of the French Fleet as he finds it has a tendency to discourage some who place great dependance upon the Assistance of it—tho he can by no means suppose the Army or any part of it in the least endangered by this Movement—the Enemy now on the Island are far inferior to this Army in Numbers and are so sensible of their inferiority that nothing can tempt them to an Action This Superiority we shall maintain so long as the Spirit and Ardour of Americans continue to be the same as it was at the Commencement of the Enterprize unless the Enemy recieve a strong Reeenforcement—this is the only Event which can oblige us to abandon any part of the Island we are now possessed of and this Event cant take place in an Instant—A Considerable Time will be required for a Fleet to come into the Harbour, come to an Anchor & land a Body of Troops sufficient to make the Number of the Enemy equal to ours, the Genl Assures the Army he has taken into Consideration Every event that can possibly happen to it & has guard[ed] in such a manner that in case of the most disagreeable Event (Viz.) that of a Retreat should take place it can be done with the utmost Safety, he is fully sensible of the Value those brave Officers Soldiers & Citizins he has the Honour to Command are to America and is determined that no rash Steps shall make a Sacrifice of them—at the same time he wishes them to place a proper Confidence in him as their Comr in Chief whose Business it is to attend to their Safety—he yet hopes the Event will ⟨pr⟩ove America able to procure that by our own Arms *which her Allies refuse to assist in Obtaining*—" (DLC:GW).

The alteration was given in Sullivan's general orders of 26 Aug., which announced that Sullivan had "the strongest reason to expect before any reinforcet arrives to oblige us to quit our present position that the French Fleet will return to cooperate with us in the reduction of the Island" and added, "It having been supposed by some persons that by the Orders of the 24th Inst. the Coma: in Chief meant to insinuate that the Departure of the French Fleet was owing to fixed determination not to assist in the present Enterprize—As the Genl would not wish to give the least Colour to ungenerous & illiberal Minds to make such unfair Interpretatio[ns] he thinks it necessary to say that as he could not possibly be acquainted with the Orders of the French Admiral he could not determine whether the removal of the Fleet was absolutely necessary or not & therefore did not mean to censure an Act which the Admirals Orders might render absolutely necessary: he however hopes that the speedy return of the Fleet will shew their attention & Regard to the Alliance form'd between us, and add to the Obligations which the Americans are already under to the French Nation.

"However mortifying the departure of the French Fleet to us at such time of Expectation we ought not too suddenly to censure the Movement or for an Act of any kind to forget the Aid & protection which has been afforded us by the French since the commencement of the present Contest" (DLC:GW).

5. This letter has not been identified.

## To Henry Laurens

Sir, White plains—Augt 25th 1778.

If it be practicable, and convenient for Congress to furnish me with some Specie (gold, as more portable, would be most convenient) valuable purposes I think would result from it. I have always found a difficulty in procuring Intelligence by the mean of Paper money. and I perceive that it increases. The period is critical & interesting, and the early knowledge of an Enemys intention, and movements too obvious to need explanation.

Having hinted to the Comee of Congress when at Valley forge this want I address this Letter to you *now* rather as a private than public one—because I do not wish to have the matter again mentioned if Congress hath been apprized of my wants & find it inconvenient to comply with them.

I have the pleasure to inform you that Colo. Laurens was well on the 23d—I have had a Letter from him of that date. with great respect & regard I have the honr to be Dr Sir Yr Most Obedt Hble Servt

Go: Washington

ADfS, DLC:GW; Varick transcript, DLC:GW. A nineteenth-century transcript, presumably made from the letter sent, shows minor verbal differences with no change of meaning (ScHi: Henry Laurens Papers).

## To Henry Laurens

Sir Head Qrs White plains Augt 25th 1778

Inclosed you will be pleased to receive a Copy of a Letter of the 23d Instant from General Sullivan, which came to hand about half after three OClock this morning, with the several papers to which it refers,

Copies of which are also transmitted.[1] By these Congress will perceive, our prospects are much changed with respect to the operations against Rhode Island, and that the issue, as things are now circumstanced, whether we look to a continuation of the Siege—to an immediate attack or a Retreat, must be attended with great difficulty and risk. I trust the wisest measures will be pursued & I will hope for the best. I have the Honor to be with the greatest respect & esteem sir Yr Most Obedt sert

Go: Washington

P.S. Genl Sullivan I think, must be under a mistake, as to the amount of the relief, which the Enemy had attempted to give from York. I have used every possible means to obtain information from time to time on this head, and I never could learn, either from Deserters or others who had been in the City, that any Troops had embarked, since the reinforcement sent up the sound long ago, except some drafts to act in the fleet as Marines.[2]

LS, in Robert Hanson Harrison's writing, DNA:PCC, item 152; Df, DLC:GW; copy, DNA:PCC, item 169; Varick transcript, DLC:GW. Congress read this letter on 28 Aug. and responded with resolutions (see *JCC*, 11:848–49).

1. The enclosed copies of Maj. Gen. John Sullivan's letter and "the several papers" are in DNA:PCC, item 152.

2. For discussion of the "reinforcement sent up the sound long ago," see Sullivan to GW, 20 July, and note 1 to that document.

*Letter not found*: from Maj. Benjamin Tallmadge, 25 Aug. 1778. On 25 Aug., GW wrote Tallmadge: "I shall be glad to see you upon the business mentioned in yours of this date."

## To Major Benjamin Tallmadge

Sir,                                    Camp [White Plains] Augt 25th 1778.

I shall be glad to see you upon the business mentioned in yours of this date.[1] If Colo. Sheldon is acquainted with W—— and the circumstances as you have related them to me, let him come also—You should be perfectly convinced of the Integrety of W—— previous to his imbarking in the business proposed—this being done I shall be happy in employing him—but there will be an impropriety in his coming with you to head Quarters, as a knowledge of that circumstance in the enemy might blast the whole design.[2]

You will let me see you this afternoon—if you can come to Dinner at three Oclock I shall be glad of Yr Companies. I am Sir Yr Very Hble Servt

Go: Washington

ALS, Lathrop C. Harper, Inc., catalog, NS no.1 (n.d.), item 113. GW's closing and signature are in the left margin of the letter.

1. Tallmadge's letter has not been found.
2. "W——" may have been Abraham Woodhull (1750–1826) of Setauket, N.Y., who by October 1778 was sending intelligence to Tallmadge under the pseudonym "Samuel Culper, Sr." Tallmadge wrote in his memoir that "This year (1778) I opened a private correspondence with some persons in New York (for Gen. Washington) which lasted through the war. . . . I kept one or more boats continually employed in crossing the Sound on this business" (Tallmadge, *Memoir*, 29).

## From Major Thomas Wickes

Huntington [Long Island, N.Y.] Augt 25th 1778
Sir                                              Tuesday Evening 7 Oclock
This moment I received Inteligence that all the Troops in Suffolk County and on Loyds are ordered to march to the Westard, the troops at Huntington marched this Morning, Tryon is on his march, this Sudden movement: is in Consequence of Some Ships Said to be french Ships in the Sound they are in the Greatest hurry, they Was Impressing teams all Last Night Tryon is Expected to be at Brookhaven this Night,[1] I am in the Woods and Without Candle Light I am Obliged to Close this Imperfect Letter. I am Your Excellencys Most obdt and Very humbe Sert
Thos Wickes

ALS, DLC:GW. The cover indicates that this letter was sent "Pr Express."

Thomas Wickes (1744–1819) had been a captain of the 1st Regiment of Suffolk County militia in May 1776 and was apparently a major at this time. He represented Suffolk County in the New York general assembly, 1777–83.

1. Lloyd Neck, on the north shore of Long Island, is about four miles north of Huntington. Brookhaven was a name used for the modern community of Setauket on the north coast of Long Island and should not be confused with the current town of Brookhaven, nearer the south coast of Long Island.

## General Orders

Head-Quarters W. Plains Wednesday Augt 26th 1778.
Parole Georgia—                          C. Signs Gibralter—Gosport.
Guards are to be placed at proper distances in front and Rear of the Brigades to see that the soldiers make use of the Vaults prepared for them; The Purity of the Air and Wholesomness of the Camp depend so much upon the observance of this order that it is expected it will be strictly attended to and every soldier severely punished who is found guilty of a breach of it.

The Brigade Quarter Masters are immediately to have racks fixed up to prevent the great Waste of·Forage, occasioned by feeding upon the ground. they are likewise to see that the Waggoners remove the dung and Litter once a Week & burn it.

The Pay-Masters who have not received Pay for their regiments for April & May are to apply to the Pay-Master General tomorrow.

The Commanding Officer of each Company is to keep an exact Size-Roll by which his men are to be drawn up in a single rank, sizing from right to left the tallest being on the right and the shortest on the left, then doubling towards the Center, the Whole is to be thrown into two Ranks the shortest in the Front and the tallest in the Rear Rank.

In all firings the Words "*Take Sight!*["] are to be substituted in Place of the Word of Command "*Present!*["]

Varick transcript, DLC:GW.

# From a Board of General Officers

White Plains, Augt 26. 1778.

Report of the Board of General Officers—

The Board recommend it to be inserted in General Orders, that half a Gill of Rice per Diem be issued, three Times a Week, in Lieu of one Quarter of a Pound of Flour; there being a large Quantity of Rice in Store; more in Proportion than Flour.

The Board also request Your Excellency to repeat, in General Orders, the strict Injunction against any Horses being kept in, or near the Camp, by Persons unauthorised to have a Horse, or Horses maintained at the Public Expence. The Officers commanding Divisions, Brigades, and Regiments, to be answerable for an exact Obedience being paid to this Order.

The Board further recommend it to your Excellency to order all Horses belonging to the United-States, now in Possession of any Person, or Persons not entitled to the same, nor allowed Forage from the Public Magazine, to be forthwith returned to the Qarter Master General, or his Deputy: and that it be forbidden all Persons whatsoever to make Use of any of the Waggon Horses as riding Horses, but by express Order in writing signed by the Officer commanding the Brigade to which such Horse or Horses may belong. This to be enjoined under a severe Penalty.

The Board, in Consequence of Your Excellency's Representation this Morning[1] are clearly of Opinion that the Words, Take Sight, be introduced into the Manual Exercise instead of the Word Present: and that in sizing the Men by Companies, the shortest Men be placed in the Front

Rank; and the tallest in the Rear Rank: each Rank to be sized from Right and Left, to the Center.

Horatio Gates<br>
president

DS, DLC:GW; Df, NHi: Gates Papers.

  1. GW's representation may have been verbal. No such letter has been found.

## From Captain Epaphras Bull

Maroneck [N.Y.]

May it Please your Excellency—        26th Augt 1778

   there has passed by this Place to the Wtward, to day 3 Sloops & one Schooner Loaded with Hay—& one Row Gally, 2 Brigs & one Sloop from the Eastward come to anchor this afternoon Just Et of Hempstead Harbour, and as far Etward as I can see, appears to be 8 or 10 Sail Vessels, believe shall be able to give an Acct of them Tomorrow.[1]

   I have the Honour to present your Excellency with 20 or 30 wt Blackfish they are now in a ⟨Car⟩, shoud be glad to know when 'twil best suit to send them up, I am your Excellencys Most Obt Hble sert

Epaps Bull

ALS, DLC:GW. Tench Tilghman docketed this letter in part: "from Capt. Bull and Lieut. Hurlbutt." George Hurlbut (c.1756–1783) of New London, Conn., who had served in 1776 as an ensign in the 19th Continental Infantry, was commissioned a cornet in the 2d Continental Dragoons in April 1777 and promoted to lieutenant in December of that year. Promoted to captain in August 1779, Hurlbut was wounded near Tarrytown on 15 July 1781, and he died of those wounds two years later. On 8 Dec. 1788 GW gave a certificate testifying to the circumstances of Hurlbut's death and stating that his heirs should be entitled to the commutation of his half pay (see *Papers, Presidential Series*, 1:107).

  1. Hempstead Harbor is the bay most immediately west of Glen Cove on the north shore of Long Island.

## From Major Alexander Clough

[New Jersey]

Sr          wedensday night 10 oClock [26 August 1778]

   I had the honour to recive your letter at ten last night,[1] at two this morning I marcht for Bergan, to collect what intelligence I could. The Gentlemen mentiond in my instructions have not made any preparation to leave the town—the waggons are on long Iseland which prevents my informent giveing a perticular Acct of them. in a few days I Expect to be more fully inform'd—On Sunday morning a detachment from the corps of Artillery with twelve field peaces march to join Genl Tryon, who is driveing cattle from the east end of Long Iseland, the Cheaf part of thayr heavy Artillery, & Ordinnances stores, are put on board transports laying at red hook, likewise a large quantity of forage. the whole of the transports are wooded, and watter'd, for six months. the above acct is conferm'd by three sailers who deserted from them last night I have not been able to learn that any regementall baggage has been put on board—The Greens are orderd to hold them selves in readiness to embark on the shortest notice, it is suposed for the west Indeas. Lord Howe saild yesterday morning from the Hook, it is said for rode Iseland, in the afternoon a heavy fireing was heard to the southward of Staten Iseland. the day before two frigates where chace't in to the Hook by a part of the french fleet. nothing has been heard of Adml Byron. two of the cork fleet are come in, and thirty are taken by the french.[2] there are no troops arive'd naither is there any expected—It is generly belived in New york the army will stay till other proposeles are made by the commisoners then to Embark with all Expedition—the Gentleman who gives me this intelligance is a person of varacity and posest of A Gentell fortune which makes me rely more on his information then on that of many others. I am your Exellencys Most Obt

A. Clough

ALS, DLC:GW. Tench Tilghman wrote "26 Augt 1778" below Clough's dateline, and Tilghman's docket for the letter conveyed the same information.
　　1. See GW to Clough, 25 August.
　　2. The "ship Sibelis, with the Cork fleet under her convoy," arrived off Sandy Hook on 25 Aug. (Rivington's *Royal Gazette*, 26 Aug.; see also Whinyates, *Services of Francis Downman*, 78; *Kemble Papers*, 1:161; and Ritchie, "New York Diary," 270).

## From Major General William Heath

Dear General　　　　　　　　　Head Quarters Boston 26th Augt 1778
　　Nearly our whole time for several weeks has been taken up in forwarding provisions, Stores &c. to Rhode Island, and in order to accelerate the operations of the Expedition we have sent to that place all the provisions that could possibly be spared from the Magazines, in particular Flour, of which upwards of 1000 Barrels have been forwarded. The unexpected destination of the Count D'Estaing's Squadron to this place will I fear be not a little embarrassing on that account, as it is reported that they are short of bread. I have wrote Mr Colt and desired him to send on a quantity of flour with the utmost expedition. The Cesar only has as yet arrived; the whole Fleet are hourly expected.[1]
　　It is truly unfortunate that circumstances would not admit this Squadron to have remained at Rhode Island to co-operate with our

Army in the reduction of that place—the prospect of which was promising—the Seige will now most probably for a time be turned into a Blockade. But it is surprising to hear the unguarded and imprudent expressions & writings of many on this occasion, the severe reflections which are thrown out I fear will give umbrage and if care is not taken wound our great & good Cause. From the unthinking Multitude some indiscreet or unguarded expressions may be expected—I wish they may be from such only.

I have offered every assistance in my power to the Officers who have already arrived. I shall extend it with every mark of respect to those who are expected. Every step is already taken to refit the fleet, a Vessel some days since was dispatched for Spars &c. I have the honor to be With the greatest respect Your Excellency's Most Obedt Servt

W. Heath

LS, DLC:GW; ADfS, MHi: Heath Papers.

1. The *César*, which had become separated from the French fleet during the storm of 11 and 12 Aug., anchored at Boston on 22 August.

## From Lieutenant George Hurlbut

New Rochel [N.Y.]
May it please your Excellency                    26th August 78

I am set down to report the occurrences of the Day—Early this morning discoverd 16 Ships, Anchored off frogs point, Several of them appeared to be very large—upon my Return, two Boat loads, of the Inhabitants of City Island, attempted to cut off my Retreat—receivd sundry shotts from them—at 2 P.M. 2 large Briggs, & Sloop, from the Eastward, Anchored off, near Huntington Harbour, near the same time, 6 Small Vessels, supposed to be foragers—went to the Eastward—I have the Honor, to be your Excellencys most Obedient Hbl. Servt

george Hurlbut,
Lieut. 2nd Regt Lt D——

ALS, CSmH: Grenville Kane Collection.

## From Brigadier General William Maxwell

Sir                              Elizth Town [N.J.] 26th Augt 1778

Your Excellency may depend on the following; as I have it from a Gentle Man of Varacity that came from Long Island yesterday Viz. Lord

How went the day before yesterday off Barren Island[1] out of the Hook and that day 4 Regts went down Long Island one of them Turnbuls, new levys, they said they were going on board of the Fleet to act as Marines but an express follow'd them that night, and they returned next morning.[2] These Troops returning gives room for speculation there, either that Rhode Island is taken, or that they give asisting of it over. above 20 pieces of Cannon was fired yesterday out of the Hook, the Colours hoisted at the light House &C. and shortly after 15 or 20 Sail was seen standing into the Hook. General Tryon is returned to Jamica from the East of the Island with every thing he could find Eatable. I am your Excellencys Most Obedt Humble Servt

Wm Maxwell

ALS, DLC:GW.

1. Barren Island is in Brooklyn at the outlet of Jamaica Bay, where Floyd Bennett airfield is now.

2. Lt. Col. George Turnbull commanded the New York Volunteers. A native of Scotland, Turnbull was commissioned as a lieutenant in the British army in February 1756 and rose to captain of the 60th Regiment of Foot in November 1765, but he sold his commission and left the army between 1774 and 1776, settling in New York. As a captain in the Loyal American Regiment, Turnbull participated in the capture of Fort Montgomery in October 1777, and he was commissioned a lieutenant colonel a few days later. He remained in command of the New York Volunteers until the end of the war. Gen. Henry Clinton's after-orders at 9 P.M. on 23 Aug. directed the New York Volunteers and the British 15th and 46th Regiments to march to New Utrecht on the morning of 24 Aug., but new orders at 3 P.M. on that date directed that the two British regiments "return again to their former Encampments as soon as convenient" (order book, 24 May 1778–2 July 1779, MiU-C: Clinton Papers).

# General Orders

Head-Quarters W. Plains Thursday August 27th 1778.
Parole New-Hampshire　　　　　　　　　C. Signs Newark Norway.

As the late Order respecting Brigade Inspectors of the day renders their duty very unequal, the Commander in Chief directs, that they be daily appointed in orders in regular rotation.

Captn John Alexander is appointed Pay-Master Lieutenant John McCullan Adjutant and Lieut. John Hughes Quarter-Master to 7th Pennsylvania Regiment[1] These appointments to bear date from the 1st day of June last when they were made.

Captain Joseph Howell of the 2nd Pennsylvania Regt is appointed Pay-Master to the same.[2]

The Colonels and Officers commanding Corps are desir'd to return to Head-Quarters, with all the Accuracy they can, a list of the names of all the Officers who have served in their respective Corps at any time since the 1st of January 1777—and the present day, in which they will specify their ranks and the dates of their Commissions; and also such promotions and removals as have happened, whether by reason of death, Resignation or from other Causes—All Corps now in service in the Continental Line are comprehended in this order.[3] The honorable the board of War want these lists & wish to obtain them as soon as they can be made out.

Half a Gill of Rice pr Ration is to be issued to the Army three times a Week in lieu of one quarter of a pound of flour which is on those days to be deducted from the usual Rations.

The General again in the most positive and express terms forbids any person whatever keeping a horse or horses in or near Camp, who are not properly authorized by the Regulations of the Army or by his special Permission to keep horses maintained at the Public Expence; The necessity of a strict Compliance with this order is obvious & Officers commanding Divisions, Brigades and Regiments will in a particular manner be responsible for the most exact obedience.

All horses belonging to the Public in the Possession of any Person not entitled to them by Public Authority are forthwith to be returned to the Quarter-Master General or his Deputy.

The making use of Waggon horses as riding horses is strictly forbidden unless by a written order signed by the Commanding Officer of the Brigade to which the horses belong; Any Person guilty of a breach of this order may depend on being severely punished.

All Persons who have horses belonging to the Public in their Possession for their own use are without fail to make return of them to the Qr Master General by saturday noon next; The utmost punctuality will be expected.[4]

After Orders.

A board of Field Officers consisting of—Lieutt Coll Cropper Major Wallace from Genl Woodford's Brigade—Coll Davis Lieutt Coll Ball from Genl Muhlenberg's—Coll Wood Majr Clark[5] from General Scott's, are to sit tomorrow to settle the relative Rank of the Field Officers and Captains of the Virginia Line; One Officer at least from each Regiment is to attend the board to give Information. The Brigadiers of the Virginia line are to appoint a board of Officers consisting of an equal number from each Brigade to settle the relative Ranks of the Subalterns.

Each of those boards are to ascertain the dates which the Commissions are to bear—and make a return of them to the Committee of Arrangement sitting at Head-Quarters that the Register may be as compleat as possible.

The Commanding Officer of the New York Brigade and the Colonels or Commanding Officers of Battalions are to attend the Committee of Arrangement tomorrow morning nine ôClock at Head-Quarters.

Varick transcript, DLC:GW.

1. John Alexander (1753–1804), who was commissioned a second lieutenant of the 6th Pennsylvania Regiment in January 1776 and promoted to first lieutenant the next month, became a captain of the 7th Pennsylvania Regiment in March 1777. He remained with the regiment through its consolidation into the 4th Pennsylvania Regiment in January 1781 but resigned in July of that year. John McCullam was commissioned an ensign of the 7th Pennsylvania Regiment in March 1777 and promoted to second lieutenant in September of that year. Promoted to first lieutenant in April 1779, he remained with the 7th (later 4th) Pennsylvania Regiment until it was disbanded on 1 Jan. 1783. Then he joined the 2d Pennsylvania Regiment, where he served until June 1783. McCullam remained regimental adjutant until June 1779. John Hughes (1754–1804), who served in 1776 as a sergeant and ensign in the 6th Pennsylvania Regiment, became an ensign of the 7th Pennsylvania Regiment in January 1777 and was promoted to second lieutenant in September of that year. Promoted to first lieutenant in April 1779, Hughes served to the close of the war.

2. Joseph Howell, Jr. (c.1750–1798), was appointed a captain of the Pennsylvania Musket Battalion in March 1776. Taken prisoner on Long Island on 27 Aug. 1776, he was exchanged on 9 Dec. 1776 and became a captain in the 2d Pennsylvania Regiment later that month. He resigned from the army in October 1778. On 27 April 1779 Congress elected Howell to be an auditor of the army. In 1783 he was appointed as a deputy to the paymaster general and commissioner of army accounts, and he became commissioner in 1788. He was accountant of the War Department, 1792–95.

3. For an example of the lists prepared pursuant to this order, see "A Return of the Commission'd Officers belonging to the Corps Commanded lately by Collonell Armand, at present Commanded by Captn Antoni Selin August 28th 1778" (DLC:GW).

4. A number of reports in response to this order can be found in DNA:PCC, item 173.

5. Jonathan Clark (1750–1811), who was commissioned a captain in the 8th Virginia Regiment on 23 Jan. 1776, became a major of the 12th Virginia Regiment in January 1778. Promoted in May 1779 to lieutenant colonel of the regiment, which had been redesignated the 8th Virginia Regiment, Clark was taken prisoner at Charleston on 12 May 1780, and he remained a prisoner on parole at the end of the war.

# From Lieutenant Caleb Brewster

Sir　　　　　　　　　　　　　　　　　　Norwalk [Conn.] August 27th 1778

When I left Long Island this Morning Governor Tryon was at Millers place with about three hundred Troops[1] and the Main body at Brookhaven about nine Miles to the Westward under the Command of Genl Delancey; The whole party consists of a thousand men. The Party under the Command of Tryon are within half a mile of the Sound, those under the Command of Delancey a mile & a half; the Parties arrived there yesterday morning and Pitched their Tents. They have large Droves of Cattle with them and are Collecting on their March all that are fit to Kill; I was so near them that I Saw them Pitch their Camp & also saw the Cattle.

The troops Stationed at Huntington & Loyds Neck have Some of them Marched to the westward, and the remainder are under Marching orders.

The Fleet That lay at Huntington harbour, Come to Sail this morning and are Standing to the Westward, in all Six and Twenty or thirty Sail; The above is the Fleet that was ordered to Rhode Island, but hearing on the Island that some of the French Fleet were coming into the Sound they have put to the Westward.[2]

On the first of this Week Several Regiments Crossed from Newyork to Brookline Ferry, and Encamped.

There is no Arrival of Admiral Byrons or the Cork Fleet at New york or any other Vessels whatever—Admiral Hows Fleet have arrived at the Hook to the Amount of Twenty Sail, three of which have got up to Town (to witt) The Isis of fifty Guns, The Renown of Sixty four, The Appollo Thirty Six. The Isis and Renown attacked two Seventy fours and are Much Shattered; The Appollo Lost all her Masts and is otherwise Much Damaged. They have taken Many of their Heavy Cannon on board at Newyork. The Transports lie in the road with their Sails Bent, are Wooding and Watering, and it is the opinion of all the Inhabitants of the Citty, that they will soon evacuate the Town. I am with all due respect your Excelencys most obedient and Humble Servt

Caleb Brewster Lieut.

ALS, DLC:GW. In this letter, Brewster was evidently reporting intelligence gathered pursuant to GW's undated directions for "particular observations to be made by persons going into N—— Y——" (see GW to Maj. Alexander Clough, 25 Aug., n.2).

1. Miller Place is on the north coast of Long Island about seven miles east of Setauket (Brookhaven).

2. British major John André, who was with the fleet that loaded troops on 27 Aug. at Whitestone, Long Island, for the relief of Rhode Island, noted in his journal for 28 Aug.: "The *Rose* and *Raven* with a considerable number of sloops and schooners joined us; their destination was Rhode Island, but in fear of falling in with the French, they had to put into Huntingdon Bay" (André, *Journal*, 85).

## From Captain Epaphras Bull

Sir                                               Maroneck [N.Y.] Augt 27th 1778
    I have to acquaint your Excellency that the two Brigs & Sloop which Anchored near Hempstead Harbour Last Night, to day made Sail &

went down, the Sloop was Armed Carrying 12 guns, the Brigs were not, but deeply Loaded, two Sloops past Wtward with Hay—the Vessels which I discovered yesterday, far Etward have made very Little Progress to day, they this Evening appeard to be Standing in to Oyster Bay, near which there is a Small Encampment, which in some of my former Reports, I made mention of to your Excellency,[1] there is about twenty five Sail of them four of which appear to be Ships—I am your Excellencys most Obt Hble Sert

Epaps Bull

ALS, DLC:GW.
1. These "former Reports" have not been identified.

## To Brigadier General Duportail

Sir,                          Head Quarters White plains 27 Augt 1778
You will proceed as speedily as convenient to the Highlands and examine the several fortifications carrying on there for the defence of the North River. When you have done this you will make me a full report of their state and progress, with your opinion of any alterations or additions which may appear to you necessary in improvement of the present plan. In doing this, you will of course consider the labor and expence which have been already incurred—the advanced season of the year & the resources of the Country for carrying any plan which may be formed into execution.

It is my wish you should also take measures without delay for executing the Instructions given you the [    ] of June last relative to a plan for the defence of the River Delaware and the city of Philadelphia[1]—in performing which, you will also view the subject in a maritime point of light; in order as far as natural circumstances will permit, to provide a secure Port, capable of excluding the enemys vessels and receiving and protecting our own or those of our allies—To this end you will make such arrangements as the state of your department and the good of the service will best warrant. I am &c.

Df, in Alexander Hamilton's writing, DLC:GW; Varick transcript, DLC:GW. The dateline and complimentary close on the draft are in Tench Tilghman's writing.
1. See GW to Duportail, 30 June.

## From Lieutenant George Hurlbut

Sir                          New Rochel, 27th Augst 78
I am set down to inform your Excellency, the two Brigs, & Sloop, I mention'd in my last,[1] have past this place, came to Anchor nere frogs

point, soon after—One Sloop of force, & three Sloops, with forrage, went to the Westward—Just before sunset, 24. Sale, came to Anchor off Auster [Oyster] Bay; three ships appeard to be of force, hope I shall be able to Report, in my next, more peticular[2]—I am with Respect your Excellencys most Obdt Hbl. Servt

Go: Hurlbut

ALS, DLC:GW.

1. See Hurlbut to GW, 26 August.

2. At Whitestone, Long Island, on 27 Aug. twenty transports embarked over 4,000 British troops destined to relieve Rhode Island. The fleet got under way between five and six in the afternoon and anchored off City Island that evening. The fleet remained at anchor until the early evening of the 28th, when the ships again got under way and sailed a few leagues westward before coming to anchor around midnight roughly opposite Rye, New York. There contrary winds forced them to remain until the morning of 30 Aug., when the fleet, which by that time consisted of thirty-two ships of war and transports accompanied by numerous small vessels, again weighed anchor (see André, *Journal*, 84–86; Gruber, *Peebles' American War*, 211–13; Lydenberg, *Robertson Diaries*, 181). Various reports sent to GW on those dates from Hurlbut, Capt. Epaphras Bull, and Brig. Gen. Charles Scott give intelligence about the fleet's movements.

*Letter not found*: from Col. William Malcom, 27 Aug. 1778. On 29 Aug., GW wrote Malcom: "I have recd yours of the 27th inclosing a weekly return of the Garrison."

# From Brigadier General William Maxwell

Sir                                    Elizth Town [N.J.] 27th August 1778

I have the pleasure to Inclose to Your Excellency Major Howels Journal.[1] I have it confirmed by another channel that the 7 Vessels of the Cork Fleet is arived, the day before yesterday; and that Lord How Sailed with his Fleet the same day to the Eastward; this is all I have at present only that I have Just got another Packet from the Commissioners to Congress and sent it on[2]—I am Your Excellencys Most Obedient Humble Servt

Wm Maxwell

ALS, DLC:GW.

1. Maj. Richard Howell's letter to Maxwell of 26 Aug. reported on ship movements from 18 to 25 Aug., of which the most significant were that on 20 Aug. "The fleet was anchor'd off the Hook & afterwards 2 frigates were sent out ⟨as⟩ suppos'd, on a Cruise of Observation"; on 21 Aug. "A large Ship anchor'd off the point . . . said to be one of Birons Fleet, but more probably one of Ld Howes, as 'twas said one large ship of his fleet was missing"; and on 25 Aug. "The fleet hove in View. . . . Observ'd 27 sail moving to the Eastward 24 suppos'd to be ships 2 snows 1 brig & a Schooner. at the same Time, a fleet of 7 sail came in from Europe—6 ships & a Brig—One only

of those Ships appeard to be a fighting Vessel And she suppos'd by some to be only an arm'd transport. I think one was a frigate with a fleet of Victuallers under Convoy: I am told that by this fleets saluting with 13 Guns & Admiral How's returning 14 Guns, there must have been an Admiral on board." Howell added other intelligence: "I am told that the french Admiral was engaged and, Night coming on, before Morning several other french Vessels were come up, which made the brittish ship retire. That a 50 attack'd a french 74 & would have carried her *but*, She fled, and the 50's Rigging being much damag'd, she could not give Chase. And that Commodre Hothman engagd a french 84 with a 50 & would have Carried her, *but* some others came to her Assistance—The Enemy at the Hook are very quiet—I sent out two men who were to pass for Deserters & Join the Wood Tories, but could not Join them from their Caution, having been deceiv'd before. Since that Measure was defeated, I now propose to go down by Night & surround a swamp in which they are from the best Intelligence, And burn their cabbins at least." On the cover he noted: "There was a heavy firing at Sea Yesterday and a ship came in dismasted supposd to be a bomb Ketch. the French are at Rhode Island" (DLC:GW).

2. For the contents of the packet of 26 Aug. from the British peace commissioners, see Henry Laurens to GW, 29 Aug., n.3.

*Letter not found*: from Brig. Gen. Peter Muhlenberg, 27 Aug. 1778. On 27 Aug., Tench Tilghman wrote Muhlenberg: "His Excellency has recd yours of this date."

*Letter not found*: to Brig. Gen. Gold Selleck Silliman, 27 Aug. 1778. On 14 Sept., Silliman wrote GW: "Your Favour of the 27th Ult. respecting a Guard at the Commissary's Stores at the Landing in this Town I received the 2d Instant."

# From Jonathan Trumbull, Sr.

Sir                                    Lebanon [Conn.] August 27th 1778
The Act of the General Assembly of this State for raising the two Battalions commanded by Colonels Enos, and McClellen provides, That the Battalions, or any Detachment therefrom, shall not be continued in actual service more than three months at any one time, to be compleated from the time they shall arrive at the place of their Destination[1]—The exigency of the case requiring, they were ordered to march by Companies, as they could be raised and equipped—of course arrived at the place of Destination at different periods of time—(viz.) between the 1st and 20th of June last. Have therefore to request Your Excellency, if the public service permit, to dismiss said Battalions, to return home together, the 5th of Septemr next, as thereby the men, who are generally farmers, will be enabled to sow their fields, and provide substance for themselves and families, another year, which, otherwise, must be untilled and neglected—many of the Militia being called into Service in the State of Rhode-Island—great part of labourers, absent, and very few to be hired.[2]

Those two Battalions to continue untill 1st March next, to have a recess as mentioned—to grant it at the time mentioned, and to all at once, may be beneficial—They may be called soon, if needful—their present station is at West Point. I am, with great Esteem & Regard Sir your Obedient humble Servant

Jonth. Trumbull

ALS, DLC:GW; LB, Ct: Trumbull Papers. The cover of the ALS is marked "Favoured ℔ Capt. [Seth] Harding."

1. Trumbull was referring to "An Act for raising two Brigades for the Defence of this State," February 1778 (*Conn. Public Records*, 1:533–35).

2. The Connecticut council of safety, in their meeting of 26 Aug., had directed Trumbull to make this request (see ibid., 2:115–16).

## From Jonathan Trumbull, Sr.

Sir                                           Lebanon [Conn.] 27th August 1778

I received your favor of the 8th instant, requesting that the Fleet under the Command of Count D'Estaing might be supplied with Water from New-London, for which I gave immediate Orders; and sundry Vessels were employed in that business, by which conclude they were, and might still have been sufficiently supplied with that very necessary article, had they continued on that Station—but alas! contrary to our expectation, the Count, with the whole of his Fleet, are with drawn, and gone to Boston to repair the Damages they recieved in the late heavy gale, and this, notwithstanding the entreaties of General Sullivan, and the other General Officers, to the contrary—of which event Your Excellency hath undoubtedly been advised before this—The consequence I fear, will be, that we shall be obliged to evacuate Rhode Island—Thus are our raised expectations, from an Expedition, which had all the appearance of Success, damped—This shews us that we ought not to place our dependence too much on foreign Aid; but may such a disappointment teach us to place our trust and confidence in that Supreme Being who governs the Universe, and can, with infinite ease, turn those things which, we are ready to conclude, are against us, eventually to our advantage, in whose all-wise disposals may we chearfully acquiesce, and rest satisfied that whatever he doth is right.

I must now beg leave to turn Your Attention to a case of peculiar, and accumulated distress—I mean the distressed situation of the Inhabitants of Westmoreland on the Susquehanna, who survived the more than barbarian cruelty of the Indians and Tories, which, in conjunction, they wreaked[1] on that unhappy place, in beginning of July last, slaying above 300 Men, and driving more than 3,000 Inhabitants, mostly Women and Children, from their before peaceful Habitations, after having stripped and plundered them of all the necessaries of Life, burning and destroying all their buildings, and carrying off all their Cattle and other Live-Stock—leaving them in the most destitute, and deplorable circumstances—a particular representation whereof hath lately been laid before me by Messrs Jenkins, Gallup and Harding— Persons of integrity, who removed from the Eastern part of this State, and settled at said Westmoreland, and had the good fortune to escape the Carnage[2]—they also inform, that at the time the Inhabitants came off, there was on the ground large and very valuable Crops of English and Indian Corn, which must inevitably be lost, unless speedy measures be taken to prevent it.

Your Excellency hath undoubtedly been made acquainted with the Distresses of this People, and felt the tenderest emotions for them, and a willingness to afford them all the relief in your power, consistent with the safety and good of the whole.

I have this day wrote to Congress on the Subject,[3] and proposed to their consideration, whether it would not be advisable that a sufficient Force, to consist of 1500, or 2,000 men, be immediately sent into that part of the Country, under whose protection the Inhabitants would return, and secure their Crops, which would be an important acquisition, and also to pursue that detestable Banditti into their own Country— chastise them for their insolence and cruelty exercised towards the innocent Inhabitants aforementioned, and effectually prevent their making any further Depredations on that, or any other of our back settlem⟨ents.⟩ Such measure, I am persuaded, would produce ⟨the⟩ happiest effects—would recommend this Affair to Your Excellency's Consideration; and wish, in case the state of the Army, and present appearances of things will permit, that Your Excellency would order a sufficient number—to be detached from the Continental Army, and employed for the purpose aforesaid. I am, with Esteem & Regard Sir your most Obedient humble Servant

Jonth. Trumbull

ALS, DLC:GW; ADfS, CtHi: Jonathan Trumbull, Sr., Papers; LB, Ct: Trumbull Papers. The cover of the ALS is marked, "Favoured ⅌ Capt. Harding." Seth Harding (1734–1814) was traveling to Philadelphia in pursuit of a naval commission and carried the letter cited in note 3 below. Where the ALS is mutilated, the characters in angle brackets have been taken from the letter-book copy.

1. Both the letter-book copy and the draft have "savagely wreaked" at this point.

2. Trumbull may have been referring to John Jenkins of the Exeter District and William Gallup (1723–1803) or Hallet Gallup of the Kingston District, each of whom signed an April 1780 petition to the Connecticut legislature praying for relief for the Wyoming refugees (*Susquehanna Company Papers*, 7:59–62). There were

a number of Hardings in the area, most notably Capt. Stephen Harding (1723–1789) of the Exeter District.

3. See Trumbull to Henry Laurens, 27–31 Aug. 1778, in DNA:PCC, item 66.

## From Major Thomas Wickes

Sir                                        Huntington [N.Y.] Augt 27th 1778

I have Just Receivd the Following Intelegence From Newyork, Yesterday morning Lord Hows fleet Consisting of about twenty Sail, went out of Sandyhook its Said he is, Bound to Rhode Island, its further Reported that two Expresses had arrived at newyork from Rhode Island, for him to Come to there releaf, one was an open boat, She Came in at the hook, Its Generaly believed by our friends in Newyork that Sir Harry Clinton is about to make a Movement, but Every thing is keept Exceeding Secret they are Getting there Waggons down to the North river they are a ⟨shewing⟩ [shoeing] there horses With the Greatest Expedition Some of there troops are Imbarking at the Narrows, there Destination is not know, Yesterday Sir Harry Clintons Baggag Was put on Board of a Vesel, and ordered to flushing, and this morning Clinton was to Cross the⟨re⟩ in order to meet his Baggage at Flushing, nothing more that is Material. I am With Respect Your Excellencys Most Obedien. and Very Humble Sert

                                                              Thos Wickes

ALS, DLC:GW. The cover indicates that this letter was sent "Pr Express."

## General Orders

                        Head-Quarters W. Plains Friday Augt 28th 1778.
Parole Hellespont—                          C. Signs Honor. Honesty—

The General observed on the 26th instant that there were several deficiencies towards a general movement of the Army—He expects every Exertion will be made to supply them without a Moment's loss of time, that the Troops may in all respects be in a perfect State of readiness for marching at the shortest notice: The several departments of the Army will make their Arrangements accordingly—The Quarter Master General in particular will endeavour to furnish a full supply of Waggons.

Officers and Soldiers will keep close to their quarters that they may at all times answer to a sudden Call.

Commanding Officers of Corps are carefully to examine the State of the men's Arms and Ammunition and will have the former in perfect order, and the latter compleat; If the quantity in their possession should be deficient they will draw a supply to make up the usual Complement.

The General finds with concern an inexcusable want of punctuality in the returns of the Cavalry—The Commanding Officers of Regiments will be responsible for the greatest exactness hereafter and may rely on it that no Apology will be admitted for neglect.

The returns of Arms and Cloathing directed in Genl orders of the 7th instant to be made to the Mustering Officers, will be omitted 'till further orders.

No Officer to appear on the Parade at Muster without his side Arms.

Varick transcript, DLC:GW.

## To the Board of War

Gentn                                    Head Qrs White plains Augt 28th 1778
Your favor of the 14th Instant has been duly received.[1]

The object which the Board have in view is desireable—and I wish it may be accomplished; however I cannot entertain a hope that accurate returns can be obtained here of the Officers who have served in the Army from the beginning of 1777 to the present time, and I am certain it will be impossible to ascertain the dates of their Commissions. The States never transmitted me lists of their appointments—and the perpetual changes which have taken place from death—resignations—the confusion of rank &c. &c. have put it out of my power to procure a competent knowledge of them. I believe the Board will not be able to form a Register with any regularity, but from the arrangemt now in contemplation; Nevertheless the Cols. & Officers commanding Corps will use, I am persuaded, their best endeavours to make the Returns requested by them, having received orders for the purpose.[2] I have the Honor to be with great respect Gentn Your Most Obedt servant

Go: Washington

Df, in Robert Hanson Harrison's writing, DLC:GW; Varick transcript, DLC:GW.
1. The board's letter of 14 Aug. has not been found.
2. See General Orders, 27 August.

## From Captain Epaphras Bull

Motts Mills [N.Y.]
Sir                          6 OClock Friday morning [28 August 1778][1]
I have to Inform your Excellency that the Fleet of Transports which lay at Frogs Neck have this morning made their appearence Round the

Point they are now lying at Anchor, they are so Intersperced amonge the Islands that it is difficult to Assertain their Number their appears to be near 20 Ships I shall Acquaint your Excellency of there first movement, the Fleet mentioned in my Report of Last Evening, at the Etward are now Coming down before the Wind their is 50 Sail which I have Counted this Morning 5 of which appears to be Ships the Others Brigs Sloops &c. I hope in a few hours to be able to give your Excellency a better Acct.

N:B. the Transports now lying near Frogs Neck, appeard thire when I first came down this morning & am not Certain whether they did not go past in the Night from the Etward tho I think it very Improbable. I have the Honour to be your Excellencys most Obt Hble servant

Epaps Bull

ALS, DLC:GW.
   1. The date is taken from a docket on the cover. James Mott (1742–1823) built a tide mill at the mouth of the Premium River in 1775.

## From Captain Epaphras Bull

Motts Mills [N.Y.]
Sir                          Friday 2 OClock P.M. [28 August 1778] [1]
   I have to acquaint your Excellency that the Fleet from the Etward have now Past this place, there was in the whole Sixty Nine Sail Viz. 6 Ships, two of them Transports, 3 appeard to be of 18 or 20 guns Each, & one which Bro't up the Rear of the whole had two Tier of guns—10 Brigs, 3 of them Armed, 21 Schooners, one of them Arm'd 6 Loaded with wood 2 with Hay, 32 Sloops, 13 Loaded with wood 2 with hay—which I believe is a pretty Exact Acct—there did not appear to be more men on board than were Necessary to work them, It was Impossable to Assertain the Force of any of them as the Air was very thick, there does not now appear any Vessel to the Etward Except the Stationed Brig in Hempstead Harbour—the Transports which came from N. York are now lying betwixt Frogs Neck & City Island Except 3 or 4 which have come up as far as Hart Island,[2] I Intend going farther below this afternoon to find out If Possable a more Exact Acct of them. Interim I have the Honour to be your Excellencys Most Obt servant

Epaps Bull

ALS, DLC:GW.
   1. The date is taken from a docket on the cover.
   2. City Island and Hart Island lie just off the Bronx shore at the far western end of Long Island Sound. Hart Island is less than a mile east of City Island.

## From Captain Epaphras Bull

Maroneck [N.Y.]

sir                          9 OClock Friday Evening [28 August 1778][1]

I have to acquaint your Excellency that I did not Inform myself any better as to the Shiping by going below, as they lie Chiefly behind the Islands, therefor was not able to discover whether there was Troops on Board or not. there appears to be 30 or 40 Sail of them, (I mean of those Transports from N. York) Chiefly Ships—Lt Hurlbut is Just Returned from Et Chester and can give no further Account of them than what I shall write which he desires me to mention it to your Excellency the Fleet which came from the Et Ward came to anchor near those from the Wtward Except the wood & forrage Vessels who past on towards N. York—at Sun set this Evening a gun was fired, upon which the whole maid Sail and are now Standing to the Et Ward, 15 Sail have already Past Whortlebury Island[2] and the others now comeing on—it is now got so dark that I am not able to discover any of them I Shall Look out for them at the dawn of the day. I am your Excellencys Most Obt Hble set

Epaps Bull

P:S. while I was at N. Roshel I discoverd between the Islands 2 Ships one of 40 guns the other of 36 whi[c]h I Suppose to be the Largest there is amonge them.

E.B.

ALS, DLC:GW.
1. The date is taken from a docket on the cover.
2. Whortleberry Island was another name for Huckleberry Island, in Long Island Sound off New Rochelle, about three miles northeast of City Island.

## To George Clinton

Dear Sir                          Head Quarters White plains 28 August 1778

By a letter received this day from Colonel Malcom I learn that the time of service for which the militia in the Highlands is engaged is very near expiring.[1] I am to request you will be pleased to order out a relief of from 500 to 1000 as expeditiously as possible. Besides the call for them to carry on the defences of the river, there is at this juncture an additional necessity for their services. Matters seem to be drawing to a crisis with the enemy and there is every appearance of their speedely making some very important movement. From various concuring accounts they seem to be in a general fermentation—They have been some days past imbarking cannon on board their transports—taking in forage &c. and yesterday an hundred and fourty sail fell down to the hook—There is no small motion of vessels in the sound, and among their troops on Long-Island. It is difficult to ascertain what these appearances indicate; but it is our duty to be at all points prepared.

I am sorry to inform you that the French fleet left Rhode Island bound to Boston the [    ] instant. Our troops were still on the Island and of course in a very precarious situation. The reasons for this conduct were—the damage suffered in the late storm; the apprehension of Byrons being on the coast, and the orders of the french king, that in case of misfortune or a superior naval force the fleet was immediately to repair to Boston, as a secure port and a place of rendezvous for any reinforcement which should be sent.

Different opinions will be entertained on the propriety of the measure; but we ought all to concur in giving it the most favourable colouring to the people—It should be ascribed to necessity resulting from the injury sustained by the storm.

If we solve the present movements of the enemy by this circumstance; one of these two solutions will appear not improbable—either that they mean to seize the opportunity for quitting the continent, or have a superior fleet on the coast, and by transfering the principal seat of the war to the Eastward, intend to operate conjointly with their sea and land force for the destruction of the french fleet.

If the latter should be their intention we must proceed Eastward—and there will be the more need of militia to reinforce the Highland garrisons. It is also possible some enterprize against this army may be in view—in that case succours of militia are equally essential. If your Excellency besides ordering out the number I have mentioned, could make any dispositions which might facilitate calling out the general body of the militia on any sudden emergency it would be a desireable circumstance. I have the honor to be with the most perfect respect and esteem Sir your most Obt & humble servt

Go: Washington

LS, in James McHenry's writing, CSmH; Df, DLC:GW; Varick transcript, DLC:GW.

1. GW was referring to Col. William Malcom's letter of 27 Aug., which has not been found.

## From Major Alexander Clough

Sr                    Hackensack [N.J.] August 28—8 OClock [1778] [1]
I have recd inteligance that Yesterday betwixt two and three in the afternoon a signell Gun was fire'd at New york upon which a hunderd and forty sail of transports fell down to the hook (this is certain thayr

numbers where told by severl persons on bergan shore) where thay are bound I am not able to lern—the day before Brass cannon was sent on board transports in the north river likewise forage the person who gives me this acct saw it.

the Jew I sent to your exellency on suspesion of being a spy returnd to new york yesterday was senit [sennight] he was seen by a person who is well acquainted with him he boasts that he has been from camp to philedelphia undiscoverd. I am your Exellencys Most Obt Hbl. Ser.

A. Clough

ALS, DLC:GW.
1. The year is taken from the endorsement on the cover.

## From Major General Nathanael Greene

Sir                    Camp near Newport [R.I.] August 28[–31] 1778

Your Excellencys favor of the 21st came to hand the evening of the 25th.

In my last I communicated to your Excellency the departure of the Count de Estainge with his fleet for Boston.[1] This disagreeable event, has as I apprehended ruined all our operations. It struck such a panic among the Militia and Volunteers that they began to desert by Shoals. The fleet no sooner set sail than they began to be alarm'd for their safety. This misfortune damp'd the hopes of our Army and gave new Spirits to that of the Enemy.

We had a very respectable force as to numbers between Eight and Nine thousand rank & file upon the ground. Out of these we attempted to select a particular Corps to possess our selves of the Enemies Lines partly by force and partly by stratagem; but we could not make up the necessary number that was thought sufficent to warrant the attempt which was 5000 including the Continental & State Troops. This body was to consist of men that had been in actual service before not less than Nine months. However the men were not to be had; and if they could have been found there was more against it than for it. Col. Laurens was to have opend the passage by landing within the Enemies Lines and geting possession of a Redoubt at the head of Eastons beach. If we had faild in the attempt the whole party must have fallen a sacrafice for their situation would have been such that there was no possibility of geting off.

I shall inclose your Excellency a plan of the Enemies Works & of their strength from the best accounts we are able to get.[2] They have never been out of their Lines since the seige began till Night before last. Col.

Bruce came out with 150 men to take off a small Piquet of ours Posted at the neck of Eastons beach, he partly succeeded in the attempt by the carelessness of the old guard, he came over after dark and lay in Ambush that when the new guard went down to take their post the Enemy came upon their backs before they discoverd them it being very dark. We lost 24 privates & two Subs.—Ten of the Piquet got off.[3]

Our strength is now reduced from 9000 to between 4 and 5000. All our heavy Cannon on garrison carriages heavy & superfluous Stores of every kind are removd to the Main & to the North end of the Island where we intend to entrench and attempt to hold it and wait the chance of events. General Hancock is gone to Boston to forward the repairs of the fleet and to prepare the mind of the Count for a speedy return. How far he will succeed I cannot pretend to say. I think it a matter of some doubt yet whether the enemy will reenforce or take off this Garrison. If they expect a superior fleet from Europe they will reenforce, but if not they will remove the Garrison.

Your Excellency may rest assurd that I have done every thing in my power to cultivate and promote a good understanding both with the Count and the Marquis and flatter myself that I am upon very good terms with them both The Marquises great thirst for glory and National attachmt often runs him into errors. However he did everything to prevail on the Admiral to cooperate with us that man could do. People censure the Admiral with great freedom and many are imprudent enough to reproach the Nation through the Admiral. General Sullivan very imprudently issueed something like a censure in General Orders, indeed it was an absolute censure. It opend the Mouths of the Army in very clamorous strains. The Genl was obligeed to explain it away in a few days[4]—The fermentation seems to be now subsiding and all things appear as if they would go smoothly on. The Marquis is going to Boston also to hasten the Counts return and if possible to get the French Troops to join the Land forces here which will more effectually interest the Count in the success of the expedition.

Five sail of British Ships has got into Newport within two Days past we have heard nor seen nothing of the Fleet of Transports your Excellency mentioned in your Letter to General Sullivan of the 23d.[5] If they arrive with a large reinforcement our Expedition is at an end. Unless it is by way of blocade and that will depend upon the French fleets being superior to that of the British.

General Sullivan has done every thing that could be expected and had the fleet cooperated with us as was at first intended and agreeable to the original plan of the expedition we must have been successful. I wish it was in my power to confirm General Sullivans prediction of the 17th but I can not flatter my self with such an agreeable issue I am sensible he is in common very sanguine but his expectations were not ill founded in the present case. We had every reason to hope for success from our numbers and from the enemies fears. Indeed General Pigot was heard to say the Garrison must fall unless they were speedily relievd by a British fleet. If we could have made a landing upon the South part of the Town two Days would have put us in compleat possession of it. Nothing was wanting to effect this but the cooperation of the fleet & french forces. The disappointment is vexatious and truly mortifying. The Garrison was so important and the reduction so certain, that I cannot with patience think of the event. The French Ship that was missing has got into Boston, the rest of the Fleet have not got there yet or at least we have no accounts of their Arrival.

We are very anxious to learn the condition of Lord Hows Fleet the French 74 that has got into Boston had an Engagement with a British 64. The Capt. & Lieut. of the former were both wounded one lost a Leg & the other an Arm.[6]

Our Troops are in pretty good health and well furnished with Provisions and every thing necessary for carrying on the Expedition.

Our approaches were pushed on with great spirit while we had any hopes of the fleets cooperateing with us; but the People lost all relish for diging after that.

People are very anxious to hear the issue of General Lees tryal various are the conjectures; but every body agrees he is not acquited.

Augt 31—Camp Tivertown [R.I.]

I wrote the foregoing and intended to have sent it by the express that went off in the morning but while I was writing I was inform'd the Express was gone and the change of situation and round of events that have since taken place, has prevented my forwarding what I had wrote as matters seemd to be coming to a crisis.

On the evening of the 29th the Army fell back to the North end of the Island. The next morning the enemy advanced upon us in two Columns upon the East & west road. Our Light Troops commanded by Col. Livingston & Col. Laurens attacked the heads of the Columns about 7 oClock in the morning, but were beat back, they were reenforced with a Regiment upon each road. The Enemy still provd too strong. General Sullivan formd the Army in order of battle and resolvd to wait their approach upon the ground we were encamped on, and sent orders to the Light troops to fall back. The Enemy came up & formd upon Quaker Hill a very strong piece of ground within about one mile & a ¼ of our Line. We were well Posted with strong works in our rear and a strong redoubt in front partly upon the right of the Line.

In this position a warm Cannonade commenced and lasted for several hours with continual Skirmishes on front of both Lines. About 2 oClock the Enemy began to advance in force upon our right as if they intended to dislodge us from the advance Redoubt. I had the command of the Right Wing after advanceing four Regts and finding the enemy still gaining ground I advanced with two more Regiments of regular Troops and a Brigade of Militia and at the same time Gen. Sullivan orderd Col. Livingston with the Light Troops under his command to advance. We soon put the Enemy to the rout and I had the pleasure to see them run in worse disorder than they did at the battle of Monmouth. Our Troops behavd with great spirit and the brigade of Militia under the command of General Lovel advanceed with great resolution and in good order and stood the fire of the Enemy with great firmness Lt Col. Livingston, Col. Jackson & Col. Henry B. Livingston did themselves great honor in the transactions of the Day but its not in my power to do justice to Col. Laurens who acted both the General & the Partizan. His command of regular Troops was small but he did every thing possible to be done by their numbers.[7] He had two most Excellent Officers with him Lt Col. Fleury & Major Talbot.

The enemy fell back to their strong ground and the Day terminated with a Cannonade & Skirmishes. Both Armies continued in their position all Day yesterday Cannonadeing each every now and then. Last Night we effected a very good retreat without the loss of men or Stores.[8]

We have not collected an account of the kild and wounded, but we judge our loss amounts to between two & three hundred and that of the Enemies to much more.

We are going to be Posted all round the Shores as a guard upon them & in that state to wait for the return of the Fleet, which by the by I think will not be in a hurry.

It is asserted that Lord How arrivd last Night with his fleet & the reenforcement mentioned in your Excellencys Letter to General Sullivan. If the report is true we got off the Island in very good season.

The Marquis went to Boston the Day before the Action and did not return until last night just as we were leaveing the Island. He went to wait upon the Admiral, to learn his further intentions and to get him to return again and compleat the expedition if possible.

I observe your Excellency thinks the enemy design to evacuate Newyork. If they should I think they will Newport also; but I am perswaded they will not neither for the present.

I would write your Excellency a more particular account of the battle & retreat, but I immagin General Sullivan & Col. Laurens has done it already. and I am myself very much unwell have had no sleep for three

Night & Days; being severely afflicted with the Asthma. I am with great respect Your Excellencys Most obedient humble Servt

Nath. Greene

ALS, DLC:GW.

1. Greene was apparently referring to his letter to GW of 22 Aug., which has not been found.

2. The plan has not been identified.

3. Capt. Frederick Mackenzie of the Royal Welch Fusiliers wrote in his diary entry of 26 Aug.: "A party of 100 Men of the 54th Regiment under the Command of Lt Colonel Bruce, went out at 8 o'Clock this Evening, in order to surprize a Picquet lately posted by the Rebels in Easton's Orchard at the East end of Easton's beach. They succeeded completely, having surrounded and brought off the whole Picquet, consisting of 2 Officers, and 30 men, 5 men excepted, who were just gone out to be posted Sentries. . . . Our party returned at 9 o'Clock, without any other loss than one man missing, supposed to have been killed" (*Mackenzie Diary*, 2:374; see also Field, *Angell Diary*, 6; Gibbs diary, 5–30 Aug., *Pa. Archives*, 1st ser., 6:735–36). Andrew Bruce, who ranked as a captain in the British army by December 1761, became a major of the 38th Infantry Regiment in July 1771, was promoted from that position to lieutenant colonel of the 54th Infantry Regiment on 10 March 1777, and remained lieutenant colonel of that regiment until at least 1786, being promoted to colonel of the army in November 1782.

4. For Maj. Gen. John Sullivan's general orders of 24 and 26 Aug., see Lafayette to GW, 25–26 Aug., n.4.

5. Greene was probably referring to GW's letter to Sullivan of 22 August. The *Sphynx, Vigilant,* and *Nautilus* from the British fleet at New York arrived at Newport on 27 Aug. (*Mackenzie Diary*, 2:376).

6. Joseph Louis, chevalier de Raimondis (1723–1792), who had ranked as capitaine de vaisseau since 1772, was captain of the *César* and lost an arm in her engagement with the *Isis* on 16 August. Lieutenant de Foucault of the régiment de Hainaut was killed (d'Estaing to French marine minister, 5 Nov., in Doniol, *Histoire de la participation de la France*, 3:457). Greene's information may have come from the *Boston-Gazette, and Country Journal*, 24 Aug., which reported on the *César*'s casualties.

7. GW quoted the text from "Our troops behavd" to this point in his private letter to Henry Laurens of 4 September.

8. For more on this battle, see John Sullivan to GW, 29 Aug., and notes to that document.

## To Major General William Heath

Dear sir                    Head Quarters [White Plains] 28 August 1778

I had the pleasure of your several favors of the 12th & 13th Instant.[1] The packet for the president of Congress, was sent forward by express.

I inclose you a letter from General Patterson respecting silk for a set of colors: You will be pleased to give directions to the clothier to have it transmitted to camp.[2] I am Sir your most Obt and very hble Servt

Go: Washington

LS, in James McHenry's writing, MHi: Heath Papers; Df, DLC:GW; Varick transcript, DLC:GW.

1. Only one letter from Heath to GW of 12 Aug. and no letters of 13 Aug. have been found. GW probably intended to acknowledge Heath's letter of 14 August.

2. GW apparently enclosed a letter from Col. Thomas Marshall to Heath of 27 Aug., which read in part: "I am directed by Brigadier Patterson, who hath Genl Washingtons desire for me to write you to have the Brigade Furnish'd with a Flight of Colours; Vizt One flagg or Standard For each Battallion as the Monuvres practised in the Army is Intirely different from what hath been practiced, in America before And the Use of Colours of more real Service then ever by the Different Moovements from large plattoons into solid Column; And then to display the Column from any part of it; as the officer shall direct—The colours are of excellent use in these Monuvres Division Colours are intirely Useless—If your Honr will direct Colo. Chase to precure them, I will desire my Sister, or Capt. Wallcutts Wife to find Silk that will Answer" (MHi: Heath Papers).

## To Major General William Heath

Dear Sir                    Head Quarters White plains 28th Augt 1778

The unfortunate circumstance of the French Fleet having left Rhode Island at so critical a moment, I am apprehensive, if not very prudently managed, will have many injurious consequences, besides merely the loss of the advantages we should have reaped from succeeding in the Expedition. It will not only tend to discourage the people, and weaken their confidence in our new alliance, but may possibly produce prejudices and resentments, which may operate against giving the Fleet such Zealous and effectual assistance in its present distress, as the exigence of affairs and our true interest demand. It will certainly be sound policy to combat these effects, and whatever private opinions may be entertained, to give the most favorable construction, of what has happened, to the public, and at the same time to put the French Fleet, as soon as possible, in condition to defend itself and be useful to us.

The departure of the Fleet from Rhode Island is not yet publicly announced here, but when it is, I intend to ascribe it to necessity, from the damage suffered in the late storm. This, it appears to me, is the Idea which ought to be generally propagated. As I doubt not the force of these Reasons will strike you equally with myself, I would recommend to you to use your utmost influence to palliate and soften matters, and induce those, whose business it is to provide succours of every kind for the fleet, to employ their utmost zeal and activity in doing it. It is our duty to make the best of our misfortune, and not to suffer passion to interfere with our interest and the public good.[1]

By several late accounts from New York there is reason to beleive the enemy are on the point of some important movement. They have been some days past embarking Cannon and other matters—and yesterday an hundred and forty transports fell down to the Hook. These and other circumstances indicate something of moment being in contemplation. Whether they meditate any enterprise against this army, mean to transfer the War elsewhere, or intend to embrace the present opportunity of evacuating the Continent is as yet uncertain. If they have a superior fleet on the Coast, it is not impossib⟨le⟩ they may change the seat of the War to the Eastward, endeavouring by a land and Sea cooperation to destroy or possess themselves of the French Fleet. With an Eye to an event of this kind, I have desired General Sullivan, if he makes good his Retreat from the Island, to disband no more of his troops than he cannot help;[2] and I would recommend to you to have an eye to it likewise, and by establishing Signals and using other proper precautions to put things in a train for calling out your Militia at the shortest notice. I am Dear Sir Your most obt & hum: Servt

Go: Washington

LS, in Tench Tilghman's writing, MHi: Heath Papers; Df, DLC:GW; Varick transcript, DLC:GW.

1. On the draft, which is in Alexander Hamilton's writing, except for the dateline in Tilghman's, the complimentary close was initially written here, but it was struck out and the following paragraph added.

2. See GW to John Sullivan, this date.

## From Lieutenant George Hurlbut

New Rochel [N.Y.]

May it please your Excellency                 28th August 78

The fleet that were Anchor'd off Frogs point mov'd up Early this Morning, came to Anchor off City Island—72. Sail past this place to day, under Convoy of 4. Ships—Chief of them appeared to be very deeply Laden, But very few had Forage on deck—above half have Anchored off Heart Island, the Remainder joind the Fleet Below—they keep Constanly passing & Repassing from one fleet to the other—from your Obd. Servt

Ge. Hurlbut

N.B. the last of the fleet past at 2 P.M.

ALS, DLC:GW.

# From Henry Laurens

Sir                                    [Philadelphia] 28 Augt [1778]

Since my last of the 20th I have had the honor of receiving Your Excellency's several favors of the 16th, 19th, 21st, 21st and 24th and of presenting them together with the several papers which accompanied them to Congress in due course.[1]

The proceedings of the General Court Martial for the trial of Major General Lee had been made an Order of the day for Wednesday the 26th, Congress then ordered the whole to be printed.[2] The work is large, and I do not expect it from the Press before the 5th of September.

At present I have only in charge to transmit to Your Excellency an Act of the 26th for settling Rations when needful, by commutation of Species.[3] I have the honor to be &c.

LB, DNA:PCC, item 13. A note on the letter-book copy indicates that this letter was carried "by [William] Jones."

In addition to the private letter that follows, Laurens wrote a second official letter to GW on this date. It reads: "I beg leave to refer Your Excellency to a letter written this Morning, and which this will accompany, and also to an Act of Congress of the present date for obtaining the advice and assistance of Baron Stuben in the Army under the command of Major General Sullivan, and for preventing the publication of the Protest of the Officers of that Army against Count d'Estaing's abandoning Rhode Island" (LB, DNA:PCC, item 13). For those acts, see *JCC*, 11:848–49.

1. Laurens had written a letter on 23 Aug. acknowledging GW's letters of 16 and 19 Aug., but the letter-book copy is marked "not sent" (DNA:PCC, item 13).

2. On 21 Aug., Congress received from GW the proceedings of Maj. Gen. Charles Lee's court-martial and ordered that they "lie on the table for the perusal of the members, to be taken into consideration on Wednesday next" (26 Aug.). Later on the 21st, Congress ordered that one hundred copies of the proceedings "be printed for the use of the members" (*JCC*, 11:824–26). Congress again took up the court-martial proceedings in October.

3. On 26 Aug., Congress resolved "That the Commander in Chief of the armies of the United States shall, in the army under his immediate command . . . settle and determine according to circumstances, the ration to be issued to the troops, from time to time, giving an over proportion of a plentiful article in lieu and in full satisfaction of such as are scarce or not to be had . . . reporting, from time to time, to the Board of War, the alterations and regulations by them respectively made in this respect" (ibid., 11:838).

# From Henry Laurens

Dear Sir                                 [Philadelphia] 28th Augt [1778]

I am indebted for Your Excellency's favors of the 20th and 25th, the former receiv'd three days since, and the latter while I was in Congress this Morning; this takes my immediate attention—I feel convinc'd that had Your Excellency named a sum in Gold and apply'd for it to Congress, an order for the Amount would have pass'd without hesitation—but from circumstances which I have more than a few times observed to attend Motions made from private Letters by Gentlemen of Merit and influence transcending far, any that I presume to claim I feared on your Account Sir, to hazard a question in the present case—there is a jealousy in the Minds of Men as unaccountable and unreasonable, as it is unnecessary to add a word more upon the subject; to contribute, however, towards forwarding Your Excellency's labours for public good, and from a mellancholly conviction of the policy and necessity for constantly prosecuting the measures for which Gold in the present critical moment is wanted, I have pack'd up a few pieces, the particulars noted below, which had been lying by me altogether useless and which do not comprehend my whole stock; these may possibly be of immediate service and I may be reimburs'd when Congress shall order a supply, which I am persuaded will be in the instant of Your Excellency's demand; be this as it may I intreat Your Excellency will permit me to insist upon the receipt and application of this mite. I do not presume to offer it to General Washington but as a loan to our Country who will repay me amply even by permitting my endeavours to serve her.

I do not remember that ever an application was made by the Camp Committee of Congress. I am more inclined to believe those Gentlemen relied on each other and that neither of them attempted the business, but I may be mistaken. I shall without waiting for a dispatch from Your Excellency to Congress which I would wish to receive seperately from all other business, and with permission to deliver or return it as occasion may require, consult a few friends on the point, and if they approve the Measure prevail on one of them to move under a proper introduction for 2 or 300 Guineas to be remitted to Your Excellency for public service. If more hundreds are necessary Your Excellency will be pleas'd to signify it, and even thousands.

I return Your Excellency my hearty thanks for the kind intimation respecting my Son, or as I now hold him, my worthy fellow Citizen, Lieut. Colonel Laurens, which came the more acceptably as full three weeks had elapsed since the date of his last Letter. I am With the most sincere Esteem & Regard Sir Your Excellency's much Obliged Humble Servant.

Two double & six single Joannes Two Doubloons Two Pistoles Eleven Guineas Contain'd in a Packet to be deliver'd by Messenger Jones.[1]

P.S. Baron Steuben was much surpris'd at the Act of Congress requesting him to repair to Rhode Island, and seems to be very apprehensive the measure will be displeasing at Head Quarters. I had been directed during the sitting of Congress to communicate the Intelligence receiv'd from General Sullivan to Monsr Girard, and to confer with that Gentleman.[2] I found at my return the Resolves on the Table.

LB, ScHi: Henry Laurens Papers. A note on the letter-book copy indicates that this letter was carried "by [William] Jones."

1. The word "Returned" was written on the manuscript with this list.

2. For the direction to Laurens and the resolution regarding Steuben, both of 28 Aug., see *JCC*, 11:848–49.

## From Brigadier General William Maxwell

Sir                                    Elizth Town [N.J.] 28th Augt 1778

I forwarded to your Excellency yesterday a Journal from Major Howel with an Acct of Lord Hows being saild to the East Ward, 6 or 7 of the Cork Fleet having arived in the Hook &Ca which is all confirmed; it is likewise confirmed that the 4 Regts returned that was going on board the Fleet. Genl Clinton is on long Islan, it is said with 8000 Men but one half is most likely as I have both informations, He was yesterday at Hamstead Plains,[1] and was to proceed to great Neck, & that 40 flat bottom'd Boats went through Helgate the day before yesterday; his destination not known. A Contract for a 100 Transports to take place verry soon. Some Querys whether they do not intend to leave New york Statten Island and Long Islan, & take post on Rhode Island; where they will be more compact. I had 5 Deserters yesterday with their Arms & accoutrements from the 27th Regt on Statten Island they came over near Amboy. I expect the 3d N: Carrolina Regt inder Coll Hogan here to night.[2] I am your Excellencys Most Obedient Humble Servant

Wm Maxwell

ALS, DLC:GW.

1. The Hempstead Plains were a grassland running from eastern Queens County through Nassau County almost to the Suffolk County border on Long Island. Described in 1670 as being sixteen miles long and four miles broad, the plains have been reduced now to a small preserve.

2. Col. James Hogun had assumed command of the 3d North Carolina Regiment in June 1778.

## From Brigadier General Charles Scott

Sir                      [Westchester County, N.Y.] 28th Augt 1778 ½ past 5

I sent You a Message By Capt. Anderson from Volentines hill informing Your Excellency of the Fleat in the sound[1] I dispatched Colos. Butler & parker from That place for Intelligence, they are Just Returnd from the Waters edg opposit them and inform me that there are about

70 Sail Chiefly Transports the Bulk of which Lyes about the west end of City Island, A considerable part of those vessils came From Frogs point. the others came from The Easter'd. But all come too at the Same Place, they Assure me there are no troops on Board. I shall continue to watch them and give You every intillegence Possable. Persons are inguaged to Go on Board. I am Your Excely Obt Servt

Chs Scott

ALS, DLC:GW.
   1. No written message of this description has been found.

## To Major General John Sullivan

Head Quarters White plains

Dear Sir                             28 Augt 1778 12 OClock Noon

   I am exceedingly anxious to hear the determination of yourself and the General Officers upon the great reverse of your prospects, since the French Fleet left you. I however think it incumbent upon me to inform you, that from a variety of intelligence, Lord Howe put to sea again on Tuesday,[1] his design no doubt to attempt the relief of New port, which will be easily effected, either by throwing in a reinforcement or withdrawing the Garrison, as I take it for granted the French Fleet would not have returned, had your protest reached them. I also yesterday received information from Long Island, that looks like a great and general move among the British Army, the real intent I have not been able to learn, but I think part of it must be meant to cooperate with their fleet, especially as many transports are drawn into the sound. You will more than probable have come to a decisive resolution either to abandon the enterprise or to attack long before this reaches you, but lest you should not, I have given you all the information that I have been able to obtain, that you may judge more fully of the propriety of remaining upon the Island under such appearances. The Wind is now contrary and if it continues a short time, this will reach you before the transports can, should they be bound Eastward.

   supposing you should remove from the Island, I desire you will keep as many of your troops together as you possibly can. We do not know the views of the enemy, should they be Eastward, you may be able with a force already collected, and the assistance of the Militia, to keep them from making much progress, untill a reinforcement from this army would join you.

   I will just add a hint, which, made use of in time, may prove important, and answer a very salutary purpose. Should the expedition fail, thro' the abandonment of the French Fleet, the Officers concerned will be apt[2] to complain loudly. But prudence dictates that we should put the best face upon the matter and, to the World, attribute the removal to Boston, to necessity. The Reasons are too obvious to need explaining. The principal one is, that our British and internal enemies would be glad to improve the least matter of complaint and disgust against and between us and our new Allies into a serious rupture. I am &c.

Df, in Tench Tilghman's writing, DLC:GW; Varick transcript, DLC:GW.

1. The previous Tuesday was 25 August.

2. At this point on the draft Tilghman wrote "and not without reason," but that phrase was struck out.

## General Orders

Head-Quarters W. Plains saturday August 29th 1778.
Parole Marlborough—          C. Signs Montcalm. Montgomery—
The board of Field-Officers appointed in orders of the 27th instant in the Virginia Line are to take into Consideration and settle Lieutt Colls Brent & Ellison's claims of rank.[1]

Colonels Wyllys, Bradley, Swift and Meigs are appointed to settle the relative rank of the Lieutt Colonels, Majors and Captains in the Connecticutt line—They are desired to meet at Colonel Wyllys's Marquee three ôClock this afternoon and make report of their proceedings to the Committee of Arrangement at Head-Quarters.

Varick transcript, DLC:GW. On this date GW's secretary James McHenry wrote Assistant Quartermaster General Charles Pettit: "The General considering the present appearances of things, and the circumstances of the enemy wishes to have an established provision of boats on the connecticut, & other rivers between this and Boston for the crossing his army in case the war should take an Eastern direction. You will be looking forward for this purpose.

"His Excellency does not conceive the boats and small craft at Norwalk altogether safe; he would therefore wish to see them, as well as all others, whether public or private property, laying along the sound, at least for some distance, collected and carryed back into creeks or rivers: You will choose Such situations as seem to give the greatest security to the boats, It may be very proper to consult with General Parsons on this head" (DLC:GW).

1. John Allison (1745–1803), who was appointed a captain of marines by the Virginia council in March 1776, became major of the 1st Virginia State Regiment in 1777. On 1 June 1778 he was appointed lieutenant colonel with a commission dated from 1 Feb. 1778, but from 7 Sept. 1778 to May 1779 he was considered supernumerary and apparently served as a major. In August 1779 he was restored to the rank of lieutenant colonel (dating from January 1779), a board of officers having ruled in May that he was entitled to that rank. Allison served at least until February 1781.

## From Major General Benedict Arnold

Dear General                                    Philada Augt 29th 1778

I was honored with your Excellencys favour of the 9th Inst. on the
15th And immediately, inclosed it to the President and Council of this
state, and requested three hundred Militia to Supply the Place of the
Continental Troops, the Next day I received a Coppy of an Act of the
Assembly of the State, which makes a requisition of Congress Necessary
before the Presidt & Council can Order Out the Militia, this Act I laid
before Congress & Inform'd them of Your Excellency's wishes to have
the Continental Troops Join the Army.[1]

Congress refer'd the Letter to the Board of Warr who have not made
their report which, (& a dearth of News,) has prevented my writeing
your Excellency before,[2] We are Just inform'd to our great Surprise
that the French Fleet have left Rhode Island and are Gone to Boston.
Many are apprehensive For General Sullivan & his Army, I think there
is little danger of his makeing good his retreat. If he does not Succeed.
I have the honor to be with the Most perfect respect & estem—Dear
General Your Excellency's Most Obedt Hble Servt

                                                      B. Arnold

ALS, DLC:GW.
    1. See Arnold to Timothy Matlack, 18 Aug. (*Pa. Archives*, 1st ser., 6:708), and
Arnold to Henry Laurens, 19 Aug. (DNA:PCC, item 162). Arnold was referring to
"An Act to regulate the Militia of the Common-Wealth of Pennsylvania," 17 March
1777, which authorized the executive council to call up the militia "in case of invasion or rebellion within this State, or in case the assistance of the militia of this
State shall be requested by Congress to assist the Continental Army in this or any
of the adjoining States" (*Pa. Laws*, 25).
    2. Congress read Arnold's letter on 20 Aug. and directed the Board of War "to
report their opinion on the necessity of an additional number of troops to the
corps of invalids, for the purpose of guards in the city of Philadelphia; and if an additional number is . . . necessary, how many and for what purposes." The board's
report of 28 Aug. was considered on 3 Sept., and Congress resolved to request that
the Pennsylvania council call up three hundred militia to serve as guards in Philadelphia (*JCC*, 11:816, 12:865). The council responded on 4 Sept. by calling militia into service (*Pa. Col. Records*, 11:568).

## From Captain Epaphras Bull

                                                Motts Mills [N.Y.]

Sir                        6 OClock Saturday morning [29 August 1778][1]

I have to Inform your Excellency that the Fleet which came to Sail
Last Night have got as far Etward as Oyster Bay where they now lie at
Anchor the wind being Rather a head, there appears to be between

60 & 70 Sail of them, (30 of them Ships) the distance is so great that I am not able to give a Particular Acct of them—I shou'd think that a Person at Horse Neck[2] or Stanford, with a good Glass might discover, If they had Troops on board.

there is no Shiping that I can desern at the Wtward of me this morning If any further movement shall Acquaint your Excellency. I am your Excellencys Mot Obt servant

Epaps Bull

P.S. some of the Smaller Vessels appear to be Runing in to Oyster Bay.

ALS, DLC:GW.

1. The cover of this letter is docketed in part "28 Augt 1778," but Saturday was 29 August.

2. Horse Neck, now Field Point, in Connecticut is the peninsula extending into Long Island Sound from Greenwich, Conn., which town was sometimes called Horseneck.

*Letter not found*: from Capt. Epaphras Bull, 29 Aug. 1778. On 30 Aug., Bull wrote to GW: "the Transport, which I mentioned as having Troops on board Last Night, appeard to have them to day"; when Bull wrote GW on the morning of Aug. 29, he had not been able to discern whether the boats were carrying troops.

## From George Clinton

Dear Sir.             Poughkeepsie [N.Y.] Augt 29th 1778.

I am this moment honored with the Receipt of your Excellency's Letter of Yesterday; In consequence of which it shall be my first Business to order out a Detachment of the Militia to strengthen the Garrisons in the Highlands; tho' I much doubt (considering the large proportion which are constantly kept out on the frontiers) whether I shall be able to march and keep out at those Posts for any considerable Time, a number larger than the least mentioned in your Excellency's Letter; especially as the Service in Garrison is not so agreable to them as that of the field At the same Time I have not the least Doubt, if any Movements of the Enemy should render it necessary that I shall be able to draw out a considerable force to join the Army immediately under your Excellency's command; and I will immediately make the necessary Disposition for that Purpose.

The People having entertained high expectations from the Operations of the Fleet and Army at Rhode Island will without Doubt be disappointed on finding that Count D'Estaign has left that Place and is gone to Boston: however I hope they will suppose it for the best; and that the Injuries the Fleet must have sustained in the late Storm has occasioned this sudden movement. I have the honor to be with the greatest Regard Your Excellency's most Obedt Servt

Geo: Clinton

LS, DLC:GW.

## To Colonel Peter Gansevoort

Sir                                   Head Quarters White plains 29 August 1778
    I have just received your favor of the 18th Instant.
    Inclosed is a copy of a letter sent you some time ago respecting the court martial you transmitted.[1]
    The spirit of desertion which possessed your soldiers was certainly very alarming and required a serious check. I hope the intention of the example you have made will be fully answered; and altho' the proceeding was not strictly in the prescribed form, yet the necessity of the case may justify the measure.
    I have spoken to Lieut. Colonel Willet on the application of the officers of the garrison. It is impossible to comply at present with their request, things are so circumstanced—but I shall take steps to releive it before winter.[2] I am Sir your Obt hble servt

Go: Washington

LS, in James McHenry's writing, NN: Gansevoort-Lansing Collection; Df, DLC:GW; Varick transcript, DLC:GW. GW signed the cover of the LS.
    1. GW enclosed a copy of his letter to Gansevoort of 13 August.
    2. For the officers' application, see Officers of the 3d New York Regiment to GW, 13 Aug.; for GW's arrangements to relieve the garrison at Fort Schuyler, see GW to George Clinton, 19 Oct., and Goose Van Schaick to GW, 1 November.

## From Lieutenant George Hurlbut

Sir                                   New Rochel [N.Y.] 29th Augst 78
    I am set don to inform your Excellency the Fleet, are now at Anchor Betwen Horse & Rye Neck[1]—the Guard Ship of 16. Guns has been Stationed, Sixteen Months, Betwen Heart, & City, Island is now with the fleet—two Briggs and a small Tender, is left in her place—a few small Sloops, are now Sailing for Newyork. I am your Excellency's most Obed. Servt

Ge. Hurlbut

ALS, DLC:GW.
    1. Rye Neck, now named Peningo Neck, extends southward into Long Island Sound from Rye, New York.

## To Thomas Johnson

Sir                                        Head Quarters White plains 29th Augt 1778
    I am honored with yours of the 12th inst.[1] I very highly approve of
the determination of your Council to reinlist the nine months Men at
this period; if it is left undone, untill the time of their service is near
expiring, it will be almost impossible to re-engage them. I, some time
ago, pointed out to Congress the expediency of[2] adopting this measure but as yet have not received their Answer. The money supplied by
the Board of treasury to the pay Master General is barely sufficient to
pay the monthly abstracts of the Army, and to defray other contingent
expences; I therefore have it not in my power to advance the state
Bounty of 40 dollars, out of the military Chest: Indeed I should not be
authorised to advance it, without the special order of Congress, did the
state of the Chest allow it. I have the Honor &c.

Df, in Tench Tilghman's writing, DLC:GW; Varick transcript, DLC:GW.
    1. See the Council of Maryland to GW, 12 August.
    2. On the draft, Tilghman completed this sentence with the words "recom-
mending this measure to the Legislatures of all the states," but Robert Hanson Harrison revised the text. GW was probably referring to comments in his letter to
Henry Laurens of 3–4 August.

## From Henry Laurens

Dear sir.                                    Philadelphia 29th Augt 1778
    I did my self the honour of writing to Your Excellency yesterday by
Jones to which I beg leave to refer.[1]
    this Morning upon enquiry I was confirmed in my belief that the for-
mer Camp Committee had made no application to Congress for Gold
or Silver to be deposited in Your Excellency's hands for public uses,
wherefore I suggested to two or three Members the necessity & utility
of establishing such a fund & prevailed upon one of the Gentlemen to
move the House for that purpose, the motion was accepted, & without
a pause, the sum of five hundred Guineas voted, these I shall presently
receive & if possible convey them to Your Excellency under the protection of Capt. Josiah Stoddard of the Light Dragoons.[2]
    I have just received new addresses to Congress from the British
Commissioners at New York—Govr Johnstone, in graceless & almost
scurrilous terms without exonerating himself from the charges alleged
against him submits to the Decree of Interdiction lately pronounced by
Congress, Nor do the Gentlemen, late his Coadjutors so highly resent
the proceedings on our part as to refuse to treat without the support of
the Governor's name.

Your Excellency will judge best from their respective performances on the present occasion, Copies of which shall accompany this Letter.[3]

I take the liberty of inclosing with the present dispatches a Letter directed to Lieutt Colo. Laurens under a flying Seal & of requesting Your Excellency to peruse a paragraph contained in it which speaks of a Monsr Galvan.[4]

Monsr Girard is exceedingly affected by the late determinations on the Water near Rhode Island & has communicated his sentiments to me with great candor. Good accounts from General Sullivan will do more towards recovering him from a slight intermittent which really seized that Gentleman immediately after he had received Monsr Chouin's Letter, than four Ounces of Bark[5]—indeed I never saw people in general more anxious than my acquaintances are, under the present suspense—within the next two hours I make no doubt there will be fifty enquirers for news within this door. I remain with the utmost Regard Dear sir Your Excellency's Obliged & hum. servt

Henry Laurens
private

ALS, DLC:GW; LB, ScHi: Henry Laurens Papers. A note on the letter-book copy indicates that this letter was carried by Josiah Stoddard.

1. Laurens was referring to his private letter to GW of 28 Aug. (second letter).

2. For Congress's order for Laurens to send GW 500 guineas, voted on 29 Aug., see *JCC*, 11:851. Josiah Stoddard (d. 1779), who took part in the expedition against Ticonderoga in May 1775, was commissioned a lieutenant of Col. Philip Burr Bradley's Connecticut State Regiment in June 1776 and was appointed a captain in the 2d Continental Light Dragoons on 31 Dec. 1776. In January 1779 Stoddard was granted a furlough to go to France for his health, but he died at Boston in August of that year.

3. The enclosed copies have not been identified. Laurens had received a cover letter by Adam Ferguson; a declaration signed by George Johnstone; another declaration signed by the other commissioners, William Eden, Henry Clinton, and Frederick Howard, earl of Carlisle; and a representation about the "unjust Detention" of the Convention Army from Eden, Clinton, and Carlisle, all dated 26 August. The representation is in DNA:PCC, item 57, while the other documents are in DLC: Peter Force Collection (copies of all four are in DNA:PCC, item 184). Both declarations respond to Congress's charges of bribery and corruption by Johnstone. Johnstone indicated that he would cease participation in the commission but characterized the charges as an "excuse" for not responding to complaints about the continued detention of the Convention Army and as "a pretext to the unhappy constituents of the Congress who are suffering under the various calamities of war, for disappointing the good effects of the commission which the real friends of America had so long requested." The other commissioners impugned French motives for entering into the treaty with America and suggested that Congress should consult colonial assemblies before rejecting the British peace overtures.

4. For Henry Laurens's letter of 29 Aug. to his son John Laurens, see *Laurens Papers*, 14:243–45. The letter explained that William Galvan, who had recently resigned his commission as a lieutenant in the 2d South Carolina Regiment, had so-

licited from Laurens letters to GW and to Maj. Gen. John Sullivan. Despite Laurens's discouragement, Galvan persisted, expressing his willingness "to act as a Volunteer," until Laurens agreed to write John Laurens on his behalf. Laurens also wrote that Silas Deane had informed him "of some very naughty tricks this young French Adventurer had play'd in Paris." Galvan, who claimed to have a commission as captain in the French army in the West Indies, remained in America, serving, according to his memorials to Congress, as a volunteer on the staffs of major generals Johann Kalb and Horatio Gates. In January 1780 he was appointed a major and inspector in the Continental army. Galvan continued to petition Congress for promotion, but he was removed from the inspectorship in March 1782 and committed suicide in July of that year.

5. The marquis de Choin's letter to Conrad-Alexandre Gérard has not been identified. For Gérard's response to the controversy, see his letter to French foreign minister Vergennes of 29 Aug. (Meng, *Despatches of Gérard*, 236–39).

## To Colonel William Malcom

Sir          Head Quarters White plains 29 Augt 1778
I have recd yours of the 27th inclosing a weekly return of the Garrison.[1] I observe that ten men of your small Regiment are upon furlough, I desire that they may be recalled as soon as the terms expire and that no more may be granted, during the active part of the Campaign. I have wrote to Govr Clinton and have desired him to call in from 500 to 1000 Militia to the Highlands, and I have no doubt of his complying to the utmost extent in his power.[2] A Lieut. Colo. Brown of a Massachusets Regt of Militia has represented to me that the Regiment is deficient in Arms and wants to draw from the Continental Store. It is very probable this Regiment is one whose time of service is near expiring, and that they now want to get hold of public Arms.[3]

I have spoke to Genl Knox upon the subject of sending more Artillery Men to Fort Arnold, he tells me, that he cannot, without leaving part of the Artillery here unmanned, possibly spare any more. I shall desire the Qr Mr Genl to make an enquiry into the disturbance among the Artificers, and know by what authority their Wages have been raised to so extravagant a sum. I am &c.

Df, in Tench Tilghman's writing, DLC:GW; Varick transcript, DLC:GW.

1. Malcom's letter has not been found, and the return has not been identified, but for a report of the troops at West Point, see Adj. Gen. Alexander Scammell's "Monthly Return of The Continental Army under the more immediate Command of His Excellency George Washington Esq." for 30 Aug. 1778 (DNA: RG 93, Revolutionary War Rolls, 1775–1783).

2. See GW to George Clinton, 28 August.

3. Abijah Brown (1736–1818) was lieutenant colonel of Col. Thomas Poor's regiment of Massachusetts militia, raised in May for defense of the North River and discharged on 20 Oct. 1778. His representation, if written, has not been found.

## From Brigadier General Samuel Holden Parsons

Dear General                                    [White Plains] 29th Augt [1778]

By my Son from Long Island, yesterday, I learn that Genl Clinton's Baggage arrivd at Flushing last Wednesday.[1] he was expected there last Thursday; about forty Field Peices had arrivd at Flushing from New York: that the Hessians at Huntington had marchd for Jamaica: that the Dragoons at Huntington had receivd Orders to march to the Narrows; but when they were ready to march were Orderd to wait for further Orders—that Orders were sent to Genl Tryon to hasten his March Westward, that his Troops were incampd Yesterday at Satacket on their Way Westward. That he heard the English Fleet saild last Wednesday, this Acct he recd from Col. Webb, and others, of our Prisoners, that the Inhabitants are anxious to have Arms & a few Men sent to them and they will Answer for Govr Tryon & his Command—That All the Vessells near the Harbour & Bay of Huntington were orderd to the Bay under Convoy of their Ships of war, whither they had loaded or not—that there were Yesterday near Seventy Sail of Vessels in Huntington Harbour mostly Square rigd Vessels.[2]

Mr Scudder, exchangd, left New York last Saturday Says he Saw from the Provost Guard a considerable Number of Small Peices of field Artillery which were removd toward Eastward which he was informd were removd to Long Island—that the British Fleet returnd much Shatterd after the late Storm; he Saw a Ship, Said to be a 50 Gun Ship dismasted lying in the East River, that most of the Artillery which was on the Fields near the Provost Guard was removd—that the Flour in the City is very musty & the Inhabitants not well supplied even with that—That Some Troops are incampd at Bushwick, a large Camp at the Fly; No English Fleet arrivd before he left the City.[3] I am yr Excelle[n]cy's h[umbl]e Servt

Saml H. Parsons

ALS, DLC:GW.

1. The previous Wednesday was 26 August. William Walter Parsons (1762–1801), Samuel Holden Parsons's eldest son, served under his father as a fifer in the 6th Connecticut Regiment from May to December 1775. He became a midshipman on the Continental frigate *Warren* and was captured by the British during the Penobscot expedition in the summer of 1779. Moved to New York City in 1780, he escaped in April of that year. After going back to sea later in 1780, he was again captured and again escaped, from the island of Saint Eustatius in the fall of 1781.

2. Most of this intelligence is also contained in a letter from Maj. Ebenezer Gray to Parsons of 27 Aug.: "The Reports from the Island this morning are that by the best Accounts from NewYork the Enemy are making every Preparation Necessary for a Removal, and probably to New Port. The Horses in N. York and are all Shod and shewing as fast as possible. the Hessians as I mentioned Yesterday have marched and

were seen at Hemstead Marchg Westward, the Light Horse at Huntington are ordered to march but had not marched Yesterday morning, their Baggage was then loaded Sir Henry Clintons Baggage was Yesterday sent to Flushing and he is to follow this Day—The shipping are all ordered from the Harbours of Long Island into the sound ready to Sail—Eight or Nine Transports have gone to Setocket supposed to take in Genl Tryon. I can't learn that he hath moved yet all the Inhabitants from 15 to 50 years of Age are stopped & detained at Huntington Fort The Wood Cutters on Loyds & Eatons neck are stopped, and the Guards are all Called of from them Necks—Lt Brewster is not yet returned from Setocket, Capt. Allen who was on the Island last Night and by whom I have the Above, will Inform you more particularly. . . . N.B. The Brittish Fleet of about 20 sail went from the Hook Yesterday supposed for New Port. They Indeaver to keep every thing as secret as possible" (DLC:GW).

3. "Mr Scudder" may have been William Smith Scudder (1739–1804) or possibly Henry Scudder (1743–1822). William Smith Scudder, who had been a private in the 2d New York Regiment in 1776 and later a whaleboat captain, was captured by Loyalists while raiding Long Island in March 1778 (see *Royal Gazette* [New York], 7 Mar.), but he was released before 30 Oct. 1778, when the New York council of appointment made him captain of the privateer *Ranger*, a commission revoked in 1781. Henry Scudder, a lieutenant in the Suffolk County, N.Y., militia, was taken prisoner at Long Island on 27 Aug. 1776. After his release, he was reputedly active in raiding Long Island to gather supplies and information about British movements. Bushwick, now within Brooklyn, is in the northeast part of Kings County, near the Queens County boundary. The Head of the Fly was located at the southern end of what was then the town of Flushing near the border of Newtown.

## From Brigadier General Charles Scott

Sir                                  [Westchester County, N.Y.] 29th August 1778.
    Inclosed is the intelligence I this moment received from Colls Butler & Parker.[1] I am your Excellencys Obedient Servt

                                                            Chs Scott

Sprague transcript, DLC:GW. Scott wrote and signed a note on the cover of the letter: "pass the Bearer to Head Quarters" (MB).
    1. The enclosure, a letter to Scott from colonels Richard Butler and Richard Parker, dated "New Rochelle [N.Y.] ½ past 10 OClock," reads: "We find the Whole fleet that lay Yesterday off City Island has weighd Anchor & are proceeding in A body toward the East end of Long Island, they movd last Evning & was About two hours in getting the whole underway, the firing that has been heard was their Signals—we have made Inquiry about troops being on board but Can get nothing Certain—one of the Inhabitants here Say that he heard they had Artillery on board—Another that Saw one moss a fisherman that goes to Long Island heard him Say that there was A Number of the Brittish troops there both Horse & foot & that he heard there that they were to go on board this fleet to Rhode Island—they Seem Intent on the voy[a]ge be it to where it will as they ar Now getting underway from opposite Horseneck, Although there is A Strong head wind, we hoped to See Moss ourselves but he is gone Afishing, therefore Shall Wait his Return if he cant be too long; the Man we want to See is out, we wait for him also—it is our Opinion that they must have

troops on board & all for Some Expedition by their different Movement, Moss has just Returnd, & Informs us that he Saw at flushing last thursday Sennight A Number of brittish troops both horse & foot that Iron had been brot from York to Shoe horses that he Saw yesterday four Vessells fited to Carry Cavarlry—& on the Sides of Some Vessells Gun-Carriage-wheels hanging & Several flat bottomd boats—which with the boats of the transports was Suffiscient to Embark as many troops as the whole Could Carry in four hours, that A horse guard was Close to the landing place Near where the Shipping lay & the other horses at Grass Near Flushing; (That Col. Hamilton and the long Island Millitia, had marchd toward the East end of the Island, before he had got there) & that there was A good deal of Provissions on board the Transports—We Shall try to Settle matters & Return as Soon as possible—if the wind falls a man will go ⟨over⟩ this Evning—" (DLC:GW).

Later on this date Scott wrote a second letter to GW enclosing "farther Intelligence from Colos. Butler & parker" (DLC:GW). That enclosure, dated from New Rochelle at "1 OClock," reads: "from Lewis Lecompte, by A woman from on board the Scorpion—Admirals Howe & Gambier with the Ships of war gone by the South passage for Rhode Island—those gone up the Sound She Says have taken the troops from L. Island all on board both Horse & foot with forage &c.

"the Guard Ship from Hampstead harbour, & the Scorpion guard Ship from City Island are Certainly gone in the fleet this womans husband is one of the Pilots—one Baxter & one other Captn with two Brigs are left at the City Island Station—we follow the woman towards Marrawneck for further Inteligence—She also Mentions that they Intend to Attack Genl Washington" (DLC:GW).

## To Brigadier General John Stark

Sir                        Head Quarters White plains 29th Augt 1778.

I have duly recd yours of the 13th 18th 19th and 21st instants to which I shall reply in course.[1] I have desired the pay Master General to appoint a deputy at Albany and to supply him with the proper Sums to pay the troops to the Northward. I have it not in my power to make you any extra allowance for your expences, an application upon that head must be made to Congress. If Capt. McKeens Company of Rangers is raised for a limited time to answer any good purpose, I have no objection to their being taken into continental pay, but if they are intended to be a permanent Corps, and to act in one particular district, I have the same objection to them, that I have to all Corps raised for local purposes, and cannot give my sanction to them, if they are upon such terms—I will desire Genl Knox to order some 2. 3 and 4 pound shot to be sent to Albany—The application for Cloathing for Colo. Whitcombs Rangers should have been made to the Cloathier General. I have not seen Lt Mott, who you say is sent down for the Cloaths, but when he arrives I will direct him in what manner to make the application in a proper manner.[2]

The appointment of a deputy Commissary in the room of Mr Winship lays intirely with the Commy General. He has been informed of

Mr Winships intended resignation, and will no doubt take care to appoint another.

I shall lay yours of the 21st respecting the Deputy Qr Mr at Albany before the Qr Mr Gen. and shall desire him to make enquiry into so extraordinary a conduct as you represent.[3] I am &c.

Df, in Tench Tilghman's writing, DLC:GW; Varick transcript, DLC:GW.
    1. Stark's letter to GW of 18 Aug. has not been found. The only identified copy of the letter here acknowledged as a letter of 13 Aug. is a printed publication in which the letter is dated 15 August. The correct date has not been determined with certainty.
    2. John Mott (1747–1831) was commissioned a second lieutenant in Capt. Thomas Lee's Independent Company of New Hampshire Rangers in December 1776. He left that company in March 1778 but apparently joined Maj. Benjamin Whitcomb's New Hampshire Rangers. In December 1778 he was stationed at Fort Ranger at Rutland in what is now Vermont.
    3. For Deputy Quartermaster General Morgan Lewis's response to the inquiry, see Lewis to GW, 11 Sept., and Charles Pettit to GW, 15 October.

## To Major General John Sullivan

Dear Sir,

Head Quarters White Plains
Aug. 29th 1778 9 oClock P.M.

I wrote to you yesterday, informing you, that a number of transports were in the sound. Last night they got under way and proceeded Eastward as far as opposite to Oyster bay; where they seem to have been stopped by the wind being contrary. There were from sixty to seventy sail. From every intelligence it appears certain, that a considerable number of troops have crossed over to Long Island; and different reports say, that they have been embarked on board the transports in the Sound. One account mentions, that Sir Henry Clinton himself is with them, with five thousand men.[1] But however these particulars may be, there can be no doubt, that every exertion is making to relieve Rhode Island. I am with great regard Dear Sir Your most Obedt Ser.

Go: Washington

P.S. About 50 of the above transports were topsail vessels.

LS, in Alexander Hamilton's writing, NhHi: Sullivan Papers; Df, DLC:GW; Varick transcript, DLC:GW.
    1. In a letter of this day dated "Saturday Morng 5 oClock," Elisha Boudinot wrote Alexander Hamilton, "The Person I mentioned to you came over last Night and informs me, that General Clinton with his whole Army has set off for Rhode Island—they are gone up the Sound and across to the East End of Long Island—there are only a small Guard left in the City—not a Canoe is suffered to pass up the East River—least it should be known, they moved with the utmost Secresy—As it might be you have not heard of this movement I send this by Express" (DLC:GW). The

intelligence was generally accurate; British officer Archibald Robertson noted in his diary for 27 Aug.: "I embarkd at Whitstone Point in Long Island along with the Commander in Chief with about 4000 men under the Command of General Grey to relieve Rhode Island" (Lydenberg, *Robertson Diaries*, 181; see also André, *Journal*, 84–85).

## From Major General John Sullivan

Head Qrs Augt 29th [1778]
Dear General,                                on the North end of R. Isl.

A Retreat to the North End of the Island[1] having been deemd adviseable (from our great diminution of Numbers) by the determination of a Council of War held the 26th Instant—I last evening gave the necessary orders for and effected a well timed & regular retreat without losing any part of my Baggage, Stores, or heavy Ordinance. The Enemy was apprizd of the Movement sometime in the Night—they had I suppose concluded that I had retreated in confusion & with Precipitation and no doubt with an expectation of my having crossd part of my Army and that the remainder wou'd become an easy Victory. In this belief, they advancd in two Columns, on the east and west roads; and vigorously attackd Colonels Livingstone and Lawrence, whose Corps were disposd of between the two Roads in front of the Army. They were warmly recievd by both those Gentlemen, whom I reinforcd occasionally, to prevent the Contests being too unequal, tho at the same time they were directed to retreat regularly and at their leisure. They strictly complyd with the order; for I scarcely remember any thing of the kind more regular—The Enemy were naturally led on to the Neighbourhood—they took post on Commanding Ground in our Front, and immediately attempted to turn our right flank—To prevent this, I detachd considerable Bodies of Infantry—Our Artillery was well servd did great execution, and contributed not a little to the Honor of the day—Skirmishing prevaild during the day & the Success of it, was determind by a warm action which lasted near an hour. The Enemy were obligd to retire in great disorder, leaving us in full possession of the Field of Action[2]—Our Loss in killd and wounded is not yet ascertaind by Returns, but is very considerable—Among the latter I have the mortification to find many valuable officers, whose Names and Rank shall be transmitted to your Excellency in my next—The Loss of the Enemy must be great[3] two of the Enemys Frigates endeavourd to enfilade our Lines; but did us no Injury[4]—I shall make it my Business to inform your Excellency as soon as possible, of such Corps and Officers who had an Opportunity of distinguishing themselves in the Action—for my whole Army only seem'd to want an Opportunity of doing themselves & Country honor—I am sorry I can not at present be more particular. I am Dr General, Yr Excellencys, most obedient and very hble servt

Jno. Sullivan

LS, DLC:GW; copy, DNA:PCC, item 160; copy, MiU-C: Clinton Papers; copy, ScHi: Henry Laurens Papers; copy (extract), PHi: Wayne Papers. The copy in DNA:PCC was enclosed with GW's letter to Henry Laurens of 1 September. Congress read the letter on 4 Sept., and it was published by their authority the next day (*JCC,* 12:880; *Pennsylvania Packet or the General Advertiser* [Philadelphia], 5 Sept.). The copy in the Clinton Papers is misdated 1777.

1. Sullivan inserted the preceding seven words on the LS.

2. The British commander at Newport, Maj. Gen. Robert Pigot, gave his report of these events in a letter to Gen. Henry Clinton of 31 Aug.: "The twenty-ninth at Break of Day it was perceived that the Enemy had retreated during the Night, upon which Major General Prescott was ordered to detach a Regiment from the Second Line under his Command over Easton's Beach towards the left Flank of the Enemy's Encampment, and a part of Brown's Corps was directed to take Possession of their Works. At the same time Brigadier General Smith was detached with the 22d & 43d Regiments, and the Flank Companies of the 38th and 54th by the East Road, Major General Lossberg marching by the West Road with the Hessian Chasseurs and the two Ansbach Regiments of Voit and Seyboth, in order if possible to annoy them in their Retreat, and upon receiving a Report from General Smith that the Rebels made a Stand and were in Force upon Quaker's Hill, I ordered the 54th, & Hessian Regiment of Huyn with Part of Brown's Corps to sustain him, but before they could arrive the perseverance of General Smith and the spirited Behaviour of the Troops had gained Possession of the strong Post on Quaker's Hill, and obliged the Enemy to retire to their Works at the North End of the Island. On hearing a smart Fire from the Chasseurs engaged on the West Road, I dispatched Colonel Fanning's Corps of Provincials to join General Lossberg, who obliged the Rebels to quit two Redoubts made to cover their Retreat, drove them before him and took possession of Turkey Hill. Towards Evening an Attempt being made by the Rebels to surround and cut off the Chasseurs who were advanced on the Left, the Regiments of Fanning & Huyn were ordered up to their Support, and after a smart Engagement with the Enemy obliged them to retreat to their Main Body on Windmill Hill. . . . After these Actions the Enemy took Post in great Numbers on Windmill Hill, and employed themselves in strengthening that advantageous Situation" (P.R.O., Colonial Office, 5/96, Military Correspondence of the British Generals; see also Davies, *Documents of the American Revolution,* 15:191–92). For other British and Hessian accounts of the day, see *Mackenzie Diary,* 2:380–85; Döhla, *Hessian Diary,* 87–88; and Prechtel, *Diary,* 26, 149. For American accounts of the battle, see Thomas Crafts to William Heath, 30 Aug. 1778, MHi: Heath Papers; "Wild Journal," 116; Field, *Angell Diary,* 8–9; Ward, "Colonel Samuel Ward," 121; Gibbs diary, 5–30 Aug., *Pa. Archives,* 1st ser., 6:736; *Independent Ledger, and the American Advertiser* (Boston), 7 Sept.; and *Connecticut Courant, and the Weekly Intelligencer* (Hartford), 8 September.

3. Pigot's official report of British casualties listed 38 killed, 210 wounded, and 12 missing for a total of 260 (P.R.O., Colonial Office, 5/96, Military Correspondence of the British Generals; see also *Remembrancer,* 7:35–36).

4. In the account of the battle that Capt. Frederick Mackenzie of the Royal Welch Fusiliers wrote in his diary for 29 Aug., he stated that "As soon as the Troops marched

out in pursuit of the Rebels, The Sphynx, and Vigilant, with the Spitfire Galley and the Privateer Brig, got under way . . . and worked up the passage between Rhode-Island and Prudence, in order to annoy the Enemy's right if there should be an opportunity. The Vigilant got up in time to have some shots at the right of the Rebels when drawn up in front of the Artillery Redoubt, but they turning some 18 prs against her from thence and from Arnold's point, she dropt lower down, and anchored with the other vessels opposite Slocum's. We were of opinion that had The Vigilant continued in the position she had gained and persisted in cannonading the Enemy's right with her 24 prs she would have galled them exceedingly, and possibly have enabled us to turn that flank. 'Tis certain there was no necessity for her moving back so soon as she did" (*Mackenzie Diary*, 2 : 383).

The captain's log of the *Vigilant* recorded that at 7 : 30 A.M. he "received orders to Weigh & try to cut off the Retreat of the Rebels at Bristol Ferry." While "working up" toward the ferry, at 10 A.M. he "Observed the British and Hessian Troops engaged with the Rebels who had posted themselves on Quaker and Windmill hills," and at 11 : 30 the ship "Stood close in & fired Several Shot to facilitate the operations of the Hessians who were by this time driveing the Rebels out of the Wood." Then, observing the Americans "turning a Work up" at Portsmouth Point, he "Stood close in and fired Several Guns with Round & Grape among those people which only disturbed them for the time. . . . At 1 P.M. Stood up as far towards Bristol Ferry as the Pilot would take Charge of the Ship the Rebels kept a Constant fire . . . from a Battery above the Ferry most of which Shot fell close on board and the rest passed over between the Mast Hd and kept fireing Shot at the Rebels posted on Wind Mill and Quaker hills." At 2 the ship again "Stood Close in" to support the Hessians, "but . . . the Rebels began a Cannonade from three 24 pounders the three first Shot hulled the Ship and the others fell all round her, received orders . . . to move." Thereafter the ship was "employed Standing off and on frequently exchangeing Shot with the Enemy. . . . At 6 the Cannonade on shore began to abate D[itt]o received orders . . . to Anchor on the Flank of the British Army during the Night with the Reprisal Brig and the Sphynx with the other two Armed Vessels stood over and Anchored under the No. end of Prudence Island" (P.R.O., Adm. 51/1037).

# From Jean-Baptiste Ternant

sir                           White plains August 29th 1778

When I accepted of the military offices proposed to me in this army, & undertook to discharge the duties of them as a volunteer, besides other motives, I had two chief objects in view: 1° to try my own self & learn from experience what I could not get with certainty from Theorical speculations, 2° to give your Excellency an opportunity of judging of my military abilities, talents &c.—how Satisfactory to you, & favorable to me this last object has been, I cannot tell, your approbation or censure about my operations having not yet come to my Knowledge— As for the first object, experience has fully Satisfied my wish, & from that experience I will draw & expose my reasons to your Excelly— I have acted four months as an Inspector, & six weeks as Dy Qr Mr Gl for the field operations with numberless difficulties to encounter, & no other means to enforce obedience to my orders but reasoning, persuasion & patience—with Those means alone, I undertook the task, & directed all my efforts towards the greatest advantage of the army—but notwithstanding my utmost exertions, I could not be half So usefull as I might have been, had I been supplied with the proper means— Those means I have fully explained several times to the heads of the departments I acted in, with their approbation & promise of taking the necessary steps, to put things on a proper footing—Without expatiating anew upon those means, I shall only mention one that seems to me indispensable: It is rank—The nature of the offices either of Inspector or Dy Qr Mr Gl for the field operations, considering, the strong exclusive prejudices of this army in favor of rank, requires inevitably a military man, invested of course with a rank superior, at least to that of his subalterns in the departments, to discharge the duties of them with any honor or satisfaction to himself, & real benefit to the service—The means mentioned before of reasoning & persuasion, which ought to be sacred in every matter either public or private, are, however, too slow & too often ineffectual for military purposes of detail, where punctuality, celerity & exactness are requisite—nothing but military authority founded upon the principles cherished in an army, I mean those of rank, can command that respect & implicit obedience to orders, which is the very soul of discipline, the criterium of all warlike operations—nay, that military authority is even necessary to give weight & consideration to reasoning & persuasion—many a times I found the first useless & the second impracticable in the discharge of my duties meerely for want of that support—I dont say that to set up any claim to a rank which my services may not perhaps deserve, but to show the impropriety of keeping any longer in the exercice of such important offices, & particularly of the last, which could be of infinite service to the army & to your Excelleny's operations, a man destitute of the necessary means for the discharge of them: Indeed, the more I think on this subject, the greater the task appears to me, & the more I doubt of my being adequate to it—Tho' I was persuaded to the contrary by the heads of these departments; however from the inaction your Excelly has left me in, for some time, I am induced to think that you dont coincide with them in opinion—In this last case I'll beg earnestly of your Excelly a candid & friendly advise of desisting from my present pursuit—the great veneration I have for your public & private virtues, the high opinion I entertain of your military character, & the preference, I make it a rule, to give to the public good over mine, will always render welcome to me, any advise of the kind—I would only require at the same time, a testimony of my having behaved in the exercice of the offices entrusted to me, as a wellmeaning member of These communities, who has used his utmost exertions, both in & out of action, to be usefull; in order that after having retired to a private & rural life no

body might question the uprightness of my public one in the army—
if on the contrary your Excelly has formed a Judgement more advantageous of my abilities than I imagine, & should think proper to continue me in the exercice of these or one of these offices, I hope you'll
consider of the indispensable necessity of my being supplied with rank
by commission, & such other means as will enable me to do the greatest good in my power—meanwhile I'll beg leave of your Excelly to
attend for a few days to my private affairs in Philadelphia. I have the
honor to be with respect your Excellency's most obedient & humble
servant

John Ternant

ALS, DLC:GW.

## General Orders

Head-Quarters W. Plains August 30th 1778.
Parole Industry—                    C. Signs Ireton. Ixworth—
The General Court Martial of the Line whereof Coll Hazen is President is dissolved and another is ordered to sit tomorrow nine oClock at
the usual place to try all such Persons as shall be brought before them.

Colonel Humpton is appointed President, Lieutt Coll Miller, Major
Thompson and a Captain from each Brigade except Nixon's Late
Larned's & Waynes are to attend as Members.[1]

Varick transcript, DLC:GW.
1. In Maj. Gen. Benjamin Lincoln's orderly book, this order continues: "all Evidences & Persons concernd to attend" (MHi: Lincoln Papers). Joseph Thompson
(1733–c.1795) of Brimfield, Mass., who had served as an ensign and lieutenant during the French and Indian War, was a captain in the Lexington Alarm of April 1775
and became a captain in Col. Timothy Danielson's Massachusetts Regiment in May
of that year. In January 1776 Thompson's company was consolidated with the 6th
Massachusetts Regiment into the 4th Continental Infantry (later designated as
Nixon's Regiment). Thompson was promoted to major in November 1776 and remained at that rank until the summer of 1779, when he was promoted to lieutenant
colonel of the 10th Massachusetts Regiment with a commission backdated to December 1777. Captured at an engagement in Westchester County on 3 Feb. 1780,
Thompson was exchanged in December 1780 and retired in January 1781.

## From Artillery Captain Lieutenants

Sir,                        Artillery Park [White Plains, N.Y.] 30th Augt 1778.
It is with the most unfeigned concern that the Captain Lieutenants
of Artillery find themselves under a real necessity of beging your Excellency's attention to their case, as they conceive themselves very sen-

sibly affected by a Resolve of the Honorable Congress passed the 27th May last.[1] They wish your Excellency to be assured that no consideration but a clear conviction of the justice they owe to their reputation could have prevailed on them to trouble you with an affair of this nature, or intrude on those moments of your Excellency's which are constantly devoted to subjects of a more public and general utility—at the same time, they pray your Excellency's indulgence, while they state the several matters of which they think they have reason to complain.

The Resolve refered to respects the Establishment and Pay of the American Army, by which we, the Captain Lieutenants of Artillery, are pointed out to the world as the only exception to the general rule observed by Congress on that occasion.

On forming the Corps of Artillery in 1776, the Pay of the Captain Lieutenants was fixed at the same rate as Captains of Infantry, and that of Captains and Field Officers at twenty five per cent more than those of equal rank in that Line, to commence the first day of January following,[2] it took place accordingly, and has been received by them ever since. Several reasons we presume might be offered in support of the propriety of this Establishment, we will only mention one: that as the nature of the service required a greater number of Officers in the Artillery under the degree of Captains, and at the same time did not allow us to rise in any other than our own Line, the appointment of Captain-Lieutenant, with the Pay of Captain in the Infantry, was considered as a compensation for the inconveniences sustained by us in having our promotion confined to such narrow limits.

Under these circumstances, and at a time when it was universally expected by the Officers of the Army that their Pay would, at least, have been continued, and which in fact is done by the Resolves refered to, as far as respects the Infantry—we, the Captain Lieutenants of Artillery, are exceedingly surprized and concernd in finding ourselves the only persons who experience a contrary treatment. The more so, as it is, by a subsequent Resolve of the same date, fixed, "That, when supernumerary Lieutenants are continued under this arrangement of the Battalions, who are to do the duty of Ensigns, they shall be intitled to hold their rank, and receive the pay such rank intitled them to receive". In this case, Lieutenants in the Infantry, though *doing duty as Ensigns*, are nevertheless intitled to their Rank and Pay as Lieutenants; while Captain-Lieutenants of Artillery, who have ever been acknowledged, respected, and obeyed as senior to any and every Lieutenant in the Line, *both as to Rank and Pay*, have had the latter reduced to the same standard with that of a Lieutenant; and are not without just apprehensions that the former also will be regarded by the Army at large as proportionably reduced.[3]

We are the more induced to apprehend consequences of this nature, as in the Resolve of the 2d of June, allowing subsistence to Officers, no notice is taken of such a Rank in the Army as Captain Lieutenants, and of course no provision made for them.[4] In this instance we know not whether to consider ourselves as intitled to subsistence at all—whether as Captains—or only as Lieutenants and Ensigns. Upon the whole, we are exceedingly at a loss indeed upon what principles to account for the exception Congress have been pleased to make in our particular case; especially as they have not extended it to that of any other Officers, even in our own Corps.

Having just mentioned these Concerns, we are happy in refering them to Your Excellency's consideration, fully convinced, that ourselves cannot be more ready to complain of grievances than Your Excellency to recommend a redress of such as may appear resonable.[5]

We beg Your Excellency's pardon for this intrusion—and are, with every Sentiment of Respect and Attachment, Your Excellency's most dutiful Servants,

| | |
|---|---|
| Isaiah Bussey | Wm Fleming Gaines |
| Ebenr Finley | Oliver Brown |
| Jonas Simonds | Daniel Gano |
| John Gridley | Thos Vose |
| Willm Power | S. Shaw |
| James Smith | Tho. Barr |
| James McClure | Edward Archbald |
| John Pryor | Geo: Fleming |
| Wm Godman | Jacob Reed |
| A. Bohannon | Thos Jackson |
| Lewis Booker | Thos Thomptson |
| Whitehead Coleman | Joseph Thomas |
| John Lillie | Philip Jones |
| | William Stevens |

DS, DLC:GW; copy, DNA:PCC, item 152; copy, DNA:PCC, item 169. The copy in item 152, which was enclosed with GW's letter to John Jay of 24 April 1779, omitted the signatures but noted that the document was "signed by 21 [27] Capt. Lieuts. being all who were at that time in camp." Ambrose Bohannon, Lewis Booker (1754–1814), Whitehead Coleman, Ebenezer Finley, William Fleming Gaines (c.1750–1797), William Godman (1754–1825), John Pryor, and James Smith (d. 1782) were in the 1st Continental Artillery; Edward Archbald, George Fleming (d. 1822), Daniel Gano (1758–1849), James McClure, William Power (1759–1835), Jacob Reed, Jonas Simonds (d. 1816), William Stevens, Joseph Thomas (d. 1804), and Thomas Thomptson (d. 1780) were with the 2d Continental Artillery; and Oliver Brown (1753–1846), Isaiah Bussey (b. 1741), John Gridley (d. 1830), Thomas Jackson (d. 1790), John Lillie, and Samuel Shaw were with the 3d Continental Artillery. Thomas Barr and Thomas Vose (d. 1810) belonged to Maj. Ebenezer Stevens's Independent Battalion of Artillery, annexed to the 3d Continental Artillery, and Philip Jones served with Capt. John Kingsbury's Independent Company of North Carolina Artillery. Coleman's promotion to captain, dated 15 Aug., apparently was not yet known, while Shaw was functioning as a brigade major and Gaines as an adjutant.

1. The captain lieutenants were referring to resolutions creating a new arrangement of the Continental army (*JCC*, 11:538–43).

2. When on 20 Dec. 1776 GW wrote then-president of Congress John Hancock to press for augmentation of the corps of artillery, he wrote that the artillerists' dissatisfaction with their pay had induced him "to promise Officers & men, that their pay should be augmented 25 ℔ Ct." Congress passed a resolution on 27 Dec. 1776 that authorized GW to recruit three regiments of artillery "and to establish their pay" (ibid., 6:1045–46).

3. The new resolutions set the pay of artillery captain lieutenants at $33⅓ per month, the same as artillery lieutenants and less than infantry captains, who received $40 per month. Infantry lieutenants (and captain lieutenants) were to be paid $26⅔ per month. For the quoted resolution, see ibid., 11:543.

4. For this resolution, see ibid., 11:560–61.

5. According to GW's letter of 24 April 1779 transmitting a copy of this to Congress and supporting the appeal, at this time he submitted the protest to the committee of arrangement, but no action was taken.


# From Captain Epaphras Bull

Sir                                   Sunday Morning 9 OClock [30 August 1778]
I have to Inform your Excellency that between 7 and 8 OClock the Fleet made Sail and Stood on to the Etward, the Transport, which I mentioned as having Troops on board Last Night, appeard to have them to day, they are now almost out of Sight.[1] I have the Honour to be your Excellencys Mot Obt Sert

Epaps Bull

ALS, DLC:GW. The date is taken from a docket on the cover.
1. Bull's letter to GW of the previous night has not been found.


# From the Continental Congress Committee of Arrangement

                                   Head Quarters Sunday at 12 o'Clock
Dear Sir                                                [30 August 1778]
It is submitted by the Committee to your Excellency's Judgement, whether it would not be better to direct an adjournment of the Court Martial, which is composed of the principal Part of the Genl officers, for a few daies untill the arrangement of the army shall be completed,

as all Information, & subject matter for the Committee to proceed upon is derived from these officers.[1]

The Committee also request your Excellency to order the attendance of Generals Poor, Patterson & Nixon, Tomorrow—They were Part of yesterday at a loss for Information, & have in Consequence thereof troubled you with the above Requests, hoping that no inconvenience may be derived from postponing the business of the Court martial, & great good result from a permanent Settlement of the Army. I am with every Sentiment of attachment & Regard yr Excellency's respectful & obedient Servant

By desire of the Committee                                    John Banister

ALS, DNA: RG 93, manuscript file no. 29350. The date is taken from an endorsement on the letter.

1. The committee was referring to the court-martial for the trial of Maj. Gen. Arthur St. Clair, constituted in the general orders of 23 August. The court, which had adjourned "till tomorrow" on 29 Aug., subsequently adjourned "by his Excellency's desire, until Thursday next" (3 Sept.) and then again "until Monday" (7 Sept.), when they resumed taking testimony (*St. Clair Court Martial*, 20).

## From Major General William Heath

Dear General                          Head Quarters Boston 30th Augt 1778
I have been honored with the receipt of yours of the 14th Instant.[1]

I beg leave to observe to your Excellency that a large Sum of Money is now due to the United States from the British Government for Supplies furnished to the Troops of the Convention and that the pay Master and Commissary to those Troops were just going for Rhode Island with the Accounts to obtain the money, when the Expedition against that place was whispered on which I stoped them. As it can now answer no purpose to permit them to go to Rhode Island I wish to be informed whether you have any objection to their going to New York, & by what rout you will have them go: To embarke at some port on the Sound or pass by the way of your Head Quarters, whether they shall proceed as soon as I receive your answer, or upon account of the present situation of our Army it will be best to delay it longer. Your Excellency will remember that Mr Commissary Clarke carried the last accounts to Philadelphia[2] and I apprehend no objection can now be made to his being sent to New York unless on account of some particular situation of our Army which leads me to request your Excellency's opinion & direction before I permi⟨t⟩ him and the pay Master to proceed. Nea⟨r⟩ Six Months Supplies are now due, the United States are the only Sufferers by so much money lying dead.

Inclosed is a Letter which I received the last night from Portsmouth with a request to forward it with care.[3]

I also take the liberty to inclose a Schedule of provisions which I received the last night from the Major of the French Fleet and said to be necessary for three Months Supply for them; but how this quantity can be procured here, especially the Flour, I cannot tell.[4] I have the Honor to be With great respect Your Excellency's Obedt Servant

W. Heath

LS, DLC:GW; ADf, MHi: Heath Papers; copy (extract), DNA:PCC, item 152; copy (extract), DNA:PCC, item 169. The extract in item 152 was enclosed with GW's letter to Henry Laurens of 7 Sept.; both extracts consist of the last paragraph and the schedule of provisions.

1. At this point on the draft, Heath wrote and struck out the following paragraph: "I am extremely Sorry to have given your Excellency so much Trouble with General Phillips's request for an Officer to go to Canada by the way of the Lakes as to write to Congress on the Subject—Your Excellency is Sensible that the Troops of the Convention, Stipulated that if they found it necessary to Send for their Clothing & other Baggage to Canada they should be permitted to do it in the most Convenient manner and the necessary Passports granted for the purpose accordingly when application was made to me for that purpose the last april I immediately gave the necessary Pass Ports for an Officer to go by the way of Hallifax—as that officer has not Since been heard off Genl Phillips wished to have another go by the way of the Lakes (that their Baggage may if Possible arrive before the Cold Season Commences) as I did not know the Situation of our Posts on that Rout it being out of my Department and whether it would be Politick or Impolitick to allow an officer to go that way I thought it my Duty to Submit the propriety of it to your Excellency and to Crave your direction as to that rout."

2. See Heath to GW, 18 Jan., and note 1 to that document.

3. The enclosure has not been identified. Thomas Martin, a Portsmouth, N.H., merchant and state legislator, had written Heath from Portsmouth on 26 Aug. that "The inclosed letter to His Excellency General Washington being of importance to a Lady" had "embolden'd" him to request Heath to forward it by "the earliest and safest conveyance" (MHi: Heath Papers).

4. The schedule of provisions reads: "1090000 lb. Bread or 1190000 lb. Flour[,] 260000 lb. Pork[,] 400 Quintals Fish[,] 240000 lb. Beans or peas[,] 5 or 6 Quintals Mustard[,] 720 Cords of Wood" (DLC:GW).


# From Lieutenant George Hurlbut

New Rochel [N.Y.]
May it please your Excellency                         30th Augst 78

this forenoon their passed by this place, Bound EstWard, Six Sloops, two Sloops, put in Hempsted Bay[1]—the rest kep on after the Fleet— in the afternoon, passed one Schooner, & two Sloops—one Sloop had Troops on board, soon after two Ships, one of 20. Guns, the other a

Transport, passed the same Course—No Guns heard in the Sound to day. I am your Excellencys very Hbl. Servt

Go. Hurlbut

ALS, DLC:GW.
  1. Hurlbut meant Hempstead Harbor.


# From Henry Laurens

Sir                                    [Philadelphia] 30th Augt [1778]

I had the honor of addressing Your Excellency twice on the 28th Instant by Jones,[1] in that which was written last, I ought more explicitly to have acknowledged the reciept and presentment to Congress of Your Excellencys favor of the 25th and of Copies of the several Papers from General Sullivan's Camp.[2]

Congress Yesterday ordered the public Treasurer to pay into my hands five hundred Guineas to be transmitted to Your Excellency to be expended at your discretion Sir, for public service.[3] These I have put under a firm cover and committed the safe conveyance and delivery of the package to the bearer of this Captain Josiah Stoddard of the 2nd Regt of Light Dragoons.

Captain Stoddard has been long soliciting Congress on behalf of himself and twelve other Memorialists of the same Regiment for a compensation equivalent to their extra expence in equipping themselves for the service in which they are engaged. The Memorial was committed and a Report made which together with divers concomitant Papers are referred to the present Committee of Arrangement at Camp who are desired by an Act of Yesterdays' date, to make necessary enquiries of Your Excellency respecting the application of Captain Stoddard, I shall therefore for Your Excellencys' information inclose with this a Copy of the abovemention'd Act.[4] I have the honor to be &c.

LB, DNA:PCC, item 13.
  1. Laurens was referring to his two official letters to GW of 28 August.
  2. Laurens was referring to GW's second letter to him of 25 Aug., which enclosed papers from Rhode Island and was read in Congress on 28 Aug. (*JCC*, 11:848).
  3. For this order of 29 Aug., see ibid., 11:851.
  4. The enclosed copy has not been identified; for the act, see ibid., 11:851–52. Stoddard's memorial and the cavalry officers' petition (neither identified) were first read in Congress on 28 July and referred to the Board of War. The board's report was laid on the table on 7 August. Two additional letters from Stoddard were laid on the table on 22 Aug. before the matter was taken up on 29 August. On 27 Oct., Congress resolved to allow $500 to "the field officers, captains, subalterns, chaplain and surgeon of the light dragoons respectively . . . to compensate the extraordinary expence of his horse and equipment, beyond that of officers of the like

rank in the infantry; provided always, that any officer receiving such sum shall be liable to refund the same if he leaves the service during the present war," which resolution was one of two suggested by the committee of arrangement's undated report on Stoddard's memorial (ibid., 11:724, 758, 819, 827, 12:1066–67; DNA: PCC, item 21).

## From Colonel William Malcom

Sir                                                   Westpoint [N.Y.] Augt 30 1778
    I hope your Excellency will not be displeased at the number of men on furlough from my Regiment, when I assure you Sir that they were Cripples for want of shoes, and had a prospect of being supply'd by their parents who live only a few miles off—I hope in a few days to remove that complaint by obtaining shoes &c. from fishkill—Not a man more shall depart from the Garrison on furlough before december with my leave.
    Mosely's and a part of Eno's Regts go to Morrow.
    I beg leave to Suggest to your Excellency that the principal part of the Connecticut troops, are enlisted for Twelve Months—Subject to be out only Three Months at a time, but liable to be called out the next day after they get home & if not, entituled to half pay—Eno's & McLelands two good Regts are I am told on this establishmt. Lt Col. Brown is off Poor's Regiment who have upwards of Six months to Serve.
    The principal part of the Militia on the West side of the River are on the Frontiers doing duty—I am therefore apprehensive that the Governor cannot comply with your Excellencys Requisition but am sure he will do all that can be expected in the present circumstances of the State.[1] I am with due Respect your Excellencys most obedient Servant
                                                                    W. Malcom

ALS, DLC:GW.
    1. For GW's request for New York militia, see his letter to Gov. George Clinton of 28 August.

## From Colonel Rufus Putnam

Sir                                          Camp White Plains 30th August 1778
    Haveing seen a list of the Massachusetts line of Colos. said to be arrangment made by a board of General Officers as they are in future to Rank, together with the Committee of arrangment being arrived in camp, I hope your Excellency will consider as a sufficient apology for my addressing you at this time on the subject of my own Rank.
    In your letter of 11th April last you say the "Massachusetts Colonels allow that I have rank in the great line of the army from the date of my

Appointment as Colonel of Engineers, but in the line of Massachusetts they contend that I only Rank from the time of my appointment to the command of a Regiment by the state.["]

However Just the reasoning may appear to some I can by no means consent to it; I have no Idea of Commanding a Colonel of one of the other States who may command a Colonel of the Massachusetts state that (by this rule) will command me, at the same time, should three officers under these Circumstances be ordered on duty together, neither of them could have the command of the whole, because they would be commanded by each other, which would introduce a scene of Confusion and Injure the service—If these gentlemen should admit that in this case the Massachusetts line of Rank should give way to the great line of the army and the Massachusetts line should be held to only when on duty with Massachusetts Officers it would Releave us very little and opens a door for the worst of Consequences,[1] as it tends in my opinion to prevent any Regular line of rank ever being established thro' the army, but admit that this would be a good Rule in future it ought to be Rejected in the present case, for till the Resolve of Congress in 1776, Ordering 88 Battalions to be Raised dureing the war and proportioning the number to each State there was no such thing as a Massachusetts line,[2] so far from it that when the Regiments were Raised for the service of the year 1776, there was pains taken to Intermix officers of different States in the same Regiment, and there was no State appointment in the army, wherefore these Gentlemens pretentions to Rank in the Massachusetts line in the present army, cannot arise from their former Rank in that line, because there was no such line, but from their former Rank in the line of the army at large, nothing I think can be more manifest than this and therefore no Reason I presume can be given why in setling the present Massachusetts Line I should not Receive equal advantage from my appointment as Colonel of Engineers, in that line, as in the great Line of the army—According to their Arguments Lt Colo. Shearman of Colo. Webbs Regt shall have no advantage of Rank in the Connecticut Line from the Majority he had in 1776, because he was under a Massachusetts Colonel, nor I from my Lt Colonelcy by reason of my serving that year under a Connecticut Colonel[3]—The Gentlemen Ranked before me in the list I have seen, and which I think ought not to be, are Colo. Shepard & Colo. Wigglesworth the one is the 3d, the other the 4th, and I am the 5th, in 1775 Colo. Shepard & I were Lt Colos. together, he then out Ranked, and had he Obtained the Regiment Immediately on the Resignation of Colo. Learned he would still commanded ⟨me⟩ but this was not the case;[4] if it should be said that his Commanding the Regt before my appointment[5], I Answer that I Commanded a Regiment in 1775 after Colo. David Brewer was dismised as long as Colo. Shepard did in 1776 before my Appointment to the Rank of Colonel, and that he did not obtain the Rank of Colonel in the Army, till near three months after I had it—therefore I cannot see the propriety of his being Arranged before me—Colonel Wigglesworth as I am informed was not in the army in 1775 the first I ever heard of him was in 1776 when he Commanded a Regiment of New Levies to the Northward; it is possible If I had Quitted the service in the fall of 1775 that I might have had one of those Regiments, I Knew a Major who was Rejected by the General Officers as a Major in 1775 who obtained one of them, and a Lt a Major in the same Regiment—I speak not this to detract from Colo. Wigglesworth I esteem him much but to shew where this Rule would carry us to if Persued.

My own Pretentions are as follows, I was four years the last war in the Actual service of my Country, the last of which I had an Ensigns Commission, I again entered the service 19th April 1775, from which time 'till the 12th of August 1776 I served as a Lt Colonel, when I was appointed Engineer with the Rank of Colonel in the army.

That under these Circumstances any Gentleman who began his service in 1776 in the manner Colo. Wigglesworth did, should be Arranged before me, I conceive to be very Injurious not only to me but all others in my situation, Exclusive of the Idea of my appointment as Colonel of Engineers.

If this Arrangment is not fully Established I pray your Excellency to take my case into Consideration and order some Measures to be taken for my obtaining Justice,[6] I am Your Excellencys Most Obedient Hble Servt

Rufus Putnam

LS, DNA: RG 93, manuscript file no. 2106; ADf, OMC.

1. At this point on the draft, Putnam wrote and struck out the following text: "it is in Short prefering State appointment to Continantal and in a degree Reverseing the order of Rank Established by the articels of War Sect. XVIII—which Sais the Continantel Shall Take Rank first althoe of a yonger date when doing duty togather and under Continantal pay and I Suppose it is for the Same Reason they have Ranked Colo. Wigelsworth Before me who had a State Colo. Commision in 1776 Before I had my apointment as Colo. of Engeneere: this arangment Injures not only me But all the othe Massachusetts Field officrs who ware Lieut. Colo. in 1775 and ware appointed to Regimets when I was."

2. Putnam was referring to Congress's resolution of 16 Sept. 1776 (*JCC*, 5:762–63).

3. As major of the 26th Continental Regiment, Isaac Sherman served under Col. Loammi Baldwin, while as lieutenant colonel of the 22d Continental Regiment, Putnam served under Col. Samuel Wyllys.

4. Ebenezer Learned resigned as colonel of the 3d Continental Regiment in May 1776, but William Shepard was not appointed to succeed him until October of that year.

5. Putnam's draft has the words "alters the case" here.

6. On the draft, Putnam continued at this point: "if this arangment is Unalterably Established: Honour the first Prinsible of a Soldier obliges me to ask a discharge which I desire your Exelency will grant or Procure Granted by Congress." GW evidently submitted Putnam's claims to a board of general officers. An undated report (docketed in part "Septr 1778") signed by generals Johann Kalb, Alexander Mc-Dougall, Samuel Holden Parsons, William Smallwood, Henry Knox, Enoch Poor, John Paterson, and William Woodford gives their opinion "that as the State of Massachusetts did not arrange the Rank of their Colonels, that Colonel Putnam ought to Stand in the Line of that State according to his continental Commission as Colo. of Engineers in Augt 76; and that Colonel Shephard ought to rank as Colonel from the Resignation of Colonel Learned and that Colo. Wigglesworth ought to be postpond in Rank to them two Gentlemen" (DNA: RG 93, manuscript file no. 2106).

## From Brigadier General Charles Scott

Sir                    [Westchester County, N.Y.] 9 oClock 30th Aug 1778

I have inteligence from York by good Authority that Seven of the Cork fleet is arived—Which Braught 600 Marins, that they war imbarking Heavy Cannon Yesterday and other Stors, 4 or 5 Brigads imbarked two days ago part of which Was from long Island, those from York Saild Out at the Hook the others eastward, all the remainder Of the fleat was taking in Stors, it is the Genl oppinion of the Inhabitance that the enemy Are about to leave New York with all possable Dispatch. But they themselves give out that they are upon Som expedition to the eastward, it is Currantly reported in York two Days ago that Genl Sullaven had withdrawn his troops from Rhod Island. I shall have farther Accts tomorrow by the very best Authority, be assurd That every possable Care shall be taken to get the Eearliest intillegence. I am Your Excellencys Obt Servt

Chs Scott

ALS, DLC:GW. Scott's signed note on the cover of this letter reads: "Pass the Bearer to Head Quarters."

## To Joseph de Valnais

Sir                    Head Quarters White plains 30th Augt 1778

I recd yours of the 18th and was not a little surprised to find it contain a request for a certificate of your services in the American Army.[1] You must be sensible that Colo. la Balme, to whom you were appointed Aid, never entered upon the duties of his Office of Inspector of Cavalry, and that consequently you could never have given any proof of your Abilities. I shall ever be ready to give testimonials of the Merit of Officers, where there services have come under my own observation;[2] but it is not to be imagined that I should sit down & write certificates for gentlemen who have afforded me no opportunities of approving their conduct. I am Sir &c. &.

Df, in Tench Tilghman's writing, DLC:GW; Varick transcript, DLC:GW.

Joseph de Valnais (1748–1826), who had served in the Garde-de-Corps of the comte d'Artois before he came to America, became French consul at Boston in January 1779 and served there until he was recalled in October 1781. He returned to France in 1783 but served again as consul at Boston, 1815–23.

1. Valnais's letter has not been found.

2. The remainder of the draft is in James McHenry's writing, with the exception of the words "their conduct," which Tilghman inserted.

*Letter not found*: from John Augustine Washington, 30 Aug. 1778. On 23 Sept., GW wrote John Augustine Washington: "Your Letter of the 30th Ulto came to my hand a few days ago."

## General Orders

Head-Quarters W. Plains Monday Augt 31st 1778.
Parole Leonidas—                                C. Signs Liberty. Law.

A board of Field-Officers to sit this afternoon in General Poor's Brigade to settle the relative Rank of the Majors and Captains in said Brigade; Colonels Hazen, Scammell & Cilley will compose the Court; One Officer at least from each Regiment to attend the board.

General Poor will appoint a Captain from each Regiment and a Field Officer as President to settle the relative rank of the subalterns.

At a Brigade General Court Martial Augt 22nd 1778—Coll Greaton President—Lieutt Welch of Coll Putnam's Regiment was tried for challenging Captain Barns to fight a Duel and for insulting and abusive language offered to him (Captain Barns) found guilty of the Charge exhibited against him & sentenced to be cashiered.[1]

The Commander in Chief is not fully satisfied that Lieutt Welch's behaviour to Captain Barns amounted to a challenge in the sense intended by the Articles of War, nevertheless his conduct was highly culpable & merited a sentence similar to that passed by the Court.

The indecent heat and fury with which he acted and the Insult and Abuse given to Captain Barns which appeared to have been unprovoked are certainly a high Impeachment of his Discretion—Nevertheless the good Character, the General has heard of him as an Officer induces Him to restore Lieutt Welch to his command.

At another Brigade General Court-Martial August 20th—Major Lee President, Captn Ewell of the 1st Virginia State Regiment was tried— 1st "For embezzling money the property of several soldiers" and 2ndly "For Embezzling Cloathing belonging to the Public"—acquitted of the 1st charge but found guilty of the 2nd—and sentenced to be reprimanded in General orders. The General disapproves the sentence; For if Captain Ewell was guilty of the Charge of embezling public Cloathing, the sentence is entirely inadequate to the offence; if he was not guilty he ought to have been acquitted—He is to be released from his Arrest.[2]

The Regimental Surgeons are to be supplied with Paper by the Brigade Qr Masters.

Varick transcript, DLC:GW.

On this date GW's secretary James McHenry wrote Assistant Quartermaster General Charles Pettit: "Circumstances have since appeared which makes some alteration necessary in the measures mentioned by his Excellency's orders in my letter of the 29th Instant.

"In case the public boats are not removed from Norwalk they may be continued there and all belonging to individuals discharged" (DLC:GW).

1. Peter Welsh (d. 1831), formerly a sergeant in Col. John Mansfield's Massachusetts Regiment and the 27th Continental Regiment, was commissioned a second lieutenant in the 5th Massachusetts Regiment in January 1777. He resigned on 30 April 1780.

2. In February 1777 John Lee, who had served as a captain in the Virginia marines in 1776, was issued a commission, dated 1 Jan. 1777, as a captain in the 1st Virginia State Regiment. He was commissioned a major of the 2d Virginia State Regiment in February 1778 and served until 1782. Thomas W. Ewell was commissioned a captain of the 1st Virginia State Regiment in January 1777 and served into 1781. Maj. Gen. Alexander McDougall's orderly book includes an additional paragraph at this point: "At a 3d Brigade General Court Martial August 30th, Lt Colonel Ford President, Lt James Ewen [Ewing], of the 2d Maryland Regiment was tried for insolent & abusive Language & acquitted" (NHi; see also Artillery Brigade orderly book, NHi).

# From Colonel Theodorick Bland

Sr                                                    Petersbgh [Va.] Augt 31st 1778

When yr order dated White Plains Augt 3d reached me, I was in Williamsburgh, whither I had gone to make application, to the Governor & Council for such horses Arms & accoutrements as had been furnished for Genl Nelsons Corps, which had now become useless to them by their being disbanded; An order for which I obtaind. Immediately on the receipt of yrs I repair to this place to put every thing in a condition, to comply with your commands as speedily as possible, I (with some of the officers) have however been so unfortunate as to be attacked with the fever and Ague, which will necessarily retard our march; but altho I did not receive yr Favor untill the 24th of August I am in hopes I shall be able to set off the whole party tomorrow or next day at furthest, and shall march them with all possible expedition to Camp. I need not Recount to you Sr the Innumerable, matters that I have to adjust here in the Course of the great and various transactions that have been for some time past under my direction nor the Embarrasment under which I labour, on account of my being streighten'd for money, and the necessity of either continuing to purchase on credit or remaining Idle on expences with the whole party for some time past. My departure on that acct occasions no small uneasiness to those of whom I have purchased many Articles, & not less to me, who have pawnd my Credit. I have however left Capt. Lewis, to see to the finishing of The Accoutrements, and to discharge the Various debts for Horses &c. which I must leave unpaid. And as yr Excellency some time ago recommended to me to have respect to recruitg a troop for that Gentn I have left Cornet White who will probably belong to that troop, & a serjeant with a few men as well to assist him in that business. as, to bring up such men & horses as may not be fit to march.[1] Capt. Lewis is at present unfortunately ill at home I have expected him here two days past, but have been disappointed. this will I fear prevent my setting off with the party, but shall not prevent my overtaking them on their march if my own health will suffer me, I hope soon again to Join the Army & am in the mean time with the greatest respect Yr Excy's Most obedt & very H. Sert

Theok Bland

ALS, DLC:GW.

1. Bland was apparently referring to GW's letter to him of 3 July. John White was commissioned a cornet in the 1st Continental Light Dragoons on 25 June 1777.

# From Lieutenant Colonel William Butler

Schohara [N.Y.]

May it please your Excellency Augt 31st 1778

Your letter of the 13th Instant I received Yesterday, my most Grateful Acknowledgment is due your Excellency for the good Opinion you are pleased to mention of me & it shall ever be my Study to Merit the Honor your Excellency has done me.[1]

Matters is Quiet here at present—Since my last[2] I have had three Scouts out consisting of about 150 Men they continued out six days &

have been on the Heads of Susquehannah & Delaware—They met with none of the Enemy during their excursions except a few Tories two of whom they took & Captn Posey left them in the Care of three of the Militia while he pursued further, upon their Attempting to escape, the Guard Fired on them & Shot one, the other escaped.[3]

In my last I Acquainted your Excellency of my parties having drove off the Cattle that were within limits of the Frequent excursions of the Enemy, which I at the same time Acquainted General Stark with, who directed them to be sold for the use of the Captors[4]—I shou'd not However have Sold them 'till your Excellencys pleasure had been known, But the Scarcity of Pasture Obliges it to be done—I have permitted none to be Sold But those Belonging to persons who are or have been in Arms against us, the rest I have ordered to be given up, & some part even to the Wives of those now with the Enemy such as Milk Cattle.

My Reason for troubling your Excellency on thi⟨s⟩ Occasion is that it is my Opinion that Genl Stark & so⟨me⟩ persons in Power in this State is not at a good Understanding—I shall therefore have regular Accounts of the Sales Kept, & the Money Accruing detain'd until your Excellencys pleasure shall be known.[5]

Inclosed I send your Excellency some intelligence I received a few days ago by a Spy.[6]

In my last I mentioned to your Excellency of my having proposed to Genl Stark a plan for Acting Offensively against the Enemy, But his Sentiments & mine in some particulars do not agree, I shall however in a few days go to Albany & Consult the Genl personally on that Subject & will inform your Excellency of the result.

The Officer sent to Camp for Cloathing is returned But had the Misfortune (having part of the Articles mentioned in his Order to receive at Fish Kilns) Not to meet with the Clothier at that place who on his Arrival there was gone to Camp—Shoes the most Material Article he has brought none, The Rifle Choir [Corps] on joining me were almost Barefoot & are now scarce able to do duty for want of Shoes, the Case is very little better with my own Regement, As my sole dependance are in these two Choirs I take the liberty to Beg your Excellency woud Order a supply. I remain with respect Yr Excellency Hble Servt

Wm Butler

ALS, DLC:GW.

1. Butler was apparently referring to GW's letter to him of 24 Aug., which replied to Butler's letter to GW of 13 August.

2. Butler was referring to his letter to GW of 13 August.

3. The shooting of Harmonus Dumond in this incident became a matter of controversy and investigation in New York. For more on the scouting expedition and the shooting, see Thomas Posey to GW, 23 Sept., and the affidavits of John Barrow,

5 Sept.; Catherine Vanwaggoner, 15 Sept.; Alexander Harper, 16 Sept.; Gabriel Long, 16 Sept.; Posey, 16 Sept.; and Alexander Ramsey, 16 Sept., enclosed with Butler's letter to GW of 27 Sept. (all DLC:GW). See also John Cantine to George Clinton, 4 Sept.; Butler to Clinton, 27 Sept., with enclosed depositions; Posey to Clinton, 23 Sept.; and Clinton to Posey, 5 Oct. (Hastings, *Clinton Papers*, 3:728–30, 4:103–11, 139–41).

4. See John Stark to Butler, 16 Aug. (Stark, *Memoir of John Stark*, 185–86).

5. On this date the Albany commissioners of sequestration wrote Butler to "make Demand of all Cattle &c., . . . excepting such as have been taken from the Enemy which they where Actually Driving of" (Hastings, *Clinton Papers*, 3:706). Butler consulted with the committee and agreed to retain the money from the sale until GW and Governor Clinton had been consulted (Butler to Clinton, 31 Aug., ibid., 3:710–11). Clinton replied that he lacked authority to resolve the dispute (Clinton to Myndert Roseboom and Flores Bancker, and to Butler, both 8 Sept., ibid., 4:11–12). GW replied in a letter to Butler of 11 September.

6. The enclosure was a copy of sworn testimony, dated 29 Aug., from John McKenzie, who stated "that on the 17th Instant he set out for Unandilla & Arrived there the 19th where he Continued until the 24th, while he was there he discoursed with a Number of his Acquaintance who had Joined the Enemy, who told him that their Numbers at Achquaga & Unandilla is about 4 or 500 White Men, & there was different Accounts concerning the Number of Indians at those places some thought 500 others 600 & others fewer.

"The Deponent was also told that [John] Butler is at Chamong with 1100 Indians—that Brandt Commands at Achquaga & that their Intentions is not to Attack the Frontiers unless the British Troops make an excursion out of York—Bread very scarce" (DLC:GW).


## To Ezekiel Cheever

Sir                               Head Quarters White plains 31st Augt 1778

I have information that there were a considerable number of Troops, on board the transports that went to the Eastward a few days ago, under the command of Genl Clinton and Lord Cornwallis. I have no doubt but the intent of this expedition was to have relieved Rhode Island, but when they find that, by the French Fleet being obliged to bear away to Boston to refit, the seige is raised, they may perhaps turn their force and views to some other object. The destruction of our Magazines of provision and military Stores is what they have aimed at thro' the whole course of this War, and I should not therefore be surprised, should they attempt to destroy Spring feild by a Coup de Main. To guard against this as much as possible, I would have you turn your attention to the sound and if you hear with certainty that a Body of troops are landed upon the Coast of Connecticut, you will begin to remove your most valuable Stores back into the Country. You will observe, that I am speaking from my apprehensions of what may happen, and not from any intelligence that the enemy have such a design. You

will not therefore be alarmed by any vague reports, but settle a correspondence with some intellige⟨nt⟩ Gentlemen upon the Coast, who
will give you such information as will justify you in beginning to remove
the stores—You will keep this matter as much to yourself as the nature
of the thing will admit. I am Sir Yr most obt Servt.

Df, in Tench Tilghman's writing, DLC:GW; Varick transcript, DLC:GW.

## To Major Alexander Clough

Sir                              Head Quarters White plains 31st Augt 1778
   It is of the utmost importance that we should ascertain whether General Clinton and Lord Cornwallis are both gone to the Eastward and
what Corps embarked in the sound and at the Hook. I would have you
make use of every endeavour to gain intelligence upon the above
points, and also of what the enemy are doing since they sent off their
detatchment. If there is any person upon whom you think you can depend, you may send him over and promise him a handsome reward if
he brings such intelligence as is really material and interesting. I have
so many reports brought me by ignorant unobserving people that they
serve to perplex more than inform. Whatever accounts you get, be
pleased to forward them to me; by comparing them with others from
different quarters they sometimes confirm intelligence. I am &c.

P.S. desire the person to make particular enquiry whether the Grenadiers and Light Infantry are gone. Keep a scout at fort Lee to observe
what ships are in the North River.

Df, in Tench Tilghman's writing, DLC:GW; Varick transcript, DLC:GW. The LS was
offered for sale in January 1918 as "a badly damaged letter" (*The Collector*, vol. 31,
no. 3, p. 28).

## To Henry Laurens

sir                   Head Qrs White plains August 31: 1778. 3 OClock P.M.
   I would take the liberty to inform Congress, that Colo. Armand is
come to camp with his Corps and has applied to me for Commissions
for his Officers. By the Resolution for establishing the Corps it was to
be officered out of the Foreigners then commissioned in our service,
who were not, nor could be provided for in any of the Regiments.[1] Instead of this, there are only three Officers in his Corps, who before
held any Commissions in our service, Viz. Lieut. Colo. Vrigney & Captains Mercley & Shafner. The Two last were only Lieutenants and are

now appointed to Captaincies, contrary it seems to me, to the spirit and intention of the Resolution. As Colo. Armand has departed from his instructions which must govern me, I am not authorised to grant the Commissions he requires—and am therefore under the necessity of troubling Congress, with the arrangement of the Corps, No. 1, as it now actually stands for their consideration & decision.[2] The Colo. founds his deviation from the Resolve upon some verbal intimation given him, that the part in question would not be insisted on.

I would also take the liberty to mention, that General Duportail lately delivered me a Memorial, in which among other things he represents, that he had made an agreement with Congress at his first appointment, that neither himself nor the other Gentlemen with him, should ever be commanded by any of the Engineers who had preceded them in our Army.[3] I could not but answer, that the Commissions of Officers were the only rule of precedency and command I had to judge by; and while others held superior appointments, I must consider them accordingly in the course of service. He gave me the inclosed Letter to you upon the subject—and is extremely anxious to have the matter placed upon a certain footing; and no doubt it will be for the good and tranquility of the service that the claim be determined as speedily as possible one way or the other.[4] At the same time I think it right to observe, that it can not be expected that Colo. Cosciusko, who has been a good while in this line and conducted himself with reputation and satisfaction will consent to act in a subordinate capacity to any of the French Gentlemen, except General Portail.

The frequent condemnations to Capital punishment, for want of some intermediate one between that and a Hundred lashes (the next highest under our present military articles)—and the necessity of frequent pardons in consequence, induced me a few days ago, to lay the matter before a Board of Officers for them to consider, whether some mode might not be devised of equal or greater efficacy for preventing crimes and punishing Delinquents when they had happened, less shocking to humanity and more advantageous to the States, than that of Capital execution. The inclosed paper No. 3 contains the opinion of the Board upon the subject, which with all deference I submit to the consideration of Congress[5]—and doubt not but they will adopt the expedient suggested, if it shall appear in any wise calculated to promote the service. I will only observe before I conclude upon this occasion, that when I called the Board to consult upon the point, there were Eleven prisoners under sentence of death and probably many more for trial, in the different guards on charges, that would affect their lives.[6]

Since I had the honor of writing you on the 25 Instant, I have not received a single line from General Sullivan. The only intelligence I have from the Eastward is from Monsr Pontjebeau.⁷ This Gentleman left Rhode-Island the 27th and arrived about Two Hours ago in Camp. From him I learn that our people were still on the Island. That it was generally thought they had made effectual provision for a retreat in case of exigency. That in the evening of that day he met Monsr preville, an Officer belonging to the Languedoc, at providence going with dispatches to Genl Sullivan, who informed him that the French fleet had got into Boston. He further adds, that Monsr Colonne, who was in company with him at providence and who had more conversation with Mr preville than he himself had, told him, that Mr preville said Count D'Estaing had sailed or was on the point of sailing again for Rhode Island with 10 Ships of the line & his Frigates.⁸ I have the Honor to be with great respect & esteem sir Yr Most Obedt servt

Go: Washington

P.S. Your favor of the 20th only came to hand just now.⁹

LS, in Robert Hanson Harrison's writing, DNA:PCC, item 152; Df, DLC:GW; copy, ScHi: Henry Laurens Papers; copy, DNA:PCC, item 169; Varick transcript, DLC:GW. Congress read this letter on 3 Sept. and referred it to the Board of War (see *JCC*, 12:862–63).

    1. For the resolution of 25 June 1778, see *JCC*, 11:644.

    2. In the enclosed undated arrangement, Armand listed the officers and wrote comments explaining their ranks (DNA:PCC, item 152).

    3. The memorial has not been identified.

    4. Duportail's letter to Laurens of 27 Aug. is in DNA:PCC, item 41. Duportail wrote that because none of the engineers commissioned prior to his arrival in America had formal training or experience, he and his French colleagues had "believed that Congress would be sensible, that it would be unjust and contradictory to ask the Court of france for Engineers and to place them in their Art under Persons who are Engineers only by name, that to do so would abase our abilities on a level with theirs, and therefore hinder our being more useful than they. Thus we required of the Congress that not any of us should be ever commanded by them." Duportail claimed that Congress had agreed and had responded by giving him command and by giving his colleagues commissions as "Coll, Lt. Coll or major *of the* Engineers, whereas the others were called only Coll Lt Coll or major Engineer." This, he asserted, was supposed to give the Frenchmen rank within the engineers, but problems had arisen, especially in the case of Colonel La Radière (who had been involved in disputes with Colonel Kosciuszko at West Point).

    5. See Proceedings of a Council of General Officers, 20–24 August.

    6. For discussion of the eleven prisoners, see General Orders, 14 Aug., and note 3, and 21 Aug., and note 1.

    7. Charles-Albert, comte de Moré de Pontgibaud (1758–1837), was serving as one of Lafayette's aides-de-camp and had been commissioned a major in February 1778. He carried Lafayette's letter to GW of 25 August.

    8. Pontgibaud had probably referred to Georges-René Pléville Le Pelley (1726–1805), a lieutenant de vaisseau on the *Languedoc*, although there was a Préville with d'Estaing's fleet: Charles-René Gras, chevalier de Préville (1732–1793), a capitaine de vaisseau since 1777 who commanded the *Engageante*. "Colonne" was prob-

ably Capt. Louis-Saint-Ange Morel, chevalier de La Colombe (1755-c.1800), another Lafayette aide-de-camp.

9. The postscript does not appear on the draft or the Varick transcript. GW was apparently acknowledging Laurens's second letter of 20 August.

## From Henry Laurens

Sir                                          [Philadelphia] 31st Augt [1778]

Yesterday I had the honor of writing to Your Excellency by Captain Josiah Stoddard who was so obliging as to take upon him the safe conduct of 500 Guineas to be lodged in Your Excellencys' hands for public service.

Be pleas'd Sir to receive here inclosed an Act of Congress of the present date for engaging in Confederal Service for three Years or during the War such of the drafts of the Militia as are at present incorporated in the Battalions of the respective States.[1]

If twenty dollars bounty shall be found insufficient to accomplish the purpose intended by the Act Your Excellency will be pleas'd to signify to Congress what sum will in Your Excellencys' opinion be necessary. I have the honor to be &c.

LB, DNA:PCC, item 13. A note on the letter-book copy indicates that this letter was carried "by [William] Jones."

1. The resolution of 31 Aug. appropriated $120,000 in Continental money, which GW was directed "to cause . . . to be paid into the hands of such trusty, active, and discreet officers as he shall think proper to appoint to recruit for the quota of the respective states, in proportion to the number of men not engaged for three years, or during the war, which each State shall have in the field" (*JCC*, 11:854).

## To Colonel William Malcom

Sir                                   Head Quarters White plains 31st Augt 1778

I have recd yours of Yesterday. I would have you inquire whether Moseley's and Enos's Regiments, who are going home, have not some public Arms among them, if they have, let them be delivered to Poors. If they have not, a return must be made of Poors deficiency. Receipts must be taken from the Officers when the Arms are delivered to them, and a strict re-delivery of them demanded when the Regiment is discharged.

Govr Clinton writes me, that he will immediately order 500 Militia to you.[1] I am &c.

Df, in Tench Tilghman's writing, DLC:GW; Varick transcript, DLC:GW.

1. See George Clinton to GW, 29 August.

## From Colonel William Malcom

Sir                            West point [N.Y.] Augt 31. 1778

Ten days ago, I called for returns from the Regiments whose lines were near expired—they made them but Acknowledge few Stores, Such as they please they deliver—I have wrote to the Q: M. General for his charges against them—and the enclosed to Colonel Stevens I expect will procure an account of the arms & ammunition they drew & which was delivered to them by him or his conductor.[1]

Your Excellencys orders on this head shall be punctually attended to—If a Sufficeint Number are not returned for Poor's Regt I shall send to Fish Kill to the armourers Shop for more.

Some of Burgoynes men behave very ill—I put them, & some other fellows under the care of one of my Officers, but I believe I shall be oblidged to Send them to the Guard House at Fish Kill.

Is Rum part of a Ration? the Militia insist for ticketts from the Commissary when they do not get their Gill. I have consider'd the matters, as discretional in the Commanding officer—and have occassionally ordered Rum to be Issued—perhaps every third or fourth day—The men on fatigue draw regularly.

Is it your Excellencys pleasure that Capt. Lewis of the Galley engage Seaman—Several have offer'd—at present I have put a few Batteaux men on board.[2]

I am getting as many old arms repaird as there are Artifficers, Waggoners &c. in Garrison—but do not mean to Issue them unless a prospect of Service.

No accounts of the Gun boats—I most respectfully am Your Excellencys most obedient Servant

                                        W. Malcom

ALS, DLC:GW.

1. The enclosure has not been identified.

2. Abraham Lewis was appointed in July 1777 to command the *Lady Washington* galley, stationed at West Point.

## To Brigadier General William Maxwell

D. Sir                          Head Qrs [White Plains] 31 Augt 1778

It is at this present crisis extremely interesting to our conduct to learn with exactness and certainty the force that is reported to have sailed for New Port by way of the Sound, & that from the Hook, and whose command they are under. It will be necessary to discover what particular corps have been embarked—what baggage—what heavy cannon and artillery and how the transports (those especially that sailed from the hook[)] were provided with provisions, whither for a long or short voyage.

You will without loosing a moment imploy the best means in your power to answer these several purposes—and in case you are possessed of intelligence on any of those subjects you will send me it as soon as possible. I have only to recommend great diligence and dispatch in this matter. I am &c.

You will send the inclosed to Col. Ogden.[1]

Df, in James McHenry's writing, DLC:GW; Varick transcript, DLC:GW.

1. This sentence was written in the left margin of the draft. GW's letter of this date to Col. Matthias Ogden reads: "I would wish in case you have carried, or can put in execution the plan for obtaining intelligence to imploy it immediately on the following objects.

"What number of troops and the particular corps have Embarked on board the transports that went up the sound, and how many in the vessels that sailed from the Hook—with what artillery and the stock of provision—whether provided in the latter for a long or short voyage—What general officers commanded—if General Clinton—or Lord Cornwallis—or both.

"I wish to have these several facts established as soon as possible, and when made known, sent me by express" (NjMoNP).

# From Brigadier General William Maxwell

Sir                                            Elizth Town [N.J.] 31st Augt 1778

Coll D'Hart having some bussiness to transact at Camp, he has obtained my leave for that purpose. I have had intiligen[c]e from New York though not d[i]rectly or by so good authority as I could wish, yet it is believed & I believe it, that a part of Birons Fleet has arived about 3 days ago Viz. five large Ships, that the Officers has been seen and spoke with in New York.[1] I have attempted to send some people for intiligence this two nights pass'd but they have deceived me both times. If the English Vessels is comin as believed I am surprised I have not had intiligence of it from Major Howel.[2] We are in great suspence here about Rhode Island & Genl Sullivan as we have heard that the French Fleet is gone to Boston & that General Clinton is gone up the sound I am. Your Excellency Most Obedt Humble Servt

                                                        Wm Maxwell

ALS, DLC:GW.

1. British engineer James Montresor noted in his journal for 28 Aug.: "Arrived six 74 Gun Ships being part of Admiral Byron's squadron" (Scull, *Montresor Journals*, 512).

2. Maxwell had apparently not yet received Maj. Richard Howell's letter to him of 30 Aug., which is now in DLC:GW. For Howell's intelligence, see GW to Vice Admiral d'Estaing, 2 Sept., n.3.

## From Joshua Mersereau

Sr                                                    Boston August 31—1778

I have Just recpd a letter from Col. Boudinot, informing me that great offence has been given, for my sending so many of the Convention officers on Parole to the enemy—and taking considerable sums of money from them for that favour.[1]

The latter I do deny—the former I had Authority for, or at least, Such as would Justify my Conduct, hoping To release our officers.

so soon as the Prisnors Taken by The Count De Estang, are secur'd and Provided for—and the Officers Prisnors of war, With The remaind⟨er⟩ of the 71 Rt in this State are Sent away—I propose Wating on your Excelency to remov⟨e⟩ any Doubts, or Charge tha[t]s been brought against me—if I have Err'd it's for Want of Judgment, I have not let one man go in Without Genl Heaths approbation. I always made it a rule to consult him first—as to the mony beg the favour, of knowing the names of the Complainants, as I am confident that there is not an officer of the Convention, can say that they have given me one Single Farthing—Capt. Vigars Made me a presant of 2 pare of Pistols, tho I never Got but 3 of them one being lost.[2]

four weeks ago part of the 71 Rt 129 men & 84 Women and Children I sent to Providence, on their Way to new Port, agreeable to Col. Boudinots orders—they were order'd back by Genl Sulivan, and not permitted to go—I apply'd to Genl Heath for permittion to Send them by New London, New Haven or some other Rout to New York—Who refer'd me to Your Excelency for Directions, Which I shall Chearfully execute.[3]

I am hiring a Prisson Ship here, for the reception of the Count De Estangs Prisnors and about 40 taken by Capt. Skimer Who Was kill'd in the engagement[4]—5 prises ariv'd this Day—a fleet is Said to be off here some say it's an English fleet others that it's a French Fleet, others that they are prises[5]—the German officers beg the favour of staying here till the privates go in also—if they are not Exchang'd Soon; there must be Chimneys built in the barn, Where the Germains and 53 Rt are kept; as it Will be too Cold Without fire in Winter, and bad building Chimneys then beg the favour of your Excelency's or Col. Baty' Direction in this case, as there is no room in the Barracks for those men, I hav⟨e⟩ been oblidg'd to make many Shifts, for Want of instrutions, it having been So

Difficult to get them; in this, out of the Way place—many letters have miscarrie'd others 6 & 8 wee⟨ks⟩ before I recpd them. I have the Honor To be your Excelency's most Obedt Hum: Servt

Joshua Mersereau

P.s. please to Direct to the Care of Genl Heath.

ALS, NN: Emmet Collection.

1. Elias Boudinot's letter to Mersereau of 27 Aug. has not been identified. For more on the complaint, see Mersereau's reply to Boudinot of 2 Sept. (NjP: Stimson-Boudinot Collection).

2. Nicholas Aylward Vigors (1755–1828) was commissioned an ensign in the British 29th Regiment in December 1769 and promoted to lieutenant in January 1772 and to captain in February 1776.

3. Mersereau announced in a letter to Maj. Gen. William Heath of 27 July that he was starting to send the 71st Regiment prisoners and that, in accordance with Heath's suggestion, he had written to inform Maj. Gen. John Sullivan. Mersereau's letter to Heath of 5 Aug. indicates that Sullivan had disapproved the movement, and Heath's letter to Mersereau of 12 Aug. suggested that Mersereau consult Elias Boudinot about what to do with the prisoners (all MHi: Heath Papers). Mersereau's request to send the prisoners to New York and Heath's reply have not been identified. For a summary, see also Mersereau to Boudinot, 31 Aug. (NjP: Stimson-Boudinot Collection). GW referred this inquiry to Commissary of Prisoners John Beatty in a letter of 26 September.

4. The *Continental Journal, and Weekly Advertiser* (Boston) of 3 Sept. reported the arrival on 31 Aug. of "the Continental Brigantine of war, General Gates, whose late commander Capt. John Skimmer of this town fell on the 3d of August, in an action with a Brigantine of 12 guns from St. John's, bound to Dominica."

5. Mersereau was referring to a report that on 30 Aug. "almost 20 Sail of Ships, many of them large, were seen off Plymouth Harbour, standing to the Northward" (*Boston Gazette, and Country Journal*, 31 Aug.).

## From Gouverneur Morris

Dear General.                    Congress [Philadelphia] 31st August 1778.

I wrote you a Letter long since which went backwards & whether it hath ever Yet got so far forwards as to reach you I am utterly incapacitated even to guess trusting however that you have got or will get it I shall not from Memory repeat what if there at all is at best but faintly traced.[1]

At present I trouble you on the Subject of recruiting your Army which is at this Moment in Debate before the House. It hath been proposed to give ten Dollars in Specie and ten Square Dollars to Recruits which I have offered and it is determined in the Negative.[2] I will not fatigue you with the Reasons opperating on my Mind they derived not inconsiderably from the probable Consequences of the Measure even upon the Army. Among others I fear to inflame the Rapacity of Soldiers with the Love by the Possession of a Metal of which we have such a plentiful Lack. However let me have your Sentiments for I can promise you a Mind open to Conviction if you differ in Opinion desirous of Information in all Cases and willing to urge your good Reasons should the Matter be again opened.

I can send you no News and therefore I shall only repeat what you knew before that I am most sincerely yours

Gouvr Morris

My Compliments to Bannister to Genl Reed to all Friends.[3]

ALS, DLC:GW.

1. Morris may have been referring to his letter to GW of 2 August.

2. For Congress's action of this date on army recruiting, see *JCC*, 11:853–54.

3. Joseph Reed and John Banister were serving on the Congress's committee of arrangement at GW's camp.

## From Major General William Phillips

Sir                    Cambridge [Mass.] August 31st 1778

I have received your very polite letter dated from White plains the 16th instant enclosing a letter to me from Sir Henry Clinton of July the 18th.[1]

I return you, Sir, my very sincere thanks for the obliging manner with which you explain your not being able to grant me passports to go to New York, and am sure if you imagined it proper for you to do, I should not fail of procuring them.

I certainly much wish to go to New York, my private Affairs are in some confusion—I have not heard from Europe of Twelve Months—have not been able to write particularly since near that time—And you will, Sir, easily imagine that under this description and in this Situation I am anxious to have A free communication by letter with my Friends and Family.

I will take a liberty with you, Sir, which I trust your good nature will excuse—It is to request your opinion whether the Congress would grant me Passports if I desired it—I will be free to own to you, Sir, of whose liberality of Sentiment I have no doubt, that I should make the request without hesitation were I in any degree led to suppose it would be granted, but it would hurt my mind to ask a favour and be refused.

I ask your pardon for giving you this trouble which the ingenuous Character you bear, in part, causes—If it is not improper for you to answer me, I may hope you will—at any rate have the goodness to excuse the liberty I have taken.

If there is nothing in the enclosed letters which Should prevent their being forwarded I will beg you will allow of it.[2] I have the honour to be,

Sir, with very great personal respect Your most obedient and very humble Servant

W. Phillips

LS, DLC:GW.
 1. Phillips received these items on 26 Aug. (see Phillips to Gen. Henry Clinton, 27 Aug., P.R.O., 30/55, Carleton Papers).
 2. The enclosed letters have not been identified.

## From Captain Thomas Posey

Schoharry [N.Y.]

May it Please your Excellency                31st Augt 1778
 I acnoledge the Rect of your Favr, bearing Date 5th Inst., incloseing a Warrent for 2500 Dollors, with a Letter for Jonathan Burrel Esqr. Assistant Paymaster Albaney.
 as my time has been much taken up with Duty, have not had the opportunity to apply for the money, however the men has not sufferd, as Got money upon my Cr. & Distributed amongst them, for which I shall acct with the Paymaster of the Rifle Regt, he Arivd here 26th Inst. with 2 months Pay,[1] If necessity Oblidges me to make use of the Warrent I Shall, If not I will Return it. I am with Respect Your Obedt Humle sert

Thomas Posey.

ALS, DLC:GW.
 1. The paymaster of the Rifle Regiment at this time was Lt. Benjamin Ashby. GW's warrant book indicates that on 8 Aug., Ashby received the pay due to "Colo. Morgans Corps" for April and May, and he received additional funds for rations due the regiment on 13 Aug. (DLC:GW). Ashby was commissioned an ensign in the 11th Virginia Regiment in November 1776, appointed regimental quartermaster in January 1777, and promoted to lieutenant in June 1777. By August 1777 he was detached for duty with the Rifle Regiment, and by January 1778 he had become paymaster for that regiment. When the Rifle Regiment was broken up in the fall of 1778, Ashby returned to his regiment, now numbered the 7th Virginia, and he served until 1783, being promoted to first lieutenant in March 1779 and transferring to the 3d Virginia Regiment in January 1781.

## From Brigadier General Charles Scott

[Westchester County, N.Y.]

Sir                31st Augt 1778 ½ past 5 oClock
 I recd Your Favour through Colo. Tilghman, Particular attention shall be paid to it,[1] Capt. Leavensworth is now on long Island for that purpose[2] But fearing he may Fail I will Dispatch a nother Person, about 8 oClock this morning Colo. Gist Fell in with a partie of the enemy

about two mile Below Philaps's hous and after exchanging a fiew Shot
they gave way leaving one killed Dead & Making three prisoners the
Colo. Returnd to his Usial post without any loss—But I am sorry To inform Your Excellency that they retalliated on us in a Very fiew hours,
Majr Steward with a partie of about forty, and Capt. Nimham with
about the Same number parted at Volentines hill and appointed to
meet at the forks of a road near the Enemys Picquet, but before or
Rather about their meeting they saw a partie of horse In front after exchanging a fiew Shot the Horse Gave way the indians persued when
they war led Into an ambucade Serounded by a large body of Horse
and foot, as was also the Majrs partie there are not more than fourteen
Indians Yet com in among the missing is Capt. Nimham his father and
the whole of the officers of that Corps, Majr Steward tells me that he
misses a Capt. Sub. & About twenty men from his partie, I am in Hopes
it is not so bad as it at Preasant appears But I cant promise my self that
it will be much Short of it[3]—I have Detached Colo. parker with Three
Hundred men to reinforce and Stay with Majr Steward this night and
endeavour to ⟨brek⟩ Up their Ambuscade in the morning. I am Your
Excys Obt Servt

Chs Scott

ALS, DLC:GW.

1. The favor has not been identified.

2. Eli Leavenworth (1748–1819) of New Haven served as a captain of the 7th
Connecticut Regiment from 6 July to 10 Dec. 1775 and as a captain of the 19th Continental Regiment throughout 1776 before becoming a captain of the 6th Connecticut Regiment in January 1777. In November 1778 he was promoted to major,
with the appointment retroactive to 18 Sept. 1777. He retired from the service in
January 1781.

3. Hessian captain Johann Ewald recorded both these engagements in his diary
for 31 Aug.: "Early today Captain Donop patrolled toward Philipse's house with
one hundred foot jägers and fifteen horse. He was scarcely half an hour away from
our outpost when he fell into an ambuscade lying in a ravine to his right, since he
had marched by his nose without taking every precaution. Two corporals and four
jägers were killed by the first fire, six wounded, and four captured. A quick flight
saved the remainder. . . . After this stroke, the enemy party turned toward East
Chester through Philipse's Manor into the area where Simcoe, Cathcart, and Emmerich were posted. These officers got wind of it and broke camp at once. Simcoe
moved to the left through the woods past the enemy party to cut off its retreat.
Cathcart and Emmerich went to meet the party with a part of their corps to draw
the enemy's attention upon themselves. They had concealed the other part, especially the cavalry, behind the hills to attack the enemy unexpectedly. . . . In the afternoon, about four o'clock, the enemy approached and began to skirmish with
our skirmishers, who withdrew, and the enemy pursued them vigorously. The cavalry of Emmerich and the Legion burst forth, charged, and drove back the enemy,
who was now attacked in the rear by Simcoe between Post's and Valentine's plantations, where he had to cross a defile.

"The Indians as well as the American defended themselves like brave men against all sides where they were attacked, so that a hot fight resulted in five or six parties where the heavily wooded terrain offered cover. By seven o'clock in the evening, however, most of the enemy were killed, partly shot dead and partly cut down by the cavalry. No Indians, especially, received quarter, including their chief called Nimham and his son, save for a few. Only two captains, one lieutenant, and some fifty men were taken prisoners. . . . The loss on the English side amounted to some forty dead without the wounded" (Ewald, *Diary*, 144–45; see also Simcoe, *Operations of the Queen's Rangers*, 83–86; Burgoyne, *Diaries of Two Ansbach Jaegers*, 45; Whinyates, *Services of Francis Downman*, 79; Baurmeister, *Revolution in America*, 205; *Royal Gazette* [New York], 2 and 5 Sept. 1778).

Abram Nimham, a Stockbridge Indian, was captain of a company of Indians who had volunteered for service in the fall of 1777 and been ordered by Congress to join Maj. Gen. Horatio Gates (*JCC*, 9:840). He and his father, Daniel Nimham (c.1726–1778), were among those killed in the engagement. The other missing captain, who was taken prisoner, was Nathan Goodale of the 5th Massachusetts Regiment (see "Vaughan Journal," 109; *Scudder Journal*, 27–28; Baldwin, *Revolutionary Journal*, 133).

## From Brigadier General John Stark

Dear General                                           Albany 31st August 1778

I Embrace this opportunity to Inform you of our Situation, the Inhabitants are daily bringing in petitions for the Losses they have Received by the Army, one Petition I send you for your Approbation, would be glad of your opinion on the Matter, I believe the House was Moved & is Still Occupied by the Troops.[1]

Lt Colo. Butler and some of his party, has been into the Enemies Country, and Brougth in, a number of Cattle, Horses, &c., which he Thinks (& I agree with him in opinion) that they are Lawfull Prises to the Captors, but the Committee of this place, Claims them, as belonging to this State, altho in the Possession of the Enemy, before Butler took them, your opinion on this Subject, may prevent a good deal of Uneasiness, between the Troops, and the Committee.[2]

I send you the Judgment of a Court Martial sent to me from Colo. Butler for your Approbation, according to the mans Behaviour I think that he ought to die, for after he had shot the Searjeant he said he would be willing to be Hanged if he could have an opportunity to kill one of the Officers.[3]

I Likewise send you one of Burgoynes men which were Included in the Convention which was Taken with the Enemy as will appear by his Crime & four Sailors taken at Crownpoint that Belonged to the Enemies Ships on the Lakes. I am sir yours with Great Respect

John Stark

LS, DLC:GW. Tench Tilghman docketed the letter in part, "Ansd"; see GW to Stark, 8 October.

1. The enclosure, which has not been identified, was probably the petition of Mrs. McNeil discussed by GW in his letter to Stark of 8 October.

2. On the dispute, see William Butler to GW, this date, and note 5 to that document.

3. Although GW replied to Stark that the court-martial proceedings "never came to hand," they are now in DLC:GW. Stark was referring to the court-martial at Schoharie, N.Y., on 21 Aug., of Richard Roach of the 4th Pennsylvania Regiment. Roach was charged with "Mutiny & Wilfully Shooting George Knox Serjeant Major to said Regiment thro' the Body, & threatning some Commissioned Officers in the Regiment with like treatment." He pled guilty and was sentenced to death, even though Knox survived the shooting.

## From Major General John Sullivan

Dear Genl                    Head Qrs Tiverton [R.I.] Augt 31st 1778

In my last[1] I promisd your Excellency to particularize such commanding Officers and Corps as more particularly distinguished themselves in the Action of the 29th Instant. I with pleasure comply with that promise.

The advancd Corps under the Command of Colonels Laurens Fleury & Major Talbot Colo. H: B. Levingstones light Troops consisting of Jackson's Corps and a detachment from the whole Army—Major General Greene and all the Genl officers & Commandants of Brigades of the first and those of Lovell's Brigade in the second Line have acquird great Honor by their Activity and spirited exertions during the day—I have likewise to inform your Excellency that in consideration of the Intilligence convey'd in your last Favor[2]—on account of a distressing diminution of Numbers from daily discharges and desertions, & in consequence of Information recievd, that the Enemy's Fleet was seen some distance off & the actual arrival of three Ships of force, which we suppose to be the Advance.[3] For these weighty Reasons, I thought proper to direct a Retreat while I had it in my Power to secure it. I therefore (after making use of some little Maneuvres, which effectually deciev'd the Enemy) gave orders about Six Clock last evening for the purpose, and before two oClock in the Morning all the Army and every thing appertaining thereto, were dissembark'd on the Main. I am confident the Enemy was not sensible of my design, nor apprizd of its execution, untill the discovery was too late to bring advantage with it; tho our Sentries were not posted one hundred and fifty Yards from those of the Enemy. I flatter myself that both the Retreat and the manner of conducting it will recieve your Excellency's Approbation—In this Expectation, I remain with great personal Regard Yr Excellency's most obedient humble Servt

Jno. Sullivan

P:S: Unfortunately for the Marquis he was prevaild upon the evening before the Action, to proceed to Boston to accelerate the Return of Count

Destiang—The Expedition with which, He perform'd this piece of Service does him honor—he arriv'd at Boston (upwards of Sixty Miles) in Seven Hours and return'd in less time—He had the Honor of bringing of the Picketts which he did with great Regularity & good order.

J.S.

I shou'd do the highest Injustice if I neglected to mention that Brigadier General Cornels indefatigable Industry in preparing for the expedition and his Conduct through the whole merit particular notice. Major Talbot who assisted me in preparing the Boats afterwards servd in Colo. Laurens's Corps deser⟨ves⟩ great praise.

Enclosd you have a Return of kill'd wounded and missing.[4]

LS, DLC:GW.

1. See Sullivan to GW, 29 August.

2. GW's letters to Sullivan of 28 and 29 Aug. contained intelligence of a British fleet departing to relieve Newport.

3. The *Sphynx* and two other ships of war arrived at Newport on 27 Aug. with news of British intentions to reinforce the post (see Maj. Gen. Robert Pigot to Gen. Henry Clinton, 31 Aug., P.R.O., Colonial Office, 5/96, Military Correspondence of the British Generals; see also Davies, *Documents of the American Revolution*, 15:191).

4. The enclosed "Return of the Killed Wounded and missing of the Army under the Command of the Honble Maj. Genl Sullivan in the Action of the 29th Augt 1778" reported 30 killed, 137 wounded, and 44 missing for a total loss of 211 officers and men (DLC:GW).

## General Orders

Head-Quarters W. Plains Tuesday Septr 1st 1778.

Parole Kingsbridge—          C. Signs Knolton Kelso.

A board of Officers will sit this day at Major Allen's Marqui to settle the rank of Captns Fenner and Read of the North Carolina Brigade[1]— Major Allen, two Captains from Nixon's and a like number from Paterson's Brigade will compose the board.

Lieutt John Bartley of the 5th Pennsylvania Regt is appointed Adjutant to the same.[2]

Thomas Dungan Ensign in the 6th Pennsylvania Regt—is appointed Pay-Master in the same.[3]

Varick transcript, DLC:GW.

1. Robert Fenner (c.1755–1816) was commissioned a lieutenant in the 2d North Carolina Regiment on 1 Jan. 1776 and promoted to captain in May 1777. He was taken prisoner at Charleston, S.C., on 12 May 1780 and served to the end of the war. After the war, he became an agent for the final settlement certificates of the North Carolina line and treasurer of the North Carolina Society of the Cincinnati. James Read (d. 1803) was commissioned an ensign of the 1st North Carolina Regiment on 4 Jan. 1776, promoted to lieutenant in July of that year, and promoted to captain in July 1777. He was taken prisoner at Charleston, S.C., in May 1780 and served to the

end of the war. The date of Fenner's commission as captain was in dispute at this time.

2. John Bartley, who was commissioned an ensign of the 3d Pennsylvania Regiment in 5 Jan. 1776 and promoted to second lieutenant in October of that year, became first lieutenant of the 5th Pennsylvania Regiment in January 1777. He was promoted to captain lieutenant in June 1779 and retired on 1 Jan. 1781.

3. Thomas Dungan (1738–1805), who was appointed paymaster of the 12th Pennsylvania Regiment in April 1777, was commissioned an ensign on 2 June 1778 and transferred to the 6th Pennsylvania Regiment in July 1778. Commissioned a second lieutenant to rank from 1 Jan. 1781, he served until June 1783, transferring to the 2d Pennsylvania Regiment in January 1783. Dungan, who graduated from the University of Pennsylvania in 1765 and was a professor of mathematics there, 1766–69, was principal of the Germantown Academy before and after his military service.

# Council of War

[White Plains, 1 September 1778]

At a Council of War held at Head Quarters in Camp at White plains Septr 1st 1778

Present

The Commander in Chief

| Major Genls | Brigadr Generls |
|---|---|
| Putnam | Nixon |
| Gates | Parsons |
| Stirling | Jas Clinton |
| Lincoln | Smallwood |
| D'Kalb | Knox |
| McDougal | Poor |
| | Paterson |
| | Wayne |
| | Woodford |
| | Muhlenburg |
| | Scott |
| | Huntington |
| | DuPortail |

The Commander in Chief states to the Council, that by a Letter of the 23d Ulto from General Sullivan, it appears that the French fleet under the command of His Excellency Vice Admiral Count D'Estaing, in consequence of damage sustained in a violent storm off the coast and from other weighty considerations, had left Rhode Island on the 21st in their way to Boston, there to refit. That by another Letter of the 29th he is informed, General Sullivan and the Troops under his command had the preceding evening retreated from the position they before occupied, to the North East end of the Island, where an Action had ensued, in which the American Troops were finally successful, though not without considerable loss.

He further informs them, that by various accounts from New York and other places, the Enemy some time since, had detached a body of about 1200 hundred men under General Tryon, on a foraging party on Long Island, which was last heard of at Setocket. That besides this, other Troops had from time to time passed over to Long Island; amounting in the whole, according to intelligence, to a considerable number. That some days since, a Fleet of about Sixty sail of Transports, great & small, had proceeded Eastward through the sound; in which it ⟨is⟩ supposed, the Troops or part of them on Long Island had embarked, and some re-por⟨ts⟩ say under the command of General Clint⟨on⟩ for the relief of Rhode Island. That if the Detachments said to have been sent to Rhode Island are really gone, the number of t⟨he⟩ Enemy's troops there, will amount to [      ] the number of those remaining at New Yor⟨k⟩ and its dependencies about 9,000.[1] That our force at this post is 12,772 rank a⟨nd⟩ file fit for duty, exclusive of men retu⟨rned⟩ on command.

His Excellency finally inform⟨s⟩ the Council, that a Gentleman who cam⟨e⟩ express from Rhode Island assures him, that he met an Officer, belonging to the Languedoc, One of the French fleet, the 27th of August in the Evening at providence, going with dispatches to General Sullivan, who informed him of the arrival of the french fleet at Boston; which had been joined by the Cæsar a 74 Gun ship, separated in the storm, and who, he also understood, mentioned that the fleet, consist-ing of ten sail of the line & three frigates, was on the point of leaving Boston or had sailed for Rhode Island—and would be there by the time of his (the Gentleman's) return.[2]

The Commander in chief having stated these facts for the consider-ation of the Council, requests their opinion,

1st   Whether any operations can be undertaken at the present junc-ture by this Army—and of what kind—Whether a movement of the whole or a princip⟨a⟩l part of it to the Eastward, will be adv⟨isa⟩ble, and afford a prospect of advantage?

2.   In case a movement to the Eastward should be thought proper, what measures and precautions should be taken for the security of the Highland passes?

3.   Or whether an attempt with such a probability of success as will justify it, can be made upon New York in it's present circumstances?[3] In determining the foregoing points—the General requests the Coun-cil will take into view the practicability of supplying the Army with pro-visions, if it should be judged expedient to move to the Eastward.

D, in Robert Hanson Harrison's writing, DLC:GW; Varick transcript, DLC:GW. Notes that Henry Knox kept of his replies to these questions state that the council was held "the eveng of Sep. 1" (NNGL: Knox Papers). There was apparently discussion that evening, and then GW requested that the generals submit written opinions. No responses have been found from James Clinton and Jedediah Huntington; the replies of the other generals are dated 2 September.

1. A British return of 15 Aug. reported almost 22,000 "Rank & file fit for duty" and more than 27,000 "Total Effectives" at New York, Staten Island, Long Island, and Paulus Hook. The force that embarked for the relief of Rhode Island numbered about 4,000 ("Recapitulation of the State of 15th August 1778" and Henry Clinton to George Germain, 15 Sept., both P.R.O., Colonial Office, 5/96, Military Correspondence of the British Generals).

2. The express rider was Charles-Albert, comte de Moré de Pontgibaud; for more on his information, see GW to Henry Laurens, 31 August.

3. See Memorandum of Campaign Plans, c.1 September.

## Memorandum of Campaign Plans

[c.1 Sept. 1778]

Scotts light Infantry 1000—A Detachment of the same Number under Wayne & the whole Commanded by Genl McDougal to Imbark at [     ] and land opposite to Morriss House at Hærlem—A Detachment of [     ] Men from this body to Land in the Cove under Fort Washington & endeavour to surprize it—some Germans to be with this party to answer if hailed in that language & signify that it is a party from Spiting devil by Water. Another Detachment to land at the Hollow between Fort Washington and the Hill at the Mouth of Spiting devil and to proceed immediately to the redoubt on the last mentioned Hill & possess themselves of it—If possible this is to be done without medling with or going near the Guards—If these detachments succeed they must turn the Cannon immediately upon the Enemy & must maintain the Works at all adventures. each party must have Artillerists with them. General McDougal is in the first place to possess himself of the chain of redoubts below Morriss & then Act from Circumstances, keeping these as places of security & retreat. This Imbarkation must be made with great secresy—the Boats must be brought from above Tarry town under cover of Night, or if brought down before the hour they are wanted appearances of getting them over to the Sound, must be throw⟨n⟩ out to create an Idea that long Island is the object—some Boats must actually be taken across to Marineck to confirm this. At the place of Imbarkation Guards are to be Stationed & Centries established to prevent any persons from prying—Guard Boats, before the Boats for Transporting Troops or the Troops themselves are put in motion are to be down a little above the Enemys advanced posts on the No. River & stop every thing moving on the Water. All the Cavalry are to be sent down before the March of the Troops are known and are to form a compleat Chain around the Enemy & suffer nothing to go in and secure all that come out & send them to me by the Road leading to Valentines. The Army to March in three Columns—the Right Wing under the Command of Genl [     ] by Philips—the left Wing by Judge Wards & Drakes—and the Second line by Valentines.[1] The right Wing is to afford a Detachment which is to endeavour to surprize the Redout No. 1—A Detacht from the 2d line is to attempt Fort Independance—& the left Wing is to furnish one for redoubt No. [     ].

AD, in GW's hand, DLC:GW. GW's note with this memorandum reads: "for Enterprise which was in contemplation but never attempted in the Campaign of 1778 when New Port was Invested and Genl Clinton went with a Force from N. Yk to relieve it."

1. The farm of Benjamin Drake (1734–1812) was about a mile north of Judge Stephen Ward's house in Eastchester township. Thomas Valentine (1722–1800) had long leased a plantation including Valentine's Hill, and in 1786, following the forfeiture of the Loyalist Frederick Philipse's estate, he purchased 286 acres.

## From a Board of General Officers

Camp White Plains September 1st 1778

Whereas the Captains of Colonel John Lamb's Battalion of Artillery, did present a Memorial to Brigadier General Knox, commanding the Artillery of the United States, bearing date the 26th day of August last, requesting, that He, and Major General McDougall together with Brigadier General Parsons, (then a Board of General Officers, appointed by the Commander in Chief, to settle the Rank of the Maryland Line,) would hear the Pretensions of the said Captains to rank relative to each other, and settle the same: And also requesting, that the said Brigadier General Knox, would apply to his Excellency, for the necessary order therefor.[1] In pursuance of the said Memorial, the Commander in Chief, was pleased to direct, that the said Board of General Officers, would settle the relative Rank of the Captains of that Battalion. The Board have had several Meetings on the Business, and received the Claims of Rank of such Captains as were present, and communicated the Pretensions of each to all of them. The Board also received Information of the Claims of those, who were absent from General Knox.

It appears that the Captains of this Corps, claim Rank on two Principles; one as being experienced Artillery Officers, the other as Senior Officers to them in the Infantry Line of the Army. The First alledge, that as a knowledge of the Science and Practice of Gunnery, is necessary to qualify them for the Artillery; and they have been at much Pains to acquire both those qualifications, and as they were not entituled to promotion, in the Infantry, it is hard and unjust, that Infantry Officers, unqualified for Artillery Corps, when compared with them, should come into their Corps, and claim Rank of them in it, by virtue of their old Infantry Commissions. On the other hand the Infantry Officers say, that as the Congress give no Preference of Rank to the Artillery Officers over those of the Infantry, it is departing from the Articles of war and degrading them, to place them Juniors in the Battali⟨on,⟩ to the Artillery Captains; and therefore that they are entituled to the rank in the Battalion, which their Senior Commissions give them.

The Board having duly considered the arguments on both Sides, and the known usage of Armies, as well as the American Articles of war, do unanimously determine, that the Officers of Artillery, before the 1st day of January 1777, *ought to take Rank in the Artillery, of any Officer before serving in the Infantry*, because their long Service in the Artillery, ought to give them prior Rank, when serving in the same Artillery Corps: But that the Captains of Artillery, who served as Officers in the Infantry, retain the Rank in the Line of the Army, which their Commissions entitule them to: This the Board conceive to be conformable to our articles of war; and to the usage of old Armies—It being a notorious Fact, that many Field Officers, in the Line of the British Army, are younger Captains in their respective Corps, and do duty in them as such, and yet command agreable to their highest Commissions, on detachment with other Corps.

Captain Mott and the other Officers of Infantry now in Colonel Lamb's Battalion, being still entituled to this Rank in the Line, will suffer no Injustice or Disgrace, by the former Artillery Officers ranking before them in their own Battalion.[2]

2dly That the Officers who served as such in the Infantry before this Battalion was formed, and now serving in it, ought to succeed next in Rank, to the former Captains of Artillery: But as the Board are not advised of the date of Captain Bliss's Infantry Commission; they determine, that Captain Mott and he, take Rank of each other, in their Corps, according to the date of their Infantry Commissions. Upon these Principles the Board beg leave to make the following Arrangement of Colonel Lamb's Captains, Vizt

| | | | |
|---|---|---|---|
| 1st Beauman | 4th Doughty | 7th Bliss | 10th Porter |
| 2d Lee | 5th Moodie[3] | 8th Walker[4] | 11th Mansfield |
| 3d Wool[5] | 6th Mott | 9th Lockwood | 12th Brown |

All which is submitted to His Excellency the Commander in Chief, by his humble Servants

Alexr McDougall
H. Knox

General Parsons agreed to this arangement, but was absent when the fair Copy was made.[6]

DS, ICHi; DS, DLC:GW. Where the document is damaged, characters have been supplied from the other DS.

At the end of the DS at ICHi, GW wrote: "The above arrangement is approved of by Go: Washington Septr 10th 1778." The DS at DLC, which has a note reading "approved by the Commander in Chief on the 10th of September," was submitted to another board of general officers ordered on 11 Sept. to settle artillery ranks. That board reported on 15 Sept.: "The board of General officers assembled by your Excellencys order to settle the relative rank of the field officers in the corps of Artillery—As also the relative rank of the Captains in Colonel Lambs Battalion of artillery—Are of opinion that the above settlement ought to be confirmed and that sd Captain's should in future take rank accordingly."

1. The memorial of 26 Aug. has not been identified. For GW's appointment of a board to settle rank in the Maryland line, see General Orders, 18 August.

2. Gershom Mott (1744–1786), who was commissioned a captain of the 1st New York Regiment on 28 June 1775 and of Col. John Nicolson's Continental Regiment in March 1776, became a captain in Lamb's 2d Continental Artillery Regiment on 1 Jan. 1777. He served to June 1783.

3. Andrew Moodie (d. 1787), who was commissioned a second lieutenant in Lamb's Independent Artillery Company in June 1775 and promoted to first lieutenant in November of that year, was taken prisoner at Quebec on 31 Dec. 1775. After his exchange, he became a captain in the 2d Continental Artillery Regiment on 1 Jan. 1777 and served to June 1783.

4. Robert Walker (c.1746–1810), who was commissioned a lieutenant in the 5th Connecticut Regiment in May 1775, was appointed a captain in Col. Samuel Elmore's Connecticut State Regiment on 15 April 1776 and became a captain in the 2d Continental Artillery Regiment on 1 Jan. 1777. He resigned in March 1781.

5. Isaiah Wool (1753–1794), who was commissioned a lieutenant in Lamb's Independent Artillery Company in August 1775 and promoted to captain lieutenant in November of that year, was captured at Quebec in December 1775. After being exchanged, he was commissioned a captain in the 2d Continental Artillery Regiment on 1 Jan. 1777. He resigned in August 1780.

6. The preceding sentence is in McDougall's writing. A similar sentence (in the scribe's writing) on the other DS reads, "General Parsons agreed to the above report but was out of Camp when presented to the Commander in Cheif."

## To George Clinton

Dr sir                                    Head Qurs White plains Sept. 1st 1778

I am extremely sorry that it is in my power to inform you, that a Captain Colson of the 5th Virginia Regiment a few days ago, violently wounded a Mr Vantassel of this State, of which he died in a little time after[1]—The moment I was apprised of it, I directed a Letter to be written & sent to Genl Muhlenburg, to whose Brigade he belonged, to have him secured, in order that he might be delivered to the Civil Magistrate, in case the wound should prove mortal, as you will perceive by the inclosed copy.[2] I have reason to believe that every exertion was used on the part of the General, to have him apprehended; but he was not able to effect it, as he kept himself out of the way, according to report, from the time he gave the wound and went off, most probably, the instant he got intelligence that Mr Vantassel was dead. Mr Colson is a native of Virginia, but whether he is gone there—or to some Seaport, to procure a passage to the West Indies, where it is said he has a Brother, seems to be a matter of doubt. I do not know the causes, which led to this unhappy accident; but I wish he could have been taken, that he might receive a regular and proper trial, in the ordinary course of Justice. If you shall think it requisite, I will chearfully join you in any expedient—or pursue any you may point out, to recover and put him into the hands of the civil authority.

My last advices from Rhode Island were of the 29th Ulto. General Sullivan informs me, by Letter of that date, that he had retreated the preceding night to the North end of the Island. That the Enemy pursued him—and the next day a warm action ensued, which lasted an Hour, in which our people obliged them to quit the Field in disorder—and with precipitation. When he wrote, he could not ascertain the loss on either side, but says it was considerable. It was a very interesting event, and I sincerely hope the next accounts I have, will announce that he & his Troops are again on the Continent. The Count D'Estaing's fleet has got to Boston. I am Dr sir with the greatest respect & regard Your Most Obedt sert

Go: Washington

LS, in Robert Hanson Harrison's writing, NN: Emmet Collection; Df, DLC:GW; Varick transcript, DLC:GW.

1. Samuel Colston (died c.1779) was commissioned a lieutenant of the 5th Virginia Regiment in February 1776 and promoted to captain in February 1777. He is recorded as having retired from the army on 14 Sept. 1778.

2. The letter to Brig. Gen. Peter Muhlenberg, which was signed by GW's aide Tench Tilghman and dated 27 Aug., reads: "His Excellency has recd yours of this date informing him of the unlucky fray between Captn Colsn and an inhabitant, by which the latter is dangerously wounded. Should the wound prove mortal the civil authority of the state will undoubtedly demand a tryal, & should the offender not be found to answer the charge they would with reason complain. His excellency therefore desires that Captn Colsn should be put into safe custody, in such manner as suits an officer of his rank until the fate of the wounded man is determined" (Df, DLC:GW; see also Hastings, *Clinton Papers*, 3:696).

## To Major General Nathanael Greene

Dear Sir                    Head Quarters White plains 1st Sepr 1778
I have had the pleasure of receiving your several letters, the last of which was of the 22d Augt.[1] I have not now time to take notice of the several arguments that were made use of, for and against the Counts quitting the Harbour of Newport and sailing for Boston. Right or

wrong, it will probably disappoint our sanguine expectations of success, and what I esteem a still worse consequence, I fear it will sow the seeds of dissention and distrust between us and our new allies, except the most prudent measures are taken to suppress the feuds and jealousies that have already arisen. I depend much upon your temper and influence to conciliate that animosity which I plainly perceive, by a letter from the Marquis, subsists between the American Officers and the French in our service.[2] This you may depend will extend itself to the Count and the officers and men of his whole Fleet, should they return to Rhode Island, except upon their arrival there, they find a reconciliation has taken place. The Marquis speaks kindly of a letter from you to him upon this subject.[3] He will therefore take any advice coming from you, in a friendly light, and if he can be pacified, the other French Gentlemen will of course be satisfied as they look up to him as their Head. The Marquis grounds his complaint upon a general order of the 24 Augt the latter part of which is certainly very impolitic[4] and upon the universal clamor that prevailed against the french Nation. I beg you will take every measure to keep the protest entered into by the General Officers, from being made public. The Congress, sensible of the ill consequences that will flow from the World's knowing of our differences, have passed a resolve to that purpose[5]—Upon the whole, my dear Sir, you can conceive my meaning better than I can express it, and I therefore fully depend upon your exerting yourself to heal all private animosities between our principal Officers and the french, and to prevent all illiberal expressions and reflections that may fall from the Army at large—[6]I have this moment recd a letter from Genl Sullivan of the 29th Augt in which he barely informs me of an Action upon that day in which he says we had the better but does not mention particulars. I am &c.

Df, in the writing of Tench Tilghman, DLC:GW; Varick transcript, DLC:GW.

1. The letters that Greene had written to GW from his departure for Rhode Island through 22 Aug. have not been found.

2. GW was referring to Lafayette's letter to him of 25 August.

3. At this point Tilghman wrote and crossed out, "You will therefore be a proper person, to go into the matter fully with him, and to point out the innumerable dangers that will arise."

4. At this point Tilghman wrote for insertion, "and upon an ungenerous mode of acting and speaking," but he crossed that phrase out. The remainder of this sentence was written in the left margin and marked for placement here.

5. For Congress's resolution of 28 Aug., see *JCC*, 11:848–49.

6. At this point Tilghman wrote but crossed out, "I have heard nothing from Rhode Island, but by report, since the 23d Augt. this leaves me in a most anxious state of uncertainty, and entirely at a loss how to form any plans."

460 September 1778

## From Major General William Heath

Dear General                    Head Quarters Boston Sept. 1st 1778
The Last Evening I received the Honor of yours of the 28th ulto.

your Excellency may be Assured of my utmost attention & Exertions as far as in my power to paliate and vindicate the Conduct of the Count DEstaing in leaving Rhode Island His Ships are now Formed in Line of Battle in Nantasket Road, at the Entrance of which on Hull and Long Island Batteries are Erecting which will afford a Cross Fire and I think Effectually prevent even a Superior Fleet Entering.[1]

I shall procure the Colours for Genl Pattersons Brigade If Possible wish to be in formed as the Letter does not, what device is to be put on the Colours or whether they are to be plain.

It will be needless for me to mention any Intelligence from Rhode Island—as you will have it more direct from Major Genl Sullivan. I have the Honor to be with the greatest respect your Excellencys most Obt Servt

W. Heath

ADfs, MHi: Heath Papers.
1. The town of Hull on Nantasket Head is about three miles east-southeast of Long Island, Massachusetts.

## From Major General William Heath

                                            Head Quarters Boston
Dear General                    Sept. 1st 1778 3 oClock P.M.
a Large Fleet of men of war are now almost up to our Light House[1] and are beyond a doubt an Enemy the alarm is Given, and the militia assembling, There are no Continental Troops here except about 40 Invalids—our Militia are as good as any but your Excy is sensible they are not like Regular Troops about Twenty Ships are in Sight & Some of them very large. I am Dear Genl in haste your obt Servt

W. Heath

ADfS, MHi: Heath Papers.
1. The lighthouse for Boston Harbor was on Little Brewster Island (also called Lighthouse Island), a little less than four miles east of Long Island at the entrance to Boston Harbor.

## To Major General Lafayette

My dear Marquis.                    White-plains Septr 1st 1778.
I have been honored with your favor of the 25th Ulto by Monsr Pontgebaud and wish my time, which at present is taken up by a Comee of Con-

gress, would permit me to go fully into the contents of it—this, however is not in my power to do. But in one word, let me say, I feel every thing that hurts the sensibility of a Gentleman; and, consequently, upon the present occasion, feel for you & for our good & great Allys the French—I feel myself hurt also at every illiberal, and unthinking reflection which may have been cast upon Count D'Estaing, or the conduct of the Fleet under his command. and lastly, I feel for my Country. Let me entreat you therefore my dear Marquis to take no exception at unmeaning expressions, uttered perhaps without Consideration, & in the first transport of disappointed hope—Every body Sir, who reasons, will acknowledge the advantages which we have derived from the French Fleet, & the Zeal of the Commander of it, but in a free, & republican Government, you cannot restrain the voice of the multitude—every Man will speak as he thinks, or more properly without thinking—consequently will judge of Effects without attending to the Causes. The censures which have been levelled at the Officers of the French Fleet, would, more than probable, have fallen in a much higher degree upon a Fleet of our own (if we had had one) in the same situation—It is the Nature of Man to be displeased with every thing that disappoints a favourite hope, or flattering project; and it is the folly of too many of them, to condemn without investigating circumstances. Let me beseech you therefore my good Sir to afford a healing hand to the wound that, unintentially, has been made. America esteems your Virtues & yr Services—and admires the principles upon which you act. Your Countrymen, in our Army, look up to you as their Patron. The Count and his Officers consider you as a man high in Rank, & high in estimation, here and in France; and I, your friend, have no doubt but that you will use your utmost endeavours to restore harmony that the honour, glory, and mutual Interest of the two Nation's may be promoted and cemented in the firmest manner. I would add mo⟨re⟩ on the subject, but am restrained for want of time & therefore shall only add, that with every sentiment of esteem & regard I am, My dear Marquis Yr Obedt Servt and Affecte friend

Go: Washington

ADfS, DLC:GW; Varick transcript, DLC:GW.

## From Major General Lafayette

My dear General                     tyver town [R.I.] 1st September 1778
   that there has been an action fought where I could have been and where I was not, is a thing which will seem as extraordinary to you as it seems so to myself—after a long journey and a longer stay from home (I mean from head quarters) the only satisfactory day I might have finds me in the middle of a town—there I had been sent, push'd, hur-

ri'd by the board of general officers, and principally by generals Sullivan and greene, who thaught I would be of a great use to the Common
Cause, and to whom I foretold the disagreable event which would happen to me—I felt in that occasion the impression of that bad star,
which some days ago has influenced the french undertakings and
which I hope will be soon Remov'd—people say to me that I do'nt
want an action more or less, but if it is not Necessary to my Reputation
of a tolerable private soldier, so at least it is to my Satisfaction, and
pleasure—however I was happy enough as to arrive before the second
Retreat, but it was not attended with such a trouble and danger as it
ought to be, had not the ennemy been So Sleepy, and then I was once
more depriv'd of my fighting expectations.

by what I have heard from Sensible, and *Candid* french gentlemen,
the action does great honor to general sullivan—he Retreated in good
order, he oppos'd very properly every effort of the ennemy, he never
Sent troops but well supported, and display'd a great Coolness during
the whole day—the evacuation I have Seen extremely well perform'd,
and *my private opinion* is that if both events are satisfactory to us, they are
very schamefull for the british generals and troops—they had indeed so
fine chances as to cut us to pieces, but they are very good people.

Now, my dear general, I must give you an account of that journey I
have pay'd so dear—the Count d'estaing arriv'd the day before in
boston—I found him much displeas'd at a protest you have heard
off, and many other circumstances which I have Reported to you[1]—I
did what I could in the occasion—but I must give the justice to the
admiral that it has not disminish'd at all his warm desire of Serving
America—we waited together on the Council, general heath, general
hancok and were very satisfied of them—the last one did much distinguish himself by his zeal on the occasion—some people in boston
were Rather disatisfied—but when they see the behaviour of the
Council, generals heath and hancok, they I hope will do the Same—I
therefore fear nothing but delays—the Mâsts are very far off, provisions difficult to be provided—the count d'estaing was Ready to Come
with his land forces and put himself under general Sullivan's orders
tho' disatisfied with the latter—but our new circumstances will alter
that design.

I beg you pardon, once more, my, dear general, for having troubl'd
and afflicted you with the account of what I had seen after the departure of the french fleet—my Confidence in you is such, that I could
not feel so warmly upon any point, without Communicating it to your
excellency—I have now the pleasure to inform you that the discontent
do'nt appear so much—the french hospital is arriv'd to boston, tho'
under difficulties which however I think I have disminish'd good deal

by sending a part of my family with them, with orders to some persons, and supplications to others to give them all assistance in theyr power— now every thing will be Right, provided the count d'estaing is Soon en- abl'd to Sail—every exertion I think ought to be employ'd for that purpose in all the Several parts of the Continent—Mâsts, bisket, water, and provisions are his wants—I long to have again the Command, or at least an equal force upon the American Seas.

by your letters to general Sullivan I aprehend that there is some gen- eral Move in the british army and that your excellency is going to send us reinforcements—god grant you may send so many as with the mili- tia will make a larger army that you might Command them yourself— I long my dear general, to be again with you, and the pleasure of Co- operating with the french fleet under your immediate orders will be the greatest I may feel—then I am sure every thing will be Right—the Count d'estaing (if Rhode island is again to be taken what I warmly wish) would be extremely happy to take it in conjunction with General Washington, and it would Remove the other inconveniences. I am now intrusted by general Sullivan with the care of warren, bristoll, and the eastern schore—it is that I am to defend a country with so few troops as are not able to defend more than a single point—I ca'nt answer that the ennemy wo'nt go where and do what they please, for I am not able to prevent any thing but a part of theyr army, and this yet must not land far from me—but I answer that if they come with equal or not much superior forces to these I may Collect, I schall flogg them pretty well— so at least I hope—my situation seems to be temporary for we expect much to hear soon from your excellency—you know mister touzard a gentleman of my family—he met with a terrible accident in the last action—for Running before all the others to take a piece of Cannon in the middle of the ennemys with the gratest excés of bravery, he was immediately covered with theyr schots, had his horse killed, and his Right arm put in pieces—he was happy enough as not to fall in theyr hands, and his life is not despaired of. Congress was going to send him a Commission of Major.

give me joy, my dear general, I schall have your picture, and Mister hancok has promis'd me a Copy of that he has in boston—he gave one to the Count d'estaing, and I never Saw a man so glad of possessing his sweet heart's picture, as the admiral was to Receive yours.

in expecting with the greatest impatience to hear from Your excel- lency which will be the general plans, and your private motions I have the honor to be with the highest Respect, the warmest, and most end- less affection dear general Your excellency's the most obedient hum- ble servant

the Marquis de lafayette

ALS, PEL. Where Lafayette edited this letter after the war, the original has been re-stored as much as possible.

1. Lafayette was referring to the American officers' protest to Vice Admiral d'Es-taing of 22 Aug., for which, see John Sullivan to GW, 23 Aug., n.2. For the "other circumstances," see Lafayette to GW, 25–26 August.

## To Henry Laurens

Head Qrs White plains Sept. 1st 1778
sir                                              11 OClock A.M.

I do myself the honor of transmitting you a Copy of a Letter I this minute received from General Sullivan.[1] I congratulate Congress on the repulse of the Enemy—and only wish our Troops may be able to effect a retreat, which seems the most eligible measure they can pur-sue, in the present situation of things. I have the Honor to be with the greatest respect & esteem sir Yr Most Obedt servt

Go: Washington

LS, in Robert Hanson Harrison's writing, DNA:PCC, item 152; Df, DLC:GW; copy, ScHi: Henry Laurens Papers; copy, PHi: Wayne Papers; copy, DNA:PCC, item 169; Varick transcript, DLC:GW. Congress read the letter on 4 Sept. and referred its en-closure to the committee of intelligence (see *JCC*, 12:880). The next day an extract of the letter was published with the enclosure by order of Congress (*Pennsylvania Packet or the General Advertiser* [Philadelphia], 5 Sept.). A transcript of this letter in the Bancroft Collection, Anthony Wayne Papers, at NN is misidentified as GW to Anthony Wayne.

1. See John Sullivan to GW, 29 August.

## To Major General John Sullivan

Dear sir.                          Head Quarters White plains 1st Septr 1778.

I have not received any letter from you since the 23d Ulto[1] which I attribute to some mishap of the messengers with whom they were sent. I was anxious to learn the determination and designs of the council of officers, that so I might be prepared for eventual measures—The suc-cess or misfortune of your army will have great influence in directing the movements and fortune of this.

The disagreement between the army under your command and the fleet has given me very singular uneasiness. The Continent at large is concerned in our cordiality, and it should be kept up by all possible means that are consistent with our honor and policy. First impressions, you know, are generally longest remembered, and will serve to fix in a great degree our national character among the French. In our conduct towards them we should remember that they are a people old in war, very strict in military etiquette, and apt to take fire when others scarcely seem warmed. Permit me to reco⟨mmend⟩ in the most particular manner, ⟨the⟩ cultivation of harmony and go⟨od⟩ agreement, and your endeavours to ⟨des⟩troy that ill humour which may ⟨have⟩ got into the officers. It is of the greatest importance, also that the minds of the soldiers and the people should know nothing of the misunderstanding, or if it has reached them that ways may be used to stop its progress and prevent its effects.

I have received from Congress the inclosed by which you will perceive their opinion with regard to keeping secret the protest of the General Officers I need add nothing on this subject.[2]

I have one thing however more to say—I make no doubt but you will do all in your power to forward the repairs of the french fleet, and in rendering it fit for service, by your recommendations for that purpose to those who can be immediately instrumental. I am Dr Sir your most Obt hble servt

Go: Washington

LS, in James McHenry's writing, NhHi: Sullivan Papers; Df, DLC:GW; Varick transcript, DLC:GW. Where the LS is now damaged, the characters in angle brackets have been supplied from an earlier photocopy of the LS in DLC:GW, series 9.

Later this day GW wrote a second letter to Sullivan, which reads: "After closing my letter to you of this date I had the satisfaction of receiving your favor of the 29 ulto dated at the Northern end of Rhode Island, and rejoice with you on the important matters it contains. I have transmitted a copy to Congress and doubt not but it will relieve them from much anxiety, and give them equal pleasure with me on the victory you have obtained" (Df, DLC:GW).

1. GW received Sullivan's letter of 23 Aug. on the morning of 25 August.

2. GW was referring to the congressional resolution of 28 Aug. (see *JCC*, 11:848–49).

## General Orders

Head-Quarters W. Plains Wednesday Septr 2nd [1778]
Parole Jedburgh—                                          C. Signs June. July—
The Court of Enquiry whereof Coll Marshal is President will assemble at ten ôClock tomorrow morning at the Presidents quarters and take into consideration a Complaint exhibited by Mr Kean Assistant Commissary of Issues against Lieutt Seldon of the 4th Virginia Regt both Parties to attend.[1]

A return of Colours in the several Regiments to be made tomorrow at Orderly time.[2]

Varick transcript, DLC:GW. Maj. Caleb Gibbs's receipt book records that on this date he received $1,000 from the paymaster general "for the use of defraying the Expence of His Excellency General Washington's family" (DLC:GW, ser. 5, vol. 27). GW's warrant book for this date records a payment of that amount "To Henry P. Livingston, Esqre, Lieut. of the Guard for his Excellency's use" (DLC:GW, ser. 5, vol. 19).

1. John Kean had been appointed as assistant commissary of issues for the staff department with the army in the field, apparently in October 1777, and he continued to serve in that post until the department of issues was eliminated in early 1782. "Lieutt Seldon" was probably Samuel Selden, who was a lieutenant of the 1st, not the 4th, Virginia Regiment. Samuel Selden, who was appointed a second lieutenant of the 1st Virginia Regiment in June 1777, was promoted to first lieutenant in June 1778 and to captain-lieutenant on 25 June 1779. Taken prisoner at Charleston on 12 May 1780, he was exchanged in November of that year and served to the close of the war, being wounded on 18 June 1781 at Ninety-Six, South Carolina.

2. Adj. Gen. Alexander Scammell compiled this data into a "Return of Colours belonging to the Several Brigades Present," dated 5 Sept. (DLC:GW). The return showed nine good and seventeen bad "Standard," thirty-five good and twelve bad "Grand Division," and one good "Regimental" colors for the fifteen brigades reporting. Scammell also noted that the 1st Pennsylvania Brigade had six colors in Pennsylvania.

## From Major Alexander Clough

Sr                                        [Hackensack, N.J.] Sept. 2d—78

I had the honour to recive your Exellencys favour yesterday, and shall use the utmost of my endavours to get the most satisfactry intelligance.[1] I think we have got it at this post, in such a chanell that we cannot faill, of getting certain information of every thing of moment, that Occurs in New york, if my conduct meets with your approbation, I shall esteem it as more then a sufficient reward for my best services—Two persons who left New york on munday night, informs me that thay are repairing thayr waggons with the greatest delligance. thay are makeing some aditions to the works on Bunkers Hill—he says four of Adml Byrons fleet is come in, he cannot tell of what force thay are, it is reported that the adml is lost—six of the cork fleet is come in, four with provisions, and two with recruits, there are not more then sixty english, the others are Hesiens, the number he cannot exactly tell, but when thay where d⟨*mutilated*⟩d there was not more then three men to a regt, Mr Eliot, the superintendent says, if this expedition to rode island should fail New york could hold out but a short time for want of provisions if it falls in our hands he is resolve'd to stay let the event be what it may, Byard delance & Mathews says the same[2] the worst sour flour is sold for five pounds a hundred—I am your Exellencys most Obt Hbl. servt

A. Clough

ALS, DLC:GW.

1. Clough was referring to GW's letter to him of 31 August.

2. Andrew Elliot (d. 1797) had been collector of customs at New York City since 1764 and was chief of the Superintendent Department established by Gen. William Howe in 1777. From 1780 to 1783 he served as lieutenant governor of Loyalist New York, acting as governor from April 1783 to the British evacuation, when he left New York. The other men were probably William Bayard, Oliver De Lancey, and David Mathews.


## To Silas Deane

Dear sir.                            Head Quartrs White plains Sept. 2d 1778
I received your favor of the 22d Ulto by Mr Webb.

The regard I have for Colo. Webb—and my wish to oblige you, would urge me most strongly to effect his release, if it were practicable; but our circumstances will not admit of it. The only rule of exchange, now existing between the two armies, is equality of rank; and unhappily, we have not a Colonel, a prisoner, in our hands. Indeed, if we had, the Enemy have other Colonels of ours, who have been much longer in captivity, and who must have a preference. As from this state, his exchange cannot now be accomplished, his enlargement must depend entirely upon the indulgence of Sr Henry Clinton, and for which I cannot sollicit, with any degree of propriety; having been obliged to refuse him requests of the same nature—and as it would lead to many inconveniences. At the same time I shall be happy, if he can obtain his parole, and from what I told Mr Jos: Webb, his Brother, I am in hopes he will interest himself through the medium of some of his British acquaintances—and that it may be granted.

With respect to news, my Letter of Yesterday to Congress, which I presume you will be informed of, contains the last from the Eastward. By General Sullivan's account the Enemy attacked him in his retreat on the 29th Ulto and after a warm action, were obliged to retire from the Field, with precipitation, and in disorder. He had not time then, to ascertain either our—or their loss. This was a very interesting event, considering his situation, and it will give me great pleasure to hear, that he and his Troops are on the main again.

I thank you much for your promised visit, and I will thank you still more for the visit itself. I shall consider it, not only as an honorable— but as a very friendly mark of your attention. I have the Honor to be with the most perfect regard & respect D. Sir Your Most Obedt servant

Go: Washington

LS, in Robert Hanson Harrison's writing, PPRF; Df, DLC:GW; Varick transcript, DLC:GW.

# From Brigadier General Duportail

General Du Portail's opinion                    [2 September 1778]

The English fleet finding itself by the arrival of six vessels greatly superior to the French fleet, it seems to me that the English may now project a decisive operation. This is to block up the port of Boston with their fleet—to embark all the troops at NewYork—conduct them to Rhode Island—debark them there and march directly towards Boston. To prevent them—this is briefly what I should think proper for us to do.

1st   To give orders to General Sullivan to take all the necessary measures to hinder their debarkation.

2   To reconnoitre a succession of positions to be occupied on the route to Boston; to have cut up, or hold himself ready to cut up, all the parallel and detour roads leading there—If any place can be found favourable for fighting the English army to have it fortified beforehand.

3—His Excellency to send towards Connecticut river three or four thousand men ready to pass when there shall be occasion and reinforce General Sullivan. That the rest of the army hold itself on such a position, that these three or four thousand men may be able to join it, in case the enemy, instead of going towards Boston should march against us; and that it may be at the same time as far advanced towards a junct⟨ion⟩ with General Sullivan, as the security of the North River will permit. I suppose that the Militia of the State of Boston are ready to assemble.

I would also propose to His Excellency with regard to myself—

That I should go immediately to General Sullivan's army to assist in choosing and fortifying a good position on the route to Boston.

When that should be done—That I should go myself to Boston to see what may be done for the defence of the town itself—I would even precede myself by Mr De la Radiere to whom I will write (if His Excellency judges it proper) to repair there immediately.

                                                            Du Portail

Translation, in Alexander Hamilton's writing, DLC:GW; ADS, in French, DLC:GW; Varick transcript of translation, DLC:GW. The date is taken from the Varick dockets on the ADS and translation. This is Duportail's response to the questions GW posed at a council of war on the evening of 1 September.

# To Vice Admiral d'Estaing

Sir,                    Head Quarters White plains 2d Sepr 1778[1]

The importance of the fleet under your command to the common cause, and the interest I take in your personal concerns would not permit me, but to be deeply affected with the information of the disappointment and injuries, you sustaind in the late unfortunate storm. I flatter myself, and I most ardently hope, my countrymen will exert themselves to give you every aid in their power, that you may as soon as possible recover from the damage you have suffered and be in a condition to renew your efforts against the common enemy.

Inclosed I do myself the honor to send you an extract from the journal, from an officer stationed in the vicinity of Black-point, to watch the motions of the enemy's fleet; which I have just receivd. He is an officer of vigilance and discernment, but from his situation it is possible he may be mistaken in the size of the ships. Part of his intelligence too from the nature of it must have been received from others, and is so far fallible.[2] I think it my duty to communicate to you as I receive it; and shall immediately give you notice of any thing that comes to my knowledge, which may either confirm or contradict.[3]

I am informed there is a considerable quantity of provisions on the way from Philadelphia for the use of your fleet—[4]part crossed the North River several days since.

you may be assured so far as it shall depend upon me, every method will be taken to forward them with dispatch. I have the honor to be With the greatest respect & esteem Sir Your most obedt serv.

Df, in Alexander Hamilton's writing, DLC:GW; Varick transcript, DLC:GW.

1. The dateline on the draft is in Tench Tilghman's writing.

2. At this point on the draft, Hamilton marked a sentence for insertion that was later struck out: "Some accounts by different channels also mention the arrival of a part of Byron's fleet."

3. GW enclosed an extract of Maj. Richard Howell's letter to William Maxwell of 30 Aug., giving his journal of ship movements from 26 to 30 Aug. (DLC:GW). Howell reported no movement on 26 or 27 Aug., but on 28 Aug. "one small Vessel came in and a large Ship thought an 84," and on 29 Aug. "Two transports went up under Convoy of a very large Ship suppos'd to be a 74 same Day 2 other Ships came in esteemd 1. 74. & one 84 went up to the Hook." Howell's entry for 30 Aug. reported: "2 ships 1 Sloop & a Brig came in not ships of Force unless one might have been a frigate And now I am to remark that one of Biron's fleet which had ⟨halted⟩ in a Gale of Wind did certainly Join Ld How & sail with him. The ships mentioned above are Birons fleet who is now in the Bay taking in water & will sail very shortly in Comp'y with a rear Admiral name unknown, who was a shore at the Hook in that Charecter. . . . It was reported in York that Rhoad Island was attack'd both by sea & land but they think they can maintain the place if our Troops do not amount to more than 40000. Certainly General Clinton was marchd to the East end of Long-Island with 8000 men there to embark on board Transports which were ready to receive them, & supposed to design for Rhoad Island. By an express to York, the french Fleet were Join'd by a small reinforcement from Chessopeak Bay 1. 50. 1. 40. & 3 frigates. I am told here that the Day before yesterday 2 ships, appeard off the Land near long-Branch, under french Co⟨lors.⟩ A ship call'd the Leviathan lays off the Hook with one tier of Guns as a Battery." Howell added information that

was probably not included in the extract: "I am in haste as my party are now on their Marc⟨h⟩ and I must over take them before Night. A fiew Days past the wood Tories attack'd a Man and robbed him. They have said they would make their fortunes tomorrow out of the Inhabitants on their way to the Sale of a Ship and Cargo at Toms River, I shall march all Night and may perhaps mar their Sport in the Morning."

4. At this point on the draft, Hamilton wrote and struck out the words "near forty waggon loads."


# From Major General Horatio Gates

[White Plains] 2d Sept. 1778

Question the First.

Whether any, or what Operations can now be undertaken?

Answer.

Want of certain intelligence of The Enemys motions, & designs; of their present Strength, and Numbers, at the posts, Stations, & Territorys, they possess; want of exact information of the State of the Army under Gen: Sullivan; want of Knowledge of what Magazine of Flour, is, or can be provided in the Eastern States; Obliges me to Confess myself, intirely at a Loss what to Determine upon the above Question; for without Sufficient light in These particulars, there is no Deciding upon so important a point.

Question the Second.

Shall the Army, or any part Thereof, move Eastward?

I apprehend this intirely depends upon the movements, & Detachments, The Enemy have made, or are about to make; These being known, and most of the Intelligence in My answer to the first Question Obtain'd, a possitive, & Determinate reply, might be given to the Second Question.

Third Question.

In case the Main Body of the Army moves Eastward, what Force is to be left for the Defence of this Country, & The passes in the Highlands?

Answer.

Here again I am at a Loss for intelligence; and can only in General Answer; That an Equal Number of Continental Troops, to Those the Enemy leave in Garrison at Their posts upon, & near York Island; Staaten Island; & the West End of Long Island; should be left, for the purposes recited in the Third Question.

Fourth Question.

Can any Attempt be made upon New York?

It was Unanimously Decided by a very Full Council of War, held at Wrights Mills in July; that an Attempt upon New York, with the whole of Our Force was improper.[1] Circumstances may be *so* altered, Since the holding that Council; as to make the Attempt immediately necessary; a Desperate Disease, must have a Desperate Remedy; The State of Our Currency; The State of Our Army; The Difficulty to recruit it next Campaign, & Furnish properly, every Sort of Magazine; may Oblige us to risque Our Fortunes upon the Events of This Summer; all which must be Submitted to The Wisdom of Congress, & Your Excellency.

Horatio Gates
Major General

ADS, DLC:GW; ADf, NHi: Gates Papers; Varick transcript, DLC:GW. This is Gates's reply to the questions posed by GW at a council of war on the evening of 1 September.

1. See Council of War, 25 July. On the draft, Gates continued at this point with text that he later struck out: "if it is resolved to Detach a large Force Eastward, will the Troops proposed to be left to Secure this Country, and the passes of the Highlands, be Adequate to such an undertaking."

## From Major General William Heath

Head Quarters Boston 2d September 1778.

Dear General

8 O'Clock A.M.

By the observations made at Hull (Nantasket) the last evening at 6 o'Clock, the Enemy's Fleet, in sight, consisted of Twenty Ships, one Sloop & one Schooner within about Two leagues, veering E.S.E., from Light house Island, 8 or 10 of them Ships of the Line (one wearing a blue Flag at her fore Top mast head)[1] 8 Frigates the others small. Between 1, & 3, O'Clock this morning 6 or 7 Cannon were fired in the Bay, and at this time, the wind being fresh at North they are not to be seen; perhaps will stand in again when the wind will permit. Whether their intention is only to block up the Count D'Estaing's Squadron until a Reinforcement arrives, or whether a landing is to be made by the Enemy at Providence or to the Southward of this place time must discover. Nine of the neighbouring Regiments of Militia are coming in for the defence of the most important Posts around the Harbour. The whole of the State Regiment of Artillery are with General Sullivan; I have wrote him to forward them here with all possible dispatch.[2]

On Yesterday a Mr Shirley, who was some time since taken by a Connecticutt Armed Vessel, a Gentlemen of Family & fortune, of whom perhaps your Excellency has heard mention made,[3] observed to some Gentlemen in conversation, on the appearance of the Fleet, that it was a matter that would not soon be over, that General Clinton would Land at Tiverton or there abouts and push his march this way; whether this

is an idle conjecture or worthy of notice you will best judge from circumstances better known to you than me.

The master of a Vessel just arrived informs that he saw yesterday
about 100 Sail of Transport standing eastward. I have the honor to be
With great respect Your Excellency's Most Obedt Servant

W. Heath

P.S. Eleven O'Clock—The Signals are again out.

Would request that your Excellency will forward the enclosed Letter
to Congress by the first Express your Excellency sends there.[4]

LS, DLC:GW; ADfS, MHi: Heath Papers.

1. Lord Richard Howe ranked as vice admiral of the blue.

2. See the two letters from Heath to Maj. Gen. John Sullivan, 1 Sept., in Hammond, *Sullivan Papers*, 2:289.

3. Heath was referring to Henry Shirley, captured by the Connecticut navy ship
*Oliver Cromwell* while aboard the privateer *Admiral Keppel* en route to Jamaica in
April 1778. For more on the capture of the *Keppel* and on Shirley's claims of im-
portance, see Hinman, *Historical Collection*, 604–6.

4. Heath's letter to Henry Laurens of this date conveyed much the same intelligence as this letter, with added information about the position of the French fleet
that Heath had sent to GW in his first letter of 1 Sept. (DNA:PCC, item 157).

## From Major General Johann Kalb

Camp at White plains 2d septembr 1778.

His Excellency The Commander in chief having laid the following
points before the Board of General officers to be considered, and to
deliver their opinion Thereon.[1]

| *Questions* | *Answers.* |
|---|---|
| 1° Whether it would be adviseable to march, this army, either part of it, or the whole, to the Eastward, if the Enemies Should re-inforce Rhode Island or land on the Con-tinent in either of the Eastern States? | Since the Enemies may with So much more ease than we, carry their Troops to and fro, as long as they are masters of the Sound it appears to me, that to follow their movements would be only harrassing and fatigueing our Army without any annoyance to them. |
| | As the Enemies divided forces in their present Situation can answer no valuable Prospect, as His Excellency observed, a short Time will clear up, whether they will continue in their present defensive Situation or collect their forces in one Place to act |

offensively, or Evacuate intirely. which
it is my opinion they will as soon as
they can conveniently do it, to Secure
their West-Indies & perhaps England
herself, rather than waste their Forces
& Money on an imaginary Conquest.

2° How to Suply the
army, if moving to
the Eastward, together
with the Troops
already there, & a
large Body of militia
the the Enemies
attempts on the
New-England States
would render
necessary, besides
Victualling the French
Fleet?

The New-England States may be able
to Suply the whole with Beef & Pork,
but the more Southern States must of
course provide all the Flour, the
Transporting of which by land
carriages will be attended with
immense but unavoidable Expenses.
for I would by no means advise to
Venture anything by Sea, though four
parts out of Five Should arrive (and
this is not to be Expected) the Fifth
part would be for the Enemies a Suply
of what they are most in need of.

Whether this army will move more
Easterly or not, I think it is highly
necessary that a considerable quantity
of flour should be Stored up as soon as
possible, in or near Connecticut State,
(in a place out of the reach of the
British Ships & land forces) for All the
above mentioned Exigencies.

3° In case this army
was to march to the
Eastward what could
be done to Secure the
Highlands?

The North River ought to be fortified
at the Points & Narrows, not only on
the Water side but also on the Land
sides, at least the most important posts,
well Suplied with Provisions, artillerie,
arms & ammunitions, & Sufficiently
Garrisoned.

4° Whether an attack
on the Enemies lines
near kings Bridge or on
New-york Island would
be eligible or proper
in the present Situation
of affairs with any
probability of Success?

It being Evident that the City of New
york can not be kept by the american
Troops I would by no means advise
Such a Attempt, which answering no
Valuable purpose must nevertheless be
attended with the loss of many Men &
perhaps other bad Consequences even
with the fairest Success.

                        The Baron de Kalb

ADS, DLC:GW; Varick transcript, DLC:GW.
1. See Council of War, 1 September.

# From Baron de Knobelauch

Philada
To His Excellency General Washington                     2d Septr 1778

I would think myself happy were I able to make to Your Excellency the first Address of my humble Respects in Words of Your national Language: The time of my travelling over the Country was too short to learn it but I shall use my endeavours to make some tolerable Progress therein.

perhaps Your Excellency are already informed by Congress that on my Memorial of the 12. Aug. they have given me Permission to repair as Volunteer to the American Camp with an Allowance of 125 Dolls. ℔ month two Rations and Forage for two Horses.[1]

In consequence of these Resolves I have the Honour to present myself to Your Excellency. My highest Wishes are to meet Opportunities to distinguish myself in the Army to become useful to the United States and by these means to render myself worthy Your kind Notice and Confidence.

I have had some Experience of the military Service to which I entred about 30 Years ago: my first Apprenticeship was made in His Prussian Majestys Seminary of War. And in his last septennial glorious War I have been present at Six decisive Battles Seventeen Encounters and two Sieges.

Anno 1762. His Prussian Majesty at the Instance of the Russian Emperor Peter 3d yielded him three Officers and I was one of that Number. From the Rank of a Staffs Captain I was advanced to that of Premier Major and received a Commission to introduce the Prussian Exercise Evolutions &ca among the Infantry and special Commissions of Major of the Exercise and Vice Commandant of Oranienbaum. After the Revolution I was by Order of the Empress retained in the Service of the Grand Duke with a pension of 800 Rubles.[2] Of this Favour I did not avail myself a long time, I sued for my Dismission and obtained it in the Caracter of Lieutenant Colonel.

Two Months after in the Spring of 1764. I entred in the King of Denmarks Service as Lieutenant Colonel in Fact, and Commander of His Majestys Regiment of Hollstein Infantry. In this Service I have under the Direction of the then Field Marshall Count de St Germain (now His most christian Majestys Minister of the War-Department) drawn the Reglement of the Exercise and Service.[3] In the last Year of my Service I had the Honour to Command the Kings Guard of Foot; an

Honour which in that Kingdom had never before been conferred upon any Foreigner. At that time her Imperial Majesty of Russia was pleased to require of the King of Dennemark to remove from his Presence a certain Count of Goertz and myself pretending that we had meddled with State Affairs against the Russian Interest,[4] Whereupon I lost the Command of the Kings Foot Guard and shortly after quitted that ungrateful Service, But the King accompanied the very honorable Letters Patent of my discharge with a present of 1200 Guineas.

All I have had the Honour to mention to Your Excellency is supported by the Original Patents or Commissions and the Discharges from the Sovereigns I have served, so as I have brought the same Originals over with me. These papers have been considered by Congress as good Evidence of the Fairness of my Caracter as an Officer And being a Stranger in this Country I offered at the same time in proof of my military Knowledge any Discourse or Commentary on some Articles relating to military affairs which Articles I have hereto subjoined. The Committee to whom Congress had referred my proposal did single out the 17. 18. & 19. of the said Articles and I have made out and delivered to them my Report accordingly.[5]

Permit me, Sir, to assure You upon Honour, that from mere Inclination without any Views of own Interest or political I have set out from my own Country to serve the United States of this, under the Command of Your Excellency, Who in all Europe is now in possession of the Reputation of one of the greatest Generals in this Age So it is that I flatter myself in the Way of Honour to attain and deserve Your Excellencys Approbation and Countenance of my Intentions.

On this Occasion I beg leave to deliver to Your Excellency a Letter of Dr Franklin and another from Mr Penet at Nantes This Gentlemen has intrusted me with the Care of his youngest Brother Mr Peter Penet to present him to You, and desired that I might become a Suitor with him to Your Excellency to place him any way in the Service.[6]

S. W. B. de Knobelauch:

LS, DLC:GW.

1. Knobelauch was apparently referring to his memorial of 27 July, on which Congress had taken action on 12 Aug. (DNA:PCC, item 78; *JCC*, 11:725, 764, 778–79). Henry Laurens enclosed a copy of the resolutions in his letter to GW of 13 August.

2. Oranienbaum, now Lomonsov, Russia, is about eighteen miles east-southeast of St. Petersburg. The name is retained for the palace there. In the summer of 1762 Czar Peter III of Russia was forced to abdicate in favor of his wife Sophie, who became Empress Catherine II (Catherine the Great). Peter was assassinated not long after.

3. Claude-Louis, comte de St.-Germain (1707–1778), who had been appointed the French secretary of state for war in October 1775, had left office in September 1777 and died in January 1778.

4. Knobelauch was probably referring to Count Karl Friedrich Adam von Goertz (1733–1797), who acted as a colonel in the Danish service before becoming a Prussian cavalry general.

5. In the enclosed undated list of "Some Articles upon which I shall communicate my Sentiments, whenever order'd thereto by the Honorable Congress," articles 17, 18, and 19 of the 30 concern "the Field Apothecary's Shop," surgeons, and hospitals (DLC:GW).

6. For Benjamin Franklin's letter to GW of 24 Aug. 1777, see Laurens to GW, 13 Aug. 1778, n.4. The letter from Pierre (Peter) Penet of Nantes has not been found. When GW wrote Henry Laurens about Penet's brother on 21 Nov., he said that Penet had "importuned me to recommend his brother to Congress for an appointment by brevet to the rank of Captain, which he observes will have no effect in this country, as his brother will immediately return to France, which he makes an essential condition of the appointment." The brother, who did not receive a commission at this time, may have been Ignace (Ignatius) Penet, who was appointed a lieutenant in Colonel Armand's legion on 6 Jan. 1781.

# From Brigadier General Henry Knox

Park Artillery [White Plains] 2d Septr 1778

I shall give my opinion on the subjects propos'd by your Excellency to your General Officers with as much brevity as they will admit.

The first is.

Whether a movement of the greater part of this Army to the Eastward under the present information and circumstances will be eligible?

I cannot see the propriety of such a measure at present, or that it could be warranted from the State of information which your Excellency gave the Council last evening. Suppose the enemies force at Rhode-Island including the reinforcement they may receive from New York to amount to 10,000 men what enterprize will this force be adequate to or what will be its object? Surely 10,000 men at this season of the Year will not attempt to penetrate the Country to Boston from Rhode Island. if they should, from what place will they probably procure the Carriages and assistance necessary to such a project? I confess I know not. It will take a great number of Carriages and Horses which cannot be procur'd from the Country contiguous to Rhode-Island. Boston will be of little value to them supposing they were possess'd of it. every body acquainted with it and its neighbourhood will know the force I have suppos'd unequal to its possession and the adjacent Country.

probably it may be urg'd that the fleet of Count DEstaing now at Boston is an object of sufficient magnitude to warrant the supposition of a combin'd operation of the British fleet and Army that Way to effect its destruction, and thereby give England the Ascendency on the Ocean during the War with France.

The probability of this supposition is founded on the existence of two circumstances, either of which being taken away or not existing must render the whole supposition groundless. Vizt The superiority of the British to the French fleet and the destruction or capture of the troops under Genl Sullivan.

If the troops get Off from the Island without much injury, they will constitute a sufficient Stamina for to collect the Force of the Country. and the experience we have had of the Militia when combin'd with the continental troops will warrant the supposition That if they are not equal to tottaly stop the March of the British troops to Boston they will be able to retard them as to give time for the greatr part of this army to arrive to their assistance—It is my opinion they will be able to stop them entirely, considering the roughness of the Country, The difficulty of Obtaining intelligence and the want of carriages to transport provisions &c.

But suppose they should overcome all difficulties and arrive at Boston. The British fleet allowing it to be superior to the french in a broad sea where the whole could act, would not be so in the Channel leading to Boston, where from its narrowness it is not possible for two ships to lead abreast, and where very few Hulks sunk which are ready prepar'd would make the approach above the Castle impossible. The reduction of Castle Island would be an ardous and extensive task too unequal to the Strength of 10,000 men who would be oblig'd besides Boston to occupy a number of Islands either of which being carried, the whole enterprize would be frustrated and in all probability the remainder made prisoners.

For these and other reasons which might be urg'd I am of opinion The Enemy have not extended their views so far as the reduction of Boston and the French fleet there.

But should General Sullivans troops be captur'd the Event would be so unfortunate to us and so advantageous to the Enemy as to ind[uce] them to undertake enterprizes of which they did not dream. A Calamity so dreadful even in supposition would demand the immediate march of the greater part of this Army to counteract the consequences which may be suppos'd to arrive from so unexpecd an incident.

There is another expedition which indeed the Enemy may undertake. That is against the Town of Providence. Their reinforcement will probably arrive at the period that General Sullivan has effected his retreat from the Island. He then will be at two days march from Providence encumberd with his heavy Cannon, which came from and are almost the only defence of that Town and all his baggage and Stores. The Enemy in full possession of the Waters, flush'd with our retreat, a formidable force at Command, their Troops ready embark'd and only three or four hours sail from Providence, a rich defenceless obnoxious Town with a considerable quantity of shipping and stores.

Under these circumstances I think the Enemy will push and destroy that Town. it may be effected without any loss or even risque in twenty four hours.

The Army under your Excellency can have no possible Agency in preventing this apprehended Evil.

2d   supposing the Army to move to the Eastward what number of troops would be necessary to secure the highlands and the Forts on Hudsons River?

The force to be left for the security of these posts and Forts should I conceive be relatively strong to those the Enemy may leave in NewYork. I suppose the Question cannot be determined with precision untill this circumstance be tolerably well ascertained.

3   Can any attack be made on the troops in NewYork under the present information and circumstances with a probability of success?

The situation of the Island of New-York is such, surrounded by Waters, as to give the party possessing the Navigation a great Superiority. The Enemy having nine thousand men have force fully adequate to its defence against our Army.

To batter their Redoubts on this side Kings Bridge would require Cannon and an Apparatus which are at a distance and which would take time to bring to this place.

To Attempt the Redoubts by Supprize would require a most perfect knowledge of their number, construction, Strength & situation. Upon the acquisition of this knowledge and the matter of risque being fully weighed against the advantages of success and the ballance preponderating in favor of the latter I should be for such an attempt. But I beleive on such a trial the reasons would be more forcible against the attempt than for it.

4th   supposing the Army to move Eastward how shall it be supplied with provision &c?

Forage for the Horses can be procur'd with ease and Meat fresh and Salted. The difficulty would be in providing bread. This can be done no otherways than by the Quarter Master General making a proper arrange[ment] of a great number of Waggons to transport it from the southern States. It may be had altho' it will require much pains and trouble. I am with the greatest respect Your Excellenys most obedient Humble Servant

H. Knox

ADS, DLC:GW; ADfS, NNGL: Knox Papers; copy, NNGL: Knox Papers; Varick transcript, DLC:GW. This is Knox's reply to the questions posed by GW at the council of war on the evening of 1 September. The draft (like the copy) has many small variations in wording but the same organization and substance as the ADS. Another document listing the questions and giving brief notes on Knox's reply to each is in NNGL: Knox Papers.

## From Lieutenant Colonel John Laurens

(Private)

Sir                                                    Providence 2d [September] [1] 1778.

I had the honor of writing to Your Excellency previous to the Action of the 29th. my letter was committed to the care of Major Gibbes—and he destroyed it as soon as the engagement commenced, to guard against accidents—As Your Excellency has already received minute accounts of the transactions of that day from those who saw them in a more collective View, than the nature of my command afforded me—any farther relation is rendered unnecessary. I shall confine myself therefore to congratulating your Excellency on the happy termination, of an expedition which at one period was threatened with the most tragical Catastrophe—The Advantages gained in the affair of Portsmouth, and the brilliant retreat which succeeded it—by doing honor to the american Arms, consoled us in some degree for the loss of our grand object—The movements which your Excellency has observed at New York—the arrival of Seventy Sail of Vessels in the Road of Newport—the appearance of twenty Sail of[f] Boston—are circumstances which keep us in suspence with respect to the enemys intentions—General Greene has requested that I would remain in this quarter 'till they can be interpreted—in the mean time—as he agrees with me that if the enemy mean to act offensively here, a few days preparation will be required—I have thought it incumbent on me, as part of the commission with which Your Excellency honored me, to wait on Count D'Estaing—and ask if he has any dispatches for Head Quarters—it will be my greatest happiness if I can be useful in explaining the causes of mutual Jealousy and Uneasiness which have subsisted between the Officers of the allied powers here—and be any ways instrumental in restoring that harmony which the common interest requires.

I foretold to the Marquis, the influence which the Counts departure from the Road of Newport wd probably have upon the minds of the people—the danger of its reviving those absurd prejudices which we inherited from the british nation—unhappily the mischief has become more extensive by the unguarded expressions of some men of rank—who listened to their chagrin rather than good policy—Reflection however begins to induce a more cautious behavior; and I am in hopes that the confidence of the people in our new allies will be restored.

The Count's Sensibility was much wounded by the manner in which the American protest was delivered to him—in a letter to Genl Sullivan he declares that this paper imposed on the Commander of the Kings Squadron the painful but necessary law of profound silence—that he had taken occasion however relatively to some other business—to acquaint him that if the Council of Boston accepted his offer—(which was to repair to Rhode Island at the Head of his land Troops & receive Genl Sullivans orders)—he would promise the most implicit obedience on · the part of his troops and set them the example of it—that the extreme sensibility which composed the french national character, in every thing that relates to their honor—required that the french commander in chief shd by his Sentiments for the American General, and by a conspicuous measure, announce that french delicacy could not be wounded in a moment of passion, which arose from disappointment felt alike by both parties—in a postscript he requests that the Marquis de la fayette may explain matters between them.[2]

the expressions of the Count's Letter are rather obscure—but by discovering an inclination to make great personal sacrifices—is in my opinion a foundation, for restoring harmony and a good understanding—Genl Sullivans Answer, I hope will improve it. I have the honor to be with the greatest attachment and respect Your Excellencys most obedt Servt

John Laurens.

If I have not taken the precaution to mark particular letters, *private*— the contents will have announced to Your Excelly which were not intended as official. if I recollect right the two first only were marked on *public Service.*

ALS, DLC:GW.

1. Laurens wrote "August," but someone crossed that out and wrote "September" above it; the docket was also changed from August to September; and the reference to "the Action of the 29th" makes it clear that September is correct.

2. The translation in Laurens's writing of Vice Admiral d'Estaing's letter to Maj. Gen. John Sullivan, dated 29 Aug., in DLC:GW, was likely sent to GW by d'Estaing on 5 September. The translation of the letter printed in Hammond, *Sullivan Papers*, 2:277–78, is dated 30 August.

# From Major General Benjamin Lincoln

Dear General                                    White Plains Sept. 2d 1778

On consideration of the several questions proposed by your Excellency to the Council, the last evening,[1] I beg leave to give it as my opinion—that the army ought to be immediately removed eastward—One division of it consisting of a number sufficient fully to reinforce the troops in the Highlands and in conjunction with them be equal to the defence of that post to be marched to Danbury and there halted untill the designs of the enemy are better known than at present—And for the sake of convenient forage & dispatch the remainder of the army I think should move in two routs towards Providence to be halted on their march or proceed as the operations of the enemy shall make it necessary—Because it appears to me that if the enemy mean to act offensively, they have it in idea either to effect the possession of the Highlands on the North River Or the town of Boston our general Magazine for many stores & asylum for our ships of war or to seek & disband the army of the United States and that many advantages will result from this movement some of them are that we shall have it in our power hereby more speedily and effectually to counteract the designs of the enemy in general—secure the North River and the Highlands—possibly be in time to succour General Sulivan, in Case he be invested or to reduce the garrison on the Island of Rhode Island in conjunction with him on the return of Count d'Estaing's fleet although the enemy may have received a reinforcement—have it in our power early to give support to the town of Boston, should it be invaded—and should the enemy mean to look up the army of the united States, we shall lead them into a strong country, and be encircled by our friend, and supported by a good militia—Though there may be many objections to a movement of this kind, indeed there are some in my own mind, yet I see none which out weigh the reasons in favor thereof. I am induced also to this measure because I see no probability of success should we attempt New York or any of the enemies posts in this vicinity.

Considering the large number of teams now employed in transporting stores from the eastern States to this camp and the many which may be procured, I have no doubt but a full supply of bread for the army may easily be obtained. I have the honor to be Dear General with the greatest regard & esteem your Excelleny Most obt servant

B: Lincoln

ALS, DLC:GW; copy, MHi: Benjamin Lincoln Papers; Varick transcript, DLC:GW.
1. See Council of War, 1 September.

## From Major General Alexander McDougall

Camp white Plains 2d Sepr 1778
His Excellency the Commander in chief of the American Army informed the Council of General officers conven'd at His quarters last night,[1] that General Sullivan with the Army under His Command had

retired on the 29th Ultimo to the North End of Rhode Island, and that the Enemy from the best information the General could obtain, had embarked about Four Thousand Troops on Board of ⟨a⟩ number of Transports in the Sound near Frogs neck, and had Sailed to the Eastward on Sunday last.[2]

That the strength of the American Army in this Camp exceeded 12,000 men; and that by advice received from Count De-Estang, then in the Harbour of Boston, He intended to return to Rhode Island, with Ten ships of the Line and three Frigates. Under this information the Commander in chief, desires the opinion of the Council on the Following points vizt 1st whether a movement of the Army to the Eastward under the present circumstance would be Eligible?

2dly   If So, what Force will be necessary to leave, for the Security of the Communication on Hudsons River?

3dly   If a movement to the Eastward should be determined on, what Probability is there of a supply of Provision for the Army?

4thly   Can any attack be made on the Troops in, and about Newyork with a probability of success? Previous to my opinion on these points, I beg leave to Enemerate Some Facts. Dire necessity obliged Lord North to declare in the British Senate, that it was impracticable to Conquor America.[3] Under the influence of this Conviction, and our Alliance with France, the Grand British Army evacuates the state of Pensylvania; and apparently changes the seat of War to the East of Hudsons River; where the American Army can be better supplied with meat than in Pensylvania; and in no danger of wanting Bread—Neither that state nor those near it could give that speedy reinforcement, to our Army, by Militia in Cases of emergency, as the New England States Can; Nor is the nature of the country So favorable in Pensylvania, for the Co-opperation of the Militia with the regular Army, as that on the East side of Hudsons River. Add to these, the long and expencive carriage to the Army of many Articles of Stores of Various kinds. The Enemy could not be ignorant of the advantage He derived in Pena, from the embarassments we laboured under. To what then is the change of His Position, to one less favourable for opperation to be ascribed? Certainly the security of His Army, until the result of the negotiation with America should be known. From this the Minister entertained great and Flattering Hopes. The Commissioners dis-appointed in the object of their Commission, and the Idea of Conquest no longer existing, a new system must be formd for the opperation of the Enemy. But no Demonstrations of the Enemy has yet marked the object of the Campaign. This I conceive is owing to there not being Sufficient time since the Commissioners received the answer of Congress, for the Minister to Form and Transmit the Plan of opperation on His unexpected disappointment. In the mean time the Enemy is endeavoring to Secure the Islands, taken into His Posesssion. Hence a reinforcement is sent to New Port, about the time Philadelphia was evacuated, and a Second attempted soon after the French Admiral appeared in those Seas; but it returned to Newyork on the French squadron's appearing before that place.[4] The Co-opperation of this Fleet with American army on Rhode Island, was so necessary to the Success of the enterprize, at the Critical moment of its Second departure, that the Enemy could be at no loss to conclude, it was owing to Some pressing distress of the French Fleet, which occationed its going from that station. on this event it was natural, for the enemy, to send such a reinforcement to Rhode Island, as would secure releif to the Garrison. Perhaps if events favor him, He may design to Sack Providence. But if even this is in Contemplation, it is utterly out of the Power of this army, or any part of it to be in time, to prevent it. However no inference can be drawn from the Sending a reinforcement to Rhode Island, or its strength, that any Capital opperation is intended on the Main in New England. For this strong reinforcement was necessary, to give certain releif to that Garrison, because the whole strength of the Enemy at Rhode Island, including this reinforcement, when arrived would not much exceed the number of General Sullivans Army. In a Country such as New England, where the People are generally So well affected to America; and where Twenty Thousand Zealous Militia may be collected in a few days; and where there is no Capital object for the Enemy, there is little Reason to fear, that He will carry the war into that Country, after relinquishing the Posession of Philadelphia, and other advantages He Had in that Quarter. It is therefore my opinion that a movement of the Army to the Eastward, under present circumstance will not be Eligible. But the Enemy may attempt a Coup de main on our stores at Springfield, or the release of General Burgoynes Army. To be ready for Such an event, it is also my opinion, that the Number of Troops which our Army in this Camp, exceed that of the Enemy in Newyork and its dependencies, should be held in perfect readiness to march to the Eastward, on the shortest notice, should the Enemy make any demonstrations to opperate on the Main in New England. This force with the Continental Troops now with General Sullivan; and the great aid which can readily be collected from the Militia will stop the progress of the Enemy, till His object for the Campaign shall be more clearly discoverd. The Condition of the Enemy in carrying on the war in this Country, will always expose him to want of regular supplies of Bread & Flour; meat is plentifully sent him from Ireland. All accounts agree, that His Army is but Illy furnished with Bread. The American Embargo and the French Cruizes will contribute to make His subsistance of this Article, still more precarious. This state will furnish Him with more Flour, than all the eastern states. And he has far less to Fear from the Militia of the former, than the Latter. If He intends to opperate in the Country, can it be supposed he will carry the War into the strongest states, where he has no chance of procuring any additional subsistence for His Troops, and Forego the advantage of the Co-opperation of His Navy, in this state. It cannot. For these Reasons I think we ought to have a sufficient Force here, to meet the Enemy in the field, otherwise; if this Army should move to the Eastward, the Enemy might take the advantage of its march, collect His Troops from Rhode Island, in four days, and get compleat Posession of Hudsons river and this state. Such a misfortune would expose our Army to great Sufferings for want of Bread. At the last Council of war held at wrights Mills, the Enemis whole Force at Newyork, Rhode Island and their Dependencies was estimated at 18,000 infantry, vizt, 14,000 at Newyork and 4000 at Rhode Island.[5] All the Force Stationed at Newyork and its dependencies may be collected in Twelve Hours, to any part of the Island, that at Rhode Island, making Large allowances may be brought to Newyork in Eight days, from the time they receive orders for that purpose. The Enemy at present Have the Command of the internal Navigation, from Sandy Hook to Rhode-Island, and probably will have it for this Campaign, from the Islands near Frogs neck, to Sandy Hook inclusive; if not from Stanford to Sandy Hook; for I do not conceive it would be prudent for the French Admiral to risque His Sqadron in the narrow part of the Sound between Connecticut, and Long Island, as Admiral Byron is daily expected in these Seas. our Force in this Camp is Stated at 12,700, and that of the Enemy in Newyork and its dependencies, (vizt long, & Staten Islands) at 10,000. From the heights on this side of Kings Bridge, to the South Point of the Island of Newyork, the Enemy have four lines of Redoubts and other works, nearly across the Island, beside Some intermediate ones, which must be forced. It cannot be imagined the Enemy will abandon these works like Poltroons. Upon the most moderate Calculation of loss, these four lines would cost us, Seven Hundd men each, Killed and wounded, which by the time we got to the environs of the City, leave us a force not superior to the Enemy. His retreat being Secure by the ships and boats, if He declined disputing the City with us, He might with ease retire to Long Island, there wait the Junction or Co-opperation of His Army from Rhode Island, and by a landing of these Troops, or the whole Army, at Pells neck,[6] Frogs Point, or Morrisenia, put us in the dangerous Position the American Army was in, the Campaign of 1776, from which it escaped by the slow movements of the Enemy. Thus after the loss of three Thousand men, we Should be obliged to relinquish the purchase of their blood; or become Prisoner by our Communication and Subsistence being Cut off.

For every Soldier of observation and experience must grant, that 10,000 Troops, well Posted on the Heights of Kings-Bridge and Mor- risena, will defeat 15,000 of equal Quality, who shall attempt to pass from york Island to westchester, when the navigation is commanded by the Power of that Army, which shall take Post on those Heights, to pre- vent an impression from York Island; as the only route, the american Army could take on Such an Event, must be on two Bridges, not Twenty five feet wide, under full command of the Smallest artillery placed on the Eastern heights. If even the Enemy was to abandon York Island, and take Post on Long Island, as He Commands the waters of the neighbourhood, it would be utterly unadviseable for our Army to take Post on the Former, because we should be exposed to the joint opper- ation of the Enemies army above mentioned. For these reasons I am against any opperations being undertaken against the Enemy now in Newyork, or its dependancies *with our present Force.*

Alexr McDougall
M. General

ADS, DLC:GW; Varick transcript, DLC:GW.

1. See Council of War, 1 September.
2. The previous Sunday was 30 August.
3. McDougall was probably referring to Lord North's speech of 19 Feb. explain- ing his proposal for a peace commission (see GW to Henry Laurens, 20 April, n.2).
4. Reinforcements of Newport included the Loyalist Prince of Wales Regiment of about four hundred men, which arrived at the city on 10 June, and about two thousand additional troops from British, Hessian, and Loyalist regiments, which arrived on 15 July.
5. See Council of War, 25 July.
6. The Pell's Neck peninsula is current Pelham Bay Park.

## To Colonel William Malcom

Sir                                            [White Plains] 2d Septr 1778
I recd your letter of the 31st Ult. with its inclosure.

The troops are intitled by a general order of the 6th August to one gill of rum or whiskey per day when *to be had*—but it was not my inten- tion that they should be allowed tickets for deficiencies.

In case the gally is of service or can be an additional security to your command, Captn Lewis may engage seamen, but upon no other con- sideration. I am Sir &c.

G—— W——

P.S. The militia are to have the same allowance in every respect as the soldiers in this army.

Df, in James McHenry's writing, DLC:GW; Varick transcript, DLC:GW.

# From Brigadier General Peter Muhlenberg

Sir                                        [White Plains] Septr 2d 1778

The uncertainty of the Enemys real Intention in transporting a part of their Army, from York to Rhode Island, renders it allmost impossible in our present Situation, to judge with propriety in what manner their Designs may, or ought to be counteracted. The Object of their Expedition must be, either to reinforce the Garrison or bring them of[f], or perhaps they intend to try their Fortune on the Main, in the Neighbourhood of Rhode Island with the best part of their Army—either of these Objects may be their Aim, but, untill it can be determind with some degree of Certainty, which of these they have in view, a Movement of this Army to the Eastward might prove very prejudicial; especially if their Object is either of the two first mentioned, for they would have time enough to take of[f] the Garrison, or Compell General Sullivan to Quit the Island, before We could possibly come to his Assistance—and as they have so great an Advantage over us, by transporting their troops by Water, They might possibly find an Opportunity to bring their whole Force to Act agt this State or any other, on the South side of the North River & cut of[f] our Communication with the Southern States, before We could be in a Condition to prevent it—Should they accomplish this; besides other ruinous Consequences, The Army would be distressd for want of Provisions, especially Bread—from this I conceive, nothing could Justify the March of the Army to the Eastward at this time, except the Army with General Sullivan should be so entangled That without the Assistance of this Army, they must fall into the Hands of the Enemy—Relative to an Expedition against York Island—as I did not understand Your Excellency meant to make a Serious Impression, I can see no desireable Object; except it is, to make a Diversion in favor of General Sullivan, but if He has left the Island, that Object Vanishes of Course—The Enemys Works on this Side Kingsbridge may probably be Wrested from them by a Coup de Main but even there the Enemy would have the Advantage. They would defend the Works so long as they thought it could be done to Advantage, & then retreat over the Bridge, which we could not prevent, so that We should only gain a post, with the loss of a Number of Men, We would not care to Occupy.

Upon the whole I conceive, That the Post which the Army at present Occupies is best Calculated for a General plan of Defence—We cover the Communication between the Southern & Eastern States—Awe the Enemy in New York & its dependencies—and can be ready at the shortest Notice to March to the Assistance of any State East or South, as the Operations of the Enemy shall make it necessary; or as soon, as their intentions shall be better known, which probably will be in a few days. I have the Honor to be Your Excellencys Most Obedt humble Servt

P: Muhlenberg.

ALS, DLC:GW; Varick transcript, DLC:GW. This is Muhlenberg's reply to the questions posed by GW at a council of war on the evening of 1 September.

## From Brigadier General John Nixon

Camp White Plains 2d Sept. 1778

May it Please your Excellency 2d Sept. 1778

The Movements of the Enemy to the Eastward Renders their Designs very Dubious. as Such: our Necessary Operations to Counter act their Designs must be very uncertain, unless we could acquire With Some Degree of Certainty their Determination. Should we find that Boston: or any part of Connecticut Should be their main Object: In that Case— a reinforcement from this army to be imediatly Detach'd to the East-ward: in My Opinion, would be highly requisite after Properly Secur-ing the Several Passes On the North river.

Considering the Situation of the Enemy, at & Near New york: Sur-rounded by waters; of which they have The entire Command; being Strongly fortified by Land; In the most advantageous manner, and the Difficulty or An attack with any Probable Success, Influences my mind to be utterly averse to Such an attempt at Present. the reasons against it, Given by the Honle Majr Genl McDougle the Last Evening—in my opinion are very Obvious.

If upon further intelligence from the Eastward, it Should be Judged Expedient to Detach part of this army to Their assistance—the great-est Difficulty in Supplying them with Provisions there, Consists—in my opinion, in the transporting the article of flower from Hence, as all other Necessary articles may be procured in that Quarter.

Upon the whole I Submit My Judgment to your Excellencys Superior Wisdom.

Jno. Nixon B.G.

ALS, DLC:GW; Varick transcript, DLC:GW. This is Nixon's reply to the questions posed by GW at a council of war on the evening of 1 September.

## From Brigadier General Samuel Holden Parsons

[White Plains] Sepr 2d 1778

Q. 1. What or whither any Operations can be undertaken with Prob-ability of Success?

2d    Shall any Part of this Army move Eastward?

3. Can any Attempts be made on the Posts at New York with a Probability of Success?

An. The Number & Strength of the Enemy. The Situation of Genl Sullivan's Army the Probable Intention of the Enemy in my Opinion ought to be known with greater Certainty before a Judgment can be given on the Subject. the Number of the Enemy's Troops at or near New York or at Rhode-Island: the Strength of their posts, & Works ought to be known with more certainty than appears in the State your Excellency gave Us before I can form an Opinion whither we can Attack them with a Probability of Success — The Strength of the Enemy at Rhode Island and the Condition of Genl Sullivan's Army before I can determine the Propriety of Moving Eastward with any part of our Force.

My General Idea of carrying on the War, is not to seperate our Force in any considerable Degree, or to follow the Enemy's Motions (leaving them in Possession of any Post of Importance) when our United Force will reduce it — if therefore our Force is now or may soon be able to reduce the Posts at & near New York I am of Opinion it ought to be attempted, without so dividing our Strength by detaching any great Part Eastward, as to prevent our Attempts on those Posts—I am the rather induc'd to this Opinion from a Beleif that the Depreciation of our Currancy, the State of our Finances, the Discontent & Anarchy of the Country, the general, just & increasing Complaints of the Army aford very little Hope of bringing so respectable a Force into the Field the next, as in the Present Year: and we have no Reason to beleive Great Britain will be in a worse State at any future Time—but if there's no Prospect of acting offensively, I am of Opinion we ought to send about 6000 or 7000 Men Eastward to join the Army under General Sullivan to Oppose the Progress of the Enemy there the Remainder about 5000 or 6000 will be sufficient to maintain the Passes of the Highlands.

The Commissary ought to send forward Flower & form a Magazine at or near Norwich as soon as possible, most of it may be sent from Norwalk by Water I think there's very little Danger.

Saml H. Parsons

ADS, DLC:GW; Varick transcript, DLC:GW. This is Parsons's reply to the questions posed by GW at a council of war on the evening of 1 September.

# From Brigadier General John Paterson

Sir                                    [White Plains] Septr 2d 1778
    The great inconvenience of transporting Flower for the Army and Navy to Rhodes Island, and the uncertainty of Genl Clintons intending

any thing more than raising the Seige in moving that Way, with the probability of his bringing his Troops from thence & collecting of them at New York, are in my Opinion sufficient Reasons against moving at present, at least until his Intentions may be known, an Attack on New York appears to me to be attended with so many difficulties and such hazard that it ought not to be attemted except a fair Opportunity should offer for a *Coup de Maine.*

I must therefore give it as my Opinion to wait where we are at present disciplining the Troops until the Operations of the Enemy shall point out to us our Duty. I am Sir with respect your Excellys most Obt humble Servant

Jno. Paterson

ALS, DLC:GW; Varick transcript, DLC:GW. This is Paterson's reply to the questions posed by GW at a council of war on the evening of 1 September.

## From Brigadier General Enoch Poor

Camp Wh. Plains September 2dt 1778
as your Excellency laid the State of your army before the Councel last Evening and Desire'd their opinyens on the following Question⟨s⟩ (Viz.)

1   whether any operations Can be carried on with a probabillity of Success against the Enemy at Present.

2   whether it will be advizeable to move to the Eastward if So how Can the Highlans on Hudson⟨'s⟩ river be Secur'd.

4   Can any attact be made on the troops at new York with a probabillity of Success.

5   if the army moves to the Eastward how will they be Supplied with Provissions.

in answer to the first Question I think if any attact is made it must be upon the troops at or near New York, whare their works are very Strong and if Carried must be Obtained with Grait loss, and the ground when obtain'd or even if the Enemy Should leave the whole Island of New York, I Cant Concive that you'd Derive any advantage by taking posession while the Enemy Command the north & East river.

as to the Second Question if you move to the Eastward I think it will be two late to afford any relief to general Sullivan as he must Either be off the Island before your troop Can reach their or fall into the Enemys hand—besides I am of apoinyon that General Clinton will Emediatly Colect all his troops to New York and Either operrate with his whole force against you upon this Ground or take them from the Continent.

as to the article of Bread it is well known that the Eastern States Scearsly raise a Supplie for its Inhabitents, and Considering the large number of the Kings Troops Billited their, togather with the united States troops I think by this time their Stores must be nearly Exspended (I mean the article of bread).

that upon waying the whole matter your Excellency laid before the Councel I think it most Advizable to remain in your present Situation untell you know sumthing more of the Intentions of the Enemy, which I think a few days will Determen—however I may differ in Sentiment do asure your Excellency that I am ready with the graitest Cheerfulness to Execute any plan of operration you in your wisdom Shall See fitt to order—I am Sir with grait respect your Excellencys most obeden⟨t⟩ & very Hue Servent

Enoch Poor.

ALS, DLC:GW; Varick transcript, DLC:GW.


## From Major General Israel Putnam

Whit plains the 2 of September 1778

as his Excelancy ginrol Washenton requsted that Each ginrol ofesor shuld transmit to him his opinyon in riteng what was beast to be don in this creticl tim whathor the army ought to move and which way I give it as my opinyon that it would not answer any good porposes to remove Estward as the Enimy have Sent such a reinforsment as is suposed to rodisland thay must have don what thay intended befor any reinforsment could posabely arive from this: and it is my opinyon a move from this towards New york would answor many good porposes for I think it must Disconsart thar plans much mor then to follow them and feteag the men with such long marches as thay can so Easley return by wartor at plesuer: and I think any plan thay may have formed against Conetecut or Boston our move towards New york will have an atendanc to Draw thar troops back again for thay never will give a cartinty for an uncartanty as they have New york now in possion thay will not give up that cartanty to try to regain Boston whare thay must be shut up much mor Closly then upon any plas upon the contenant which thar own Experonc tels them. I am your Exelancys most Obedant humbel Sarvant

Israel Putnam

ADS, DLC:GW; Varick transcript, DLC:GW. This is Putnam's reply to the questions posed by GW at a council of war on the evening of 1 September.

## From Brigadier General Charles Scott

Sir                                 [near White Plains] 2d Sept. 1778
   I am Sorry to inform You that I have not been able to get any Intelligence worth Your attention since The Rect of Your Instructions.[1] Colo. Butler returnd last evning who tells me it is next to an impossability to get a proper person to go on long Island, I Have Still out Colo. Grayham & Capt. Levengsworth I hope they may bring somthing. Inclosd Your Excellency will Receive a Paper of the 29th. I am Your Excellencys Obt Servt

                                                      Chs Scott

ALS, DLC:GW. GW's aide-de-camp Richard Kidder Meade wrote to Scott later on this date: "His Excy received your favor accompanied by a news Paper.
   "From the pretty frequent desertion of the Corps under Colo. Gist's command, & the absolute necessity of their being chosen men in every respect—His Excellency wishes you to attend particularly to the appointment of them—so as to have such as may be fully depended on" (DLC:GW).
   1. The instructions, apparently transmitted in a letter from Tench Tilghman of 31 Aug., have not been identified.

## From Brigadier General Charles Scott

Sir                                 [near White Plains] Sept. 2d 1778
   Having Considerd the several Matters Your Excellency Laid before the board of officers last evening. I am of opinion that No relief be Sent from this armey to Rhode Island unless Some farther Intelligence should Warrant it, which in all probability the Event of a few Days will determine I have no Idea of any Valuable purposes Being answer'd by even taking posession (If we could do so) of the enemys works at and about Kings Bridg. when they can when ever they please force us to leave them, I am therfore of oppinion that nothing aught to be attempted there I am Your Excellencys Obt Servt

                                                      Chs Scott

ALS, DLC:GW; Varick transcript, DLC:GW.

## From Brigadier General William Smallwood

Dear Sir                          Camp White Plains 2d September 1778
   I am clearly of opinion no movements or Opperations in this army ought to be undertaken, 'till we can with more Certainty ascertain the designs of the Enemy, which from their present Manœuvres, and the

aspect before us, is difficult to limit, with any degree of precission, so as to render our movements secure, or to hold up any great prospect of success; they must have had two objects in view in going to Rhode Island, either (as Circumstances might require) to intercept General Sullivan and his army during the absence of the Count de Estaing, or to relieve and bring off their Garrison, should Sullivan have debarked on the main, and there should be a probability of the Count's speedy return to his Station, in either instance they have it evidently in their power to evade our pursuit, or relief, from the Superior Advantages they derive from their fleet, and their future opperations must be Governed, and must be more or less inlarged or confined in their prospect of the Arrival of a Superior Naval force, which in the event must determine our Conduct, the impediment and risk which our Army must encounter (from Particular Circumstances which your Excellency can be no stranger to) in going to Rhode Island or New York, in the present instance to me appear if not insuperable at least to promise but a slender prospect of any Material Success, because in either instance our Endeavours after much fatigue and risk, may be frustrated, and rendered abhortive, by a slight exertion of theirs, and in the first might open a prospect up Hudsons river which might be very flattering to them; and no less distructive to us, by cutting off our resources for a time from the Southward, and from their Superior Land and Naval force, and the Advantages derived from the latter, might with great facility by a sudden and rapid Movement, endanger any body of forces which we could spare to Garrison the Highlands, before we could come to their relief, admitting our Supplies to be ample in the Interim, which to me is doubtfull, and in the latter Instance, by making an attempt on New York, our Supplies might not only be intercepted, but the force now at Rhode Island getting in our rear, might render the situation of our forces Critical & Alarming; I am therefore for waiting the event a few days when Circumstances may enable us to act with more precission. I have the Honor to be with great regard Your Excellencys most Obdt Hble Servt

W. Smallwood

LS, DLC:GW; Varick transcript, DLC:GW. This is Smallwood's reply to the questions posed by GW at a council of war on the evening of 1 September.

## From Major General Stirling

Camp White plains September 2d 1778.
On Considering the Several Questions Stated by your Excellency Yesterday to your General Officers[1] I am of Opinion,

That any Attempt on the troops on New York Island must be *futile* and *extremly dangerous*. Futile because, if we could drive the troops from that Island, and they should retire either to their Ships or to Long Island, our acquisition would be Useless; especially while the Enemy have a Naval force there and we none.

Dangerous because, 1st Wee know not with any Certainty what troops are on the Island, and Consequently the Event of an Attack on it Uncertain; the probability is, that it would be attended with such a loss of Troops as this Army ought not to risque. 2dly because this Army would be thrown into Such a Scituation, that if the Enemy with their force returning from Rhode Island, Joined by those now at New York should land at frogs point or any other good landing in the Sound, and take post on this Side of Kings bridge; it would infalliably be Cut off from their provision, and in Short from all further Connection with the Continent.

That an immediate Movement of this Army to the Eastward is unecessary and must be Attended with many disadvantages.

Wee have as yet received no advices that the Enemy have made such preparations as will enable them immediately to operate on the Continent; it is most probable they have not. should we move, and they afterwards return with their whole force, they might force the passage of the high lands, and be Masters of all the Country West of Hudsons River before we could possibly return to Oppose them.

We have no Magazines of bread or flower formed near that line of March. the Country is not a Bread Country, and Cannot Subsist an Army in that Essential Article, untill a Supply can be brought from other parts. This necessarily makes it proper to Collect Magazines of that Article, and to form them in that Country previous to the March of an Army into it.

It therefore seems Judicious to keep the Army in *this Neighbourhood* 'till such Magazines can be formed, or 'till we find by our advices of the Motions of the Enemy, it becomes Necessary for some important purpose to Change our ground.

When I say this Neighbourhood I do not mean the Identical spot we are now encamped upon: for I have my Suspicions that we are now too low down in the *Cul de Sac*. for Supposeing the Enemy should retire with their whole force from Rhode Island, should land at Norwalk and be Joined with their whole force from Nyork Meeting them either thro' the Sound or by way of Long Island: would not this Army be so hem'd in that it would be difficult to gain the Enemy's Right, or to Maintain itself in provisions, especially if the Enemy should push a few small ships up Hudsons River even so far as to Kings ferry. I would therefore

Suggest the propriety of looking out in time for some ground fitting to encamp on, further in our Rear.

I take the liberty here of Mentioning that I think there is too much flower brought to Tarry Town, it is a precious Article, and I fear may be Cut off. The Army should by that Communication receive enough to Subsist upon, whatever can be Collected more than that should be Stored Elsewhere; if we have a large stock on hand here, it will in Case of a Movement be lost for want of Teams to Carry it off.[2]

The Secureing the passage of Hudsons River thro' the Highlands is of the Utmost importance, and in Case of a Movement of this Army to the Eastward; a proper force should be left for that purpose in the Vicinity of the works at West point; what Number of Troops will be Competent I can form no Judgment of, as I do not know the Nature of nor the State of those works.

Stirling,

ALS, DLC:GW; Varick transcript, DLC:GW.

Subsequently, probably about 4 Sept., Stirling revised his ideas on the basis of additional intelligence about British movements and wrote a second opinion. That undated and unsigned document was docketed by Varick's transcribers with a date of "Septr 2nd 1778," but it mentions the appearance of British forces off New London, which did not occur until the afternoon of 3 Sept., and Maj. Gen. John Sullivan's retreat to the mainland, news of which reached GW on 4 September. Whether the two opinions were submitted separately or together has not been determined. The second opinion reads: "Since I had the Honor of giveing my Opinion on the Subject wch I shall suppose is now before us, the face of Affairs is greatly Changed, every such Change most probably will alter our opinions, of what ought to be the immediate movements of the Army.

"After General Sullivan had happily Effected his retreat from R. Island, & Sir Henry Clinton had arrived there with a Strong detachment of the best troops in his Arrmy, and Lord Howe had arrived off Boston Harbour and blocked the Counte de Estainge in. I will Confess it was my Opinion that the Enemy would have made the destru[c]tion of the french fleet their first grand object, especially as Sir Henry might Cooperate there with his whole Army; a few Ships being Suffecient to Secure Rhode Isle & New york; then become useless to this Army.

"Sir Henry Clinton haveing left Rhode Island, and was as I am informed so far on his return as New London—I must Conclude they have something Else in Veiw.

"If they mean to Continue the war in America they Cannot now have any other object, than the destruction of this Army, If that is their Object, they will never attack us in front as we are now posted. they can land in our rear and with their whole force can operate there, while with their Shipping they Annoy the Navigation of Hudsons River. while this is possible, I think the Army should be moved further Northerly towards Danbury, where it Can have a possition more Secure to itself, and equally Convenient to protect the pass of the Highlands and more so in Communicating with the Country from whence it is to receive its provision" (DLC:GW).

1. See Council of War, 1 September.

2. On 5 Sept., GW's aide-de-camp Tench Tilghman wrote Assistant Commissary

General of Purchases Royal Flint: "His Excellency has been informed that there is a considerable quantity of Flour at Tarry town, which he looks upon as a very unsafe place, considering the ease with which the Enemy may run up a Vessel of Force. He would never wish more Flour or any other provision to be lodged there at one time than can be immediately brought forward to the Army, especially at this time when our stay is very uncertain" (DLC:GW).

## From Major General John Sullivan

Dear General                    Head Quarters Providence Septr 2d ⟨1778⟩
   I am informed by Genl He[a]th & the Council of B⟨os⟩ton that an English fleet has anchord off the Harbour of Boston & from the accounts you gave me of Lord Howes Fleet suppose it to be the same sent in to block up Count Destiang that the Reinforcement detachd to the Relief of Rhode-Island might meet with no Interruption in its passage [1]—What seems to give credibility to the Supposition is, that the Reinforcement has actually arrivd. I have the honor to be Sir, with the most exalted Esteem Yr Excellencys, very hble Servt

                                                        Jno. Sullivan

LS, DLC:GW.
   1. For the accounts of the fleet, see GW's letters to Sullivan of 28 and 29 August. For Maj. Gen. William Heath's letters to Sullivan of 1 Sept., see Hammond, *Sullivan Papers*, 2:289.

## To Jean-Baptiste Ternant

Sir,                        Head Quarters [White Plains] Septr 2d 1778
   I received your letter of the 29th of August, which hurry of business has prevented my answering before.
   You express an opinion that rank is essential to a proper and effectual discharge of the duties of your station from the respect and authority it commands, which you seem to think are unattainable without it—The abuses formerly existing from a lavish distribution of rank in the departments of the staff obliged me to exert my utmost influence to have all rank out of the line of the army abolished [1]—Whatever may be my opinion of the merit of an individual, I cannot recommend a deviation from a general principle in his favour. I should incur by doing it the charge of inconsistency and partiality—It would be made a precedent for a similar claim, at least throughout the department to which he belongs, if it did not extend to others—These could not be complied with without overturning the whole system, we have been

labouring to establish, and could not be refused without exciting much clamour and dissatisfaction. I am aware, that a distinction may be made between the civil and military branches of the department; but this distinction has been hitherto unknown in our army, and the ideas now familiar could not easily be changed.

I am sensible of the prejudice in favour of rank; but I cannot agree with you, that it is essential to authority—Your authority must be founded in the nature of your office, not in the degree of rank you may hold. In your transactions with the officers of the line, the rank you would expect or which could be given you would be of little efficacy; because as obedience on the principle of rank can only be demanded from inferiors in rank the extent of your authority from that source would be too limited to answer any material end—With respect to your subalterns in office, they are all of course *officially* under your direction and controul; and I will engage to support you in enforcing obedience, whenever it may be necessary, by all the means commonly used in armies.

With respect to the office you first acted in—there are some arrangements now in contemplation with Congress which if adopted, will put it out of my power to employ you again in that line—Agreeable to that, the inspectors must be taken from the line of the army.[2]

You intimate an apprehension that your conduct may not have met my approbation—I take pleasure in assuring you of your mistake— Justice and inclination induce me to acknowlege, that in the different capacities in which you have officiated you have distinguished yourself as an officer of intelligence zeal and activity, and have rendered valuable services. I shall be happy, it may be agreeable to you to continue in the line you are in, from a full conviction of your usefulness. I am with esteem Sir Your most Obedt servant.

Df, in Alexander Hamilton's writing, DLC:GW; Varick transcript, DLC:GW.

1. For an expression of GW's views, see GW to a Continental Congress Camp Committee, 29 Jan. 1778. Congress had resolved on 29 May "That no persons, hereafter appointed upon the civil staff of the army, shall hold or be entitled to any rank in the army by virtue of such staff appointment" (*JCC*, 11:555).

2. Congress had asked GW to give his opinion of a pending report about army inspectors; see Henry Laurens to GW, 20 Aug., and note 2, and GW to Laurens, 12 Sept., and note 1.

## From Lund Washington

Dr Sir                Mount Vernon Septmbr 2d 1778

Your Letter of the 15th Augst is at Hand, with respect to the Lands therein mentiond (Marshalls & Barrys) in my endeavours to Purchase them, I shall make use of every art in my power to prevent them from putg too great a price on them, & if in the Bargain I can prevail on them to take Negroes Value'd as they now sell, I will. I went over to Marshalls on Monday,[1] with design to tell him I had recieved an answer from you—and in the course of our conversation endeavour to find out what he woud realy take for his Land, but first to give him to understand that you did not want it to live on as Custis did Alexanders, therefore he had no right to expect such a price for it—but he was gone from home & not to return for several Days again. you again say you wish to get quit of negroes, before the rect of this you will find that in a former Letter I have desired that you will tell me in plain terms, whether I shall sell your Negroes at Publick sale or not, & how many of them & indeed Who.[2] I was sufficiently Hurt before from my own reflections, to know that you had for several years lost your Crops of Wheat, and that I had nothing to sell at the present High prices that wou'd enable me to purchase a favourate tract of Land for you, altho at such an uncommon price. but when I find you seemingly to Lament your inability to purchase and that from the above cause, (not makeg any thing from your estate,) I am more so, believe me nothing wou'd mortify me more than that those Lands shoud be sold to any other than your self. as to the last crop of wheat made, it is worse if Possible than any of the former, at the Ferry Plantation it is so totally destroyd that it cannot be sew'd, not one grain in a Hundred woud come up— I want to sew the Fields if for no other purpose, to serve as pasture in Winter for sheep, Calves, Colts &c.—there surely must be an End to the Fly,[3] as there is to the Catterpilla, Locust, and many other insects, and if so, the wheat we sew may turn out well, yet I am not for dependg on it, but shall prepare at every place for a Tobacco Crop—I had some time past determine'd upon makeg Tobacco at Morrises & Davys, your last Letter puts me upon it at the other places, no great Crop may be expected, but all that can be done I believe will be done towards makeg as much as possible—altho we are seldom without rain three days together, and our mill swamp is over our shews almost every where in Water, yet are we Ditchg of it, and I am determined to keep on altho the people in the Ditch are up to their knees in mud & water when that is properly done I expect it will yield a very great Crop of Tobacco—this leads me to relate to you the Death of one of the most Valuable Slaves you Possessd Cooper James[4]—I had put the Coopers to assist Davy & his people in Ditchg the swamp—on saturday they had retired from the Ditch and were at there Dinners—Jim finishd his meal before the Rest, & went from them towards the mill Race which was within 50 yds of where they were setg. when they had finishd, they calld for Jim, but his not answerg made Ben:[5] go the way he went to see where he was, he found Jims Breeches Layg by the Race, callg for him several times & his not answerg made them believe he was drownd in the Race, for by this time the Rest of the people had joind him, Davy excepted who it seems was at his House getg his Dinner, Ben immediately got in to the Race to search for him & by the Ac[coun]t given me had like to have been drownd also, the place is Deep & he went down several times before the others pulld him out—they then got a hookd pole & drag'd for him (Jim), by this time Davy returnd & wasted much time in the same fruitless attempt—he then Run off to inform me of what had hapne'd—I orderd him back as fast as Possible to Draw the gate in the Race that the water might run off thinkg perhaps he might be saved if found in time I soon followd my self so as to get there as soon as Davy, we were long before we coud get the gate drawn, a stone or some thing being got in to it in such a Manner as to prevent its moveg—but when accomplishd, I soon found Jim by makeg Davy & Jack go into the Pond & search for him—but our attempts to recover him were fruitless for he had been too long in the Water—coud they but have thought to draw the gate instead of wasteg time by dragg for him & then run[nin]g to me, by which 3 Hours at least was lost, perhaps he might have been saved, as I have heard of such things being done—or had they plunged immediately in to the water after him, but after the fright Ben got they were affraid all of them was to be drown'd—the conjecture is, the day being very warm, James went in the Race to Bathe himself, within about 20 feet from where he got in, the water is when the Race is full, (which was the case then) 7 or 8 feet deep & altho they all say Jim was well acquainted with that place, yet there he got drownd—to look at the place you woud think hardly possible, for the willows grow thick on the Bank hanging over the water, it appears to me the least exertion whatever wou'd save one, for the place where the water is deep is not more than Six feet wide & as the mill was not going, the Race gates down, there was no current to put him out of his way, it seems he coud not swim a stroke & was always remarkable fearful of water never venterg above his waiste. if you remember the Race crosses a Hollow in the old Field near the Mill near to the House Alton, formerly lived in, & ponds up some distance from the Race, to form the Bank where the Race crosses this Hollow, a Ditch was dug for the purpose of getg earth, & not that it was necessary to convey the water along there, it was that this Valuable slave lost his life.

But this was not the only accident that befell us that Day, Carpenter James by a stroke from his Broad axe has given himself such a wound a cross the ankle & heel, that I expect it will be several Months before he will be well enough to do any thing in his way again.[6]

I Re[ceive]d from Captn Lewis £200 for the Phaeton which was the price agreed for before it was diliverd. Congress haveg permited the People of Boston to import some Flour for their own Consumption,[7] afforded me an opportunity of sellg the Flour I made last year, 236 Barrels, when the warm weather came on it was emptied in the loft & has been frequently turn'd since, yet it was a little sour but from the scarcity of Flour, and the great want, of the Bostonians, I got what I askd for it 30/ pr C.—the Amt of sales upwards of £700. part of the Wheat that made the above Flour I purchased at a Dollar pr Bushel. the Wheat was Bad & the Flour is nothing More than Common.

Whoever has wheat to sell this year will I expect not take less than 10 or 12/ pr Bushel for it, but even at that price if it can be got a Miller may make great profit for Flour will sell very high, 40 pr C. I make no doubt may be got—you are never fond of Speculating therefore I expect will be agnst purchasing & unwilling to give a certainty for an uncertainty. if so I will endeavour to manufacture for those who will, they giveg so much pr C. Bushels, or pr Bushel, as may be agreed on let me know Your sentiments upon the above.

Wm Roberts & myself have had some talk about his continuing here longer—he like most others, says his wages will not purchase him cloaths—& I, in return tell him his services are not adequate to his wages, this he says is not his fault, for if we wou'd supply the Mill with Wheat the Profits woud afford wages to the Miller—I gave him to understand that I woud not encrease his Wages, nor did I believe you woud. I cannot tell what it is he expects, for I had before intinded in this Letter to write to you respectg him, therefore was determined to come to no agreement whatever with him until I had given you a state of the matter, & you had determined therein what you woud do. I told him I shoud refer the Matter wholy to you in this Letter—he sd he woud right to you, & a few days past gave me the Inclosed for you.[8]

Roberts has Faults—he is fond of Drinkg too much & when in Liquor is apt to be ill natured, and at times neglects his Duty by being absent & drinkg. altho an excellent worckman yet he seldom lays his Hands on any thing more than the immediate & absolutely necessary repairs of the mill, there are many things that he might do that is not done, they are put off from time to time until the year is expired, & then they are mention'd, as necessary to be done next year, & made use of as an argument why it wou'd be more to your advantage to employ him than another, because few millers are millrights & can do what he can, He is fond of Horse swaping, & new objects generally draw the attention more than the old, consequently his time is taken up in that way when he might be doing some thing or other of more service to you He has now two or three mares which he has pickd up this summer by chafferg one way or other, I believe by what he said to me, he wants to winter two of them at your expence, & be permitted to let them run in your pastures & to raise Colts from them.

Roberts is very clever provided the mill was always kept in Wheat, I believe there are few millers so good as he is, he is Active & industrious & keeps every thing in order—but we have had little done by him since you left us—except what little Flour we have made he has made one new Water wheel & done some other repairs in the Mill, has assisted in makeg & repairg the Tumbling Dams at Piny & Dogue Run, made a gate & Dam in the Race Frequently attended the mendg the Race &c.,[9] indeed I shoud do him injustice not to say that he is not only very clever in all such repairs, but very ready to attend the mendg them. whether his perfections or imperfections predominate I cannot say, I leave you to determine, and say whether you will employ him or provide another, for I suppose one must be had. I am of opinion if Roberts & you part he will repent it, & be anxious after one years experience to come again shoud you want him on your own terms—he now lives comfortable and well at no expence for provisions except a few Luxuries—he raises great Quantitys of Fowls, rather more than he consumes these he sells altho contrary to his agreement, for by that he was to raise for his own consumption only[10]—but he says it is very Hard after takeg the pains his wife does that they shoud not be permitted to dispose of the overplus, for the purpose of getg sugar, Coffee &c.

you perhaps may expect me to give my opinion with respect to keepg Roberts—If a Miller cou'd be got of a more Happy disposition than Roberts (for he is a strange temperd man) for less wages, (I think his too high) it certainly woud be preferable, for a Millers being a Millright, Cooper, or any thing, if he does not worck at these things when not employd in the Mill, signifys nothing—shoud you think of partg with him, woud it not be well for you to write to some of your Pensylvania acquaintance to look out for a miller for you. you ask if pens will not do to cure Tobacco in, I answer yes, But it takes as much Timber to make them as to make Houses, & at Best they are but a makeshift, for often with driveg Rains the Tobacco gets weather Beaten & Hurt, but they must be your only Chance, for you have not nails nor time to Build Houses—I am sorry, very sorry that the French Admiral was oblige to go in pursuit of Lord Howe, before the conquest of Rhode Island was accomplishd, But I hope all will End well & that Rhode Iland is before this taken, & all the men on it Prisoners, that Lord Howe has got a Drubg & that the time is approachg fast when I shall hear you are in new york, with Clinton & the Detestable Johnstone your prisoners, I hate that man for his attempt to Bribe men who I hope will for ever be above corruption.[11] I have not Lost altogether the £300 which I told you the Pork woud bring that I Lost—I had it clean'd & smoakd and have sold it in Bacon to the amt of (with two of the Barrels one of Beef the other Porck) £195.7.6—the remainder altho it will not sell the negroes are fond off—still I look upon the loss to be £104.12.6—for as to its being eat is nothing to the purpose.

I fear I shall not be able to get any worckman to Asist Lanphier, if so the coverd ways will not get done[12]—our people are sickly many of them having Agues & Fever—we have so much wet weather that we are over run with grass Weeds &c.—never was there in my remembrance in the Month of August such Pasturage but whether it will Fatten Cattle &c.—or not is by some a doubt—it raind all yesterday & looks likely enough to do the same to day.

I shall conclude this long Epistle by assureg you that I always have been, and still am anxious to do every think in my power for your interest, & shall most Heartily set about prepareg for to make a Crop of Tobacco next year—we have neither apples nor Peaches this year—I am done with makeg any more Experiments of the Corn stalk for it will not quit cost. Am your sincere Friend & affectionate Hbl. servt

Lund Washington

I Rob'd your Trunk of this Quire of paper at the time I did, which was about ten days past there was not to be got in alexandria without it was in ⟨mutilated⟩ of other goods by whole sale ⟨mutilated⟩.

ALS, ViMtV. Below the postscript of this letter, GW wrote, "Clear Swamp at Morris's."

1. The previous Monday was 31 August.

2. This letter has not been identified.

3. The "Fly" was probably a reference to the "Fly-Weevil" or moth described in Landon Carter's "Observations concerning the Fly-Weevil, that destroys the wheat, with some useful discoveries and conclusions, concerning the propagation and progress of that pernicious insect, and the methods to be used to prevent the destruction of the grain by it," *Transactions of the American Philosophical Society, Held at Philadelphia for Promoting Useful Knowledge*, 1 (1769–71), 205–17.

4. Cooper James may have been the James who appears as a tradesman on GW's tithable lists of June 1773 and 1774. That man was probably purchased from Robert Washington in April 1773 (*Papers, Colonial Series*, 9:224, 238, 10:137).

5. Ben, who was a slave at GW's Mill farm by 1773, became the miller by 1786 and remained in that capacity until GW's death (Memorandum List of Tithables, c.9 June 1773, *Papers, Colonial Series*, 9:238; *Diaries*, 4:279; Washington's Slave List, [June 1799], *Papers, Retirement Series*, 4:527–42).

6. Carpenter James (born c.1759), owned by GW, appears on his 1786 slave list at the home plantation and on his 1799 slave list at the Muddy Hole farm (*Diaries*, 4:278; *Papers, Retirement Series*, 4:528). He may have been the boy James whom GW purchased from Thomas Moore in 1770 (see Ledger A, 204). In 1796 GW wrote

of James: "He is a very worthless fellow; indeed I have sometimes suspected that he cuts himself on purpose to lay up. for something or another of this sort is constantly happening to him—In Harvest, he is sure to get a cut in the beginning of it, so as to lay him up during the continuance of it" (GW to William Pearce, 20 March 1796, DLC:GW; see also *Diaries,* 5:3).

7. Lund Washington may have been referring to Congress's resolution of 14 Jan. 1778, which directed the Massachusetts board of war to purchase 15,000 barrels of flour from the middle or southern department to fill eastern magazines (*JCC,* 10:48–49).

8. The enclosed letter has not been found.

9. In the spring of 1770 GW began construction of a new mill on the west bank of Dogue Run near where the road from Gum Spring to Colchester crossed that creek. To supply water to the new mill, which was larger than and downstream of his old mill, he constructed two dams, one on Dogue Run a short distance above where it is joined by Piney Branch and the second on Piney Branch a few hundred yards above its mouth. The mill race, which was west of Dogue Run, connected the two dams and then continued roughly parallel to Dogue Run until it reached the new mill about two miles below (see *Diaries,* 2:218, 222).

10. For William Roberts's agreement to work as GW's miller, 13 Oct. 1770, see *Papers, Colonial Series,* 8:395–96.

11. For the charge that British commissioner George Johnstone had attempted to bribe congressmen Joseph Reed and Robert Morris to support the British peace proposals, see Henry Laurens to GW, 13 Aug., n.6.

12. The construction of the two covered walkways leading from the Mount Vernon mansion house to the north and south dependencies remained uncompleted in December (see GW to Lund Washington, 18 Dec.).

## From Brigadier General Anthony Wayne

Sir                               Camp at White Plains 2nd Sepr 1778.

In Obedience to your Excellencies Desire I have Maturely Considered the Questions which you were pleased to put to the Board of General Officers yesterday, the purport of which was

1st  Whether it will be Advisable to make a Movement with the Whole or any part of this Army to the Eastward.

2nd  If such a move should be thought proper how is this Army to be Supplied—& what force will be necessary for the Defence of the passes at the High Land & north River.

3rd  Whether an Attempt can be made with any probability of Success on New York In the Absence of so great a part of the Enemies forces.

As to the first, I can't Conceive what Advantage we should Derive from any Movement to the Eastward *at this time*—on the Contrary would we not by a Movement that way give an Opening to the Enemy to cut off all our Supplies of Bread & flower by possessing themselves of the passes of the North River, and leave us the more Distressed for want of Provision by the Additional Consumption of the French Fleet & Army—and when they found us far Advanced Eastward they might with great facility Return up the Sound to New York & thus Harrass us at pleasure.

In my Opinion the Enemy have but two moves to make i.e. the Withdrawing their troops from Rhode Island & Seeking this Army in force—Otherwise to leave the Continent; for by three years Experience they find that the possession of a State, tends little to the Subjugation of America, whilst we have an Army in the field.

But should Boston & *De Estang's* fleet be their Object (as some Gentlemen Suppose) then our possition is the most favourable that we could wish for making a Capital push at New York—without the Danger of loosing the passes of the north River, or of being *Enclosed in our Rear.*

I am therefore clearly of Opinion that we should Remain in this Camp & take the first Opening to Strike the Enemy in the Vicinity of Kings Bridge, the mode & manner of this Attempt your Excellency will best Determine.

In the Interim every possible Exertion should be used to Collect a large Quantity of flower & Bread on this side the north River—as well as Materials for Barracks in case the Enemy Continue on the Continent. I am with every Sentiment of Esteem your Excellencies most Obt & very Hume Sevt

Anty Wayne B.G.

ALS, DLC:GW; ADfS, PHi: Wayne Papers; Varick transcript, DLC:GW. The arrangement of the words of the draft varies from that of the ALS, but the content is essentially the same. This letter answers the questions posed by GW at a council of war on the evening of 1 September.

## From Brigadier General William Woodford

Dr Genl                                   Camp [White Plains] 2d Septr 1778.
     I cannot see any valuable purpose that would be answer'd by an attack upon New York, which we could not keep after we had gain'd it, without a superiority by Water.

Was the Commissary able to supply us with Bread for such a March, I would advise against moveing the greatest part of this Army to the Eastward in the present situation of affairs, but would recommend it to your Excellency to waite a few Days before any Capital Step is taken— & in the mean time to put two or three Brigades in motion for the Eastward. with much respect I am Your Excellencys Most Obedt Servt
                                                    Wm Woodford

ALS, DLC:GW; Varick transcript, DLC:GW. This is Woodford's answer to questions posed by GW at a council of war on the evening of 1 September.

## General Orders

Head-Quarters W. Plains Thursday Septr 3rd 1778.
Parole Languedoc—                           C. Signs Leech. Ludlow.
The troop to beat at 7 ôClock and the Guards to be on the Grand Parade at 8 in the morning 'till further orders—All the Drums and Fifes of the Right Wing, Second Line and Left Wing to attend the Parade in Rotation; Those of the Right Wing tomorrow.
The Inspector of Music will daily attend the Parade.

Varick transcript, DLC:GW.
On this date GW's aide-de-camp Tench Tilghman wrote to Assistant Commissary General of Purchases Royal Flint: "The uncertainty of the operations of the enemy renders it necessary that we should be prepared to move either up the North River or to the Eastward as may be necessary. You have already established Magazines of Bread upon the communication between this and Fishkills, and His Excellency desires that you may immediately establish others between this and providence upon the upper and lower Road, those upon the lower, as far from the sound as convenience will admit. The Quantities need not be great, only sufficient to support the Army upon the march and untill supplies can be brought forward" (DLC:GW).
Tilghman also wrote a letter directed to Robert Erskine (Tilghman wrote "William Erskine") or William Scull of the army's geography department: "His Excellency desires that you will permit General Wayne to take a Copy of the surveys that you have already made, and of your additions" (PHi: Wayne Papers).

## From Ezekiel Cheever

Hond Sir                              Springfield [Mass.] Sepbr 3. 1778
I have the honor to acknowledge the receipt of your Excellencys Letter the 31st ulto and observe the Contents & will take all necessary precautions respecting the Same. Will write immediately to his Excelly Govr Trumbull to give me the earliest Notice in Case the Enemy Should make a Landing upon the Coast of Connecticut, and If He apprehends it adviseable or necessary to remove the public Stores from this Place; to grant me as many Teams as possible for the purpose.
Yesterday I recd an order from Genl Heath to Send to Boston with the utmost dispatch, 100,000 on Cart'gs. 4 doz. portfires Four Tons Cannon Powder all wch is gone forward, His honrs letter is Dated the 31st ulto. He Sayes a Fleet of Ships are now in our Bay, But who or what

they are is yet unknown—perhaps they are the Ships your Excellency mentions ever Solictous Sir for your Health & Prosperity—I have the Honor to be your Excellencys Obedt Hume Servt

Ezekl Cheever D.C.G. M. Stores

ALS, DLC:GW. Cheever wrote on the cover that this letter was "favd by mr Lewis Dunn."

## To Vice Admiral d'Estaing

Sir,                              Head Quarters White Plains Septr 3d 1778
    I had the honor of writing to you yesterday communicating the intelligence I had received of the arrival of four large ships of war at the *Hook*—I have just received a New York paper of the 1st instant announcing the arrival of Admiral Parker with six ships of the line. I send it you inclosed.[1] With every sentiment of respect & esteem, I have the honor to be Sir Your most Obedt servant

Go: Washington

LS, in Alexander Hamilton's writing, FrPNA: Marine, B4, I46; DfS, DLC:GW.
    At "2 OClock P.M." on this date, GW wrote Rhode Island governor William Greene: "I take the liberty of transmitting to your care, a Letter for His Excellency Admiral Count D'Estaing, which I request the favor of you to forward to him by the earliest Express. It contains an account of the arrival of Rear Admiral parker at Sandy Hook on Friday last with Six ships of the line" (Df, DLC:GW). GW's letter to d'Estaing apparently reached Boston on 5 Sept. (see *Independent Ledger, and the American Advertiser* [Boston], 7 Sept.).
    1. The enclosed newspaper, most likely an issue of the *Royal American Gazette*, has not been identified. Hyde Parker, Sr. (1714–1782), who was promoted to rear admiral on 23 Jan. 1778, was second in command to Vice Admiral John Byron. His ship, the *Royal Oak*, was among six warships that arrived at Sandy Hook on 28 August.

## From Major General Lafayette

                              Camp Near Bristol [R.I.]
My dear General                    the 3d September 1778
    I Can't let Mons. de la Neuville go to headquarters without Recalling to Your Excellency's memory an inhabitant of the Eastern Rhode island schore, who long much to be again united with you, and Conceive now great hopes from Sir henry Clinton's motion to Newport, that you will Come to oppose him in person—I think if we mean to oppose the

ennemy in this quarter that more troops are absolutely necessary, for we are not able to do any thing in our Scattered Situation—I Confess I am myself very uneasy in this quarter, and fear that those people will put in theyr heads to take some of our batteries &ca which if properly attak'd will be difficult to prevent, and I am upon a little tongue of land where in case of an alarm a long stay might be very dangerous—but we'll do for the best.

I am told that the ennemy is going to Evacuate Newyork—my policy leads Me to believe that some troops will be sent to hallifax, to the west indias, and Canada—that Canada I aprehend will be your occupation of next winter and spring—this idea, my dear general, alters a plan I had to Make a voyage home, in some Months, for as long as you fight I want to fight along with you, and I much desire to see your excellency in quebec Next Summer.

Mons. de la Neuville is going to head quarters—that gentleman I have a Great Regard for on account of his politeness, Candor, and military merit—I am very happy that he might deserve your excellency's approbation—I will take his brother in my family—Mons. touzard's arm is in pretty good Situation. With the most tender affection and highest Respect I have the honor to be dear general Your excellency's the most obedient humble Servant

the Marquis de lafayette

ALS, PEL. Where Lafayette edited this letter after the war, the original has been restored as much as possible.

## From Brigadier General Charles Scott

Sir                                    [Westchester County, N.Y.] 3d of Sept. 1778
    Capt. Levensworth returnd last Night but Was not able to procure any Intelligence Material, he Is again gon to meet another person whom he expects from Whitestone, Colo. Grayham also expects to meet a person from New York this Day. So soon as it can possably be had I will Transmit it to Your Excellency. Inclosd You'l Receive a York paper of Yesterdays date.[1] I am Your Excellency's Obt Servant

Chs Scott

ALS, DLC:GW.
    1. Scott probably sent an issue of James Rivington's *Royal Gazette*.

## From Major General John Sullivan

My Dear General,                          Providence September 3d 1778
    I had Last night the honor of Receiving your Excellenceys Favor of
the first Instant & impatiently wait your Excellenceys Sentiments on
The Steps I have taken Since the 29th ult. an Account of which has
been Transmitted by Major Morris.[1]
    The Justice of the observations in your Excellenceys Letter Respect-
ing the Departure of the French Fleet are So obvious That if a Consciousness of my Duty to yield implicit obedience to your Excellenceys
Commands did not Ever make that obedience a pleasure The Reasoning alone must have pointed out the part I have to Act—I have the
pleasure to Inform your Excellencey That Though the first Struggles
of passion on So important a Disappointment were Scarcly to be Restrained: Yet in a few Days by Taking advantage of the Subsiding passion I found means to Restore the former harmony between the American & French officers of the Army. The Count DEstaing & myself are
in the Same friendship as heretofore. The Reason of the Protest[2] has
been Explained to him & he is now perfectly Satisfied he has offered to
come on with his Land Forces & do every thing which I may Request of
him & his Troops but This Step has become unnecessary—The Reason of Drawing the Protest was this: The Count himself wished to Remain with us but was by his Captains overruled in Council as Deviating
from the voice of his Council would be attended with ill Consequences
to him in Case of misfortune it was Supposed that The protest might
Justify his Deviating from the voice of the Council & Acting a part agreable to his own Sentiments & those of the Coopperating Army. prudence Dictated it as our Duty to keep it Secret from all but him your
Excey & the Congress & no publication of it was Ever thought of on our
part & your Excy may Rely on my Exertions to prevent it—Every thing
in my power Shall be Done for Repairing the Injury Sustained by the
French Fleet. The Fleet off Boston Harbor of which I gave your Excy
an Account yesterday are Eight Ships of the Line ten Frigates one
Sloop & a Schooner There can be no Doubt of its being Lord Howes
Fleet watching the motions of the French Fleet to facilitate the Relief
of Rhode Island & perhaps to Cover the Retreat of the British Army
from Rhode Island & New York to other places where they are more
needed. Those Ships were out of Sight yesterday morning Eight of
Clock but I hear they afterward hove in Sight again. The Report here
is That Six thousand Troops have arrived at Newport. I know they are
numerous but cannot as yet ascertain the number[3] your Excellencey
will please to Transmit Copy of This Letter to Congress & believe me

to be with Every Sentiment of gratitude Respect & Esteem your Excellenceys most obedt & very Humble Servant

Jno. Sullivan

ALS, DLC:GW; copy, DNA:PCC, item 152; copy, ScHi: Henry Laurens Papers; copy, DNA:PCC, item 169. The copy in DNA:PCC, item 152, was enclosed in GW to Henry Laurens, 4–5 September.

1. Sullivan was referring to his letter to GW of 31 August.

2. For the American officers' protest to Vice Admiral d'Estaing of 22 Aug., see John Sullivan to GW, 23 Aug., n.2.

3. The roughly four thousand British troops that arrived to relieve Newport on 1 Sept. did not disembark. They sailed off on the evening of 2 Sept. (see *Mackenzie Diary*, 2:389–91; Lydenberg, *Robertson Diaries*, 181).

# General Orders

Head-Quarters White Plains Friday Septr 4th 1778.

Parole                                                                C. Signs

At a General Court Martial of the Line of which Coll Hazen was President—Captain Norwood of the 4th Maryland Regiment appeared before the Court charg'd with—1st—Publickly declaring and implying that he did not regard the Censure of the Commander in Chief, because the Facts set forth on his trial, to Him, were mis-stated—2ndly—With Conduct unbecoming an Officer and Gentleman in suggesting publickly that the Facts were mis-represented; which has an implied tendency to reflect on His Excellency, on the Court Martial, on General Smallwood or on the whole.[1]

3rdly—With declaring that General Smallwood has been guilty of partiality in his Case—That the General was no Gentleman and that he would make it his business to declare publickly ["]that General Smallwood was a partial Man and no Gentleman"—plead not guilty of the first and second charges—Captain Norwood requested the Court not to proceed on an examination of the third charge exhibited against him unless he was permitted to lay before them those facts which had occasioned the Expressions he had used relative to the Character of General Smallwood in this Case—he said he could justify them.

As such an Enquiry would lead to the trial of General Smallwood, which the Court do not think themselves authorized to enter on—and as passing sentence on Captain Norwood for Expressions he has made use of without hearing his reasons for those Expressions might do injustice to that Gentleman; The Court are unanimously of Opinion that they cannot with Propriety, enter into an Enquiry of said charge exhibited against Captain Norwood.

At the particular request of General Smallwood the Court deferred hearing the Witnesses on the 1st & 2nd charges exhibited against Captain Norwood 'till they should be empowered to try him for the 3rd likewise—The Court adjour[n]s 'till tomorrow 9 oClock.

Moses Hazen Colonel President.

Head Quarters August 22nd 1778.

Sirs—I have read and considered the proceedings of the Court Martial in the Case of Captain Norwood.

If our military constitution does not authorise the Court to investigate the 3rd charge exhibited against him, and to determine upon the same, and on the defence he offers, no Power can be derived from Me for the purpose—However I am of opinion that they have a Jurisdiction in the Case, and that tho' a trial before such a Court, may in it's consequences and operation bring in question the Character of a General Officer, yet that this Circumstance will not supercede their power of Enquiry as to the matters in charge, as they are not to pass sentence against the General Officer.

This I deliver as mere matter of opinion and without the least design or wish to influence the Court to proceed in the Case of Captain Norwood, if their sentiments are still the same respecting the Incompetency of their Power. I am Sir your most obedient Servant

Geo. Washington

Coll Moses Hazen President of the Court Martial now sitting—

Saturday August 22nd 1778

The Court of which Coll Hazen is President met after intermediate Adjournments.

A letter from His Excellency General Washington to the President respecting a former determination of the Court Martial, that they could not with Propriety enter into an investigation of the third Article in charge exhibited by General Smallwood against Captain Norwood, was laid before the Court.

They reconsidered their former decision & still remained of Opinion that it was founded on Military Principles & that they could not depart from it.

Captain Norwood observed to the Court that he had been arraigned before them, that he had plead to that part of his charge which they tho't themselves competent to proceed on and that he now insisted on being tried on those Articles of the Charge exhibited against him, to which he had already plead.

The Court were of opinion that as Captain Norwood had plead to his charge, he had a right to insist on his trial and determined that they would proceed to an Investigation of the two first Articles of the Charge exhibited against Captn Norwood—The Court adjourns 'till Monday morning next 9 ôClock.

The Court having met on Monday the 24th adjourn'd 'till the day following and then proceeded to an investigation of the two first Charges exhibited against Captain Norwood as before recited.

General Smallwood made an objection to the Court's proceeding on the two first Articles of the charge exhibited against Captain Norwood, unless they would include the whole of the charge, in which Case he was willing to give Captain Norwood the fullest Power of justifying those Expressions with which he was charged. The Court after considering the objection made by General Smallwood to their proceeding farther in the Case of Captain Norwood, were of opinion that it was inadmissible, since stoping their proceedings in consequence of this objection, would be supposing they had no right to continue them and consequently that any officer who has arrested another possesses the power of preventing the Supreme Military Court in the American Army from examining into the Merits of the Charge—The Court then proceeded to hear the Witnesses on the two first Charges and came to the following determination.

The Court having considered the Charges and the Evidence are of Opinion that Captain Norwood did say that he did not regard, or did not mind the Censure of the Commander in Chief, because the Facts stated to Him on his (Captain Norwood's) trial were mis-represented, and are farther of opinion that this Expression had a tendency (tho' Captain Norwood could not mean it) to reflect on His Excellency as well as on General Smallwood—The Court find Captain Norwood guilty of breaches of the 5th Article of 18th Section and of the 2nd Article of 2nd Section of the Articles of War & do sentence him to be reprimanded in general Orders.[2]

The Court acquit Captain Norwood of unofficer- and ungentleman-like behaviour and of reflecting on the Court-Martial.

Moses Hazen President.

The Commander in Chief finds himself under the disagreeable necessity of disapproving the proceedings of the Court because they have not tried all the charges exhibited before them—On each Fact agreeable to Precedent and common usage they ought to have given either a sentence of Acquittal or Condemnation; To this end their power & Jurisdiction seem to have been fully competent. The third Charge from it's very nature implied a right of Justification in the prisoner and could not be discriminated in Point of reason from either of the preceding ones or any other—The matter in question between the Parties in this instance was the Character and conduct of one of them—the Prisoner by the strongest Implication acknowledges he had made the charge as stated and if permitted would justify it.

General Smallwood on the other hand consented and declared himself willing that he should have the fullest Power of doing it—This circumstance supposing there had been room for doubt before respecting the Court's authority to try the matter was sufficient to remove every objection—Captain Norwood still remains in Arrest and is to be tried on the several charges exhibited against him.

At the same Court Joseph Askins a soldier of the 5th Pennsylvania Regiment was tried for desertion twice—2ndly for making his escape from a Guard and endeavoring to desert to the Enemy found guilty of the charges exhibited against him & sentenced to receive one hundred lashes.[3]

Also Peter Wood of the 1st New-York Regiment was tried for Robbery and Desertion—acquitted of the charge of Robbery but found guilty of desertion & sentenced to receive one hundred lashes.[4] The Commander in Chief approves the sentences and orders them to be put in Execution tomorrow morning at the head of the Regiments to which said Askins and Wood belong.

Varick transcript, DLC:GW.

The orders for this date in the orderly book of the artillery brigade begin: "Returns of Blankets actually wanted in the Sevl Regts & Corps to be made immediately & given in at the Orderly Office" (NHi; see also Maj. Gen. Benjamin Lincoln's orderly book, MHi: Lincoln Papers).

1. For discussion of Capt. Edward Norwood's initial court-martial of 2 June, see William Smallwood to GW, 8 June; for GW's censure of Norwood, see General Orders, 11 June.

2. Article 2 of section 2 authorized punishment of "Any officer or soldier who shall behave himself with contempt or disrespect towards the general, or other commander in chief . . . or shall speak words tending to his hurt or dishonor." Article 5 of section 18 authorized punishment for "disorders and neglects . . . to the prejudice of good order and military discipline" not mentioned in the other articles (*JCC*, 5:789, 807; Smallwood, *Trials*, 33–37).

3. Joseph Orskin was a private in Capt. William Oldham's company of the 5th Pennsylvania Regiment. He deserted again in December 1778, rejoined the regiment in May 1779, and deserted in July 1779.

4. Peter Wood, who enlisted for three years' service as a private in the 1st New York Regiment on 1 Feb. 1778, deserted on 15 April. He returned to the regiment in August but deserted again in October.

## From Captain Epaphras Bull

Sir                                          Maroneck [N.Y.] 4th Sepr 1778

I have to Inform your Excellency that at Sunset this Evening, came from the Wtward one 20 gun Ship one Brig & 2 Schooners, the Latter being so far in the Rear of the Ship 'twas dark before they came up, therefore cou'd not 'tell whether they were armed or not Can send your Excellency a Mess of Black fish whenever 'tis agreable they are now in Cur.[1] I have the Honor to be your Excellencys Mot Obt Sert

Epaps Bull

ALS, DLC:GW.

1. Bull may have meant "cure."

## To Colonel Lambert Cadwalader

Dear Sir                              H. Qers [White Plains] 4 Sepr 1778

I am pressed by a number of causes to beg your determination on a point which is likely to give rise to much disquietude in the Pennsylvania line. The officers consider the retention of your commission as an obstacle to their rise, while it is urged that you are not viewed by the enemy as a prisoner of war.[1]

It appears to me that the workings of a delicate sentiment should never be discouraged, tho we do not find men much inclined to favor its operation against their own rank. But this is not the principal consideration your liberty is supposed to be the price of General Prescots obligation to your Father which it is thought implied no inactivity whatsoever on your part.[2] The circumstances of the transaction which came to my knowledge I must confess led me to think in the same manner—And The inclosed letter will also explain the judgement of the comissioners of arrangement on this subject.[3] I wish to have your decision as soon as possible; and should it be to return to the army I shall consider it a fortunate circumstance to the service.[4] I am Sir with much esteem your most Obt &.

G. W——n

Df, in James McHenry's writing, DLC:GW; Varick transcript, DLC:GW.

1. Cadwalader had been captured on 16 Nov. 1776 and almost immediately released, but he had not been formally exchanged. Meanwhile, in December 1776 he had been appointed colonel of the 4th Pennsylvania Regiment.

2. On 30 Jan. 1776 Congress requested that Dr. Thomas Cadwalader (c.1707–1779) of Philadelphia, Lambert Cadwalader's father, examine British brigadier general Richard Prescott, then a prisoner of war. Dr. Cadwalader's reports led to Prescott's removal from the jail to "proper lodging," and later Prescott, who had been exchanged, was instrumental in securing Lambert Cadwalader's release from captivity (*JCC*, 4:101, 112).

3. The enclosed letter has not been identified, but it apparently stated that Cadwalader should be ordered to join his regiment (see Cadwalader to GW, 7 Oct.).

4. The draft originally continued, "However if you are prevented by any delicacy of thinking I know it cannot be easily changed—But should it arise from an opinion that you are regarded by the enemy as their prisoner, I need not inform you that the proper steps to bring the matter to a certainty will be to desire an explanation from General Clinton or those who were immediately concerned in the transaction," but after slightly revising that text, McHenry crossed it out.

## From Major Alexander Clough

Sr                        [Hackensack, N.J.] Sepr 4th [1778] 12 OClock—
I am inform'd by a person from New York, that the 27th Regt have sent thayr Baggage on board the Britania transport, three companys of Artillery are orderd on board the Howe, the Officers Baggage is sent on board—Another informs me thayr waggons are repair'd, and the horses are shoeing in every part of the town—Major tenpeny is order'd to raise a Corps of horse. I am Your Excellency[s] Most Obt Hbl. Servt

A. Clough

ALS, DLC:GW. The year is taken from the endorsement on the cover.

## To Colonel James Hogun

Sir                                        Head Quarters White plains 4 Sepr 1778

Since the orders sent to you last Evening,[1] I have seen the surgeon General, who wishes to have the innoculation of your Regiment put off at present, especially as there is not the least danger of infection. You will therefore march to Fort Arnold at West point and there put yourself under the command of Colo. Malcom and assist in carrying on the Works at that post, untill Arms and Accoutrements can be provided. I am Sir Your most ob.

Df, in Tench Tilghman's writing, DLC:GW; Varick transcript, DLC:GW.
1. These orders have not been identified.

## From Major General Jabez Huntington

Honrd Sir          New London [Conn.] 4th Sepr 1778, 1 OClock P.M.

Yesterday 2 O'Clock P.M. this Quarter was Alarmed by the Appearence of a British Fleet from the Eastward which Appeared to be making an Attempt to Gaine this Harbour. the Wind then at North. at 6 O'Clock the whole Fleet Came to Anchor, About a Mild from the Enterence of the Harbour.[1]

I Arived here Early this Morning & have Reconoiter'd them as near as possible find they Consist of About Fifty Sail Six of which Appear to be Frigats the other Transports Row Gallies &c. they Appear to be full of Troops. I have Ordered the 3d & 5th Brigade of Militia into this Place. they are now Collecting fast.[2]

the Fleet still Continue the Position in which they Anchor'd Last Evning Notwithstanding the wind is now Favourable for them to proceed Either East or West.[3]

it Remains Very Uncertain what there Design may be but with the Present Appearences I thought Proper to Acquaint your Excellency. Interem Remaine your Excellency's Most Obedt & Most Humb. Servant

Jz Huntington

ALS, DLC:GW.

Jabez Huntington (1719–1786), a member of the Connecticut council of safety, was appointed second major general of Connecticut militia in December 1776, became first major general in May 1777, and served until May 1779.

1. An account of the movements of British forces commanded by Maj. Gen. Charles Grey, "Published by Authority" in the *Royal Gazette* (New York) of 12 Sept., stated that after the American forces retreated from Rhode Island, "Major General

Gray turned his thoughts towards New-London, where he hoped to surprize a number of privateers. When he arrived off that harbour, not more than three or four small vessels were discovered in it, the General therefore would not risque the lives of any of the brave felows under his command for so inadequate an object. Having anchored there for some hours in order to draw the attention of the Rebels to that point, he again set sail" and destroyed stores at the towns of Bedford and Fairhaven, Massachusetts. The account of this alarm in the *Connecticut Gazette; and the Universal Intelligencer* (New London), 11 Sept., attributed the fleet's failure to enter the harbor to "the Wind and Tide being against them," which is in more accord with the account given by British major John André, who wrote in his journal for 3 Sept. that the British intended "to have landed the Troops and proceeded immediately to destroy what shipping or stores to be found; but Captain Fanshaw . . . asserting that the Troops could not be landed that evening . . . It therefor became a matter of deliberation whether the Troops should be landed next day, after giving the Enemy so much time to collect force and to remove whatever was valuable; and it was thought more advisable, after having spread an alarm here, to proceed to New Bedford in Buzzard's Bay" (André, *Journal*, 87).

2. The *Connecticut Gazette* stated that "Expresses were sent into the neighbouring Towns for Assistance, and by Friday Evening [4 Sept.] about 4000 Troops, well equipt, had arrived in New-London and Groton, and the Roads were crowded with others who continued to march from Towns more remote, till they were countermanded."

3. According to the *Connecticut Gazette*, the fleet began sailing from its menacing position "between 4 and 5 o'Clock Friday Afternoon."

## To Henry Laurens

Sir                                  Head Qrs White plains Sept. 4 1778

I had the pleasure to hear this morning by a Letter from General Sullivan of the 31st Ulto, that he had effected a retreat to the main, the preceding night, without any loss, either of men or Stores. As he has written to Congress fully upon the subject, and I feel their anxiety to hear it, I shall not detain Major Morris longer than to observe, that I think the retreat a most fortunate—lucky and well timed event.[1]

Major Morris informs me he has heard that Lord Howe was off Boston with his fleet—and it appears by a New York paper of the 2d, that Rear Admiral Parker arrived at Sandy Hook on this day week, with Six Ships of the line of Seventy four guns each, which is corroborated by other accounts. I transmitted the intelligence to His Excellency, Count D'Estaing yesterday, and the day before—as it acquired more and more the appearance of certainty[2] as I have regularly done every occur[renc]e, interesting to his Fleet, & our Operations. I have the Honor to be with the greatest respect & esteem sir Yr Most Obedt Servt

Go: Washington

LS, in Robert Hanson Harrison's writing, DNA:PCC, item 152; Df, DLC:GW; copy, DNA:PCC, item 169; Varick transcript, DLC:GW. GW signed the cover of the LS.

Congress read this letter on 7 Sept. and referred the enclosure to the committee of intelligence (see *JCC*, 12:884–85).

1. For Maj. Gen. John Sullivan's letter to Laurens of 31 Aug., see DNA:PCC, item 160; see also *Laurens Papers*, 14:248–54.

2. GW wrote the text from this point to the complimentary closing of the LS; that clause does not appear on the draft or Varick transcript.

## To Henry Laurens

Dear Sir,                                                    White plains—Sep. 4th 1778

I am your debtor for two Letters bearing date the 28th & 29th Ulto[1]—The contents shall be the subject of a future address.

Feeling myself interested in every occurrance that tends to the honor of your worthy Son; and sensible of the pleasure it must give you to hear his Just plaudit, I take the liberty of transcribing a paragraph of General Greens Letter to me (giving some Acct of the conduct of particular Officers in the action on Rhode Island):

"Our Troops behaved with great spirit, and the Brigade of Militia under the Command of Genl Lovel advanced with great resolution, and in good order; and stood the fire of the Enemy with great firmness— Lt Colo. Livingston, Colo. Jackson, & Colo. H.B. Livingston did themselves great honor in the transactions of the day. But it is not in my power to do justice to Colo. Laurens, who acted both the Genl & Partizan—His command of regular Troops was small, but he did every thing possible to be done, by their numbers."[2]

Major Morris affords me too good an oppertunity of returning your paper parcel of gold, sent me by Messenger Jones, to pass by—& therefore I embrace it—A more particular acknowledgement of, and thanks for this favor, shall, as I have promised before, be conveyed in my next—At present I shall only assure you—& with the most perfect truth I can do it, that with every sentiment of regard and Affection, I have the Honor to be Dr Sir, Yr Most Obedt & Obligd Servt

Go: Washington

ALS, CSmH; ADfS, DLC:GW; copy, ScHi: Henry Laurens Papers; Varick transcript, DLC:GW.

1. GW was acknowledging Laurens's private letter of 28 August.

2. GW was quoting from Nathanael Greene's letter of 28–31 August.

## To Henry Laurens

Sir                                                    Head Qrs White plains Septr 4th[–5] 1778

I have been duly honored with your favors of the 28th, and that of the 30th Ulto with the several Inclosures, to which they refer.[1]

Congress may rely, that I will use every possible means in my power to conciliate any differences that may have arisen, in consequence of the Count D'Estaings going to Boston—and to prevent a publication of the protest upon the occasion. Several days before the receipt of the Resolution, I had written to the Eastward; urging the necessity of harmony—and the expediency of affording the Admiral every assistance to refit his Ships. This I repeated after the Resolution came to hand[2]—and I have also taken opportunities to request all the General Officers here, to place the matter in the most favorable point of view, whenever they hear it mentioned.

The Five Hundred Guineas, which Congress were pleased to order,[3] came safe to hand—and shall be appropriated to the purposes they intended, and as the exigency of the service may require. For want of supplies of this sort, we have been very deficient in intelligence, in many important and interesting points. In some cases, no consideration in paper money has been found sufficient to effect, even, an engagement to procure it; and where it has been otherwise, the terms of service, on account of the depreciation, have been high—if not exorbitant.

The designs of the Enemy, as to their future movements, remain yet entirely unfolded; but the expectation of their leaving the Continent is daily decreasing. The hurricane season seems opposed to their going to the West Indies—and the passage to Europe in a little time will become more and more dangerous. Besides these, there is another circumstance of some weight, if true, to induce a belief that they mean to stay. It appears by the papers, that part of the Regiments lately raised in Britain, are ordered to Hallifax.[4] If the troops here were intended to be recalled, it would seem, that some of them would be sent to reinforce that Garrison, sooner than troops from England or Scotland; and hence I think it may be presumed, that another Campaign will take place in America, especially if Administration are disappointed in their expectations from the commission. Where the theatre of War may be, must be a matter of conjecture, but as it is an acknowledged fact, that an Army acting in the Eastern States must derive flour for it's support, from those more Western, I submit to Congress the expediency, and in my opinion the necessity, of establishing without loss of time, Magazines of this Article at convenient places, removed from the Sound, in Connecticut & Massachussets. I am the more induced to wish an early consideration of this point, as by a sudden move of the Army, should events make it necessary, the departments of Commissary & Quarter Master would be greatly distressed. Nor would such Magazines, I should immagine, be attended with any considerable loss, though the Army should not operate in that Quarter, as the flour would answer occasionally for our Shipping and the surplus might, in all probability, be otherwise readily disposed of.[5]

I take the liberty of transmitting to Congress, a Memorial I received from the Reverend Mr Tetard. From the certificates annexed to it, he appears to be a Man of great merit—and from every account he has suffered in the extreme, in the present contest. His attachment—services and misfortunes seem to give him a claim to a generous notice; but according to the now establishment of the Army, it is not in my power to make any provision for him. I therefore recommend his case to the attention and consideration of Congress.[6]

6 OClock P.M. I this minute received a Letter from General Sullivan, of which the Inclosure, No. 2, is a Copy.[7] I shall be exceedingly happy, if a perfect reconciliation has taken place between him and the Count and all the Officers. His Letter will shew some of the reasons that led to the protest and that it was the hope of our Officers, that it would have operated as a justification to the Admiral, to return against the sentiments of his Council, especially as it coincided, as it is said, with his own inclination. I had these reasons from another hand, when the protest first came.[8]

Septr 5. I was duly honored yesterday evening, with your favor of the 31st Ulto—Though it is not expressed in the Resolution of that date, that any other bounty is to be given to the Men who engage for three years or during the War, than Twenty Dollars, I shall take it for granted they are to receive the usual allowances of Cloathing & Land. There are several Continental Troops, whose time of service will expire at the end of the fall or during the Winter. I shall consider these within the meaning and operation of the Resolve, though they are not mentioned—and shall direct every necessary measure to be taken to reinlist them. From the exorbitant State—Town and Substitute bounties, I am very doubtful whether Twenty Dollars will be found sufficient to engage so great a proportion either of the Draughts or Continentals, as was at first apprehended. Our failure in the enterprize against Rhode Island will have it's weight and every day, from the approach of the fall and Winter, will add new difficulties. As it is a work of the most essential importance, I will order it to be begun, the instant the Money arrives; and lest on experiment, the sum should prove too small, I would submit it to Congress, whether it will not be expedient to pass another Resolve, authorising a further bounty of Ten Dollars, to be used as circumstances may make it necessary. This can remain a secret, and will not be carried into execution, but in case of evident necessity. I feel very much interested upon the occasion, and have submitted this mode, that there may not be the least possible delay in attempting to engage the men, under a second expedient, if the first should not succeed.[9] The Articles of Cloathing and blankets should also employ the utmost attention to provide them. We are now in great want, particularly of the latter, there not being less than [      ] actually wanted at this moment.[10] I have the honor to be with the greatest respect & esteem sir Yr Most Obedt servt

Go: Washington

P.S. The return of Blankets has not come in and therefore I cannot ascertain the deficiency by this conveyance.

LS, in Robert Hanson Harrison's writing, DNA:PCC, item 152; Df, DLC:GW; copy, ScHi: Henry Laurens Papers; copy, DNA:PCC, item 169; Varick transcript, DLC:GW. Congress read this letter on 8 Sept. (see *JCC*, 12:889).

1. GW was acknowledging Laurens's two public letters of 28 August.
2. See GW to John Sullivan, 28 Aug. and 1 Sept. (first letter). For the protest to d'Estaing, see Sullivan to GW, 23 Aug., n.2; for Congress's resolution on that subject, see *JCC*, 11:848–49.
3. For the order of 29 Aug., see ibid., 11:851.
4. The *Royal Gazette* (New York) of 19 Aug., for example, carried a report of "23 transports, having Major-General Tryon's [70th Regiment of Foot], and two Highland regiments, in all 3000 Men," bound for Halifax.
5. On 8 Sept., Congress referred this suggestion to a committee formed earlier that day to consider letters discussing military supplies and impending shortages of flour and wheat (*JCC*, 12:889).
6. John Peter Têtard (1722–1787), who had earlier served as a minister for the French Protestant Church at Charleston, S.C., and the Fordham Manor Reformed Dutch Church in New York, was operating a boarding school at his residence near King's Bridge, N.Y., when he was appointed in July 1775 to serve as French interpreter for Maj. Gen. Philip Schuyler and as a chaplain of New York troops. In November 1776 Têtard was appointed chaplain to the 4th New York Regiment, and he remained on the rolls of that regiment until August 1778, although he was not with the unit after September 1777, being on furlough and absent sick. In April 1782 Têtard was appointed clerk to Secretary for Foreign Affairs Robert R. Livingston, a post he held until Livingston's resignation in June 1783. He was subsequently appointed professor of French language at Columbia College in May 1784. Têtard's memorial has not been identified, but he evidently asked for financial assistance, citing his services with the American army in Canada and the damage done by the British army to his property at King's Bridge (see Robert R. Livingston to president of Congress, 2 Dec. 1782, DNA:PCC, item 79, and Têtard's memorial to Congress of 8 May 1783, DNA:PCC, item 42). Congress referred the memorial to a committee consisting of William Duer, John Harvie, and James Lovell (ibid., 12:891), but no record of subsequent action has been found.
7. The enclosed copy of Maj. Gen. John Sullivan's letter to GW of 3 Sept. is with this letter in DNA:PCC, item 152.
8. See John Laurens to GW, 23 August.
9. Congress passed a resolve to this effect on 8 Sept. (ibid., 12:889–90).
10. Congress referred this issue to the Board of War, which was directed "to make use of the most vigorous exertions for transporting to camp the ready made cloathing stored in the eastern states" and for "procuring and forwarding" the blankets "necessary to make up the deficiency" (ibid., 12:891).

# From Pierre-Charles L'Enfant

Sir                                    White Plains, September the 4th 1778

It is with the greatest surprize that I have read in the New York papers, the pretended Translation of a Letter I had written to a Friend of mine in Europe.[1]

Of all the little, mean Tricks the English makes use of to sow dissentions among their Adversaries, This is indeed the most odious and abominable. They have most Villainously abused of the Liberty of a Translator, and have artfully altered the Words and Phrases of my Letter to a most horrid performance.

Your Excellency may remain assured, that the real Letter I wrote to my Friend was nothing but a faithful Exposition of the real State of the Army. I wondered with him that with so few means, and so little Experience, the Americans had been able to withstand the flower of the British Troops. But all the injurious reflections, and Even hazarded Expressions that are artfully thrown in the Translation, they are certainly the Work of a newspaper writer, hired undoubtedly by Government for Such inequitous purposes.

I dare hope however, Sir, that my Conduct since I have the honor to serve in the Army under your Command, and my Zeal in sharing All their labours and dangers, has convinced fully, that I have never been able to Entertain sentiments such as Mr Rivington gives me.[2] I Shall haste to insert in the publick papers an Explicit disavowal of my Letter, such as it is translated in the New York Gazette.[3] And as Your Excellency's Esteem is infinitely precious to me, I beg you will accept of my Justification, & render Justice to my Sentiments. I have the honor to be With great respect Sir Your Excellency's Most obedient and most humble servant

P. L'Enfant

ALS, DLC:GW.

1. The translation of a letter dated 3 Nov. 1777 "To Mons. L'Ogett, at the Castle of Chaville, near Versailles, road to Paris," appeared in the *Royal Gazette* (New York) of 10 June 1778. In the letter, L'Enfant complained that "the Congress have refused complying with any of their promises, and have been guilty of a breach of justice and good faith, by refusing to comply with their engagements, and in addition to our misfortunes we found ourselves without resources by the death of the unhappy Monsieur De Coudraye." While he was "determin'd to stay this winter with the army and act as a volunteer, that I may be under no obligations to the Congress," L'Enfant announced his "intention of returning to you in the spring." Considering military matters, L'Enfant pointed out that the defeat of Burgoyne's army more than made up for the losses of Fort Ticonderoga and Philadelphia but claimed that the Americans had "been fortunate, and not more brave on that account, for to speak freely of them, they are cowards of the first order, beginning with their officers who have no one point of honour, they are all haughty, there is

no discipline throughout their army, all is disorder, they resemble the beggars we see in the court yards before our hospitals, some naked, others covered with rags; they are scared at the least noise, and ever ready for flight, they never face their enemy, but, as soon as they have thrown in their fire they run and hide themselves in the woods, and leave their leaders destitute of assistance."

2. James Rivington (1724–1802), a London-born bookseller and printer, commenced publishing *Rivington's New-York Gazette* in 1773, and at this time he was publishing the *Royal Gazette*.

3. No published disavowal has been identified.

## From Cornet James Paton

Sir                                    Marenock [N.Y.] Septr 4th 1778

I have to inform your Excellency, that this forenoon, I Observed three Sloops & 2 Schooners from Cow Bay[1] the Schooners and Sloop Appeared to be Armed, Came to off City Island in Company with Several Vessels on that Station before the Other Sloops Stood for N. York, About the middle of the Afternoon Came one Brigg from the West, and Came too off City Island, About Sun ⟨Or⟩ Half an Hour high Observed 1 frigate of 20 Guns and One Arm'd Brigg from the Westward Stood East, when Past City Island fired a Gun, when the Brigg two Schooners, and Sloop Made Sail and Stood After them some Small Boats Appeared from the West but the Evening prevented me making any Discovery. I have the honor to be your Excellencys humble servt

Jas Paton

ALS, DLC:GW.

James Paton (d. 1816) enlisted in the 2d Continental Light Dragoons in February 1777 and served as a corporal and sergeant before being promoted to cornet in October 1777. He did not obtain his commission as second lieutenant, dated from June 1778, until after November 1778. He resigned the commission in May 1779.

1. Cow Bay, now called Manhasset Bay, is the inlet west of Port Washington, Long Island.

## From Major General John Sullivan

Dear General                          Head Qrs Providence Septr 4th 78

I am sorry to inform your Excellency of a Disscontent which at present prevails among the Officers of Webbs and Sherburnes Regiments—They have lately been so clamorous as to verge towards quitting the Service, & I am really apprehensive, that we shall lose many valuable Officers by Resignations if a speedy Redress is not had for

their Grievances. Their uneassiness seems to have arisen from comparing their Situation with that of those Regiments, which are ac-
knowledgd and provided for by their Respective States, at a considerable discount while they are considerd as belonging to no particular
State, & are neglected by the whole—Many of them (if we may judge
from their Appearance,) have great reason to complain—Your Excellency will be pleasd to mention this Circumstance to Congress & use
your Influence for a more liberal Provision for those Officers & Men
who have in our late Action so greatly distinguishd themselves. I have
the honor to be, with the utmost Regard Yr Excellencys most obedt
humble Servt

Jno. Sullivan

LS, DLC:GW.

## From Jean-Baptiste Ternant

sir                                            White Plains september 4, 1778.
    your Excellency's kind answer was handed to me yesterday eve-
ning[1]—from the Idea I entertain of a good military constitution, I am,
& have always been sensible of the necessity of limiting rank to the line
of an army, & of the dangerous impropriety of lavishing it to men mer-
cantilely or otherwise civily employed in the Staff departments; nor did
I ever think of proposing any direct or indirect deviation of this principle in favor of myself or any body else—It is true I Spoke of having
military business transacted by military men, & so far your Excelly
seems to be *aware* of the distinction that should be made between the
civil & military branches of the department I have lately acted in—if
the familiar grown Ideas of this army about the matter are a Sufficient
ground for not ratifying what is So different in other services & So opposite in this, to the true principles of military science, your Excellency
knows best—I am very sorry to find that arrangements of Congress, or
of any body else, will prevent my being any longer employed in the Inspection, after having cheerfully encountered & surmounted the
difficulties which opposed its success, & gone through the most toil-
some & fastiduous details of it—As for my continuing any longer in the
line I am at present in; was the office a military one & on a proper footing, I would; & had it not been represented & offered to me as such, I
would not have accepted of it—for—when I undertook the laborious
task of the Inspection; when I exposed myself to danger in several occasions; when I took pains to exercise the office of Dy Q. Mr upon military principles, my intention was to share the toils & glory attached to

the defense of the cause of America, which glory I could not arrive to, but by being a military man, & deserving by real services, what constitutes him—I am sorry all my endeavours could not get me any other reward but a kind of a Clerkship in the Qr Mr's department. if I must resume a civil employment; I'll try to get one which may be more honorable or profitable to me, & if possible more beneficial to the community—I'll have the honour to call tomorrow morning at head quarters, to take my leave of your Excellency & beg the necessary passes for my journey to Philadelphia. I have the honor to be with respect your Excellency's most obedient & humble servt

John Ternant

ALS, DLC:GW.
    1. See GW to Ternant, 2 September.


# General Orders

Head-Quarters White-Plains saturday Septr 5th 1778.
Parole Mount-Joy—                    C. Signs Maroneck Milton—
The General expects agreeable to former orders that the whole Army is now prepared to move at the shortest notice[1]—Circumstances may, very soon make it necessary.

Coll Chambers is appointed to relieve Colonel Craige who is now Superintending the hospitals in Pennsylvania.

Varick transcript, DLC:GW.
    1. See General Orders, 28 August.

*Letter not found*: from the Board of War, 5 Sept. 1778. On 14 Sept., GW wrote the board: "On sunday night I had the honor to receive your favors of the 5th & 7th Instant."


# From Vice Admiral d'Estaing

Sir.                              [Boston] 5th September 1778.
I have the honor of transmitting to Your Excellency a copy of the account which I have rendered Congress, in my letter to His Excellency Mr henry Laurens.[1]

Men who like you found and support empires, have the same privileges as those who govern them—the admiration and confidence which you inspire—ensures them to you—and it is a homage which my heart pays you with eagerness—I annex to this packet a copy of the Protest and my letter to Genl Sullivan in consequence of it—I hope you will find in the latter a proof of my being devoted to the common cause, and the union of the two nations.[2] it is but too common for those who exercise an art, which is not known by every body—and such as Naval War, to be judged with a degree of prejudice—especially when such prejudice is supported by the interested opinion of some individuals, who tho good pilots and worthy men in other respects have no idea of what a squadron is—however successfully they may have acquitted themselves in conducting small barks—it likewise no uncommon thing to give way to ones passion—Every man is not a Washington, nor like him a Fabius during a Campaign—to reassume the character of Cæsar or Alexander at Monmouth and in every engagement. it was for a great Statesman such as Mr Hancock good policy which dictates reason and never injuries, to put so respectable a name as his to the protest, because as a General Officer he could not dispense with following the example of him who commanded—and because tho he subscribed the words "hitherto esteemed" he certainly suppressed many others—his conduct in rendering us the greatest services, the valuable and flattering present which he has been so kind as to make me—in your portrait—are marks of his sentiments which he entertains for us. You will pardon me for having a good opinion of my own way of thinking, when it coincides with Your Excellencys—this has been the case Sir, for at the very time that you recommended in a letter, to suppress the [      ][3] which often arise from ill-success. I offered and was ready at the head of a Regiment to go and serve under Genl Sullivan, as I formerly did under Marshal Saxe, in the war which finished in 48. I would not take this step at present under the idea of reinforcing an army, with such a handful of men—or Of proving what is already known—viz.—that the french Nation can sacrifice life with a good grace. but I was anxious to demonstrate that my nation could not have been offended by a vivacity—and that he who had the honor of commanding it in America was & would be all his life, one of the most affectionate and zealous Servants of the United States.

I have this moment received a letter from Mr de chouin, of the 2d inst: which confirms the arrival of Admiral Byrons Squadron[4]—the point now is to divine the projects which their naval superiority may probably give rise to.

I am endeavouring with the permission of council, to render the batteries which defend Nantasket Road, as respectable as possible—if I should withdraw to Kings Road, I might be blocked up there, and the possession of the islands without, would give the enemy considerable advantages over me[5]—As I have not the assistance of any American Troops in guarding the islands and peninsulas, they are but illy defended—if the enemy are enterprising they may force me by sea—and then the Ships with which they attack me, and my own may remain there—if they disembark on the continent, doubtless their superior numbers will make them masters of the adjacent posts, which are but feebly occupied—by me—the loss of the Squadron would easily follow, it might be burned without difficulty or danger—and Boston would certainly be much exposed—It appears to me that this Metropolis may be menaced, and ought to be well defended—I will do whatever lies in my power in the Road—but if the coast is left defenceless, I shall be driven from the Road, or my Vessels will be burnt by the enemys possessing themselves of the peninsulas. Perhaps the English may design to winter in our Southern Colonies—Masts arrived yesterday from Portsmouth, they must be made—provisions and water must be procured, before we think of sacrificing ourselves and going to defend them—if any point of the territory of the United States is attacked, I shall act in the same manner on the first requisition made by Your Excellency—because in the eyes of the King, there exists no difference between what belongs to him and what is the property of his allies.

In order to counteract the enemy's projects, it is essential to penetrate them without loss of time—it is impossible to employ money more usefully than on this object—and I would readily engage for the Kings Share of the expence of Spies—[6] in order to act is essential to have intelligence. I have the honor to be &ca.

Translation, in John Laurens's writing, DLC:GW; LS, in French, DLC:GW.

1. Both an LS copy, in French, and a translation by John Laurens of d'Estaing's letter to Henry Laurens of 26 Aug. are in DLC:GW (see also *Laurens Papers*, 14:222–33). D'Estaing summarized events since his arrival in July, giving greatest attention to justifying his course of action during the Newport siege.

2. A copy of the protest of 22 Aug., signed by d'Estaing as "bon pour copie conforme a l'originale," is in DLC:GW. The text of d'Estaing's copy has minor variations from the copy sent to GW by Maj. Gen. John Sullivan (see Sullivan to GW, 23 Aug., n.2), most notably an underline of the phrase "hitherto Esteem'd Allies." A copy (in French) of d'Estaing's letter to Sullivan, dated 29 Aug., was marked by d'Estaing, "bon pour copie." D'Estaing probably also enclosed John Laurens's translation of that letter (both DLC:GW). Laurens had summarized the text in his letter to GW of 2 September.

3. Here Laurens did not render the French word, "propos," which evidently had reference to the protest of 22 August. GW's recommendation on the subject was sent in his first letter to Sullivan of 1 September.

4. The marquis de Choin's letter to d'Estaing of 2 Sept. enclosed another copy of the Howell journal that GW had sent to d'Estaing earlier that day. In a postscript, Choin added that deserters just arrived from New York confirmed the information (FrPNA: Marine, B4, I44).

5. A committee from the Massachusetts council had a "private conference" with d'Estaing about military affairs on 30 Aug., and on 1 Sept. the council granted him permission "to Land Such and so many of your Troops as you may judge Expedient . . . on Hull Long Island or Such other Points or Islands as you may think best

Situated for the defence of your Squadron." By 3 Sept., d'Estaing had "erected very formidable works on George's Island, in which . . . he has mounted near 100 cannon, of heavy mettal, which he took from his fleet" (William Heath to d'Estaing, 1 Sept., MHi: Heath Papers; *Continental Journal, and Weekly Advertiser* [Boston], 3 Sept.). King Road was the channel north of Spectacle Island within Boston Harbor.

6. At this point in the translation, Laurens did not render text that appears in the French LS. It reads: "on Repousse quelque fois par L'offensive, et attaquer, est souvent la meilleure facon de Se deffendre; mais" (sometimes one repels by the offensive, and attacking is often the best way to defend oneself; but).

## From Major General William Heath

Dear General                                    Head Quarters Boston Sept. 5th 1778
Nothing worthy of notice has Transpired Since I had the honor to write you on the Second Inst. whether the British Fleet that came and looked at the French Squadron are gone to Hallifax, or to Newport or are Still Cruizing off is Unknown, a Considerable firing of Cannon was heard off in the Bay this morning.

Upon the receipt of your Excellencys Letters this morning for the Count DEstaing, I immediately dispatched them to him by an Express Boat.[1] The Station of his Ships, and the Position of the Batteries which He has Opened renders his Situation I think fully Safe & Secure on the water Side—The masts and Spars that were Sent for arrived yesterday from the Eastward the Utmost endeavours are in exercise for refitting the Fleet with Expedition. I have the Honor to be with the greatest respect your Excellencys most Obt Hbble Servt

W. Heath

P.S. let me request the favor that the letters addressed to the Hon. the president may be forwarded by the first express going Philadelphia.[2]

ALS, DLC:GW. This letter was docketed in part, "ansd," but no reply has been identified.

1. Heath was apparently referring to GW's letters to Vice Admiral d'Estaing of 2 and 3 September.

2. Heath's letter to Henry Laurens of "7 oClock P.M." this date conveyed much the same information as this letter (DNA:PCC, item 157).

## From James Hill

Worthy General                                    Wmsburg [Va.] the 5th Sepr 1778
Mr Custis Have thought proper to alter His estate in such a manner that it woud not suit me To look after it any longer provided he was willing tho it appears to me as tho he was not. However by not recceiveing a line from You Respectg Yours that I have under my Care was deter-

mind unless you & he agree'd on terms for him to have taken it—I woud acontinued it untill you returnd provided you had no objection; at what you thought reasonable tho expect by what I have heard he purposes to take it—I intended to awrote by him out to You but my business was Such at that time I had no opportunity, till he Set out; Youl please to rembr you told me in our agremt to do the best I coud with Mr Custis's Estate & provided the Estate improved you'd increase the Lay which I was exceeding Willing in case it did not I woud ⟨ne⟩ver askd for 1 farthing More but you well Know Sir, You purchased two more plantations which enlarged the Estates considerably & made it more Troublesome them being purchased much out of order for Croping[1] & woud Heartely Wish You to see the Estate now & you Know the order it was in When I took it & woud Wish to have Your opinion what yo. thought I deserved; & as to the Profits Asaveg Hope he will have no reason to complain tho I have had the misfortune for Several Years to loose the Wheat by Weavle;[2] have made it up by Stock &c., which was all the Way I had to dispose of it, & now have the Estate in General in as good order for Croping as any Estate in the Colloney; for Tobo Wheat or any thing he Chuses to go upon for I have never sufferd the Tobo lands to be put in Corne or in wheat oats &c., till I got every plantation inclosed & thirded & is now with Slight run[nin]g over with Dung capable of bringing choice Tobo which hope Youl refer to Some Gent. that you can confide in that is a Judge & hear what they Say, & if they dont think that what Ive mentiond to you is as I say; I dont desire one farthing otherwise hope youl Allow me agreable to the difference of money when it took aRise; I agree'd to take the Lay Vollentine had which I have b⟨een⟩ Credibly informd he never gave An Acct for butter Sold & had Shugar found for his familys Use the Rum &c., that the butter &c. was Given up for his Wifes Trouble in doctorg lookg After Sping & this much I never Mentiond to yo. before,[3] Mr Custis Says he is Willg to Allow what you think right & am Shure I am; & was you To abeen privy to Every Transaction of mine Ive renerd Accts for Every farthing Receivd & for every Article therefore hope if this was the Case With Vollentine Youl make me Some Allowance; & please to mention what you are willg to Give for yr own Since the Rise of Specia & am Sattisfyed With what ever yo. think reasonable as I am abt closeing my Accts what money I have of yours Shoud be Glad to Know if You woud have it put in the Continantal Loan office or Sent up by Mr Posey to Mr Washgton I woud apaid it to your Ladye but coud not get it in time enough Mr Custis & my Self agreed to leave my Wages to Colo. Basset & Mr Webb[4] & they Allowd me 150£ for 2 Years & 175 for this But Mr Webb now Says he realy thought I only managed 3 plantations Near Wmsbg I shoud asupposed that they woud allow⟨d⟩ me the Value of

100£ Specia—for I have had the Trouble on me to make Sail of every plantations Crops in Wmsbg & there deliver it in order to get the Highest prisees delvd it in Small quantityes Which was aVast deel more trouble to me—Your Answer if possable to the Above requests by the first Oppertunity will ever be Acknowledged the greatest favour done.[5] Yr Mo. Obt & Mo. Hble St

Jas Hill

P.S. I am Now abt Sellg Yr Beeves we have lost None with the Distempr as Yet.St

J. H.

Youl plea⟨s⟩e to informe me the Qty of Stock Mr Custis wants Left he has Accts of the whole as Davenp[or]t tells me; otherwise, I[']ll inform You by my Next.

ALS, DLC:GW.

1. On 17 Mar. 1772 GW contracted with Hill to manage "all" of John Parke Custis's plantations and other business, as well as GW's "Plantation in King William, Lotts in Williamsburg &ca" (*Papers, Colonial Series*, 9:21). In 1773 GW purchased for Custis from William Black two plantations: Romancoke, containing about 1,780 acres adjacent to GW's dower plantation called Claiborne's in King William County, and Pleasant Hill, consisting of about 2,000 acres in King and Queen County (see GW to Robert Cary & Company, 10 Nov. 1773, and notes 3, 4, and 6 to that document, ibid., 9:374–380). For GW's recollection of the effect of those purchases on the agreement, see his reply to Hill of 27 October.

2. Hill was probably referring to the "Fly-Weevil" or moth (see Lund Washington to GW, 2 Sept., n.3).

3. Before his death, Joseph Valentine (d. 1771) was employed as steward of Daniel Parke Custis's estate and then manager of the dower lands of John Parke Custis and GW. His wife was named Mary.

4. Hill was referring to Burwell Bassett and probably George Webb.

5. In GW's letter to Hill of 27 Oct., he replied that, having rented his plantation in King William County to Custis, he had no further need for Hill's services.

## From Henry Laurens

Sir                      [Philadelphia] 5th September [1778]

My last was dated the 31st Ulto forwarded by Messenger Jones, since which I have had the honor of receiving and presenting to Congress Your Excellencys dispatches, one of that date and one of the 3d Instant,[1] the first is committed to the Board of War & remains there.

This will be accompanied by two Acts of Congress of the 3d Instant.

1. An Act for raising a Corps of troops by the name of the German Volunteers—for granting the Pay and Subsistence of a Lieutenant to Lieutenant Charles Juliat a Volunteer in the Infantry of General Pu-

laski's Legion—for appointing Monsr Girard to the Rank of a Lieutenant of Dragoons by Brevet to serve at his own expence[2]—for laying aside the intended Expedition against the Seneca and other Indians, and for authorizing Your Excellency to pursue proper Measures for defending the frontiers against the incursions of those Indians.[3]

2. An Act for guarding this City by 300 Militia in place of the Confederal Troops who are to join the Main Army. I have the honor to be &c.[4]

LB, DNA:PCC, item 13. A note on the letter-book copy indicates that this letter was carried "by [Joseph] Burwell."

1. Laurens evidently meant to refer to GW's letters to him of 31 Aug. and 1 Sept., read in Congress on 3 and 4 Sept. (*JCC*, 12:862, 880); no letter of 3 Sept. has been found.

2. Karl Josef Juliat (born c.1760), formerly a lieutenant in the Landgrave Regiment, had deserted and approached Congress with a letter of recommendation from Maj. Gen. Johann Kalb. He deserted from Pulaski's Legion in New Jersey on 14 Oct. 1778, and Pulaski attributed an attack on his troops the next day to information supplied the enemy forces by Juliat (see Casimir Pulaski to Laurens, 16 and 18 Oct., DNA:PCC, item 164). Juliat subsequently served with Capt. Ernest Frederick von Diemar's Corps of Hussars before returning to Europe in January 1781. Gérard de St. Elme served as a volunteer captain in Pulaski's Legion, and Congress granted him the brevet rank of major when he returned to France in February 1779 (ibid., 13:182–83).

3. For this act, see ibid., 12:866–68.

4. For this act, see ibid., 12:865.

## To Gouverneur Morris

Dear Sir,                                   White-plains Sepr 5th 1778.

I was yesterday favoured with your Letter of the 31st Ulto—The one you allude to, came to hand about five days before.

I thank you for your very polite and friendly appeal, upon the Subject of half bounty in solid Coin. The measure, I have no doubt, would produce an Instant benefit, so far as the engaging drafts &ca might be concerned; but I am certain, many mischievous and pernicious consequences would flow from it—It would have a tendency to depreciate our paper money, which is already of little[1] value—and give rise to infinite difficulties and irremoveable inconveniences. Nothing after this would do but gold or Silver. All would demand it—and none would consider the impracticability of its being furnished. The Soldiers seeing the manifest difference in the value between that and paper— that the former would procure, at least, five or Six fold as much as the latter, would become dissatisfied—they would reason upon the subject—and in fine cast their views to desertion (*at least*) as a very probable and the only expedient from whence it might be derived and similar & greater advantages arise.

As the Express is now waiting, I will not enter upon a long detail— or into an enumeration of the evils that would result from the Grant. I am satisfied they would be many & of an obstinate & injurious kind; and that they would far over ballance in their operation & effect, any present good. We have no prospect of procuring Gold & Silver to discharge more than a mere scruple of our demand. It is therefore our interest & truest policy to give a currency—to fix a value, as far as it may be practicable, upon all occasions, upon that which is to be the medium of our internal commerce, and the support of the War. I am Dr Sir Yrs Very Affectionately

Go: Washington

ALS, NNC; Df, DLC:GW; Varick transcript, DLC:GW.

    1. GW first wrote "no," which was the word on Robert Hanson Harrison's draft, before substituting "little."

## To Major General John Sullivan

Dear Sir              Head Quarters White plains 5[–6] Sepr 1778

    I have recd yours of the 31st ulto by Major Morris and of the 2d and 3d instants by Express. At the same time that the former relieved us from infinite anxiety upon your account, it served to convince—that the enemy felt the weight of their repulse, by their permitting you to pass the River without the least interruption. I sincerely congratulate you not only upon your safe retreat, but upon the success of our Arms upon the 29 Augt and I beg you will present my thanks to the Officers of all Ranks and to the troops for their gallant behaviour upon that day. I am exceedingly happy to find by yours of the 3d that harmony is again reestablished between our Army and our Allies. I have transmitted a Copy of your letter to Congress[1] and I am certain it will afford them pleasure.

    I have been informed that you were obliged to draw all the Arms from the Magazine at Spring feild to put into the hands of the Militia.[2] If this has been the case, I entreat you to make use of all possible means to have them returned, when the Militia are disbanded, and lodged again in the Magazine. A large Regiment arrived a few days ago from North Carolina, unarmed, and we have none to supply them.[3] Besides this, there is a considerable deficiency in the other parts of the Army. I beg you will upon no account or pretence suffer them to turn their backs upon you, before they have delivered their Arms and other stores, for if they once carry them out of your sight, it wi⟨ll⟩ be impossible to recover them.

6th Sepr    I have recd yours of the 4th respecting the complaints of Colo. Sherburnes & Colo. Webbs officers. Their circumstances are similar to those of all the other 16 additional Battalions. What will be determined upon in regard to those Battalions I do not know, but I imagine the Committee for arranging the Army upon the new establishment, who are now sitting here, will have direction from Congress[4] concerning them. As soon as they come to any resolution, that affects them, I will communicate it. I am &c.

Df, in Tench Tilghman's writing, DLC:GW; Varick transcript, DLC:GW.
1. See GW to Henry Laurens, 4–5 September.
2. The source of GW's information has not been determined.
3. GW was referring to the 3d North Carolina Regiment, commanded by Col. James Hogun. The monthly return for September reports 564 men in the regiment (Lesser, *Sinews of Independence*, 85).
4. On the draft, Tilghman first continued this sentence with the words "either to put them upon some certain and permanent footing, or," but he struck out that text and inserted the two words that follow.

## From Major General John Sullivan

Dear General                                    Head Qrs Providence 5th 78 Septr
    Since my last, Two N. Hampshire Volunteers (who were capturd in Rhode Island & since exchangd) have brought out a Newport Gazette containing the following Intelligence—"That Sir Harry Clinton with the Troops arrivd there on Tuesday last & saild again on the 2d Instant["][1]—I have it likewise from General Cornell who is station'd at Tiverton, that the British Fleet had saild passd Newport & were turning Seconnet Point, steering eastwards—Their destination not known—General Clinton from every Account is on board—I have the honor to be with great Respect, Yr Excellencys Most obedient & hble sert

                                                            Jno. Sullivan

P.S: Those Gentlemen Volunteers likewise assure me, that one hundred and Six Waggons were brought into Newport after the action, With the wounded. that the smallest Number killd (by their own Accounts) were three hundred (that including both their Loss amounted to 1000 or 1500[)][2]—J.S.

LS, DLC:GW.
1. The preceding Tuesday was 1 September. The *Newport Gazette* was established by John Howe in January 1777 and ceased publication in October 1779.
2. On 10 Sept. the *Continental Journal, and Weekly Advertiser* (Boston) reported information given at Boston by exchanged prisoners "Captains Hart and Fernald, and Mr. Neal McIntyre of Portsmouth . . . that 306 of the enemy were killed in the late engagement there, and about 700 wounded. They also say . . . that Gen. Clinton had arrived there from New York, but instead of leaving a reinforcement, he

took away some of the best troops on the island." The "Captains" were privates John Hart and William Furnald of Capt. John Langdon's Company of Light Horse Volunteers, to which McIntyre also belonged (see Hammond, *Rolls of Soldiers*, 2:579; and *New Hampshire Gazette. Or, State Journal and General Advertiser* [Exeter], 18 Aug. 1778).

## General Orders

                      Head-Quarters White-Plains sunday Septr 6th 78.
Parole Narragansett—                C. Signs Newtown—Nottingham.
    The General Court-Martial whereof Majr Genl Lincoln is President stands adjourned to the New-Din[in]g room.
    The Court whereof Coll Humpton is President will meet at the President's quarters.

Varick transcript, DLC:GW. In the artillery brigade orderly book, these appear as "Genl After Orders," along with an additional sentence: "The Auditors office is kept at Mr. Treddels in purchase Street, enquire at the pay Master Genls" (NHi). Other orderly books, such as that of Maj. Gen. Benjamin Lincoln, have only the routine detachment orders on this date (MHi: Lincoln Papers).

## To Major General William Heath

Dear Sir                  Head Quarters White plains 6th Sepr 1778
    I have been favd with yours of the 26th and 30th August, and 1st and 2d instants. I am glad to find that your sentiments, respecting the reception that ought to be given to the Count D'Estaing and his Officers, corresponded with mine, and that you had taken proper Steps to prepare for refitting his fleet, previous to the receipt of my letter[1]—As the Rhode Island expedition is now at an end, I can see no objection to Mr Commissary Clarkes going thither, and if he should have occasion to go from thence to New York to settle his accounts and procure Money, he may do it without any disadvantage to us.
    I do not know what device Genl patterson will chuse to have upon his Colours. I will speak to him and desire him to inform you.[2]
    The fleet that has appeared off Boston, consists only of Men of War, and I imagine is intended to block up the Count. I have just recd a letter from New London, which informs me, that about fifty sail of transports, with troops on Board, appeared off that Harbour, bound Westward.[3] Whether they are only bringing back the late Reinforcement, or have withdrawn the Garrison of Newport intirely I do not yet know: But at any rate, it serves to evince, that they have no intent against Boston by land. It will however be prudent to man all the Batteries to aid and protect the Counts Fleet against a superior British Squadron.

September 1778

A Company of Artificers at Springfeild will apply for a suit of Cloaths each, part of their annual Bounty. They were inlisted upon those terms, and you will therefore be pleased to give orders to the Cloathier to supply them. I am Dear Sir Your most obt Servt

Go: Washington

LS, in Tench Tilghman's writing, MHi: Heath Papers; Df, DLC:GW; Varick transcript, DLC:GW.

1. GW was referring to his letter to Heath of 28 August.

2. On 17 Sept., Maj. Tobias Fernald wrote Heath at the request of Brig. Gen. John Paterson, sending "the Devices for the Standard of each Battalion in his Brigade" (MHi: Heath Papers).

3. See Jabez Huntington to GW, 4 September.

## To Major General Jabez Huntington

Sir,                              Head Quarters [White Plains] Septr 6th 1778

I had the pleasure of your letter of the 4th Instant.

It is probable the Fleet you mention is part of the one which passed through the Sound some time ago, for the relief of Rhode Island, now on its return to new York. But if any thing serious is designed in your quarter, it must soon be determined. I thank you for the early information—and am Sir Yr Most Obet Servt

Go: Washington

LS, in Richard Kidder Meade's writing, InU: U.S. History Mss; Df, DLC:GW; Varick transcript, DLC:GW.

*Letter not found*: from Richard Henry Lee, 6 Sept. 1778. On 23 Sept., GW wrote Lee: "Your favor of the 6th Instt did not get to my hands till the 18th."

*Letter not found*: from officers of the 2nd Maryland Brigade, 6 Sept. 1778. On 7 Sept., GW wrote the officers: "I was just now favd with your letter of yesterday."

## From Brigadier General Charles Scott

Sir                              [Westchester County, N.Y.] 6th Sept. 1778

Capt. Croghan Waits on Your Excellency for the Hard Money.

nothing extraordinary this morning. I am Your Excellencys Obt Servt

Chs Scott

ALS, DLC:GW. Below Scott's signature, GW wrote out a receipt, which was signed by Capt. William Croghan: "Septr 6th 1778. Then received Twenty five Guineas of

Geo. Washington to be delivered to Brigr Genl Scott." According to GW's expense account, the money was sent to Scott "to enable him to engage some of the Inhabitants betwn him and the Enemy to watch their Movements & apprize him of them to pre[ve]nt surprizes" (DLC:GW, ser. 5, vol. 22). For discussion of Scott's expenditure of the money, see his letter to GW of 23 September. On 25 Sept., Scott was given an additional 25 guineas "for the like purposes," and he was sent another 25 guineas on 22 Oct. (GW's Revolutionary War expense account, DLC:GW, ser. 5, vol. 22).

*Letter not found*: from Maj. Gen. John Sullivan, 6 Sept. 1778. On 9 Sept., GW wrote Sullivan: "I am favd with yours of the 5th and 6th."

## To Jonathan Trumbull, Sr.

Dear Sir                      Head Quarters [White Plains] 6th Septemr—1778
     I had the satisfaction of your two favors, both of the 27th ulto.

     The Battalions of Colo. Enos [&] McClellan, I am informed by Colonel Malcom,[1] who commands where they were stationed, were to be discharged, and I suppose they are now on their way home.

     The violent gale which dissipated the two Fleets when on the point of engaging, and the withdrawing of the Count D'Estaing to Boston, may appear to us as real misfortunes—but with you I consider storms and victory under the direction of a wise providence, who, no doubt, directs them for the best of purposes, and to bring round the greatest degree of happiness to the greatest number of his people.

     I feel with you for the unfortunate Frontiers exposed to all the inroads of an Enemy, whose natural barbarity in War, has been encreased by the Arts & influence of a civilized nation. I had early ordered for the defence of the Inhabitants Colonel Hartley's Regiment—Colo. Butler's—Colo. Olden's, with the remains of Morgan's Rifle Corps[2]—These, I believe, have been of considerable service—but I am unhappy in not having it in my power to afford them at present, a more compleat and sufficient security, from this Army, for the purpose you mention of carrying the War into the Enemy's Country—It is of the utmost importance to maintain the force now in the Field, and even to encrease it as far as possible. However, as soon as circumstances will admit of putting a more comprehensive plan into execution, I shall be ready to give it all kind of furtherance in my power. I am, Dear Sir your most Obedient Servant

G. Washington

LB, Ct: Trumbull Papers; Df, DLC:GW; Varick transcript, DLC:GW.
     1. GW may be referring to Col. William Malcom's letter to him of 30 August. On the draft, James McHenry finished this sentence with the words "who commands at West pt were in readiness to return before the receipt of your letter; and I suppose they are now on their way home."

2. For GW's orders to Lt. Col. William Butler's 4th Pennsylvania Regiment and Morgan's Rifle Corps, see GW to Brig. Gen. John Stark, 18 July, and note 1. Also in July, Col. Thomas Hartley's Additional Continental Regiment had been ordered to the frontier by the Board of War (see Benedict Arnold to GW, 30 July, and note 1). Col. Ichabod Alden's 7th Massachusetts Regiment had been ordered to the frontier by Stark earlier in July (see Horatio Gates to GW, 13 July, and note 3).

*Letter not found*: from Philip Van Rensselaer, c.6 Sept. 1778. On 14 Sept., Horatio Gates wrote Van Rensselaer: "I thank you for your obliging letter by Quin. . . . Your letter to the General, and that to the Board of War, with the Return, were immediately forwarded to Head-Quarters" (Van Rensselaer, *Annals of the Van Rensselaers*, 184). Van Rensselaer's letter to Gates carried by James Quinn was dated 6 Sept. (NHi: Gates Papers).

## To Nicholas Way

sir                                                  White Plains Septr 6: 1778

In the Brig. Symmetry, taken in the course of the last Winter at Wilmington, there were several Medical manuscripts, belonging to a Mr Boyce, Surgeon of the 15th British Regiment—For these Mr Boyce applied to me and obtained my promise that they should be returned.[1] I am now much concerned to find, that after so much time has elapsed— and after his politeness, in consenting that they might be copied, that they have not been sent him and that there are some difficulties made against doing it. I am told the Manuscripts are at present in your hands; If it is the case, Sir, I must request the favor of you to transmit 'em either to me or to General Smallwood by the first safe conveyance, that they may be sent to New York by a flag. I am sir Yr Most Obedt servt

Go: Washington

Df, in the writing of Robert Hanson Harrison, DLC:GW; Varick transcript, DLC:GW.

1. For the capture of the *Symmetry*, see William Smallwood to GW, 30 Dec. 1777, and note 3; for discussion of the medical manuscripts of Robert Boyes, see GW to Smallwood, 23 Jan. 1778, and note 4.

## General Orders

Head-Quarters White-Plains Monday Septr 7th 1778.
Parole Halesworth—                          C. Signs Harlow Heden.

For the present and until the Circumstances of the Army will admit of a more perfect Arrangement it is to be divided and commanded as follows, viz. Woodford's, Muhlenberg's and Scott's Brigades by Major General Putnam—Poor's, Late Larned's & Paterson's by Major General Gates; Wayne's, 2nd Pennsylvania and Clintons by Major General Lord

Stirling. Parsons's and Huntington's Brigades by Major General Lincoln—Smallwood's and 2nd Maryland by Major General Baron De Kalb—Nixon's & North-Carolina by Major General McDougall.

The Commanding Officers of Brigades are to call for exact returns of the number of Waggons appropriated thereto respectively, and with the Quarter Master General or his Assistants see that each Regiment has its due proportion agreeable to former Regulation in this matter— If any Corps is incumbered with heavy baggage it is to be immediately removed. The board of Officers ordered to determine the claims between Lieutt Coll Brent & Ellison to command in the 1st Virginia State Regiment, are of Opinion that Lieutt Coll Brent resume his former Command in the same.[1]

Varick transcript, DLC:GW.
  1. For the order to the board, see General Orders, 29 August.

*Letter not found*: from the Board of War, 7 Sept. 1778. On 14 Sept., GW wrote the board: "On sunday night I had the honor to receive your favors of the 5th & 7th Instant."

## From George Clinton

Dear Sir,                              Poughkeepsie [N.Y.] 7th Sep'r 1778.
  I have received your Excellency's Letters of the 27th of last Month & 1st Instant.[1] I am greatly concerned for the Unhappy Fate of Van Tassel, who I am informed always maintained a good Charecter & his Familly have afforded many Proofs of their Attachment to the Cause of their Country in which some of them have been great Sufferers. At the same Time as Capt. Colson has already Quit the Army Until It can be discovered to what Place he is gone I think it will be most prudent to make as little stir about the Matter as possible. When this is the Case, if your Excellency's aid in securing him shall be necessary, I will take the Liberty of asking it. In the mean Time your Excellency will please to accept my warmest acknowledgments for the Regard you have paid to the Rights of the Civil Authority.

  Before Mr. Smith left the Country, he applied to me concerning his Male Servants, which the Commissioners did not conceive themselves authorized to permit him to take with him as they might be imployed to fight against their Country. The Slaves he might have sold if he had pleased. The white Servants he mentions in his Letter to your Excellency, tho they are hardy Scotch Hierlings in whom he has no Property, yet I promised to send them into him in Exchange for any Two subjects of this State in the Power of the Enemy which he shoud procure to be sent out for that Purpose. This being the Case I cant help thinking Mr. Smith's Letter to your Excellency complaining of Injustice in the Commissioners as well as his Request of having his Servants sent into him not only exceptionable but very unjust & unreasonable. I am with the highest Respect Your Excellency's Most Obed't Serv't

G.C.

*Public Papers of George Clinton*, 4:6–7.
1. No letter from GW to Clinton of 27 Aug. has been found; this is probably a reference to GW's letter of 21 Aug., which forwarded the complaints of William Smith (see GW to Smith, 21 Aug., n.2).

## To Henry Laurens

sir.                                        Head Qrs White plains Sept. 7th 1778

I take the liberty of laying before Congress the inclosed Copies of a paragraph and Schedule, contained in a Letter from General Heath, which I lately received.[1] These will apprize Congress, if they are not already informed, of the supplies of provision and wood wanted by the Count D'Estaing; and will naturally lead to a consideration of the ways and means to be pursued for furnishing them, as soon as possible.

Since I had the honor of addressing you on the 4th and 5th Instant, I have obtained a Return of the Blankets which are now deficient.[2] This and the fast approach of the Fall will suggest, the necessity of the most vigorous exertions being used to procure 'em. Not a night will pass from this time, without the Soldiers feeling the want. I have the Honor to be with the greatest respect & esteem sir Your Most Obedt servant

Go: Washington

LS, in Robert Hanson Harrison's writing, DNA:PCC, item 152; Df, DLC:GW; copy, DNA:PCC, item 169; Varick transcript, DLC:GW. Congress read this letter on 10 Sept. and referred it to the Board of War (see *JCC*, 12:896).
1. The enclosure consisted of the last paragraph and schedule of provisions from Maj. Gen. William Heath's letter to GW of 30 August.
2. The "Return of Blankets, wanting in the several Brigades at White Plains," dated 6 Sept. and signed by Adj. Gen. Alexander Scammell, reported 11,067 blankets needed (DNA:PCC, item 152).

## To Colonel William Malcom

Sir,                                        [White Plains, 7 September 1778][1]

Brigadier General Du Portail Chief Engineer is by my orders on a visit to the posts in the Highlands, to examine into the state of the fortifications carrying on there. It is my wish that Col: Koshiosko may comminicate every thing to this Gentleman, who is at the Head of the department, which he may find requisite for the purpose he is sent upon. I am persuaded you will show him every proper attention. I am Sir Yr Most Obedt ser.

Df, in Alexander Hamilton's writing, DLC:GW; Varick transcript, DLC:GW.
  1. The date is based on the Varick docket, which is consistent with Malcom's letter to GW of 10 September.

*Letter not found*: from Capt. Edward Norwood, 7 Sept. 1778. On 7 Sept., GW wrote Norwood: "Your favor of this date has been duly received."

## To Captain Edward Norwood

sir                     Head Qrs [White Plains] Septr 7th 1778
  Your favor of this date has been duly received.[1]
  I have already given my reasons in General Orders, for disapproving the proceedings of the Court Martial in your case, and therefore I need not repeat them.[2] I will only observe that they appeared to me, to be contrary to precedent and common usage—and totally irregular and incompleat. Under this persuasion I could not but continue your arrest. The matters in charge against you had never been tried.
  With respect to any reflection on myself I believe you never intended One and I am concerned that my name is mentioned in any of the charges. This circumstance however has not, nor will it have I assure you, the least possible influence on my Judgement in deciding on your case. You will be tried by a Constitutional and General Court Martial— the One now sitting—and I doubt not agreable to the Articles of War and the customs of the Army.[3] I am sorry your arrest has been of such long continuance; but it has been occasioned in a great measure, by the New and peculiar difficulties that have occurred in the course of the proceedings under It. I am sir Yr Most Obedt servt
                                        Go: Washington

Df, in the writing of Robert Hanson Harrison, DLC:GW; Varick transcript, DLC:GW.
  1. Norwood's letter of 7 Sept. has not been found.
  2. See General Orders, 4 September.
  3. For the verdict of this court-martial, see General Orders, 29 September.

## To Officers of the Second Maryland Brigade

Gentlemen              Head Quarters [White Plains] 7th Sepr 1778
  I was just now favd with your letter of yesterday.[1]
  Tho' I would willingly grant a request coming from so respectable a number of Officers, yet in the instance of your present application, I

cannot do it, without incurring a charge of impropriety, and staying the course of Justice. Captain Norwood has been arrested by General Smallwood for an injury done his character—He has pursued the constitutional mode of redress—the matter has never been tried—nor the prosecution relinquished by the party. I am sorry that he should have been longer in arrest than what is customary, but it has proceeded from the new and peculiar difficulties that have occurred in his Case.[2] I am Gentlemen with great Respect and Esteem Your most obt Servt

Go: Washington

LS, in Tench Tilghman's writing, PHi: Dreer Collection; Df, DLC:GW; Varick transcript, DLC:GW.

1. This letter has not been found.

2. At this point on the draft, Robert Hanson Harrison wrote and crossed out a sentence reading: "I have not the smallest enmity or charge against him, and as far as my Judgement directs me, he shall have equal & ⟨strict justice⟩."

## To Charles Pettit

Sir                              Head Quarters White plains 7th Sept. 1778

I imagine you must stand in need of assistance in your Office at this time, by reason of Genl Greens absence, and Mr Ternant and Maj: Forsyth's having left the department. I therefore think it adviseable and expedient that Colo. Hay should be immediately called down from the Highlands, more especially as it is probable that the Army may be under the necessity of changing its present position in a short time. Genl Gates informs me that there is also a Major Chattinet, a deputy Quarter Master at Fort Arnold, who is remarkably active, especially in the Waggon department, and as he can be spared from that post, be pleased to order him down likewise.[1]

If the Enemy continue in New York this Winter, we shall be obliged to quarter a considerable Force at and in the vicinity of the Highland posts. I would therefore have you immediately contract for a quantity of Boards, Plank, Scantlin and Nails for the purpose of building Barracks. As I cannot ascertain the number of men that will be stationed there, I cannot say precisely what quantity of materials will be necessary; but I beleive you need not be afraid of over doing the matter, as they will always be useful for other purposes—Colo. Biddle should be advised in time of the probability of a considerable post's being established in the Highlands this Winter, that he may form his Magazines of Forage contiguous to them. He should also be desired to draw his Forage from between the present encampment and the Enemy, that we may leave the Country as bare as possible, should we remove[2]—no time shd be lost in doing this.

I shall, in the orders of this day, direct the Brigadiers to call for exact returns of the Waggons in their Brigades, and allot them to the Regiments in proportion to their numbers. I am apt to beleive that there will be upon the whole a deficiency of Waggons for Baggage, and I would therefore wish you to be endeavouring to procure a supply for them. In a word I would wish you to have your whole department so arranged that the whole Army may move at the shortest notice[3]—it will not be advisable to keep more Stores in your line at this Post than what are absolutely necessary for immediate use. I am &ca.

Df, in Tench Tilghman's writing, DLC:GW; Varick transcript, DLC:GW.

1. Francis Chandonet (1752–1810) was commissioned an ensign in the 1st New Hampshire Regiment in November 1776 and remained on the rolls of that regiment until at least April 1778, but from September 1777 to April 1778 he was on command at Albany, acting as a subordinate to Deputy Quartermaster General Udny Hay, and he likely commenced service as a quartermaster as early as July 1777. When precisely he was ordered to West Point has not been determined. Chandonet continued to work with Hay into 1781.

2. The remainder of this paragraph is in GW's writing.

3. From here to the closing, the writing is GW's.

*Letter not found*: from Brig. Gen. John Stark, 7 Sept. 1778. On 8 Oct., GW wrote Stark: "I have been favd with yours of the 31st Augt and 7th 15th and 28th Septemr."

## General Orders

Head-Quarters W. Plains Tuesday Septr 8th 1778.
Parole Oakingham—                    C. Signs Orton Onslow.

The Colonels and Commanding Officers of Corps are to cause Company rolls to be made out with all possible expedition, comprehending the names of their men actually in the Field, on Command and in hospitals and particularly noting the time for which they are engaged to serve—These rolls are to be regimentally bound up and delivered to the Brigadiers or officers commanding Brigades who are to transmit them to Head-Quarters as soon as they have obtain'd full returns of their respective Commands.

The General expects that there will be the most pointed and expeditious compliance with this order.

His Excellency the Commander in Chief is pleased to accept the following report of the Court of Enquiry whereof Coll Marshall was President.

It is the opinion of the Court that Lieutt Selden throughout the whole of his Conduct towards Commissionary Kean was uniform— That the Conversation relative to Sword and Pistol did not amo[u]nt to a Challenge; And as the Commissary was indulged to stay in the same Apartment with the Officer of the Guard or to go any where within his sentries that there appears nothing unjustifiable in the Conduct of Lieutt Seldon. Likewise by consent of Coll Davis & Doctor Brown it is published, "That the Muster in which the Doctor was mentioned as superceded was founded upon a mistaken Supposition of Facts, and that he was not actually superceded."

Varick transcript, DLC:GW.

## From Vice Admiral d'Estaing

Sir—                                            [Boston Road] The 8th Septem. 1778.

The Letter which Colo. Laurens was pleased to take charge of for Your Excellency contains the expression of my acknowledgements for the Letter which M. De Choin announced to me, and which was delivered to me the evening of the same day.[1] I hastened to give an anticipated answer to it, for we are generally eager to speak, what we sensibly feel—The Extract of Major Howels Journal, by coming to me duplicate, has but too well confirmed the report made by three of my ships, of the Arrival of Admiral Byrons Squadron.

This Deposition and the certainty of Genl Sullivans Army being reduced to Six thousand men including a Majority of Militia—by the departure of three thousand while I was employed in pursuing Lord Howe—will doubtless appear to you the principal reasons for a conduct, the melancholy motives of which I have already amply explained.

It was impossible to disarm Vessels while it was required of them to repulse or attack General Howes Squadron—It was still less so when it was reinforced by the arrival of Byrons fleet, and the enemys naval force acquired by that event, so considerable a degree of Superiority— It was not less difficult to persuade oneself that Six thousand men well intrenched—and with a fort before which trenches had been opened—could be carried in four and twenty hours or in two days— the bravery with which your troops effected a retreat, the Victory which they gained over superior numbers in the open field—have acquired them new Glory—the merit of the matter is established, by taking the number of men for granted[2]—Your Excellency is doubtless instructed as to this point: you have the means of judging of the possibilities and estimating whether the military calculations have been grounded on false principles—their object ought to be, not to sacrifice the Kings Squadron but when it can be attended with evident utility to Allies who are so dear to him.

You have just proved Sir, that this is your way of thinking—in sending me a detail of the naval reinforcement which has been discovered at New York.

Upon the kind and number of Ships—their condition—their compact or detached State—the insight which may be gained of their designs—will depend our offensive or defensive plans—it appears to me therefore that good Spies must be the basis of all—permit me incessantly to repeat my sollicitations, and offers of money to gain this important end.

The Uncertainty in which we are respecting the measures of the British—after the atrocious destruction of Bedford[3]—makes me doubt whether this Letter will reach you soon—Lt Colonel Fleury who is so kind as to take charge of it, will perhaps be detained by the hopes of giving new proofs of his zeal courage and talents—To fight the enemy is the only circumstance, that can retard in this excellent officer what all those who serve under Your Excellency call their happiness—I mean the returning to increase the number of your Soldiers and admirers—M. de fleury, is if it can be possible, more penetrated with this Sentiment than any one—and I love him the more for it—It is General Sullivans part to inform you and testify all that I am told he did while he was second to Col. Laurens.[4] The accounts given me, made me form the project, when I thought of recommencing the Young Man, & the Colonel, of emulating these Gentlemen, or rather of following their example. Permit me particularly to recommend to your kindness Mr de fleury; he is a useful frenchmen—and when occasion offers I should be very happy to serve with him—and he is calculated for establishing that union between individuals which subsists between our Nations. I have the honor to be &c.

Translation, in John Laurens's writing, DLC:GW; LS (in French), DLC:GW; Df (in French), FrPNA: Marine, B4, I46; copy (in French), FrPNA: Marine, B4, I46; copy (extract, in French), FrPBN. The extract commences with the reference to Howell's journal and ends with the text translated as "You have just proved Sir, that this is your way of thinking."

1. D'Estaing was referring to his letter to GW of 5 Sept. and GW's letter to him of 2 September.

2. The preceding fifteen words are a translation of the French "C'est en faire sentir tout Le prix, que de convenir du veritable nombre des soldats."

3. D'Estaing was referring to a raid of New Bedford and Fairhaven, Mass., by British troops led by Gen. Charles Grey on 5 and 6 September. Grey's account of the action, "Published by Authority" in the *Royal Gazette* (New York), 12 Sept., says that on the evening of 5 Sept. he "arrived off Dartmouth river in Buzzard's-Bay. The troops were landed immediately, and proceeded to the town of Bedford, where they destroyed several vessels, and many rich stores, without opposition. They then proceeded to the mills above the town, where they burnt a considerable

number of vessels; and having crossed the river, demolished all the stores at Fair-Haven; the Rebels having abandoned their Fort near this last town, a party was detached to it, who destroyed eleven pieces of cannon, and blew up the magazine. The troops then proceeded to Sconticut Neck, where they were re-imbarked by 12 o'clock on the 6th, having had only six men wounded by some random shots which were fired by a few stragglers at a great distance. Above seventy sail of vessels, among which were some privateers, were destroyed in this expedition" (see also Grey to Clinton, 6 Sept., and Grey to Clinton, 18 Sept., with a return of vessels and stores destroyed, P.R.O., Colonial Office, 5/96, Military Correspondence of the British Generals; André, *Journal*, 88–90, 94–96; Gruber, *Peebles' American War*, 215–16). The perspective of the American defenders is given in a letter published in the *Independent Ledger, and the American Advertiser* (Boston), 14 Sept., from an officer of Col. Thomas Crafts's regiment stationed at Bedford. News of the fleet's arrival reached him at 3 P.M. on 5 September. "The fleet consisting of 47 sail, anchored in the harbour, landed their troops, who were advancing upon me with the greatest rapidity." The officer, "having but fifteen men," could only retreat, with losses among those who attempted to bring off baggage and provisions and keep watch on the enemy's movements. Another account in the *Boston-Gazette, and Country Journal*, 14 Sept., reported that "by sunset all the warehouses, and many dwelling-houses there, were in flames, and the rest plundered. About one half of the whole, with their contents, is burnt, together with all the shipping in the harbour, except a few vessels at some distance up. . . . they then marched by moon light, up to the head of the river, about four miles; and thence down on the east side, to Fair-Haven . . . plundering the houses, and burning many of them as they went." A briefer report, widely reprinted, appeared in the *Continental Journal, and Weekly Advertiser* (Boston), 10 September.

4. D'Estaing was referring to Fleury's part in the engagement of 29 Aug. at Rhode Island.

# From Vice Admiral d'Estaing

Sir                                          Boston Road 8th Septem. 1778.

I receive the Letter which Your Excellency did me the honor to write the 3d of this month—and the New York paper which you deigned to annex to it—as I presume that Lieut. Col. Fleury is not gone, I endeavour to avail myself of this opportunity to add new thanks to those which I entreated you to accept the homage of this morning.

The Division of Six Ships under Rear Admiral Parker appears to me to be the strongest half of the Squadron announced under Admiral Byrons orders—the rest may have joined Admiral Howe at Sea, or perhaps is not yet arrived—or perhaps these five other Ships may have been destined for the Southern States, or the Windward or Leeward Islands. I hope the goodness of Your Excellency will assist me constantly, in throwing light upon facts which are to influence our measures—mine will always have for their ruling principle whatever you shall esteem most useful to the General Good—One of the greatest happiness in all circumstances is that of obtaining the opinion of those we revere.

I have the honor to be respectfully Your Excellencys—most obedt & most hble Servt.

Translation, in John Laurens's writing, DLC:GW; LS (in French), DLC:GW; Df (in French), FrPNA: Marine, B4, I46; copy (in French), FrPNA: Marine, B4, I46. The LS was docketed in part, "Recd 12th & acknowledged."

## From Brigadier General Charles Scott

Sir                        [Westchester County, N.Y.] 8th Sept. 1778
   I am unhappy to inform You that the Enemy had returnd before our partie was able to Reach them, Be assurd that every exertion was made To intercept them, the attention of our partie was so Taken up with the two Columns on Wards & Volentons Roads that it was impossable to git intelligence of That partie sooner than we did, they had passed by East Chester near two Hour before our partie got There, they had with them Five of Colo. Sheldons And about Twenty Continental Horses the inhabitance Say that they had som horsmen Prisoners about 4 or 5. their partie Consisted of about one Hundred Horse and the Same number of foot They passed up through the fields without Touching On any Road. But returnd Boldly along the road Through East Chester.[1] I am Your Excellencys obt Servt

                                                      Chs Scott

ALS, DLC:GW.
   1. GW's aide-de-camp Alexander Hamilton wrote Maj. Gen. Horatio Gates on this date: "His Excellency desires me to inform you that having received information of the enemy's being out advanced this side of Wards House, He thought it prudent to put the troops quietly under arms and has sent orders to the several Brigades for this purpose" (NHi: Gates Papers). Sgt. Maj. Benjamin Gilbert of the 5th Massachusetts Regiment recorded in his diary for 8 Sept.: "In the morning the Reglars Came out of York in four Collums and Allarmd the whole Camp. Colo. Greatons Regt Sat off to meet them and a Regt. from Each Bgd but they went Back into York again" (Symmes, *Gilbert Diary*, 36; see also "Vaughan Journal," 110; Baldwin, *Revolutionary Journal*, 134). The Hessian staff officer Carl Leopold Baurmeister recorded in his dispatch of 13 Sept. that "Colonel Simcoe, chief of the Queen's Rangers, and Emmerich's and Lord Cathcart's light troops patrolled from late in the night of the 7th to the 8th of this month. Simcoe went to Mamaroneck and New Rochelle and on his return passed close to the left wing of the enemy light infantry under General Scott in the vicinity of Valentine's Hill, where he captured one corporal, five dragoons, and a commissary. General Scott's report so stirred the entire camp at White Plains that the men took down their tents and packed their baggage, and Washington reinforced all outposts with artillery" (Baurmeister, *Revolution in America*, 212). The *New-York Gazette: and the Weekly Mercury*, 14 Sept., reported that the troops captured "two Commissaries of Forage, with 6 Light Dragoons, and sundry Horses."

*Letter not found*: from Capt. Thomas Young Seymour, c.8 Sept. 1778. Seymour wrote GW on 9 Sept.: "The two Ships mentioned in my last, to have come to anchor, close under Long-Island shore, passed City Island early this morning, and stood for New york."

## General Orders

Head-Quarters White-Plains Wednesday Septr 9th 1778.
Parole Glastenbury—                    C. Signs Graves-end. Grantham.
The following resolutions of the Committee of Arrangement respecting rank in the Army are published at their Request.

The Committee of Arrangement after mature Consideration of the many disputes of rank, subsisting in the Army of the United-States have agreed to the following resolutions founded upon a report made by a board of General Officers of the whole line (vizt).[1]

1st—That the relative rank in the Continental Line of the Army between all Colonels and Inferior Officers of different States, between like Officers of Infantry and those of horse and Artillery appointed under the Authority of Congress by Virtue of a resolution of the 16th of September *1776*,[2] or by Virtue of any subsequent Resolution, prior to the 1st of January 1777—shall be deemed to have their Commissions dated on the day last mentioned, and their relative rank with respect to each other in the Continental line of the Army shall be determined from their rank prior to the 16th of September 1776.

This rule shall not be considered to affect the rank of the Line within any State or within the Corps of Artillery, Horse, or among the sixteen Additional Battalions where the rank hath been or shall be settled; but as there is a difficulty in settling the rank of the Line of Artillery by reason of the peculiar Circumstances attending some Appointments in that Corps—it is recommended that the general rule now to be established for the great line of the Army should be the rule to determine the relative rank within the particular line of Artillery so far as their rank remains unsettled.

2ndly—That in determining rank between Officers of different States previous to the 16th of September 1776. preference should be given in the first instance to Continental Commissions, and to State Commissions of those Corps which have been incorporated into the Continental Army, the latter being considered as Continental from the time of their entering the Continental service: That in the second instance Preference shall be given to Commissions in the New-Levies and Flying Camp—That in the third Place Commissions in Militia be considered where they have served in the Continental Army for the space of one Month at least.

3rd—That all Colonels and Inferior-Officers appointed to vacancies since the 5th of January 1777—shall take rank from their Right in Succession to such Vacancies.

4th—That in all Cases where the rank between two Officers of different States is equal, or between an Officer of State Troops and one of Cavalry, Artillery or the Additional Battalions, their Seniority is to be determined by Lot.

5th That a resignation entirely precludes any Claim of benefit from former rank, under a new appointment.

6th—Adjutants, Pay Masters and Quarter Masters taken from the line shall be again admitted into it in the rank they would have been entitled to had they continued in the Line, and such Adjutants, Pay Masters & Quarter Masters not taken from the Line may be admitted into the line in such Subaltern Ranks as by a signed Certificate from the Field Officers of their respective Corps they shall be deemed competent to.[3]

7th—The rules above laid down for the determination of rank between Officers of different States are to govern between Officers of the same State unless where a rule has been laid down by the State or rank already settled, in which Case it is not the Intention of the Committee to interfere.

Signed in behalf of the Committee of Arrangement

Jos[ep]h Reed Chairmain

At a General Court Martial August 31st 1778, Coll Humpton President, Adjutant Verrier of Coll Patten's Regiment was tried for—"Cruelly & unnecessarily beating the Fife-Major of the same Regiment while in the execution of his duty"—The Court are of opinion that Adjutant Verrier is guilty of beating the Fife Major unnecessarily but not cruelly and sentence him to be reprimanded by the Commanding Officer of the Brigade to which he belongs in presence of the Officers of the Brigade.[4]

The Commander in Chief approves the sentence and orders it to take place tomorrow morning.

At the same Court Samuel Bond Assistant Waggon Master was tried for 1st "Picking a Lock; breaking into a public store and taking from thence rum and Candles" which he appropriated to his own use, found guilty of the charges exhibited against him and sentenced to receive fifty lashes and to return to the Regiment from which he was taken. The General remits the stripes & orders said Bond to return to the Regiment from which he was taken.

The Commander in Chief is pleased to confirm the following Opinions of a Division General Court Martial whereof Lieutt Colonel Miller was President held in the Pennsylvania Line August the 30th 1778. Lieutenant McFarlin of the 1st Pennsylvania Regiment tried for unmercifully beating James Welch—soldier of the 7th Pennsylvania Regiment without Provocation.[5]

The Court are unanimously of opinion that Lieutt McFarlin did not unmercifully beat James Welch and that he had sufficient Provocation to strike him The Court therefore acquit him of the Charges.

At the same Court by Adjournment Septr 4th Mr Allen Quarter-Master to the 2nd Pennsylvania Brigade was tried for Disobedience of General Orders and neglect of duty to the Detriment of the Service and endangering the health of the Officers and Men—The Court are unanimously of Opinion that Mr Allen is not guilty and acquit him of the Charges.

Varick transcript, DLC:GW.

1. The report of the board of general officers, dated 7 Sept. and signed by generals Horatio Gates, Johann Kalb, Alexander McDougall, Samuel Holden Parsons, William Smallwood, Henry Knox, Enoch Poor, John Paterson, William Woodford, and Jedediah Huntington, gives the first five rules stated below. The board made one recommendation that does not appear here: "To avoid Confusion & perplexity which have arose from Brevet Rank—it is earnestly recommended by the Board that no more Brevets be given except to Officers in the Line or in Cases of very eminent Services" (DLC:GW).

2. For Congress's resolution of 16 Sept. 1776, see *JCC*, 5:762–63.

3. After receiving the board's initial report, the committee on 7 Sept. asked the board to determine "What Rank in the Line shall now be given to Officers of the Staff who have had Rank annexed to their Offices by a Resolve of Congress as Paymasters &c.—and whether when such Rank is given it implys a Right to command according to that Rank in the Line of Succession in the Army of the United States," and received the preceding paragraph as their reply (DLC:GW).

4. James Verrier, who was appointed adjutant of the 5th North Carolina Regiment in October 1776, was commissioned an ensign in August 1777. At this time he ranked as an ensign and served as adjutant in Col. John Patten's 2d North Carolina Regiment, which he had probably joined in June 1778. The fife major of that regiment was Thomas Tiack (Tyack), who had enlisted for the war in June 1777.

5. James McFarlane (1751–1794) was commissioned a second lieutenant of the 1st Pennsylvania Regiment on 13 May 1777 and promoted to first lieutenant on 21 March 1778. He remained a lieutenant of that regiment until the end of the war, serving in 1783 as regimental quartermaster. A resident of Washington County, Pa., McFarlane joined in the Whiskey Rebellion and was killed during that insurrection. James Welch enlisted in the 7th Pennsylvania Regiment in February 1777 and remained a private in that regiment at least through October 1780.

*Letter not found*: from the Board of War, 9 Sept. 1778. On 19 Sept., GW wrote the Board of War: "I have been honoured with the Boards Letter of the 9th Inst." In a report of the Board of War to Congress on clothing, 5 Oct. 1778, they stated: "In a letter of the 9th [to GW] we suggested that the drafts were not intitled to new cloathing—that where necessity obliged us to clothe them, it might be done out of the old cloaths, which we proposed should be laid up on issuing the new." Elsewhere in the report, the board stated that they had written GW on 9 Sept. informing him of steps taken to clothe Col. George Baylor's dragoon regiment "and suggesting the expediency of supplying all the horse, wanting cloathing, in the same way" (DNA:PCC, item 147).

# To the Officer Commanding Militia at Hackensack New Bridge

Sir                 Head Quarters [White Plains] 9 Sept. 1778

Major Clough, who commands at Hackinsack, is under the necessity of sometimes allowing persons to carry small matters into New York, and to bring a few goods out, that he may the better obtain intelligence. The persons employed in that way are sometimes stopped by your guards, under suspicion that they are carrying on a contraband trade. You will therefore be pleased to give orders to your officers not to detain or molest any person shewing a pass from Major Clough. I am &c.

Df, in Tench Tilghman's writing, DLC:GW; Varick transcript, DLC:GW.

## To Charles Pettit

Sir                  Head Quarters [White Plains] 9th Sepr 1778

I have more reason for thinking that the Army will have occasion to remove from its present position shortly, than when I wrote to you two days ago. I therefore desire you will immediately send off all the supernumerary Stores of your department. I think it would save land carriage if they were transported by water above the posts in the Highlands, and removed from thence more inland, at leisure. The Ox teams you mentioned should be collected as quick as possible, as I mean to remove the sick, and all the spare stores of every department from this Ground. I am &c.

Df, in Tench Tilghman's writing, DLC:GW; Varick transcript, DLC:GW.

## From Brigadier General Charles Scott

Sir              [Westchester County, N.Y.] 9th Sept. 1778

I have the unhappiness to inform You that Desertion still prevails among my Corps, we Seldom Send a Detachment on the line, But we loose one or two. and last night Deserted From this Camp three Serjants and 29 privats of Colo. Grayhams Regt of Militia, whom I am much afraid has gon to the enemy. as three of them are taken up by one of my Picquets making that way, this togather with those Inlisted in the Waggon Department has reduced That Regement from a 171 to about thirty, but Fiew of them fit for Duty, indeed war they able to do duty I should be very unwilling to trust Them. this togather with the loss of Armands Corps will in Som measure Prevent my Covouring this Country as Well as I Could Wish, without Fatiguing the men Very much.

Since my Taking the Comd at this post I Have lost By Desertion Sickness & other ways Near three hundred men, the Guards indispensably Necessary as well for the Security of the Grand armey, as this Corps, leads me to wish they may be replaced, the loss of Armads horses Is sevearly felt. Since their departure we Have been obligd to furnish a Strong patroll on the Sawmill River & Albany Roads, but In order to ease the men I had Just posted majr Washington for that Purpose, whilst majr Lee would do the like Duty on the East Side of the Brunx. But had orders from the Adjutant Genl Last night for majr Washington to return to his Regt, if it is not Indispensably Necessary that he should do So, I should be proud he Could Stay if it was But a fiew days untill I could make some other Disposition. I am Your Excellencys Obt Servt

Chs Scott

ALS, DLC:GW. Scott's signed note on the cover reads: "Suffer the bearer to pass to Head Quarters."

GW's aide Richard Kidder Meade replied to Scott: "His Excy Commands me to acknowledge the receipt of your favor of this date & express his uneasiness at the frequent Desertions from your Corps—He however rests satisfied that you take the necessary steps to prevent it, & apprehend them when it happens—Agreeable to your request you have permission to detain Majr Washington some time longer, of this the Adjt Genl will have immediate notice, as also to replace the loss of your Original command by Detachments from the Line" (DLC:GW).

## From Captain Thomas Young Seymour

Rye Neck [N.Y.]

May it please your Excellency                      Sepr 9th 1778

The two Ships mentioned in my last, to have come to anchor, close under Long-Island shore, passed City Island early this morning, and stood for New york [1]—Sun an hour high this afternoon hove in sight a Large Fleet from the Eastward, which continued to increase till darkness prevented a further discovery—In the Morning, I hope to be able, to give your Excellency a more satisfactory account of the Matter—I am with due respect your Excellency's most Obedt Servt

Thos y. Seymour

ALS, DLC:GW.

1. Seymour's previous letter has not been found. The *Royal Gazette* (New York), 9 Sept., noted that "one of his Majesty's ships, with a fine new brigantine privateer of 20 guns and 87 men," arrived the previous night, "five days from Boston."

## To William Shippen, Jr.

Sir                      Head Quarters [White Plains] 9th Sepr 1778

It is more than probable, from some late maneuvres of the Enemy, that the Army will have occasion to move from its present position to the Eastward. I therefore desire that the most immediate measures may be fallen upon to remove the sick of the Army at least as far as Danbury.[1] The Hospital established at Bedford will for the above Reasons be too much exposed and should therefore be immediately removed also as far as Danbury. The Quarter Master General will, upon application, afford all the assistance in his power, towards procuring Waggons for the removal of the patients and Hospital Stores. I am.

Df, in Tench Tilghman's writing, DLC:GW; Varick transcript, DLC:GW.

1. A return of the sick in the army at White Plains for 7 Sept. gives a total of 1,458 men. A return of the sick and wounded in eastern department military hospitals for September and October shows 107 admitted at Bedford, N.Y., and 938 admitted at Danbury, Conn., with a note that seems to indicate that 435 of the Danbury admissions came from Bedford. The same return records 294 soldiers remaining at Danbury, none at Bedford (DNA: RG 93, Revolutionary War Rolls, 1775–1783).

## To Major General John Sullivan

Dear Sir                          Head Quarters White plains 9th Sepr 1778

I am favd with yours of the 5th and 6th[1] I hope the loss of the enemy mentioned in the former may prove true.

I cannot at present account for the intent of the landing at Bedford, if they mean to act seriously to the Eastward, I think it will occasion a removal of their whole force from New York. Many accounts from thence say that an evacuation is intended, but I cannot learn that they have yet made sufficient demonstrations to render the thing certain. I hope your next will give me such further information of the operations of the Enemy, as will serve [in] some measure to direct me as to what ought to be the disposition of this Army. I am &c.

Df, in Tench Tilghman's writing, DLC:GW; Varick transcript, DLC:GW.

1. Sullivan's letter to GW of 6 Sept. has not been found.

## General Orders

Head-Quarters W. Plains Thursday Septr 10th 1778.

Parole Palmyra—                          C. Signs Poland. Pittsfield.

The Committee of Arrangement having requested that a board of Officers may sit not connected with the Artillery to settle the rank and Precedence of the Colonels and the Seniority of the Regiments in that Line;[1] All the General Officers in Camp except Brigadier General Knox are to meet at 4 oClock tomorrow afternoon at the New-Dining Room for these Purposes where the Parties interested will attend.

The board will be furnished with such Resolutions upon the subject as the Commander in Chief is possessed of.

Varick transcript, DLC:GW.
1. See the Continental Congress Committee of Arrangement to GW, this date.

## From a Board of Officers

[White Plains, 10 September 1778]

At the request of His Excellency General Washington, we the Sub-scribers met to consider, and Report, upon the best ways, and means, for the Invasion, & possession of Canada. Camp—at White plains September the 10th 1778.

This Campaign is drawing to a close, and we have great reason to hope for a happy Issue thereof.

The union of Canada, on which depends a permanent peace with the Indians—The Advantages resulting from their Trade—The security of our Frontiers—and the evasion of the extended limits of Canada by the late Quebec Bill,[1] will, we hope, in due time, have its full weight in the great scale of politicks.

The taking possession of the upper part of Canada, would give the Canadian⟨s⟩ an Opportunity to unite, join the American Arms, and assist in expelling the British Tyrants from that Country; the easy Communications to which, are strongly barred by a powerfull Navigation in the possession of the Enemy, on Lakes Champlain, and Ontario—Yet, there are other Communications, which are scarcely known in that Country, and by few in any of the United States of America. From Newbury at Co'os, to St Johns in Canada, is not more than Ninety Miles: From Newbury, to the Settlements on Masca River in Canada, is about the same distance—And from the said Settlements on the River Masca, to St Dinnes on the Sorrel River, the heart of Canada, and the very Grainery of that Country, is only Nine Miles.[2] From the Settlements on the upper part of Connecticut River, (Seventy five Miles above Newbury,) to St Francois on the River St Laurence, is only Seventy five miles. St Dinnes is forty two miles from St John's, and St Francois is about seventy. Either of these three Routs are practicable, and may be opened for a Wheel Carriage with five Hundred good men, in One Month, at a proper season of the Year.

The next thing to be considered, is the force necessary to send on such an expedition, and the means of subsisting an Army on their march, as well as in Canada, and the proper season of the Year to undertake such an expedition. To which we answer, that the force necessary, will depend on that of the Enemy now in Arms in Canada; which is pretty well ascertained; tho' great care should be taken, to obtain *certain* Intelligence respecting that, as well as to know if any Reinforcements are expected.

Should no Reinforcements be sent into that Country, a Winter's Expedition may be practicable, prudent, and attended with great Success. On the other hand, should a strong Reinforcement be sent into Canada this season, it might render a winter's expedition into that Country imprudent; and if attempted, unsuccessfull—The Month of January will be the proper time for a winter's Expedition, as the Snow is not then so deep, or difficult to break through. The Month of July, or August, is the time to Cross the woods in the Summer; in that Season, any body of men whatever, may be thrown, by either of these Routs, into Canada: and whether by a Winter, or Summer's Campaign, Beef must carry itself, and the Oxen may in the Winter be Yoked in Sleighs, and Loaded with Stores. A small quantity of Flour may be transported across the Woods, in Sleighs, Waggons, or on pack Horses: It is presumed that Canada will be able to furnish an Ample Supply of Bread.

The Settlements on Connecticut River, abounds in plenty of Provissions of every kind: The transportation by water, from Hartford to Newbury, is not difficult for Batteaus, or other small Boats—the distance is about 190 Miles, in which are short carrying places. It would however be a great saving, to lay in magazines of Provissions, and Forage, at Newbury; which ought to be purchased up Immediately.

The Settlements on the Connecticut River, from No. 4 upwards,[3] are able to furnish from Ten to Twenty Thousand Bushells Wheat—and to lay up at least Two Thousands Barrels Salt provissions. Newbury can furnish the greatest part of this quantity, with at least Three Hundred Tons of Hay, and Five Thousands Bushells Oats. If the Wheat is not purchased up immediately, it will be taken, as usual, for the markets of Boston, Salem, newbury port, & Portsmouth: The Hay & Oats will be expended, or Stock retained by the Inhabitants, for that purpose, and the other provissions, will be Drove elsewhere to market. All which is most respectfully Submitted to Your Excellency, by

> Horatio Gates Major General
> Jacob Bayley Brigadier General
> Moses Hazen Col:

DS, in Horatio Gates's writing, DLC:GW; copy, DNA:PCC, item 152; copy, DNA:PCC, item 169. The copy in PCC, item 152, was enclosed in GW's second letter to Henry Laurens of 12 September.

1. The Quebec Act of 1774 extended Canada's boundaries south to the Ohio River and west to the Mississippi River.

2. The Sorel River, now called the Richelieu River, runs north from Lake Champlain to enter the St. Lawrence River at Sorel, Quebec. The Yamaska River, east of the Sorel River, follows a similar northward path, entering the St. Lawrence River near St. François du Lac, Quebec.

3. Charlestown, N.H., was designated number 4 when Massachusetts laid out townships along the Connecticut River's east bank in 1735.

# From Major John Clark, Jr.

Audrs Office [Harrison's Purchase, N.Y.]
May it please your Excellency                         10th Septr 1778

A difficulty has arisen between the Officers of the State of Newhampshire & me, in settling their Accounts: The State some time since, transmitted to the Board of Treasury a list of Monies advanced to the Officers, including the Continental Bounties, which have since been transmitted to me:[1] I have called upon the Officers & they alledge they ought not to be charged with those sums—as the State intended those sums in lieu of Cloathing: for my own part I wish that justice shou'd be done, but it seems to me that the money advanced, was that belonging *to the United States* and as such ought to be accounted for, or why wou'd the State have transmitted those Accounts? the settling them with me don't preclude the Officers from obtaining what was voted by the State, but *the evil* at present, is they have not Money sufficient to pay the Soldiers the Subsistence due them—I am loth to trouble you, but am so situated that I conceive I cannot admit what they alledge in their defence, you will observe that even the Resolve of the House of Representatives say they shall hereafter account for the sums advanced them, as the Accounts on Oath cou'd not then be lodged with the Board of War. I am in haste with the greatest Respect your Excellencies Most obedt

Jno. Clark Junr Audr of Accts

ALS, DLC:GW.

GW's aide Robert Hanson Harrison replied to Clark: "His Excellency has been favoured with your Letter of this date respecting the New Hampshire Officers. As they are now under marching orders and have not an opportunity of applying to the Council of the State to get further & full satisfaction about the Money in dispute; and as stopping it out of their accounts for their own and their Mens subsistence at this time will be injurious to the service—The General desires, that they may be paid without a deduction of the sum transmitted by the State to the Board of Treasury & by them forwarded to you as advanced the Officrs on Contl account. At the same time you will give no release exonerating them from the charge or that will preclude a settlement at a future day when circumstances will admit of a full investigation of the points in Question" (DLC:GW).

1. The list has not been identified, but the sums involved are suggested by a letter from New Hampshire president Meshech Weare to Henry Laurens of 18 Sept., enclosing the state's account against the United States. Weare explained: "In Said Charge is Included £41,000 Expended for Cloathing & other necessaries, and Transportation for the three Battallions raised in New Hampshire for the Continental Service now in General Washingtons Army, Some part of which was in Such necessaries as the Soldiers are to pay for at the price they were Sold when they enlisted, which will Refund back but a meer Trifle to the State" (DNA:PCC, item 64).

## From the Continental Congress
## Committee of Arrangement

Sir          Head Qrs [White Plains] 10 [September] 1778.

Before a proper arrangement can take place in the Line of Artillery, it is the opinion of the Committee that a dispute Subsisting between Cols. Harrison Lamb & Crane respectively should be settled; they therefore request the Subject of this difference may be referred to a board of officers, of some other Corps, as soon as it may be convenient. We are with the highest Respect your Excellency's Most Obed. Servants

Jos: Reed
Chairman of the Committee

P.S. The Committee also request that the Board will at the same Time determine the Seniority of the Regimts.

LS, DLC:GW. The letter is dated 10 April, but the docket apparently reads, "10 Septr 1778." GW's general orders of 10 Sept. mention this request and direct a board of general officers to convene on 11 September. On that date GW gave information about the dispute to the board, and their decisions were reported in GW's general orders of 15 September.

## To Major General Horatio Gates

Sir,          [White Plains, 10 September 1778]

The superiority of naval force, which the enemy at present possess over our allies, rendering it not improbable, that they may be tempted to undertake a co-operation, by sea and land, for the capture or destruction of the French fleet, in the Port of Boston, it appears expedient, that our dispositions, so far as is consistent with the other important objects of our attention, should be calculated as much as possible to afford succour in that quarter. In persuance of this principle and other motives of weight which will occur to you; You are to proceed with the division under your command towards Danbury, taking the route by *Kings Street* and *Bedford*, and making slow and easy marches. You will begin your march tomorrow morning, and halt at some convenient place within six or eight miles of this Camp. Intelligence may be received in the course of the day, which may decide the measure of your future progress; but, if you have no further advice from me, You are to continue your route by proportionable stages to the place of your destination.

For your supplies of provision, forage and other necessaries on the march, You will be pleased to make the necessary arrangements with the Quarter Master—and Commissary-Generals. Given at Head Quarters White Plains the 10th of Septemr 1778.

Go: Washington

LS, in Alexander Hamilton's writing, NHi: Gates Papers; Df, DLC:GW; Varick transcript, DLC:GW

At 9 P.M. on 9 Sept., GW's secretary Robert Hanson Harrison had written Adj. Gen. Alexander Scammell: "His Excellency desires, that you will issue Orders immediately to Generals Poor & Patterson & to the Officer commanding the Brigade, late Learned's) to be in readiness to march at 9 OClock tomorrow morning, with their respective Brigades and all their Baggage. He also desires that you will communicate this to General Gates to night" (NHi: Gates Papers). On this date GW's aide-de-camp Tench Tilghman wrote Gates: "Orders were last Evening given to the Brigades of Poor, Patterson and Learned to hold themselves in readiness to march this morning. His Excellency would be glad to see you respecting their destination and Route" (NHi: Gates Papers). However, that movement was postponed. Sgt. Maj. Benjamin Gilbert of the 5th Massachusetts Regiment noted in his diary for this date: "Genl Gates Division had orders to march at 9 oClock in the morning but some dispute arising among the Genls they pitcht their Tents again in the after noon" (Symmes, *Gilbert Diary*, 36).

## From Major Ebenezer Gray

Sir                                   ⟨Norw⟩alk [Conn.] Septr 10th 1778
     Having received certain Intelligence that about Forty Refugees from this State were Commissioned by Govr Tryon to Cruise in the Sound in Eight Whale Boats and that their Place of Rendezvous was in Huntington Harbour about one mile & a half from the Town and Two mile from the Fort[1] I formed a little Expedition against them with the assistance of some People from Long Iland who had fled to this Place for safety, which I put in Execution the Night before last and returned yesterday to this Place, in which I have taken thirteen Prisoners, all, except one, formerly Inhabitants in this State, and have fled to the Enemy as they say from Principle, not daring to oppose King George in any matter, Eight of them belong to the Privateer whale Boats, the other five are Enemies to the present Constitution of the Country from Principle as they say & have been, (some of them) skulking to and from the Iland for some purposes they don't chuse to own, Ten of the thirteen were taken at a House after pretty smart Fire from the House, in which Three of their Ringleaders were killed, their Names were Isaac Coffin, Peter Lyon of Reading & Mattw Mallet of Stratford Captains of the Whale Boats. I was so unfortunate as not to find any more of the Party, the remainder having Just gone to Loyds Neck.[2]
     I have them under Guard here and shall wait your Excellenys orders

respecting them, should have sent them to Head Quarters, but Genl Parsons advised to give your Excelleny this Information and wait for further Direction. I am with proper Respects your Excelly Obedt Humbe Servt

Ebenr Gray Majr Comg at this Post

P.S. I forgot to mention that I found a Brig Sloop & small Schooner aground on the Beach which I ordered to be burned, and one whale Boat which I took Lt Deney the Bearer was with the Party and will give your Excelly any further that is necessary.[3]

ALS, DLC:GW.

1. Gray was evidently referring to Fort Slongo, east of Huntington Bay at the present town of Fort Salonga, Long Island.

2. Brief reports of this raid appeared in the *Norwich Packet*, 14 Sept.; the *Connecticut Courant* (Hartford), 15 Sept.; and the *Connecticut Journal* (New Haven), 16 Sept.; the names of the prisoners were listed in the *Independent Chronicle. And the Universal Advertiser* (Boston), 17 September. According to a notice in Rivington's *Royal Gazette* (New York), 19 Sept., the Americans "landed at Oak Neck, in Huntington, Long-Island, and attacked the house of the Widow Chicester." Isaac Coffin was reportedly from Woodbury, Connecticut. Lt. Peter Lyon of the 4th Regiment of Connecticut militia, who had subscribed to the Redding Association of Loyalists in February 1775, was ordered before the Connecticut assembly in June 1776 for disobedience of orders. In March 1777 the Redding selectmen, noting that he had "put and Continues to hold and Screen himself under the Protection of the Ministerial Army," began proceedings for the seizure of his estate (*Rivington's New-York Gazetteer; or the Connecticut, Hudson's River, New-Jersey, and Quebec Weekly Advertiser*, 20 April 1775; Grumman, *Revolutionary Soldiers of Redding*, 199–200). Matthew Mallet may have been the man appointed in June 1778 as quartermaster for Andreas Emmerich's Chasseurs, a mixed Loyalist and Hessian corps.

3. The postscript was written on the cover. John Denny, who was commissioned an ensign in the 1st New York Regiment in July 1776 and promoted to second lieutenant in November of that year, was on command at Norwalk in August and September 1778. He resigned from the army in October 1778.

## From Major General William Heath

Dear Genl                       Head Quarters Boston Sepr 10th 1778

Enclosed I do myself the honor to transmit the Commission of Capt. R. Allen late of Colo. Aldens Regiment who had your Excellency permission to Resign.[1]

Colo. Lee some time since received leave from Congress to resign his commission in the army[2]—The time when the resignation was to take place I have settled with him but have not taken his Commission as his accounts are not settled—He informs me that he is ready for a settlement and desires to be directed with whom and where it is to be done.

The night before last an unhappy affray happened here between a number of American and French sailors—some French Officers who were near the place attempting to quell the disturbance were much wounded one I fear mortally—The guards instantly turn'd out to suppress the riot but the Rioters dispersed before the guard arrived at the place Every step has been taken to discover and apprehend the persons concerned and to satisfy the French Gentlemen who appeared much alarmed on the occassion and in particular that their Officers should be insulted & wounded—The conduct of the Council has been very spirited[3] The guards patroled the streets the last night to prevent further disturbance—The Count D'Estaing has assured me this Day he is fully satisfyed the Inhabitants had no hand in the affray[4]—The enemies fleet who landed a number of their troops at Bedford on saturday night[5] is still hovering on that coast and doubtless have intentions of further mischief—Measures are taken to call in the Militia should an attempt be made this way and sentinels constantly kept at the several Beacons to give timely notice—If the situation of the army is such as will admit two or three of the Continental Battallions to come this way it would be of infinite service greatly spirit the Militia and be a basis for them to build upon Your Excellency is fully sensible should such an event happen how necessary it would be and how much advantage might be expected from it. I have the honor to be with the greatest respect your Excellencys most Obedt Servant

W. Heath

LS, DLC:GW; AdfS, MHi: Heath Papers. Tench Tilghman docketed the cover of the LS, in part, "Ansd 22d."

1. The enclosed commission of Capt. Robert Allen has not been identified. For his permission to resign, see GW to Heath, 8 April, and note 3 to that document.

2. For Congress's resolution of 24 June accepting the resignation of Col. William Raymond Lee, see *JCC,* 11:640.

3. On 9 Sept. the Massachusetts council issued a proclamation calling for all justices of the peace, sheriffs and deputies, and other civil officers "to use their utmost Endeavours for discovering, apprehending and bringing to Justice" persons involved in the "high handed Affray or Riot happening in this Town on the last Evening, wherein several Persons have been badly wounded, and one or more, it is feared, mortally so" (*Continental Journal, and Weekly Advertiser* [Boston], 10 Sept.; see also *Boston-Gazette, and Country Journal,* 14 Sept.). An account of the riot printed in the *Independent Ledger, and the American Advertiser* (Boston), 14 Sept., claimed that it was begun "by seamen captur'd in British vessels, and some of Burgoyne's army, who had inlisted in privateers just ready to sail. A body of these fellows, demanded, we are told, bread of the French bakers, who were employed for the supplying the Count D'Estaing's fleet; being refused, they fell upon the bakers with clubs, and beat them in a most outrageous manner. Two officers of the Count's being apprized of the tumult, and attempting to compose the fray, were greatly wounded; one of them is a person of distinguished family and rank." Vice

Admiral d'Estaing's report of 5 Nov. to the French marine secretary confirms that the dispute began at the bakery and that Lieutenant de Vaisseau Grégoire Le Henault de Saint-Sauveur was killed and Lieutenant de Vaisseau Georges-René Pléville Le Pelley wounded when they tried to intervene (Doniol, *Histoire de la participation de la France*, 3:460; see also comte de Breugnon to [Sartine], 10 Aug., in Stevens, *Facsimiles*, vol. 23, no. 1974).

4. For d'Estaing's letter to Heath of 10 Sept. (MHi: Heath Papers), see "Heath Papers," 4:269–71.

5. For discussion of the British landing at New Bedford, Mass., on the evening of 5 Sept., see Vice Admiral d'Estaing to GW, 8 Sept., and note 3 to that document.

## From Major General Johann Kalb

Camp White plains Septer 10th 1778

In obedience to your Excellency's orders for the opinion of the Board of M. Gls respecting the next Winterquarters.[1]

It appears to me that they should be taken in the State of New-york, on North River either on the left Bank or on both Sides, at the Distance of about 40 Miles from the Enemies Lines at kings Bridge, if they keep their present position. for the following reasons.

1st Because 'tis important to Secure Said River and prevent the Enemies of fortifying themselves thereon, they would thereby with the assistance of the Tories, cut off, or at least render difficult & precarious the communication between the Eastern & Southern States, if the American Army was quartered in any other of the United States.

2dly Because it will be required for the Exercising the army, that the Men Should not be too much fatigued by frequent Detachments & Strong Picket Guards, which would be unavoidable if near the Enemy.

3dly For the Conveniency of providing feed for the Horses & Provisions for the army, in forming Magazins & Stores near the intended Ground, while the Roads are yet good and the River open.

It is also my opinion that for the better Police, order & Discipline of the Troops, the army should be quartered as closely as possible, but no Towns being near the herelaid down distance, it will be necessary to Hutt again great part of the army, Therefore a sufficient Quantity of Timber & Boards ought to be provided without loss of Time, that no green wood may be employed, as being unwholsom. providing the Hutts with Straw for the Men to Lay on, and to renew it from Time to Time would also cont[r]ibute to the health of the Men.

The Posts of kings ferry & West points ought to be peculiarly Secured against the Enemy's Ships & Even on their out Sides in case of a Landing.

The Baron de Kalb

ADS, DLC:GW; Varick transcript, DLC:GW.
  1. No such orders have been identified.


# From Henry Laurens

Sir                                            [Philadelphia] 10th Septr [1778]
      Since my last of the 5th by Burwell, I have had the honor of receiv-
ing and presenting to Congress Your Excellency's favors of the 4th and
[      ] Inst. together with Copy of Major General Sullivan's Letter of
the 31st Ulto and other Papers referred to.[1]
      Your Excellency will be pleased to receive under the present Cover
the following Acts of Congress.
      1. of the 4th Inst. for allowing 3 Dollars per day for the expence of
Officers ordered to a distance from Camp upon extra Services.
      2. of the 8th for augmenting the Continental Bounty to Recruits en-
listing for 3 Years or during the War.
      3. for expressing the sense of Congress respecting the late Retreat
from Rhode Island, and the Action there the 29th Ulto.[2] I have the
honor to be With the highest Respect & Esteem &c.

LB, DNA:PCC, item 13. A note on the letter-book copy indicates that this letter was
carried "by Dodd." William Dodd was employed as messenger for Congress by John
Hancock in 1777, and he continued in that duty at least until December 1778. This
was probably the letter that Laurens sent with his letter to GW of 12 Sept., where it
is referred to as "a Letter of the 9th."
  1. Laurens was evidently referring to GW's official letters to him of 4 Sept. and
4–5 September.
  2. The enclosed copies of these resolutions of 4, 8, and 9 Sept. have not been
identified. For their texts, see *JCC*, 12:878, 889–90, 894–95.


# From Colonel William Malcom

Sir                                            West Point [N.Y.] sept. 10th 1778
      Herewith are inclosed the weekly return of the Garrison.[1]
      General Duportail arrived yesterday I wish it had been six weeks
sooner—Koscuiszko is not returned from the plains, but the General
has been shewn all the works—Your Excellency may depend that I will
shew him every proper Attention. To morrow I go up to Windsor with
him—He has already laugh'd at Stephens mills and I wish to have him
view the Chiveaux De Freize scheme—that my conduct in withdrawing the Workmen, & materials therefrom may be sanctify'd by so good
an authority—If I could obtain the regulations concerning the Al-

lowance of Rations to Artificers & other appendages of the Army it would deliver me from a world of trouble—the Commissary General sent one Establishment to the Commissary here—and Baldwin sends another for what is called his corps—so that If I abide by the General Orders of August 6th one sett plagues me—and if I take notice of Baldwins, another sett does the same—if Col. Baldwin had not interfer'd the Order of August 6th wou'd have continued in effect without any difficulty.

I have been under the Necessity of sending six of the fellows brought here by Mr Lovell, back to Fishkill—In my Opinion they had better be set at large.[2]

Mr Pettitt wrote for my Qr Mastr yesterday—he said by your Excellency's Order[3]—I desired Col. Hay to expostulate on that Subject—I flatter myself that he will be able to offer such reasons as will prevail with your Excellency not to insist on his removal—I have only that Man of the department in the Garrison—who manages Waggoners &c.—without any trouble to me and much to the Advantage of the service—and as I have taken a great deal of pains to learn him his business during the summer I hope to have the benefit of my trouble.

Only about thirty Militia of this State came in—of which I have received no return.

Does your Excellency know that the Arms which went from this Garrison to be repair'd at Fishkill, & which I depended on having brought back, are order'd to camp—There are 400 repaird arms expected from Albany—may I have them for the Carolina troops? There is a very good Armourer's shop at Fishkills and Mr Allen a good Man to conduct it—Yet the method is to send the Arms to Albany to be repaired, and then bro't back—by which means a great deal of time is lost and Expence occasion'd—Shall I write to Genl Stark for half a dozen Gun Smiths to employ at Fiskill? I have the Honor to be Your Excellencys, Most Obedient and very humble Servt

W. Malcom

LS, DLC:GW.

1. The enclosed return has not been identified. For the totals reported, see the "Weekly Return of The Continental Army under the more immediate command of His Excellency George Washington Esquire," 12 Sept. 1778 (DNA: RG 93, Revolutionary War Rolls, 1775–1783).

2. See GW to James Lovell, Jr., 30 July.

3. See GW to Charles Pettit, 7 September.

## From Charles Pettit

Sir                                      Camp [White Plains] 10th Septr 1778
   Colonel Hay is just arrived; and, having met a Letter from me at
Tarry Town, has sent off an Express from thence to order Vessels for
conveying the Sick to Fishkill.
   As there is no absolute certainty of the Teams expected from Connecticut coming in so soon as your Excellency wishes to have them employed, it may be best to impress some of the Teams of this State between this and Fishkill. Col. Hay informs me there are many Persons
who, either from being Quakers or from Disaffection never serve the
Publick voluntarily, and whom their better disposed Neighbours wish
to see called upon; if your Excellency thinks it proper to have Teams
impressed, a Number might be collected in the Course of a Day or two
amongst the People I have described; but your Excellency's written Authority will be necessary for such Purpose. I have the Honr to be Your
Excellency's most obedt hume Servt
                                              Chas Pettit A.Q.M.G.

LS, DLC:GW. The cover is docketed, in part, "press Warrt granted."

## From Charles Pettit

Sir                                    Camp, White Plains 10th Septr 1778
   The Scarcity of Forage, and the Reluctance with which the Farmers
part with what they have to spare, has, for some Time past, filled me
with more alarming Apprehensions than I have felt on account of any
other Branch of the Quarter Master's Department. The necessary Consumption of Forage, not only in and about the Army, but for the numerous Teams employed in the inland Transportation of Provisions
and Stores, has so far exhausted the Resourse⟨s⟩ of former Crops that
every Farmer in the Middle States discerns that the Demand for Grain
is equal, if not more than equal, to all that can possibly be furnished,
and of course that the Purchasers, whether for publick or private Use,
must of necessity pay whatever Price shall be insisted on. The Discretion of each Individual is therefore the only Boundary to the Price demanded. Hence we find it impossible, without the Interposition of legislative Authority, to adhere steadily to any fixed Price, and at the same
Time obtain the necessary Supplies. For although many of the better
disposed among the Farmers would be willing to sell their Forage at the
present current Prices if they were not apprehensive their more avari-
cious Neighbours would obtain a higher Price for theirs; yet while they
see Prices constantly rising and unbounded, they are unwilling to pre-

clude themselves from the Advantages which Experie⟨nce⟩ has taught them may be obtained by with-holding their Commodities from the present Market. This increases the Avidity of the Demand, and of course obliges the Purchase⟨r⟩ to submit to the Terms imposed by the Seller. The enormo⟨us⟩ Increase of the Publick Expenditures, though perhaps the greatest, is but one of the Evils which must attend the permitting the Prices of Grain to continue rising witho⟨ut⟩ any other Limitation than the capricious Discretion of the Sellers of it. The Mischief is increased both in Size and Velocity by every Step it advances, and must, if permitted to continue, produce the most pernicious Consequences. On the other Hand, if the Legislatures of the respective States will give us their Aid, by fixing a Table of Prices between Individuals and the Publick, & establishing a legal Mode, as well for the obtaining at such Prices what each Individual can spare, as for ascertaining the Quantity which may be taken in Case of Dispute; I imagine the Quantity of Grain in the Country will be found more adequate to the Demand than present Appearances indicate.

From the Scarcity, whether real or artificial, which we now feel, and have for some Time past experienced in the States northward of Chesapeak Bay, we have been under a Necessity of drawing considerable Quantities of Grain from Virginia, Maryland and Delaware; the Transportation of which not only enhances the Price, but, by employing more Teams in the publick Service, increases the Consumption. If therefore the Inhabitants of the States more contiguous to the Army could be induced to deliver, in a short Time, what they can with Propriety spare, it would not only enable us to form our Magazines in due Season, but might authorize us to relax our Demand on the distant Places from whence Supplies are transported at so great an Expence.

I take the Liberty of troubling your Excellency with these Facts and Observations, together with a Letter from Colonel Biddle, Commissary Genl of Forage, which is inclosed herewith,[1] on a Confidence that a Representation of the Matter from your Excellency to the Legislatures of the respective States, either immediatly or through Congress, will be the most likely way to have the Business speedily and effectually attended to, and to procure it that Dispatch which it's Importance demands. I have the Honour to be, with the greatest Respect, Your Excellency's most obedient & most humble Servant

Chas Pettit A.Q.M.G.

LS, DLC:GW; copy, M-Ar: Revolution Letters, 1778; copy, R-Ar: Letters to the Governor; copy, PHarH: Records of Pennsylvania's Revolutionary Governments, 1775–1790; copy, Nj-Ar: Miscellaneous Correspondence; copy, DNA:PCC, item 192; LB, Ct: Trumbull Papers. The copies were enclosed in GW to Jeremiah Dummer Powell, to William Greene, to George Bryan, and to William Livingston,

22 Sept., and GW to Henry Laurens, 23 September. Another copy (see Hastings, *Clinton Papers*, 4:22–24) was enclosed in GW's letter to George Clinton of 22 Sept., and a copy (not identified) was enclosed in GW's letter to Jonathan Trumbull, Sr., of that date.

1. Clement Biddle had written to Pettit on 6 Sept. that "The Consumption of Forage is so great and from the distance it is brought subject to so many delays and disapointments that I wish to fall on every method that will be most likely to ensure a certain & regular Supply—At this time we draw considerable quantities of Corn and Oats from Virginia and Maryland by the way of the head of Elk to Trenton & thence by land to this Camp—the same from the Delaware States—and these supplies must be continued as long as the Season will permit, the middle States being much drained. however I think much more might be drawn from Pennsylvania Jersey, York and Connecticut if the Legislatures of those States would take effectual measures to bring out their Hay & Grain for the use of the Army, and we shall have Occasion for all that can possibly be spared from each of those States to subsist our Horses." He pointed out that his agents in New Jersey, Pennsylvania, New York, and Connecticut all complained "of the great prices demanded . . . and all agree that from various Causes the Forage is not brought to market. the absence of the Militia in service in some places has been one Cause of their not threshing and in many the Expectation of a rising price induces them to keep it back—some Measures are necessary to bring them to thresh & deliver all that can be spared for the use of the Army." Noting that "limiting a generous price beyond which they would not have an Expectation of a rise would have a good Effect," Biddle proposed that GW "should be informed of this and be requested to write to the different Legislatures to take the most Effectual Measures to assist my Agents in the different Districts in the Collection of Forage, by limiting the prices & enforcing a Delivery of the Hay & Grain that can be spared at stated periods, also in furnishing Carriages to hawl the same in their respective States to such places as it may be wanted at." Biddle also suggested that "it may be necessary to make an application to the Legislatures of Delaware, Maryland & Virginia on the same Occasion as the Conveniency of water Carriage from & the greater Abundance of Corn & Oats in those states as well as the insufficiency of Grain in the Others will make it necessary to draw largely from them." Biddle agreed with Pettit that "Ox Teams would be a great relief if they Could be procured as the Oxen could be subsisted on Grass & a very little Hay," but he warned, "There is so little Grain thresh'd in this & the adjoining States & our present situation requiring immediate supplies, there is no time to be lost in adopting some method to get the Farmers to work" (DLC:GW).

# From Brigadier General Charles Scott

Sir                               [Westchester County, N.Y.] 10th Sept. 78

I recd Your orders through Colo. Meade which Shall be immedeatly attended to. Capt. Leavenworth is now on the Sound In persute of Intilligence I make no doubt He will be able to give Some Acct of the Fleat You mention.[1] Exclusive of this I Shall this moment Send Colos. Butler Parker & Grayham Some of them I make no doubt Will be able

Learn with Certainty whether they have troops on Board. my Corps Shall be in Perfect Readiness to march On the Shortest notice. I am Your Excellencys Obt Servant

Chs Scott

ALS, DLC:GW.

1. Scott is most likely referring not to Richard Kidder Meade's letter of 9 Sept. in reply to Scott's letter to GW of that date, but rather to another letter from Meade that has not been found. GW was apparently seeking information about the fleet mentioned in Thomas Young Seymour's letter to him of 9 September.

## From Major General John Sullivan

Dear General                Providence Septemr 10th 1778

I can only Inform you at present that the Enemy have Left Bedford but are Still Hovering Round the Shore they have Burnt ten Dwelling Houses all the Stores & all the vessels but one in Bedford Sir Henry Clinton Left them at New London & Returned to New york in a Frigate Major General Gray Commands the Party which Consists of one Regt of Light Infantry & one of Granadiers of Six hundred men Each And two Brigades Consisting of Eight Regiments viz. the 15: 42, 33d: 64: 17: 37 46th & 44th a Searjent has Deserted from them with an orderly Book which gives this Information. Lord Howe with a Fleet of Seventeen Sail of the Line is Standing off & on before Newport Harbor— from the Declaration of the Inhabitants of Newport of a Number of prisoners Exchanged & from the Declarations of Gentlemen who have been on the Island as well as the Similar Declarations of a Number of Deserters the Enemy had between a Thousand & fifteen hundred killed & wounded in the Action of the 29th a Woman who Lived in the Hospital & is said to be a Woman of veracity Says She Saw the Returns of the Surgeon which Amounted to a Thousand & Sixty one[1] it is agreed on all hands that Three hundred & twenty were killed & mortally wounded on the field. I beg your Excellency to Transmit a Copy of this Letter to Congress & believe me to be with the most profound Respect your Excellenceys most obedt Servt

Jno. Sullivan

ALS, DLC:GW. GW enclosed a copy of this with his first letter to Henry Laurens of 12 Sept., and it was subsequently published in newspapers by order of Congress (*Pennsylvania Evening Post*, 16 Sept., and others).

1. The published version of this letter altered the preceding sentence to hide the sex of Sullivan's informant. Whether the copy that GW sent to Congress was altered has not been determined.

# From Major Thomas Wickes

Sir                                                   Huntington [N.Y.] Septr 10th 1778
    I have Certain Accompts that the Enemy at Newyork are Putting Large Quantitys of Lead on Board there Transports, and the Coopers are Very Bussy in Over haling and Reparing there Water Casks, I was further Informed that days was Appointed to Sell there horses but I have not heard Whether they Sold any, there Sick is Removing down to the ferry, from out of the Country, A man is Sent to Loyds Neck to Pay off all the Wood Cutters and Carter that have been Imployd, but I did not Learn Whether he was to discharge them, an Intire Imbargo is Laid on all Vessels none is allowd, not the Wood botes to Leave the City, Its the Oppinion of our Friends on the Island and in Newyork that they are Preparing to Leave Newyork, but Tryon tells the torys and Friends to Goverment as he Calls them, that a Large Reinforcement Will be here Soon, at Least ten thousand, that they are Under Convoy of Admiral Birumb, Since Tryon hath Swore the People its Very difficult Gitting People to Go to Newyork, most of those that I sent to Newyork are either Prisoners or have fled into the Woods to Secret themselves, to Prevent being Prisoners, The Inclosed is a Copy of the Oath that Tryon Obliges the Inhabitants to take, or to Pay five Pounds and Quit the Island Imediately.[1] I am Sir With Due Respect Your Excellencys Most Obdient and Very Humbl. Sert
                                                               Thos Wickes

ALS, DLC:GW.
    1. The oath asked a resident of "Southold Township" to swear "to bare faith and true Allegance" to the king "& that he Will not directly or Indirectly openly or Secretly, aid, abet, councel, Shelter or Conceal, any of his Majestys Enemys, and those of his Goverment, or Molest or betray the Friends of Goverment but that he will behave himself Peaceably and Quietly, as a Faithful subject of his Majisty and his Goverment" (DLC:GW). Tryon reported to the British secretary of state for the colonies that the oath was "administered to all the inhabitants on the north side of the island, giving them the alternative either to take the oath or remove with their families and furniture to Connecticut. Not one of the whole chose the latter, even the hottest rebels said my proposal was generous and took the oath, which convinces me that the acrimony of opposition is much softened by the late concessions of government" (Tryon to Lord George Germain, 5 Sept., in Davies, *Documents of the American Revolution*, 15:198).

# General Orders

                          Head-Quarters W. Plains Friday Septembr 11th 1778.
Parole Frankfort—                              C. Signs Freetown. Falkland.
    The General Court-Martial whereof Coll Humpton is President is to sit tomorrow nine ôClock at the new Dining Room—Lieutt Coll Reg-

nier is appointed a Member, *vice* Lieutt Colonel Mellin—Nixon's and the 1st Pennsylvania Brigades each give a Captain in the room of those who have marched.

The Drum and Fife Majors of the Regiments on the Ground are to attend at the Inspector of Musick's tent in the rear of the Park tomorrow morning ten ôClock to receive his Instructions.

Varick transcript, DLC:GW.

On this date GW's aide-de-camp Richard Kidder Meade wrote Brig. Gen. Jedediah Huntington: "Lieutenant Solomon [Hendricks] who commands the remaining part of the Stockbridge Indians has requested His Excellency to discharge four of their Tribe who are in your Brigade—As they behaved well and were unfortunate in a late action His Excy is inclined to indulge them, & if it meets with your approbation He requests that you will discharge the above number, the particular ones will be pointed out to you by the Lieut. who will deliver this" (DGC:GW).

## To Brigadier General Jacob Bayley

Sir                                        [White Plains, 11 September 1778]
I am to request that you immediately employ Proper Persons to gain the most Authentic Intelligence from Canada of the several matters hereinafter mentioned vizt

First—What Force is now in Arms in that Country.

Secondly—If any Reinforcement has arrived in Canada the Summer past, & if any are expected to arrive this Season.

Third—In what State of Defence are the Garrisons, and how are the Troops posted in that Country.

Fourth—Are any Canadians in Arms there, if so, are they Compell'd to it, or is it from their own Choice, & what number.

Fifth—The General Sentiments of the People with respect to American Politics and that of the Clergy in particular.

Sixthly—The Disposition of the Indians in the Neighbourhood of Canada.

Seventhly—who is the Governor and Principal Magistrate in that Country.

Eighthly—If there is a plentiful, or short Crop, there, and what may be the Price of Grain.

Ninthly—If the Canadians have been disarmed by any Authority from Government, or not.

Tenthly—Whether the Canadians wou'd chuse to reunite with the Independent States of America.[1]

If you find a favorable Account, from Credible People on the matters herein mentioned, and as your Situation is so distant from hence, you may in the Month of November next imploy a part of Colo. Bedels

Regimt, shou'd it be continued, or a small number of other good men, in Cutting a Road from your House into Canada which you with others, have reported unto me to be practicable. Your reasonable Expences in this Service will be allowed You—You will from Time to Time Transmit to me an Account of your Proceedings with all the Intelligence you shall Collect. Given at Head Quarters White Plains Sepr 11th 1778.

Go: Washington

Copy, MHi: Heath Papers; Df, DLC:GW; Varick transcript, DLC:GW. The copy, which is in the hand of Bayley's scribe, was enclosed to Maj. Gen. William Heath by Bayley in his letter of 21 Oct. (MHi: Heath Papers).

1. On 13 Oct., Bayley wrote Col. Timothy Bedel, directing him to "immediately proceed to the Upper Co'os with Joseph Lewis [Gill] and provide a proper person to go with him among the Indians," where "Lewis" and his companion were to seek answers to these questions (Hammond, *Rolls of Soldiers*, 4:276).

## To a Board of General Officers

Gentn                         Head Qrs [White Plains] Septr 11: 1778.
    The Book you will herewith receive contains the Journals and proceedings of Congress for the year 1776.[1] Among these—and agreable to the pages marked below, you will find all the Resolutions that I am possessed of, respecting the Regiments and Officers of Artillery now in Camp—and also the establishment of the Army for 1777. I have the Honor to be with great respect and esteem Genn Yr Most Obedt servant

G.W.

Page 17. Capn Lamb promoted
        357–8 Establishment of Army for 1777.
        479. A Regiment of Artillery ordered to be raised in Virga
        487—Officers appointed to the Regt
        515—Three regiments of Artillery to be raised &c.[2]

P.S. I wish you also to settle the relative rank of all the Artillery field Officers now present.

G.W.

Df, in Robert Hanson Harrison's writing, DLC:GW; Varick transcript, DLC:GW.

1. GW sent *Journals of the Continental Congress. Containing the Proceedings from January 1, 1776, to January 1, 1777* (York, Pa., 1778). This volume, printed by John Dunlap, was the second volume of journals published by order of Congress.

2. GW was referring the board to resolutions of 9 Jan., 16 Sept., 26 Nov., 30 Nov., and 27 Dec. 1776 (see *JCC*, 4:43, 5:762–63, 6:981, 995, 1045–46).

# From a Board of General Officers

[White Plains, c.11 September 1778]

The board of General officers to whom your Excellency was pleased to refer a draught of a number of resolves transmitted to your perusal and observations there on by Congress relative to the appointment of an Inspector General &c.[1] have attentively considered the same and view with concern that resolves so dangerous in their consequences to the safety of the united States as some of them are & so derogatory to the officrs of the army in general should ever have been penned and with surprise that they should have been thought to have merited the attention of the Congress and offer the following remarks, & some of the reasons among many which pointed us to them.

Remarks on the first Resolve. That in all future appointments the Inspector General be taken from the line of the army and have such rank as he hold, in that line.

Because many inconveniencies have been experiencd in the army from rank being given to men not in the proper line thereof.

On the 2d Resolve and in lieu thereof. The duty of the Inspector Genl shall be to direct the exercise of the troops in the manual evolutions & manœuvers for the service on guard, detachment camp and garrison duty—That he shall review the troops at such time & place and receive such return of them as the commander in chief shall from time to time direct and shall confine himself at such reviews to the inspection of the men their arms accoutriments clothing and exercise only—And in exercising the troops in the manual evolutions and manœuvres he shall govern him self by no other system of rules and regulations but such as shall be agreed on by himself in conjunction or in council with a board of General officers appointed for that purpose & be approved of by the commander in chief which are to be transmitted to the board of war with all convenient dispatch.

Because that although we have the utmost confidence in the wisdom and integrity of the present commander in chief, yet the time may come when the armies of America may, unhappily, be commanded by a Genl of a very different character.

Because the returns of the army should be in the hands of the commander in chief only or to such as he shall communicate them, as the safety of the army & the liberties of this country may be in danger in certain circumstances should their strength by negligence or other wise be disclosed.

Because a great part of the resolve is unnecessary as officers are already appointed to the several parts of the duty therein pointed out, and who from their perticular connection with the troops must be best quallified for the discharge of it—and because it is depriving the present officers of corps of part of that duty which in all services would devolve upon them and will thereby render them cheap & contemptable as they will be held up, either as unequall to their duty or wanting in attention to the faithfull discharge of it.

On the 3d Resolve. Unnecessary.

Because the senior sub-inspector may do all the duty assigned to the assistant inspector and thereby avoid multiplying offices & rank—And because[2] the assistant Inspector General must be the oldest Colonel of the army who may probably be unfit for the office or a young Colonel or a person not in the line must be promoted out of their proper course which would occasion disgust.

On the 4th Resolve. That there be one Lieutenant colonel of cavalry one Lieutenant colonel of Light troops & four lieutenant colonels of infantry appointed as sub inspectors all of whom are to receive their instructions from the Inspector General relative to the exercise of the troops in the manual evolutions & manœuvres for the purpose of regulating the service on guard detachment camp and garrison duty. And that on the death or removal of the inspector general the senior sub inspector shall do the duty of the inspector General untill an other shall be appointed by Congress.

On the 5th Resolve. That Brigade inspectors be appointed from time to time by the commander in chief from the line of their respective Brigades as hath been practised heretofore.

Because annexing the office of Brigade inspectors to that of Majors of Brigade will be depriving the Brigadiers of a necessary officer and at the very time when he hath the most need of his services viz. forming the Brigade speedily for action and changing its position as circumstances may require to which duty an aid taken from the line of subalterns will probably be incompetent and because the Brigade majors have lately been taken from the Captains of the lines.

On the 6th Resolve. Unnecessary—For the above reasons.

On the 7th Resolve. That the Inspector General & sub-Inspectors hold command in the line according to their ranks and appointments therein abstracted from their office of inspectors by which they are to have no comand in the line whatever, that they shall be exempt from all common detached camp and garrison dutis that they may attend more carefully to those of the Inspection.

On the 8th Resolve. The first paragraph unnecessary—The second provided in the 2d Resolve.

On the 9th Resolve. Unnecessary, excepting the last paragraph.

Because to suppose that in the army every officer will not be treated with that respect due to his rank & office is an implied & unmerited reflection and because provision is made for part of this resolve in the second resolve.

On the 10th Resolve. Unnecessary.

Because there is provision therefor in the rules and regulations made for the better government of the army, besides should it be adopted it would convey a reflection and a want of confidence in those in whom those powers are already more propely vested from their acquaintance and immediate connection with the troops, but be fraught with other inconveniences as it will be establishing a kind inquisitional authority totally inconsistant with the good of the service.

On the 11th Resolve. The right of appointment undoubtedly in the Congress.

On the 12th Resolve. Unnecessary.

On the 13th Resolve. That General Washing[ton] be desired to appoint the sub Inspectors before mentioned and that he add to their Number or diminish as future circumstances and his judgment shall derect.

Upon the whole it is painful to the board to observe that if the resolutions in question should be passed into ordinan[c]es it would form a new fangled system of power running through the line of the army uncontrouled and unchecked totally inconsistent with that chain of connection and dependence which is the foundation and support of all military establishment.

But the board observe with pleasure that resolutions containing matters of so great importance have not received the sanction of Congress untill the Commander in chief had been consulted.

|                   | Jno. Nixon        | P: Muhlenberg.  |
| ----------------- | ----------------- | --------------- |
| Israel Putnam     | Saml H. Parsons   | J. Huntington   |
| Horatio Gates     | James Clinton     |                 |
| The Baron de Kalb. | W. Smallwood     |                 |
| B. Lincoln        | H. Knox           |                 |
| Alexr McDougall   | Enoch Poor        |                 |
|                   | Wm Woodford       |                 |

LS, DLC:GW. GW's first letter to Henry Laurens of 12 Sept. indicates that he received the resolutions under consideration on 31 Aug. and completed his review of them on 11 September. The board's report was most likely submitted about the time of GW's completion of the review.

1. For the resolutions, transmitted with Henry Laurens's second letter to GW of 20 Aug., see *JCC*, 11:819–23.

2. The remainder of this paragraph was written just above the signatures on the last page of the letter and marked for inclusion at this point.

## To Lieutenant Colonel William Butler

Sir                              Head Quarters White plains 11th Sept. 1778

I am glad to find by your letters of the 31st Augt that matters continued so quiet upon the Frontier.

It appears to me that the money, arising from the sale of Cattle belonging to those in the interest of the enemy, belongs to the Captors. But I beg you will proceed in these matters with the caution which you have used in the first instance, otherwise the soldiers for the sake of plunder will seize every thing under the denomination of its being Tory property.

I shall give orders to the Cloathier Genl to send up some shoes to Albany for your detachment. They will go to the Care of General Stark who I suppose can forward them to you. I am Sir Yr most obt Servt.

Df, in Tench Tilghman's writing, DLC:GW; Varick transcript, DLC:GW.

## To Vice Admiral d'Estaing

Head Quarters [White Plains]
Sir.                              11[–12]th September 1778.[1]

I have had the honor of receiving Your Excellencys Letter of the 5th inst: accompanied by a copy of two letters to Congress and General Sullivan—The confidence which you have been pleased to shew me in communicating these papers, engage my sincere thanks—if the deepest regret, that the best concerted enterprises and bravest exertions should have been rendered fruitless by a disaster which human prudence is incapable of foreseeing or preventing, can alleviate disappointment; you may be assured that the whole continent sympathises with you—it will be a consolation to you to reflect that the thinking part of mankind do not form their judgement from events; and that their equity will ever attach equal glory to those actions which deserve success, as to those which have been crowned with it—It is in the trying circumstances to which Your Excellency has been exposed, that the virtues of a great mind are displayed in their brightest lustre—and that the Generals Character is better known than in the moment of victory—it was yours by every title which can give it—and the adverse element which robbed you of your prize, can never deprive you of the glory due to you—And tho' your Success has not been equal to your expectations—yet you have the satisfaction to reflect that you have done essential service to the common cause.

I exceedingly lament that in addition to our misfortunes, ther⟨e⟩ has been the least suspension of harmo⟨ny⟩ and good understanding between the Generals of allied nations, whose vie⟨ws⟩ must like their interests be the same—on the first intimation of it I employ⟨ed⟩ my influence in restoring what I regard as essential to the permanen⟨ce⟩ of an Union founded on mutual inclination, and the strongest ties of reciprocal advantage—Your Excellencys offer to the Council of Boston had a powerful tendency to promote the same end, and was a distinguished proof of your zeal and magnanimity.

The present superiority of the enemy in naval force, must for a time suspend all plans of offensive cooperation, between us—it is not easy to foresee what change may take place by the arrival of succours to you from Europe—or what opening the enemy may give you to resume your activity—in this moment therefore every consultation on this subject would be premature—but it is of infinite importance that we should take all the means that our circumstances will allow for the defence of a Squadron, which is so pretious to the common cause of France and America, and which may have become a capital object with the enemy—Whether this really is the case can be only matter of conjecture; the original intention of the reinforcement sent to Rhode Island[2] was obviously the relief of the garrison at that post—I have to lament that tho seasonably advised of the movement, it was utterly out of my power to counteract it—a naval force alone could have defeated the attempt—how far their views may since have been enlarged by the arrival of Byrons Fleet, Your Excellency will be best able to judge. Previous to this event I believe General Clinton was waiting orders from his court for the conduct he was to pursue—in the mean time embarking his stores and heavy baggage in order to be the better prepared for a prompt evacuation if his instructions should require it—but as the present posture of affairs may induce a change of operations, and tempt them to carry the war eastward for the ruin of your Squadron; it will as I observed before, be necessary for us to prepare for opposing such an Enterpr⟨ise⟩—I am unhappy that our situation will not admit of our contributing more effectually to this valuable end—but assure you at the same time, that whatever can be attempted without losing sight of objects equally essential to the interests of the two nations—shall be put in execution.

A Candid View of our Affairs which I am going to exhibit, will make you a judge of the difficulties under which we labour.

Almost all our supplies of flour, and no inconsiderable part of our meat, are drawn from the States westward of Hudsons River—this renders a secure communication across that River indispensibly necessary not only to the support of the Army, but the valuable Squadron of His most Christian Majesty, if it should be blocked up by a superior fleet—

the enemy being masters of that navigation would interrupt this essential intercourse between the States—they have been sensible of these advantages, and by the attempts which they have made to bring about a Separation of the Eastern from the other States[3]—have always obliged us besides garrisoning the forts that immediately defend the passage—to keep a force at least equal to that, which they have kept in New York and its dependencies—and it is incumbent upon us at this time to have a greater force in this quarter than usual, from the concentred State of the enemys Strength and the uncertainty of their designs—in addition to this it is to be observed that they derive an inestimable advantage from the facility of transporting their troops from one point to another—these rapid movements enable them to give us uneasiness for remote unguarded posts, in attempting to succour which we should be exposed to ruinous marches, and after all perhaps be the dupes of a feint—if they could by any demonstration in another part, draw our attention and strength from this important point, and by anticipating our return possess themselves of it—the consequences would be fatal[4] to the Army & Fleet.

Our dispositions therefore, must have equal regard to cooperating with you, in a defensive plan—and securing the North River—which the remoteness of the two objects from each other renders peculiarly difficult—Immediately upon the change which happened in the State of your naval affairs—my attention was directed to conciliating these two great ends—the necessity of transporting magazines collected relatively to our present position—and making new arrangements for ulterior operations, has hitherto been productive of delay—these points are now nearly accomplished and I hope in a day or two to begin a general movement of the Army eastward—as a commencement of this, one division marched this morning under Major General Gates towards Danbury—and the rest of the army will follow as speedily as possible.

The following is a general idea of my disposition—the Army will be thrown into several divisions—one of which consisting of a force equal to the Enemys in New York, will be about thirty miles in the rear of my present Camp—and in the vicinity of the North River with a view to its defence—the others will be pushed on at different stages, as far towards Connecticut River, as can be done consistently with preserving a communication, and having them within supporting distance of each other—so that when occasion requires, they may form a junction, either for thei⟨r⟩ own immediate defence, or to oppos⟨e⟩ any attempts that may be made on the North River—the facility which the enemy have of collecting their whole force, and turning it against any point they please, will restrain us from extending ourselves so far, as will either expose us to be beaten in detachment, or endanger the securi⟨ty⟩ of the North River.

This disposition will place the American Forces as much in measure, for assisting in the defence of your Squadron and the Tow⟨n⟩ of Boston, as is consistent with the other great objects of our care.

It does not appear to me probable that the enemy would hazard the penetrating to Boston by land, with the force which they at present have to the Eastward—I am rather inclined to believe that they will draw together their whole land and naval strength to give the greater probability of success—in order to this New York must be evacuated, an event which cannot take place without being announced by circumstances impossible to conceal—and I have reason to hope that the time which must necessarily be exhausted in embarking and transporting their troops and stores, would be sufficient for me to advance a considerable part of my army in measure for opposing them.

The observations which Your Excellency makes relative to the necessity of having intelligent spies, are perfectly just—every measure that circumstances would admit has been taken to answer this valuable end, and has in general been as good as could be expected from the situation of the enemy.

The distance at which we are from our posts of observation in the first instance, and the long journey which is afterwards to be performed before a letter can reach Your Excellency—hinder my communicating intelligence with such celerity as I could wish—the letter which I sent giving an account of Lord Howes Movement, was dispatched as soon as the fact was ascertained—but it did not arrive 'till you had gone to Sea in pursuit of the british Squadron.[5]

As Your Excellency does not mention the Letters which I last had the honor of writing to you, I apprehend some delay or miscarriage—their dates are the 2d and 3d inst.

The sincere esteem and regard which I feel for Your Excellency, make me set the highest value upon every expression of friendship with which you are pleased to honor me—I entreat you to accept the warmest returns on my part.

I shall count it a singular felicity if in the course of possible operations above alluded to, personal intercourse should afford me the means of cultivating a closer intimacy with you—and of proving to you more particularly the respect and attachment with which I have the honor to be Your Excellencys most obedient and most humble Servt.

Go: Washington

P.S. My dispatches were going to be closed, when Your Excellencys Letter of the 8th was delivered me; I detain the express to acknowledge the receipt of it.

The State of Byrons Fleet from the bes⟨t⟩ intelligence I have been able to obtain is as follows—*6* Ships—the names of whi⟨ch⟩ are mentioned in the Gazette which I had the honor of transmitting the 3d inst., have arrived at New York with very sickly Crew⟨s.⟩ 2. vizt the Cornwall of 74 and Monmouth of 64 had joined Lord Howe—2. one of which the Admirals Ship, missing—one had put back to Portsmouth⁶—Of lord Howes Squadron a 64 and 50 are at New York.

LS, in John Laurens's writing, FrPNA: Marine, B4, I46; Df, DLC:GW; copy (extract), FrPBN; Varick transcript, DLC:GW. The extract corresponds to the first paragraph of the LS.

　　1. According to the docket on d'Estaing's second letter of 8 Sept., acknowledged in the postscript below, it was received on 12 September.

　　2. GW inserted the word "Island."

　　3. At this point the draft continued with the words "and the facility which their superiority by Sea had hitherto given him."

　　4. Laurens put a period at this point, but GW added the words following.

　　5. GW was referring to his letter to d'Estaing of 8 August.

　　6. The remainder of the postscript does not appear on the draft.

# From Major General Horatio Gates

Sir　　　　　　　　　　　　　　　　　　　　　　11th September 1778

　　I earnestly entreat your Excellency will be pleased to permit Col: Kuscuiusco to be The Engineer to serve with The Troops marching under my Command; if I had not an Affectionate regard for This amiable Foreigner, I should upon no Account have made this my request—The out Works at West point are in a manner finish'd & the Body of the place in such forwardness, as to put it in The power of The Two Engineers now There, to compleat the whole with the utmost Facility; I am sorry it is not your Excellencys pleasure to allow Colonel Hay to go with me.[1] I *must* think, that his being in the Advance of your Army would perhaps be of more benefit to it than his remaining here; should Your Excellencys March to the Eastward take place. The Troops halt this Evening about Three Miles from hence, I shall be with them at Bedford by tomorrow noon, any Commands before then, I shall with pleasure receive here, or on the Way. I am Your Excellencys most Obedient Humble Servant

　　　　　　　　　　　　　　　　　　　　　　　　　　　　Horatio Gates

ALS, DLC:GW; Df, NHi: Gates Papers.

　　1. Assistant Quartermaster General Charles Pettit wrote Gates on this date, in part: "the Situation of the Quarter Masters Department at present makes Col. Hay's

Assistance so highly necessary to me that it would be with great Reluctance I should part with him were I to consult my own Feelings only; and on mentioning the Matter to His Excellency he was pleased to forbid it in Terms the most explicit" (NHi: Gates Papers).

## To Major General Horatio Gates

sir                                    Head Qrs [White Plains] 11 Septr 1778
I have been favoured with your Letter of this date.

I am always willing to grant requests where I think the good of the service will admit of it, and I am particularly so, when the requests are urged by Others besides the party, in whose behalf they are made. However, in the present instance of your application, I cannot do it with any degree of propriety, as I conceive. Colo. Kosciusko has had the chief direction and superintendence of the Works at West point, and it is my desire, that he should remain to carry them on. New plans & alterations at this time, would be attended with many inconveniences, and protract the defences of the River. These possibly in some degree, might take place in case of his absence, under the management of Another Engineer. With respect to Colo. Hay, he will be of very essential service here, and I cannot consent to his leaving Camp, while the Army continues in its present position and under it's present circumstances. I am Sir Your Most Obedt servt

Go: Washington

LS, in Robert Hanson Harrison's writing, NHi: Gates Papers; Df, DLC:GW; Varick transcript, DLC:GW.

## From Colonel Morgan Lewis

Albany 11th Sepr 1778
It gives me Pain to be under the Necessity of addressing your Excellency on so disagreeable a Subject, as an attempt made by Brigr General Stark, not only to injure me in your Opinion, but even to strike at the Foundation of my character as a Servant of the Public.

That the charges in General Star⟨k's⟩ Letter to your Excellency (Copy of which was transmitted me by Charles Pettit Esqr:) are without Foundation and untrue,[1] I am convinced will be made appear to your Excellency's Sa⟨tis⟩faction; nor am I at a Loss for the Source that urged the General to his illeberal method of Revenge.

My Office being of a Nature tha⟨t⟩ required the Strictest attention to my Duty an⟨d⟩ the nicest Circumspection to avoid Complain⟨ts⟩ from either Civil or Military, I flatter Myself my Conduct which has hitherto bee⟨n⟩ unimpeached, *saving by General Stark*, will be approved of by the unanimous Testimony of the most respectable Bodies in this Department and your Excellency from the Proofs inclosed to Mr Pettit, which he will have the Honor to lay before you,[2] will perceive the Malevolence which induced the General to transmit your Excellency such Gross Misrepresentations. I have the Honor to be most respectfully— Your Excellency's Obt Servt

M. Lewis

ALS, N. Where the document is now frayed, characters have been taken from a typescript made in 1907 (NN: Miscellaneous & Personal Miscellaneous Folders).

1. Lewis was referring to Brig. Gen. John Stark's letter to GW of 21 August.

2. Lewis's letter to Charles Pettit dated 9 Sept., which enclosed certificates of his conduct from Deputy Commissary General of Purchases Jacob Cuyler, 9 Sept., and thirty-eight Albany citizens, 10 Sept., as well as other documents, was sent to GW by Pettit on 15 October.

## To Colonel William Malcom

Sir            Head Quarters [White Plains] 11th Sepr 1778.

I am favd with yours of the 10th with the weekly Returns of the Garrison.

By a special agreement with the Artificers, they draw larger Rations than the Soldiers, you are therefore to allow them, what Colo. Baldwin's draw here, which I think is 1½ lb. Bread or Flour 1½ lb. Meat and half a pint of Rum ℔ day.

Altho' your Qr Mr would be very useful here at present, yet Colo. Hay has pointed out the difficulties the Garrison would be under for want of him, in such a manner, that I must consent to his staying.

You will detain the four hundred repaired Arms expected from Albany, for the use of Colo. Hogans Regiment, and desire as many more to be sent down as will complete them. The armourers shop is, I am told, in very fine order at Albany, and I would not therefore wish to break in upon it, by drawing off the hands.[1] I would rather you should endeavour to find a few Gun Smiths among your own men and put them under the direction of Mr Allen at Fishkill to repair the Arms of the Garrison. I am &c.

Df, in Tench Tilghman's writing, DLC:GW; Varick transcript, DLC:GW.

1. This information apparently came from Maj. Gen. Horatio Gates, who wrote Philip Van Rensselaer on 14 Sept.: "I have in the strongest manner recommended the Armory at Albany to the protection and encouragement of His Excellency General Washington" (Van Rensselaer, *Annals of the Van Rensselaers*, 184).

## From Major General John Sullivan

My Dear General                    Providence septemr 11th 1778
   I was honored with your Excellenceys favor of the 5th Instant yesterday 12 of Clock. also That of the 9th Last night at Eleven. It gives me & the officers here Infinite Satisfaction that your Excellencey has approved our Conduct—I am at a Loss to guess the Designs of the Enemy in this Quarter General Gray with his Fleet are Standing off & on before Bedford Harbor The Day before yesterday a number of vessels Supposed to be Twenty were out of Newport and Stood westward. yesterday upward of thirty Sail went out of the Harbor about twenty Small ones went Eastward the Residue Stood to the Southward[1]—Colo. Peabody who is Stationed on the western Shore writes me that all the Ships & other vessels are out of the Harbor They have been taking heavy Cannons & Stores on board for Some time past—They have taken no pains to Lay up Forage & Some of their movements Seem to Indicate an Evacuation what are their Real Intentions cannot at present be Divined I Shall keep your Excellencey Constantly advised of Every movement & have the honor to be with the greatest affection & Esteem your Excellenceys most obedient & very Humble Servant

                                        Jno. Sullivan

ALS, DLC:GW.
   1. British officer Frederick Mackenzie at Newport, R.I., wrote in his diary for 10 Sept.: "The Ships under Commadore [William] Hotham sailed this Morning for New York. A number of small vessels sailed at the same time for Martha's Vineyard, for Stock." According to Mackenzie's entry for 9 Sept., Hotham's vessels carried naval stores and the officers, seamen, and marines belonging to the British vessels burned at Rhode Island, to "be distributed to the ships of Admiral Byrons fleet" (*Mackenzie Diary*, 2:394).

## General Orders

                    Head-Quarters White Plains Saturday Septr 12th 1778.
Parole Rockingham                    C. Signs  Rye. Rippon
   The troop, retreat &c. to be beat in the following manner—The Drums Call to begin at the Artillery Park a quarter of an hour before beating off and to run thro' the Right and Left Wing and second line and be returned into the Park again.
   The next signal to be three Taps from the Park runing thro' and to be return'd in the same manner—Then the whole beat off at the hour appointed for the respective Beats: Every Fifer and Drummer to be ready to beat off after the Drummer's Call is beat before the Taps are received.

The hours of Exercise in the afternoon are altered from four to six ôClock.

The Court-Martial whereof Coll Humpton is Presidt will sit tomorrow morning nine ôClock at the Presidents quarters near the Provost—The Members are desired to attend punctually.

The General Officers off duty agreeable to Orders of the 10th instant are desired to meet this afternoon four ôClock at the New-Dining Room, for the Purpose therein mentioned—The Field Officers of the Artillery will attend the board at that time.

A Subaltern and sixteen men from each Brigade to be paraded tomorrow morning on the Grand Parade where they will receive particular Orders to patrole the Vicinity of the Camp to pick up all public and other horses that may have stragled away.

A Surgeon and a proportionable number of Officers with a sufficiency of well men will hold themselves in readiness to assist the sick to Terrytown and from thence in boats to Fish-Kills-Hospitals—The Officers will see that the sick draw three days provisions.

The Brigade Surgeons to settle this Piece of duty among themselves or in failure—to be appointed by the Commander of the Brigade. The Surgeons for this service will immediately deliver to the Surgeon General at the Hospital tents the number of sick in each Brigade that the Waggons may be sent to transport them as soon as the boats are ready to receive them.

A Vessel is waiting at Terrytown for the Reception of such heavy baggage as is ordered to be sent off to transport it to Fish-Kill where it will be carefully stored. The Officers will send it in Waggons to Terrytown between this and tomorrow noon—They are desired to mark their Names on their own Baggage.

A Field Officer from Genl Muhlenberg's Brigade is appointed to Superintend the Hospitals in Pennsylvania under the direction of Coll Chambers.

Varick transcript, DLC:GW.

On this date John Mitchell, deputy quartermaster general at Philadelphia, wrote to Assistant Quartermaster General Charles Pettit regarding supplies procured for GW: "I have now sent the Seats, Tacks & Brass Nails for 18 Camp Stools, two Pair Pistols, Holsters, Saddle Cloths, one Dozen Common knives & forks, two Copper wash hand Basons & one Copper Urinal for His Excellency I have got the China, Cups, Saucers &c. and two large China Bowls for His Excellency but the case is not yet finished I expect it will be neat & hope it will please—the 2 Mustard went some time ago—have not been able to get the Bearskin, Table Cloths & best Knives & Forks yet; but hope soon to procure them no pains shall be wanting to procure every thing he desires or wishes for." On an attached list of the items, Mitchell mentioned that letter paper, quills, wafers, "British ink powder," and pencils were included in the box and that he had been unable to acquire "smaller Brass

Nails." Also, "the Saddle &c. for his Excellency went in July & hope has got safe" (DLC:GW).

## From John Clark, Jr. and James Johnston

Harrison's Purchase [N.Y.] [1] Auditors Office
May it please your Excellency.                    Septr 12th 1778.

In virtue of a Resolve of Congress of the 3rd Inst:, We have digested a Plan for setling the accounts of back rations: as also a hint to the Officers, on the subject of settling their Accots agreeable to your late order; and directions for the Regimental paymaster's *of the line*: all of which, are intended to promote the public good; and facilitate the settling and adjusting the Accounts of the Army. We beg leave to submit them to your consideration, and hope (if not inconsistent with good policy) the inclosed may be inserted in the next General Orders.[2] We have the honor to be with the greatest attachment and respect Sir Your Most Obedt Humble Servts

Jno. Clark Junr
Jas Johnston Audrs

P.S. Col. Harrison's Letters of the 10th 11th & 12th Inst. have been received and attended to.[3]

LS, DLC:GW. Robert Hanson Harrison docketed the cover of the letter, in part, "ansd verbally."

Congress elected James Johnston auditor of accounts at the main army on 3 Sept. 1778, and he remained at that post in 1781.

1. The northern end of Harrison's Purchase, near Purchase, N.Y., is about three miles east of White Plains; the southern end, near Harrison, N.Y., is about five miles southeast of White Plains.

2. The resolution of 3 Sept. authorized the auditors to settle rations accounts "upon the oath of the party, and such other evidence as the circumstances of the case will admit" when certificates of issuing commissaries could not be obtained (*JCC*, 12:863). In the enclosed plan, the auditors quoted the resolution and directed "that all accounts of back rations be made up to the first of September Instant, and those of each Regiment collected in form of a regimental Abstract. . . . The accounts being attested to before the Brigadier . . . and forwarded with the regimental abstract will be allowed." The auditors also referred all officers to GW's general orders of 25 July regarding the settlement of accounts, threatening that those who failed to comply within one month would "be proceeded against Agreeable to the Resolves of Congress" (DLC:GW).

3. For Robert Hanson Harrison's letter to Clark of 10 Sept., see Clark to GW, 10 Sept., source note. The letters of 11 and 12 Sept. have not been identified.

## From Major Alexander Clough

Sr                    [Hackensack, N.J.] Sept. 12th 78 12 OClock
   Three french merchants who have been prisoners in New york four
months, but had the liberty of the town—informs me, that Gnl Clinton went over to long Island on wedensday last,[1] it is suposed to see
those troops he carry'd up the sound, which are now encamp't, he is
expected back in a few days, thay continue to embark thayr cannon,
and ordinance stores, a body of troops are likewise embarkt, but he
knows not the number—another who left new york the last night, con-
ferms the above account, and further adds, thay prest upwards of seven
hundered the last tusday, and wedensday, & it still continuas very hot,
it is given out that two thousand is wanted, the european merchants are
selling of thayr goods by vandue at a very low rate, he gave me the following instance that a sadle & bridle, which would have been sold two
months ago for six pounds, may now be bought for four dollors, all
other goods are sold in the same proportion, thay have been employ'd
in this manner somthing better then a week—whithin these three days
orders have been isue'd for all the market boats to be brought in from
Long Island, he says further there as been near three thousand head
of cattle drove from the east end of Long Island, which thay are now
killing, salting, & packing in Barrels, to the southward of Hamstead—
bread is sold for sixteen pence sterling a pound. I am your Exellencys
most Obt Hbl. Servt

                                                        A. Clough

ALS, DLC:GW.
   1. The previous Wednesday was 9 September.


## From Major General Horatio Gates

Sir                                                 12th Septr 1778
   I am this moment Hond with your Commands by Letter from Lieut.
Col. Hamilton, & shall halt as you direct near Bedford.[1] I am Sir Your
most Obedt Humble Servant

                                                        Horatio Gates

ALS, DLC:GW.
   1. Alexander Hamilton's letter to Gates of this date reads: "His Excellency commands me to inform you, that he has received advice, that the enemy, who had
made a debarkation at Bedford [Mass.], after burning the little town, had reim-
barked their troops and were hovering about the Coast. He does not think it expedient that you shou'd advance too far from the army and therefore desires, that

you will halt near Bedford [N.Y.] 'till you hear further from him" (NHi: Gates Papers). Another letter of this date, from GW to Gates, conveys similar orders: "From intelligence this moment come to hand, I think it prudent that the Troops under your Command should halt, I have therefore to desire that you will encamp whereever this may meet you, and there wait until you recieve further orders" (LS, NHi: Gates Papers).

## From Major General William Heath

Dear General                    Head Quarters Boston Sepr 1[2]th[1] 1778

I have received the honor of yours of the 6th instant;[2] and have given orders for the Artificers at Springfield to be cloath'd, agreeable to your direction.

This moment[3] the Continental sloop of war, commanded by Capn John Rathburn arrived in this Port from a cruise, and gives the inclosed intelligence[4]—Whether this fleet was from Europe, and what is calld the Glasgow fleet[5]—or whether they were from Cannada—of which I think there may be at least some probability is uncertain—I thought it my duty to give your Exellency the earliest notice of it.

I would request that the Letter addressed to the Hon. the President of Congress may be sent by your first Express to Philadelphia and ask your Excellency's pardon for giveing you the trouble.[6] I have the honor to be with the greatest Respect your Excellencys most Obedt Servt

W. Heath

LS, DLC:GW; ADfS, MHi: Heath Papers.

1. Heath wrote "11th" on the LS, but the draft and both enclosures are dated 12 September.

2. Heath received GW's letter of 6 Sept. on 10 Sept. (see Heath's second letter to Maj. Gen. William Phillips of that date, P.R.O., 30/55, Carleton Papers).

3. On the draft, Heath wrote "morning."

4. According to newspaper reports, the *Providence* returned to Boston on 11 Sept. (*Boston-Gazette. And Country Journal*, 14 Sept.). The enclosed intelligence, dated 12 Sept., reported: "That on the 7th Ulto about Ten Leagues from Louisbourg, He fell in with 30 Sail of Transports Standing to the Westward, One of Which He engaged from Sun sit till 12 oClock at night when he quited her—Supposes there were 200 Men Highlanders on Board—The Transports were all armed Apprehends they mounted from Ten to Fourteen Guns each and were under Convoy of the Aurora Frigate—About the 30th of Augt Capt. Rathburn put into Port Roswell [Roseway] about 25 Leagues West of Halifax to repair his Mast. He was informed by the People there that five thousand Troops had arrived at Hallifax" (DLC:GW). Capt. John Peck Rathbun (1746–1782) was appointed to command the sloop *Providence* in April 1777 and remained in command of that vessel until 1779, when he assumed command of the Continental frigate *Queen of France*. Captured at Charleston in May 1780, Rathbun had been exchanged by February 1781, and he assumed command of the letter-of-marque brigantine *Wexford* in August 1781. That vessel was

taken by the British frigate *Recovery* in September 1781, and Rathbun was eventually confined in a British prison, where he took ill and died.

5. The *Continental Journal, and Weekly Advertiser* (Boston) of 10 Sept. printed a report from London, 2 July, that "Upwards of 8000 men have embarked from Glasgow within the last two months."

6. Heath's letter to Henry Laurens of 12 Sept. conveyed Rathbun's intelligence (DNA:PCC, item 157).

## From Major General William Heath

Dear General                    Head Quarters Boston Sept. 12th 1778
    The Inclosed I have Just received, the Gentlemen are here on furlough from Major General Sullivan, I mentioned to them that as the Regt was with General Sullivan, it would have been proper for them to have Applied to him, They acquaint me that they mention'd it to the General before they left providence and that He advised them to apply to your Excellency through me I fear the greater part of the Officers of the Same Regt intend to apply for leave to resign their Commissions.[1]

    Colo. Cheever in Consequence of pressing Orders from Genl Knox has Just Sent here for a number of Arms to Compleat one Thousand Stand which he has wrote to have forwarded immediately, I have been obliged to obtain the loan of 300 from the State. I have the Honor to be with the greatest respect your Excellencys most Obt Servt

                                                    W. Heath

ALS, DLC:GW; ADfS, MHi: Heath Papers.
    1. Heath enclosed letters of 12 Sept. from Capt. Nathaniel Jarvis and Adj. James Carew of Col. Henry Jackson's Additional Continental Regiment. Both men requested that Heath write GW to allow them to resign, Jarvis citing "Bussiness . . . which has suffered exceedingly by my absence" and Carew citing business, family affairs, and a "Constitution . . . by no means equal to the fatigues of a Camp" (both DLC:GW).

## To Henry Laurens

sir                          Head Quarters White plains Septr 12 1778
    I do myself the honor of returning to Congress the report of their Committee on the subject of an Inspectorship, transmitted in your Letter of the 20th Ulto, which was not received till the 31st—with such observations as have occurred to me, in considering the matter, and which I have made with a freedom, that I trust will be agreable to Congress.[1] I wish it had been in my power to have returned it before; but

the intervention of a variety of other important business from time to time, obliged me to postpone a conclusion upon the points till yesterday. I have already, in a Letter of the 26th of July, delivered my sentiments upon the consequences that would attend the Baron Steuben's being appointed to an actual and permanent command in the line and therefore, and I will not trouble Congress with a repetition of them; however, I will take the liberty to add, that I am more and more convinced, that what I then said upon the occasion was well founded; and that I am certain such a measure will produce at least, infinite discontents and disquietudes among the General Officers.

I have also had the Honor to receive your favor of the 5th Inst., with the several papers to which it refers. These shall have my attention as far as practicable. I hope all the Confederal troops are on the march from Philadelphia—and if they are not, that immediate orders will be given for their joining the Army.

The Inclosed copy of a Letter from General Sullivan of the 10th Instant, will inform Congress, that the Enemy have not relinquished their burning plans, and that in this way they have destroyed several Houses—Stores and Vessels at and near Bedford. I was advised on Wednesday night, that a body of them, consisting of four or five Thousand, under General Grey had made a landing in that quarter, and were intrenching.[2] In consequence of this, and from an apprehension that General Clinton might possibly mean to operate at the Eastward and form some project in concert with Lord Howe against the Count D'Estaing's Squadron, I determined to move the troops from this ground to a Rear position, better calculated to afford support to the Works on the North river, in case an attempt should be made against them, and at the same time more convenient for forwarding Detachments to the Eastward, if the Enemy point their operations that way. I was the more induced to come to this determination, as most of the accounts from New York seemed to lead to a belief, as they still do, that a considerable movement was & is in contemplation, if not an entire evacuation of the City, and this by water. Besides these reasons, the principal Objects for taking post here do not now exist. One was to create every possible jealousy, in favor of the expedition against Rhode Island; another—the consuming the forage within its vicinity and towards Kings bridge &c. The former is now over—and the latter in a great degree accomplished. I have the Honor to be with great respect & esteem sir Your Most Obedt Servt

Go: Washington

LS, in Robert Hanson Harrison's writing, DNA:PCC, item 152; Df, DLC:GW; copy, DNA:PCC, item 169; Varick transcript, DLC:GW. This letter was read in Congress on 14 Sept., and its enclosures were referred to committees on 15 Sept. (see *JCC*, 12:913–14).

1. The copy of the report that GW returned here has not been identified, but the draft of his observations, which is in Robert Hanson Harrison's writing with one phrase added by GW, includes the texts of the thirteen resolves (DLC:GW; for the report, see also *JCC*, 11:819–23). The undated observations sent to Congress, which are in Tench Tilghman's writing, read as follows: "Observation on 1st Resolve. This seems to imply that a new Officer shall be created for this special purpose, on whom, the Rank, Pay and Rations of Major General shall be conferred as appendages of the office. But it would be preferable, when circumstances will permit, to take the Inspector General from the officers already in the line of the Army, and to give it the more weight and respect, it would be proper to appoint him from among the Major Generals. This however can only apply in future appointments, as Baron Steuben has already been elected to the office, and his Talents and services give him a title to continue in it.

"Observation on 2d Resolve  The first period of this Resolve is unexceptionable, and comprehends all the objects of the Inspectorship, consistent with the present establishment of the Army. From the beginning of the second period vizt 'that he shall also review &c.' to the end of the third paragraph concluding with these words 'the means of redress' all the duties of the Muster Master are delineated with some additions relating to the [']inspection of Tents and Camp equipage' and 'advising in what manner deficiences in the Articles of Cloathing, Arms, Accoutrements, Tents and Camp utensils may be supplied and future loss as much as possible prevented' and reporting to the Commander in Chief 'any error or defect which appears in the administration or discipline of the troops *with the means of redress.*' Either the department of Muster Master must be abolished, or that part of the establishmt for the Inspectorate must be abridged, for to have two departments with precisely the same duties and objects, would be irregular and inconsistent. But it might answer good purposes to invest the inspector with some occasional powers of a similar kind, which may be an inducement to the Muster Masters to execute their office with the greater circumspection and exactness, in order to which, instead of that part of the Resolve before described, I would propose the following 'That the Inspector and his Assistants shall review the Troops at *such times and places* and receive *such returns* for that purpose, as the *Commander in Chief* or *Commanding Officer in the department shall direct,* at which reviews, he or they shall inspect the number and condition of the Men—their discipline and exercise, and the state of their Arms, accoutrements and Cloaths, observing what of these Articles have been lost or spoiled since the last review, and, as near as possible, by what means, and reporting the same with the deficiencies and neglects to the Commmander in Chief and to the Board of War.'

"The fourth paragraph is not agreeable to practice, nor is there any necessity for it.

"The fifth paragraph needs no alteration, But the sixth is entirely improper. Troops should never be under Arms but with the knowledge and authority of the commander in Chief, or of the Officer immediately commanding the Corps to be under Arms. A contrariety of orders and Views might otherwise frequently ensue; and it would also be derogatory to the Officers commanding Wings—divisions and Brigades, and make them but little more than Cyphers, to have their Men subject to be ordered under Arms, whenever it shall be the pleasure of the Inspector General and his Assistants.

"Observation on 3d Resolve  It is not essential there should be an Assist. Inspector General unless to act in a separate department, where there is a large body of Troops employed. But as this is a contingent service, the appointments to answer it may be occasional—The Inspector General, with a proper Number of Subinspectors, will suffice with the main Army; and in case of the Absence or removal of the Inspector General, the oldest subinspector may officiate. When an assistant Inspector General may be necessary, he should be taken from the line of Brigadiers, and may be only temporary. A multiplication of Rank & Offices should, in every case, be avoided as much as possible.

"Observation on 4th Resolve   The number of Inspectors should have relation to the distributions of the Army into brigades—divisions—Wings and lines. Each Brigade will require a Brigade Inspector, and besides these, it may suffice to have a subinspector for the light Troops, another for the Cavalry and three others for the three Grand divisions of the Army—vizt the Right and Left Wings and the second line. The number can be increased hereafter if found necessary.

"Instead of the words 'relative to the discipline, order and exercise,['] the words 'relative to the department' will be more precise and definite.

"Observation on 5th Resolve   This Regulation will be extremely proper with these alterations—that he shall be *one* of the Majors in the Brigade, and instead of doing duty in the line in time of Action, that he shall assist the Brigadier by executing his orders for performing the necessary maneuvres of the Brigade.

"In order that the Gentlemen at present officiating in the capacity of Brigade Majors, who have no other existence in the line of the Army, may not be thrown out of employ, they may remain in character of Aides de Camp to their respective Brigadiers with their present Rank, Pay and Rations.

"Observation on 6th Resolve   This is a proper Regulation—under the restrictions contained in the observations on Resolve No. 5. and securing to the Aides to the Brigadiers, their right of succession and promotion in their Regiments as usual.

"Observation on 7th Resolve. In time of action, the Inspectors may be as usefully employed as at other times, by assisting in the execution of the field Maneuvres; and it seems more advancive of the service, that they should act in this Capacity, than that they should be invested with actual command in the line. When circumstances will permit, it may be allowable for them to hold commands; but it should not be made a general principle. And the priviledge should only extend to those, the nature of whose appointment would otherwise intitle them to it.

"It should be clearly expressed, that the Officers appointed in the Inspectorship from the line, should retain their Rank and places in the Corps, and their right of succession and promotion in the same manner as if they had not assumed the Office.

"The present allowance to the sub and Brigade Inspectors is deemed sufficient. The Inspector Genl may receive in addition to the pay of his Rank [      ] Dollars ℔ month, and the Asst Inspector General when there is a necessity for one [      ] Dollars.

"Observations on 8th Resolve   The Inspector Generals assistants shall also be subject to the Officers commanding Divisions and Brigades to which they are attached, under the principles established. All Regulations ought to be finally ratified by Congress, till which however, from the exigency of the service, they might be practiced upon as temporary expedients liable to be rejected, altered, amended or confirmed as Congress shall judge proper.

"Observation on 9th Resolve   The whole of this Resolve had better be omitted—Some parts of it are exceptionable and the whole too much in detail. The part that is not exceptionable is rather an object of military arrangement with the Officer commanding the Troops, than of a particular act of State.

"Observation on 10 Resolve. This Resolve had better be omitted. It would establish a species of inquisition, which would render the Office and person exercising it odious, and would serve to renew and keep alive a number of complaints and quarrels, which would otherwise be buried in oblivion. It is unnecessary, because there are ample means already provided by the constitution of the Army for hearing complaints and redressing grievances.

"11th Resolve. This needs no comment.

"12th Resolve    See Remarks on 3d Resolve.

"Observation on 13 Resolve    It is expedient that there should be a power in the Commander in Chief or Officer commanding in a separate department to increase or diminish the number of subinspectors, as the exigency of the service shall require.

"General observations.

"In general it may be remarked, that this plan of the Inspectorship is upon too extensive a scale and comprehends powers so numerous and enlarged, as will naturally expose it to the jealousy and disapprobation of the Army, and will be really injurious to the Rights of the superior Officers in general. It extends to almost every part of the arrangement, management and government of troops, except in the actual operations in the Field: and by giving a legislative authority to the Inspector General, in forming Rules and Regulations for the Army, and an executive authority to him and his assistants to carry the same into practice, independent on every officer in the Army but the commander in chief, throws almost the whole administration into their hands. This not only places the other Officers on a very unimportant footing; but subverts the fundamental principle on which all military establishments turn. Agreeable to this principle a Colonel is supreme in his Regiment and responsible for its discipline, order, equipment &ca. A Brigadier in his Brigade in like manner, and so upwards. particular Officers and sets of Officers may be appointed in aid of these, but they must be subordinate and dependant—Thus the Adjutant charged with the detail &ca of the Regiment is subordinate to his Colonel. By the same Rule the Brigade Inspector should be dependant on his Brigadier, the subinspector to his Major General or the Officer commanding the division to which he is attached. If this is not the Case, the authority of these Officers in their respective Corps is reduced to a shadow and no man of spirit will continue in the service.

"The Rules and Regulations established in the first instance with the approbation of the Commander in Chief are binding in the whole Army. The particular Officers commanding Divisions Brigades &ca are answerable for the execution of them within the limits of their respective commands. The Inspector General is to see that the principles laid down are adhered to—to point out any neglects or deviations he may perceive—and if they are not rectified to make report to the Commandr in Chief. This principle is to pervade the whole department, but in a manner consistent with the Rights and powers of other Officers" (DNA:PCC, item 152).

2. The previous Wednesday was 9 September. The information may have come in John Sullivan's letter to GW of 6 Sept., which has not been found (see Sullivan to William Heath, 6 Sept., in Hammond, *Sullivan Papers*, 2:310, and GW to Sullivan, 9 Sept.).

# To Henry Laurens

Sir,                        Head Quarters White Plains September 12th 1778

Inclosed, I have the honor to transmit Congress a copy of the report of a Board of Officers, who were appointed by me to consider what would be the most eligible plan for invading Canada; in case our future prospects and circumstances should justify the entreprise.[1] The pains which General Gates has, for some time past, taken to inform himself on the subject, and the knowlege, which General Bailey and Col: Hazen possess of the country, induced me to make choice of these Gentlemen. It appears to me, that the mode recommended by them, for an expedition of this kind, is liable to fewest objections, and, though attended with many difficulties, affords a reasonable prospect of success. The great naval force of the enemy on the lakes is, in my opinion, an almost insurmountable obstacle to any attempt to penetrate by the ordinary communications.

The expediency of the undertaking in a military point of view will depend on the enemy's evacuating these states and on the reinforcements they may send into Canada. While they keep their present footing, we shall find employment enough in defending ourselves, without meditating conquests; or if they send a large addition of strength into that country, it may require greater force and more abundant supplies on our part, to effect its reduction, than our resources may perhaps admit. But if they should leave us, and their other exigencies should oblige them to neglect Canada, we may derive essential advantage, from a successful expedition there; and if it should be thought adviseable, there is no time to be lost in making preparations, particularly if the idea of carrying it on in Winter be persued.

The great importance of the object both in a military and political light demands the sanction and concurrence of Congress, before any steps can be taken, towards, it with propriety. The peculiar preparations, which will be necessary, from the peculiar nature of the interprise is an additional motive with me, for requesting thus early, their determination; as a considerable expence must be incurred in procuring several articles which would not be requisite, but on this occasion. The soldiery must be clad in a particular manner to fit them for enduring the inclemencies of an active winter-campaign—a number of snow shoes must be provided and extraordinary means of transportation, to convey our stores and baggage through a country covered with snow, and, a great part of it, hitherto unexplored.

Congress will perceive, that valuable Magazines, both of provision and forage, may be laid up in the upper settlements on Connecticut River—I have given directions for this purpose; because if the expedition in question should be carried into execution, they will be indispensible; if it should not, they will still be very beneficial for supplying the army, especially if the war should be tranferred Eastward, which there are many powerful reasons to expect.

I shall not trouble Congress with more extensive details on the subject, as Colonel Hazen who will have the honor of delivering this, will be able to satisfy any inquiries they may be pleased to make. With the greatest respect and esteem I have the honor to be Sir Your most Obedt servant

Go: Washington

LS, in Alexander Hamilton's writing, DNA:PCC, item 152; Df, DLC:GW; copy, DNA:PCC, item 169; Varick transcript, DLC:GW. GW signed the cover of the LS, which is docketed in part, "Read 15. Referred to Mr Lee, Mr Drayton" (see *JCC*, 12:914).

1. See a Board of Officers to GW, 10 September.

## To Henry Laurens

Dear Sir, White-plains Septr 12th 1778.

A few days ago I wrote, in haste, a Letter to you by Major Morris, and took the liberty of returning the gold you were so obliging as to send me by Jones[1]—For your kind intention of forwarding that sum, and goodness in bringing Congress acquainted with my want of specie you will please to accept my sincere and hearty thanks—These are also due to you for your polite attention in forwarding, for my perusal, the late exhibitions of Governor Johnstone, and his brethren in Commission[2]— That of the former is really a curious performance—He trys to convince you, that he is not at all hurt by, or offended at, the interdiction of Congress—and, that he is not in a passion; while he exhibits abundant proof that he is cut to the quick, and biting his fingers in an agony of passion.

Your Letter to Colo. Laurens respecting Monsr Galvan was forwarded to Rhode Island while he was on his return from Boston, by which means he missed it—This Gentn (if he may be so called, Monsr Galvan) waited on me a few days ago, and met with the reception due to his merit & conduct to you.[3] The beginning of the next paragraph of that Letter,[4] excited my curiosity to pursue it to the end, and to my shame, was reminded of my inattention to your favor of the 18th of June, which coming to hand upon my march thro Jersey, and being laid by to be acknowledged at a time of more liezure, was entirely forgot[5] till your enquiry after the Letters from Messrs Oswald & Manning recalled it to my recollection—I now return these Letters, together with Govr Johnstones, & a tender of my thanks for the favor of perusing them. I am convinced that no apology can be more agreeable to you, in excuse for my neglect, than a plain narrative of the truth—& this I have offered.

I am sorry to find by your favor of the 29th Ulto that Monsr Gerard was indisposed—I hope his disorder was not of long continuance, & that he is now perfectly recovered. Having often heard this Gentleman spoken of as a well wisher to, and promoter of the rights of America, I have placed him among the number of those we ought to revere—

Should you therefore see no impropriety in my (being a stranger to Monsr Gerard) presenting compliments to him, I would give you the trouble of doing this, and of assuring him, that I could wish to be considered (by him) as one of his admirers. With every sentiment of esteem & regard I am Dr Sir Yr oblig'd & affecte Hble Servt

Go: Washington

ALS, PPRF; ADfS, DLC:GW; Varick transcript, DLC:GW. The ALS is docketed in part, "Received 15th."

1. GW was referring to his private letter to Laurens of 4 Sept. (second letter).
2. See Laurens to GW, 29 August.
3. John Laurens discussed William Galvan's reception when he wrote his father on 15 Sept.: "The Genl asked me in private whether this was not the person alluded to in your letter; I told him he was; the General then left the room without taking any further notice of him" (Laurens, *Army Correspondence*, 224).
4. Laurens had sent his letter to John Laurens of 29 Aug. open for GW's perusal. The paragraph to which GW refers reads: "When I was at York town I sent Letters which I had receiv'd thro' Governor Johnstone from my friends Mr. Oswald and Mr. Manning either to Your General or to yourself for perusal. I request you, my dear Son, return them as soon as you can" (*Laurens Papers*, 14:244). Henry Laurens had enclosed the letters written to him by William Manning, 11 April, and Richard Oswald, 12 April (ibid., 13:103–5, 107–13), with his letter to GW of 18 June.
5. On the draft, the remainder of this paragraph, after revisions, reads: "till reminded thereof by your enquiry after the Letters from Messrs Manning & Oswald which I then, and not till then recollected had been sent for my perusal. I now return them & Govr Johnstone's Letter with my thanks for the favor of the perusal of them. I am convinced that no appology to you can be of equal weight with the recital of a fact—I must therefore take shame to myself & acknowledge that this is the truth which I have here related—I hope no inconvenience has arisen from the detention of these Letters contrary to my intention & much more so to my wish."

## From Henry Laurens

Sir                                    [Philadelphia] 12th Septr [1778]

This will be accompanied by a Letter of the 9th, since which I have had the honor of presenting to Congress Your Excellency's favor of the 7th which the house were pleased to commit to the Board of War.[1]

My present duty is to transmit to Your Excellency the undermentioned Acts of Congress which will be found within the present inclosure.

1. An Act of the 11th Septr for removing if necessary the Troops of the Convention of Saratoga—for obtaining Passports for American Vessels to transport Provision and fuel for the said troops—for establishing Magazines of Provision [in] the Eastern States—for removing the Cavalry now with the Main Army if their service can be dispensed with, to places where they can be best subsisted, and for reducing the number of Horses kept by Officers in the Army.[2]

2. Duplicate of the Act of the 13th of January last refer'd to in the Act above mention'd.[3] I have the honor to be &c.

P.S. since writing the above I have been directed to transmit an Act of Congress of the 4th Inst. Resolving that no Ratification of the Convention of Saratoga not equivalent to the terms prescribed in the Act of the 8 January last can be accepted which Act will be found inclosed with this & Your Excellency is requested to transmit it to the British Commissioners at New York[4]—And this Instant the Secretary has brot me an Act of the present date for regulating the purchase of forage & other purposes therein mentioned which will be also inclosed.[5]

By an unanimous ballot in Congress on the 10th Inst. General John Cadwalader was appointed Brigadr & Commr of the Cavalry in the service of the United States & on the 9th a Brevet to rank Lieutt Colo. granted to Maj. Lewis Morris.[6]

LB, DNA:PCC, item 13. A note on the letter book indicates that this letter was carried "by Dodd."

1. Laurens was probably referring to his letter to GW of 10 September. No letter of 9 Sept. has been found. GW's letter to Laurens of 7 Sept. was read in Congress on 10 Sept. (see *JCC*, 12:896).

2. For this act, see ibid., 12:901–3; the enclosed copy has not been identified.

3. The resolution of 13 Jan. 1778 directed GW to require Gen. William Howe to provide "proper passports for vessels to transport salted meat, flour, and fuel to Boston, necessary for the subsistence of Lieutenant General Burgoyne's army" and to inform Howe that if Howe refused, "these states . . . shall think themselves at liberty to remove or separate the said army" (ibid., 10:45).

4. For the act of 4 Sept., see ibid., 12:880. The act of 11 Sept. directed that certified copies of the resolutions of 4 and 11 Sept. and 13 Jan. be sent to Gen. Henry Clinton. For the act of 8 Jan., see ibid., 10:35.

5. In the act of 12 Sept., Congress resolved "That the quarter master general be directed to order the commissary of forage to give immediate directions to his deputies and assistants not to purchase any wheat for forage, except in the vicinity of camp, unless in cases of absolute necessity"; that the commissary general of purchases should give orders to his assistants "forthwith to deliver to the commissary of forage, and his deputies, the bad wheat and offals of wheat, which they at present have, or hereafter may have," and order the purchasers "not to purchase, in future damaged wheat"; and "That the quarter master general be directed to consult with the Commander in Chief, whether a reduction of the stationary teams cannot be made . . . or whether ox-teams cannot . . . be substituted in a great measure for horse-teams," and to execute those changes if GW so advised (ibid., 12:906–7).

6. For these acts, see ibid., 12:897 and 894.

## From Brigadier General William Maxwell

Sir                                      Elizth Town [N.Y.] 12th Sepr 1778
    I have some thing to lay before your Excellency which is far from being agreeable and I do ashure you that I have done every thing in my

power to prevent it, unless I had put your orders to me into publick Orders here. I have herewith sen you the proceedings of a General Court Martial where two Capts. is tryed for disobedience of Orders. I think the Evidence is quite full especialy agains Capn Burrows, but you will see what the Judgment is, it does not signify to try them here for the crime of stoping persons going out to make discoverys the lower Officers has got a notion that there is a traid carryed on by it, and as Coll Og[d]en Dayton & Barber procured the people for that purpose they thought they were serving them selves, you must know that persons going on that errand must have some thing with them for an excuse, this was all that was done, they took the Boat several times going in and found nothing of consequence.[1]

They took her 2 or 3 nights after each other when your Excellency wanted Intiligence most. I have not aproved of the Court Martial but sent it to your Excellency for Your Perusal and direction and am Sr Your Most Obedient Humble Servant

Wm Maxwell

N.B. Coll Ogdens Letter of last night I kept till this morning to send it by Mr Armstrong.[2]

ALS, DLC:GW.

1. The enclosed proceedings have not been identified. GW's general orders of 14 Sept. approved the "not guilty" verdicts for captains John Burrowes and Alexander Mitchell, and GW's secretary Robert Hanson Harrison informed Maxwell in a letter of 17 Sept. (DLC:GW). Burrowes, who had been a captain in Col. David Forman's Additional Continental Regiment since its formation in January 1777, became a captain in Col. Oliver Spencer's Additional Continental Regiment in April 1779 and was promoted to major in July of that year. He retired from service when that regiment was disbanded in January 1781. Mitchell, of Gloucester County, was appointed a first lieutenant in the 4th New Jersey Regiment in November 1776 and was promoted to captain in November 1777. He transferred to the 1st New Jersey Regiment in July 1778 and served in that regiment to the end of the war.

2. Col. Matthias Ogden's letter has not been identified.

## From Brigadier General Charles Scott

Sir                                    [Philipseborough, N.Y.] 12th Sept. 1778

I am led to believe that the enemy are at the Very eve of a Movement. the Several Persons Sent in for intelligence, who was to Have been Back (Some Yesterday and others the Day before) are not Yet returnd, I am told that they are all good people. this togather with What Colo. Gist tells me about a person that He Sent in with Markiting being stoped at the out lines Contrary to the Usual costom Leavs it no longer a doubt about the others Being detaind. the Colo. also informs me that There are Colected in Spiking Deavil Creek, Upwards of a hundred Boats, within a fiew Days. Colos. Butler Grayham & Capt. Leavenworth will all be out again to day in order To meet those persons already sent in and in Case of Faliour provide others for the Same Purpose, I am so indisposd that I cant attend to this business in person, but rest assurd that every thing possable shall be don To gain the earliest intelligence which shall Be immediatly Transmited to You. I am Your Excellencys Obt Servt

Chs Scott

ALS, DLC:GW. Also on this date, Scott wrote a brief note to GW transmitting "a letter this minut Recd from Capt. Leavenworth" (DLC:GW). In that enclosure, dated "half Past 8 Oclock 12th se:," Capt. Eli Leavenworth informed Scott: "My Man has not return'd has sent me word he Cant get by the Shiping before 12th Oclock this evening, but that he shall ⟨an⟩swer my Expectation. I am inform'd by a person who left him, there has been an action to the Esward, at a place they think Call'd Sing-sing, report it turn'd in favour British troops a number of troops are Call'd for from New York to go there and are Imbarck'd some of them will Come through Hell Gate this Day. I am further inform'd fifteen hundred Hessians are Coming to Re-Inforce at King Bridge beg your Hon: woud not sent any Body on this Post for I shall have the whole on it very soon if not discovered" (DLC:GW). In the dateline Scott's location is taken from the address on Leavenworth's letter.

## To Major General John Sullivan

Dear Sir                              Head Quarters White plains 12th Sepr 1778
    Yours of the 10th came to hand late last night. The intentions of the Enemy are yet very mysterious. From the expression of your letter, I take it for granted that General Gray had embarked again after destroying Bedford; and by his hovering about the Coast, and Lord Howe's coming round again to New port, I cannot but think, that they mean something more than a diversion or deception. The destruction of the Count D'Estaings Fleet is an object of the greatest magnitude, but as that cannot be easily effected, while they lay in the Harbour of Boston, without a cooperation by land and water, I am apprehensive that they mean to possess themselves of such Grounds in the neighbourhood of Boston, as will enable them to carry such a plan into execution. Whether they would do this by landing at a distance and marching thro' the Country, or by possessing themselves at once of part of the harbour, I cannot determine. I must therefore recommend it to you to keep the strictest watch upon the motions of the Enemy, and if you find them inclining towards Boston, endeavour, with your own force and what you can collect upon the occasion, to prevent them from taking such positions as will favor their designs upon the Fleet.

Upon a supposition that the Enemy mean to operate to the East-ward, I have already advanced three Brigades some distance from the main Body of the Army, ready to move forward, should there be occasion; and I intend to place the whole in such a position, in a day or two, that they may either march to the Eastward, or be within supporting distance of the posts upon the North River, as appearances may require.

I shall govern myself chiefly in my motions, by the advices I receive from you. I therefore most earnestly intreat you to be very clear and explicit in your information, and to let me hear from you every day—tho' there may be nothing material to communicate, yet it releives me from a state of anxiety, which a suspension of intelligence naturally creates.

I would not have you attempt, in the present situation of affairs, to divide your force too much in order to cover every part of the Country, and as the Enemy have now the superiority by sea, I recommend it to you by all means to keep out of Necks or narrow peices of land with any considerable Bodies of Men. Small guards posted at the most likely places of descent are all that ought to be expected from you. In one of my late letters I mentioned the necessity of taking the public Arms out of the Hands of the disbanded Militia.[1] I cannot help repeating the necessity again, because I find our public Magazines are unable to supply the wants of the Army, notwithstanding the great importations of last year. Be pleased to forward my letter to Count D'Estaing with the greatest expedition to whom be pleased to communicate every move of the enemy by land or water, as far as they come under your observation.[2] I am &c.

Df, in Tench Tilghman's writing, DLC:GW; Varick transcript, DLC:GW.

1. See GW to Sullivan, 5–6 September.
2. GW was referring to his letter to Vice Admiral d'Estaing of 11–12 September.

*Letter not found*: from Brig. Gen. William Woodford, 12 Sept. 1778. A letter of 12 Sept. from Woodford to GW was offered for sale by the Anderson Auction Company, *Library of the Late Adrian H. Joline of New York City. Part 5: American Autographs . . . to Be Sold April 28 and 29, 1915*, entry 621. The catalog quotes one sentence of the letter, which requested a leave of absence for Lt. Col. John Cropper: "If your Excellency has no objection, he can be spared from his Regt. which Col. Morgan commands."

## General Orders

Head-Quarters W. Plains Sunday Septr 13th 1778.
Parole Eugene— C. Signs Eastown Elk.

The Commander in Chief directs that such of the sick in Camp who are able to walk may be immediately sent off towards Peeks-Kill under careful Officers who will march them moderately and attend carefully to their Accommodation; They are to take their Arms and Accoutrements with them; Their Packs to be sent to Terrytown and transported by Water to Fish Kill—Boats will meet this part of the sick at Peeks-Kill to convey them to Fish Kill.

At a General Court-Martial whereof Coll Humpton was President Septr 4th 1778—John Pooler Private in the second Regiment of Light Dragoons tried 1st for Desertion—2ndly Selling his Continental Cloathing—3rdly Stealing a horse and Saddle found guilty of breaches of the 1st Article 6th Section, of 3rd Article 12th section and of 5th Article of 18th Section of the Articles of War and sentenced to receive one hundred lashes and to serve on board such Frigate as His Excellency shall direct during the term for which he is inlisted.[1]

His Excellency remits the service on board a Frigate but approves the remainder of the sentence and orders it to be put in execution tomorrow morning at the head of the Regiment to which he belongs.

Varick transcript, DLC:GW.

1. John Pooler, a Salisbury, Conn., farmer who apparently enlisted in the 2d Continental Dragoon Regiment in July 1778, deserted on 9 Aug. 1778. Article 1, section 6, of the articles of war prescribed death or "other punishment" as penalty for desertion; article 3, section 12, prescribed imprisonment or corporal punishment for a soldier convicted of "having sold, lost or spoiled, through neglect, his horse, arms, clothes or accoutrements"; and article 5, section 18, authorized discretionary punishment for "All crimes not capital, and all disorders and neglects . . . to the prejudice of good order and military discipline" not mentioned in the other articles ( *JCC*, 5:792, 796, 807).

# From Brigadier General Duportail

White Plains 13th [September][1] 1778
Memoir on the works made in the Highlands

The works, which are in hand at West Point and some inconsiderable ones, which it is necessary to add to them, will, with the help of the chain, perfectly fulfil the object which is proposed, that of hindering the enemy's remounting the North River.

Fort Putnam, which is, as it were, the key of all the others may be rendered almost impregnable. There is indeed a height, which commands it, but besides that this height may be taken possession of with a redoubt, it would be very difficult for an enemy, even when master of it to bring heavy cannon there. Besides it would be too far to make a breach. This fort has nothing to fear, but a bombardment, or escalade. with respect to a bombardment, the mean to render it ineffectual is to have bomb-broofs sufficient for three fourths of the Garrison, magazines hospital &c.—I am told Col: Koshiusko proposes, at this time to begin one; but which will not suit more than 70 or 80 men. This is far from sufficient. There must be another, the place and size of which, I have pointed out to the Captain who conducts the works. It will contain about two hundred men—with respect to the escalade, to prevent its success, the side of the fort which looks towards the river and is the most accessible, as well as that which looks towards Fort Arnold, must be raised a great deal more than it is, and besides the palisades and chevaux de frises, abaties must be made in front. The roof of the great bomb-proof, which I propose, may be made use of to collect the rain and conduct it into the Cistern. This will always be a small resource.

Fort Willis[2] does not appear to me well traced. It ought to be put entirely upon the declivity which looks towards the River, the face next Fort Putnam following the ridge of the eminence. In this manner, it would have overlooked equally all the valley between Fort Putnam and itself and all its interior would have been under cover of Fort Putnam; the face next the river would have extended to the very border of the declivity; and the work in every respect would have been a great deal stronger. In its present position it is too large its parapet makes too great a circuit. It will be best perhaps to rebuild this fort altogether; if this is not done, to remedy its inconveniences, the face opposite Fort Putnam must be raised not so as to cover the interior, which I am told Col. Kosciousko proposes, because it must be prodigiously elevated to answer that purpose—[3]but instead of this, I would prolong the eminence which is in the middle of the work, and improve it into a Traverse, to extend the whole length of the work—I would then reject a third of the work on the South, as altogether useless—the bomb-proof will be backed by the traverse abovementioned.

I should have prefered to the Redans which are in front of the Redout Willis, on the south side, and which require for their defence four or five hundred man—a small inclosed work to secure the possession of the eminence and protect the batteries in front—but for the present, matters may be left as they are.

Fort Arnold appears to me to be pretty well situated and traced—but if the intention of Col. Kosciousko is to leave the sides next the River at the present height—(as appears to be the case) I cannot approve it—they are exceedingly liable to an escalade—it is proper to elevate them, and even to make a small covert way without, having good palisades in front, to secure the body of the place against all Surprise.

The Scantlin for the Bomb proofs appears to me too feeble—the top will be almost flat—What is made of earth ought to have been of Masonry or bricks—however I forbear enlarging upon this subject, because time will hardly admit of a Remedy—the Stuff being Squared,

and ready to be put together—observing only that the work should be
sunk more in order to furnish a greater thickness of earth for the roof.

There is below Fort Putnam,[4] a battery nearly round, which is extremely well placed for battering the Vessels which should approach
the Chain—but its situation likewise exposes it to the fire of the
Ships—at least as it is much advanced, the fire of the tops would injure
the Gunners, and the more, as by the form of the battery they are collected within a very small Space—it appears to me advisable, to raise
the parapet of this battery several feet—and to cover the embrasures
from the top of one Merlon to another—so as not to interfere with the
working of the Guns—altho it is equally necessary to secure the Chain
on the left-hand Shore of the River—it seems to have been little attended to—there is no enclosed work on this side to hinder the enemy
from debarking a sufficient number of men to get possession of the
ground and cut the Chain. there is only a battery which may answer
some good ends—but cannot prevent the enemy from doing as abovementioned—With three small works we shall render this point perfectly secure—the *first* to be place⟨d⟩ where the block house of fort independence stood[5]—it is sufficient for it to contain abou⟨t⟩ sixty
men—its end is to afford an immedia⟨te⟩ defence to the Chain and its
extremity—against a hardy enterprise, which a few men are engaged
sometimes to undertake by dint of money or other recompences—the
parapets ought to be of wood in order to take less room—and
sufficiently elevated to cover the area.

the *second* Redout should be placed on a steep eminence which commands all the other rising grounds in the island.

the *third* on an eminence in the rear of the newly constructed battery—these two Redouts ought to be made for 150 men or 200 at most.

There was a battery, the remains of which are still in existence, (below Fort Independence)[6]—it was perfectly well placed for battering
the enemys Ships—it ought to be rebuilt, with a strong parapet of
earth—and as this battery is low and exceedingly exposed to a plung-
ing fire from the Tops of Ships—the parapets must be high, and terminated by a Roof of thick plank for the protection of the Canoniers—
this battery as well as that which is just finished, will be interlocked by
the three Redouts—and be in perfect safety—With these works we
shall be completely masters of the Island.

As to the Chain itself, I would not have it floating on the Surface of
the Water—which exposes it to be laid hold of by machines prepared
for the purpose, on board the Vessels that may approach—but the
greatest danger arising from this would be the breaking it by Cannon
Shot—when a vast number comes to be fired on both sides in a con-

test between the enemys Ships and the batteries—I should think it
more eligible therefore to suspend the Chain three feet below the surface of the water—because as the greatest number of the Shots bound
when they strike the water—there would be so many ineffectual with
respect to it—besides, the matter would be very easily executed—by
placing the floats above instead of below the Chain—and having another chain made fast at each end to the great one, and carried above
the floats—by these means the great Chain may be supported at the
depth which is judge⟨d⟩ suitable—if a shot should carry away the
Chain, by which the great one is made fast to the floats—the whole
mischief that would result, would be, that the Chain in that place
would douse a few feet more.

There are so many accidents by which an iron Chain may be broken,
that it would be prudent to have a stout cable in reserve to supply its
place in part, for a time.

Every thing that I have explained being finished—1800 men will
render us completely masters of the River, and put us out of reach of
the enemys enterprises—At least, the Resistance that may be made will
allow ample time for the arrival of Succours, however remote the Army
may be.

The following is the Distribution of these troops as nearly as can be
judged—

| | |
|---|---|
| In Fort [Arnold] [7] | 700 |
| Willis Redout | 200 |
| Fort Putnam | 400 |
| Small Work above Fort Putnam | 100 |
| For the Works on the Island or | |
|     Peninsula, on the left-hand Shore | 400 |
| | 1800 |

At the present moment, if we except the batteries against Ships—the
works are not in a state of defence—but a little time would be
sufficient for completing fort Putnam, which is the most important—
the Redouts on the island on the left-hand Shore—are likewise objects
of the first attention.

His Excellency had ordered me to give him an account of the expences arising from all these works to the present time—it is not in my
power to present any thing on this subject, not having seen Col.
Kosciousko, who alone is possessed of these facts—I am going to write
to him for this purpose.

I was likewise at New Windsor—The River appears to me very wide
in this part for a defence of Chevaux de frise—besides the Chevaux de
frise themselves appear to me to be very weak—and I can with

difficulty persuade myself, that a Ship would be much embarrassed by them—And indeed until West point is completed—I do not think we should occupy ourselves about New Windsor—I shall therefore forbear adding any thing farther relative to it.

Duportail.

Translation, DLC:GW; ADS (in French), DLC:GW. On a separate scrap of paper following the translation is written a related text that does not appear to be translated from the French; it reads: "One hundred pieces of Cannon—(twenty fours and eighteens) including those already here—will be wanted.

"The number of Artillery men—exclusive of the eighteen hundred men required to garrison the Forts & man the works—may be estimated at Six Hundred."

1. The month is taken from the docket on the translation. Although the French text is dated "13 aout," 13 Sept. is almost certainly the correct date. Duportail was ordered to undertake a survey of West Point defenses on 27 Aug. and arrived there on 9 Sept.; his report was delivered to GW before 19 September. Moreover, John Laurens, who translated most of the document, was in Rhode Island on 13 Aug. and remained there until early September.

2. In this and subsequent references to "Fort Willis" or "Willis Redoubt," Duportail may have meant Fort Webb (see Miller, Lockey, and Visconti, *Highland Fortress*, 130).

3. The text preceding this note is in Alexander Hamilton's writing, but the remainder of the translation is in John Laurens's writing.

4. Duportail probably meant Fort Arnold (see also note 7).

5. Duportail wrote "fort de l'independance," but he was apparently referring to Fort Constitution.

6. Duportail was evidently referring to Fort Constitution.

7. Laurens originally wrote "In Fort Putnam," which agrees with the French text, but he crossed out "Putnam" and added a note that reads: "fort Arnold probably."

## To Major General Horatio Gates

Sir                           Head Quarters [White Plains] 13th Septr 1778

As it is more than probable that the road Leading to Danberry is out of order, I would wish you to send a party under a proper Officer to repair it, as far as that place, that should you receive orders to move on, you may have as little hindrance as possible.[1] I am Sir Yr Mo. Obet Sert

Go: Washington

LS, in Richard Kidder Meade's writing, NHi: Gates Papers; Df, DLC:GW; Varick transcript, DLC:GW.

1. Brig. Gen. Enoch Poor, at "Camp Bedford," wrote Gates on this date: "Inclose'd is the letter Sent you by his Excellencey, if it is your pleasure that I Send an officer and a party of men to Danbuary to morrow morning youl pleas to give me orders for that purpus, but as you have Sent the Artificiers it I think it will answer the Desine of the order" (NHi: Gates Papers).

## To Major General William Heath

Dear Sir,                          Head Quarters White Plains Sepr 13. 1778

I have just received advice from the Board of War, that they have given directions to Mr Fletcher, to send forward to Springfield and Hartford all the ready made cloathing in his possession, there to be sorted and repacked previous to their coming to Camp, except a few particular articles, which are ordered immediately on; and to deliver Messrs Otis and Andrews all the Cloths, woolens linnens and other goods, to be made up by them, as expeditiously as possible, for a further supply.[1]

The necessities of the army and the experience we have had of the total mismanagement, too common in the manner of transporting cloathing to camp, by which great delay and loss have been incurred— induce me to desire your particular attention and assistance in the matter. The importance in this advanced season of losing no time and sparing no pains to supply the exigencies of the soldiery, in so essential an article, is too obvious, and I am persuaded too interesting to your own feelings, to need being inforced by a single argument. I would wish you to call upon Mr Fletcher to know what means he is employing to answer the views of the Board; and if they do not appear to you perfectly adequate, to concert with him any additional measures, you may think adviseable. The necessity is urgent and the exertions should be proportioned.

I have written to General Greene directing him to instruct his assistants in Boston, that they may strain every nerve to give the most effectual aid.[2] There is a number of return-waggons both in the Commissary's and Quarter Master's line, which may be made use of on the occasion, and be a saving of expence to the public. But though this resource should be well improved, in a business of such moment, it ought not wholly to be relied on. It is my anxious wish, the cloathing may come on with the greatest dispatch, and as much together as circumstances will permit; and for this purpose every expedient ought to be used to provide a sufficient number of waggons—hiring them if to be had, or if not, calling in the aid of the civil authority to impress, or otherwise procure them in the most certain and expeditious mode.

It hath been too much a practice hitherto to send on the cloathing in small parcels, without a guard or conductor to take care of them. The consequences have been, in every case, loss of time, in many cases, the loss of the cloathing itself, which being scattered about at different places on the road, has often been converted to private use. To obviate this—I request your care to have trusty persons appointed to conduct the cloathing, to the respective depositaries, furnished with proper guards—to facilitate which, it will be necessary to send it on in large parcels.

I should also be glad, you would call upon Messrs Otis and Andrews and know what measures they are taking for making up the articles intrusted to their care—and to give them all the advice and assistance in your power. In every step you take, however, you are to be cautious not to contravene the directions of the Board of War; but to promote and accelerate their execution. With great esteem and regard I am Sir Your most Obedt servant

Go: Washington

LS, in Alexander Hamilton's writing, MHi: Heath Papers; Df, DLC:GW; Varick transcript, DLC:GW. On the draft, the date was changed from "13" to "14," and the transcript is dated "Septr 14th."

1. This information, sent in an unfound letter from the Board of War of 5 Sept., was received on the night of 13 September. The Massachusetts council on 17 July appointed Samuel Fletcher to take charge of the clothing then arriving from France, pursuant to Congress's resolution of 28 May. In mid-August a letter from Fletcher had led the Board of War to conclude that it would be best to store the made-up items at Hartford, and they sought and received from Congress authority to do what they deemed "expedient and best adapted to present circumstances" with the clothing (Board of War to Henry Laurens, 14 Aug., and Board of War report on clothing, 5 Oct., DNA:PCC, item 147; *JCC*, 11:548–49, 811; Jeremiah Dummer Powell to Fletcher, 17 July, *Documentary History of Maine*, 16:39).

2. See GW to Nathanael Greene, 14 September.

## To Patrick Henry

Dear Sir                         Head Quarters White plains 13 Sepr 1778

I have been honored with yours of the 21st Augt inclosing a letter for Capt. Henry, whose ill state of health obliged him to quit the service about three weeks past. I therefore return you the letter.[1]

I wrote to you the 23d May last, and inclosed you a Return of the number of the drafts, under the old and new law,[2] who had actually joined the Army. I did this that the Assembly might see what Counties had been deficient in sending forward their quotas. Having never recd an answer, I am apprehensive that the letter and papers may have miscarried. If they have never reached you, be pleased to signify it, and I will furnish duplicates. I have the honor to be &c.

Df, in Tench Tilghman's writing, DLC:GW; Varick transcript, DLC:GW.

1. Neither Henry's letter to GW of 21 Aug. nor its enclosure has been found. John Henry (1757–1791), Patrick Henry's son, was appointed a cornet in the 1st Continental Dragoons in June 1776 and promoted to lieutenant in December of that year, but he resigned from the dragoons in February 1777 to take an appointment as captain in the 1st Continental Artillery Regiment. He resigned from the army on 27 Aug. 1778.

2. For the two laws, passed in the May 1777 and October 1777 sessions of the Virginia general assembly, see Hening, 9:275–80, 337–49.

## From Brigadier General Charles Scott

[Westchester County, N.Y.]

Sir                    ½ past 11 oClock Sept. 13th 1778

I have this moment Intelligence from Colo. Gist That, by a Deserter he is informd that there are about Five thousand of the enemy Coming out, two thousand On the Albany road & three thousand on Mile square Road. the deserter says that he belong'd to one of the Parties. in consequince of this I have put every thing In the Greatest readiness to receive them. mean time I Have orderd Majr Lee & Majr Tammage to keep Out Strong Patrolling parties, on the Right and left of our incampment and also infront. if I should Hear with Certainty that they Mean to reach my Camp I shall Fier three Musquets as an alarm Which May be heard at Head Quarters, (I think) But least it Should not a horsman Shall be dispatched To give You the Earliest Intelligence possable.[1] I am Your Excellencys Obt Servt

Chs Scott

ALS, DLC:GW. Scott signed a note on the cover: "Suffer the Hors man to pass to Head Quarter."

1. This intelligence was received at night. Private Zebulon Vaughan of the 5th Massachusetts Regiment noted in his journal for 14 Sept., "Last Night thare was a larom [alarm] in Camp desarter Come to us and informed that five thousand was on thar march to give us Batel Now it is 8 in mor [morning] of th Clock and thay are not Come all ouer Sick Sent of [off] to the Horspitel" ("Vaughan Journal," 110). Sgt. Maj. Benjamin Gilbert of the same regiment recorded on 14 Sept. that the alarm occurred "About two hours before Day" (Symmes, *Gilbert Diary*, 36–37).

GW's aide-de-camp John Laurens evidently replied to Scott at "¼ after 1 Oclock" on the morning of 14 Sept.: "His Excellency desires that you will immediately as it shall appear to you that the enemy have a serious design of advancing—despatch a horseman to Col Carlton who commands at Tarry Town—to give him notice of it if he has any oarsmen in his party, he will send them on board the Batteaus & Vessels to assist in getting them off.

"The General desires that you will inquire particularly of the Deserter, whether any Troops have crossed lately from Long Island—or whether any have come on this side Kings bridge and the adjacent posts—as Forts Washington, Independence &c." (Kirkland, *Letters on the American Revolution*, 1:40, dated [5 May 1777]).

## To Major General John Sullivan

Dear Sir            Head Quarters [White Plains] 13th Septem. 1778

I duly received your favor of the 11th Inst.

Repeated accounts from different quarters, announce some great and general movement on the part of the enemy—And tho' the facts with which I have been hitherto furnished are not sufficiently pointed to determine clearly whether the result may be an attack on this army, an enterprise against the french Squadron—or finally a simple evacuation of N. York unconnected with any offensive operation in the territories of the United States—yet the conduct of General Gray, & return of Genl Clinton to N.Y. without troops, require us to be very particularly on our guard against any operations which they may meditate eastward.

The immediate embodying of the Militia might be attended with the disadvantages of a heavy expence, to the State—and disgusting the men by premature Service—but it will be of the utmost importance, to have every preparatory Step taken for collecting them on the Shortest Notice—The establishing known Signals for this purpose in every proper place—that an alarm may be rapidly communicated—is an object of the first attention—every thing that regards provision, Amunition and the means of transporting them, I suppose to be already in a proper train.

I need not suggest to you how important it will be to give powerful opposition to the enemys first attempts, and by checking their progress afford the more time for the arrival of Troops from this Army—but persuaded that your foresight & activity will make the best use of the means you have, I remain &c.

Df, in John Laurens's writing, DLC:GW; Varick transcript, DLC:GW.


# From Major General John Sullivan

My Dear General                    Providence Septemr 13th 1778

I have nothing new in this Quarter Since my Last[1] The Pilots who waited on Count D Estaing call for Six Dollars pr Day I Should be glad to know whether the Sum ought to be allowd or whether I am to pay them or Send them to the Count.

Many officers of Jacksons Detachment want to Resign as there is a great Surplusage of them I think it would be no Injury to the Service. I think also that if the three Regiments[2] were Incorporated into one it would be a great Saving of Expence to the publick. I wish to know your Excellenceys mind upon the Several points & have the Honor to be with the most profound Respect your Excellenceys most obedt Servt

Jno. Sullivan

ALS, DLC:GW.

1. Sullivan was referring to his letter to GW of 11 September.

2. Sullivan was referring to the Additional Continental Regiments commanded by colonels David Henley, Henry Jackson, and William Raymond Lee.

# General Orders

Head-Quarters W. Plains Monday Septr 14th 1778.
Parole St Augustine—                    C. Signs Salem. Sandown.

The Consumption of Ammunition in this Army considering there has been no Action nor any extraordinary weather to injure Cartridges in good tents, has for the two last Months been beyond description; but this is not to be wondered at when the Camp is continually disturbed both within it's own limits and Vicinity by a disorderly firing—So many orders have been given to correct this Abuse, and induce the Exertions of the Officers to prevent it, punish delinquents and make their men attentive to preserving their Ammunition, that it gives the General real Pain to be compell'd to a further Repetition; but finding himself hitherto disappointed he positively requires that Officers Commanding Companies will in future keep an exact account of the Cartridges delivered their men, charging six pence for every Cartridge which cannot be satisfactorily accounted for besides administring Corporal Punishment for neglect and disobedience. This order is to be regularly read to the men once a Week in Presence of a Commissioned Officer to obviate every Plea of Ignorance.

At a General Court Martial in Maxwell's Brigade Septr 4th 1778—Coll Shreve President, Captn Mitchel of the 4th New Jersey Regiment was tried for willfully disobeying positive, Express written Orders on the night of the first of September. The Court are unanimously of opinion the Charge is not supported, but that he behaved like a careful, vigilant, active Officer and do therefore acquit him with honor.

At the same Court Septr 5th Capt. Burroughs of late Forman's Regiment was tried for disobeying positive written General Orders on the night of the 2nd of September and persisting in the same: The Court likewise acquit him of the Charges with honor.

His Excellency the Commander in Chief confirms the Opinion of the Court.

At a General Court-Martial in Nixon's Brigade September the 12th—1778—Lieutt Coll Loring President Captn Daniels of Coll Nixon's Regiment was tried for Inattention to his duty while under Arms[1]—The Court are of opinion that the Charge is not supported and that he be acquitted with honor. The Commander in Chief confirms the Opinion of the Court.

After orders September 14th 1778.

At a General Court Martial held in the Highlands January the 13th 1778—by order of Major Genl Putnam whereof Coll Henry Sherburne was President—Matthias Colbhart of Rye in the State of New-York was tried for holding a Correspondence with the Enemy of the

United States, living as a Spy among the Continental Troops and inlisting and persuading them to desert to the British Army, found guilty
of the whole Charge alledg'd against him and in particular of a breach
of the 19th Article of the 13th section of the Articles of War[2] and therefore sentenced to be punished with Death—by hanging him by the
Neck until he is dead.

Which Sentence was approved of by Major General Putnam. His Excellency the Commander in Chief orders him to be executed tomorrow morning nine ô Clock on Gallows Hill.

Varick transcript, DLC:GW.

On this date, GW, acting with the committee of arrangement ( John Banister and
Roger Sherman), signed a document commending the services of brevet Lt. Col.
Ebenezer Stevens and recommending "his appointment to hold effectually a Lieutenant Colonels Commission in the Artillery with the Pay of that office from the
date of his Brevet Commission, and that he be entitled to the first vacancy that may
fall in the Line." The recommendation was needed because the decision "to in-
corporate the three independant Companies into an incomplete Battalion of Artillery" had deprived Stevens "of a Command to which he was much attached"
(DNA:PCC, item 59). Congress included that recommendation in its resolutions of
24 Nov. 1778 on the army arrangement ( *JCC*, 12:1158).

1. Jotham Loring (c.1740–1820) of Hingham, Mass., who served as a captain in
the Lexington Alarm, was commissioned in May 1775 as a captain in William
Heath's Regiment of Massachusetts state troops. He remained with the unit
through various consolidations and redesignations, becoming major of the 24th
Continental Infantry in January 1776 and lieutenant colonel in November 1776.
He was court-martialed and dismissed from what was then the 3d Massachusetts
Regiment in August 1779. Japhet Daniels (1738–1805) was commissioned a lieutenant in Col. Joseph Read's Regiment of Massachusetts state troops in May 1775
and remained with the unit (redesignated the 13th Continental Regiment) until
January 1777, when he became a captain of the 6th Massachusetts Regiment. He
served until June 1783.

2. This article authorized a death penalty for those "convicted of holding correspondence with, or giving intelligence to the enemy, either directly or indirectly"
( *JCC*, 5:799).

## To the Board of War

Gentn                              Head Qrs White plains Septr 14: 1778

On sunday night I had the honor to receive your favors of the 5th &
7th Instant, with the papers to which they refer.[1]

It gave me great pleasure to find, that we were on so respectable a
footing in the General articles of Cloathing, and I would fain hope, if
we can once get the Troops tolerably supplied, that we shall in future,
by proper & timely exertions always keep them well and suitably pro-

vided.[2] I have written to Mess. Otis & Andrews urging the necessity of the strictest attention to the points severally enjoined them—and also to General Heath, to give every possible assistance to have the Cloathing forwarded, under the care of proper persons to be employed for the purpose.[3] For want of a regulation of this sort, It has come on, when it came at all, in the strangest manner; and the loss I am persuaded has been immense. I have also written to General Greene requesting that he will use his endeavours to expedite the Transportation.[4] The deficiency in Hats, besides taking off much from the appearance of the Men, will be an essential want, in case they cannot be procured. I do not know how good or extensive the Boards prospects may be of obtaining supplies at philadelphia, and from the southern States; but I should think, if the order to the Agents in this instance as well as for Blankets—Stockings and Shoes, was enlarged, no injury would arise from it, as the demand is almost constant.[5] And here I will take occasion to submit to the Boards consideration, whether it will not be greatly to the advantage of the States, to enter into Contracts for the Article of Shoes. It appears to me, that this would produce not only large & certain supplies but such as would be good. I have been told that A Mr Henry in Lancaster would contract for a considerable number and so of others in Jersey and I dare say there are persons in every State, who would engage in the business—and that it might be conducted by an easy and profitable barter of Hides for Shoes, compared to the prices usually paid and the waste of the former. The Board's idea of having all the new Cloathing delivered at one time is certainly right—and the measure will be attended with many valuable consequences. I also think the depositing of the old in proper places of security a beneficial expedient.[6] With respect to overalls, Woollen ones for the Winter and Linnen of a proper quality for the Summer, in my opinion, are much to be desired for the Troops. They look well and neat and in the summer at least they will remove the difficulty of furnishing Stockings; In the winter, both Overalls and Stockings should be provided if it can be done, as is the case in the British Army—but if it can not, Socks made out of the Old Cloaths, might in some degree answer as a substitute for the latter. I perceive the Board have directed Overalls instead of Breeches as far as the quantity & quality of the Cloth to be made up will admit—This I wish them to make a standing rule. I have desired Mr Otis & Andrews to make a distinction in the Cloaths for the Sergeants—to let them be superior in quality to that of the Soldiers—and to be more in the Style of Officers. For want of this and some encouraging designating marks, we have been very deficient in this useful & essential order of men in our Army. I have also suggested to them, that the Drummers & fifers should be uniformed differently from the Soldiers of their Regiment. The Board I observe have not considered themselves at liberty to direct the purchase of Mittens. These in case of a late Campaign or a Winter expedition will be of great service—and I would recommend the procuring a good many.[7]

I do not find from the Invoice nor from the Copies of the Letters which the Board have been pleased to transmit me, that there is any provision of Cloathing for the Officers.[8] I wish some measures could be pursued for this purpose. At present, it is with infinite difficulty that an Officer can procure necessaries to make him appear decent—and when he can, it is at the expence of all his pay.[9]

I would also take the liberty to mention to the Board, that we are in great want of Cartouch Boxes. At this time we have many Men without any—and a large proportion of those we have in use, serve but for little more than to spoil ammunition. This is an object worthy of consideration—and I am well persuaded the waste of Cartridges in the course of a Campaign, independent of their utility, and the inconveniences experienced for want of them, is equal nearly in value to the sum necessary to procure a competent supply. The Board are acquainted with the best patterns and the quality of the leather of which they ought to be made; and I trust they will direct the most expeditious measures to be pursued for furnishing the Army with them.

The prisoners confined in Easton jail, were committed by an Officer who had the charge of conducting a party to Valley forge, for mutinous conduct and attempting to escape, as he reported to me.[10] If they could be employed at philadelphia or about the River defences, it would be the best way of disposing of them. To bring them to the Army—would be to afford them an opportunity of deserting with their arms and cloathing—and perhaps of seducing many others. I have the Honor &c.

G.W.

Df, in Robert Hanson Harrison's writing, DLC:GW; Varick transcript, DLC:GW.

1. The board's letters to GW of 5 and 7 Sept. have not been found. According to the board's report to Congress on clothing, 5 Oct., the letter of 5 Sept. was "giving him the state of our cloathing, & making some proposals for the regular & economical distribution of it" (DNA:PCC, item 147). The preceding Sunday was 13 September.

2. Harrison wrote a sentence here that was later stricken from the draft: "Your letters to Messrs Otis and Andrews & to Mr Fletcher contain very useful and ⟨material⟩ directions—and my only concern is that the Board did not take the matter up a little sooner."

3. See GW to Otis & Andrews, this date, and GW to Maj. Gen. William Heath, 13 September.

4. See GW to Maj. Gen. Nathanael Greene, this date.

5. In the board's report on clothing of 5 Oct., they wrote that in consequence of the preceding passage, "we on the 22d directed them [Otis & Andrews] to purchase 10,000 hats[,] 30,000 pr hose[,] 20,000 pr shoes including the former orders. . . . The 5000 blankets before ordered we judged sufficient" (DNA:PCC, item 147).

6. At this point on the draft, Harrison continued with text that was struck out: "yet I am not certain of the operation it may have on the minds of the soldiery as they will consider both their property."

7. The board on 22 Sept. ordered Otis & Andrews to purchase 20,000 pairs of mittens (Board of War report to Congress on clothing, 5 Oct., DNA:PCC, item 147).

8. These items have not been identified.

9. Harrison's draft continued at this point with text that was stricken: "Hence there arises a sort of unconsequential feeling—a want of proper pride—an indifference to the service—and in fine a disposition, at least, to resign his Commission. I will not enlarge upon this Head—or the propriety of Cloathing and the enormous charges which attend the getting it, If Cloathing could be furnished them in an easy way & on tolerable terms, I am certain, the public would derive advantages from it. I have the Honor &c. Go: Washington."

10. GW was probably referring to the imprisonment in April of men being marched to the main army by Col. David Henley (see GW to Heath, 29 April).

## From Richard Caswell

Sir                                    North Carolina 14th September 1778

The General Assembly in may last directed a French Regiment to be raised in this State for the Service of the United States & directed Commissions to issue to the Officers necessary to Command such Regiment among whom was Monsr Sureau Duviviear appointed Major,[1] the impracticability of raising which Regiment appeared to the General Assembly in their late Session in August last, when they thought propper to disband the privates that were inlisted and declered the State had no further Service for the Officers,[2] Mr Duvivire who will have the Honor of presenting this letter Behaved extreamly well in his Station whilst imployed here, which indues me to take the Liberty of recommending him to your Excellency Notice.[3] I have the Honor to be with the utmost respect & regard—Sir your Excellency's Most Obdt & very Humble Servt

Richard Caswell

ADfS, Nc-Ar: Governor's Papers; LB, Nc-Ar: Governors' Letterbooks.

1. Sureau Duvivier petitioned the legislature in April 1778 for permission to raise a regiment of foreign troops on the Continental or provincial establishment and was then denied, probably because the legislature was already considering a similar proposal from a Monsieur Chariol. After Chariol's proposal was approved, he appointed Duvivier as major of the new regiment (*N.C. State Records*, 12:563,

590, 674, 691–93, 699, 728, 13:129). Sureau Duvivier, who was from Guadeloupe, petitioned Congress in April 1779 "to be Continued in his post of Major in the Continental Service," but the petition was rejected (Sureau Duvivier to Congress, c.19 April 1779, DNA:PCC, item 41; *JCC*, 13:472–73).

2. On 18 Aug. the North Carolina legislature resolved to disband Chariol's regiment, "as a sufficient number of privates of the French Nation can not be obtained to compleat the said regiment within this State or the vicinity thereof" (*N.C. State Records*, 12:873–74).

3. Caswell wrote another letter to GW on this date, introducing James Montflorence, a captain in the regiment, and on 22 Sept. he wrote three more letters of introduction to GW for officers of the regiment (all Nc-Ar: Governors' Letterbooks).

## From Major Alexander Clough

Sr                              [Hackensack, N.J.] Sept. 14th 78 7 OClock
On Satterday[1] Orders where given in New york, for one hundred and fifty transports to be got ready to sail at an hours warning, Gnl Clinton is on his march with his army for New york—the above intelligance may be depended on—the whole are employ'd in cleaning thayr vescells—It is reported that ten thousand are to embark for the Northward. I am Your Exelencys Most Obt

                                                A. Clough

ALS, DLC:GW.
   1. The previous Saturday was 12 September.

## To Samuel Fletcher

Sir                      Head Quarters White plains 14 Sept. 1778
   The Board of War have favd me with a Copy of their letter to you of the 20th Augt by which I find that they had directed you to forward all the ready made cloathing to Springfeild and Harford there to be opened, aired and Assorted, and the Blankets, Shoes Stockings and shirts to Camp.[1]
   The intent of the Board is to put the whole Army in compleat new uniform as early as possible in October, and to call in the old cloathing to be appropriated to other purposes. As their orders to you were pressing, I hope that considerable progress has been already made in forwarding the Goods to the places directed, but lest you should have met with difficulties in procuring Waggons, I have wrote to Genl Heath and the Quarter Master General to afford you all the assistance in their power.[2] I expect you will derive considerable advantage from the re-

turning Teams which have carried provision to the Fleet and Army at Boston.

I observe that the Board had directed you to deliver all the unmade Cloths and linens to Mess[r]s Otis and Andrews, to be by them made up into proper Cloathing for the Army. When finished and packed up, they will put them under your care to be forwarded after the others.

Vast quantities of cloathing have been lost during the course of last winter, in the passage from Boston to Valley forge, for want of proper persons to attend and conduct the Waggons, and see the delivery of the goods at the place of destination: to remedy this evil, I have likewise desired General Heath and the Qr Mr to appoint active persons, whose Business it shall be to attend every detachment of Waggons, and see that they neither loiter upon the way or lose any part of their loading. It is of the greatest consequence to the Healths of the Troops that the Blankets should reach them as quick as possible, and I therefore desire that they and the shoes may be first forwarded, with orders to come immediately to the Army. The season also requires that the Men should be in their new Cloathing as early as possible in next month. I therefore hope that no exertion on your part will be wanting to have it lodged at the places directed, and properly assorted for delivery to the Deputy Cloathiers. I am &.

Df, in Tench Tilghman's writing, DLC:GW; Varick transcript, DLC:GW.

1. This letter has not been identified.
2. See GW to Maj. Gen. William Heath, 13 Sept., and to Maj. Gen. Nathanael Greene, this date.

## To Major General Nathanael Greene

Dear Sir,                    Head Quarters White Plains Sepr 14th 1778

The Board of War have advised me of a large quantity of ready made cloathing for the use of the army, in possession of Mr Samuel Fletcher of Boston; which they have ordered to be immediately sent on to Springfield and Hartford in the first instance and afterwards to the army. You are aware of the mismanagement there has been in the manner of transporting cloathing, which has commonly been brought forward in small parcels, without guards or conductors; a mode always productive of delay frequently of loss—An apprehension of similar mismanagement in the present case and an anxiety to have the necessities of the troops at this advanced season, supplied as speedily as possible—have induced me to call the attention of General Heath to the matter. I have directed him, in conjunction with your assistants, to employ every resource for hastening the transportation[1]—Agreeable to this idea, I would wish you to make every arrangement you can in your department, for that purpose. Good use should be made of the return waggons on the occasion,[2] but in an affair of such consequence every additional resource, that may promote dispatch should be improved.

The wants of the army and the season of the year are sufficient motives for every exertion to bring on so valuable a supply of cloathing; but there is at this juncture a further reason for it, of the greatest weight. Congress have come to a resolution to inlist all the drafts in service, for the Continental bounty to serve during the war[3]—It is the opinion of the officers, that if the cloathing was on the spot, so that every reinlisted man could be furnished in hand with a good suit of cloaths, it would have a most powerful influence in promoting the success of that resolution. So many promises have been made to the men, which have never been fulfilled, that they will now trust to nothing but actual performance. If you think your going to Boston will be serviceable, it will be perfectly agreeable to me. With the greatest regard and esteem, I am Dear Sir Yr Most Obedt Serv.

Df, in Alexander Hamilton's writing, DLC:GW; Varick transcript, DLC:GW. In Greene's reply of 19 Sept., he acknowledged a letter of 15 September. Whether Greene miswrote or the letter sent was dated 15 Sept. has not been determined.

1. See GW to Maj. Gen. William Heath, 13 September.

2. Before revising the text, Hamilton wrote at this point on the draft, "but a business of such importance ought not to depend wholly upon them; every expedient that may promote dispatch should be added."

3. GW was referring to a resolution of 31 Aug. (see *JCC*, 11:854).

## From William Livingston

Dear Sir                                    Brunswick [N.J.] 14. Sepr 1778

I just now arrived in this City, & there find Capt. Costigan just arrived on parole—I learn that an express is already gone from him to Collo. Lowrie[1]—I was almost tempted to send him to your Excellency to prevent any Interview between him & Lowrie, whom I take to be one of the most artful man living—But to take a man Prisoner, & thus to bring him into disgrace, when for any thing I know, he may be innocent, I think would rather be a rash step, and probably exeed my authority— I therefore give your Excellency the earliest notice of his being here, & intend to send this by express to General Maxwell, with request to him to dispatch it to the commanding officer at hackinsack[2]—I am with the highest esteem Dear Sir your Excellencys most obedient humble Servt

Wil: Livingston

ALS, DLC:GW.

1. Livingston may have been referring to Col. Thomas Lowrey, who was later accused of aiding the British by his son-in-law, the Loyalist Thomas Skelton (see Jones, *Loyalists of New Jersey*, 189–91).

2. A note on the cover reads, "To be sent by the commanding officer of the light Dragoons at Hackinsack. Governor Livingston."

## From Brigadier General William Maxwell

Sir,                          Elizth Town [N.J.] 14th Septr 1778 Evening

I believe I can inform you Excellency that Lord How is returned to New york with the whole or greatest part of his Fleet. This I had last night from N.Y. and to day confirmed by Major Howel so far that 29 Sail went in.[1] The Brest Fleet is much talked of but no one knows where it is. It is said that with Genl Clinton came Lord Cornwalles & Sir Wm Arskin but that the Troops they took with them was left at Rhode Island or Connanicut with General Grant My Informant says there was a Council of General Officers held in New York yesterday it was thought on Bussiness of the utmost importance to them selves, supposed about their sittuation a Packet is expected in hourly when it is thought they will declare their Intensions, to move off. Three Regts was to leave Statten Island to day or to Morrow whether to embarque or go to New York not known. Viz. the 10th 27th & 55th Regts. Any of the Transports that wanted repair was geting it This is all I can gather at present[2] and Am Your Excellencys Most Obedient Humble Servant

Wm Maxwell

ALS, DLC:GW. Maxwell wrote and signed a note on the cover, which reads, "To be forwd by Express."

1. British naval captain Henry Duncan, with Howe's fleet, recorded that they returned to New York "the afternoon of the 11th September" ("Journals of Henry Duncan," 164). When GW received this letter on the morning of 17 Sept., his secretary Robert Hanson Harrison wrote Maxwell to request clarification of "Whether the 29 Sail . . . were Ships of War & of what size" (DLC:GW).

2. Col. Matthias Ogden wrote and signed a note on the back of this letter, stating that "General Maxwell's acct is agreeable to mine except that of Genl Clintons troops having remained at, or in the vicinity of Rhode Island, the greatest part have certainly returned.

"The account of Byrons death is contradicted—It is reported that Lord Howe is going home."

## To Otis & Andrews

Gentn                          Head Quarters White plains 14th Sepr 1778

I have been honored with a letter from the Board of War accompanied by the Copy of one from the Board to you of the 20th August.[1]

They desire me to give you such further directions as I may judge proper and essential to the good of the service, but their instructions are so full, that I have very little to amend or to add. In making up regimental Cloathing in future, I must desire that a difference may be made between the Serjeants suits and those for the privates, both as to fineness of Cloth and mode of finishing. Nothing contributes more to keep up that distinction which ought to subsist between the non-commissioned Officer and the soldier than a difference in point of dress. The Cloathing of the Drums and Fifes should also be characteristic of the Regt to which they belong, that is, the Ground of the Coat of the same Colour as the Regimental facing—The Board have with great propriety remarked upon the usual scantiness of the Cloaths and I beg that it may be particularly attended to.

We are often unable to alter or even to mend the Cloaths of the soldiers for want of Thread; I could therefore wish that you would purchase a quantity of coloured threads and send them forward to the Deputy Cloathier General who attends the Army, to be distributed among the regimental Quarter Masters.[2]

The approaching season demands that no time should be lost in having the Cloathing made up and ready for the Troops. I must therefore urge your utmost exertions in that respect.

I observe that the Board of War have instructed you to have all the Cloths fit for overhalls made up into that kind of Garment, and I must desire that you will in future, except you have orders to the contrary, endeavour to have a sufficiency of them, both for winter and summer wear instead of Breeches. The superior advantages of them in point of convenience, and warmth and coolness, at the different seasons is too obvious to need commenting upon.[3]

Taking it for granted that the charge of forwarding the Cloathing when made up, devolves upon Mr Fletcher, I have wrote to him upon the subject, and have desired Genl Heath and the Quarter Master General to give him every assistance in procuring fresh teams and taking advantage of those returning, which have carried supplies to the Fleet and Army at Boston.[4]

I would recommend it to you to pack all the Uniforms of different Colours in separate Parcels, marking upon the package the number and Colour of the Contents.

General Knox will send an Officer with a return of the uniforms and other Cloathing still deficient for the Corps of Artillery. Be pleased to attend to it and make up the quantity called for by him. I am &c.

Df, in Tench Tilghman's writing, DLC:GW; Varick transcript, DLC:GW.

1. Neither the Board of War's letter to GW of 5 Sept. nor the enclosed copy has been found.

2. The assistant clothier general with the army at White Plains was Daniel Kemper.

3. The preceding paragraph was written as the last paragraph of the draft but marked for placement at this point.

4. See GW to Maj. Gen. William Heath, 13 Sept., and to Samuel Fletcher and to Maj. Gen. Nathanael Greene, this date.


## From Brigadier General Charles Scott

[Westchester County, N.Y.]
Sir                Monday Morning Sun rise [14 September 1778]

I this moment recd a Note from Majr Tallmadge who informs me that his patroles Are Just returnd, who has been on all the roads Between the Brunnx and North river, the one on the albany road proceeded down almost as Fare as Phillips's Hous that on Sawmill River as low as fowlers[1] then Crossed the ridge To the Mile Square road five miles below this, Nither of which has obtaind the least intellags. of any Movement of the enemy. I have heard Nothing from Majr Lee who is on the east side of the Brunx, the deserter is Just reached my Camp who Seams to give but a lame Acct. He knows nothing of any troops Coming from long Island. he says that Some red Coats and greens Moved over the Bridg Last evening to Join Those troops on this Side, he Supposes when all togather amounted to about 2000, who He Says was on their March when he came off I this moment recd a Message from Majr Lee who informs me that his patrolls is allso Returnd without any intelligence of the enemy. I am Your Excellencys Obt Servant

Chs Scott

ALS, DLC:GW. Scott signed a note on the cover to "Suffer the B⟨e⟩arer to pass." The date is taken from the docket.

1. Benjamin Fowler (1715–1786) was a Philipse Manor leaseholder. In 1786 he purchased the 305 acres of forfeited Loyalist land on which he resided, located between the Sawmill River and Sprain Brook, about two miles north-northwest of Valentine's Hill.


## From Brigadier General Gold Selleck Silliman

Sir                Fairfield [Conn.] Septemr 14th 1778

Your Favour of the 27th Ult. respecting a Guard at the Commissary's Stores at the Landing in this Town I received the 2d Instant, inclosed in One from Mr Squier.[1] He desires me to have the Guard constantly kept up through the Summer. Whereupon I immediately gave Orders to an Ensign to inlist the Number of Men requested with One Serjeant, and One Corporal, to mount a Guard at the Store and to remain on

Duty untill the first of January unless sooner discharged; and directed him to apply to Mr Squier for Provisions Cookeing Utensills &c. The Ensign had very good Success in inlisting his Men, and has had a Guard mounted for some time past tho his Number is not yet compleated. Our present Circumstances are such that to have ordered a Detachment to have been made would not have answered the End. But the Ensign was with me on Saturday last and told me that Mr Squier had refused to furnish his Men with Provisions &c. I prevailed with him to keep his Men on Duty, till I could write Your Excellency on the Subject and have Your Answer. I first wrote Mr Squier on the Subject, but he has not thought proper to give me any Answer at all. I have therefore to desire Your Excellency to give the Necessary Orders respecting Provisions for the Men, for I have none for them, and they cant be expected to remain on Duty without. This Store stands in a Place that is very much exposed to the Enemy. A 20 Gun Ship may Anchor within a Mile of it, & her Boats may come directly to the Store & destroy it notwithstanding such a small Guard as this is. I am of Opinion that there ought to be at that Place a Captain's Command at least. But this in our exhausted State it would be extreamly difficult to raise here. Might not the Continental Troops at Norwalk be posted in this Town with equal Advantage and save the Trouble & Expence of a Guard from the Militia?[2] I am Your Excellency's Most Obedient & Most Humble Servant

G. Selleck Silliman

ALS, DLC:GW.

1. Neither letter has been found. Samuel Squire (1715–1801), who represented Fairfield in the Connecticut general assembly, 1774–80, was appointed a state commissary at Fairfield in 1775.

2. GW replied to Silliman on 22 Sept.: "I yesterday recd yours of the 14th. Inclosed you have an order to Mr Squires the Commissary to supply the Guard with provision. The Guard at Norwalk answers a particular purpose and cannot therefore be removed at present to Fairfeild" (Df, DLC:GW).

## From Major General John Sullivan

Dear General                  Providence Septemr 14th 1778

I was this morning Honoured with your Excellencys favor of the 12th Instant; The Directions in which I Shall Carefully Comply with & give Constant & the most Explicit Information of Every thing which may occur in this Department. I Inclose your Excellencey a piece of Intelligence Reced from General Heath this morning.[1] There is a Rumor here that an Express is arrived at Boston Informing that the Enemy has Landed at Falmouth Casco Bay & Burnt the remaining part of the

Town.[2] I have not been able to find out how it came or what party of the Enemy was Employd in this Laudable Business or Even how far the Report may be Relied on. General Gray with his Fleet has been gone from Bedford Several Days it is possible that he might have done it but he must have been favored with remarkable good winds. Lord Howes Fleet was a few Days agow Anchored under Block Island they are Cruising about Block Island Sound Constantly for what purpose I know not. A man has Arrived at this place (one Jacob Westcoat) who Governor Bowen Says is a man of great veracity[3] he Says that he Sailed from the west Indias with an English Fleet of Merchantmen bound home—under Convoy That the vessel he was on was Cleared out for Hallifax That after parting from the Fleet & Coming upon this Coast They were brought to by a Privateer from New york The Captain was ordered on Board with his papers which being Examined the vessel was Suffered to proceed The Captain of the Privateer Informed the Captain of the merchantman That the Enemy was going to Evacuate New york & bring all their Land and Naval Force against Boston to possess themselves of That Town and Destroy the French Fleet—I make no Doubt of the Captain of the Privateer having given this Information but how far his Authority is to be Relied on your Excellencey will Determine This is all the Information I have in this Department I Shall write your Excellencey Every Day in future—The Arms are all taken out of the hands of the Militia And Shall be forwarded to Springfield with all possible Dispatch I have the honor to be Dear General with the greatest Respect your Excellenceys most obedt Servt

Jno. Sullivan

ALS, DLC:GW. A note on the cover indicates that this letter was sent "pr Express."

1. For discussion of the intelligence from John Peck Rathbun, see Maj. Gen. William Heath's first letter to GW of 12 Sept., n.4. There are two copies in DLC:GW.

2. Falmouth, in what is now Maine, had been largely destroyed by a British raid in October 1775. The source of this rumor was probably the presence near Falmouth, Mass., of the British fleet carrying Maj. Gen. Charles Grey's troops (see William Heath to GW, 15 Sept., and for more detail on the British movements, Gruber, *Peebles' American War*, 217–18).

3. Jabez Bowen (1739–1815) of Providence was elected deputy governor of Rhode Island in May 1778 and remained in that post until 1786. Jacob Westcott, a mariner, was master of the Rhode Island privateer *Sally* in 1782.

# Appendix: Routine Documents Omitted from This Volume

These documents, which include routine letters of introduction and recommendation, routine administrative correspondence, routine letters of resignation, and personal appeals to which GW made no significant reply, will ultimately be placed in the electronic edition of the Washington Papers.

To Mrs. Ross, 6 July 1778 (ADS, NHi: George and Martha Washington Papers).

From Colonel Israel Angell, 13 July 1778 (LS, DNA: RG 93, manuscript file no. 15649).

From Colonel Benjamin Tupper, 12 Aug. 1778 (ALS, DNA: RG 93, manuscript file no. 2358).

From Colonel Michael Jackson, 13 Aug. 1778 (ALS, DNA: RG 93, manuscript file no. 2235).

From Major Benjamin Titcomb, 22 Aug. 1778 (ALS, DNA: RG 93, manuscript file no. 3330).

From Brigadier General Jedediah Huntington, 25 Aug. 1778 (LS, DNA: RG 93, manuscript file no. 751).

From Lieutenant Colonel John Nevill, 25 Aug. 1778 (LS, DNA: RG 93, manuscript file no. 18001).

From Captain Solomon Strong, 25 Aug. 1778 (LS, DNA: RG 93, manuscript file no. 751).

From Major Benjamin Titcomb, 27 Aug. 1778 (LS, DNA: RG 93, manuscript file no. 3325).

From Major Benjamin Titcomb, 28 Aug. 1778 (LS, DNA: RG 93, manuscript file no. 3329).

From Captain Thomas Paterson, c.4 Sept. 1778 (ALS, DNA: RG 93, manuscript file no. 4027).

From Captain Thomas West, 9 Sept. 1778 (ALS, DNA: RG 93, manuscript file no. 31624).

From Lieutenant James Black, 10 Sept. 1778 (ALS, DNA: RG 93, manuscript file no. 31452).

From Captain John Nice, 11 Sept. 1778 (*Pa. Mag.*, 16 [1892]: 400).

From William Woodford, 11 Sept. 1778 (ALS, DNA: RG 93, vol. 169, Commissions, 1775–1778).

From Lieutenant Colonel Ebenezer Stevens, 13 Sept. 1778 (ALS, DNA: RG 93, manuscript file no. 18192).

From Captain Mountjoy Bayly, 14 Sept. 1778 (ALS, DLC:GW).

# Index

Adam, Robert (*see* 14:449): agent for John Parke Custis, 79

Adams, Daniel Jenifer (*see* 1:338, 3: 116, 6:557): on detachment, 241; land transactions, 316–17; *letters from*: to GW, 84

Adams, Peter (*see* 15:378): *letters from*: to GW, 84

Adams, Samuel (*see* 1:26): on congressional committee, 304

Additional Continental Regiments. *See* Continental army

Adjutant general, 91; British, 327; deputies, 251–52; duties, 254–55, 263, 335; gives orders, 217, 548. *See also* Scammell, Alexander

*Admiral Keppel* (British privateer), 472

Aides-de-camp: appointments of, 106, 145–46; and brigade majors, 585; British, 8–9, 327; French, 39; of general officers, 21, 29, 46, 64, 95, 138, 199, 440–41; orders sent by, 4, 64; pay of, 310; sent to French fleet, 68, 74, 88–90, 125, 127; sent to Rhode Island, 137; used as messengers, 30, 133. *See also* Hamilton, Alexander; Harrison, Robert Hanson; Laurens, John; McHenry, James; Meade, Richard Kidder; Tilghman, Tench

*Aimable* (French frigate), 47, 246

Albany (N.Y.), 101, 111, 120, 149, 192, 287, 314, 436; arms repair at, 559, 576; artillery at, 65; commissaries at, 330–31; Commissioners of Indian Affairs at, 85; Indians at, 86, 184, 275–76; magazine at, 229; paymaster at, 65, 256, 313, 416, 447; prisoners at, 114, 214, 256; rendezvous point, 183, 222; shoes sent to, 570; support of soldiers' wives at, 214, 256; quartermasters at, 539; complaints about, 417, 575–76; troops at, 30, 66, 75, 113, 145, 157, 196; unrest among, 76

Albany County (N.Y.): commissioners for conspiracies, 108, 113–14, 129; commissioners of sequestration, 437, 449

Albany Road: British troop movements on, 601; patrols on, 547, 613

*Alcmene* (French frigate), 47, 246, 251

Alden, Ichabod (*see* 1:432): and command on N.Y. frontier, 257, 287; regiment, 65, 149, 287, 314, 349, 533–34, 555

Alden, Roger (*see* 14:299): *letters from*: to Jeremiah Wadsworth, 240

Alexander, Garrard (*see* 15:99): land transactions, 77–79, 230, 232

Alexander, John: appointed paymaster, 382; id., 384

Alexander, Philip: id., 79; land transactions, 78–79

Alexander, Robert (*see* 8:602; 15:99), 497; Custis debt to, 231; land transactions, 77–79, 230, 232

Alexander, William. *See* Stirling, Lord

Alexander the Great: compared to GW, 523

Alexandria (Va.), 501

Allen, —— (armorer), 559, 576

Allen, —— (capt.), 415

Allen, Ethan (*see* 2:22, 3:196): and citizens banished by Vermont, 108; and New York frontier defense, 66; *letters from*: to Horatio Gates, 111; to John Stark, 111

Allen, James (Mass.; *see* 12:682): tried by court-martial, 545

Allen, Jonathan (d. 1780; *see* 4:406): on board of officers, 451

Allen, Robert (*see* 14:424): resignation, 555

Allen, William (Va. recruiting officer), 148

Allentown (Pa.): British army at, 3

Allison, John: id., 407; on detachment, 241; rank and rank disputes, 407, 535